THE ENCYCLOPEDIA OF THE
FBI'S
TEN MOST
WANTED LIST

1950 to Present

THE ENCYCLOPEDIA OF THE
FBI'S TEN MOST WANTED LIST

1950 to Present

Duane Swierczynski

Checkmark Books®
An imprint of Facts On File, Inc.

The Encyclopedia of the FBI's Ten Most Wanted List, 1950 to Present

Checkmark Books
An imprint of Facts On File, Inc.
132 West 31st Street
New York NY 10001

Library of Congress Cataloging-in-Publication Data

Swierczynski, Duane
The encyclopedia of the FBI's ten most wanted list, 1950 to present / Duane Swierczynski
p. cm.
Includes bibliographical references and index
ISBN 0-8160-4560-7 (alk. paper) — ISBN 0-8160-4561-5 (pbk.: alk. paper)
1. Criminals—United States—Portraits. 2. Criminals—United States—Biography.
3. Fugitives from justice—United States—Portraits. 4. Fugitives from justice—United States—Biography.
5. United States—Federal Bureau of Investigation. I. Title
HV6786.S95 2003
364.1'092'2—dc21

2003005971

Checkmark Books are available at special discounts when purchased in bulk quantities for businesses, associations, institutions, or sales promotions. Please call our Special Sales Department in New York at (212) 967-8800 or (800) 322-8755.

You can find Facts On File on the World Wide Web at http://www.factsonfile.com

Cover design by Cathy Rincon
Text design by James Scotto-Lavino

Printed in the United States of America

VB FOF 10 9 8 7 6 5 4 3 2 1

This book is printed on acid-free paper.

This book is for Walter and Barbara Swierczynski.

I spent many years on the run, but you never
stopped making me feel most wanted.

Contents

Acknowledgments

Here are my Top Ten Acknowledgments: (#1) Meredith, Parker, and Sarah Swierczynski, who understood when I had to go on the lam for long periods of time during the writing of this book. (#2) Gary Goldstein, who put me on the lineup. (#3) April White, who not only served as my research chief for this project, but went far beyond the call of duty, journeying deep into the strange lands of dusty FBI archives, Freedom of Information Act Requests, and the U.S. Library of Congress. This book literally could have not been finished without her. She runs an excellent resource for writers at www.KnowMore Research.com. (#4) David Hale Smith, a known associate of writers, editors, and other lowlifes. Approach with extreme caution. (#5) James Chambers, the most patient man on the face of the Earth. He stuck with me on this project, even though I remained at large longer than most Top Ten fugitives. (#6) Ernie Porter of the FBI's Fugitive Publicity Unit, who was gracious with every annoying question, and extremely helpful in finding the answers. (#7) Linda Vizi of the Philadelphia FBI office, who gave me great insights into the inner workings of the Top Ten program. (#8) Richard Rys, for late night fugitive missions in Liberty City. (#9) Ron Geraci for his contagious enthusiasm. And finally (#10), Deacon Luke Elijah, for his spiritual guidance. Also be on the lookout for Patrick Michael Mitchell, Tracy Reynolds, Rex Tomb, Loren Feldman, Jordan Matus, Larry Platt, Tom McGrath, Jimmy and Sharon Allen, Paul and Cindy Barsky, Bro. Gerry Molyneaux, Lynne Texter, Michael Newton, Jason Rekulak, Valentine O'Connor, Louis Wojciechowski, Joel Fogelson, and all of my friends and family.

"Give me your worst":
An Introduction

It was February 1949. A United Press crime reporter was looking for something to fill a column. Then an idea popped into his head, and he called an FBI agent he knew. "If the FBI could catch the nation's 10 worst criminals," asked the reporter, "who would they be?" A few days later, the FBI sent the reporter a list of 10 men, along with their photographs and details. The headline "FBI's 'MOST-WANTED FUGITIVES' NAMED" screamed across the front page of the *Washington Daily News* on February 7, 1949. The story:

The FBI today listed 10 men as the most-wanted fugitives not at large. They are two accused murderers, four escaped convicts, a bank robber, and three confidence men. There are about 5,700 fugitives from justice in this country. Of these, the FBI said it considered these to be the 10 most potentially dangerous. The FBI does not label any one of them as "Public Enemy No. 1." But in response to a United Press inquiry, it compiled the list in the hope that this may lead to their arrest. Anyone knowing the whereabouts of these men should communicate immediately with the nearest FBI office or the local police.

Following this brief introduction were 10 stark, black-and-white photographs of men. Some looked straight into the camera, practically daring you to blink first. Two of the men wore faint smiles; another looked like he was snickering at some private joke. One rotund balding man was shown with his jaw clamped down on a pipe, looking off into the distance. Still others had cold, dead stares, utterly devoid of humanity. These 10 men were the public faces of crime in 1949. Names were named, along with birthplaces, brief descriptions of their criminal offenses, and last—but not least—their height and weight.

The byline belonged to a writer named James F. Donovan; but it is still unclear if he is the wire service reporter who first asked the FBI to "give me your worst." (Other accounts name the reporter as "Sam Fogg.") The byline didn't matter: those 10 felonious mugs did. The article was an instant sensation, capturing the public's imagination. For the first time ordinary civilians felt empowered to do something about the violent crime that has been on the rise in their towns and neighborhoods. All they had to do was take a closer look at these mug shots, then see if anybody around fit the description. Might a vicious killer be hiding in the boardinghouse next door? Working at the gas station down the street? Sitting one barstool away? That single list of 10 resulted in so much media coverage and public support—not to mention the capture of two fugitives—that FBI director J. Edgar Hoover institutionalized the "Top Ten" the very next year.

Wanted posters are nothing new; Americans have been eyeing the mug shots of suspicious individuals since the time of the Old West. And rankings aren't new either. Back in the 1930s, Depression-era newspaper readers thrilled to stories of the FBI's "G-Men" duking it out with "Public Enemy No. 1," be it Al Capone or Al Karpis or whoever Hoover had decided fit the bill. However, this was the first time the FBI laid out 10 bad guys at once, and actually asked for the public's assistance. It was the FBI's most shining public relations moment, and the Ten Most Wanted list became one of the most successful law enforcement tools in the country.

From its inception on March 14, 1950, through January 2000, a total of 458 bad guys have made the FBI's Most Wanted list. An astounding 94 percent have been captured. The first "Top Tenner" (as the Feds refer to them) was caught only two days after the list was announced. Others turned themselves in within *hours* of making the list. "Once we placed fugitives on the Top Ten, publicity was such that they'd even call in to surrender," said Agent Carter DeLoach, Hoover's number three man in the 1950s and 1960s. During the first year of the program, seven Top Tenners were caught; four of them thanks to tips from the public. In 1968 alone a record 33 fugitives were brought to justice.

The complete list of Top Tenners—which you'll find in the pages to follow—reads like a rouges' gallery from Hell. On it you'll find charming psycho Ted Bundy, Martin Luther King Jr. assassin James Earl Ray, controversial murderer Leonard Peltier, World Trade Center bomber Ramzi Ahmed Yousef, glam spree-killer Andrew Cunanan, and this generation's most feared name: Usama Bin Laden. Over the past 50 years, the types of Top Tenners have changed with the times. In the 1950s the list was full of murderers and bank robbers; in the '60s you'd find political subversives, black militants, and antiwar radicals; in the '70s terrorists and organized crime leaders; in the '80s drug lords; recently terrorists and abortion-clinic gunmen. "At any given time, the Ten Most Wanted is a snapshot of America's crime concerns," explained Rex Tomb, current head of the Fugitive Publicity Unit.

If you need more proof that the FBI's Ten Most Wanted list is one of the most effective fugitive-nabbing tools since the invention of the snitch, check out the Top Ten's imitators. Since 1950 countless other law enforcement agencies have adopted their own Top Ten lists, including the Bureau of Alcohol, Tobacco and Firearms (ATF), the Drug Enforcement Agency (DEA), U.S. Customs, U.S. Marshals—which boasts a "Top 15" list—even Interpol, the international police agency. In early October 2001 President George W. Bush unveiled the latest incarnation of the Top Ten list: the Most Wanted Terrorist list. When unveiled, this list included 22 suspected terrorists who were badly sought in the days after the September 11, 2001, disaster.

Even people who don't like the FBI very much have a grudging respect for the Ten Most Wanted program. "The Ten Mutts Wanted? It's about the only thing concerning the Feebs we pay any attention to," one New York City detective told reporter Bob Drury in *Details* magazine. "I got lots of beefs with the Feebs. But the Top Ten ain't one of them. They do a damn good job with that." Fugitives, too, have publicly praised the Top Ten list—even ones who have appeared on it. "You fellows sure did a good job," said armed robber Robert William Schuette (#155) after his capture. "I'm glad it's over. I know the FBI," said Edwin Sandford Garrison (#122), a two-time Top Ten fugitive. "You can't fool the FBI for very long."

HOW TO MAKE THE TOP TEN LIST

In the 1969 Woody Allen movie *Take the Money and Run*, Woody's fictional wife complains about her husband's disappointing criminal career. "I think if he'd been a successful criminal, he would have felt better," she says. "You know, he never made the Ten Most Wanted list. It's very unfair voting. It's who you know."

Er . . . not quite.

The Ten Most Wanted list is by no means a popularity contest. (Or even the inverse of a popularity contest.) There's no checklist of atrocities—x number of murders, x number of drug deals—you have to commit to qualify. Making the list is often a matter of being the right perp at the right time.

Then again, not just any old thug can make the Ten Most Wanted. For starters, you must be wanted on federal charges—a bank robbery, kidnapping, or by crossing state lines with stolen goods. Or you have to be a murderer, rapist, or thief who's fled across state lines and committed an unlawful flight to avoid prosecution (UFAP). That last bit is important in terms of getting noticed by the FBI, and it's just what it sounds like: You think you're going to be pinched for something, so you skip out of town, and across state lines. Crossing a state line is what makes it a federal, not local, matter.

Those are just the qualifications to make your case a so-called federal case. The official criteria for the Ten Most Wanted, according to the FBI:

1. The fugitive must be a particularly dangerous menace to society.
2. Nationwide publicity will assist in apprehending the fugitive.

The first criteria—"a dangerous menace to society"—is fairly subjective, and depends on the crime concerns at the moment. Back in the early 1970s, for example, young radicals were seen as a particular threat against American society, so those types of fugitives were given precedence. As of this book's printing, terrorists and child molesters seem to be on the FBI's mind a lot. Equally as important as the *type* of crime is the *frequency* of the crime. One big drug deal might make you a bad guy, but maybe not Top

Ten material. A series of drug deals over a decade that involved the deaths of innocent people? There are no certainties, but you're getting warmer.

The second criteria—"nationwide publicity"—is just as subjective. It's basically a judgment call. Will taking this case public help or harm the case? Before the FBI proceeds with naming someone to the Top Ten list, they always clear it with prosecutors at the federal and local levels, just to make sure that publicity in the case won't screw up any future prosecutions. Or maybe there's already enough publicity out there, which is why you won't find Charles Manson, Patty Hearst, or O. J. Simpson on the Top Ten. At the time, all had generated plenty of publicity on their own. (True, Ted Bundy's name sticks out among the 460-plus members of the list so far, but back when he was added to the list, he was unknown to the public at large.)

Still, thousands of perps fit those requirements every year. To make the Top Ten, you *really* have to stand out: You must remain at large and continue to pose a threat to the American public. It helps if you've killed people—especially a cop or a federal agent, or a child. It certainly helps if you've escaped federal prison more than once. You must also frustrate an FBI field agent to such a degree that he is compelled to convince his bosses in D.C.—with a report and case file thicker than a Stephen King novel—that worldwide publicity is the last, best chance they have to nail you.

Whenever there's a slot open on the Top Ten, the Criminal Investigative Division (CID) contacts all 56 FBI field offices and asks them to submit candidates. Choosing the worst of the worst is up to each field office. "To get one of your fugitives on the Top Ten list, you were a salesperson," 25-year FBI veteran Clinton Van Zandt told National Public Radio in 2000. "You had to present this person in the most negative light, and you have to make that case to the nines, and you have to make it better than anybody else makes the case if you're going to get your fugitive on there."

Special agents at the CID wade through the hundreds of nominees to come up with the few lucky winners—"the ones who jump out at you," explained Robert Bryant, currently the FBI's assistant director of the CID and the man with the next-to-final say on the Ten Most Wanted. The CID's selection is then sent to the FBI's deputy director for final approval, and a Top Tenner is born. A press conference is held; posters are distributed to law enforcement agencies big and small across the United States; your photo and vitals are posted to the Internet in many places.

Once you make the list, congratulations. The pressure on you will never end. Your name, image, and vital stats will be sent to all 56 FBI field offices, as well as to countless police stations and post offices. John Walsh may talk about you on TV. Your cartoon likeness will appear in the Dick Tracy comic strip. Your image may even appear in the most random special interest magazines. Back in the 1960s the FBI put the photo of Benjamin Hoskins Paddock (#302) in *The Sporting News* after learning he was a big fan of stock-car racing. Your height, weight, tattoos, scars, and most insignificant marks will become fodder of the general public.

You will never be "bumped" from the list by a more heinous criminal. In fact, if need be, the FBI will add an 11th or 12th person to the Ten Most Wanted (called "a special addition.") In fact, there are only three ways off the list:

1. You are captured or killed.
2. The charges against you have been dismissed.
3. You no longer fit "Top Ten" criteria.

In other words: Unless a court of law decides to dismiss your case, there will be thousands of federal agents who will put in countless feverish hours of overtime until you are captured, surrendered, or dead.

Then another slot opens up, and the process begins all over again. "A lot of work goes into these Top Ten announcements," explains Special Agent Linda Vizi in the FBI's Philadelphia field office. "If bang, you catch 'em, means bang, you gotta do another one."

As you'll see in the profiles that follow, there are many ways to get nabbed if you're a Top Tenner. You could violate some minor traffic law, leading to your arrest and fingerprint check. (However, over the years many Top Ten fugitives have been arrested and released on bail before the fingerprint check could come back with a "hit.") You could choose to visit old friends, neighbors, or your mother. (More than one Top Tenner has been nabbed by an FBI stakeout covering home turf—this is why the birthplace is always listed on the fugitive's wanted poster.) The most popular way, of course, is to be recognized by someone who's seen your face on a wanted poster somewhere. Nine of the first 20 fugitives put on the Top Ten list were caught thanks to eagle-eyed citizens; over the years

134 fugitives have been captured thanks to tips from the public.

Sounds fairly straightforward, doesn't it? But there are still some popular myths about the Top Ten list:

Myth #1. The Top Ten is ranked in some kind of order. Some people believe that the Top Ten starts with the "most dangerous" and works its way down to "well, not exactly the most dangerous." This is untrue. All fugitives are equally wanted, which is why there are no numbers assigned to the fugitives other than their identification order number, which is a number assigned to all federal fugitives. Or their ranking in Top Ten history, as in "the 458th fugitive to ever make the list."

Myth #2. Hide long enough, and the FBI will stop looking for you. This is not true. Alleged cop killer Donald Eugene Webb (#375) has been on the list since 1981, and he remains the holy grail of the Top Ten list—the fugitive the FBI most wants to bust. Webb has single-handedly skewed the statistics for average days at large: Before Webb it was 154 days; today it's 314 days. The only way out for Webb is if prosecutors in Pennsylvania (where he allegedly shot a police chief to death) decide to give up on the case. While it's true that a handful of Top Tenners were removed from the list when process was dismissed, it's no guarantee. The only other way out is death, which is how 10 other Top Tenners between 1950 and 2000 made it off the list.

Myth #3. You have to kill a cop or an FBI agent to make the list. It doesn't hurt, but as you'll see, the history of the Top Ten is populated by all manner of criminals, including thieves, confidence men, murderers, racketeers, drug dealers, rapists, and terrorists. Sadly, there are plenty of cop killers out there who haven't made the Top Ten list.

Myth #4. If you're "most wanted" by the FBI, you're automatically on the "Ten Most Wanted" list. Not true, but it's easy to see how this can get confusing. Every month the FBI highlights a new crew of "most wanted" fugitives on its website (www.fbi.gov), culled from the 56 field offices around the country. However, these are not members of the official *Ten* Most Wanted list. Basically, there are three general layers of FBI fugitives: 1. the ordinary, garden-variety wanted; 2. the most wanted; and finally 3. the Ten Most Wanted. It's kind of like Little League, then the Minors, and finally, the Major League. All are equally wanted by the Feds; the only difference is the amount of publicity thrown at them.

Myth #5. The FBI throws up "easy" guys on the list. This was a criticism hurled at the FBI in the early days of the program when it seemed to be catching Top Tenners every other week. Critics said that it was simply J. Edgar Hoover, looking to boost his public image with a series of high-profile captures of "easy" crooks. Conspiracy theorists might have a field day with this one, but simply put, the history of the list doesn't support this notion. There have been too many fugitives who were too difficult to catch, and the ones who were "easy" were usually caught thanks to a tip from the public, which is the whole point of the list in the first place. Take a look at the fugitives of the 1990s—there are only 29 of them—and see how "easy" those guys are to catch. If anything, the FBI seems to train its sights on fugitives increasingly difficult to catch every year.

THE POWER OF TEN

The Ten Most Wanted list is all about numbers: days on the run, height, weight, age, spot on the list. Here are 20 other interesting numbers that have emerged over 50 years of Ten Most Wanted history:

7	number of women who have appeared on the list
6	number of fugitives who have appeared on the list twice
37.4	average age of a Top Tenner
5'10"	average height of a Top Tenner
168.5	average weight of a Top Tenner
316	average number of days fugitives spend on the list
2	shortest fugitive run, in hours
6,800	longest fugitive run, in days (and still counting)
11	number of times the FBI has made a "special addition" to the Ten Most Wanted list, pushing the number above 10
16	the most fugitives ever to appear on the Top Ten list at once
13	number of fugitives captured thanks to magazine articles
3	number of fugitives captured thanks to radio broadcasts
21	number of fugitives captured thanks to TV shows

134	number of fugitives captured thanks to tips from the public
9	number of fugitives killed during capture
10	number of fugitives who died before capture
21	number of fugitives who surrendered before capture
25	number of fugitives captured in foreign countries
47	number of U.S. states where fugitives have been captured (the missing states: Alaska, Maine, and Delaware.)
1,000	average number of miles from the crime scene from where a fugitive is arrested

THE FUTURE OF THE TEN MOST WANTED

Will the Top Ten list survive into the 21st century? Some experts think not, thanks to an increasingly indifferent public. "Americans are bombarded with so many messages of caution and alarm and fear that they have become desensitized and simply don't respond," said Jack Levin, director of the Program for the Study of Violence at Northeastern University in Boston, to *USA Today*. "We are in the age of information overload, especially in the wake of 9-11. Who's going to worry about being on the lookout for a serial rapist when there are dirty bombs and anthrax and ricin and hijacked airplanes to worry about? Even the U.S. Postal Service stopped putting up Ten Most Wanted posters in their lobbies back in the mid-1990s. "We researched this and found that very few people, if any, had been caught in recent years as a result of post office display," a spokeswoman for the Postal Service told *USA Today*. "So now post offices keep a copy, but you have to ask for it."

Technology is the other threat, according to others. Eventually computers with face-recognition software will be able to pluck out a fugitive's mug from a sea of faces far more easily than even the keenest beat cop could. In the future all that might be needed is a series of surveillance cameras—rather than a series of wanted posters—to track down America's worst.

The FBI, of course, is nowhere near ready to abandon one of its most popular weapons in its war against crime. In the past 15 years the Ten Most Wanted program has been energized by two different mediums: television, thanks to such popular shows as *America's Most Wanted,* and the Internet. Post office? Not if the posters for the Ten Most Wanted list are available at www.fbi.gov. Filing a tip is even easier than it's ever been, thanks to the FBI's website. Even after 50 plus years, the Top Ten list still has the ability to focus the eyes of a nation on a type of crime, at least, if not on a particular criminal.

Not bad for an offhanded request made by a wire reporter looking to fill column inches back in 1949.

RESEARCHING THIS BOOK

For the nearly 500 profiles in this book, I relied heavily on two sources: 1. bulletins, placards, identification orders, and posters direct from the FBI's files—in some cases, obtained by filing a Freedom of Information Act request—and 2. contemporary newspaper and magazine accounts. (In multiple cases, a fugitive's identification order was sealed, most often because the fugitive was still living. As a result, some of the fugitive profiles in this book lack "vital stats" such as height and weight, birth date, and criminal background.) Still, I tried to use as much information direct from the FBI as possible and hope that it has resulted in the most accurate data.

I am also thankful for two other existing books about the Ten Most Wanted program: *FBI Most Wanted: An Encyclopedia* by Michael and Judy Ann Newton (Garland, 1989) and *Most Wanted: A History of the FBI's Most Wanted List* by Mark Sabljack and Martin H. Greenburg (Bonanza, 1990). Both titles helped me flesh out scarce details on many of the older fugitives, and I'm grateful to all four authors, as well as to the countless reporters and writers who contributed to stories about Top Ten fugitives to various newspapers and magazines over the years. Their frontline digging enabled me to compile a more complete picture of 50 years of Top Ten history.

I hope you enjoy this roundup of the FBI's Most Wanted. If you have information for future editions of this book, do not hesitate to contact me at duane.swier@verizon.net.

FUGITIVES
OF THE 1950s

Introduction

Ah, the 1950s: simpler times, simpler crimes. Or so it seemed. Even though the list was populated with car thieves, bank robbers, and con men, there was still room for creepy harbingers of felonies to come. Freddy Tenuto (#14), Giachino Anthony Baccolla (#25), Dominic Scialo (#106), and Angelo Luigi Pero (#107) were all associates of the New York mob, but the FBI wouldn't actually acknowledge the existence of a "Mafia" until years later. And Isaie Aldy Beausoleil (#33) was a cross-dressing killer whose story seems ripped right out of a Thomas Harris novel.

Still, the Ten Most Wanted list enjoyed a wholesome, all-American beginning. The list was launched on March 14, 1950, with a new Top Tenner added every day for 10 days after that. Just four days later came the Top Ten's first bona fide success with the capture of William Nesbit (#3). You couldn't have scripted a better story: Nesbit, a heister linked to the bombing murder of his associates, was captured by a real-life version of the Hardy Boys—a pair of bright teenage boys who had spotted the fugitives skulking around a nearby cave. Not all of the Top Ten captures to follow would be as dramatic, but the arrest of Nesbit sent a clear message to the American public: This Top Ten list works—thanks to you.

Other notable fugitives of this decade included 1930s-era heister Thomas Holden (#1), gentleman bank robber Willie Sutton (#11), Dutch Schultz numbers man Edwin Garrison (#59), home invader Franklin James Wilson (#60), disappearing killer David Daniel Keegan (#78), two-timer Nick George Montos (#37 and #94), and Brink's robbers James Ignatius Faherty (#95) and Thomas Francis Richardson (#96).

1. THOMAS JAMES HOLDEN, bank robber, murderer

LISTED: March 14, 1950
CAUGHT: June 23, 1951
DESCRIPTION: Born April 22, 1899, in Chicago, Illinois. Five feet 8 1/2 inches, with dark brown hair and blue eyes. Nickname: "Tough" Tommy.

Number One With a Bullet. Holden's was the first name on J. Edgar Hoover's new list of March 1950, but he wasn't a newbie to the world of crime. His career dated back to the 1920s, when he was convicted of robbing a mail train. In 1930 he escaped from Leavenworth Prison and eventually hooked up with a virtual all-star team of Depression-era crime: bank robbers Harvey Bailey, Verne Miller, Frank Keating, and Frank Nash. Golfing was big with the 1930s heist men. After a string of lucrative heists in 1932, the four met up for a couple of holes at the Old Mission Golf Course, a public course in Kansas City. Little did Holden know that the FBI was wise to their nine-iron addiction and had been snooping around public courses for months.

Holden, Bailey, and Keating had just finished putting out when they heard a voice behind them.

"Hold it, boys."

An FBI agent popped out of the trees along with six other cops. The golfers were arrested without resistance. After all, it's hard to conceal a pistol in your finest golf duds. Holden was put on ice until

November 28, 1947. By that time all of the 1930s heist men were either dead or in prison. The world had moved on. Holden returned to Chicago and picked up where he'd left off with his wife, Lillian, and their two boys. He didn't quite know what to do with himself, so he spent a lot of time brooding and drinking in the local taverns. What does a former bank robber do for a follow-up act anyway?

Nothing.

On June 5, 1949, police found two men and a woman shot to death in an apartment on Chicago's West Side. The murder weapon, a .38 revolver, was found in a dresser with four shells spent. The woman was Mrs. Thomas Holden, and the two men were her brothers. There had been a Holden family party that evening, and apparently it had gone horribly wrong. Thomas Holden was nowhere to be found.

Nearly a year later, when J. Edgar Hoover decided to create a special "Most Wanted" list of the most notorious criminals in America, Holden's name popped up almost immediately. He was a throwback to the 1930s—Hoover had made his name duking it out with the Depression-era heisters—but he was also symbolic of the unrepentant criminal that the Top Ten list was designed to catch. "Thomas James Holden is one man whose freedom in society is a menace to every man, woman and child in America," read the FBI press release. On March 14, 1950, Holden was named to the newly created list.

It took a little over a year, but Holden was finally caught after an Oregon resident saw the fugitive's photo in the paper. Holden had been working as "John McCullough" in Beaverton, Oregon, doing plaster work. Holden was convicted of murder and sent to the Illinois state prison.

INTERESTING FUGITIVE FACT:
Holden didn't receive hard time because of a bum ticker. After his capture in 1951, he died of his heart condition after only two years in jail.

2. MORLEY VERNON KING, murderer

LISTED: March 15, 1950
CAUGHT: October 31, 1951
DESCRIPTION: Born in Wheeling, West Virginia. King's right leg is shorter than the left, forcing him to walk with a limp.

The Killer from Casablanca. The maid noticed the "Do Not Disturb" sign on Morley King's door. When the sign still hung the next day, the maid asked

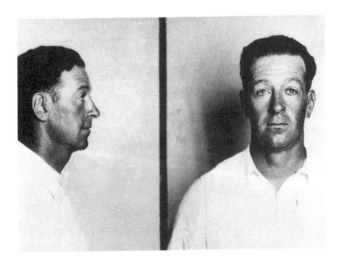

Thomas Holden, a career criminal from the 1920s, became the first fugitive posted to the FBI's "Ten Most Wanted" list in 1950.

King if he wanted his room cleaned. He asked if she could leave it alone for a few days. Soon after, another hotel employee detected a weird smell coming from the room. That's just a new perfume and shaving cream, King explained.

King and his wife, Helen, had been staying at the San Luis Obispo, California, hotel for a few months, with Morley running the hotel kitchen. Then suddenly, on July 8, 1947, King left the hotel and the area. The next day the hotel staff finally forced their way into the room to see what had been going on. They found nothing in the room. But they did find something under the hotel's back porch. It was a steamer trunk containing the body of Helen King. She had been strangled to death with a man's scarf and apparently had been rotting away in the trunk for six days. Three days later, a warrant was issued charging King with murder. But King had disappeared, and he was no stranger to travel. He ran away from home at the age of 15, and spent his adolescence bumming his way through Europe, eventually landing in Casablanca, Morocco, where he met and married Helen in 1931. King ran a restaurant in New Orleans for a while before moving his wife out to the American Southwest in the mid-1940s, bouncing from restaurant to restaurant. He became the second addition to the Top Ten list on March 15, 1951.

Fortunately, the FBI didn't have to scour Europe to find their man. On Halloween 1950 agents found King working under the alias "William Wilson" in a Philadelphia seafood house, shucking oysters. He was sent back to California and sentenced to life in prison. Nobody knows why King decided to do away with his Casablancan bride; some people reported that the couple had bickered incessantly in the months preceding Helen's murder. Here's looking at you, King.

INTERESTING FUGITIVE FACT:
King could say "I hid my wife's corpse in a trunk under the porch" fluently in four different languages.

3. WILLIAM RAYMOND NESBIT, burglar, murderer

LISTED: March 16, 1950
CAUGHT: March 18, 1950
DESCRIPTION: Born June 1, 1899, in Marshalltown, Iowa. Five feet five inches, 160 pounds, with brown-gray hair and brown eyes. Occupations: box maker, butcher, electrician's helper, laborer, and shoemaker. Boil scar on neck, scar above left eye, and an irregular scar on his left forearm. Nesbit is left-handed. Aliases: Lee Bradley, Patrick R. Davis, William R. Nesbeth, Harry Reeves, Gilbert Renard, and Frank Raymond Smith.

The First Capture. Nesbit was living in a cave near St. Paul, Minnesota, when he suddenly became one of the most notorious criminals in the United States.

He had already been famous once, having participated in one of the more spectacular crimes in Sioux City, Iowa's, history—a $37,000 jewel heist on New Year's Eve in 1936. A short while later, things turned ugly when two gang members started arguing while trying to steal dynamite from a powder house, and one ended up with a bullet in his gut. When the fallen crook's girlfriend started screaming, another member of the gang beat her on the head with a hammer and another shot her. The three remaining gang members decided to dispose of the evidence. But how? Hasty preparations were made to dispose of them with dynamite. Bodies were stacked, and a fuse was lit. By the time the three surviving crooks were five miles away from the scene, the dynamite finally blew. There was more bang, however, than the crooks had bargained for. They unwittingly set off 3,500 pounds of dynamite and 7,000 pounds of black powder, and the resulting explosion destroyed $20,000 worth of plate glass in downtown Sioux Falls five miles away and reportedly could be heard 50 miles away.

William Nesbit was one of the gang members, though nobody could pin either murder on him personally—and according to testimony from the other gang members, he wasn't to blame. Still, he was slapped with a life sentence, later reduced to 20 years. He would have been out sometime in the 1950s, but Nesbit couldn't wait. He bolted from prison in 1946 and stayed on the lam for four years.

Life on the run wasn't easy. By Thanksgiving 1949, Nesbit was making his home in an abandoned cave along the Mississippi River. Local boys from St. Paul started to befriend "Ray," who they thought was a down-on-his-luck bum who had wild stories to tell about his adventures. James Lewis and his buddy James Radeck, 13, were among Ray's biggest fans. That was until March 17, when Lewis came home from school and noticed a piece of newspaper on the kitchen floor. His mother had just scrubbed and waxed the floor and had tossed random pieces of the *St. Paul Dispatch* down to cover it. Lewis was shocked when he saw the face of his homeless buddy, "Ray," looking back up at him.

Lewis took the article to Radeck to confirm his suspicions, but he couldn't be sure. They decided to take one last look the next day. Arming themselves with a plastic atomic ray gun and a slingshot, the teens wandered down to the cave. Ray was hiding inside. They still weren't positive about the identification, so Lewis and Radeck decided to force him out of his cave. Using a perverse genius for mischief that only teen boys seem to possess, they got the idea to shove snow down a stovepipe that Ray had rigged in the cave. Smoke started pouring out of the front of the cave, and soon Ray came stumbling out. Lewis and Radeck took one hard look and knew they had their man. They ran to fetch police, who came back and took Ray Nesbit into custody. It was the first official capture of the new Top Ten list, and it had been made possible by two kids from St. Paul, Minnesota, armed with a ray gun and a slingshot.

INTERESTING FUGITIVE FACT:
Lewis and Radeck were later rewarded with a trip to Washington, D.C., to meet J. Edgar Hoover. A reporter asked if the boys were frightened as they approached the cave. Lewis said: "Naw, I wasn't scared. We could have handled him."

4. HENRY RANDOLPH MITCHELL, robber

LISTED: March 17, 1950
REMOVED FROM LIST: July 18, 1958
DESCRIPTION: Born in 1895. Five feet 5 1/2 inches tall, 155 pounds.

Little Mitch Beats the Rap.   Nobody knew it at the time, but the fourth man to make the original roster of the Ten Most Wanted would eventually become an anomaly—the rare fugitive who would actually evade capture.

Allegedly, Mitchell was part of a duo that knocked over a bank in Wiliston, Florida, on January 21, 1948. The robbers forced the employees to the floor at gunpoint, then helped themselves to $10,353 in the cash box. FBI agents interviewed bank employees later and discovered that the two men resembled two recent guests at the Florida State Penitentiary—one of them being Henry Randolph Mitchell, a gambling nut nicknamed "Little Mitch," who robbed to support his pony habit. Mitchell's partner was quickly arrested, but Mitchell stayed on

Process dismissed. Mitchell was placed on the list two days after its inception and was the only person on the original list still at large when process was dismissed.

the lam and eventually became the fourth fugitive on the new Ten Most Wanted list.

Eight years later, when Mitchell would have been 63 years old, there wasn't a trace of him. Mitchell remained on the list as dozens of new fugitives joined him on posters tacked up in post offices across the country. Still nothing. Finally, the Federal District Court at Jacksonville, Florida, threw in the towel and federal process was dismissed. Only then was Mitchell begrudgingly removed from the Top Ten. Nobody knows what ever became of Little Mitch, but some theorized that he welshed on too big a loan and other criminals took justice into their own hands.

INTERESTING FUGITIVE FACT:
Mitchell was never charged with the Wiliston robbery, but his record did include bad check passing, grand larceny, narcotics violations, breaking and entering, and forgery.

5. OMAR AUGUST PINSON, burglar, murderer

LISTED: March 18, 1950
CAUGHT: August 28, 1952
DESCRIPTION: Born in Iowa. Alias: Joseph Anthony Dorian.

Dead Man Running. If you lived in a private home on the West Coast in the 1940s and happened to own a gun, you were among burglar Omar Pinson's favorite targets. He was extremely skilled at sneak-thievery and loved it when the occupants of the house owned a weapon—they were extremely easy to exchange for cash. But Pinson's love of guns backfired on the night of April 25, 1947. He had been sneaking back to his truck when an Oregon State police officer named Delmond Rondeau stopped him. Pinson whipped out a .32-20 automatic and started blasting at Rondeau, fatally wounding him. Pinson made his escape, bursting through a police blockade and hopping a freight train, but was captured before the train could make it out of Oregon. Convicted of first-degree murder, Pinson was sentenced to life in prison at the Oregon State Penitentiary.

Two years later, on May 30, 1949, Pinson and a fellow inmate made their escape. The other inmate was caught four months later and grilled about the whereabouts of Pinson. He told investigating FBI agents that Pinson had caught a couple of slugs during the escape and subsequently died. The fellow con did the honorable thing and buried his buddy's body in a shallow grave near Kellogg, Idaho. Oddly, the convict also told the Ohio police a different story: that Pinson had died of gangrene poisoning and was buried near Salem, Oregon. Meanwhile, Omar Pinson was alive and well, and back in business for himself under the name Joseph Anthony Dorian. Soon even this alias was being sought in connection with a series of West Coast burglaries. FBI agents made the connection and identified Dorian as Pinson. (The search parties looking for Pinson's shallow grave were relieved of their grim duty.) By that time Pinson had adopted yet another alias—Sam Cignitti—and three new partners. The gang was caught trying to knock over a hardware store in Polson, Montana. Two crooks were nabbed and hastily identified their ringleader's real name. Pinson was made the fifth member of the fledgling Ten Most Wanted list on March 18, 1950.

Pinson was finally caught after he adopted still another alias—"D.C. Audell"—and purchased a 1942 Ford in South Dakota. (Salesmen remembered that the buyer matched Pinson's description.) A statewide alert was issued, and Pinson was caught in an FBI sting while trying to register that car in person on August 28, 1950. But the sneak-thief had one ruse left in him. Pinson asked a special agent for a glass of water, only to throw the glass in his face and then tried to run for it. Agents grabbed Pinson before he made it to his 1942 Ford, which contained a rifle, a shotgun, and two revolvers.

INTERESTING FUGITIVE FACT:
Even in prison Pinson stuck to the story that he had been buried alive by his fellow escapee. "I went out of my head from a fever. The man told me I was going to die and asked me what he should do. I remember telling him to bury me." Pinson claimed waking up later in a shallow ditch with a blanket of sticks and stones. "I don't know how long I laid there," he said.

6. LEE EMORY DOWNS, robber

LISTED: March 20, 1950
CAUGHT: April 7, 1950
DESCRIPTION: Born April 2, 1906, in Butte, Montana. Six feet, 167 pounds, with brown hair and blue eyes. Occupations: presser, salesman, jewelry engraver, barber, bartender. Downs has a scar on the right side of his upper lip, a cut scar on his forehead, freckles on his forehead and face, a scar on his upper right arm, a round burn scar on his inner right forearm, a scar on his inner left wrist, and both little fingers are deformed at the second joint. His upper teeth are false. Aliases: Emery Lee Downs, C.E. Gardner, Harold Gordon, Lee Harrington, Lee Landers, Ed Morris, Charles Murphy, Lee Murphy, Frank Ralston, and "Gabe."

Trailer Park Takedown. A pair of heisters brazenly entered the office of a telephone company in San Jose, California, near midnight, subdued and tied up the employees, then helped themselves to $10,800 inside a safe. Later, a hogtied employee told police that she had noticed a 1948 beige Oldsmobile parked outside immediately before the robbery. The car traced to one "C.E. Gardner," which was an alias of none other than Lee Downs, a veteran hold-up man thought to be connected to a series of clever burglaries and robberies up and down the Pacific coastline. By the time the first Ten Most Wanted list was being compiled, Downs's name emerged as a natural candidate.

Indeed, Downs was clever. By the time he made the Top Ten he had long abandoned his favored stomping grounds—the West Coast—and hid out with his wife in Florida. Still, he wasn't *that* clever. FBI agents traced him to a trailer park in Daytona Beach, Florida, anyway. Downs was arrested while working on his 1949 Lincoln automobile, having long since traded in the telltale Olds. But he wasn't about to trade in his criminal ways. Inside Downs's trailer, arresting officers found two pistols, six rifles, nine sticks of dynamite, 12 fuses, and two bulging leather suitcases full of bullets. Downs was returned to San Jose and convicted of robbery.

INTERESTING FUGITIVE FACT:
In 1968, shortly after being paroled, Downs tried to rob the Colombian consulate in San Francisco. Downs grossly underestimated the Colombian security guard's prowess with a crowbar, and he was quickly—not to mention painfully—subdued, then returned to jail for parole violation.

7. ORBA ELMER JACKSON, armed robber

LISTED: March 21, 1950
CAUGHT: March 23, 1950
DESCRIPTION: Born in Missouri in 1906.

The Last Picture Show. Orba Jackson grew up a farmer, got tired of the hardscrabble life of livestock and dirt, turned his hand to crime, but eventually ended up right back where he started: among the livestock and the dirt. By the age of 18, Jackson had boosted his first car. But by 30 Jackson had really hit the big time, pistol-whipping the owner of a store near Poplar Bluff, Missouri, before cleaning out the till. But it was a poor target. The store also happened to serve as a U.S. Post Office, and it's a federal offense to knock over a post office. Jackson was convicted of assault and armed robbery, and shipped off to Leavenworth to serve a 25-year hitch.

Eleven years later, Jackson was transferred to a Leavenworth "honor farm"—a less secure facility where prisoners toiled with livestock and dirt. Jackson was apparently overcome with an unpleasant bout of déjà vu, for three weeks later the convict turned up missing during a prisoner headcount. He stayed hidden for three years until the brand-new Top Ten list came into existence, and when that happened, Jackson would last only three more days. A citizen who lived near Portland, Oregon, had previously written the FBI

a letter complaining about a "suspicious character" seen working at a nearby poultry farm. When Jackson was named to the Top Ten and a short profile of him ran in the *Portland Oregonian*, the citizen became convinced. The poultry worker was, in truth, one of the most wanted men in America. After years spent desperately trying to escape the farm, Jackson had resigned himself to the lifestyle once again. Jackson was quickly arrested and returned to the prison. On the bright side, Jackson wouldn't have to toil on a farm anytime in the near future.

INTERESTING FUGITIVE FACT:
Fellow poultry farm workers in Portland considered Jackson to be a "perfect gentleman."

8. GLEN ROY WRIGHT, armed robber

LISTED: March 22, 1950
CAUGHT: December 13, 1950
DESCRIPTION: Born March 16, 1899, in Malvern, Arkansas. Five feet 8 1/2 inches tall, 130 pounds, with gray hair and blue eyes. Occupations: laborer, plumber, steam fitter, tool dresser, and welder. Wright has a gunshot wound on outer left forearm five inches above his wrist, a cut scar on the left side of his chin, and a cut scar on the cheek near his left eye. Aliases: J.R. Dare, Jack Dare, Jack Hudson, Roy Hudson, and Glen LeRoy Wright.

The Smoking Gun. Pity Glen Wright. He was locked away during the gunslinging, bank-robbing afternoons of the 1930s, having worked with such Depression-era luminaries as Alvin Karpis and Fred Barker, and not hesitated to unload hot lead at police when it came down to it. When he was finally pinned down, Wright tried to use a sawed-off shotgun to discourage his pursuers, but to no avail. Put on ice in 1934, Wright had to wait 14 years before he could make his escape from the Oklahoma State Penitentiary. By then the glory days of bank robbing were over, and a new law enforcement tool was waiting to be unveiled. After a year and a half of life as a fugitive, Wright became number eight on the new Ten Most Wanted list.

Nine months later, a mysterious tipster told the FBI that Wright would be at a particular drug store in Salina, Kansas, on December 13. Wright was arrested without a fight and shipped back to Oklahoma to complete his life sentence. For Glen Wright, however, there wasn't much of a life left to serve. He died on May 7, 1954.

The tipster who ratted on Wright was never publicly identified.

9. HENRY HARLAND SHELTON, kidnapper, car thief

LISTED: March 23, 1950
CAUGHT: June 23, 1950

Road Trip. The FBI caught up with Henry Shelton outside of a bar. "Come on, fella," said one agent. "It's over."

"That's what you think," Shelton replied and reached for the .45 caliber pistol he had tucked under his belt. But the agents already had their weapons drawn, and they fired first. Shelton bucked, twisted, and collapsed. Number nine had been taken down, and it had been the most violent arrest in the Top Ten's short history. Fugitives weren't liking the extra attention, and many to follow would take Shelton's lead and swear not to be taken alive.

Shelton was a bank robber who managed to pop out of the Michigan House of Correction and Branch Prison on September 5, 1949, along with a fellow con named Sam Lieb. The pair hid in the woods for 12 days, then got desperate and decided to hijack a citizen. They chose an electrical worker from Amasa, Michigan, who stepped outside of his workplace for a midnight meal and suddenly found himself sandwiched between two foul-smelling, slightly crazed criminals who threatened to carve him up with a knife unless he drove them away. Shelton and Lieb directed the worker to drive them to Illinois, then Wisconsin, back to Illinois, and finally to Indiana. By then, the second morning after his abduction, the electrical worker had decided he'd had enough. He ran from the car during a meal break in Montmorenci, Indiana, and managed to alert Indiana state police. Meanwhile, Shelton and Lieb hit the road again and would steal three more cars at knifepoint before Lieb was finally caught. Shelton slipped away somehow and managed to stay hidden throughout the fall and winter.

Then came spring, and the creation of the Top Ten list, and suddenly there was more heat on Shelton than he could handle. FBI agents learned that there was a certain bar in Indianapolis that Shelton liked to frequent, and on June 23—exactly three months after he was named to the list—agents cornered him at the tavern. As it turned out, Shelton survived his wounds and later pled guilty to kidnapping and car theft charges. He was sentenced to 50 years in prison.

Shelton, with two FBI bullets in his body, had a beer and couple of cigarettes before being hauled away.

10. MORRIS GURALNICK, attempted murderer

LISTED: March 24, 1950
CAUGHT: December 15, 1950
DESCRIPTION: Born on New York City's Lower East Side. Five feet four inches tall, 138 pounds. Guralnick has a broken nose, two upper front teeth missing, and a sloping forehead. Previous occupations: popcorn vendor and candy maker.

The Finger-Man. In April 1948, after nearly stabbing his girlfriend to death, Morris Guralnick apparently still had some steam to blow off. Arresting officers worked hard to subdue the violent, spitting-mad Guralnick, but even *then* he wasn't finished. The would-be killer craned his neck forward and chomped down on the finger of one of the cops, severing it from the hand. Either he wanted to blow off steam, or he'd skipped a few meals. Police threw Guralnick in the Ulster County Jail at Kingston, New York. But just three months later Guralnick teamed up with a gang of four other inmates, ripped apart the prison's plumbing system, then used the broken pipes to brutally assault two prison guards. The four accomplices were quickly rounded up, but Guralnick stayed on the lam for nearly two years before becoming number ten on the newly minted Top Ten list, which is ironic, considering the fugitive left his earliest victim with only nine fingers.

Meanwhile, Guralnick had hightailed it to Madison, Wisconsin, and tried to hide himself among the racks of a clothing store where he'd found a low-paying job. But one of the store's customers thought Guralnick's dome-shaped head looked familiar; he looked an awful lot like one of the fugitives pictured in a *Coronet* magazine article. An FBI agent and Madison cop teamed up to make the arrest, and true to form, Guralnick bitterly resisted. In the end the collar was made without another finger lost. Number 10 was extradited back to New York.

INTERESTING FUGITIVE FACT:
According to Guralnick's wanted poster he was a "wild-eyed person" and a "constant menace to society."

11. WILLIE SUTTON, bank robber

LISTED: March 20, 1950
CAUGHT: February 18, 1952
DESCRIPTION: Born June 30, 1901, in Brooklyn, New York. Five feet, eight inches tall, 150 pounds, with brown hair and blue eyes. Occupations: clerk, driller, florist, gardener, stenographer, hospital porter. Sutton smokes cigarettes in moderation, is a continuous user of chewing gum, dresses neatly and conservatively, wears or carries gloves no matter the season, is soft spoken and courteous in manner, and may be wearing tinted glasses to disguise appearance. Aliases: William Bowles, James Clayton, Richard Courtney, Leo Holland, Julian Loring, Edward Lynch, "Slick Willie," and "Willie the Actor."

Prince of Thieves. William Francis Sutton's quip about robbing banks—"Because that's where the money is"—has appeared in hundreds of articles about banks. Actually, Sutton never said it. He later admitted that the quip came from a snarky newspaper man, and Sutton never thought to dispute ownership. "If anyone had asked me, I would have said it. Anyone would have said it."

Sutton always knew where the money was; at first the problem was getting to it. The first bank Willie Sutton tried to rob, Ozone Park National Bank in Queens, was an unmitigated disaster. Sutton took all night to chop through a concrete floor to gain access to the vault, and by the time he did, he only had 15 minutes to burn through the vault before the bank opened up in the morning. Ten minutes later, two bank employees were standing outside, ready to open the joint. Sutton had to abandon his expensive tools and the robbery. To make matters worse, an oxygen tank—the kind used for safe-burning torches—was traced to his partner, Eddie Wilson, two weeks later. Sutton was linked to Wilson the morning of the attempted caper, and on April 5, 1926, he was found guilty of burglary in the third degree and attempted grand larceny. Sutton was headed to Sing Sing state prison.

After winning parole in 1929, Sutton found himself trying to make an honest living—along with a new bride—on the eve of the Great Depression. Sutton was laid off from his landscaping job a week after his wife told him she was pregnant. "Right there, I began to think about making money the way I knew best," wrote Sutton.

Sutton started kicking around the shortcomings of the Ozone Park heist and remembered the two employees lingering outside, ready to open the bank.

Why chop through inches of concrete and steel, Sutton thought, when the waiting employees could be forced to open the vault at gunpoint? Why not *be* the employees? "That is the answer," wrote Sutton. "A uniform provided automatic entrée. Ring the bell and you could walk right in." Hence Willie "The Actor" was born. Sutton used theatrical costume houses to outfit himself with enough disguises—cop, mailman, fireman, security guard—to make the Village People jealous.

Next Sutton went looking for a partner and found one in Jack Bassett, a trustworthy prison buddy who had been sprung from Dannemora and was looking for work. Now it was time to test run for the Method. On October 28, 1930, Sutton disguised himself as a Western Union delivery man and knocked over the M. Rosenthal and Sons jewelry store, which was on Broadway between 50th and 51st Streets—practically in the heart of Times Square. He bagged $150,000 worth of gems and jewelry, which he fenced through the infamous Dutch Schultz, who was running most of the rackets in the city. "I doubt very much that there could be a recital of crime so daring in New York," a judge would later say.

Sutton and Bassett considered themselves ready for a bank. Sutton had been eyeing one in Jamaica, Queens, and he set himself to study it more closely, specifically the comings and goings of its employees. Sutton called the bank and asked for the name of the manager. He sent himself a Western Union telegram just to get the envelope, and typed up a phony telegram to the bank manager. Presto—a key prop was ready. "I was beginning to think of this as a drama, with myself as director and main actor," Sutton recalled. Together with Bassett, Sutton carefully rehearsed their roles.

The morning of the robbery Sutton whipped out his makeup box for the first time and spent time flattening his nose and lightening his complexion. Then he donned a Western Union uniform and paid the bank a visit an hour before it was set to open. After the guard entered, Sutton waited a minute, then knocked on the door. It opened a cautious inch or two, but when the guard saw the uniform he opened it all the way.

"I got a telegram for the boss," Sutton cheerfully announced.

When the guard took Sutton's offered clipboard and pencil, Sutton reached down and took the guard's gun. Jack Bassett appeared with another gun and closed the bank door behind him. The show had begun.

Thirty minutes later, the first bank employee arrived, exactly as Sutton had expected. "It's a wonderful day, Fred," he called to the guard.

"That's what you think," replied the guard.

When the manager arrived, Sutton approached him with the gun. "All I want you to do is open the vault. It would be very silly to refuse."

Apparently the manager agreed with Sutton's logic. He opened the vault without complaint. Sutton helped himself to $48,000 in crisp new bills, then told the frightened employees that a third man was waiting outside. If anyone bolted after them, they'd get shot. Of course employees could use the phone to call the cops, but that didn't bother Sutton, since he knew it would take the first squad car at least 10 minutes to respond. Sutton and Bassett would be long gone by then. The drama was an amazing success, with Sutton giving himself rave reviews. "This," Sutton decided, "would be my technique from now on."

Willie the Actor, along with Bassett, used a variety of rouses and disguises—postal worker, cop, window cleaner with sponge—on at least a dozen more banks. It became fun to spot some of the code signals bank guards and managers used to warn one another in case of trouble. For instance, window blinds might be pulled halfway up until the bank guard pulled them up all the way, giving the signal that all was fine. Once Sutton told a bank guard to turn up the calendar in the front window. "I thought he was going to fall right through the floor," recalled Sutton.

The technique was wonderful, but trouble came from the best supporting actor. Bassett, flush with money for the first time in a long time, felt rich enough to start cheating on his wife. When the wife got wise to his tomcatting, she turned both Bassett and Sutton in to the cops. "Me? A rob-ber?" Sutton protested, trying to play the part of the innocent rube. "I'm not a rob-ber." But fingerprints matched up; Sutton was indeed the robber they were looking for. Sutton was sent back to Sing Sing in June 1931, five years after he'd left it. A year and a half later, Sutton made his first prison escape when he fit two nine-foot ladders together and scaled the wall.

Eager to resume the drama, Sutton hooked up with his old pal Eddie Wilson and a new robber named Joe Perlango to rob the Corn Exchange Bank, on 110th Street between Amsterdam Avenue and Broadway, which netted the trio $30,000. Not the take of a lifetime, but it was enough to move to another city and make a new start for himself.

New York City cops were too wise to the Sutton technique, so after New Year's 1933, Sutton moved

A bank robber, Sutton was arrested in Brooklyn, New York, without incident. He was spotted by a citizen who had seen Sutton's wanted flyer and notified the local police after seeing Sutton on the subway in New York City.

to West Philadelphia, where he found an apartment for himself and his new girlfriend, Olga. (Sutton's wife, Louise, had already left him.) Eddie Wilson would bring his girlfriend down to visit, and the foursome watched football games at nearby Franklin Field on the University of Pennsylvania campus. But all the while Sutton was casing his new city for a juicy target and found one at the Corn Exchange Bank at 60th and Market, not far from a busy elevated train station. "We'd been lucky with one Corn Exchange," Sutton reasoned, "we might be lucky with another."

Sutton noticed that the bank's mail slot was fairly small, so he rented a postal worker's uniform and made up a phony package that couldn't possibly fit it. Then on January 15, 1934, Sutton took his package in a leather pouch to the bank an hour before it opened. A tired-looking guard peeked through the glass and decided to let him in. Sutton pulled his gun, and his two partners—Wilson and Perlango—entered behind him. As bank employees would enter for the money, the three would round them up and tell them to behave or risk a bullet. When the manager finally arrived, Sutton forced him to open the vault and put $160,000 in cash into his leather pouch. As they were about to make their getaway, Sutton was surprised to see that customers had already begun to line up outside. Sutton sent Wilson and Perlango outside to their getaway car and told the customers it'd only be a few more minutes. When he heard the car start up, he exited the bank, locking the door behind him. "Just another minute," he told the puzzled customers. Who was this guy?

The next day the newspaper supplied the answer: Law enforcement officials branded the Corn Exchange Bank heist a Willie Sutton job. "They recognized my technique, all right," recalled Sutton, "and according to newspapers, police of both cities were searching intensively for me." However, the law found Wilson and Perlango first and engaged in a brief shootout in New York City that would leave Wilson blinded by a bullet to the head. The squeeze was put on Perlango, who told them exactly where to find Willie the Actor.

A 15-man team of NYPD and Philly cops armed with tommy guns stormed Sutton's West Philly apartment and arrested him on February 5, 1934. He was sentenced to 25 to 50 years at Eastern State Penitentiary, an old prison known for keeping inmates in solitary confinement. "From its birth the Eastern State Pen had a bad name," wrote Sutton, who would be a guest of the prison for over a decade. Entering during the height of the Depression, Sutton would pop out—quite literally—at the tail end of World War II.

On April 3, 1945, Sutton and 11 other convicts performed a daring escape from the prison, tunneling under the huge walls and right up onto Fairmount Avenue, a busy city thoroughfare. Unfortunately for Sutton, two beat cops happened to be walking by across the street and rounded up the escapees. Sutton was given a life term and transferred to another tough Philly jail: Holmesburg Prison. On February 10, 1947, Willie Sutton and four other prisoners stole a set of guard uniforms and marched across the yard with two huge ladders.

Spotlights swung in their direction. Sutton cried out, "It's okay!"

The bluff was lame, but it bought Sutton and his friends enough time to scale the wall, hijack an early morning milk truck, and race toward downtown Philadelphia. The group split up, and hours later Sutton ducked out of the cold snow and hitched a ride from a kindly man who was headed to Princeton, New Jersey. The man had a late-edition paper on the seat next to him. Sutton glanced over and saw his own face staring back at him.

"I hear they got all of 'em by now," the driver said cheerfully.

"I'm glad of that," Sutton said.

After getting dropped off in Princeton, Sutton wandered in the snowy dark all night, thinking the cops would find his frozen corpse in the middle of New Jersey. Luckily, another drive gave him a lift all the way to the Bronx, and soon Sutton set himself up

with a new alias—"Eddie Lynch"—and a new job as an orderly at a hospital for the infirm on Staten Island. The job left him with enough time to take trains and wander odd corners of New York City, and before long Sutton was getting that old feeling again.

On a walk through Sunnyside, Queens, Sutton passed the Manufacturer's Trust Company. "Almost unconsciously my mind photographed the bank entrance, the condition of its roof, the depth of the plot on which it was situated, and the number of people who were going in and out of the establishment," recalled Sutton.

On March 9, 1950, the Manufacturer's Trust Company in Sunnyside was hit, and the three bandits got away with $63,933.

Weekdays, "Eddie Lynch" cleaned hospital halls with a mop; on weekends, Willie Sutton and some bank robbing buddies mopped up at small banks in New York and New Jersey. It was the perfect cover. Once a nurse saw Willie Sutton's photograph in the New York *Daily News* after he had landed on the FBI's Ten Most Wanted list and confronted him. "Hello, Willie Sutton."

"What did you call me?" Sutton asked.

"I'm calling you Willie Sutton. Here's your picture in the paper."

"You kidding me?" Sutton laughed. "You think I'd be working in this dump at ninety dollars a month if I was this person?"

Of course he would.

In late February 1952, Sutton was riding the BMT subway when he noticed a young guy giving him strange looks. Sutton's eyes darted down to the guy's shoes; they were black suede. No cop—even a plainclothesman—would be caught dead in black suede "hepcat" shoes. He shrugged off the incident as paranoia. When he left the station, Sutton walked to his car and discovered his battery had died. He started to change it himself when two cops approached and asked if he needed help.

"This damn battery's gone sour," Sutton said.

"Let's see your license."

The bank robber handed over the papers, which seemed to satisfy the officers. Sutton continued to fiddle with the battery.

Unbeknownst to Sutton, that young man with the black suede shoes had trailed Sutton as he emerged from the BMT, and tipped off the two cops who had approached him. They promptly ran to the station house to grab a detective, and before long Sutton heard a voice behind him.

"You'd better come to the station house with us."

Sutton turned. One of the original cops was standing there, along with a detective. "Why?"

"You look like Willie Sutton."

"Do I look like a bank robber to you?" Sutton replied.

"That's the point. Come on."

Once in a custody, after a fingerprint check, Sutton admitted who he was.

The tipster was 24-year-old Arnold Shuster, who had seen Willie the Actor's mug on an FBI Ten Most Wanted poster. Shuster was immediately famous, which turned out to be the worst thing that could have happened to him. A local mob chieftain named Albert Anastasia watched a TV report featuring Shuster and immediately launched into a blind rage. He didn't know Sutton, nor particularly care that he had been captured. Something else bugged him. "I hate squealers!" he reportedly screamed. "Hit that guy!" Apparently one of his underlings took the request seriously, and on March 8, 1952, an unknown gunman pumped four bullets into Shuster's head and two into his stomach. Shuster was only 10 steps away from his own front door. The primary suspect: FREDERICK J. TENUTO (Top Tenners #14; see later in this section), who had been along with Sutton for both his Eastern State breakout attempt and the Holmesburg escape.

Nevertheless, Sutton insisted he had nothing to do with Shuster's murder. There was good reason to believe him; he had never so much as laid a finger on bank employees during any of his heists. Then again, there was that tricky matter of the Sutton-Tenuto connection. A loyal criminal buddy might have felt it a matter of honor to ice Shuster—and an opportunity to make a little cash from the Anastasia contract. It was a dead-end proposition for Tenuto either way; he was later believed to be gunned down by fellow mobsters, who thought that killing a civilian betrayed their own code of ethics. His body has never been found.

Willie Sutton was sentenced to 30 years in prison, and there would be no more escapes—the kind that required a shovel or ladder, anyway. Sutton, suffering from emphysema and clogged leg arteries, was shown mercy and released from Attica on Christmas Eve 1969. A year later, he was paid to appear in a TV commercial promoting the New Britain, Connecticut, Bank and Trust Company's credit cards and subsequently wrote the more candid of his two biographies, 1976's *Where the Money Was*. (The previous bio, *I, Willie Sutton*, was co-written by Quentin Reynolds and published in 1953.) The

Actor took his final bow in Spring Hill, Florida, on November 2, 1980.

INTERESTING FUGITIVE FACT:
Open a medical textbook and there's a good chance you'll find "Sutton's Law," which was inspired by the bank robber. In short, it means that it's never a bad idea to look at the simplest answer when diagnosing a patient. The term originated with a doctor from Yale who used the alleged Sutton quip—"Because that's where the money is"—with medical interns who were overlooking the obvious.

12. STEPHEN WILLIAM DAVENPORT, murderer, robber

LISTED: April 4, 1950
CAUGHT: May 5, 1950
DESCRIPTION: Born in Iowa. Alias: William Stephen Daniels.

Most Wanted Bum. Most cop killers, they lock them up and forget where they put the key for 50, 60, 70 years. Not Stephen Davenport. He was cornered by Hammond, Indiana, cops after a robbery gone awry in 1929 and tried to shoot his way to freedom. One police officer was killed in the shootout, and Davenport was sentenced to spend the rest of his life behind bars. Somehow he earned parole less than 20 years into his sentence.

Did Davenport take this amazing break and try to make a run at the straight life? No. Next the police found Davenport was boosting stolen cars, and he was tossed into the U.S. penitentiary at Leavenworth. He didn't wait around for parole this time. Using razor blades, Davenport managed to saw through bars and squeeze out of prison in July 1949. Less than a year later, the Top Ten list was created, and Davenport was named as the 12th member in early April 1950. His arrest only a month later might be seen as a kind of cosmic payback. Davenport had been hiding out as a bum in Las Vegas, where local cops picked him up for vagrancy. Davenport claimed to be "William Stephen Daniels," but a fingerprint check revealed the truth—that this "bum" was one of the most hunted criminals in the country. Davenport, fresh out of lucky breaks, was returned to Leavenworth.

INTERESTING FUGITIVE FACT:
Davenport deserted the U.S. Army in the 1920s and received jail time for the offense.

13. HENRY CLAY TOLLETT, armed robber

LISTED: April 11, 1950
CAUGHT: June 4, 1951
DESCRIPTION: Born July 21, 1894, in Howard County, Arkansas. Five feet 8 1/2 inches tall, 180 pounds, with gray hair (often dyed black) and brown eyes. Occupations: barber, butcher, farmer, makeup artist. Tollett has an appendectomy scar, walks with a slouch, and has tattoos—"Henry-Goldie-Clay," a black cat, and the number 13—on his left calf. Aliases: Clay Henry Tollett, Claye Tollett, Howard Web, Frank Woods, and "Seminole."

Flushed Tollett. Henry Tollett was serving a 25-year hitch for bank robbery at the U.S. penitentiary at McNeil Island in Washington, but escaped on November 22, 1949. His trick: the old hide-in-the-prison-delivery-truck ploy. (In this case, it was a shipment of convict-crafted furniture.) If it was simply a matter of skipping on a quarter-century sentence, the FBI might not have bothered with Tollett. But the fugitive had nearly 30 years of violent robbery experience, along with assorted weapons and kidnapping charges. When Tollett was named to the Top Ten list in April 1950, the FBI advised law enforcement agents that Tollett was fond of carrying two hidden guns: one in a special pocket of his left sleeve and another under the front seat of his car. More than a year after Tollett made the list, the FBI tracked him to California, and that state's highway patrol spotted him in a stolen car near Redding on June 4, 1951. Fortunately, the CHiPpers heeded the advice on Tollett's wanted poster and approached him with caution, because Tollett popped out of the car looking for a gunfight. The fugitive was fatally wounded in the ensuing shootout.

INTERESTING FUGITIVE FACT:
Tollett had an odd-shaped head, like a criminal right out of a Dick Tracy comic strip. The top of his head was so flat, you could almost rest a cup of coffee (and saucer) on top.

14. FREDERICK J. TENUTO, murderer

LISTED: May 24, 1950
REMOVED FROM LIST: March 9, 1964
DESCRIPTION: Born January 20, 1915, in Philadelphia, Pennsylvania. Five feet five inches, 143 pounds, with black hair and dark brown eyes. Occupations: butcher's helper, sheet metal worker, laborer. Scars and marks: imperfect tattoo: "S.J." on left forearm, imperfect tattoo on right forearm which may be "ANA" or "ANNA," or "AMA," a small brown mole on right cheek, 1-1/2 inch scar over right eye. Tenuto has suffered from a recurring skin eruption. Aliases: Leonard Durham, Leonard Durken, John Thomas Lestella, Frank Pinto, Durso Thornberry, "St. John," "St. Johnny," "The Angel," and others.

Freddy Got the Finger-Man. Freddy Tenuto was a South Philly tough guy full of contradictions. He liked a sharp suit, but somehow always managed to look rumpled and sloppy. He was fond of booze, but couldn't handle it. Though he would eventually become affiliated with the top East Coast mobsters, he would also pull a two-bit stickup for beer money.

Contradictions or not, Tenuto was consistent about one thing: running afoul of the law. He was in and out of reform schools for burglary, robbery, and in the words of the police, just being a "suspicious person" in general. As he matured, the crimes became more serious—a dairy stickup here, a Railway Express truck boost there. Then on March 11, 1940, two Philly boys named William O'Neill and Dominic DeCaro were duking it out in a neighborhood tavern when DeCaro left to get his father, James, who was mob related. This frightened O'Neill, who in turn fetched Tenuto—known around the nabe as a rough customer—to watch his back. O'Neill and Tenuto were the first guys to return, according to a profile of Tenuto in *Reader's Digest*. O'Neill hung out front, while Tenuto hid in a room in the back. A short while later, the elder DeCaro entered the bar. "I'm looking for a guy named O'Neill."

"I can get a message to him," the bartender said.

DeCaro pulled out a pistol. "Tell him that when I see him, I'll give him six of these."

O'Neill, of course, was in the room, watching DeCaro threaten to ventilate him. Still hidden in the back, Tenuto made a noise. "It's the cops," said O'Neill walking up to DeCaro. "You'd better not let them catch you with that gun," he said in the friendliest voice he could muster. "Give it to me and I'll get rid of it."

DeCaro thought that was a good idea—he was too closely associated with the underworld to be caught in a bar with a gun. He handed O'Neill the gun, and O'Neill promptly turned it on him.

From outside Dominic DeCaro saw what was going on, then rushed inside with a gun and started blasting away at O'Neill, who caught a slug in the back. That was Tenuto's cue. He emerged with a .38 revolver and started firing at father and son. James DeCaro was killed on the scene, and young Dominic suffered serious injuries. Tenuto fled, but was rounded up two days later and sentenced to 10 to 20 years at the Graterford State Penitentiary.

Over the next seven years Tenuto dedicated himself to busting out. In late September 1942, he and a fellow convict constructed two dummies with paper heads and hair clipped from a brush. Then they took a ladder they had fashioned from old sections of pipe, propped it against the prison wall, then climbed over to freedom. Almost. The pipe ladder worked with the trip up, but broke apart on the trip down. Both cons tumbled 30 feet, injuring their feet on the hard ground below. It didn't take much to round them up within 24 hours of the escape. Next Tenuto was shipped over to the infamous Eastern State Penitentiary near downtown Philadelphia. Another guest of Eastern State at the same time was bank robber extraordinaire—and future Top Tenner—WILLIE SUTTON. On April 3, 1945, Tenuto, Sutton, and other cons used a secret tunnel they'd built to escape to Fairmount Avenue outside. (For more details, see Sutton's profile, #11.) Most of the escapees were rounded up right away, but Tenuto somehow scrambled through the streets of Philadelphia and made his way to New York City . . . for about seven weeks. For a third time, Tenuto was thrown into a different jail. This time, it was Holmesburg Prison in Northeast Philadelphia. Oddly enough, his old escape buddy Willie Sutton was also in residence. On February 10, 1947, Tenuto and Sutton gave it another go, this time deciding to use two ladders to go over the wall instead of under it. Third time was a charm—Sutton and Tenuto both escaped for the long haul. On May 24, 1950, Tenuto became the 14th addition to the Ten Most Wanted list.

Tenuto was assumed to have evaded the FBI for a new record—14 years. That is, until Joe Valachi made his infamous confessions about the inner workings of the Mafia in the early 1960s, and it was revealed that Tenuto didn't escape after all. The way Valachi told it, Tenuto ran up to New York, asked the local mob for protection, and quickly found himself working as a hit man for Brooklyn mob boss Albert Anastasia. One day Anastasia saw the news that a rat named Arnold Shuster had pointed cops in Willie Sutton's direction. (For more, see entry #11.)

"I hate squealers!" he reportedly screamed. "Hit that guy!"

Valachi said the job fell to Tenuto, who allegedly pumped four bullets into Shuster. But Anastasia also wanted to cover his tracks—it wasn't considered couth for the mob to be whacking innocent straights—and ordered Tenuto dead, too. Best as Valachi could say, Tenuto was buried double-decker, Mafia style: his corpse hidden in a special coffin compartment beneath the corpse of another person who had been buried legit.

In light of this new information the FBI stopped looking for Freddy Tenuto. (Federal process was dismissed in Philadelphia, Pennsylvania, by a U.S. district judge.) Was Freddy whacked? Or was he one of the few fugitives to find a way to beat the Ten Most Wanted list? We'll probably never know.

INTERESTING FUGITIVE FACT:
The author's grandfather, Louis Wojciechowski, grew up with Tenuto in South Philadelphia. "Know him?" Wojciechowski asks. "Guy still owes me five bucks." (Good luck getting that fiver, Grandpop.)

15. THOMAS KLING, bank robber

LISTED: July 17, 1950
CAUGHT: February 20, 1952
DESCRIPTION: Born in 1906 in New York City. Alias: "Mad Dog."

Friend of Willie. Thomas Kling, a one-time enforcer for waterfront unions in New York, had the incredible luck to team up with one of the most talented bank robbers of the 20th century, WILLIE SUTTON. Kling also had the misfortune of meeting up with Sutton toward the end of his career and ended up taking the big fall just two days after Sutton. Even in criminal careers, timing can mean everything.

Sutton and Kling's joint caper was the robbery of $63,942 from the Sunnyside branch of the Manufacturer's Trust Company in Queens on March 9, 1950. The heist started promptly at 8 A.M., with a third accomplice named John De Venuta acting as getaway driver. Sutton knew that the same bank guard, James Weston, always opened the bank doors at the same time, after stopping at the corner newsstand for his morning paper. The three men got out of the car, with De Venuta leading the way. He pressed a gun into Weston's back, snarling, "Just keep walking, and you won't get hurt." Sutton caught up with Weston. "I'll take it from here," he told De Venuta. The guard was tied to a radiator, and two rows of

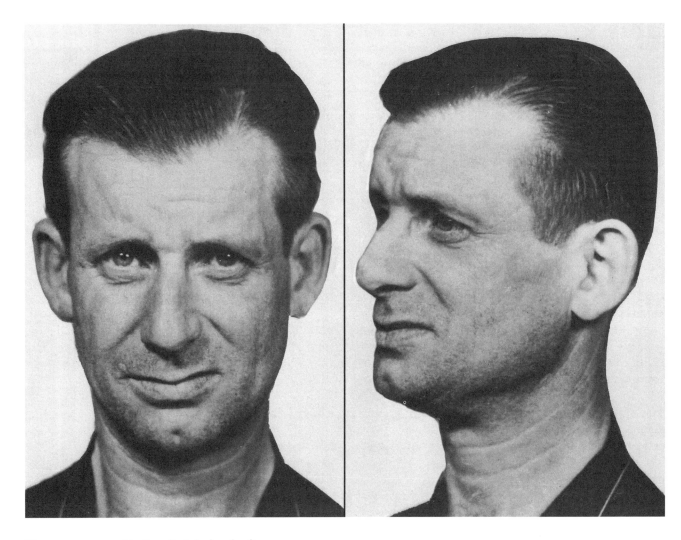

Kling was arrested in New York by local police.

chairs were carefully lined up in the bank lobby. As bank employees entered, they were led to the chairs, as if being ushered to their seats at a film premiere. The vault was opened, cash boxes were dumped into a sack that Kling had supplied, and the trio made their getaway. A smooth heist, in typical Willie Sutton style. Kling and De Venuta were more than happy to be along just for the ride.

The only problem: A few days after the heist, the FBI announced the creation of the Ten Most Wanted list. Sutton was named to the list as number 11, and not long after a spot opened up just for Kling, his number two man. Oddly enough, Kling stayed on the lam as long as Sutton did. On February 18, 1952, a 24-year-old Brooklyn man named Arnold Shuster fingered Sutton to the cops, and just two days later the cops descended upon Kling in his 18th Street

apartment in Manhattan. (Whether or not Sutton ratted out Kling is unknown.) De Venuta ended up turning state's evidence against his former partners, who both were slapped with prison terms of 29 years. Sutton's name would go down in bank robbery history, while Kling's exists only as a footnote.

INTERESTING FUGITIVE FACT:
Kling's first recorded arrest took place in 1916, when Kling was 10 years old.

16. MEYER DEMBIN, bank robber

LISTED: September 5, 1950
CAUGHT: November 26, 1951
DESCRIPTION: Born on New York City's Lower East Side.

Out of the Past. In 1935 Meyer Dembin and three accomplices knocked over a bank in Sparkill, New York, stealing $20,000. Two of the robbers were arrested quickly, and a third was nabbed 11 years later. But by 1950, Dembin—who had a history of knockovers and jewel heists since running with the gangs of the Lower East Side—remained at large. The trail had gone hopelessly cold; some thought he might be dead. Still, the FBI thought it might be a good idea to add Dembin to the newly created Ten Most Wanted list. Could the public turn up the criminal who had managed to elude the FBI for so long?

The answer was yes—sort of. Dembin had been on the lam in Mexico, leading a straight life as a rug merchant. He had popped back up into San Diego to broker a legit deal and saw his face among the Ten Most Wanted in a local newspaper. "In his heyday, Dembin had been so tough a character that between crimes he served as a bodyguard," observed the *Saturday Evening Post* in 1953. "But now the thought of having to fear recognition in every passer-by's eyes was too much for him." The suddenly unnerved Dembin returned to his hometown of New York City and peacefully surrendered to the U.S. attorney there.

INTERESTING FUGITIVE FACT:
Some FBI agents believe that Dembin actually hadn't gone straight and linked him to a series of bank robberies in the Southwest.

17. COURTNEY TOWNSHEND TAYLOR, con artist

LISTED: January 18, 1951
CAUGHT: February 16, 1951
DESCRIPTION: Born June 22, 1908, in East Hartford, Connecticut. Five feet 10 inches, 220 pounds, with brown hair and eyes. Occupations: clerk accountant. Scars and marks: a tattoo of cupid or kewpie doll and "Jerry" on forearm. Aliases: James Anderson, Glen C. Baker, Jacob S. Deane, Robert S. Dikeman, Justin B. Hart, Ralph G. Howard, Richard N. Howard, Carlton H. Hunt, David A. King, Homer D. Nevin, Henry J. Pate, Curtis N. Reid, Edward S. Sims, Joseph M. Vossley, Wilson B. Walker, among others.

Taylor Made. Even though he was a thick, meaty guy who looked like a mob legbreaker, Courtney Taylor was involved in a nonviolent criminal enterprise: paperhanging—that is, fake check writing. "This is all the gun I need," he was fond of saying, holding up a fountain pen. He was right. By the time Taylor was named to the Top Ten list, he had written more than 225 rubber checks worth more than $100,000 in over 100 cities. But you can't just turn off such a compulsion, even after every law enforcement agency in the country has started looking for you. Taylor was nabbed on a vacation trip in Alabama after a jeweler recognized his mug from a wanted flyer. Sending his clerk to follow Taylor, the jeweler called the FBI and police. Within 25 minutes Taylor was surrounded by agents, eager to discuss more than 225 pieces of business with him. He was eventually sentenced to 15 years in prison.

INTERESTING FUGITIVE FACT:
Taylor occasionally wore a mustache and eyeglasses to mask his appearance and had a removable upper bridge.

18. JOSEPH FRANKLIN BENT, robber

LISTED: January 9, 1951
CAUGHT: August 29, 1952
ALIASES: Charles Rayborn, Coal Frederick Redmond.

Get Bent. Joseph Bent was one of the hardest-to-catch fugitives in the history of the Ten Most Wanted program. That's mainly because Bent was so prolific a stickup artist, the FBI originally thought they were chasing three separate crooks.

As far as the FBI knew, Joe Bent was wanted for a long list of stickups, most spectacularly a July 24, 1949, supermarket heist in San Diego that netted Bent and his accomplice $2,150. That wasn't the spectacular part; the getaway was. A motorcycle cop followed them during the getaway, and Bent started blasting at him with a shotgun. Later, the accomplice was pinched and confessed that Bent was on a bus headed for Santa Barbara the next morning. The police barely missed Bent, who hopped off the bus, stole a car, and went screeching out of town. An hour later, cops found the abandoned car on the edge of the Mojave Desert. Footsteps and a trail of blood led cops into the desert. A mile out, the cops expected to find Bent either dead or mortally injured. After all, it was 105 degrees and based on the trail of blood, Bent wasn't doing too well when he started the trip. But instead of a dying crook, the cops found a gray suit and maroon shirt buried neatly in the sand, as well as wrapping paper and twine. Somehow Bent had wandered out there, changed into new duds, buried the old, then mysteriously vanished. There were no footprints leading anywhere else.

In early 1950 the FBI started looking for a robber named Charles "Hap" Rayborn, who was pulling stickups in Wyoming, Colorado, and New Mexico. In the fall of 1950 the FBI issued a wanted poster for Coal Frederick Redmond, a robber based in Granite Falls, Washington, who was suspected of robberies in New Orleans, Baton Rouge, Cincinnati, Minneapolis, and New York City.

Joe Bent made it to the Top Ten list in early January 1951, but it took agents the following 16 months to piece together fingerprints, evidence, and eyewitness accounts to figure out that Bent was actually Rayborn and Redmond, too. Amazing as it was, Bent had been hopping around the country, pulling heists in no discernible patterns, seemingly allowing whimsy to lead the way. He had an equally amazing lucky streak, facing arrest at least twice, but each time taking advantage of a nearby car and hightailing it away.

In August 1951, Bent/Rayborn/Redmond appeared to pull his last heist, stealing $3,198 from a supermarket in Des Moines, Iowa. Then nothing. A year passed; had the prolific stickup artist been stricken by a criminal form of writer's block? Then a resident of Anchorage, Alaska, saw Bent's picture in an issue of *Pageant* magazine, called the FBI, and told them Bent was last seen in Monterrey, Mexico. As ridiculous as the tip sounded—Alaska isn't exactly next door to Mexico—it checked out, and the trail led agents to an apartment in Texas City, Texas. There Bent had holed up with a dark-haired beauty. Late in the evening of August 29, 1952, a team of agents swarmed around Bent as he hopped out of a cab. Here's how it went down, according to the FBI report:

"Bent made a darting motion with his hands toward his belt, wheeled and ran south between two small buildings. Two agents pursued him. He circled a small frame building and attempted to cut back to his car. In doing so, he approached two other agents who were coming at him. Again, he made a motion with his hands toward his trousers, as though attempting to draw a weapon. One of the agents fired one shot, striking the fugitive in the left leg midway between the knee and hip. Bent continued to run for approximately 50 feet, when he was finally forced to the ground (with a diving football tackle) by an agent. While still struggling violently, Bent was handcuffed and restrained, after which he completely relaxed into submission. He (finally) admitted his identity and was brought to a clinic, where his bullet wound was treated."

As it turned out, Bent wasn't even armed. But it would be his last escape.

INTERESTING FUGITIVE FACT:
In 1946 Bent had another amazing escape—he was freed from the U.S. penitentiary at Leavenworth after a legal technicality overturned a conviction for robbing a post office. Later, a higher court reversed the decision and ordered Bent thrown back behind bars. "They'll never get me alive," he told friends and went on the run before officers could bring him back.

19. HARRY H. BURTON, alleged murderer

LISTED: March 9, 1951
CAUGHT: February 7, 1952
DESCRIPTION: Born December 14, 1902, in Clinton, Kentucky. Five feet 10 inches, 190 pounds, with brown hair and gray eyes. Occupations: automobile salesman, welder. Scars and marks: a bullet wound scar behind right ear, operation scar behind left ear, two blotch scars on right side of neck, small black marks on face resembling powder marks resulting from explosion while welding. Remarks: Burton reportedly wears pancake makeup to hide scars on his face. Alias: Harry Halliburton.

Harry's Alibi. Was Harry Burton the pancake-faced killer-bandit? To this day, nobody's sure. In October 1947, a team of tough guys held up a private party in Los Angeles, ordering the tipsy revelers to eat carpet and surrender their purses and wallets. One guest, Robert Crane, made the mistake of lifting his head and received a bullet through the skull. The robbers fled, but one guest noticed that one of them wore a lot of pancake makeup. That fit the freakish description of longtime heist man Harry Burton, who received a set of scars from a welding mishap and tried to cover it up with enough stage makeup to make the Phantom of the Opera jealous. The LAPD tried to bring in Burton on their own, but after three years enlisted the help of the FBI and their new Top Ten list. Burton was announced almost exactly a year after the list was created. Burton was finally arrested a year later in Cody, Wyoming, by the local sheriff and FBI. His arrest was thanks to the *True Detective Mysteries* radio show, which broadcast an episode about Burton, and the scarred fugitive's neighbors put two and two together. When it came time to try Burton, however, two witnesses testified that at the time of the L.A.

robbery the scarred robber was at his dying mother's bedside. The jury acquitted him.

INTERESTING FUGITIVE FACT:
Burton was no angel. His record, dating back to 1921, included a score of forgery and robbery beefs.

20. JOSEPH PAUL CATO, murderer

LISTED: June 27, 1951
CAUGHT: June 21, 1951
DESCRIPTION: Born in 1903. Nickname: "Flat Top."

The Original Cato. Phyllis McCullough was young when she married a firefighter and gave birth to their first child. The relationship didn't

Brancato surrendered to the FBI in San Francisco, California, after seeing the INS story in the *San Francisco Call-Bulletin*.

quite work out, and eventually she found herself dating Joe Cato, a tough-talking gangster type. He wasn't exactly a dreamboat, either, so she searched elsewhere for love, finding it in a taxi driver named Herb Wellander. Cato found out about it. On March 22, 1946, Cato shot and killed McCullough in a jealous rage. He withdrew $7,000 from his bank account, then fled San Francisco and disappeared, and from there the law lost track of him. Meanwhile, Cato hooked up with the Los Angeles syndicate boys and found work as a trigger man. (It is widely believed that Cato was the guy who pumped bullets into rival gangster Mickey Cohen's right-hand man, Neddie Herbert.) By the time Cato was being considered for the Top Ten list more than five years later, he was getting married under the name "Joseph Royale Lombardo" and ostensibly working as a machine shearer in Cleveland. Acting on a tip, FBI agents swarmed the manufacturing plant and arrested him. "In spite of his boasts that he would never be taken alive," said FBI agent Ray J. Abbaticchio Jr. to a *San Francisco Chronicle* reporter, "he put up only a slight struggle. He was not armed."

INTERESTING FUGITIVE FACT:
Cato was the first Top Tenner to be arrested before formally being announced to the list. (He was rubber-stamped by J. Edgar Hoover, however, so he counts.)

21. ANTHONY BRANCATO, robber

LISTED: June 27, 1951
CAUGHT: June 29, 1951
DESCRIPTION: Born July 18, 1914, in Kansas City, Missouri. Five feet eight inches tall, 170 pounds, with black receding hair and brown eyes. Occupations: mechanic, machinist. Scars and marks: two-inch scar on right knee, small scar right wrist, scar on right hand at base of fingers, burn scar on lower right arm, cut scar on little finger right hand, small scar on left side of upper lip, two-inch scar about nose between eyes. Remarks: Brancato has a prominent nose and usually wears horn-rimmed glasses. Aliases: Giovanni Brancato, Tony Brancato, Tony Brancatto, Tony Brancato.

Double Down. In May 1951, Tony Brancato robbed the Flamingo Casino in Las Vegas—yes, that Flamingo Casino—with three accomplices. The take was only $3,500, but it was enough to propel L.A.-based Brancato to the FBI's Ten Most Wanted list a month later. That's because Brancato's criminal record, which dated back to the 1930s, was full of robbery, gambling, drug, bootlegging, and murder beefs—a total of 46 arrests. The Flamingo heist tipped the scales for Brancato, and apparently the national attention was too much. Just two days after the announcement, Brancato and his lawyer walked into FBI headquarters and surrendered. Brancato didn't intend to stay surrendered, however; he'd brought along $10,000 to post bail and turned to leave the building, most likely feeling proud of himself. That's when Nevada cops showed up to arrest him on a state warrant, and the ex-Top Tenner was all out of cash.

INTERESTING FUGITIVE FACT:
At one point, Brancato was a suspect in the sniper slaying of Bugsy Siegel, who practically invented Las Vegas.

22. FREDERICK EMERSON PETERS, con artist

LISTED: July 2, 1951
CAUGHT: January 15, 1952
DESCRIPTION: Born September 28, 1885, in West Salem, Ohio. Five feet eight inches tall, 160 pounds with gray hair and blue eyes. Occupations: advertising agent, book salesman, as well as some experience in journalistic work. Peters is a smooth talker and frequently claims to be a physician or college professor. Aliases: Dr. Ernest E. Baker, Frederick V. Chase, Dr. A. B. Davis, Alan de Palme, Russell Erskine, Philip Fleming, Dean Hanson, Robert U. Johnson, Dudley Nicoll, P. W. Payne, Fred. C. Pillsbury, Richard E. Wainwright, among many, many others.

The Writer. Fred Peters had so many aliases bouncing around in his head it was a wonder he never developed a split personality. Cons and bad-check writing was his game, and he frequently claimed to be a doctor, a college professor—and at one point, even Franklin D. Roosevelt—to pull his scams. By the time Peters had reached his mid-60s, the federal government had had enough of his swindles and impersonations, and the FBI added his name to the Ten Most Wanted list in July 1952. Six months later, two FBI agents were in the lobby of a Washington D.C. hotel when one of them thought he recognized a face from the Top Ten list. The agents approached the man, who claimed to be "Paul Carpenter," and was in from New York to discuss the possibility of a music festival in Uruguay with members of the U.S. State Department. The

agents said fine. We'll take you there. Once "Carpenter" arrived at the State Department, he snapped his fingers and remembered that he was supposed to meet with the Pan American Union, not the State Department. But by that point Peters was all out of lines. A fingerprint check later, the agents knew they'd bagged a Top Tenner.

INTERESTING FUGITIVE FACT:
Peters would routinely con his own parents, sending them a terse telegram informing them that their son had been found dead and that $100 was required to send the body home. Mr. and Mrs. Peters would immediately wire the money.

23. ERNEST TAIT, burglar, safecracker

LISTED: July 11, 1951
CAUGHT: July 12, 1951
DESCRIPTION: Born January 1, 1911, in Indianapolis, Indiana. Six feet 1/2 inch tall, 163 pounds with dark brown hair and brown eyes. Education: eighth grade. Occupations: laborer, automobile mechanic. Scars and marks: several small moles on forearms, five vertical scars below left knee, vertical scar between nose and upper lip. Characteristics: Has high cheek bones and thick lips; reported to have impediment in speech. Subject is believed to be armed and very dangerous. He has escaped several times, recently after a running gun battle with police officers. Aliases: Theodore Lawrence, Ted Malloy, Theodore Malloy, Ted Maloy, Emil Tait, Ernest Tate, Ernest Willhelm, George Wilson, Ted Wilson.

Fried Chicken. It was 10:15 P.M. on July 11, 1951. Ernie Tait sat himself down at a diner in Coral Gables, Florida, and ordered a fried chicken dinner and coffee. Then he pulled out a newspaper and started to skim the headlines. The waiter brought the food, but Tait hardly touched it. His eyes bugged out at the newspaper. "Right away," he told police later, "I knew I was done."

What Tait saw was his own name added to the Ten Most Wanted list. Tait quietly dropped his napkin, slid out of his chair, then made a beeline for the exit.

Tait was a veteran safecracker who had picked the wrong box to beat on April Fool's Day 1951. That night he and an accomplice named Richard Schmidt were getting ready to pop a safe in New Castle, Indiana, when two cops surprised them in the act. Tait whipped out a pistol and started blasting, hoping he could shoot his way to freedom. Cops returned fire, killing Schmidt and winging Tait in his left arm. Tait kept pressing the trigger, but his gun clicked empty. There was only one thing left to do: run for it. Tait burst past the police and high-tailed it three blocks to the getaway car. A cop caught up with him, but Tait spun around and heaved a knee into his pursuer's genitals. Once inside the car, the safecracker pounded the gas and drove to Indianapolis, where he abandoned the car and promptly disappeared.

Tait was named to the Ten Most Wanted a little over three months later. That same night Tait saw his announcement while eating fried chicken in Coral Gables, Florida. After Tait bolted, the owner of the restaurant, Lewis Hillsberg, picked up a copy of the paper and recognized the fugitive. Hillsberg called the FBI, as did a local jeweler and haberdasher, who both saw Tait, too. Once the FBI has a fugitive pinned down in a certain region, they start working his habits. Where does he like to go? Horse races? Taverns? Brothels? Does the fugitive have any interesting hobbies? Vices? Fetishes? In Tait's case an obsession with cars was the link the FBI needed to capture him. One witness in Coral Gables spotted Tait in a late-model car. Knowing that the obsessive fugitive would probably want to have it serviced at some point, agents passed out Tait's photo to every possible auto dealer in the Miami–Coral Gables area. It was a long shot, but sometimes long shots pay off. In this case, it did—just 17 hours after Lewis Hillsberg watched Tait leave his restaurant.

At about 3:45 P.M. on July 12 a service manager named Hugh O. Chaney called the FBI and said he thought Tait was in his motor shop.

"If there's any way you can safely stall until our agents arrive," said the FBI agent on the phone, "we'd appreciate it."

"Don't worry," said Chaney, according to a story in the *Saturday Evening Post*. "We've already taken care of that."

When agents arrived, they found Tait, hands in pockets, looking up at his car, which was suspended high on the auto shop hoist.

"Are you James Marsh?"

"Yes," Tait replied.

"Are you also Ernest Tait?"

Tait hesitated, then held out his wrists for the handcuffs. "O.K. Let's go." He might have been thinking about his twin loaded .45s, but they were up in the car, out of reach.

24. OLLIE GENE EMBRY, bank robber

LISTED: July 25, 1951
CAUGHT: August 5, 1951
DESCRIPTION: Born in 1929 in Harrisburg, Arkansas.

The Busted Radiator. Ollie Embry carried pistols on his hip and shoulder—he liked the way they looked. His first arrest came at the tender age of 15, and over the next few years he racked up convictions for highway robbery, grand theft, transportation of stolen cars, and attempted burglary in California and Oklahoma. At the age of 22, Embry signed on for what would be his biggest gig yet: a daylight bank robbery. The target was the Monroe National Bank in Columbia, Illinois, and he and three accomplices planned the heist in exacting detail, from the imbedded nails they drove into the ground to discourage pursuit to the three cars they used to make their getaway. On February 6, 1951, Embry and his gang were successful, stealing $8,943 from the vault and speeding away. But a tip from a neighbor led police to one of the robbers—the teenaged getaway driver—who quickly gave the identities of his partners. Two were nabbed; only Embry remained at large. A few months later, he was named to the Top Ten list.

Once on the list, however, it was only a matter of 10 days before his capture. A Kansas City resident happened to notice that the guy pumping gas at a nearby filling station looked an awful lot like a guy he saw on a poster. That citizen notified a local cop, James Messick, who then called the FBI. The G-men knew Embry always carried pistols on him, so they came up with a ruse that would allow them to bring in their man without bullets flying everywhere. Special Agent Lee Bordman drove up to the station and complained about a busted radiator. Embry put the car up on the rack to take a look, and the FBI swiftly made their arrest. Embry didn't resist—and he didn't have any guns on him, either. He was returned to Illinois to face the bank robbery charges.

25. GIACHINO ANTHONY BACCOLLA, alleged murderer

LISTED: August 20, 1951
CAUGHT: December 10, 1951
DESCRIPTION: Born 1917 in Paterson, New Jersey. Baccolla is an extremely dangerous criminal who may kill without the slightest provocation.

Silence the Jeweler. You're a mobster. You know two thugs who knocked over a jeweler and stole $25,000 worth of merchandise. Now the jeweler wants to testify. You have to protect your boys. What do you do? Hire someone like Giachino Baccolla, a New York City–based slab of mob muscle who also did a little narcotics smuggling on the side. In May 1951, Detroit jeweler Albert Swartz was gunned down just a week before he was due to testify against two Chicago gangsters who stole from him. Baccolla was quickly identified as the triggerman, and he went into hiding at an Ulsterville, New York, boardinghouse. On August 20, he was named to the Ten Most Wanted list. The very next day Baccolla split from Ulsterville and decided to hide in New York City. The FBI rounded up William C. Cottone (a.k.a. "Willie Greco"), the man who'd hidden Baccolla, and after staking out some of Baccolla's usual city haunts arrested their man on December 10. A few days after Christmas 1952 Baccolla received a present: He was acquitted of the murder charges. Unfortunately for Baccolla, however, he had already been convicted of smuggling drugs out of Mexico and was sentenced to seven years in jail.

INTERESTING FUGITIVE FACT:
Baccolla was a former professional boxer.

26. RAYMOND EDWARD YOUNG, armed robber

LISTED: November 12, 1951
CAUGHT: November 16, 1951
DESCRIPTION: Native of Lincoln, Nebraska. Alias: Donald Sherman.

Steal the Bread. Ray Young pulled a bunch of burglaries in California in the 1940s and was finally slapped with a five-year-to-life sentence at the California state prison in Soledad. One of his prison duties included helping out with a crew that fought forest fires, and on August 31, 1948, Young saw his last chance out and slipped away in the confusion of smoke and brush. A month later, an acquaintance of Young's claimed that he was in Los Angeles, and that the two had gotten into a scuffle. Young fired six bullets at his former pal—fortunately, none of them hit—and disappeared again. By late October Young was still in Los Angeles and apparently up to his old tricks. A suspicious cop pulled Young's car over, and the fugitive panicked. He blasted away at the cop, striking him in the leg, then took off on foot. As it turned out, the car was stolen and hidden inside were the proceeds from a number of recent L.A. burglaries. Seemingly, Young had disappeared for good. Three years passed. Finally, in November 1951, law enforcement officials convinced the FBI to name Young to the newly minted Ten Most Wanted list.

Four days later, the FBI found their man.

Young had been hiding in Denver, hard at work. He had been there since December 1948 and immediately decided to try a run at the straight life. Young married a Denver woman in late February 1949 and found two jobs to support them both. By day Young delivered messages by motorcycle for a local mortuary. By night Young slaved away at a bakery, loading fresh loaves of bread onto awaiting delivery trucks. (Young had gone from sneak-thieving bread to baking it.) When Denver FBI agent George Burton showed up on a Friday evening to arrest Young—who had been living under the alias Donald Sherman—he offered no resistance and immediately admitted his true identity. "I'm going straight," Young insisted. Young's neighbors agreed and even petitioned the governor of Colorado to stop his extradition to California. It didn't work.

INTERESTING FUGITIVE FACT:
Young tried to rob a bank when he was 20 years old.

27. JOHN THOMAS HILL, murderer

LISTED: December 10, 1951
CAUGHT: August 16, 1952
DESCRIPTION: Born in 1903 in Maryland. Terribly ferocious when drunk. Known to occasionally pose as a doctor.

Hill the Hammer. "He wouldn't hesitate to kill anyone to further his own interests," read John Hill's FBI wanted poster. It would be hard to refute that statement. In 1926 Hill was convicted of breaking into a woman's bedroom and stabbing her in the stomach while she slept. He was also once accused of trying to drown a woman by plunging her head into a tub of water, and by 1950 was even charged with trying to slay his own nephew.

But the crime that landed Hill on the Top Ten list occurred on March 19, 1950—ironically enough, just around the time the list was created. That's when Hill and five accomplices robbed a 70-year-old shopkeeper in Willoughby, Maryland. They took turns beating the elderly merchant with the blunt end of an axe he had behind the counter, then fled with a small amount of money. The shopkeeper died from his injuries. Police immediately rounded up the five accomplices, but Hill somehow slipped through the dragnet. He made his way to his mother-in-law's house in Portsmouth, Virginia, where his estranged wife was living. At first Hill and the ex got along fairly well. Then booze entered the picture and suddenly Hill was reminded of all the reasons his wife was estranged in the first place. In an alcohol-fueled rage, Hill took an ice pick and jabbed at her head and chest five times, then fled. Amazingly, she survived her wounds and named her husband as her attacker. A year and a half later, with no sign of the Hill, his name was added to the Ten Most Wanted list.

After making the list, there was word that he was in Albany, New York, working as a short order cook. A short while later, he worked in a junkyard in Detroit, using the alias "James Smith." But the FBI finally pinned him down in Hamtramck, Michigan, thanks to an anonymous tipster who saw Hill's poster. Hill was sleeping in a rooming house when agents, led by chief agent James A. Robey, raided at 5:30 A.M. Robey questioned his suspect, who meekly admitted: "You've got the right man." Police found a butcher knife hidden in the room. Hill later confessed to the slaying of the Willoughby shopkeeper and was charged with murder and felonious assault.

INTERESTING FUGITIVE FACT:
Hill used to work as an oyster dredger and had stopped attending school around third grade.

28. GEORGE HEROUX, bank robber

LISTED: December 19, 1951
CAUGHT: July 25, 1952
DESCRIPTION: Born in 1930.

You're Coming with Me, Copper. George Arthur Heroux was desperate. He was wanted by the FBI, thanks to the little matter of two big-ticket bank robberies in Missouri and Kansas, and now two cops

Heroux was arrested in El Portal, Florida, by local police following a police department investigation.

were knocking on the door—his door in suburban El Portal, Florida, where he'd been hiding out for the past few months. Heroux took his gun and opened the door. He forced the stunned cops, El Portal police chief Barron Shields and patrol officer Robert Dubray, back into their own vehicle to drive away. Soon much of the El Portal police force was in hot pursuit, and a nervous Heroux started trading bullets with them from the backseat.

It all started with those two big heists. Heroux had been robbing banks for years, but none with paydays this large. Along with GERHARD PUFF (see #30), Heroux hit the South Side Bank in Kansas City on October 10, 1951, then followed up that job on November 23 by stealing $62,000 from the Johnson County National Bank in Prairie Village, Kansas. Heroux made the Ten Most Wanted list just weeks later; his accomplice Puff would have to wait over a month for an open spot.

Heroux and Puff had temporarily separated while on the lam in Florida, and now Heroux was in this strange predicament—squad cars chasing another squad car, with a Top Ten fugitive in the backseat, blasting away. Finally, Police Chief Shields decided he'd had enough. He jerked the steering wheel to the right and rammed into a tree. The blow stunned Heroux long enough for the cops to disarm him. Heroux was arrested and immediately questioned about the whereabouts of his partner, Puff. Heroux refused to say anything, but as it turned out, accidentally dropped a hint that would lead to Puff's arrest. (See below for more.)

INTERESTING FUGITIVE FACT:
A year later, Heroux pulled a little scam to get out of solitary confinement. In July 1953, while languishing in a Miami jail, Heroux promised that he would at long last testify against his partner. He was given a trip to New York City to meet with the assistant U.S. attorney working the case, but then changed his mind—he wanted to testify *for* Puff, not against him. Heroux was shipped back to finish out his 40-year sentence, but at least the ploy got him out of stir for a while. "[Heroux received] a happy holiday in the comparative luxury of the Tombs here last week, all at Government expense," wrote columnist Meyer Berger in *The New York Times.*

29. SYDNEY GORDON MARTIN, murderer

LISTED: January 7, 1952
CAUGHT: November 27, 1953
DESCRIPTION: Born June 18, 1922, in Longmeadow, Massachusetts. Five feet six inches tall, 145 pounds, with curly dark brown hair and blue eyes. Occupations: laborer, farmer, cook, dishwasher, pantryman. Scars and marks: burn scar on left cheek, three-inch scar on palm of left hand. Aliases: William Jesse Bishop, Sid Martin, William Gordon Martin. Subject is armed and should be considered extremely dangerous. He has attempted to commit suicide in the past.

A Crushing Blow. Sydney Martin didn't like playing by the rules. Not the army's rules in World War II—he deserted twice and eventually was dishonorably discharged. And not society's rules, either. On June 1, 1950, Martin shot and bludgeoned a Massachusetts farmer right outside of his home, just to steal a measly $440 the farmer had tucked away inside. (Amazingly, the farmer lived.) Martin was arrested just 17 days later and confessed. But apparently Martin's confession didn't come from a sense of remorse for his crime. Just two and a half months later, while awaiting trial, Martin busted out of prison. On January 7 he was named to the Top Ten list and stayed on the list for nearly two years. He might have stayed longer, if not for a story in the *Saturday Evening Post,* which had run a huge feature on the Ten Most Wanted program. A reader recognized Martin from his mug shot, and the vicious fugitive was quickly arrested without incident and shipped back to Massachusetts to face life in prison.

INTERESTING FUGITIVE FACT:
According to the FBI bulletin, Martin had the "nervous habit of running his hands through his hair, and walking with his head bowed."

30. GERHARD PUFF, bank robber

LISTED: January 28, 1952
CAUGHT: July 26, 1953

The Ambush. GEORGE HEROUX (#28) and Gerhard Arthur Puff were bank-robbing partners. Both would have made the Ten Most Wanted list at the same time, if not for the fact that there was only room for one. As it turned out, that really didn't matter, since both were apprehended within 36 hours of each other. Although Heroux steadfastly refused to rat out his partner, he inadvertently dropped the hint that would lead to Puff's arrest.

The hint? That Heroux and Puff had stayed in the same New York City hotel—the Congress Hotel, on West 69th Street—the previous weekend. The FBI quickly dispatched a team and created an ambush for Puff, who was still checked in at the hotel along with his new bride and Heroux's wife of a year and a half. The five-man team watched the two women leave with suitcases (they turned out to be full of weapons and ammunition) and then observed Puff entering the hotel. Something must have struck him as odd though, because Puff sneaked back down a staircase and surprised FBI Special Agent Joseph J. Brock, who had been hiding behind a frosted pane of glass separating the lobby from a back hallway. Puff took his automatic pistol and pumped five bullets into 44-year-old Agent Brock—a married father of three—and then raced into the lobby. One of the other agents hidden there shot the fleeing fugitive in the leg and then swooped in to make the arrest. Brock died of his wounds, which meant that Puff now had a

Due to an FBI investigation, Puff was arrested in New York City by the FBI.

first-degree murder charge added to his bank robbery charges. The robbers' brides were also arrested and charged with harboring a fugitive and being accessories after the fact to a bank robbery.

INTERESTING FUGITIVE FACT:
Puff's alias on the hotel register was "J. Burns," while Heroux's was "John Hanson."

31. THOMAS EDWARD YOUNG, bank robber

LISTED: February 21, 1952
CAUGHT: September 23, 1952
DESCRIPTION: Born in 1919. Six feet one inch tall, 230 pounds.

Thomas and Margaret. The names don't have quite the same ring as Bonnie and Clyde, but Thomas Young and his wife, Margaret, operated in much the same fashion—stealing cars and knocking over banks and post offices and anything else they thought might contain a few bucks. Instead of a 1934 Ford V-8, the Youngs used the ultimate 1950s family road-tripping vehicle: a car hitched to a one-ton trailer, which is where the couple kept matching pairs of rifles, shotguns, and an ammunition case. (It is not known if the weapons were marked HIS and HERS.) The burglary of a Santana, Kansas, bank propelled the two to the Ten Most Wanted list in February 1952, and the Youngs were forced to use their car-and-trailer to hide from the FBI in various trailer camps and national parks. Some Idaho residents recognized the Youngs from the posters that hung in the post office, and by late September FBI agents were combing the Boise National Forest. The fugitive couple tried to ram their way through a roadblock, but were discouraged by the sheer number of gun barrels pointed in their direction.

"Drop it!" yelled an agent.

"Shoot the bastard, Tom! Shoot them, shoot them!" yelled Margaret, according to the *Saturday Evening Post*.

Young surrendered without resistance anyway, making the Youngs' last encounter with law enforcement very different from Bonnie and Clyde's. In other words, they lived.

INTERESTING FUGITIVE FACT:
Even though Margaret Young played the Bonnie to Thomas Young's Clyde, she was not added to the Top Ten list. It would be nearly 20 years before the list would include its first female fugitive.

32. KENNETH LEE MAURER, murderer

LISTED: February 27, 1952
CAUGHT: January 8, 1953
DESCRIPTION: Born December 16, 1932, in Dearborn, Michigan. Five feet 10 inches, 150 pounds, with dark brown hair and blue eyes. Occupations: tree trimmer, gardener, store clerk. Remarks: Maurer has noticeable freckles, protruding ears, teeth slightly protruding, is stoop-shouldered, is interested in Boy Scout lore in which he is thoroughly trained, and is also fond of all forms of horticulture. Maurer is being sought for multiple murders. He may be armed and should be considered dangerous. He has displayed occasional fits of temper in the past and extreme care should be exercised in approaching him.

WANTED BY THE FBI

UNLAWFUL FLIGHT TO AVOID PROSECUTION (MURDER)

Photograph taken 1949   Photograph taken 1950

KENNETH LEE MAURER

DESCRIPTION

Age 18, born December 16, 1932, Dearborn, Michigan; Height, 5'10"; Weight, 150 pounds; Build, slender; Eyes, blue; Hair, dark brown; Complexion, medium; Race, white; Nationality, American; Education, tenth grade; Occupations, tree trimmer, gardener, store clerk. Remarks, has noticeable freckles, protruding ears, teeth slightly protruding, is stoop-shouldered, is interested in Boy Scout lore in which he is thoroughly trained, is fond of all forms of horticulture. FBI Number 929,302 A

Fingerprint Classification: No fingerprints available.

CAUTION

MAURER IS BEING SOUGHT FOR MULTIPLE MURDERS. HE MAY BE ARMED AND SHOULD BE CONSIDERED DANGEROUS. HE HAS DISPLAYED OCCASIONAL FITS OF TEMPER IN THE PAST AND EXTREME CARE SHOULD BE EXERCISED IN APPROACHING HIM.

A complaint was filed before a U. S. District Judge, December 3, 1951, at Detroit, Michigan, charging Maurer with a violation of Title 18, U. S. Code, Section 1073, in that he fled from the state of Michigan to avoid prosecution for the crime of murder.

If you are in possession of any information regarding the whereabouts of this individual, please communicate with the undersigned, or with the nearest office of the Federal Bureau of Investigation, U. S. Department of Justice, the local address and telephone number of which are set forth on the reverse side of this notice.

JOHN EDGAR HOOVER, DIRECTOR
FEDERAL BUREAU OF INVESTIGATION
UNITED STATES DEPARTMENT OF JUSTICE
WASHINGTON, D. C.
TELEPHONE, NATIONAL 7117

Wanted Flyer No. 81
December 7, 1951

Maurer, working at a local cabinet shop, was arrested in Miami, Florida, after several customers saw his published photograph and contacted the FBI. Because of Maurer's fear of flying, he was allowed to return to Detroit by train to face murder charges.

The Boy Scout. Kenneth Maurer was a huge believer in the Boy Scouts of America and their various survival techniques. Apparently, however, Maurer never earned a merit badge in family relations. On one crisp November night in 1951 Maurer took his Boy Scout knife and stabbed his mother 36 times, then hacked his own 11-year-old sister four times. Both died from their wounds, leaving Kenneth's father to come home from work and discover a bloody slaughterhouse inside his otherwise quiet Detroit home. At first Kenneth was thought to be a kidnap victim, but missing photographs from family albums—all photos with Kenneth in them—forced investigators to shift gears and consider the horrific possibility: that the 18-year-old had snapped and butchered his own family.

A manhunt ensued, with various tips indicating that the teen slayer had fled south to Florida. Maurer was named to the Ten Most Wanted list the following February. It wasn't until a year later when several Miami-area shoppers noticed that the young fellow who seemed so handy with a saw at the cabinet shop looked a lot like this awful Maurer guy. FBI agents arrived at the shop a day later and confirmed that "John Arthur Blotz" was actually Maurer. The killer confessed to his mother's slaying, but claimed he didn't remember butchering his sister. Either way, Maurer was committed to an insane asylum, where he remained until he went missing on May 12, 1964, only to be found dead in a reservoir near the asylum grounds. It is still not known if the death was accidental or a suicide.

INTERESTING FUGITIVE FACT:
Because Maurer had a morbid fear of flying, he was allowed to return to Detroit by train to face his murder charges.

33. ISAIE ALDY BEAUSOLEIL, murderer

LISTED: March 3, 1952
CAUGHT: June 25, 1953
DESCRIPTION: Born April 21, 1902, in Simcoe County, Ontario, Canada. Five feet 10 inches tall, 170 pounds, with dark brown hair and brown eyes. Occupations: store clerk, auto mechanic. Scars and marks: deep dimple in point of chin, diagonal scar at first joint of left little finger. Aliases: Albert C. Amos, Aldie Beausoleil, Aldie Isaic Beausoleil, Aldie Isis Beausoleil, Antoine Beausoliel, Charlie Beausoliel, G. Martin, "Al" and "Frenchy." Beausoleil is reported to always carry firearms, and he is considered to be extremely dangerous.

Fugitive Looks Like a Lady. Top Tenners will do anything to evade capture. Just ask Isaie Beausoleil, whose fugitive disguise will forever go down in FBI history.

Beausoleil was a Canadian who pulled a variety of crimes—bootlegging, payroll robbery—since the late 1920s, bouncing back and forth between the United States and Canada. In August 1949, however, Beausoleil became the prime suspect in the murder of a 47-year-old Canadian woman who was found beaten to death in a Monroe County, Michigan, culvert. The FBI almost caught up with him in Massachusetts in 1950, but the fugitive ducked out a back door at the last minute, leaving his half-eaten dinner on the table. He moved to Chicago under the name "Raymond Blair" and not long after was named to the Top Ten. The publicity bugged Beausoleil—everywhere he went, he saw his own face looking back from the pages of a newspaper or a poster on a wall. At some point the fugitive had a brainstorm. People everywhere were looking for Isaie Beausoleil. What if he became someone else? Namely, Rita Bennett?

From that moment on, one of the most hunted criminals in the United States dressed up like a woman—heels, lipstick, bra padding, the works—every time he set foot out of his Chicago apartment. (Beausoleil was not a handsome man. In drag he was downright horrific.) Sure, it made dating tough, but it kept the G-men away. Or so he thought. The outlandish outfit disturbed some Chicago beachgoers along North Avenue who called the cops to report a "pervert" in the ladies' room. A park policewoman stepped inside, frisked "Rita Bennett," and noticed something quite odd about her chest. It was too puffy, even for a poorly endowed woman. And what was up with that squeaky voice? A wig removal here, a fingerprint check there, and Rita Bennett morphed back into Isaie Beausoleil, federal fugitive.

INTERESTING FUGITIVE FACT:
In 1951 a Wisconsin gas station attendant claimed to see Beausoleil sitting in the back of a car next to "a young boy with a bullet hole in his forehead." It turned out to be a hoax.

34. LEONARD JOSEPH ZALUTSKY, armed robber, cop killer

LISTED: August 5, 1952
CAUGHT: September 8, 1952
DESCRIPTION: Born in Pennsylvania.

Bad Eye's Last Run. Some fugitives are known as "rabbits"—men who can't seem to adjust to life behind bars and will stop at nothing to escape. Zalutsky was a rabbit six times over. From 1937 through 1951 Zalutsky, nicknamed "Bad Eye," thanks to his tough looks, escaped from jails or prison camps half a dozen times, and the last was arguably the worst. In September 1951 Zalutsky and a convict buddy fire-bombed the guard tower at Florida's Raiford penitentiary, then held the prison's dentist and his wife hostage until they could make their escape. A year later, Zalutsky was named to the Ten Most Wanted list, and it took only a month before two residents of Beaver Falls, Pennsylvania, recognized "Dominic Bulaski" as the escape artist pictured in the wanted posters hanging in the local post office.

INTERESTING FUGITIVE FACT:
Zalutsky pulled his first burglary—and jail term—at age 16.

35. WILLIAM MERLE MARTIN, cop killer

LISTED: August 11, 1952
CAUGHT: August 30, 1952
DESCRIPTION: Born in St. Louis, Missouri, in 1909.

Three Days and Two Bologna Sandwiches. June 23, 1952. The report of a stolen farm truck had just come in when the two Olathe, Kansas, sheriff's deputies saw the same truck driving toward them. As the cops tried to force the truck to a halt, the driver whipped out a revolver and started blasting away. Deputy Willard Carver took a bullet to the head and died instantly. The renegade truck slowed down for a moment while a passenger jumped out, then sped away. Carver's partner arrested the passenger, who coughed up the name of the driver: William Merle Martin.

Martin was a car thief and burglar who had just been paroled in May. Now he had a cop killing on his rap sheet, and the Missouri native made the Top Ten list in early August. Seventeen days later, the Missouri Highway Patrol spotted a car matching the description of a stolen vehicle—a car believed to have been boosted by Martin. The patrolmen offered pursuit, and Martin ran into a ditch 40 miles west of St. Louis. The fugitive was on foot. Every available trooper was summoned to form a tight cordon around the woods of western St. Louis. Three days passed, but no Martin. The manhunt was finally called off when it was believed that Martin had slipped through their trap, and it was announced that all troopers would be taken off the hunt and reassigned to police the highways in anticipation of the Labor Day holidays.

Martin had indeed managed to slip through their trap, making his way through 17 miles of hell. "I wanted to get as far from the wrecked car as possible so it would take more people to find me," Martin later told a reporter. "I bet I fell 30 feet half a dozen times. You get in those woods at night and in 30 minutes you don't know where you are."

Tired, hungry, and ripped up from sharp branches, Martin finally emerged from the woods and stole a car—which just so happened to belong to a Jefferson County sheriff—then hauled ass into St. Louis. Big mistake. Two St. Louis patrolmen saw the speeding Ford coupe and pulled it over. They were joined by two more cops, and Martin knew he'd had it. He surrendered meekly and was given two bologna sandwiches, the first food he'd eaten in three days.

INTERESTING FUGITIVE FACT:
Martin was once arrested for stealing chickens in Oklahoma.

36. JAMES EDDIE DIGGS, alleged murderer

LISTED: August 27, 1952
REMOVED FROM LIST: December 14, 1961
DESCRIPTION: Born in North Carolina. Six feet tall, 160 pounds.

Daddy Gone. James Diggs represents a rarity on the Ten Most Wanted list: a true mystery. Nearly a decade after making the list, Diggs was unceremoniously removed—there were simply too many other bad guys who needed the attention, and the trail had gone hopelessly cold. (Federal process was dismissed in Norfolk, Virginia.) To this day, nobody knows whatever happened to Diggs. His alleged crimes were equally mysterious. On May 26, 1949, the Diggs household in Norfolk, Virginia, was rocked by shotgun blasts. Police found Diggs's wife, Ruth, shot twice, and the two boys—James Jr. and Alfonso—with three gunshot wounds each. All three were dead, the house covered in blood. James Diggs was missing. Over the years, Diggs's sterling reputation as a hard-working family man had been tarnished by arrests for drunkenness and reports of Diggs's womanizing and loud arguments in the Diggs household.

A few days after the grisly triple murder, a North Carolina cop pulled over a suspicious vehicle. Instead of producing identification, a man who would later be identified as James Diggs allegedly pulled a pistol and shot the cop in the mouth. He fled into the nearby woods and hasn't been seen since.

INTERESTING FUGITIVE FACT:
During World War II, Diggs was the neighborhood air raid warden, in charge of warning his neighbors in case of enemy attack.

37. NICK GEORGE MONTOS, armed robber

LISTED: September 8, 1952
CAUGHT: August 23, 1954
DESCRIPTION: Born in Tampa, Florida, in 1916. Five feet five inches tall, 140 pounds.

Repeat Offender. Nick Montos deserves a spot in the Ten Most Wanted Hall of Shame for one reason: He was the first fugitive to make the list twice. (This trick would be repeated by other fugitives later.) But Montos didn't stop there—he continued to rack up convictions and jail time well into the 1990s. "His FBI rap sheet reads like a book," said one county prosecutor in 1995. "He's been in prison or jail in virtually every state east of the Mississippi at one time or another." We'll come back to Mr. Montos's later exploits in his next entry (see #94); now let's see where the magic began.

That would be age 14, when young Nick was pinched for possessing stolen property. Car theft, burglary, and grand larceny followed in the 1930s and 1940s, as did numerous prison escapes. But Montos's first high-profile crime took place on August 11, 1951, when Montos and two other thugs—one of them being ROBERT BENTON MATHUS (#47)—broke into the home of an elderly brother and sister and merciless pistol-whipped and robbed them. Somehow the sister managed to free herself and phone the cops, and a high-speed chase ensued. Montos and Mathus bailed out of the car, while their getaway driver smacked into a tree and was subsequently arrested. The pair wished each other luck, divided the $1,000 pay day from the old folks, and split up. A year later, Montos made the Top Ten and actually managed to stay free for nearly two years—quite an impressive run for a small-time hood. He was finally captured in Chicago after he sat in his car, waiting for a freight train to finish passing. Two

G-men spotted the car, made a quick I.D., and arrested him. Montos was shipped back to Mississippi to finish one of his many jail sentences.

Oddly enough, Montos's final crime—in 1995—involved a 73-year-old woman. The really strange part was that Montos was 78 years old, and apparently he hadn't learned a thing since the 1950s. The woman was the owner of an antique shop, and Montos subdued and tied her up while he helped himself to her cash. Once again a Montos victim was able to slip out of her bindings and tripped a silent alarm. Then the 73-year-old grandmother grabbed an aluminum baseball bat and started beating Montos with it. "I don't take any crap from anybody," the woman later told a reporter. "I beat the hell out of him."

INTERESTING FUGITIVE FACT:
Montos was 18 years old when he made his first prison break.

38. THEODORE RICHARD BYRD JR., bogus check passer

LISTED: September 10, 1952
CAUGHT: February 21, 1953
DESCRIPTION: Born in 1926 in Oklahoma City. Six feet tall, 170 pounds, with dark brown wavy hair and blue-gray eyes. Previous occupations: bus driver, chauffeur, cook, telegrapher, radio repairman, laborer, hotel clerk, and taxi driver. At this stage of his lawless career, Byrd is reportedly armed and should be considered dangerous.

Deposits and Withdrawals. In 1951 Ted Byrd had a fairly clever bank scam going. He'd use bogus checks to set up bank accounts for fictitious companies, then invent various characters to go and cash checks from these fictitious companies. "He frequently poses as an oil operator, lawyer, doctor or printing-concern owner," read the FBI bulletin on Byrd. "To give a convincing air to his assumed position, he exhibits spurious identification cards and fictitious membership cards, bearing his name or alias and the designation of some legitimate organization." In other words, Byrd had a wallet full of fake I.D. and bogus business cards to go along with those rubber checks.

By the time the bank caught up with the flurry of bad checks, Byrd would have already skipped town. During one trip to Oklahoma City, Byrd cashed 20 bad checks for $3,578. Later he cashed a bad check for $7,500 in Albuquerque, New Mexico, and then another $7,500 in Phoenix, Arizona, the very next day. Over a 14-month period, Byrd used his pen and aliases to steal over $40,000, all the while hopping from city to city with his wife and two young children. He was named to the Ten Most Wanted list in September 1952.

Five months later, Byrd himself bounced. The bad check artist was relaxing with a cup of hot joe in a Phoenix coffee shop when a man named Robert Harvey recognized him. Harvey just so happened to be an off-duty FBI clerk who had prepared and mailed Byrd's Ten Most Wanted poster the previous September. The clerk rubbed his eyes to make sure he wasn't seeing things, then ran to the nearby police station and summoned help. Byrd was arrested and deposited into a jail cell.

INTERESTING FUGITIVE FACT:
The FBI bulletin notes that Byrd "dresses very neatly and is a smooth, impressive conversationalist."

39. HARDEN COLLINS KEMPER, car thief

LISTED: September 17, 1952
CAUGHT: January 1, 1953
DESCRIPTION: Born in 1902.

Should Old Acquaintance Be Forgot. In the 1950 the biggest "chop shop" in the American Southwest was located in Taos, New Mexico, and run by that state's stolen car king, Harden Kemper. Authorities believe that Kemper "processed" nearly 60 cars between 1950 and 1951—in other words, he had his gang steal autos from neighboring states to be resold in New Mexico. Kemper's auto theft ring was the culmination of years of criminal training, starting in 1926 and including forgery and violations of the White Slave Traffic Act. In March 1951 the FBI broke Kemper's ring and charged its kingpin with conspiracy to violate the law against interstate transportation of stolen motor vehicles. Kemper made bail, however, and promptly skipped town. He'd worked too hard in his criminal endeavors to take a fall now. He was named to the Top Ten list in September 1952.

The fall holidays blurred by, and New Year's Day 1953 there was a knock at Kemper's new home in Glendale, Arizona. Actually, make that "Harvey Charley Kennedy's" new home. It didn't matter. An Arizona highway patrolman recognized Kemper from his wanted poster, and the FBI converged on the first of the year to make the arrest. Kemper had

been living there with his two adult sons and making $100 a week as a car mechanic.

INTERESTING FUGITIVE FACT:
Kemper was fond of cowboy clothes and wore fringe and boots whenever he had the chance.

40. JOHN JOSEPH BRENNAN, bank robber

LISTED: October 6, 1952
CAUGHT: January 23, 1953
DESCRIPTION: Born in 1920.

41. CHARLES PATRICK SHUE, bank robber

LISTED: January 15, 1953
CAUGHT: February 13, 1953
DESCRIPTION: Born in 1926.

Four for the Money. The four-man gang that hit the Bank of Lyons in Lyons, Illinois, knew what they were doing. "The robbers really knew our setup," said R. C. Belasick, the bank's assistant cashier. "They knew we were not busy at the time, and they knew just where to go for the money. All the money was taken out of the cages—none from the vault." Dressed as railroad workers, the four robbers hit at precisely 3:45 P.M. on Friday, August 1, 1952, just 15 minutes before workers from local industrial plants would start hitting the bank to cash their weekly paychecks. In short, the bank was fat with money. Three men herded the 13 employees and five customers into the back, while the fourth man scooped up $39,998.78 from the cashiers' drawers. Within three minutes the men were already outside and making their getaway in a 1950 model Ford. A sharp-eyed employee, hidden away in a rear office, managed to place a call to the police, but by the time squad cars arrived, the robbers had wrapped up the heist and were gone.

Two of the four—George Ellis, 27, and Richard Westerhausen, 32—were rounded up fairly quickly and offered up the names of their partners: John Brennan, a 33-year-old ex-con who spent practically half of his life behind bars, and Charles Shue, who had a rap sheet full of felony arrests for burglary, auto theft, and armed robbery. When leads began to run dry, the Lyons police department turned to the FBI. Brennan made the Top Ten list two months later, while Shue would have to wait three more months for an open spot. They wouldn't have to wait long to be caught, however.

Brennan, who vowed that he would "never be taken alive," was pinned down in a Cicero, Illinois, tavern, thanks to a tip from an informant. He and his wife were relaxing with a couple of drinks, Brennan self-assured that his disguise—thick horn-rimmed glasses—would be enough to fool cops. Around the same time, the FBI heard reports that Shue was hanging around his 17-year-old sister-in-law in Cicero. Agents missed him by five minutes one night in early February. A few days later, Shue was spotted in Los Angeles by a resident who recognized the bank robber's photo in a newspaper. Agents picked up his car, complete with Missouri plates, after it made a U-turn in an alley. Shue gave up without a fight. He had neither a gun nor a single dollar from the Lyons heist on him.

INTERESTING FUGITIVES FACT:
Both Brennan and Shue started their careers as teenage hoodlums, with their first arrests at ages 15 and 17, respectively.

42. LAWSON DAVID SHIRK BUTLER, armed robber

LISTED: January 22, 1953
CAUGHT: April 21, 1953
DESCRIPTION: Born July 22, 1910, in Berkeley, California. Five feet eight inches tall, 170 pounds, with dark brown hair and blue eyes. Occupations: cook, laborer, clerk, seaman, writer, sheepherder. Scars and marks: 1 1/2-inch horizontal scar on back of left hand, three-inch scar on left shoulder blade, tattoos of one dot on back of left ring finger and two dots on back of left forearm, brown birth mark on right hip. Aliases: J. C. Bonney, Jack Bonney, Jack Bonnie, Lawson Donald Butler, Charles Hamblin, Chuck Hamlin, Edward Hammon, "Bud." Butler is probably armed and should be considered extremely dangerous.

Third Time's a Charm. Lawson Butler, a lone wolf stickup man, wanted out of prison *bad*. He had just begun a 10-year stint in an Oregon jail, and after that, the state of California wanted a long appointment with him. A bust-out was the only sane option. For his first escape attempt, Butler tried an old classic: saw through the bars. But the bars were too thick, and the convict's arms quickly tired out. The second time he secretly tapped some pepper into his fist, then tossed it into the face of a guard while being taken to a courtroom. The only thing that tactic gained him was a severe beating. But the third escape attempt finally worked. On February 8, 1952, Butler took advantage of a fog and scaled a wall. It was hours before a guard realized what had happened, but by that time Butler was a memory. The U.S. commissioner at Portland, Oregon, charged Butler with unlawful flight to avoid confinement, and about a year later, the FBI decided he was Top Ten–worthy. A few months later, a tipster pinpointed Butler—now living as "Albert Caine"—in Los Angeles, and a group of FBI agents scooped him up and returned him to prison. His time (and then some) was there, waiting for him.

INTERESTING FUGITIVE FACT:
Butler never worked with a team. He preferred to pull jobs himself.

43. JOSEPH JAMES BRLETIC, armed robber

LISTED: February 8, 1953
CAUGHT: February 10, 1953
DESCRIPTION: Nicknamed "Zump." Investigation has shown that this criminal, posing under the alias of Frank Garfolo, worked as a pin boy at bowling alleys and as a gambling "shill" at gambling places in Las Vegas.

Four Years and Two Days. Joe Brletic must have thought he'd beaten the system. In 1948 the drinker and gambler pulled a bunch of stickups and got himself cuffed and convicted in St. Louis, Missouri, only to escape a month later from the county prison and disappear. He lammed out to Lancaster, California, and adopted a new name—"Jimmy Rizzo"—a new family (a wife and two daughters), and even a new hobby—bowling—that would keep his mind off gambling. Brletic enjoyed his new straight life for over four years and perhaps thought the worst was behind him. But the FBI never forgot about Joe Brletic, even if few at the Bureau could pronounce his last name. The fugitive made the Top Ten list on February 8th. The next day a resident of Lancaster, California, recognized "Jimmy" as "Joey." On February 10th the FBI arrived to arrest him. It was one of those Ten Most Wanted success stories that made the program seem worth every dime. Brletic may not have shared that opinion.

INTERESTING FUGITIVE FACT:
Brletic once worked as a pinsetter in a bowling alley.

44. DAVID DALLAS TAYLOR, murderer

LISTED: March 3, 1953
CAUGHT: March 26, 1953
DESCRIPTION: Born in 1927. Alias: Billy Jackson Eaton.

The Hairpin. Nothing could seem to keep David Taylor behind bars. In 1948 he was willing to slay a guard to bust out of a prison in Jasper, Alabama, where he was serving a hitch for grand larceny. He was recaptured and slapped with an additional 20 years for the murder. Two years later he snuck out of another prison by hiding in a dump truck, but was recaptured seven months later. Finally, in September 1952, Taylor pulled his greatest escape. While being transported to a prison in Killby, Alabama, the handcuffed convict broke free from the guards and leaped from a moving train. Somehow he managed to land and roll into some underbrush without snapping his neck. Still, there was that little matter of the handcuffs. Taylor had found a hairpin on the train and used it to pick the lock and free himself. He stayed hidden in the underbrush until nightfall, then made his way to another passing train—a freight train—and hitched a ride to Knoxville, Tennessee, and from there, hopped a bus due for Chicago. The following March, the FBI got tired of Taylor's constant escapes. The airplane-eared murderer was put on the Top Ten list in early March.

FBI agents picked up Taylor's trail and traced him to Chicago. They didn't know he had been there for months, working construction jobs with the Morris Handler Company, Inc., and saving up to buy a restaurant. By chance two G-men spotted Taylor driving past the corner of Wilson and Sheridan in the North Side and hammered the gas pedal. Taylor saw his pursuers and speeded up, hoping to lose them. He raced up behind a city bus, then passed it on the left—right into opposing traffic. Too bad another bus was headed right for Taylor, which forced him to jump on his brakes. A row of cars stopped at a red light prevented his escape to the left. He surrendered to the FBI, admitted his identity, and was eventually returned to Alabama—maximum security this time.

INTERESTING FUGITIVE FACT:
While at large in Chicago, Taylor married a 17-year-old girl he met in a neighborhood restaurant. She claimed not to know a thing about Taylor's criminal past.

45. PERLIE MILLER, armed robber

LISTED: March 4, 1953
CAUGHT: March 5, 1953
DESCRIPTION: Born in 1922 in Wayland, Massachusetts. Alias: Leroy Miller.

Miller Time. It was May 17, 1948. Car thief and armed robber Perlie Miller, stuck in a prison work camp in Yancey County, North Carolina, decided enough was enough. He grabbed a large rock, hoisted it over his head, brained a guard, and then led six of his convict pals out to freedom. For those six the freedom was short lived—they were quickly rounded up. But Miller managed to elude authorities for years . . . until he was named to the Top Ten list in March 1953. Then the one-time army deserter kept his freedom for only 24 hours. As it turned out, Miller had hightailed it to New Hampshire not long after his '48 break. By March 1953 he was working nights at a local diner and had just applied for a job at a local manufacturing company. It was a run at the straight life, but Miller never forgot he was a fugitive—he'd dyed his hair jet black (from light brown). That didn't help matters much once Miller made the Top Ten. A diner customer recognized the fugitive and reported him to the police. The FBI was put in the novel position of announcing a Top Tenner one day, then announcing his capture the very next. Miller's new neighbors were surprised, not the least of all his live-in lover. Even the nearby police department in Dover, New Hampshire, said that he had never come to their attention as a suspicious character.

INTERESTING FUGITIVE FACT:
Miller had tried to break out of prison twice before—once in 1943, and another time in August 1947. The third time, apparently, was the charm.

46. FRED WILLIAM BOWERMAN, bank robber

LISTED: March 5, 1953
CAUGHT: April 24, 1953
DESCRIPTION: Born January 8, 1893, in Pipestone Township, Berrien County, Michigan. Five feet tall, 147 pounds with gray hair and blue/gray eyes. May wear glasses. Occupations: machinist, toolmaker. Scars and marks: 1 1/2-inch cut scar lower right cheek and jaw, tattoos on arms including horseshoe, butterfly, shield, tattoo of bracelet on left wrist. Aliases: Fred Boone, Fred Booth. Bowerman should be considered armed and dangerous.

Old Man Running. In some alternate universe, Fred Bowerman is probably just as famous as Al Karpis, Harvey Bailey, "Baby Face" Nelson, and John Dillinger. He was a veteran bank robber and contemporary of the famed gunmen of the Great Depression, but for some reason never made headlines in his youth. An unrepentant heister, Bowerman was in and out of jail for robberies throughout the 1930s and 1940s. By the time Bowerman was pulling down a jug jack in South Bend, Indiana, in September 1952, he was already pushing 60. But that South Bend job spelled the beginning of the end. Bowerman's gang stole $53,000 from the stickup, but also left behind a bank employee with a bullet wound. The following March Bowerman earned the attention of the agency that had gunned down or jailed all of his contemporaries: the FBI. He was named to the Top Ten on March 5, 1953.

A little over a month later, Bowerman received the slam-bang career finish that had previously eluded him: a hellzapoppin bank heist gone bloodily wrong. The target was a St. Louis bank, and the haul was nice, $140,000. But a quick-witted employee tripped a silent alarm, and by the time Bowerman and his three accomplices were ready to split, dozens of armed cops were outside waiting for him. Bowerman decided to shoot it out. The cops retaliated with bullets and tear gas, and before long the gang was split up and trying to blast their way to safety. The 60-year-old heister caught a bullet in the lungs and collapsed; another robber was shot trying to reach for another pistol when he was pummeled and handcuffed. The third bandit shot himself rather than give up, and a fourth—a one-time college football star—actually slipped away and stayed at large for three days before police caught him. To the end Bowerman fought the law. He gave a fake name to cops and was probably trying like hell to plot his escape when he died from his bullet wound a week after the heist.

INTERESTING FUGITIVE FACT:
Bowerman is one of the few bank robbers of that era to make it to his sixth decade, even though he didn't quite make it through that decade.

47. ROBERT BENTON MATHUS, armed robber

LISTED: March 16, 1953
CAUGHT: March 19, 1953
DESCRIPTION: Born March 25, 1927, in Birmingham, Alabama. Six feet, 158 pounds, with brown hair and brown eyes.

Occupations: electrician's helper, tool grinder, welder. Scars and marks: V-shaped scar on back of right hand, gunshot scar on right upper arm, small scar on forehead. Aliases: Robert Benton Mathis, Robert Ben Mathus, Robert B. Mothers. Mathus has been convicted previously for carrying concealed weapons. He is armed and should be considered extremely dangerous.

The Other Half. Bob Mathus was the partner of NICK GEORGE MONTOS (#37) on their violent robbery of an elderly couple in Georgia. After Montos and Mathus escaped from Georgia, they split, Montos heading north to Chicago and Mathus heading south to Lafayette, Louisiana. Mathus adopted a new name, "Robert Conway," and set about blending into his new environment. Mathus watched his partner make the Top Ten list in September 1952 and probably exhaled a sigh of relief when there was no room left on the list. That changed when PERLIE MILLER (#45) was scooped up in 24 hours, and the pudgy-faced fugitive was catapulted to the Ten Most Wanted on March 16. Like Miller, Mathus didn't last long. A Lafayette resident read a story about Mathus in the local paper and tipped off the local cops, who in turned called in the FBI. The arresting agents found weapons and burglary tools in Mathus's hideout and returned him to Georgia to face the music.

INTERESTING FUGITIVE FACT:
Mathus was first pinched at age 16 for carrying a concealed gun.

48. FLOYD ALLEN HILL, armed robber

LISTED: March 30, 1953
CAUGHT: April 18, 1953
DESCRIPTION: Born May 29, 1912, in Fort Worth, Texas. Six feet 2 1/2 inches, 192 pounds, with blue eyes and wavy dark brown hair that is turning gray. Occupations: truck driver, cleaner, painter, farmer, barber, tailor, salesman. Scars and marks: cut scar on upper center forehead, noticeable raised flesh mole above outer corner left eyebrow, tattoo of a rose outside upper right arm, dimple in chin. Aliases: Clyde John Cole, J. C. Cole, Floyd Alton Hill, Floyd C. Hill, Jess Hill, Jess O'Dell, Jessee O'Dell, Jack Winters, "Iron Jaw," and "Tex." Hill is known to be armed and should be considered extremely dangerous. He has escaped custody in the past and once entangled in a running gun battle with law enforcement officers attempting to apprehend him.

Cuban Heels. Some crooks rob banks. Some pick on innocent people on the street. Still others might choose supermarkets, loan offices, or even gas stations. Floyd Hill didn't think in terms of usual robberies. On October 3, 1952, Hill and three accomplices pulled off what might be considered a combination con game/armed robbery. They pretended to be weapons dealers and agreed to meet with Cuban revolutionaries who wanted to buy guns to overthrow Fulgencio Batista and reinstate President Carlos Prio Socarras. The meeting place was the luxurious Western Hills Hotel in Fort Worth, Texas. The two Cubans sat inside their cabana, waiting for their contact to arrive. Instead, three gunmen burst in and subdued them, binding their hands and feet with wire. A tall man wearing a hood and carrying a Thompson submachine gun entered the room, then promptly relieved the revolutionaries of the $280,000 they had brought along. The man in the hood? Floyd Hill.

Hill didn't get involved in international robbery scams overnight. "I got kicked out of my home by a stepfather when I was 10 years old," he told a reporter later. "I hung around with older men, and learned to be a criminal from them." Car thefts, burglaries, and armed robberies followed, as did stints in Alcatraz. The Cuban caper, though, was the highlight of his career. After the loot was split up, Hill immediately buried his share (some $120,000), but was lured back to the spot by his third wife a month later. Hill was cuffed and shipped off to Tarrant County jail. This worried Hill—there were too many angry Cubans running around, probably gunning for his head—so he decided to make a break for it. "It wasn't a jail break at all," Hill said later. "I just walked out. Those boys [younger prisoners] who went with me had no idea what was going on. I left with my hat and my coat and a pocket full of $100 bills. Now you know, in a real jail break, you don't get your hat and coat." (Later, it was revealed that Hill had inside help.) A month and a half later, Hill made the Top Ten list. Again, though, he was ratted out, and FBI agents swarmed down on the Dallas home where friends were keeping him hidden. Hill was slapped with a 20-year sentence.

Amazingly, this is where the heister's life seems to have completely turned around. He forgot about guns and money and turned to art and literature. Hill—called a model prisoner by his jailers—was paroled in 1969, moved to California, married a 21-year-old model named Tinna, and died from cancer

two years later. "Floyd Hill was a hoodlum," said Dr. James Beto, former head of the Texas prison system, "but a high-class one."

INTERESTING FUGITIVE FACT:
While in prison Hill completed over 1,000 oil paintings of landscapes, farm animals, and fellow prisoners. "I've never served time," he said. "I make time serve me."

49. JOSEPH LEVY, scam artist

LISTED: May 1, 1953
CAUGHT: April 30, 1953
DESCRIPTION: Born March 16, 1897, in New York, New York. Five feet seven inches, 150 to 175 pounds, with blue eyes and gray hair, with a bald spot on crown of head. Occupation: male nurse. Scars and marks: Small wen on left eyebrow, scar over right eye, red mole on left cheek, scar back of left hand, scar back of right hand, 1/2-inch scar left palm (among others). Defective hearing left ear, bushy eyebrows, protruding eyes, dentures, protruding upper front teeth, chain cigar smoker, horse race fan. Aliases: Sidney Berger, Maurice W. Cohen, Gideon E. Doswell, Julius Fleishman, Nathan Goldstein, Samuel Hoffman, Earl Kaufman, Dr. Leonard Levins, Harold Morrison, Ralph W. Newman, Roy W. Phillips, Simon Strauss, among others.

The Day Before. "Levy ran wild through the boudoirs of the Midwest for a decade, swindling close to a million before making the FBI's most-wanted list and being captured by agents at the fifty-dollar window at Churchill Downs," writes Jay Robert Nash in *Hustlers and Con Men* (1976). Levy was apprehended in Louisville, Kentucky, one day prior to the public announcement of being placed on the Top Ten list. FBI agents recognized him from the Top Ten material sent to the field office for the announcement. Levy denied his identity at first, claiming he was "Morris Goldsmith." But the agents persisted, and he finally confessed. "When you dance, you have to pay the piper," he said, "and this is the end of the road for me." Despite being captured before the formal announcement, Levy is still considered an official member of the list.

INTERESTING FUGITIVE FACT:
According to Levy's FBI poster, he was a "well-dressed name-dropper who claims acquaintanceship with government and national figures."

WANTED
BY THE FBI

IDENTIFICATION
ORDER NO. 2573
March 4, 1953

F.P.C. 14 M 9 U IOM 10
          M 2 U IOI

ARNOLD HINSON,

FBI No. 1,048,012

with aliases: S. B. GRAY, ALEC HENSON, LEO CHARLES HILL, ALEC HINSON, ARNOLD ALEXANDER HINSON, MIKE L. HINSON, J. M. MONCRIEF, RAYMOND D. SLATTERY, G. S. TODD, STEVE TODD, "AL," "RED" AND OTHERS

UNLAWFUL FLIGHT TO AVOID PROSECUTION (MURDER)

Hinson was apprehended by special agents in the downtown area of Memphis, Tennessee.

50. ARNOLD HINSON, murderer

LISTED: May 4, 1953
CAUGHT: November 7, 1953
DESCRIPTION: Born January 23, 1913, in Jacksonville, Florida. Five feet eight inches, 180 pounds, with brown hair and blue eyes. Occupations: welder, electrician, painter, mechanic, shipyard worker, ranch hand, foundry laborer. Scars and marks: one-inch cut scar above right eye, one-inch dent scar center forehead, pitted scar between eyebrows, scar at outer angle left eye, shot through left hand, scar on right muscle above elbow outer back, large scar left knee, scar right kneecap. Aliases: S. B. Gray, Alec Henson, Leo Charles Hill, Alec Hinson, Arnold Alexander Hinson, Mike L. Hinson, J. M. Moncrief, Raymond D. Slattery, G. S. Todd, Steve Todd, "Al," "Red," and others.

Crazy 50. The 50th member of the Top Ten list, Arnold Hinson was special: He is one of the few fugitives from the 1950s to be certified "psychotic" by psychiatrists at a prison hospital in Atlanta, Georgia. His crimes weren't necessarily horrific—mostly car thefts, with a little grand larceny and prison breaks thrown in for good measure. (The FBI would later refer to him as a "nomadic car thief.") It was Hinson's violent attitude that alarmed the shrinks in 1945, when they examined him. But just three years later, prison officials thought Hinson was fit to re-enter society. Their judgment seemed correct for a while. Hinson settled down, got married, and seemed to be cured.

That was until June 17, 1952, when cops discovered a ranch hand named Edward Howard beaten, shot, and dumped in a Montana field. He had been last seen drinking with Hinson and his wife, Judy, the night before. Hinson was suspect number one, and in less than a year his name would appear in the Top Ten list. Hinson and his wife were finally spotted by an FBI agent on November 7, 1953. They were relaxing in a car in downtown Memphis, reading newspapers, when G-men with guns surrounded them. Contrary to his diagnosis, the "psychotic" Hinson surrendered without a fight and later pled guilty to Howard's murder.

INTERESTING FUGITIVE FACT:
There was one last flight left in the 50th fugitive. In January 1964 Hinson broke out of a prison mental ward and managed to stay free for three days until he was recaptured.

WANTED BY THE FBI

UNLAWFUL FLIGHT TO AVOID PROSECUTION (MURDER)

Photographs taken May 8, 1952   Photograph taken January 20, 1948

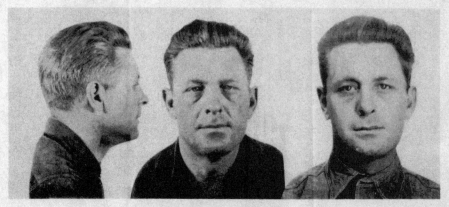

ARNOLD HINSON

with aliases: S. B. Gray, Alec Henson, Leo Charles Hill, Alec Hinson, Arnold Alexander Hinson, Mike L. Hinson, J. M. Moncrief, Raymond D. Slattery, G. S. Todd, Steve Todd, "Al," "Red" and others

DESCRIPTION

Age 40, born January 23, 1913, Jacksonville, Florida; Height, 5'8"; Weight, 180 pounds; Build, stocky; Hair, brown; Eyes, blue; Complexion, medium; Race, white; Nationality, American; Occupations, welder, electrician, painter, mechanic, shipyard worker, ranch hand, foundry laborer, service station attendant; Scars and marks, 1" cut scar above right eye, 1" dent scar center forehead, pitted scar between eyebrows, ½" scar over outer corner of right brow, scar at outer angle left eye, shot through left hand, 2" oblique scar at left elbow, front, ½" oblique scar on base of right thumb rear, scar on right muscle above elbow outer back, large scar left knee, scar right kneecap. FBI No. 1,048,012

Fingerprint Classification: $\dfrac{14\ \text{M}\ 9\ \text{U}\ \text{IOM}\ 10}{\text{M}\ 2\ \text{U}\ \text{IOI}}$

CRIMINAL RECORD

Hinson has been convicted previously for violation of the National Motor Vehicle Theft Act, grand larceny, and larceny of auto.

CAUTION

HINSON IS BELIEVED ARMED AND SHOULD BE CONSIDERED EXTREMELY DANGEROUS.

A complaint was filed before a U. S. Commissioner at Great Falls, Montana, on June 20, 1952, charging Hinson with a violation of Title 18, U. S. Code, Section 1073, in that he fled from the State of Montana to avoid prosecution for the crime of murder.

If you are in possession of any information regarding the whereabouts of this individual, please communicate with the undersigned, or with the nearest office of the Federal Bureau of Investigation, U. S. Department of Justice, the local address and telephone number of which are set forth on the reverse side of this notice.

Wanted Flyer No. 119
April 28, 1953

JOHN EDGAR HOOVER, DIRECTOR
FEDERAL BUREAU OF INVESTIGATION
UNITED STATES DEPARTMENT OF JUSTICE
WASHINGTON 25, D. C.
TELEPHONE, NATIONAL 8-7117

Arnold Hinson—murderer.

51. GORDON LEE COOPER, armed robber

LISTED: May 11, 1953
CAUGHT: June 11, 1953
DESCRIPTION: Born January 27, 1921, in Painton, Missouri. Five feet 9 1/2 inches, 140 pounds, with brown curly hair and blue eyes. Occupations: baker, oiler, musician, kitchen helper. Scars and marks: shot scar on right leg above knee, dull tattoo marks on left forearm. Sometimes wears mustache. Aliases: Leo Cooper, Lloyd Lee Cooper, Tom Cooper, David Gordon Cruper, Gordon Cruper, Frank Powers, Tommy Thompson, William Tommy Thompson. Cooper is probably armed and should be considered extremely dangerous. He once escaped from jail after severely beating a law enforcement officer.

Confessin' Cooper. When the FBI agents capture a Top Ten fugitive, they're usually prepared for protestations, claims of innocence, and even cries of "You've got the wrong guy!" That wasn't the case with the arrest of Top Tenner Gordon Cooper in June 1953. He had been sought for a host of robbery and burglary charges, plus a nasty prison escape that left a prison guard beaten and bloodied, as well as a fellow escapee with a broken leg. (Both Cooper and his buddy had shimmied down an elevator shaft; Cooper made it, while the other guy slipped and fell.) The Top Ten publicity put Cooper in the Missouri newspapers, and in exactly a month agents were able to spot Cooper as he was driving around St. Louis. They pulled him over, took away his sawed-off shotgun, then put him behind bars. Apparently not content with the list of charges already against him, Cooper started to blab about other crimes he'd perpetrated in St. Louis, including the robbery of a Catholic charity for $396. Prosecutors had plenty to convict Cooper for robbery and assault, which earned him a life sentence.

INTERESTING FUGITIVE FACT:
Years later, Cooper shivved a fellow inmate and earned another life sentence for the murder.

52. FLEET ROBERT CURRENT, armed robber

LISTED: May 18, 1953
CAUGHT: July 12, 1953
DESCRIPTION: Current suffers from a severe case of tuberculosis; the fugitive has a gaunt and sickly appearance.

Bad Apple. Fleet Current didn't let a bad case of tuberculosis—or a bizarre first name—dissuade him from an amped-up life of crime. For nearly ten years Current had been the master of oddball stickup jobs, with a restaurant ($1,500) here, a tavern ($2,500) there, and even a dairy ($22,000) and a hotel ($275) now and again. He also had an oddball appearance—a very prominent Adam's apple, which supplied his nickname, "the Apple." By the time the Apple earned the attention of the FBI in January 1953, he was working up to the big leagues: bank robbery. Current was named to the Top Ten in May 1953, and the very next month he and two accomplices robbed the American Trust Company in Oakland, California, for $5,148. It wasn't a huge score, but the heat (and TB) was beginning to be too great a burden to bear. The Apple lammed out for Nebraska, hoping that hiding in the middle of nowhere would

Current was arrested after an FBI investigation on an Omaha, Nebraska, street corner.

keep the FBI off his back. It didn't work. A tipster led FBI agents to Current's new neighborhood, where they discovered the stickup artist without a gun, but with a new teenage bride. He was shipped back to California to face a large number of oddball robbery charges.

INTERESTING FUGITIVE FACT:
Minneapolis police once called Current's robbery of a loan company "the smoothest stickup in a generation."

53. DONALD CHARLES FITTERER, murderer

LISTED: June 8, 1953
CAUGHT: June 21, 1953
DESCRIPTION: Born March 17, 1925, in Burlington, Iowa. Five feet eight inches, 155 to 160 pounds, with light brown hair and blue eyes. Occupations: plumber, machinist, truck driver. Scars and marks: large cut scar and two smaller cut scars on left arm, tattoos of nude woman on left forearm and heart pierced by dagger on right forearm. Aliases: Art Barry, Donald Davis, Wayne Davis, Donald Charles Fetterer, Donald Charles Fitter, Wayne Fitterer, Dale Johnson, Dale Russell, Charles Valley, and others.

Crossing Guard.   It was an anonymous call, but it yielded an oddly precise tip. Donald Fitterer, the caller said, would be crossing the San Francisco-Oakland Bay Bridge on June 21st between 3:30 and 4:00 P.M., alone in a gray 1952 sedan. Fitterer had just been named to the Top Ten list two weeks previous; somebody clearly wanted this guy caught. The Iowa native had a long record of robbery and forgery beefs and made the list after allegedly pumping an Illinois grocer full of bullets following a barroom fight. (The grocer, Charles Harrison, was found in a ditch just outside of Denmark, Iowa.) Police caught Fitterer's accomplice in the murder—Pat Russell—but Fitterer remained free.

Sure enough, Fitterer was crossing the bridge at precisely the time the tipster had said he would. He was arrested by an armed team of G-men and California state troopers. Later, it would be revealed that the tipster had reported Fitterer to the FBI after hearing a description on a *True Detective* radio broadcast, but it's not clear how he knew Fitterer would be crossing that bridge that afternoon.

INTERESTING FUGITIVE FACT:
Fitterer racked up his first arrest at age nine.

54. JOHN RALEIGH COOKE, armed robber

LISTED: June 22, 1953
CAUGHT: October 20, 1953
DESCRIPTION: Born in 1923 in Fitchburgh, Massachusetts.

Thirty Feet to the Slammer.   A Detroit deputy sheriff named Ray Tessier was approached by a friend one day in late October. "There's something odd about this new guy on the welding team over at Ten and One Half Mile," he told his sheriff buddy. When Tessier went to the construction site, he was able to I.D. the young man, thanks to a poster he'd seen recently. That man was John Raleigh Cooke, the only remaining fugitive from a team of four bandits who had staged a crime spree in Massachusetts. Cooke was on the FBI's Ten Most Wanted list.

The highlight of this spree was a home invasion/kidnapping that, in retrospect, was hardly worth the effort. In September 1952 Cooke and three accomplices raided the home of Joseph A. Cayouett, a 79-year-old café owner in Chlemsford, Massachusetts, holding Cayouett, his housekeeper, and her husband hostage while they tore the house apart, looking for jewels or cash. There was nothing worth stealing, so the men forced Cayouett to his own café—which was open for business at the time—to take $300 from his own register. The four fled the scene with little more than chump change. Three were quickly rounded up, but Cooke stayed free. On June 22, 1953, he made the Top Ten.

Months later, Sheriff Tessier summoned the FBI, and a squad of G-men were waiting for Cooke as he descended a 30-foot ladder to take his lunch break. He surrendered with a sheepish smile on his face. "It is a relief to be caught," he said. "I knew it was coming, but I didn't know when."

INTERESTING FUGITIVE FACT:
Cooke was a repeat parole violator.

55. JACK GORDON WHITE, armed robber

LISTED: July 6, 1953
CAUGHT: August 27, 1953
DESCRIPTION: Born in 1919 in Atlanta, Georgia. Aliases: Zach Ralph Taylor, Jay Balton, Buddy Clark, E. M. Day, Jay Gordan, James Gordan, Jay Gordon, Jack B. White, and "Buddy."

One Last Knockover.   Jack White, a veteran stickup man, had been on the Ten Most Wanted list for about a month and found himself in desperate need of cash. The G-men had been dogging him every step of the way, from the Carolinas to Washington State until finally in Seattle, where maybe his luck would change. As he would later tell investigators, he came to the city to find a "whisky store to knock over." But he never got the chance. White was recognized by a cop within hours of arriving in Seattle.

Officer E. L. Parker followed White around, but was unable to call for backup since he had no radio in his car. White shook him, but Parker immediately pulled over and called it in to his superiors, who in turn called the FBI. A city-wide manhunt was launched, with cops and FBI agents sealing off all possible escape routes out of Seattle. Soon after, an agent spotted White turning onto Alaskan Way, and after a brief chase, White gave up and pulled to the curb. He had a .38 tucked under his driver's seat, but gave up without a fight.

After his arrest, the FBI started to tally White's holdups since escaping from a state prison camp in Loxahatchee, Florida, in August 1952. (The fugitive had been serving a 30-year sentence for grand larceny, armed robbery, and breaking and entering.) Apparently White wasted no time getting back into business for himself. He estimated that he'd robbed about 38 joints—mostly small-time scores at liquor stores and gas stations. Going for the 39th had done him in.

INTERESTING FUGITIVE FACT:
White didn't show in Washington State at random; his wife and 8-year-old daughter had been living there.

56. ALEX RICHARD BRYANT, armed robber

LISTED: July 14, 1953
CAUGHT: January 26, 1954
DESCRIPTION: Born in 1905 in Chicago. Five feet eight inches tall, 150 pounds. Alias: Edward F. Lawson.

"When I Married Ed, I Knew It Would Last." The scene was right out of a Hollywood tearjerker. Alex Bryant, 48, clutched his wife, both of them kissing and crying in the courtroom while flashbulbs popped and reporters swirled about them, recording the scene. Minutes later, the wife was pleading to U.S. commissioner Howard V. Calverley. "Keep my husband in this state," she said. "His escape may have

been drastic, but what man wouldn't take such measures? He served 22 years in prison. Isn't that enough?"

Bryant had indeed served over two decades in the Michigan State Penitentiary, but on January 24, 1952, he held a makeshift knife to a guard's throat and broke out. (Bryant had been sentenced to life after a number of gas station and grocery store robberies in 1929.) He stole a prison guard's station wagon, crossed the state line into Ohio, then eventually made his way out to Los Angeles and started a new life. Under the name Edward F. Lawson, he married, found a job, and worked at a freight company. "Lawson's" wife, Gladys, 27, gave birth to their daughter in August 1953. Just a month before that happy day, however, Bryant had been named to the FBI's Ten Most Wanted list. Bryant was simultaneously a new father and one of the most fiercely hunted men in the country.

That came to an end in early 1954, when FBI agents finally tracked Bryant down and arrested him on the streets of downtown L.A. His new wife was shocked—"Oh no! Are you sure? There must be some kind of mistake!" she told the agents—but stood by her man. "He's a wonderful husband and father," she told the commissioner. "His spare time was devoted to the baby and me, to our friends, our home and garden. I'm going to do everything in my power to help him." Unfortunately, even the love of a good woman wasn't enough to save Bryant. He was returned to Michigan to complete his sentence.

INTERESTING FUGITIVE FACT:
Gladys Lawson's first marriage ended badly. But she had nothing but praise for her second husband, even if he never told her his real name. "When I married Ed," she said, "I knew it would last."

57. GEORGE WILLIAM KRENDICH, murderer

LISTED: July 22, 1953
FOUND DEAD: October 11, 1953
DESCRIPTION: Born September 7, 1923, in Akron, Ohio. Six feet tall, 175 pounds, with brown crew cut hair and brown eyes. Occupations: machinist, turret lathe operator, airplane pilot. Scars and marks: small scar under left eye. Krendich bowls and plays golf, and occasionally rents light planes for local flights. He is also able to speak Serbian. Krendich should be considered dangerous. He is being sought for a brutal murder.

One Dark Night. George Krendich's story is something right out of a John D. MacDonald thriller. He was the son of Serbian immigrants and a World War II vet, flying planes for the U.S. Army Air Force, and after the war he kept flying planes for fun. No rap sheet, no arrests. In fact, Kendrich was a fine, upstanding citizen until April 27, 1951, when a pregnant woman named Juanita Bailey went missing from her home in Akron. A few weeks later, Bailey's dead body was dredged up from a nearby creek, and fingerprints matched Krendich's. (Even though Krendich had a clean record, all military personnel have fingerprints on file.) The pilot was nowhere to be found. On December 10, 1951, a U.S. commissioner in Lexington, Kentucky, charged Krendich with avoiding prosecution for the crime of murder. A year and a half later, Krendich was still at large. He was named to the Top Ten List in July 1953.

There were some clues left along his getaway trail—a cashed check here, a sighting there. But the trail ended unexpectedly in early October 1953, when some hunters in North Dakota made a grisly discovery—George Krendrich's decomposing corpse inside his Jeep. Krendich had attached a rubber hose from the exhaust pipe inserted into the driver's side window. The local coroner estimated Krendich had been dead for three weeks, an apparent suicide. Was it guilt for Juanita Bailey's savage murder, or was Krendich just tired of running? Either way, the Feds were just as happy to close the book on this one.

INTERESTING FUGITIVE FACT:
Krendich was either unaware or simply didn't care that he had landed on the Bureau's Top Ten list. While on the run, he freely cashed his paychecks, which ultimately put federal agents hot on his trail.

58. LLOYD REED RUSSELL, armed robber

LISTED: September 8, 1953
KILLED: August 3, 1954
DESCRIPTION: Born in Ohio in 1921. Five feet 5 1/2
    inches tall, 147 pounds. Russell wears a hat to cover
    his baldness.

Dead Alias. August 3, 1954. Two Washington State sheriff's officers pulled up to the blue Cadillac, which was sitting in the parking lot in front of Rosauer's market in Spokane. A tip had just been received: Two gunmen in the blue Cadillac were the

guys who had robbed $30,000 from another supermarket a few weeks back. But the Caddy looked empty. Cautiously, Officer George Kallas approached the car and shined his flashlight into it. "Good Lord!" he yelled, jumping backward. "They're in there and they've got guns!"

Kallas ran for cover behind a parked car just in the nick of time; the gunmen in the Caddy started firing. Kallas and his partner, Wes Adams, returned fire, shattering the rear window. (An innocent bystander was sitting in the parked car that served as the officer's shield; when a reporter asked if he was lying on the floor of the car, the man replied: "You're not just a-whistling I was.") One of the gunmen ran for it, but both Kallas and Adams took careful aim and shot the fleeing bandit in the head. His accomplice, 22-year-old Norman J. Wyatt, was pulled out of the car and arrested. At first the dead man was revealed to be Raymond M. Kidd. But then came a surprise: Kidd was just an alias for Lloyd Reed Russell, a member of the FBI's Ten Most Wanted list since the previous September.

Russell was only 32 at the time of his death, but he had been racking up convictions for armed stick-ups and robberies for years. What propelled him to the Top Ten, however, was a penchant for violent prison busts. The first was from an Ohio penitentiary in 1950; in the manhunt that followed, Russell plugged a cop and was deposited in the Michigan state prison at Marquette. Three years later, on May 22, 1953, Russell and six other inmates staged another violent bust-out, armed with shivs and hacksaws. All other escapees were rounded up, save Russell. The next thing anyone knew, Russell had become Kidd and teamed up with Wyatt to hit supermarkets. The truth was not revealed, though, until after his death.

INTERESTING FUGITIVE FACT:
Russell came from a family of criminals, including a convict brother who helped him escape from that Ohio prison in 1950.

59. EDWIN SANFORD GARRISON, robber, murderer

LISTED: October 26, 1953
CAUGHT: November 3, 1953
DESCRIPTION: Born March 25, 1900, in Newport, Kentucky.
    Five feet 9 1/2 inches tall, 137 to 143 pounds, with gray
    hair and blue eyes. Occupations: accountant, bookkeeper,

auditor. Scars and marks: burn scar lower right leg, burn scar lower left leg. Wears false teeth, occasionally drinks to excess, reportedly can perform complicated arithmetical problems. Aliases: James Brown, George Coleman, James Gardner, Edwin Garretson, Edward Sanford Garrison, Gary Garrison, George E. Garrison, George E. Garry, George E. Martin, George Walker, George E. Williams, George Walter Williams, "Brownie," and others. Garrison reportedly will violently resist arrest. He has a record of several escapes from penal institutions and has been armed while arrested.

Readin', Robbin', and Arithmetic. Given his numerous (though mostly unimaginative) aliases and his even more numerous scars, one doesn't have to be a licensed criminologist to ascertain that Edwin Sanford Garrison was the proverbial bad egg. Though he was a late bloomer, criminally speaking—he took his first pinch at the age of 25 in 1925—Garrison made up for lost time. He was jugged off and on for burglary, armed robbery, kidnapping, and grand larceny. By 1929 Garrison sported a quite impressive criminal résumé. Garrison, it turned out, was a math wizard, and in crime as with any business timing is everything. His skills with numbers were in high demand with the fledgling national crime syndicate. Garrison went to work for no less than crime mastermind Dutch Schultz, rigging odds at local racetracks in and around Kentucky, then a wide open criminal paradise.

Schultz's assassination in October 1935 ended Garrison's accounting career for the mob. (Rumor has it that Garrison was en route to New York City to deliver a wad of racetrack cash to Schultz personally the very night the Dutchman and four of his boys were massacred, but missed his train, thus saving himself a similar fate.) Garrison wasn't unemployed for long. He went to work for Cleveland's infamous Mayfield Road Gang, headed by future Las Vegas big shot Moe Dalitz. In February 1936 the Cleveland syndicate tried to muscle in on Pete Schmidt's Beverly Hills Club, a popular and very profitable "rug joint" in Newport, Kentucky. Schmidt resisted their advances, and the Cleveland crew burned the club to the ground. Unfortunately, the child of a maintenance worker died in the blaze, and Edwin "Brownie" Garrison was chosen to take the rap.

A stand-up guy, Garrison served his time without protest and upon his release from prison was given a nice soft job in a nightclub by his Cleveland bosses. Garrison's saga might have ended there, but old habits die hard. Brownie made his way to Alabama and became a one-man crime wave, pulling off a series of lucrative robberies. He was caught and handed a life sentence. On August 27, 1952, Garrison and 11 other inmates broke out of the penitentiary in Atmore, Alabama. (It was Garrison's third jailbreak.) He became a member in good standing on the Ten Most Wanted list on October 26, 1953.

Brownie sought refuge in the safety of Covington, Kentucky, which was then controlled lock, stock, and sheriff by the Cleveland syndicate. The heat from the Bureau became too great, however, and it was strongly suggested to Garrison by the Mayfield Road boys that he hang his hat in another city. Garrison opted for Detroit, Michigan, where he had friends, but some well-meaning neighbors in the Motor City ultimately tipped off the Feds. On November 3, 1953, four heavily armed G-men paid Garrison a visit. He surrendered without incident and was resigned to his fate, saying, "I knew I'd be caught eventually."

INTERESTING FUGITIVE FACT:
While most professional criminals support themselves on the lam by stealing and robbing, Garrison earned his way by working as an income tax consultant. It pays to have a trade.

60. FRANKLIN JAMES WILSON, armed robber

LISTED: November 2, 1953
CAUGHT: January 18, 1954
DESCRIPTION: Born in Chicago in 1904. Six feet, 210 pounds, with thinning gray hair. He has an oblique scar at the right corner of his mouth and a cut scar on the end of his nose.

Big Boy Closes the Deal. A lone gunman burst into the Wolfners' posh Chicago apartment during breakfast. It was August 4, 1951. At 8:15 A.M., John Piech walked up the rear stairs of the apartment—which consisted of a first floor and a basement—then startled the family housekeeper, who was sweeping the back porch. Piech pointed his pistol at her and forced her into the kitchen. There Piech found Walter Wolfner, 52, along with his 19-year-old daughter Patricia and her 11-month-old son Gary, who were visiting from St. Louis. So far it was the perfect home invasion of the perfect target: Walter and his wife, Violet, were the owners of the St. Louis Cardinals, and Piech knew there was a safe in the basement packed with football cash. The element of surprise was on Piech's side.

However, he didn't expect Wolfner to bolt from the kitchen and into his bedroom, grabbing his .38 revolver from a bureau drawer. Piech and Wolfner blasted shots back and forth at each other until Piech heard Wolfner's gun clicking. It had jammed. The veteran stickup man easily disarmed and subdued Wolfner, then forced him to the front door. Piech's three armed accomplices were there waiting. Meanwhile, the housekeeper took advantage of the confusion to rush out and call the police from a neighboring apartment, then slipped back in. (Within minutes, 12 squad cars with 50 cops were summoned to the Wolfner place.) By the time the housekeeper was back, Piech and his gang were herding everybody into the Wolfner basement. It was time to get what they came for.

Then police sirens filled the morning air. The robbers panicked.

One cop burst in past the front door, and one of the robbers used the brave housekeeper as a shield, slowly making his way to the basement entrance. He then smacked her on the head with his gun and fled down the stairs. Another robber raced down the hall and out the back door. The job was obviously going sour; it was time to split. Two Chicago cops were there, waiting for him. The robber's name was Franklin Wilson.

Wilson's accomplices had regrouped with their lone hostage, Wolfner, in the basement. It was a standoff. The Chicago P.D. decided to use Wilson to talk some sense into his buddies. Detective Clarence Gersch grabbed Wilson by the arm and made his way into the apartment, using the robber a shield. Then the cop nudged Wilson.

"This is a closed deal," shouted Wilson. "There must be 100 coppers here. They've got the house surrounded, and they're going to use tear gas."

Someone shouted back, "Big Boy! Get out of here or we'll kill you, too!" (Wilson's nickname was "Big Boy," and for good reason: He was a thick slab of a man.)

Still, Big Boy's plea seemed to work. Within 15 minutes—and some heated argument in the basement—two more robbers came up and surrendered: Rene Bergamin, 40, and Michael Spans, 37, along with their hostage, Wolfner. (Mrs. Wolfner had also been in the house, in the basement, but she slipped outside before she could be taken hostage along with her husband.) That left Piech

alone in the apartment. Police swept the area, looking for weapons or additional gunmen—they still weren't sure if the raiding party totaled three or four. Two detectives, William Donovan and Thomas Babbington, were assigned to scour the basement. "We had gone just a few feet," Babbington told the *Chicago Tribune*, "and there he was. Before I could move, the robber fired a shot that went right past my head. I grabbed him and we rolled over, but his hands were still free. Then Donovan shoved his revolver against the robber's side and fired three times." Piech, with three slugs in his heart, died.

The siege was over. Piech's idea had gone bust in more ways than one: There was no safe full of cash in the basement. The most the robbers managed to gather up was a diamond ring worth $3,000 and $1,300 in cash, but this was later recovered. The three surviving bandits were charged with a host of crimes. While his two accomplices stayed put behind bars, Franklin Wilson posted $30,000 in bail and promptly disappeared. Wilson had already served two hitches in prison, and had been paroled just one month before the Wolfner home invasion. A little over two years later, Wilson was put on the Most Wanted list.

Wilson should have steered clear of his hometown, but that's exactly where the FBI found him in January 1954. Wilson surrendered meekly to arrest agents at the Lenox Hotel. During an interview following the arrest Wilson blamed the Top Ten publicity for his early capture.

INTERESTING FUGITIVE FACT:
Wilson had been at large for so long, the original robbery charges against him had lapsed and needed to be reinstated.

61. CHARLES E. JOHNSON, robber

LISTED: November 12, 1953
CAUGHT: December 28, 1954
DESCRIPTION: Born 1908, New York City. Occupation: steel worker.

Have a Holly, Jolly, Christmas. Charlie Johnson at the time of his arrest in late 1954 was sporting a pencil-thin mustache, a receding hairline, and thick glasses that made him look less like a criminal and more like a middle-class insurance salesman or bookkeeper.

Johnson was apprehended in Central Islip, Long Island, New York, after a citizen recognized him from a magazine article in the November 14, 1953 issue of the *Saturday Evening Post.*

But make no mistake. Charles Johnson was a career criminal. His took his first pinch in 1921, at the age of 13, for a small–time robbery. Between 1934 and 1952 he'd spent all but six months of his life in one prison or another. He was sentenced as an adult for a botched robbery in 1934 and sentenced to a term of four to eight years in Sing Sing. A failed escape attempt, in which he shot a cop, resulted in his transfer to Dannemora Prison in upstate New York, affectionately nicknamed "Siberia" by hardened cons for its harsh conditions.

Johnson was back on the street by late 1952 and not surprisingly went right back to his criminal career. In late August of that year Johnson and four of his pals ripped off a guy who'd robbed a North

Carolina bank of $50,000. It was the perfect crime— it wasn't like the victim was going to complain to the police. What the victim did do, however, was finger Johnson and his friends as the men who'd stolen his ill-gotten booty when the cops arrested him for the bank robbery. Johnson made the Most Wanted list on November 12, 1954 for receiving stolen property.

In the 18 months he was a fugitive, Johnson settled in Central Islip, Long Island, then a nondescript Suffolk County bedroom community. A squadron of FBI agents and local lawmen surrounded his house and took him into custody without incident three days after Christmas 1954. When Johnson was unable to raise the $25,000 bail, he was remanded to the Federal House of Detention in Manhattan to await extradition to North Carolina to stand trial.

INTERESTING FUGITIVE FACT:
Charlie Johnson's 15 minutes of fame occurred when a piece about him was published in the *Saturday Evening Post* (which regularly printed profiles of the FBI's Ten Most Wanted) in late 1954. It also brought Johnson unwanted attention. A nosy neighbor recognized Johnson's photo in the magazine and tipped off the law.

62. THOMAS JACKSON MASSINGALE, kidnapper

LISTED: November 18, 1953
CAUGHT: November 26, 1953

Saturday Evening Pest. A native of Kansas, Tommy Massingale probably saw one too many crime movies as a youth. In October 1952 he was sent to the state reformatory in Hutchinson, Kansas, for his part in a robbery. Eight months later, in a scene straight from the classic 1949 Cagney flick *White Heat,* Massingale and two other inmates made good their escape, knocking one guard out with a club and using two others as human shields, making their way to the front gate and freedom.

Massingale and his fellow cons made their way to Wichita, where they freed their hostages and stole another car. Now the subjects of a nationwide manhunt, the fugitives headed due south and were spotted by cops in New Mexico. A rip-snorting car chase ensued, but Massingale and his pals managed to escape even though the Guadalupe County cops were firing large amounts of lead at them.

The fugitives split up. Massingale's companions were nabbed a short time later and extradited back to Kansas, where they were handed sentences of 60 years apiece for kidnapping. Massingale was more fortunate and managed to vanish. He was added to the Most Wanted list on November 18, 1953.

A week later, the FBI got a tip that Massingale was hiding out in the town of Las Vegas in eastern New Mexico. One of the locals had seen Tommy's mug shot in the November 24, 1953, edition of the *Saturday Evening Post*. Massingale was nailed two days later in a rundown motel and quickly dispatched back to Kansas, where he was hit with a grand total of 140 years of prison time on charges ranging from assault with a deadly weapon to kidnapping, escape, and auto theft.

INTERESTING FUGITIVE FACT:
Tommy Massingale was none too surprised when the Feds caught up with him at the Las Vegas, New Mexico, motel where he was hiding out. "It was a good run while it lasted," he said to the agents when they nabbed him.

63. PETER EDWARD KENZIK, armed robber, murderer

LISTED: December 7, 1953
CAUGHT: January 26, 1955
DESCRIPTION: Born June 29, 1907, Pittsburgh, Pennsylvania (not verified). Medium build, 145–165 pounds. Occupations: tailor, sailor, fireman, merchant seaman, and valet in various Chicago hotels. Scars and marks: scar across bridge of nose, burn scar left forearm, burn scar outer side of right elbow. Aliases: Joseph Kamnynski, Frank J. Kenzik, Peter Edward Miller, Bud Peterson, "Pete."

Mama's Boy. A minor league punk who loved the booze, Peter Edward Kenzik sported a blue tattoo in the shape of a headstone that affectionately read "In Memory of Mother" on his right forearm. Kenzik may have also loved Mother, but his wife was a different story—he tried to stab her to death. He was handed a term of one to 20 years at the state prison farm in New London, Ohio, but escaped in March 1948. He remained loose for the next five years until, on March 13, 1953, his estranged wife was found stabbed to death in her Chicago home. Kenzik was charged with the murder and in December of that year was added to the Bureau's Ten Most Wanted list.

Kenzik wasn't all that hard to find—FBI flyers listed him as a heavy boozer, known "to frequent saloons, taverns, and dance halls." Also, his upper left-hand tooth was reported to be missing. On January 26, 1955, police in San Diego, California, picked him up for public drunkenness. A check of his fingerprints earned Kenzik a one-way ticket back to Chicago to face the murder charge.

INTERESTING FUGITIVE FACT:
Kenzik picked up a few extra bucks as an amateur boxer, which might explain the loss of his front tooth and made him easier for cops to identify.

64. THOMAS EVERETT DICKERSON, robber

LISTED: December 10, 1953
CAUGHT: December 21, 1953
DESCRIPTION: Born 1926, West Virginia (not verified).

A Few Not-So-Good Men. Thomas Dickerson had problems with authority. He was booted out of a Virginia military school in 1939 as a chronic juvenile delinquent and soon after embarked on a none-too-successful life of crime. He was handed a 10- to 25-year stretch for an Ohio robbery and was paroled in early 1953. That summer, in July, with his moll behind the wheel of the car, he robbed a loan company in Bethesda, Maryland, and was nabbed the very next day in Arlington, Virginia.

If nothing else, Tommy Dickerson knew how to exploit the system. In jail awaiting trial, he first tried suicide. When he botched this, he tried a hunger strike. Though the local law authorities were unmoved, they nonetheless transferred him to the state mental hospital in Cantonsville. Tommy escaped the next day and was added to the Most Wanted list on December 10, 1953. Dickerson's kin back in West Virginia—no strangers to crime themselves—came to his rescue. Tommy, accompanied by a sympathetic uncle, made his way to Verdunsville, West Virginia, where relatives lived. The FBI was one step ahead of them and arrested them the moment they arrived, taking them without a struggle.

INTERESTING FUGITIVE FACT:
Thomas Dickerson had no problem with resorting to violence when the need arose. In his escape from the state mental hospital in Virginia, he beat a guard half to death.

65. CHESTER LEE DAVENPORT, cattle rustler

LISTED: January 6, 1954
CAUGHT: January 7, 1954
DESCRIPTION: Born in Oklahoma.

He Wore a Yellow Jumpsuit. Chester Lee Davenport wasn't really bad; folks in and around Oklahoma might describe Chester and his brother, Norman, as free-spirited, not criminals as criminals go. The law, however, took a dimmer view. The Davenport boys fancied themselves modern-day cowboys like the ones they saw in the Wild Bill Elliot and Gene Autry movies they enjoyed in their youth. By the time they grew into adulthood, however, there were few true men of the Wild West to be found anywhere. Chester and Norman rectified this situation by becoming cattle rustlers. By all reports they were pretty good at it, stealing beef all over Oklahoma and Texas and even Arkansas. They were first pinched for the crime in 1950, in Idabell, Oklahoma.

In the old days they would have been strung up and hanged by an irate posse. Not so in the second half of the 20th century. Instead, they were granted bail, which they promptly jumped, remaining at large well into 1951. They were surprised by a state trooper, who they overpowered, but were apprehended not long after. Chester Lee and Norman were each handed a 25-year sentence for assaulting an officer of the law. Chester was a pretty fair ballplayer. In the summer of 1953, the prison ball team was driven to a neighboring jail for a match. The diamond was located conveniently outside the prison walls. Chester Lee, not one to let an opportunity pass, simply strolled off the field and escaped. In the months that followed, Davenport, accompanied by his wife and young son, hotfooted it west to Sacramento, California, using the name Floyd Walker. Given his experience with cows of all kinds, he easily found work on a dairy farm and was a valued employee.

Chester Lee had been named to the Most Wanted list on January 6, 1954. A local veterinarian recognized Chester Lee's mug shot, and he was captured by the Feds on January 7. Unlike his childhood celluloid heroes, however, Chester Lee Davenport did not ride off into the sunset. Instead, he was driven back to prison.

INTERESTING FUGITIVE FACT:
When apprehended by federal agents, who had surrounded the barn where he was working, Chester Lee Davenport was contentedly milking a cow, a somewhat humiliating end for a tough hombre who considered himself something of an outlaw.

66. ALEX WHITMORE, robber

LISTED: January 11, 1954
CAUGHT: May 10, 1954

Hatchet Face. Alex Whitmore earned his place on the Top Ten list for picking up a hitchhiker. While hitching is generally viewed as a crime for the one doing the hiking, not the one doing the picking up, Whitmore made this particular ride count in a big way. Whitmore had no serious criminal record to speak of when he picked up Norfolk, Virginia, resident Ralph Williams on August 14, 1950. Whitmore threatened Williams with a hatchet, demanding his money. Williams brandished a knife and fought back, but his was a losing battle. Though Williams got in a few solid slashes, the hatchet proved mightier than the knife. Whitmore delivered several savage blows to his victim, subduing him. When he dumped Williams on the side road, leaving him for dead, Whitmore drove off with a watch, a couple of cheap rings, three cigarette lighters, and a whopping $18 in cash.

Problem was, Williams wasn't quite dead when the cops found him. He ID'd Whitmore, and the whacko hatchet man was arrested the same evening. He was taken to a local hospital for treatment of the knife wounds and managed to escape a few hours later. He remained at large and ended up on the Most Wanted list January 11, 1954.

For the next four months Whitmore stayed one jump ahead of the law, hopping from Florida to Texas, Mexico, and Los Angeles. He was apprehended by federal agents in Tacoma, Washington, on May 10, 1954.

INTERESTING FUGITIVE FACT:
When he was caught, Whitmore attempted to downplay his most wanted status, claiming, "I wasn't exactly hiding." He knew it was just a matter of time before he was nabbed, but added, "I was just putting it off as long as I could."

67. EVERETT LOWELL KRUEGER, burglar, car thief

LISTED: January 25, 1954
CAUGHT: February 15, 1954
DESCRIPTION: Born August 3, 1922, in Laramie, Wyoming. Five feet 11 inches tall, 150–160 pounds. Occupations:

truck driver, auto mechanic, laborer, carpenter, ranch hand, restaurant busboy. Scars and marks: flesh mole near right cheekbone, five-inch vertical scar outer part of left forearm, scar on left elbow, 3/4-inch vertical scar inside of left wrist, cut scar on inner part of terminal joint of middle finger of left hand, tattoo of initials "E.K." on outer part of upper left arm, bullet scar on upper right arm near shoulder, cut scar inside base of right hand, 3/4-inch diagonal scar at second joint on right thumb. Slightly stooped-shouldered.

You're in the Army Now. You're Not in the Army Now. Given his supposed birthplace of Laramie, Wyoming, in another era Everett Krueger might have been a gunslinger or Western outlaw. Unfortunately, the days of the Wild West were long past when Everett embarked at age 14 on a criminal career. He was deemed by the local court as an incorrigible youth and was tossed into the Wyoming Industrial School, a reform school, in 1936. He was paroled the next year, but was arrested barely two years later in 1939 in Nebraska for carrying a concealed weapon. It was right back to Wyoming Industrial for young Everett. He was paroled in February 1940; records show he joined the army seven months later. Army life proved no more to Krueger's liking than prison life, however, and he went AWOL, stealing a car for this purpose.

Krueger was given four years' probation for this crime. He made his way back to Wyoming—Casper this time—and promptly reverted to type, robbing a number of local businesses. He was caught, slapped with four years, and this time was sent to the much tougher federal lockup in Englewood, Colorado.

He was paroled in November 1943. Now, with the country at the peak of World War II and suffering a severe man shortage, the army welcomed Krueger back. His second hitch seemed to agree with him more, and he was honorably discharged in May 1946. Back in freeside, Krueger spent the next two years in and out of Wyoming prisons for a series of botched robberies, his last attempt earning him a five-year sentence. He escaped from prison, but was recaptured shortly thereafter. He agreed to mental testing and spent 30 days in a VA hospital, whereupon his sentence was commuted. By March 1950, though, he was back in the slammer, serving two years, then was paroled in January 1952. Career criminal that he was (and not a very competent one), Krueger was back inside the Big House ten months later, this time for helping a buddy escape from a local jail in Jackson, Wyoming.

Krueger pleaded insanity, but prison shrinks were singularly unimpressed, and he was returned to prison to await trial. On May 8, 1953, Krueger and two buddies overpowered a guard and crashed out in his car. Krueger and his pals abandoned the guard's car in Idaho and stole a pickup truck. With this act of thievery, Krueger made the big time. He was charged with a federal crime (transporting a stolen vehicle across state lines) and was named to the Top Tenners in January 1954, having remained at large for almost nine months.

Krueger's luck ran out in February 1954, when he was nabbed by federal agents in Las Cruces, New Mexico, before he could lam it over the border into Mexico.

INTERESTING FUGITIVE FACT:
After Kreuger escaped from jail in Jackson with his two buddies, a cop in nearby Driggs, Iowa, spotted the fugitives and went off in hot pursuit. In a scene worthy of the Keystone Kops, the Iowa patrolman was forced to abandon the chase after slamming into a deer. The patrolman was uninjured; the deer was less fortunate, dying at the scene.

68. APEE HAMP CHAPMAN, murderer, robber

LISTED: February 3, 1954
CAUGHT: February 10, 1954
DESCRIPTION: Born August 9, 1919, Greenwood County, South Carolina. Occupations: longshoreman, laborer. Scars and marks: cut scars on nose, chin, left buttock.

Waiter, There's a Corpse in My Soup. While not exactly the worst criminal in Greenwood County's black community, Apee Hamp Chapman got into enough minor scrapes through his hobbies of crap shooting and pool playing. He managed to avoid any serious jail time until December 1939, when he was arrested for burglary and sentenced to 10 years in prison at the State Industrial School in Huntingdon, Pennsylvania.

He was paroled a year later and worked as a laborer and longshoreman all through World War II, when skilled or even unskilled labor was at a premium. His weaknesses for crap games and billiards continued. November 1949 found Apee Hamp Chapman plunging more deeply into crime. With an accomplice he knocked over a Philadelphia construction payroll office for $11,000. The accomplice was caught and quickly named Chapman as his partner.

Chapman managed to stay free, and by 1953 he was married and living in Cleveland, Ohio. The marriage was not a happy one, if the events of February 8 are any indication.

Over dinner at the home of some friends, Chapman and his wife got into a nasty screaming match. The reasons for the argument are lost to history, but not the results. Chapman stormed out of the apartment and returned an hour later, gun in hand. He pumped two bullets into his wife, killing her instantly. When the other guests tried to intervene, Chapman ungraciously killed the hostess and seriously wounded two others before fleeing. Chapman robbed a Norfolk, Virginia, grocery store of $1,600 in November 1953 and beat through a police cordon to make good his escape. He made the Most Wanted list on February 3, 1954. He was nailed in Silver Spring, Maryland, a week later, on February 10. At the time of his arrest, he was sporting a chrome-plated .45 automatic.

INTERESTING FUGITIVE FACT:
By all indications, Apee was a sore loser; he sported nasty knife scars on his face and butt as a result of several altercations.

69. NELSON ROBERT DUNCAN, burglar, car thief

LISTED: February 8, 1954
CAUGHT: May 21, 1954
DESCRIPTION: Born March 27, 1921, Chattanooga, Tennessee (not verified). Five feet six inches tall, 135 pounds, with reddish hair and brown eyes. Occupations: used car dealer, hotel bellboy, construction worker, truck driver, lathe operator. Scars and marks: mole on right cheek, pit scar near outer corner left eye, two pit scars on left cheek, freckles on face and forehead. Known to sometimes sport a mustache and dye his hair black. Aliases: R. S. Bailey, Jessie Donald Buckner, Robert Nelson Duncan, Joseph H. Dunham, John Patrick Dunigan, Howard Dunning, W. H. Dunning, Jean E. Harper, Gene E. Jackson, Jack Robert Pittman. Considered armed and extremely dangerous. Reportedly armed with a small pistol carried in a shoulder holster and an automatic pistol carried in his belt. Also known to carry pistol in glove compartment of his car and a sawed-off shotgun at his feet.

I Can Get It for You Wholesale. Though he resembled a maniacal Don Knotts, Nelson Duncan was nothing like jittery Deputy Barney Fife. Duncan was reported to be the mastermind of an interstate auto theft ring. Working out of Atlanta, Georgia, Duncan

was also an accomplished safecracker and burglar. In short, Duncan was a career criminal, and a fairly successful one at that despite having earned cutesy nicknames like "Little Red" and "Peewee." Though he spent his fair share of time boardin' with the warden, Duncan managed to practice his craft relatively unmolested by the law (save for the usual pinch) until the November 1949 robbery of the Grant Field stadium ticket office in Atlanta. The take was a whopping $2,000. As the wheels of justice turn slowly, it took almost five years for Duncan to make the Bureau's Ten Most Wanted list, which he did in February 1954.

A smarter criminal, knowing he'd made the Bureau's major leagues, would have promptly left town for greener and safer pastures. Not Nelson Duncan. He remained in his beloved Atlanta until May 1954, when he was popped in the middle of robbing the safe of a local grocery store. He was nailed on a host of state and federal charges and sent away for good.

INTERESTING FUGITIVE FACT:
Duncan managed to bust out of no less than two maximum-security prisons.

70. CHARLES FALZONE, robber, kidnapper

LISTED: February 24, 1954
CAUGHT: August 17, 1955

Take My Wife . . . Please. Massachusetts-born Charles Falzone was in and out of trouble with the law with an arrest record dating back to 1932. He was paroled from the Massachusetts State Reformatory in 1944, where he'd been serving time for burglary and armed robbery. Deciding he was none too popular in his home state, Falzone made his way down to North Tonawanda, New York, a suburb of Buffalo, where he got a job in a shipyard.

In May 1947, deciding that honest employment was for suckers, Falzone ripped off the company payroll, about $6,000, and kidnapped two coworkers to use as hostages should the need arise. He dumped them outside of Buffalo. Whether he was confident that he'd pulled off the crime of the century or just plain didn't care if the law was after him is unclear, but Falzone stayed in Buffalo. That June he met and later married a widow who was evidently unaware of his criminal past. The couple moved to New Bedford, Pennsylvania. Falzone changed his name to James LaSalle and went to work as a carpenter.

Fate closed in on Charles Falzone. He'd been added to the Most Wanted list on February 24, 1954, almost six years after his robbery/kidnapping, though it didn't appear that the Feds were expending much energy looking for him. In June 1955, however, Falzone's wife spotted his wanted poster in the local post office. When confronted with this, Falzone tried to bluster it out with lies and denials. When his bride wouldn't shut up about it, though, Falzone threatened to kill both her and her daughter. Fearing for her life, Falzone's missus dropped a dime on him. On August 17, 1955, FBI agents moved in and arrested him.

INTERESTING FUGITIVE FACT:
When Charles Falzone threatened to kill his wife for her incessant nagging about his checkered past, it was no idle threat; Falzone was fond of firearms. When federal agents arrested him, they found 13 pistols, seven rifles, and one shotgun stashed in his house.

71. BASIL KINGSLEY BECK, suspected murderer, robber

LISTED: March 1, 1954
CAUGHT: March 3, 1954
DESCRIPTION: Born March 1, 1933, in Grand Rapids, Michigan. Five feet 11 inches tall, 160 pounds. Occupations: painter, laborer. Scars and marks: cut scar on inside right pinkie, circular burn scar on back of right hand, burn scar at base of thumb of right hand, burn scar on right leg, birthmark on lower left side of back, mole on face. Aliases: Basis Kingsley Beck, Rasis Kingsley Beck, Tommy Kingsley, Mr. Starr, Freddie Welsh, Joseph Welsh, Tommy Welsh, and "Base."

Basil Faulty. Slightly resembling an undernourished Arnold Schwarzenegger in a July 1953 prison mug shot, Basil Kingsley Beck—Base to his friends, if he had any—spent his formative years, ages 11 through 16, in a series of brutal Oklahoma reform schools, which no doubt added fuel to the fire of his criminal tendencies. Upon graduation, Beck decided to pursue a life of crime, an avocation for which, thanks to the Oklahoma penal system, he was now uniquely qualified.

His next stop was Kansas City, where he was promptly suspected of burglary in September 1953. He made his way to Arkansas, but was nabbed by police and returned to Kansas to await trial. He and three fellow inmates broke out of the Oswego jail before he could go to trial. Wisely deciding that his best bet was to put as much mileage between himself

and the state of Kansas, Beck made his way east to Philadelphia. He was linked to a murder there, though details are unknown. He resurfaced in Milwaukee, Wisconsin, in November 1953, where he burglarized a restaurant. The Bureau handed Beck a thoughtful 21st birthday present, placing him on the Most Wanted List on March 1, 1954.

The Feds were aware that Beck had spent time in San Pablo, California, sometime during his fugitive days in June 1953 and had a hunch he might return. Their persistence paid off. Beck was working at an auto-wrecking yard and was nabbed without incident when agents boxed him in at an intersection.

INTERESTING FUGITIVE FACT:
Though he was captured without a single bullet being fired, Beck liked to brag, according to his FBI wanted poster, that "he would shoot himself rather than return to prison." The best-laid plans of mice and men notwithstanding, Beck went back up the river bullet free.

72. JAMES WILLIAM LOFTON, armed robber

LISTED: March 16, 1954
CAUGHT: March 17, 1954
DESCRIPTION: Born Owassa, Alabama.

Wascally Wabbit. As good as he was at getting himself thrown into various prisons in and around Montgomery County, Alabama, Jimmy Lofton was almost as good at escaping from them. He was described by local law enforcement as a "rabbit," one who excelled at breaking out of prison camps, usually ones located in the dense Alabama swamps. By all accounts, he'd escaped from half a dozen Alabama jails and work farms.

By the summer of 1952 Lofton was looking at almost 35 years of jail time for any number of robberies and assorted mayhem. That August Lofton and 10 other inmates escaped from the prison in Atmore, Alabama. The 10 inmates were rounded up in short order, but Lofton, the most experienced of the bunch, stayed gone. Nineteen months later, on March 16, 1954, he was named to the Most Wanted list. A tip led FBI agents and local cops to Morgan City, Louisiana. Under the alias of Fred Moore, Lofton was nabbed at a shell crushing plant, where he'd found gainful employment. He was promptly dispatched back to Alabama, where more jail—and possibly one more escape—awaited him.

The Atmore jailbreak of 1952 was a gutsy one. Lofton and his 10 companions used a hydraulic jack to smash the prison door, enabling them to tunnel out into the surrounding countryside.

73. CLARENCE DYE, armed robber

LISTED: March 8, 1954
CAUGHT: August 3, 1955

Do or Dye. Clarence Dye was a small-timer who pulled a string of unsuccessful robberies throughout the Depression-era South until one, in West Virginia, earned him 10 years behind bars. Released in late 1943, he managed to eke out a living through some nickel-and-dime robberies. By 1946 Dye figured he needed some help. Hitting the town of Akron, Ohio, in 1946, Dye and his equally inept accomplice, Orris Gaines, successfully robbed a restaurant. Encouraged, they attempted to rob a second eatery on July 29, but this time things didn't go quite so smoothly. The restaurant owner pulled a gun of his own and started blasting. Gaines was killed on the spot. Dye wounded the owner before escaping with a small amount of cash. Gus Ballas, the restaurant owner, quickly identified him as the second robber.

Dye remained at large for almost eight years before the Bureau got around to adding him to the Most Wanted list, which they did on March 8, 1954. By this time Dye had relocated to Milwaukee, Wisconsin, where he worked a number of odd jobs, including chef at a country club, and managed to keep his nose relatively clean. Nonetheless, the law moved in and arrested him on August 3, 1955.

INTERESTING FUGITIVE FACT:
For a change, it wasn't the Feds who nabbed Clarence Dye. Milwaukee city detectives made the pinch after receiving a tip that Dye was known to frequent a local nightspot.

74. STERLING GROOM, murderer

LISTED: April 2, 1954
CAUGHT: April 21, 1954

Voice of Groom. Sterling Groom murdered a Virginia woman in 1934 and was sentenced to life in prison. He was paroled in 1951, and by December of that year he was jugged again, for larceny this time, in Orange County, Virginia. He escaped on December 15, 1951, and two days later tried to rob a general store in the Virginia town of Winston. For good measure, he strangled the storeowner. Remaining at large, Groom was named to the Most Wanted list on April 2, 1954. Groom was working at a foundry in Baltimore, Maryland, when a coworker spotted his wanted poster at the post office and alerted authorities. Agents arrested him at his place of employment on April 21; Groom maintained his innocence, but his fingerprints ultimately gave him away.

INTERESTING FUGITIVE FACT:
Groom used the alias John Waugh while hiding in Baltimore.

75. RAYMOND LOUIS OWEN MENARD, robber, burglar

LISTED: April 3, 1954
CAUGHT: April 5, 1954
DESCRIPTION: Born August 27, 1926, St. Louis, Missouri. Five feet five inches tall, 140 pounds. Build: medium. Occupations: hospital orderly, laborer. Scars and marks: small cut scar under left eye, scar on right thumb, scar on left leg, tattoos including "Amphibian Forces" and shield with "USN" on outside of right upper arm; dancing girl above rose and banner with bird on right outer forearm; banner with rose on right inner forearm; rose and banner with "Mother" and anchor and banner with "RLM" on outside of left upper arm; bird and dagger on left outer forearm; American flag and "USA" on left inner forearm. Aliases: Raymond Louis Menard Jr., Raymond Lewis Menard Jr., Raymond Owens Louis Menard.

Tats R Us. In addition to being lousy at inventing aliases, Raymond Louis Owen Menard's name was probably the biggest thing about him. At a mere five feet five inches, Menard in his mug shot resembles one of the Bowery Boys after a five-day bender. Fond of tattoos, as his description makes clear, Menard served in the U.S. Navy seemingly without incident; at least, no records exist proving otherwise.

What separated Menard from the gaggle of veteran pug-uglies and two-bit small timers he associated with was an ability to reinvent himself when necessary. He went from simple robbery to much more lucrative safecracking. He was in and out of prison between 1948 and 1953 on convictions of robbery, burglary, and intent to rob. Despite his small stature,

WANTED BY THE FBI

UNLAWFUL FLIGHT TO AVOID PROSECUTION (BURGLARY)

Photographs taken July, 1953

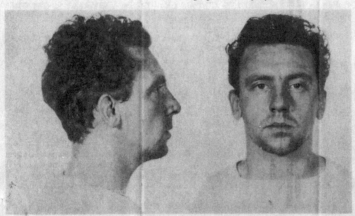

RAYMOND LOUIS OWEN MENARD

with aliases: Raymond Louis Owen Manard, Raymond Lewis Menard, Jr., Raymond Louis Menard, Jr., Raymond Louis Owens Menard

DESCRIPTION

Age 27, born August 27, 1926, St. Louis, Missouri; Height, 5'5"; Weight, 140 pounds; Build, medium; Hair, brown; Eyes, gray; Complexion, ruddy; Race, white; Nationality, American; Occupations, hospital orderly, laborer; Scars and marks, small cut scar under left eye, scar on right thumb, scar on left leg, tattoos including "Amphibian Forces" and shield with "USN" on outside of right upper arm, dancing girl above rose and banner with bird on right outer forearm, banner with rose on right inner forearm, rose and banner with "Mother" and anchor and banner with "RLM" on outside of left upper arm, bird and dagger on left outer forearm, American flag and "USA" on left inner forearm. FBI No. 4,718,227

Fingerprint Classification: $\dfrac{8\ S\ 1\ T\ II\ 4}{S\ 1\ T\ II}$ Ref: $\dfrac{U}{T}$

CRIMINAL RECORD

Menard has been convicted for robbery, burglary and assault with intent to rob.

CAUTION

MENARD IS PROBABLY ARMED AND SHOULD BE CONSIDERED EXTREMELY DANGEROUS. HE REPORTEDLY HAS STATED THAT HE WILL NEVER BE TAKEN ALIVE AS LONG AS HE HAS A GUN.

A complaint was filed before a U. S. Commissioner at St. Louis, Missouri, on February 10, 1954, charging Menard with violating Title 18, U. S. Code, Section 1073, in that he fled from the State of Missouri to avoid prosecution for the crime of burglary.

If you are in possession of any information regarding the whereabouts of this individual, please communicate with the undersigned, or with the nearest office of the Federal Bureau of Investigation, U. S. Department of Justice, the local address and telephone number of which are set forth on the reverse side of this notice. For ready reference, the telephone number of the FBI office covering this territory is listed below:

Wanted Flyer No. 152
April 27, 1954

JOHN EDGAR HOOVER, DIRECTOR
FEDERAL BUREAU OF INVESTIGATION
UNITED STATES DEPARTMENT OF JUSTICE
WASHINGTON 25, D. C.
TELEPHONE, NATIONAL 8-7117

Menard was arrested in New Orleans, Louisiana, by local police after a citizen recognized a photograph in a local newspaper.

Menard possessed both criminal cunning and solid leadership skills. By early 1953 he was heading up his own criminal gang in his hometown of St. Louis, pulling off an impressive 30 capers in one year's time. It was enough to bring him to the attention of federal agents, who busted 14 members of the gang in February 1954.

With this, Menard was wise enough to realize that St. Louis was getting a little too hot. Accompanied by his wife, he fled south to that Shangri-La of crime, New Orleans. Where women were concerned, Ray Menard was ahead of his time; long before the era of women's lib, he happily sent his wife out to work—as an exotic dancer in a Big Easy saloon.

On April 3, 1954, Menard was inducted onto the Ten Most Wanted Hall of Fame. Two days later, after his photo was published in a local New Orleans newspaper, a neighbor dropped a dime on him. Agents surrounded the apartment and apprehended Menard and his wife without incident.

INTERESTING FUGITIVE FACT:

Like BASIL KINGSLEY BECK a few years before him, Menard went on record as stating he would "never be taken alive as long as he had a gun." But taken alive he was—and whether he was packing heat at the time or not is open to debate.

76. JOHN ALFRED HOPKINS, armed robber

LISTED: May 18, 1954
CAUGHT: June 7, 1954

Roll Along, Prairie Moon. A native of Spokane, Washington, Johnny Hopkins maintained a busy but mostly uninspired criminal existence, consisting of crimes ranging from burglary to forgery. He escaped from police custody on his way to a court appearance in Los Angeles and surfaced in Fort Worth, Texas, a month later, where he was quickly arrested. He was returned to California and spent some time in San Quentin before being paroled in 1942.

Dreaming of riches far beyond the grasp of a petty criminal, Hopkins tried his hand at gold mining in the Vulture Mountains of Arizona. The rewards were virtually nonexistent as they were for even the most determined prospector, so he decided to return to a life of crime. In Wickenburg, Arizona, Hopkins shot it out with the town marshal, who caught him trying to rob a drugstore. Both men were wounded; the mar-

shal ultimately died, but not before tagging Hopkins as the shooter. Johnny was tried, convicted, and sentenced to life in the harsh state penitentiary in Florence, Arizona.

He continued to get into trouble even behind bars. What Hopkins needed, prison officials decided, was a hobby. And what a hobby he chose.

Hopkins thought it might be fun to build something—like a vehicle. He scavenged parts from the prison machine shop and assembled a functioning jeep. His pet project turned out so well that Hopkins, along with another inmate, decided to take it for a test drive. They drove it straight out of the prison and into Phoenix on November 30, 1953, where they ditched it and stole another car to complete their successful getaway. Hopkins made the Most Wanted list on May 18, 1954. Three weeks later, federal agents found him in the desolate mining town of Beowawe, outside the Cortez Mountains. Hopkins was working as a gold miner once more when he was arrested on June 7, 1954. His luck as a prospector was no better than his luck as a fugitive.

INTERESTING FUGITIVE FACT:

During his stay in the penitentiary in Florence, Arizona, Hopkins did not cease his criminal activities. Figuring he had nothing to lose, Hopkins was involved in a plot, along with 10 other inmates, to defraud the Internal Revenue Service. The inmates filed fraudulent income tax returns to obtain large refunds. The caper earned him even more prison time.

77. OTTO AUSTIN LOEL, murderer

LISTED: May 21, 1954
CAUGHT: January 17, 1955
DESCRIPTION: Born October 28, 1910, in Waverly, Ohio. Five feet 10 inches tall, 160 pounds. Occupations: molder, foundry worker, mariner, farmer, machinist's helper. Scars and marks: half-inch scar on right thigh, one-inch scar on right knee, two scars left forearm, tattoos on both forearms. Has false teeth which he seldom wears, making cheeks appear sunken. Reportedly drinks alcoholic drinks to excess; frequently wears western-type clothing. Reportedly speaks Chinese and frequents Chinese restaurants. Has hobby of gunsmithing. No aliases.

Fortune Kooky. His sinister, hollowed-cheeked appearance notwithstanding, Otto Austin Loel was married five times, or claimed to have been married five times, once to a young Chinese girl he supposedly "purchased" from her parents. He was dubbed a "social reject" by court psychiatrists. He joined the U.S. Navy, but his stint was short-lived—he was booted out of the fleet on a bad conduct discharge. For several years, he roamed the Far East and returned stateside in the late 1940s. When drunk, which apparently was often, he delighted barflies with exotic tales of his experiences, claiming at various times to be an opium dealer and mink dealer in China, and a lumberjack in Oregon.

A consummate conman, Loel in 1948 actually talked his way into a job as a police chief in the small town of Sandy, Oregon. Whether Sandy's crime rate went up or down during his tenure as a lawman is unknown. What is known, however, is that by 1954 Loel was out of a job and had somehow talked a frustrated housewife from Compton, California, one Elizabeth Henderson, into running off with him. The two had met in a tavern. Telling her dimwit husband that she was traveling east to visit some of her relatives, and that she and Loel were merely sharing the expenses, off she went.

Henderson's vacation was cut short when her half nude body was found decorated with 13 stab wounds in an Oklahoma City hotel room on January 10, 1955. For an ex-lawman, Otto Loel was extremely sloppy when it came to murder. He left behind a butcher knife with his fingerprints on it at the scene of the crime. He was named to the Ten Most Wanted list on May 21, 1954.

Loel was arrested by local police in Sanford, Florida, on January 17, 1955. Returned to Oklahoma City to stand trial, he pleaded insanity. The local shrinks disagreed, finding him sane, if an "oddball." With the insanity option gone, Loel switched his plea to self-defense, claiming Henderson had lured him into an act of sexual perversion. "I went haywire," Loel insisted. The jury didn't buy his story, though, and Loel was convicted of murder on October 22, 1955. He was subsequently executed for Henderson's murder, proclaiming his innocence to the end.

INTERESTING FUGITIVE FACT:

Loel's crimes were those of passion, not profit. When he was nabbed for Henderson's murder, cops in Sanford, Florida, found him hiding in a local city dump, living in a crude shack made out of palmetto leaves.

78. DAVID DANIEL KEEGAN, murderer, robber

LISTED: June 21, 1954
CAUGHT: Never
DESCRIPTION: Born: September 28, 1918. Five feet 11 inches tall, 159 pounds. Occupations: saloon owner, bartender, cab driver. Alias: Burt Williams.

Last Call. David Daniel Keegan is the one who got away. He served in the U.S. Navy during World War II and returned to civilian life in his native Iowa in late 1945. He drifted into the saloon business—a very good thing for a man who liked the booze as much as Keegan did. For most of the next decade he owned or co-owned a number of watering holes and was, his customers liked to kid, his own best customer. It was rumored that he owned a piece of a local whorehouse as well. Though there are no records of Keegan being arrested, much less convicted, it's not hard to surmise that any number of crimes was planned in the backrooms of his gin mills by the local criminal elements. One such crime that occurred on a nippy night in 1954 landed Keegan on the Most Wanted list.

Someone got a tip that a farmer, William Edwards, from nearby Mondamin, Iowa, kept a safe in his house with a good deal of money in it. On February 22 Keegan and two of his stooges wearing black masks and brandishing guns burst into the Edwards home, where Edwards's sister and another woman were also present. The armed intruders forced Edwards into the bedroom where the safe was located. Edwards, either fearing for the ladies or his money, pulled a move and things got a little physical. Either Keegan or one of his pals pumped two bullets into Edwards, killing him instantly. Leaving the terrified women unharmed, Keegan and his crew, toting the safe, beat a hasty retreat.

The safe was found the next day outside of Sioux City, North Dakota. Reportedly $9,000 in cash was missing; another $8,000 in bonds was left behind. The brazen crooks, either giddy with glee over the fairly sizable score or just plain piss drunk, got a little sloppy. They abandoned the getaway car, but didn't bother to remove the license plates. The car, found by cops the morning after the murder/robbery, was registered to one Daniel David Keegan.

Keegan's witless partners were taken by Sioux City cops on February 24. Keegan and the $9,000, however, had vanished "faster than a fart in a tailwind," said one law enforcement official. There was still no trace of Keegan when he was named to the Most Wanted list on June 21, 1954. By that time Keegan's coattails couldn't be seen for the dust; neither he nor his ill-gotten $9,000 were ever apprehended. In December 1963 the Bureau relegated Keegan's case to the cold file. As of this book's publication, Danny Keegan is still at large. Or dead.

INTERESTING FUGITIVE FACT:
Unknown, though there are probably plenty, since Keegan was never caught.

79. WALTER JAMES WILKINSON, kidnapper, armed robber

LISTED: August 17, 1954
CAUGHT: January 12, 1955
DESCRIPTION: Born May 1924, Troy, New York. Five feet nine inches tall, 165 pounds. Occupations: mechanic, seaman, taxi driver. Scars and marks: tattoo of "Molly" on left forearm. Known to wear mustache. Aliases: Walter Rogers.

Melonhead of Troy. While the wide-open, lawless streets of New York City may hold the record for the number one spot in breeding criminals, it doesn't hold the monopoly. The upstate town of Troy, New York, a stone's throw from the state capital of Albany, managed to squirt out a few of their own. Walter J. Wilkinson is proof positive that crime thrives outside of Manhattan, the Bronx, and Brooklyn.

Not much is known about Wilkinson's early years, but by 1954, at the age of 30, Wilkinson was the head of a merry band of merciless thugs who robbed and pillaged their way through Troy, Albany, and several other New York State towns. In Corinth, New York, Wilkinson and his mob kidnapped a supermarket manager and forced him to open the store's safe. The gang fled with a whopping $2,000, but not before they locked the hapless manager inside the store's freezer.

The next morning supermarket employees found their manager in the freezer. Slightly chilled but still alive, the manager identified Wilkinson as one of the perps. By this time the law had enough on Wilkinson to hang a number of burglary and armed robbery charges on him, and he was named to the Most Wanted list on August 17, 1954.

Wilkinson wisely decided to put some distance between himself and upstate New York. To that end, he headed west and sought anonymity in Los Angeles, rightly assuming, as have millions before and

since, that one more cheeseball in L.A. would hardly go noticed.

The fugitive found work as a busboy in a swanky country club, keeping his nose relatively clean. Three months later, however, a coworker saw Wilkinson's published photo and fingered him to the Bureau. When the law moved in, he offered no resistance, even though he was toting a loaded automatic pistol. "It didn't take you too long," Wilkinson said. "I know how you guys work."

INTERESTING FUGITIVE FACT:
Somewhere between New York and California Wilkinson, showing the lack of imagination that kept him a small-timer for most of his criminal career, adopted the alias "Walter Rogers."

80. JOHN HARRY ALLEN, armed robber

LISTED: September 7, 1954
CAUGHT: December 21, 1954
DESCRIPTION: Born November 10, 1909, Carroll County, Tennessee.

The Great Escaper. John Henry Allen was a good ol' boy from rural Tennessee who was only a fair criminal, but when it came to breaking out of prison, he had few equals. He logged his first jail break in Pocatello, Idaho, in 1927, at the age of 18, when he was arrested for auto theft and highway robbery. In April 1932 he was sentenced to a 15-year stretch for armed robbery and sent to the state pen in Nashville, Tennessee. He hung around for eight years and managed to break out in May 1940. He robbed his way west for the next four months and was arrested once more in Kansas. He was finally paroled in 1949, but his time behind bars had only steeled his resolve to become a better criminal.

By December 1950 John Harry was back to his old tricks. He robbed a grocery store, along with an accomplice, and escaped. He was picked up in Mississippi by the highway patrol after a shoot-out and sent back to Alabama, where he was handed a sentence of 35 years. He escaped two years later, in April 1952.

Johnny Allen wasn't one to let any grass grow under his feet. He went west and robbed a gas station in Fargo, North Dakota. He was nabbed the next day in Grand Forks and sentenced to 15 to 25 years in the state pen in Bismarck. In September 1952 he escaped. He surfaced in Kansas in December of that year, where he'd embarked on yet another robbery spree. He was arrested and jugged and sent to the state penitentiary. Again he scaled a wall and escaped on March 25, 1954.

Allen continued robbing his way through Kansas and Arkansas, making the Most Wanted list on September 7, 1954. He was nabbed in Fort Smith, Arkansas, four months later, on December 21, 1954, and returned to Kansas to serve out what had amounted to 140 years worth of prison sentences. Records show no further bust-outs from this point on.

INTERESTING FUGITIVE FACT:
While on the lam, John Harry Allen liked to relax by going to the movies. On July 29, 1954, he cruised into a drive-in theater in Coffeyville, Kansas, to enjoy a double feature. When the show ended, he robbed the box office.

81. GEORGE LESTER BELEW, forger

LISTED: January 14, 1955
CAUGHT: January 24, 1955
DESCRIPTION: Born October 31, 1913, Mountain View, Missouri (not verified). Five feet 11 inches tall, 160–170 pounds. Occupations: nurse, clerk, artist, laborer, mechanic, farmer. Scars and marks: 1/2-inch diagonal scar beneath point of chin, scar on bridge of nose. Tattoos: faded scroll on upper right arm, two roses, "Mother Rose Of My" with small heart beneath on lower right arm, heart pierced by dagger entwined with the banner "Death Before Dishonor" on lower left arm. Aliases: Art Anderson, F. C. Anderson, George E. Anderson, C. H. Bennett, E. H. Benton, M.D., Fred C. Boweman, Fred C. Duperson Jr., Fred C. Eckerson, Fred Hanson Jr., Fred E. Hastings, Fred R. Hewlett, Henry E. Marshall, Frederick Peterson, R. B. Robertson Jr., Fred R. Sancaster Jr., C. H. Stanley Jr., Earl P. Stevenson Jr., Earl C. Tidball Jr., Roy E. Tompkins Jr., John W. Wallenta, and others.

Checks and Imbalances. George Lester Belew was, in criminal parlance, a "writer." That is, his particular M.O. was writing checks, all of them as worthless as the paper they were written on. Belew's avocation also likely accounts for his numerous aliases, some of which show a degree of creative thought, most notably "Earl C. Tidball" and "Fred C. Duperson."

Not much is known about his first 40 years of existence, though judging from a tattoo that read "Death Before Dishonor," it's safe to assume Belew spent some time as a U.S. Marine. His Most Wanted photo, taken sometime in July 1951 (the time of his first recorded arrest), when Belew was 38 years old,

shows a man who appears to be of above-average intelligence—no mental giant, but no hulking homicidal jitterbug, either. The charge was writing a check against his account in a Fargo, North Dakota, bank. The problem was, a shrewd judge pointed out, Belew had no account in the bank. He was given a brief sentence, but upon his release from jail Belew reverted to type and continued papering the Midwest with bogus checks. He was jugged again in Hays, Kansas, on July 30, 1954.

As this was at least his second offense and would draw a much harsher sentence, Belew opted to break out of jail. On August 4 he bushwhacked a guard and made his escape via a stolen car. With this rash act, Belew made his bones; he was dropped onto the Most Wanted list in early January 1955 for the twin acts of assaulting an officer of the law and transporting a stolen car over state lines. By this time he had managed to avoid capture for almost six months.

On January 24, Belew, along with his wife and another couple—Belew's sister- and brother-in-law—checked into a Champaign, Illinois, motel. Belew registered as Dr. Clyde C. Hoyt, but the clerk was suspicious. Dr. Hoyt seemed overly nervous—hardly appropriate bedside manner for a rural Illinois sawbones. Motel owners at that time made it a habit of accumulating Most Wanted posters. A number of guests at these less than four-star establishments who gave phony names were either philandering husbands or fugitives from justice. After consulting a stack of posters and seeing the good doctor on one of them, the clerk dropped a dime. Belew was nabbed by Federal agents that night; his wife and in-laws were charged with aiding and abetting. Belew was returned to Kansas and was convicted on a number of counts, including forgery, assault, and jailbreaking.

INTERESTING FUGITIVE FACT:
When Belew and his companions were arrested, agents also found a tackle box that contained the tools of Belew's trade: a kit for printing phony payroll checks and phony ID cards used to cash those checks.

82. KENNETH DARRELL CARPENTER, bank robber

LISTED: January 31, 1955
CAUGHT: February 4, 1955
DESCRIPTION: Born July 20, 1912, Wyandot, Ohio. Five feet 11 inches tall, 152 pounds. Occupations: semi-skilled machinist, truck driver, cook, musician. Scars and marks:

small cut scar center of upper lip, one-inch horizontal scar and one-inch vertical scar at base of left thumb. Tattoos include "True Love" on fingers of right hand, script initials A. L. on right wrist, cupid on lower left forearm. Remarks: Has had mastoidectomy performed on left ear. Aliases: Kenneth Lamar, "Kenny."

Crime on My Hands. Kenneth Darrell Carpenter was an arch criminal, pure and simple. His first arrest came for contributing to the delinquency of a minor—the A. L. tattooed on his right wrist? One will never know. What is known is that in November 1937 at the age of 26, Carpenter was pinched for car theft and sentenced to one to 20 years in an Ohio reformatory. Ten months later, in September 1938, he escaped but was apprehended in four days. He was paroled a year and half later, in January 1940, and quickly reverted to form. Carpenter was strongly suspected of participating in a string of gas station robberies in and around northern Ohio and was finally nailed, along with an accomplice, both of them heavily armed, near Toledo, in December 1940.

This time around Carpenter was handed a sentence of between one and 25 years. He served almost five years before crashing out of prison once again in February 1945 and was captured 11 months later. Whether Carpenter was a model prisoner in between jailbreaks is unknown, but by August 1949 it was decided Carpenter had paid his debt to society, and he was paroled.

A two-time loser by this time, Carpenter resumed his criminal escapades. Deciding that gas station robberies were small potatoes, he tried his hand at bank robbery, with middling results. His first attempted bank heist, in Mount Blanchard, Ohio, netted him a paltry $395. Even more humiliating, he was nailed the very same day for the robbery. This time the charges were federal, and in early 1950 an angry judge sent him off to the queen mother of prisons, Leavenworth—this time for seven years of very hard labor.

Carpenter was back on the streets by October 1954 and picked up where he'd left off. A month later, along with a buddy named Leroy Adolph, he hit a liquor store/gas station in Independence, Kansas. Their take was evidently small, for two weeks later in Oswego, Carpenter and Adolph successfully took down a bank (using guns this time—Carpenter favored a .32 automatic pistol) for an excellent $9,300. Carpenter was plenty tough—that much seems abundantly clear—but he wasn't the sharpest tool in the shed. His fingerprints and Adolph's were found inside the Oswego bank.

Leroy Adolph was nabbed in Webb City, Missouri, in December 1954 and went up the river with a harsh 15-year sentence. Carpenter was still at large when he was named to the Most Wanted list on January 31, 1955. Agents tracked him down to East Arlington, Tennessee, four days later, and it was back to Leavenworth for Kenneth Darrell Carpenter.

INTERESTING FUGITIVE FACT:
In lieu of a gun, Carpenter robbed the Mount Blanchard bank by brandishing a vial of nitroglycerine—later revealed to be plain H_2O—until the terrified teller handed over the booty.

83. FLENOY PAYNE, murderer, robber

LISTED: February 2, 1955
CAUGHT: March 11, 1958
DESCRIPTION: Born July 18, 1909, Scott, Mississippi.

Payne in the Neck. Along with an accomplice, Flenoy Payne shot and killed a grocer in Greenville, Mississippi, on February 7, 1933. The grocer was white; Payne and his pal were black. That he didn't find himself at the end of a rope—this was Depression-era Mississippi, after all—is a small miracle in itself. He was paroled in 1942. He worked as a cotton picker and earned a few extra bucks gambling. By 1949 he was living in Toledo, Ohio. On May 4 of that year Payne shot and seriously wounded a woman he'd been living with, and her estranged husband as well. He fled back to Mississippi. Trouble followed. He shot and killed a man over a gambling debt in August 1953 and skipped town. He made the Top Ten list on February 2, 1955. Federal agents nabbed him in Arkansas on March 11, 1958. He was returned to Mississippi, where he was convicted of murder.

INTERESTING FUGITIVE FACT:
Unlike most Top Tenners, Payne spent three years at large before federal agents got around to arresting him.

84. PALMER JULIUS MORSET, armed robber

LISTED: February 7, 1955
CAUGHT: March 2, 1956

Back Home in Indiana. Palmer Morset started out as a horse thief in his native Nebraska and had graduated to armed robbery by 1935. For the latter, he served a stretch in Joliet Prison, getting paroled in 1940. Morset spent the 1940s pulling off a variety of armed robberies. By 1950 Chicago police suspected him of masterminding a series of finance company robberies. On March 20 of that year his luck ran out and he was indicted on four counts. This being Chicago, armed robbery was considered child's play. Bail was actually set, and Palmer Morset managed to post it. Not surprisingly, he never got around to showing up for his trial. Instead, he skipped town. He made the Top Ten list on February 7, 1955, almost five years after disappearing. Federal agents caught up with him a month later on March 2, 1956.

INTERESTING FUGITIVE FACT:
After beating it out of Chicago in early 1951, Palmer Morset decided to go straight. He changed his name to Thomas Rooney, married and found gainful employment as a salesman, settling in Indianapolis, Indiana. Federal agents found him anyway.

85. PATRICK EUGENE MCDERMOTT, murderer

LISTED: February 9, 1955
CAUGHT: July 19, 1955
DESCRIPTION: Born September 13, 1898, Dunlo, Pennsylvania. Five feet 4 1/2 inches tall, 172 pounds. Occupations: hospital technician, machinist, barber, automobile parts salesman, sign painter, composer of crossword puzzles. Scars and marks: one-inch oblique scar over left eyebrow; tip of left index finger amputated. Tattoo of red and blue bulldog on right forearm. Remarks: has complete set of upper and lower dentures, which he may not be wearing; occasionally wears glasses; is interested in astrology, has in the past composed crossword puzzles.

Your Moon Is in the House of Pancakes. Not many members of the Most Wanted Society possess a fascination with astrology or compose crossword puzzles in their spare time. But such a man was Patrick Eugene McDermott, an eighth grade dropout with a near-genius I.Q., a man who might have walked the straight and narrow in life if it just hadn't been for those darn violent outbursts.

In addition to his skills as a puzzle maker, McDermott also was self-taught in chemistry, hematology, and bacteriology. He even created, the story goes, a medical technique that aided in faster detection of tuberculosis. Whether McDermott acquired these skills behind bars or on freeside is unclear. For all of this McDermott had his dark side. His first recorded brush with the law occurred in 1922, while he was serving in the army. He was convicted of grand larceny and court-martialed (the details are also unclear) and was placed into the stockade. That tinhorn joint couldn't hold him, however, and McDermott promptly escaped. He was nabbed in short order, but by this time the army wanted no part of him, and he did the rest of his stint in the much more secure Atlanta Penitentiary.

He was released a few years later with a sparkling new set of dentures and a rotten attitude toward society. For a man obsessed with astology, McDermott proved blind when it came to reading his own future. Prohibition was in full swing by this time, the peak of the Roaring Twenties, and McDermott's violent streak made him perfect for bootlegging and a life of crime. He worked with a number of Ohio hooch gangs and wasn't shy about pulling a trigger when necessary, and sometimes even when not.

A crusading newspaper editor named Donald Mellett of the Canton, Ohio, *Daily News* proved to be Patrick McDermott's undoing. As with most crusading newspaper editors, Mellett's tireless print campaign against sin and police department corruption earned him a fair amount of enemies in the Ohio underworld. Buttinskies like Mellett were bad for mob business. McDermott was chosen to do something about it.

On July 16, 1926, Don Mellett was ambushed as he parked his car in his garage at home and was dead before he hit the cold concrete. McDermott and his goon squad were quickly tagged with the crime. McDermott was arrested, tried, and found guilty of first-degree murder in a trial that also brought down the head of the bootlegging gang and the Canton chief of police. McDermott was handed a life sentence and sent to the state prison in Columbus.

From all indications Paddy McDermott was a patient man. He served 18 years of his sentence before he escaped from the slammer, on November 28, 1954. In his haste, however, McDermott neglected to formulate a plan once he was outside the prison. Records show he abducted a hapless cab driver and eventually made his way to Chicago, where he vanished. He made the Top Tenners on February 9, 1955, the charge being unlawful flight to avoid confinement.

The territory between Chicago and New York was thick with safe houses where a fugitive could lie low. Syndicate hospitality, though, had its limits when the federal heat became too great. It was strongly urged that McDermott keep moving and follow Horace Greeley's advice in reverse: "Go East, Young Man." In New York City on July 20, 1955, agents caught up with Patrick Eugene McDermott. True to form, he was working as an ambulance driver at the time of his arrest. He offered no resistance and was sent back to prison and his horoscopes.

INTERESTING FUGITIVE FACT:
Paddy McDermott was so adept in writing crosswords that his puzzles, when completed, revealed a horoscope, much to the delight of his readers.

86. GARLAND WILLIAM DANIELS, forger, car thief

LISTED: February 9, 1955
CAUGHT: March 29, 1955
DESCRIPTION: Born November 4, 1904, Henderson, North Carolina. Five feet eight inches tall, 175 to 190 pounds. Occupations: salesman, seaman, clerk, baker, and accountant. Scars and marks: jagged 1 1/2-inch cut scar on neck below left ear, one-inch scar inside left hand, line scar back of base joint of left middle finger, line scar inner right wrist. Tattoos: heart pierced by dagger and initials G. W. D on left forearm, and sailor's head on right forearm. Remarks: may be wearing small mustache, has deep dimple in chin, sometimes wears glasses. Aliases: R. B. Abbott, Floyd Babcock, C. C. Brun, George Dillon, J. B. Everton, James B. King, William Lee, James Mason, Robert Thomas Peabody, Jimmy Vernon, "Flash," and others.

Thunder Road. Only the finest car thieves earn a nickname like "Flash." Garland Daniels earned the moniker by being able to steal a car faster than anyone in his Dixie hometown of Henderson, North Carolina. Nobody could boost a jalopy like ol' Garland. Considering his primary source of income, it was probably for the best.

A notorious forger and paperhanger (someone who passes bad checks), Garland Daniels used a series of creative pseudonyms and spread enough bad paper and stole enough cars to earn him jail time by 1950 in prisons all across the United States, including California, Kansas, Maryland, Connecticut, and even in Washington, D.C. There was never any shortage either of things to charge Daniels with, be it forgery, auto theft, carrying a concealed weapon, and violating the federal Stolen Property

Act. By this time as well, Daniels was also a full-blown dope addict.

He was sentenced to seven years in a Florida prison for any number of these charges in 1951. Some anonymous prison official took pity on Gar Daniels, as he was transferred to the U.S. Public Health Service Hospital in Lexington, Kentucky, where his addiction might be treated. Though better than a steamy Florida hellhole, Daniels found his new Kentucky digs not to his liking and broke out in November 1951. Now a free man, he managed to ply his trade unencumbered for the next four years. On February 19, 1955, he earned Most Wanted status.

His travels took him to Los Angeles, the citadel of West Coast crime. A neighbor spotted Daniels's FBI mug shot in a newspaper and fingered him to the law. He was captured as he tried to vault over a backyard fence. Daniels was returned to Florida—no minimum security rehab center this time—and served out the remainder of his sentence. He was released and moved to Texas, where he died in 1965.

INTERESTING FUGITIVE FACT:
Daniels was so drug-addled he had to go through rehab before entering prison.

87. DANIEL WILLIAM O'CONNOR, burglar

LISTED: April 11, 1955
CAUGHT: December 26, 1958
DESCRIPTION: Born 1928. Aliases: Clarence O'Connor, Arthur Nelson, others.

The Paper Hanger. Danny O'Connor joined the army at age 18 in 1946, but hated it. Even in the pre-Vietnam years, draft dodgers and deserters alike sought safe haven in Canada. He ended up in a Canadian jail in 1948 on a two-year stretch for burglary.

Daniel William O'Connor's criminal specialty was passing bad checks. Between 1953 and 1955 O'Connor hung enough bad paper to reforest half of the Pacific Northwest. O'Connor plied his trade in Montana, Oregon, North Dakota, and all over British Columbia, dragging his road-weary wife and two children along. On May 14, 1953, things got ugly. O'Connor administered a severe pistol-whipping to a Canadian Mountie after being stopped for questioning. O'Connor left the badly beaten officer for dead in a roadside ditch. O'Connor headed south into Montana and passed half a dozen more bad checks between Butte and Great Falls. He was added to the Most Wanted list on April 11, 1955, on federal charges of transporting stolen property across state lines.

Whether O'Connor was aware that he was the subject of the FBI's attention is open to question, but he was smart enough to lie low for the next three years. He settled with his family in El Cajon, a modest California suburb, and stayed out of trouble for three years, though it appears likely that his neighbors regarded him with a degree of uncertainty. There was just something *not right* about that Arthur Nelson, the alias O'Connor adopted for his entry into the straight life. On December 26, 1955, their suspicions proved correct. Local cops busted O'Connor for stealing a $15 kiddie trailer. Fingerprints ID'd O'Connor as the toy thief. They also led federal agents to El Cajon, where O'Connor was arrested and returned to Montana to stand trial.

INTERESTING FUGITIVE FACT:
When it came to forging a new identity, Danny O'Connor wasn't content to merely use an alias. For his new life Danny had a tattoo burned into his left arm, dyed his hair red, and chopped it short. He gained 60 pounds and grew a bushy mustache. His new look was for naught. He got caught anyway.

88. JACK HARVEY RAYMOND, forger, embezzler

LISTED: August 8, 1955
CAUGHT: October 14, 1955

Things to Do in Denver When You're Broke. Jack Raymond was a small-time career criminal who was sentenced to life imprisonment in late 1953. In February 1954 he slipped away from prison guards transporting him to Walla Walla Prison. Once free, he supported himself by passing government checks he manufactured (without the government's consent), rubber-stamping his alias, Lou J. Ames, on them. The caper worked well enough from Montana to Southern California, though it did bring Raymond to the attention of the Secret Service. He made the Most Wanted list on August 8, 1955.

Federal agents circulated posters for Jack Harvey Raymond/Lou J. Ames all across the western third of the United States. In Denver on October 14, 1955, Raymond was made by a grocery store manager when he tried to pass a bad check. Cops arrested him after a chase in which Raymond totaled his car and tried to flee on foot.

INTERESTING FUGITIVE FACT:
Denver was a hotbed of Most Wanted activity in the second week of October 1955. A week earlier FBI agents had nabbed DANIEL EVERHART (#89.)

89. DANIEL EVERHART, burglar, car thief

LISTED: August 17, 1955
CAUGHT: October 9, 1955
DESCRIPTION: Born February 22, 1925, Akron, Ohio. Five feet nine inches tall, 135 to 145 pounds. Occupations: taxi driver, laborer, truck driver, clerk. Scars and marks: numerous pit scars on face, appendectomy scar, tattoo of "Betty" on outer part of left forearm. Aliases: Daniel Abraham Everhart, Thomas Jacobs, George R. Murphy, Carl Myers, "Dan," "Danny."

Brother, Can You Spare a Crime? "All them Everhart boys were bad," was the cry in and around Akron, Ohio, and one look at the combined rap sheets of the Everhart clan proved this beyond any doubt. By the time little Danny took his first pinch—he was all of 12 at the time—two of his brothers were already doing hard time in various Ohio slammers and a third had hanged himself in his jail cell. If there's any truth to the old adage that the apple doesn't fall far from the tree, then it's safe to say Daniel Abram Everhart landed somewhere close to the trunk.

Danny Everhart's mug shots, dated December 1949 and April 1950, respectively, could have been a Hollywood casting director's dream. Everhart was the epitome of the cold-hearted, shifty-eyed gunsel portrayed variously by Elisha Cook Jr., Lee Van Cleef, Jack Elam, or John Ireland, mainstays of any number of 1950s film noir classics who ended up dead in the last reel.

By 1955, in between stints as a cabby, day laborer, and truck driver, Everhart was wanted by police for a host of burglaries, armed robberies, and even one attempted murder for his participation in a shoot-out with local cops. The "Caution" notation on his Most Wanted poster reads, "Everhart may be armed with a .32 caliber automatic pistol and should be considered extremely dangerous. He reportedly has fired at pursuing officers and has remarked that he will not be arrested alive. He has previously escaped from custody."

With his addition to the Most Wanted on August 17, 1955, Everhart decided that Akron was becoming a little too hot for his liking. Two months later, he popped up in Denver, Colorado, down on his luck and flat broke. Rousted by cops accustomed to checking out the new vagrants along Skid Row, Everhart was asked to identify himself. Everhart, the man who vowed never to be taken alive, tried to make a break for it, but the beat cops were faster, tackling him and slapping the cuffs on his skinny wrists. A quick check of fingerprints ended Everhart's freedom. He was turned over to FBI agents and hustled back to Akron, where he enjoyed a family reunion of sorts with his two brothers in the penitentiary.

INTERESTING FUGITIVE FACT:
According to his Most Wanted poster Everhart's criminal record included "operating a motor vehicle without the owner's consent." In less polite parlance, he was a car thief. Either that or he had some very trusting friends.

90. CHARLES EDWARD RANELS, kidnapper, armed robber

LISTED: September 25, 1955
CAUGHT: December 16, 1956
DESCRIPTION: Born April 14, 1922, Conroe, Texas. Five feet 7 1/2 inches tall, 150 pounds. Occupations: bookkeeper, truck driver, fireman. Scars and marks: cut scar left eyebrow, cut scar middle of upper lip, cut scar on bridge of nose, small scar side of forehead near hairline, cut scar inside of right elbow. Tattoos: bird with "Love" on outer side of left upper arm; heart and "T. L." on outer side of left forearm; bird and "T. M. L" on inner left forearm; skull, clasped hands, and "R. A. Charlie" on outer side of right upper arm; dagger and scroll with "C. R. and Tinnie" on inner right forearm; "HARD" on backs of fingers of right hand, and "LUCK" on backs of fingers of left hand. Aliases: H. L. Boyer, John L. Boyer, H. L. Cameron, Charles H. Mercer, T. A. Nelson, Charles Renals.

Hard Luck, Hard Time. As criminals go, Charles Edward Ranels was well above average. In a four-month period between February and May 1955, Ranels, with the help of a pal, heisted almost $69,000 in bank and supermarket robberies, not a bad chunk of change for that time. Ranels was a native of Conroe, a small central Texas town near Waco. Hit harder than most during the Great Depression, Conroe was a hardscrabble burg that produced hardscrabble citizens. Charlie Ranels was picked up for stealing a car when he was 15 and sent off to a state institution for

juvenile delinquents. Reform school, as it was for most young'uns, was an ideal criminal breeding ground. By 1954 he had spent almost half of his 33 years in a number of Texas state prisons for kidnapping, robbery, and car theft. He spent his time behind bars getting himself tattooed and alternately carved up in knife and jagged bottle fights.

Back in freeside in October of that year, Charlie Ranels had had himself a bellyful of Texas and was ready for more fertile territory. With his partner, Ranels took a supermarket in Louisville, Kentucky, for $3,000. Charlie was just warming up. Two and a half weeks later, Ranels and Co. hit the big time, cleaning out a Louisville bank of almost $35,000.

Deciding $38,000 would hold him for the time being, Ranels lay low for the next seven months. Somewhere along the line he and his unknown partner went their separate ways. Ranels single-handedly robbed a bank in Lonoke, Kentucky, on May 27, 1955, hauling away almost $10,000 in cash and $15,000 in unsigned travelers checks. With this the Bureau sat up and took notice; Ranels was named to the Most Wanted list on September 25, 1955.

Obviously aware that few bank robbers lived long enough to spend their purloined loot, Ranels wisely planned for his retirement. To this end he sent his moll, identified as one "Opal May," down to the tiny town of Dew Drop, Arkansas, 20 miles southeast of Little Rock, with enough money to buy the couple a nice little grocery store. Ranels in the meantime decided on one last score. On January 9, 1956, he withdrew $11,000 from the bank in Monticello, Arkansas. He hightailed it back to Opal May and the grocery store, where he enjoyed nearly a year of freedom.

In flyspeck towns, people gossip. In Dew Drop they gossiped about the scary-looking man who was married to Opal May—he looked a lot like that man on "one of them Wanted Posters." On December 16, 1956, Ranels's dream of peaceful anonymity was shattered when Federal agents, toting Tommy guns and the latest fashions from Smith & Wesson, surrounded his farmhouse just as he and the missus were sitting down to dinner. As he was cuffed and led away, he said to the agents, in an understatement Franz Kafka would have envied, "I know you'd get me, so I decided to hide out."

INTERESTING FUGITIVE FACT:
With the Monticello, Arkansas, robbery, Ranels got a little sloppy. He wore no mask, but even if he had,

the tattoos on his hands were a dead giveaway. Bank employees couldn't help but notice the words *hard* branded on the fingers of his right hand and *luck* branded on the fingers of his left, making identification pretty much a no-brainer.

91. THURMAN ARTHUR GREEN, robber

LISTED: October 24, 1955
CAUGHT: February 16, 1956

Not Easy Being Green. Thurman Arthur Green might have been an upstanding member of society had the situation been right. Unfortunately, the situation wasn't right. He was in and out of prisons from Chicago to Walla Walla, Washington. By spring 1954, he was serving a six-year stretch for armed robbery. Records show the take was less than $100; the unusually harsh sentence indicated that this was hardly his first robbery.

On May 21, 1954, with less than a year left on his sentence, Green came down with a bad case of cell fever. Along with two other inmates, he escaped Walla Walla by crawling under a fence and stealing a car. The trio got as far as Iowa, where Green's accomplices were nabbed in the town of Creston. Green remained at large and was named to the Most Wanted list on October 24, 1955.

In December Green arrived in Nashville, Tennessee, and decided to stay, his criminal instincts telling him that the heat was off. He adopted the name Frank DuMonte and found honest labor in a foundry and worked hard, missing only one day of work in almost a year. He found a nice girl and married her, and the couple moved into a comfortable apartment complex. The story might have ended there, with Thurman Green ending his days as a hard worker and good husband, had not his neighbors gotten nosy. Several of them recognized Green's mug on a Most Wanted poster and ratted him out to the Feds. Sensing that the law was closing in on him, Green sent his wife to Knoxville and, nursing a toothache, settled in to wait for the inevitable knock on the door. It came on February 16, 1956.

INTERESTING FUGITIVE FACT:
Never at a loss for words, even if they were the wrong ones, Thurman Green calmly informed the arresting agents, "I was expecting you yesterday."

92. JOHN ALLEN KENDRICK, murderer

LISTED: November 2, 1955
CAUGHT: December 5, 1955
DESCRIPTION: Born February 17, 1897, Washington, D.C. (not verified). Five feet seven inches tall, 202 pounds. Occupations: taxi driver, chauffeur, construction worker, painter, steam fitter, tailor, welder, laborer. Scars and marks: pit mark on center of forehead; scar on chin; 3/4-inch oblique scar on inner side of left wrist, cut scar on inner side of left forearm above wrist; one-inch vertical scar on palm of left hand. Remarks: reportedly walks with a rolling gait. Aliases: John H. Diggs, John J. Dugan, John Dugen, John Henric, John Kendric, John Nolan Kendrick, John Allen Kendricks, John Kendrix, John Kenericks, John L. Lee, John J. Murphy, John O'Brien, Sam W. Thompson, Frank Wilson, John J. Wilson, among others.

Johnny B. Not Good. In the minds of most Americans, the words *crime* and *Washington, D.C.* are synonymous. However, not all criminal behavior in our nation's capital is limited to the chicanery of congressmen and senators with degrees from Harvard. John Allen Kendrick is a fine example.

Born in or around Foggy Bottom in 1897 (the exact location has never been verified), Kendrick scored his first major arrest for larceny and murder in Baltimore in 1923. He plea-bargained the charges down to just plain larceny and assault and drew five years in the pen. He served most of them—no time off for good behavior for Johnny Kendrick—and was released on December 4, 1928. Fourteen months later, in February 1930, he was sent up for two and a half years for carrying a concealed weapon. A smarter felon would have done the 30 months standing on his

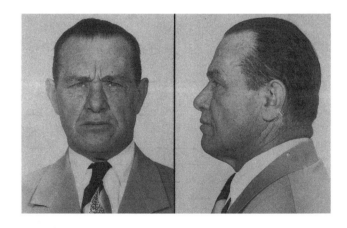

Murderer John Allen Kendrick, arrested in Chicago, Illinois

head, but John Kendrick was not particularly smart. He broke out of prison instead in September 1931, only 10 months shy of completing his sentence.

While on the lam, he shot a cop in Washington, D.C., in March 1932 and was handed a much-deserved sentence of 10 years in the federal reformatory in Lorton, Virginia. Iron bars do not a prison make; 16 months later, in July 1933, Kendrick escaped once again. His abilities with a machine gun and smaller but just-as-deadly *pistolas* earned him a position with the notorious, kill-crazy Tri-State Gang, a band of hardened crooks, thugs, and holdup artists who plundered their way through Pennsylvania, Maryland, Virginia, and North Carolina. (Technically speaking, they should have been called the Quad-State Gang, but it's doubtful that Kendrick and his associates cared much about this minor oversight.)

In June 1934 Kendrick was nabbed in Johnson City, Tennessee, long a haven for on-the-run criminals. He was returned to the reformatory in Lorton, but not for long. Johnny Kendrick had earned his ticket to the Big Time. He was transferred to Alcatraz, where he served six and half years of hard time. For reasons one shudders to speculate, he was shipped off to Leavenworth in July 1941 to finish his federal sentence. That out of the way, he was sent off to a federal pen in New Jersey to finish out an interrupted federal rap. He was finally paroled in June 1943.

Kendrick managed to keep his nose relatively clean until June 1947, when he was arrested and later convicted of shooting a fellow hood in Washington, D.C. It was back to Leavenworth for the next seven years, until March 1954. He was almost 58 years old, but age did not mellow Johnny Kendrick; if anything, he was worse. Back in Washington, D.C., nine months after getting sprung from Leavenworth, Johnny tried to empty his pistol into someone, hitting his victim at least once, in the throat. Hoover's boys added Kendrick to the Most Wanted list on November 2, 1955.

Kendrick made his way to Chicago, where federal agents nailed him a month later, without incident on December 5, 1955. He was returned to Washington, D.C., to stand trial once more, a procedure that was fast becoming a bad habit. This time, however, the judge took no chances. He sent John Allen Kendrick up the lazy river forever.

INTERESTING FUGITIVE FACT:
Johnny, like most hardened criminals, liked the booze. His Most Wanted poster dated October 24, 1955, carries this description, which was obviously penned by a failed English major: "[Kendrick] reportedly drinks to excess on which occasions he exhibits an ungovernable temper."

93. JOSEPH JAMES BAGNOLA, murderer, armed robber

LISTED: December 19, 1955
CAUGHT: December 31, 1955
DESCRIPTION: Born 1916, Chicago, Illinois.

That Toddlin' Town. Chicago turns out criminals faster than Philadelphia turns out cheese steaks. Joey Bagnola was a product of the merciless South Side. By the age of 16 he was serving time for petty larceny. By 1940 he was paroled after serving five years on an armed robbery conviction. It was back to the Windy City, where Bagnola became a 24-year-old hitman for the Chicago syndicate. There were a number of first-rate executioners in the Chicago mob in those days, and competition for murder contracts was fierce. Bagnola supplemented his income pulling off some armed robberies and a couple of nonsyndicate hits.

In the spring of 1950 Bagnola was approached by three goons from the New Orleans mob, who made him an offer he couldn't refuse. Word on the street was a Chicago used-car dealer had a huge amount of money stashed somewhere on the premises of the establishment, which also doubled as the car dealer's home. With two of the New Orleans hoods outside keeping the getaway car running, Bagnola and the third hood broke into the dealer's apartment and found a cool $50,000 and some expensive jewelry. When the car dealer resisted, he was beaten and tossed down a flight of stars, killing him on the spot.

Bagnola and the New Orleans crew split the take and went their separate ways. The Dixie mobsters were apprehended between May 1952 and April 1953; Joey remained at large. He earned Most Wanted honors on December 19, 1955. Federal agents tagged him on New Year's Eve 1955. Instead of gurgling champagne to celebrate, Bagnola chugged weak jailhouse java instead.

INTERESTING FUGITIVE FACT:
It's safe to assume Bagnola never left the mob-protected safety of Chicago during the years between 1950 and 1955. He went on his merry Mafia way until he landed on the Most Wanted list. Federal heat

Mug shot of armed robber James Faherty

was much hotter than local heat, and Bagnola was quickly apprehended.

94. NICK GEORGE MONTOS, armed robber

LISTED: March 2, 1956
CAUGHT: March 28, 1956
DESCRIPTION: Born in Tampa, Florida, in 1916. Five feet five inches tall, 140 pounds.

Twice as Not Nice. Nicky Montos had a talent for getting himself on the FBI's Ten Most Wanted list. In Nicky's case he landed on the list twice, the first time in 1952 for the violent robbery of an elderly couple in Georgia. Montos was serving time at the Parchman, Mississippi, prison farm for an unrelated crime when he escaped, along with fellow inmate Robert Jones, on January 10, 1956. The duo sawed

through a door latch with a hacksaw and tossed blankets over the barbed wire fence to make good their escape. Montos made the Most Wanted list, for the second time, on March 2, 1956.

The heat was on. Montos and Jones made it to a Memphis, Tennessee, motel but were identified by the clerk, who alerted authorities on March 28. It took a big mess of tear gas to flush the fugitives from the motel room. Montos pleaded guilty to a number of charges and was handed an eight-year prison stretch. Jones was given six years for possession of illegal weapons.

Nicky Montos's problems did not end with his guilty plea. He was shipped to Georgia to stand trial for assaulting and robbing the elderly couple. A hard judge sentenced Montos to death. Miraculously, Montos won an appeal based on a couple of legal technicalities, but authorities were not about to let him walk away a free man. He was retried in 1957 and found guilty. This time around he got 10 to 20 years in stir.

INTERESTING FUGITIVE FACT:
When it came to the life of a fugitive, Nicky Montos didn't believe in traveling light. At the time of his arrest at the Memphis motel federal agents retrieved seven guns, three bottles of assorted narcotics, body armor, and almost $5,000 in cash.

95. JAMES IGNATIUS FAHERTY, armed robber

LISTED: March 19, 1956
CAUGHT: May 16, 1956

96. THOMAS FRANCIS RICHARDSON, armed robber

LISTED: April 12, 1956
CAUGHT: May 16, 1956

I've Got My Loot to Keep Me Warm. James Faherty. Tommy Richardson. James "Specs" O'Keefe. Carlton O'Brien. Joe Banfield. Stanley Gusciora. Vincent Costa. Michael Geagan. Anthony Pino. Henry Baker. Joe McGinnis. Adolph "Jazz" Maffie. They were small-time Italian and Irish crooks, petty thieves, grifters, and hustlers from Boston's North End. Individually they were barely competent enough to rob a blind man. Together they managed to steal almost $3 million in what was the largest haul in American history—the Great Brink's Robbery of January 17, 1950.

It seemed like a good idea at the time: Grab what they could from the Brink's North Terminal Garage on the corner of Prince and Commercial Streets, then lie low for six years until the statute of limitations ran out. A half-assed plan to be sure, and it all went sour within a year or two, but that came later.

The caper was meticulously planned to ensure maximum success. The boys spent more than a year laying it out. They broke into the Brink's garage at night (unbeknownst to midnight watchmen and guards), where huge sums of money were deposited nightly in the company vaults on the far end of the second floor. The planners measured distances, navigated neighborhood fences, escape routes, checked which ways the doors swung in and out, and even removed crucial locks from which they had new keys made up. No detail big or small was over-looked. Several members of the gang broke into a security company to study blueprints of the alarm system utilized by Brink's. They put together makeshift but nonetheless convincing Brink's uniforms. They even had a dry run shortly after Christmas 1949, then chose January 17 as B-Day, when stores of Brink's cash would be at their largest.

It was all over in 15 minutes. The Boston bandits made their way through the Prince Street entrance, through the deserted counting room, then through the cage door opposite the safety room, and hit the vault with guns drawn. Terrified employees gave it up on the spot. By the time the gang finished cleaning out the safe, $1,218,211 in cash, plus another $1,557,183 in checks and securities, were heisted. Jimmy Faherty, Tommy Richardson, and the rest of their buddies got away without a shot being fired. There was plenty of cash to go around, more than enough in fact—the haul exceeded all of their puny expectations. A cool hundred thou apiece, more or less, plus whatever the securities could be peddled for on the street.

James "Specs" O'Keefe got greedy first. He demanded an additional 60 grand for his part in the caper. His request was promptly denied. Specs skulked off threatening retribution, and that was enough for the others. Even worse, he was called up on a special grand jury investigation into the crime a year after the robbery and spilled his guts, dropping enough dimes to telephone Seattle, Washington. He named five of his accomplices in the robbery; all were cited for contempt of court when they declined to testify.

Faherty, Richardson, and the others wanted Specs gone, and to their credit they hired the best man in the business to make him go away. Elmer "Trigger" Burke was an accomplished hitman from Hell's Kitchen, New York, who worked primarily for the Syndicate in his hometown but wasn't averse to traveling to a job if the price was right. He cornered Specs O'Keefe on a deserted Boston street late on June 16, 1954, and sprayed machine-gun fire at him, wounding him in the arm and chest. Leaving O'Keefe for dead, Trigger Burke departed the scene. Specs survived (one of the few times, if any, that Elmer Burke bungled a hit) and started singing. By this time, more than four years after the robbery that made headlines the world over, the FBI had spent an estimated $25 million on the investigation. They were hot to nail someone—anyone—for the heist. Specs O'Keefe was handed a two-year sentence on an unrelated weapons charge, the best the law could muster. Specs was determined not to be the fall guy

After an FBI investigation, Richardson was arrested in Boston, Massachusetts, with Faherty (#95).

Warren Oates, Peter Boyle, and Paul Sorvino, and was directed by William Friedkin, red-hot off the success of *The Exorcist*. *The Brink's Job* opened to favorable reviews and was played mostly for laughs. Two of the surviving heisters were invited to the world premiere in Boston. Seventy-year-old Adolph "Jazz" Maffie thought the picture was okay, but was slightly put off by the flick's light-hearted tone. "That was hard work, that kind of job," he commented.

Tommy Richardson, then 72, was more philosophical. "I'm glad they made something light out of it," he said. "People need a few laughs these days."

INTERESTING FUGITIVE FACT:
After the botched O'Keefe hit, Elmer "Trigger" Burke unwisely hung around Boston to carry out another assignment. He bumped off a local hoodlum, one George O'Brien, the very next day. He was arrested for this crime the same night but managed to escape from a Boston prison with the able assistance of two friends on the outside, a break that electrified the nation. He remained at large for a year, when he was nabbed in a South Carolina bus station. Convicted in 1952, Burke died in the electric chair on January 9, 1958. His last meal consisted of a big steak and half a dozen cigars. He spent the last hours of his life reviewing more than 150 newspaper clippings of his exploits. He urged the warden to preserve them. "For history's sake," Burke said.

and in 1955 fingered each of his partners in crime. Joe Banfield was dead by this time, and Stanley Gusciora was already serving a 20-year stretch for armed robbery in Pennsylvania. By January 12, 1956, all but Faherty and Richardson—childhood pals who took their first pinch together in 1934—had been rounded up and handed life sentences.

Faherty made the Most Wanted list on March 19, 1956; Richardson was listed three weeks later, on April 12. Though the heat in and around the Boston area was intense, neither Faherty nor Richardson could stay away from their lifelong homes. On May 16, 25 FBI agents nabbed the duo without incident. $5,000 in cash was found in the apartment where Faherty and Richardson were hiding out. It was the only loot ever recovered from the robbery. Like their friends, they were tried and convicted and handed life sentences. Give or take, all of the Brink's boys were paroled after 14 years.

In 1978 a movie chronicling the gang's exploits was released. *The Brink's Job* starred Peter Falk,

97. EUGENE FRANCIS NEWMAN, car thief, burglar

LISTED: May 28, 1956
PROCESS DISMISSED: June 11, 1965
DESCRIPTION: Born October 3, 1928, Brooklyn, New York (not verified). Five feet eight inches tall, 170 to 180 pounds. Occupations: bricklayer, clerk, construction worker, counterman, laborer. Scars and marks: one-inch scar of right eye; two smalls scars back of right hand; small scar center of left cheek; birthmark on upper part of left arm, mole on left index finger. Tattoos: "Danny" and heart on outside of right forearm, number "13" within dotted circle on back of left hand at base of thumb. Aliases: Elvin James Hall, Daniel Joseph Lyons, James Salemski, James Salermerio, James Salerno, Daniel J. Sheridan, James Sheridan, "Jim."

When Irish Eyes Are Scowling. Often referred to as the "city of homes and churches," Brooklyn, New York, can also add one more to the list: criminals.

Brooklyn and New York in general mass-produce criminals faster than Hershey pops out chocolate bars. A child of the Great Depression, Eugene Newman learned to steal at an early age. He pilfered what he could from poor family members and ran around with the bad kids on the block. By age 15 he was long lost to the streets, taking his first pinch for petty larceny. He was sent away to the state reformatory in New Hampton, New York. The year was 1943, World War II was raging, and the navy needed a few good men. Anything was better than the reformatory, so, using the name Daniel Lyons, Newman enlisted.

The military and Eugene Newman were mismatched from the start. Criminals rarely take orders gracefully, and Brooklyn boys by nature are bad sailors, hating any water that doesn't come out of a seltzer bottle. Newman went AWOL in August 1945 and was nabbed by the shore patrol shortly after. He was court-martialed and sent up for a year. By this time, in late 1946, the war was over and the navy decided to make Eugene Newman someone else's problem. He was sent packing with a bad-conduct discharge and returned to the land that knew him best, Brooklyn.

Not much had changed in the old neighborhood since Newman had gone away three years earlier. He attempted to go straight, or at least gave it the old reform school try, taking the typical odd jobs of bricklayer, restaurant counterman, day laborer. The lure of easy money, though, proved too great, and Eugene took his first major pinch for burglary in April 1947. When his trial came up six months later—justice moves slowly in New York City—an impatient judge handed him ten hard years in the state reformatory in Elmira, New York.

Newman served two years and was paroled shortly before Christmas Day, 1949. He returned to his old haunts and dropped out of the sight of the law until February 1951, when he was caught trying to steal a government car. By the time he had served his sentence for that crime, and another for parole violation, it was 1955. But Newman wasn't through with crime. In fact, he was planning his biggest caper yet.

On August 3, 1955, an armored car drove back from a race track in Ontario, loaded with half a million American and Canadian dollars. Eugene Newman was with two accomplices in Buffalo, New York, waiting for it. When the drivers climbed out of the cab, Newman shot one of them, as if to teach them a lesson about compliance. But the wounded driver managed to crawl away undetected and sounded a company alarm. Newman and his bandits panicked, leaving the money behind and kick-starting a wild chase that would end in a residential section of Buffalo, where police finally surrounded the bandits with tear gas and pistols. Despite the odds, Newman managed to squeak by and elude his pursuers.

Nearly nine months later there was still no sign of Newman, and he was named to the Top Ten list. Unfortunately, the massive publicity generated by the list did not help flush Newman from his hiding spot. The bandit became a fixture on the list for nine years until it was decided that a case against Newman could never be successfully prosecuted. He was removed from the list on June 11, 1965.

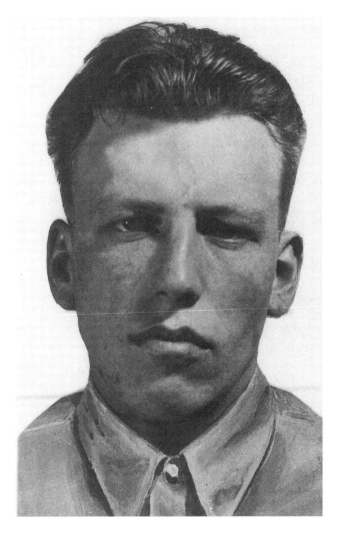

Federal process for Newman was dismissed in Buffalo, New York.

INTERESTING FUGITIVE FACT:
Newman launched his life of crime when he was in grade school, stealing cash from his own family.

98. CARMINE DIBIASE, gangster

LISTED: May 28, 1956
CAUGHT: August 28, 1958

Leave the Gun. Take the Cannoli. You didn't want to mess with Carmine DiBiase. He had a bad temper and besides, he was a made member of the Vito Genovese crime family, at that time one of the biggest and most powerful of the New York outfits. DiBiase took his orders directly from Anthony "Tony Bender" Strollo, Genovese's number one man.

Carmine was an earner—he made lots of money for la Famiglia Genovese through such rackets as shylocking, extortion, drug dealing, and a host of other enterprises. He was also assigned to do a hit every now and then. Killings didn't bother Carmine. In fact, he killed for free, which is where his problems began.

In December 1951 at a social club on Little Italy's Mulberry Street (the nerve center of La Cosa Nostra), DiBiase got into an argument with an associate, Michael Errichiello. Over money more than likely, though it didn't take much to set these guys off. DiBiase left but returned a few hours later, this time packing heat. He pumped three bullets into Errichiello's head, killing him instantly. DiBiase then shot a witness, Rocco Tisi, who was in the wrong place at the wrong time.

Tisi survived and was faced with a dilemma: either rat out DiBiase or be arrested for withholding information about a murder. Tisi opted to rat DiBiase out, which was technically against Mafia rules and for which Tisi would ultimately pay with his life a few years later. DiBiase in the meantime disappeared into the New York underworld. By the time the Feds got around to adding him to the Most Wanted list, on March 28, 1956, DiBiase was weary of hiding out. No doubt spurred on by promises by mob bosses that he'd be protected, DiBiase surrendered to the FBI on August 28, 1958.

Big mistake. He was tried, convicted of murder, and sentenced to the electric chair. Mob lawyers filed an appeal, and he was retried. This time around—thanks to some skillful jury tampering—DiBiase was acquitted and was quickly back in circulation in Little Italy. Along the way DiBiase switched alliances from the Genovese crime family to the Profaci family, which became the Colombo family after Profaci's death in 1964.

DiBiase was identified as one of the hitters who assassinated Crazy Joe Gallo outside of Umberto's Clam House on April 6, 1972, a mob rubout that has become the stuff of legend. (Gallo's killing was payback for any number of Mafia infractions, not the least of which was his attempted assassination of family boss Joe Colombo.) Charges were filed against DiBiase, but he was nowhere to be found. Word on the street was that Carmine was made to "sleep with the fishes"—mob slang, as any fan of *The Godfather* can tell you, for whacking someone. Apparently mob bosses were concerned that DiBiase would name names if arrested for the Gallo hit and made Carmine go away permanently.

INTERESTING FUGITIVE FACT:
Carmine DiBiase was not exactly loved by some of the lower-level street soldiers in his mob crew. He reportedly demanded that one soldier kill his own wife because the soldier was spending too much time with her and his family.

99. BEN GOLDEN MCCOLLUM, murderer

LISTED: January 4, 1957
CAUGHT: March 7, 1958
DESCRIPTION: Born in Kentucky.

Golden Boy. A Kentucky native, Ben McCollum robbed two Oklahoma banks of $7,000 in 1929 and was sent to McAlester penitentiary. McCollum was not a model prisoner. He slaughtered two fellow inmates with a homemade knife. He was sentenced three times to fry in Old Sparky and was given stays of execution each time. McCollum knew that given his irritable temper he'd be pushing up daisies in the local bone yard sooner or later. He escaped from prison on May 1, 1954, and made it onto the Most Wanted list on January 4, 1957.

He spent the next year on the lam and eventually settled in Indianapolis, Indiana, where he found honest employment (going by the alias George Napier) in a hospital that treated tuberculosis patients. He was a good, solid worker, so much so that he requested and was granted a new gig at the Indiana state school for the blind. Unfortunately, McCollum's life on freeside ended when an employee recognized his mug shot from a Wanted poster. Federal agents nabbed him in a rooming house on March 7, 1958, and he was returned to McAlester to finish out his sentence.

INTERESTING FUGITIVE FACT:
McCollum's 1929 sentence was unusually harsh—40 years.

100. ALFRED JAMES WHITE, burglar

LISTED: January 14, 1957
CAUGHT: January 24, 1957

The Slow and the Furious. By 1940 Alfred James White had been in and out of prison for crimes ranging from burglary to bank robbery to auto theft. If crime is indeed a business, then Alfred White qualified for the Kiwanis Club Criminal of the Year award.

In the summer of 1954 White was surprised by local police in Hamlin, West Virginia, as he attempted to burglarize a lumberyard. He managed to escape by diving into a river and swimming downstream, but cops lifted his fingerprints and he was quickly identified. It took two and half years for the FBI to add his name to the Most Wanted list (on January 14, 1957). In the interim he kept on the move, even buying a car and trailer for this purpose. He worked odd jobs and kept largely to himself, spurning everything but the most distant friendships, and he was fond of hanging out at airports and watching planes take off and land for hours on end.

White was going by the alias Frank Shaw and living in a transient hotel in Memphis, Tennessee, when

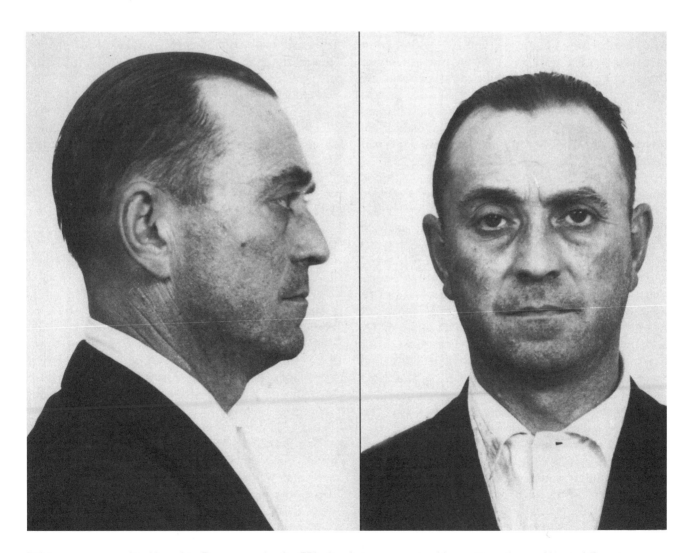

White was arrested in Memphis, Tennessee, by the FBI after being recognized by a citizen from a Wanted flyer.

a tip led FBI agents to close in on him. He offered no resistance, but, like most fugitives, he liked to be prepared for any contingency. When the agents searched his car and trailer, they found a number of pistols, a sawed-off shotgun, plenty of ammo, and a bag of the tools of his burglary trade. It was enough to send him packing straight back to prison.

INTERESTING FUGITIVE FACT:
White told arresting agents that he had considered surrendering several months before he was caught— all because, as a Most Wanted felon, he could not use his health insurance for an injury he'd sustained.

101. ROBERT L. GREEN, burglar

LISTED: February 11, 1957
CAUGHT: February 13, 1957

The Goldbricker. Some men are born great. Some men achieve greatness. And some men have greatness thrust upon them. Others, like Bobby Green, are born losers.

Green's teenage years were cluttered with arrests for minor offenses. He tried to straighten himself out by joining the army, but like many future felons, was dishonorably discharged. He then took a stab at marriage, in California, hoping the love of a good woman would do the trick. It didn't. Bobby decided to try his luck in Utah, but a combination of bad luck and stupidity ended in a combined 25-year prison stretch for burglary and armed robbery. He was no happier in prison than he was on freeside, and on September 7, 1954, he escaped from the penitentiary at Draper to accompaniment of bullets whizzing by his ears. In 1955 he was in Minneapolis, Minnesota, where he attempted to go straight. He adopted the alias Floyd Baker and went to work for a liquor distributor. He was a good employee, so much so that he landed an even better gig at a drum and barrel company. His employer had nothing but good things to say about him: "A fine worker," is how he described Bobby Green.

Along the way Green took himself another bride and became a father. He took yet another job at a plumbing supply company, but unlike the first two this one didn't work out as well. He was perpetually foul tempered, accused of not performing and, according to his supervisor, "wouldn't look you in the eye." Green quit the job "saving me the trouble of firing him," the supervisor said.

Needing money, he knocked over a gas station, making off with a small amount of cash and a loaded pistol. Then, on February 4, 1957, he embarked on a one-man crime spree, albeit a minor-league one. He burglarized his last place of employment, an apartment house where he'd once lived, and a downtown Minneapolis office building. He stole dictation machines, typewriters, a radio, a camera, and a clock. Hardly a king's ransom, but it was enough to bring him to the attention of the law, who by now had ID'd him as an escaped criminal. He was added to the Most Wanted list on February 11, 1957. His photo was published in the *Minneapolis Star* the next day, sealing his fate. Green decided it was time to leave town for good, having sent his wife and child up to Wisconsin to stay with her family weeks before.

Unfamiliar with the ways of the FBI and unaware that the Feds had every airport and bus and train station in town covered, on February 13 he attempted to board a Greyhound to Milwaukee. Feds nabbed him on the spot.

INTERESTING FUGITIVE FACT:
Not without a degree of vanity, Bobby Green also stole an electric razor during his week-long crime spree. Unlike the other stolen items, Green didn't pawn it, keeping it for himself.

102. GEORGE EDWARD COLE, murderer

LISTED: February 25, 1957
CAUGHT: July 6, 1959
DESCRIPTION: Born in Philadelphia.

Cole Slawed. George Cole was a native of Philadelphia, but decided to ply his criminal trade in California, figuring the spoils were more abundant. Unfortunately, it didn't quite work out that way. Cole spent time in Folsom and San Quentin for robbery. Not long after his release from prison, on December 30, 1956, Cole and a sidekick, Tommy Hamrick, attempted to rob a saloon outside of San Francisco. Things went sour, however, when an off-duty cop, Frank Lacey, tried to stop the robbery and was shot and killed. Cole and Hamrick fled empty-handed, but not before Cole was ID'd as the shooter.

Hamrick was picked up first and confirmed to cops that Cole was indeed Lacey's killer. (He was ultimately given a life sentence for accessory to

Lacey's murder.) Cole packed up his faithful moll, Yvonne Conley, and tried to put as much distance between himself and San Francisco. FBI agents traced them first to Wyoming and then to Nebraska, but by the time they hit Omaha, the trail had gone cold. Cole was added to the Most Wanted list on February 25, 1957.

In the meantime, posing as Mr. and Mrs. James Walker, the couple settled in Des Moines, Iowa, where Cole earned enough from working two jobs to open his own service station. Conley was taking medication for a bad case of cirrhosis of the liver, information known to federal authorities. Checking prescriptions filed at drugstores from coast to coast, FBI agents eventually narrowed down the search and on July 6 descended on Des Moines. James Walker at first attempted to deny he was George Cole, but a fingerprint check indicated otherwise. The couple was returned to San Francisco. Yvonne Conley was jugged for harboring a fugitive, while Cole went on trial for Lacey's murder. He was ultimately convicted and handed a sentence of five years to life in his alma mater, San Quentin.

INTERESTING FUGITIVE FACT:
During his murder trial George Cole tried to weasel out of admitting his guilt in Lacey's murder, weakly maintaining, "It's possible I did it, but I don't remember." The jury didn't buy it—they give Cole a guilty verdict.

103. EUGENE RUSSELL MCCRACKEN, murderer

LISTED: March 26, 1958
CAUGHT: March 27, 1958

McCracked. Another good ol' boy gone bad, Eugene McCracken was locked up in a county jail in Bristol, Tennessee, when he escaped, killing a lawman from neighboring Kingsport two days later during a shoot-out. McCracken was given a life sentence and spent the next 15 years behind bars in the state pen in Nashville. In October 1955 he crashed out of prison and managed to stay free for almost two and a half years. He was placed on the Most Wanted list on March 26, 1958.

By this time he had settled in Baltimore, Maryland, and had married a nice local girl when his photo was printed in the *Baltimore News-Post;* after it appeared, four people called into local FBI headquarters and identified McCracken, who was going

by the name Richard Kirkman. He was arrested without incident and returned to Tennessee to finish out his sentence.

INTERESTING FUGITIVE FACT:
While hiding, McCracken worked as a nurse.

104. FRANK AUBREY LEFTWICH, thief, armed robber

LISTED: April 4, 1958
CAUGHT: April 18, 1958
DESCRIPTION: Born February 23, 1922, Surry County, North Carolina. Six feet one inch tall, 173 to 185 pounds. Occupations: boiler maker, laborer, welder. Scars and marks: one-inch scar left side of forehead near hairline; quarter-inch scar above right eyebrow; scar on nose, four-inch L-shaped irregular scar on right wrist; two-inch scar on left wrist; four-inch operation scar on abdomen. Remarks: reportedly may become violent when intoxicated and is reported to be deceptively strong and muscular. Aliases: Archibald Hamlin, Archie Hamlin, Aubrey Frank Leftwich, Frank A. Leftwich, Frank Aubry Leftwich.

Cracker Like Me. Frank Leftwich hated authority of any kind, whether it was a parent with a leather strap or a cop with a billy club. A not-so-good ol' boy from rural North Carolina, he took his first pinch at the age of 19, in 1941, for breaking into a house in Richmond, Virginia. He was handed a one-year sentence. In 1943, with Uncle Sam's talent pool for soldiers to fight in World War II rapidly shrinking, Leftwich—tall and amazingly strong—was conscripted into the army. His attitude toward authority had improved little, and between June 1943 and July 1945 he was prosecuted five times for going AWOL and spent more than his share of time in the stockade.

It was hardasses like Frank Aubrey Leftwich that author E. M. Nathanson undoubtedly had in mind when he penned his 1963 novel *The Dirty Dozen*. In one incident while serving in the army, a female saloon owner shot him in the arm in self-defense after Frank had had one too many and got a little rowdy. Drinking and Frank Leftwich were a rotten combination, as evidenced in April 1945, when he and two buddies stole an army truck and went on a drunken joyride through the streets of Mt. Airy, North Carolina, destroying the vehicle in the process.

The army brass were not amused, and Leftwich was handed a three-year sentence for theft of government property. In August 1947 he was given a conditional release and dumped into freeside to wreak more havoc. He returned to his native North Carolina, and for the next three years he worked at odd jobs, drank too much, and fought with anyone who pissed him off—which was practically everyone he met. In April 1950 in Lumberton, local cops picked him up for public drunkenness but failed to search him properly. During the booking process, Leftwich pulled out a .25 caliber pistol and started firing at the arresting officers, seriously wounding one. The cops weren't fond of being shot at, especially in the sanctity of the station house, and returned fire. Leftwich took a bullet in the belly and went down for the count.

A lesser man might not have survived his wounds, but Leftwich came from solid pioneer stock and regained his health enough to be convicted of assault with intent to kill. He was given six to 10 years in the slammer, where he never had to worry about a nomination for Most Popular Inmate. He still maintained a hatred of authority and clashed with guards and his fellow prisoners alike. A violent prison brawl left him with a severely fractured skull, and he was plagued with dizzy spells and brain-splitting headaches from that day on.

He escaped from prison in October 1952, but was nabbed two months later in Bay City, Michigan, in a bar, not surprisingly. Almost two years later to the day—October 19, 1954—Leftwich escaped once again and this time managed to stay free for almost two and a half years. He surfaced in Delaware, but managed to slip away. A warrant was issued charging Leftwich with unlawful flight to avoid confinement, and he was named to the Most Wanted list on April 4, 1958. Though his Wanted poster claimed that Leftwich "reportedly may have suicidal tendencies," he apparently never acted on them. Instead, he went to Chicago. He was working as a welder and going by the reasonably creative alias of Ralph Calvin McDonald when the Feds arrested him on April 18, 1958. Despite his frequent boasts that the cops would never take him alive, Leftwich was unarmed and went along peacefully enough.

INTERESTING FUGITIVE FACT:
Frank Aubrey Leftwich might have remained on the lam forever had he not chosen to give himself away in an act of what was either brazen boldness or jaw-dropping stupidity. On April 14, 1958, Frankie's name surfaced on the Feds' watch list when he strolled into a Georgetown, Delaware, courthouse and paid a fine of $200—for drunk driving.

105. QUAY CLEON KILBURN, bank robber

LISTED: April 16, 1958
CAUGHT: June 2, 1958

Quay Pigeon. Quay Cleon Kilburn was a career felon who spent almost half of his first 34 years in the slammer for a variety of offenses ranging from auto theft to passing bad checks. While serving in the military, he was busted for stealing uniforms and selling them at a very reduced discount. A Utah bank robbery earned him more jail time in Leavenworth after he was booted out of the service, and he was paroled in early 1956. It wasn't long, however, before Kilburn was wanted for violating his parole, and he was named to the Most Wanted list on April 16, 1958.

A tip led federal agents to Long Beach, California, where they questioned one Clay Kilborn, who was sporting a phony moustache and even phonier ID cards. Agents weren't having any; they arrested Kilburn and shipped him straight back to Leavenworth.

INTERESTING FUGITIVE FACT:
Kilburn tried to throw arresting agents off the scent by maintaining the prints on his ID card differed from the prints they had on file for him. And the prints *were* different—Kilburn used his big toe for the ID card print. Agents weren't fooled.

106. DOMINICK SCIALO, gangster

LISTED: May 9, 1958
CAUGHT: July 27, 1959
DESCRIPTION: Born July 11, 1927, Brooklyn, New York. Six feet, 190 pounds. Occupations: chauffeur, laborer, mechanic, part owner of a candy store/luncheonette, truck driver. Scars and marks: three-inch scar outer corner of left eye; several pockmarks on right side of face; six-inch scar on abdomen. Remarks: Flashy dresser, prefers large cars, reportedly considers himself a ladies' man, a good dancer and likes to patronize dance halls, reportedly must refrain from drinking heavily and eating spicy foods due to an injury of his liver caused by gunshot. Is reportedly a racetrack and baseball fan. Aliases: Mimi Anthony Scialo, "Mimi."

107. ANGELO LUIGI PERO, gangster

LISTED: June 16, 1958
CAUGHT: December 2, 1960
DESCRIPTION: Born June 20, 1905, New York City. Five feet three inches tall, 180 pounds. Occupations: claims adjuster, cook, electrician's helper, farm hand, plumber's helper, sewing machine operator. Scars and marks: mole center of forehead; one-inch scar outer corner of right eye; several moles on neck, chest and back. Remarks: conservative dresser, round-shouldered, speaks slowly, occasional drinker with preference for scotch and water. Pigeon fancier, reportedly a racetrack and fight fan. May be suffering from injured right ankle.

It's Personal, Not Business. It takes that special something extra for a couple of low-level goodfellas to make the Most Wanted list. Dominick "Mimi" Scialo and Angelo Pero had that something extra and then some. Their exact Mafia family affiliation, whether Bonanno, Genovese, or Anastasia, is lost to history—Mimi and Angie were active in the years before Joe Valachi's revelations exposed New York's five-family Mafia hierarchy. Suffice to say that Scialo and Pero were loyal and efficient foot soldiers in La Cosa Nostra. In other words, they followed orders. If their *capo* said break some legs, they broke some legs. If the order was to whack someone, you could consider yourself whacked.

They were a study in contrasts. Mimi Scialo was darkly handsome in a *goombah* sort of way and favored flashy pinstripe suits, the attire of choice for many a Brooklyn wiseguy. Pero was short, squatty, and no feast for the eyes, cursed as he was with ugly moles on his forehead and neck. Unlike Scialo, the more seasoned Pero preferred less ostentatious attire, all the better to remain low key. Scialo liked the ladies and hung out in nightclubs and dance halls. Pero, a product of the tenements, preferred the popular hobby of raising pigeons. Scialo had to watch his diet; as a result of a nasty bullet wound to his liver, he had to curtail his intake of garlicky marinara sauce, veal piccata, and hard liquor. Pero liked scotch and water and was reportedly an excellent Italian cook, likely the result of "going to the mattresses" more than once.

Mimi Scialo was a part owner of a candy store/luncheonette, one of the street corner hangouts that were the lifeblood of every New York City neighborhood. In addition to serving up egg creams, liverwurst sandwiches, and selling the *Brooklyn Eagle* and the *Daily News,* the neighborhood candy store served as unofficial headquarters for the local mobsters. It was in these establishments where bookies took fifty-cent bets, shylock loans were made, and numerous crimes were planned.

The year was 1958. A connected nightclub owner in Framingham, Massachusetts, wanted his place torched—the joint was losing money and he wanted the insurance. ("Jewish lightning," as arson was then called.) For sensitive jobs like this, it was always better to use out-of-town talent, those less likely to get caught. The order came down to Scialo and Pero to handle the assignment, but they did not choose wisely. They paid a couple of incompetent amateurs, Alexander Menditto and Bugsy Garofalo, $500 to go up to Beantown and do the job.

The two *gavones* botched it, leaving ample evidence (like empty gas cans) strewn all about to attest to their crime. The insurance company wasn't buying it. "If Eisenhower owned the place, we wouldn't pay," they said.

Scialo and Pero wanted their $500 back. Menditto and Garofalo refused to repay the money, which earned the foolhardy young gangsters a death sentence. On March 16, 1958, Scialo, Pero, and two other Brooklyn hoodlums took Menditto and Garofalo for the proverbial one-way ride. Cops found Menditto lying in a gutter, blood spurting from several bullet holes. Miraculously, he was still alive. Garofalo was less fortunate—cops found his bullet-riddled carcass the next day, March 17.

Menditto lingered for more than a week, and, proving himself to be less than a "stand-up" guy, spilled what was left of his guts to the cops. On his deathbed he fingered his four abductors. Two of them, a couple of local torpedoes named Louis Espositio and Tommy Caizzo, were picked up and questioned. Cops got little from them, and they were quickly released for lack of evidence. Mimi Scialo and Angie Pero, on the other hand, wisely comprehended that this was one rap that would be tough to beat and dropped from sight. Scialo made it onto the Most Wanted list on May 9, 1958; five weeks later, on June 16, 1958, Pero was added to the list.

The boys had friends in high places. Armed with the best lawyers that syndicate money could buy, not to mention a dearth of witnesses, Scialo was confident enough to surrender to the FBI on July 27, 1959. Pero did the same, and by Christmas 1960 the U.S. attorney for the Eastern District of New York tossed out the federal warrants against both men.

INTERESTING FUGITIVE FACT:
Though there was federal paper issued on both men, it's highly unlikely the fugitives ever strayed far from their usual haunts in Brooklyn and Manhattan for the 14 months they were wanted. Both boroughs were lousy with safe houses and hideouts with all the comforts of home. In those heady days the Mob took care of their own.

108. FREDERICK GRANT DUNN, burglar, bank robber

LISTED: June 17, 1958
CAUGHT: September 8, 1959
DESCRIPTION: Born May 13, 1905, Sioux City, Iowa. Five feet 9 1/2 inches tall, 150 pounds. Occupations: shoemaker, railroad shop worker, salesman. Scars and marks: round scar above left ear; scar left side of nose; scar over right eye; small cut scar above left eyebrow; cut scar on upper lip; mole on right side of throat; scar on left middle finger; scar on right index finger. Aliases: Fred Carlson, Fritz Dunn, Freddie Dynn, Freddie Gunn, William Haney, Fred Mathison, Fred Matterson, Robert Bartlett Nolan, Robert Bartlett Noland, others.

Frederick the Not-So-Great. In his Most Wanted mug shot, Freddie Dunn at the age of 52 resembled not so much a hardened criminal but rather a meek, unassuming bespectacled clerk and devoted family man. He was, in reality, a career felon who took his first pinch for breaking and entering at the age of 14, in 1919.

He was sent to the Iowa State Training School for Boys, a pleasant-sounding name for what was little more than a juvenile prison. He remained there for the next five years and was discharged in 1924. Two months later, he turned up in Gayville, South Dakota, where he was arrested for knocking over a general store with two accomplices. Shopkeepers in South Dakota, where frontier justice still reigned, didn't cotton to being robbed. The grizzled old proprietor grabbed a shotgun and started spitting lead, hitting one of Dunn's pals in the eye. Dunn and his now half-blind friend were convicted of burglary in November 1924 and were given sentences of five years apiece.

Dunn was paroled in 1927 and resurfaced in Omaha, Nebraska, and was quickly nabbed for violating said parole. He was returned to the state pen in South Dakota to serve out the balance of his sentence and was freed in August 1929. He returned to his native Iowa, but freedom was fleeting. He was connected to a bank robbery in the town of Salix. A few weeks later, Dunn and another accomplice knocked over a store in his hometown of Sioux City. Four months later, in early 1930, he took a second bank in Sioux City. With Iowa becoming too hot, Dunn fled to Chicago, by now a popular refuge for criminals. It was here that Dunn was arrested in February 1930, and he was returned to Iowa to stand trial. A three-time loser and then some by now, Dunn knew that any judge worth his salt would toss the book at him. With a gun smuggled into his cell by a friend, Dunn and another inmate broke out, shooting the jailer in the thigh in the process. He was nabbed the same day when lawmen cornered him in an alleyway. After a pitched gun battle he surrendered.

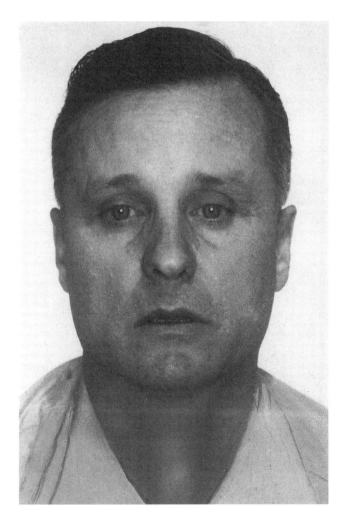

A farmer located skeletal remains along a stream bank near Ellsworth, Kansas, and contacted the sheriff. The remains were sent to the FBI Lab and identified as Dunn.

This time around the angry judge didn't just throw the book at Dunn; he tossed the entire library. Dunn was sentenced to 40 years for the bank robberies and for good measure, handed an additional 30 years for assault with intent to kill. He was sent to the state prison at Fort Madison, Iowa, in March 1930.

Whether Freddie Dunn was a model prisoner isn't known, but authorities either felt he was sufficiently rehabilitated or they were just tired of looking at him; either way, he was paroled in June 1941. Like most cons, Dunn exaggerated his criminal deeds and was convinced, according to some reports, that he was the reincarnation of John Dillinger. If so, he did not share Dillinger's talent for picking more lucrative paydays. In July 1942 Dunn and two others took a bank in Portis, Kansas, for a piddling take of less than $3,000, locking the sole teller inside the vault. The teller managed to escape and, wielding a mean shotgun, fired at the fleeing bandits, wounding one of them. Their car swerved out of control and flipped, rolling over three times. The robbers were at least smart enough to have a second getaway car waiting—as were a couple of their lady friends—and they managed to escape.

Three weeks later, on July 21, Dunn and company were picked up in Denver, Colorado. The three men were handed sentences of 15 years apiece; their molls each landed six years apiece. At 36 Freddie Dunn was older, but no wiser. Prior to the actual sentencing prison officials found hacksaw blades in Dunn's cell. He had no choice but to confess to planning a breakout. This time around authorities decided stronger measures were necessary where Dunn was concerned. He was sent to Leavenworth, this time for 10 years.

By the time he was paroled in November 1952, Dunn had spent most of his 47 years behind bars. Cooler heads would have called it quits on crime, but not Dunn. He continued his lawless ways and was nailed in January 1954 for possession of firearms. It was back to Leavenworth until August 1957. Barely two months passed before Dunn was a wanted man again—for burglary in Iowa and Kansas. He was caught again in Russell, Kansas, for robbing a general store. Dunn was once and forever a small-time crook.

He escaped from the hick town jail in Sylvan Grove, Kansas, on January 11, 1958, and named to the Most Wanted list on June 17, 1958. This time, however, Dunn stayed out of sight, but not because he had gotten better at dodging the law. On September 8, 1959, his skeletal remains were found

near Ellsworth, Kansas. Cause of death was debatable, but the smart money was on murder. His Wanted poster described him as "frugal," which can also be construed as cheap. There's a good chance he was killed over an unfair division of spoils.

INTERESTING FUGITIVE FACT:
During one robbery in Sioux City, Iowa, Freddie Dunn supposedly fired his gun into the ceiling to get everyone's attention. It worked, but only to a point—the take was a paltry $67.

109. FRANK LAWRENCE SPRENZ, robber, airplane thief

LISTED: September 10, 1958
CAUGHT: April 15, 1959
DESCRIPTION: Born February 13, 1930, Akron, Ohio. Five feet 10 inches tall, 185 to 192 pounds. Occupations: auto mechanic, clerk-typist, construction worker, painter, lifeguard. Scars and marks: one-inch cut scar over on chin; little finger of right hand crooked at first joint. Remarks: May wear toupee; reportedly likes to wear Ivy League clothing; is said to be studious and soft-spoken, but inclined to brag and enjoys being the "big shot"; enjoys working on old cars and is an avid gun trader. Aliases: James Heil, Frank Lawrence Spence, Frank Lawrence Spentz Jr., Frank Lawrence Sprence, Frank Lawrence Sprence, Frank Larry Sprentz, Harold Scali, others.

That Magnificent Man in His Flying Machine. He was a tricky one, that Frank Sprenz. Most criminals steal cars. Frankie also stole cars, but unlike most criminals, he also stole a plane or two.

Like many teenagers of the World War II generation, he lied about his age (he was all of 15) and enlisted in the U.S. Army in 1945. Whether he was driven by patriotism or was facing jail time for some youthful offense is unknown, but he was in fact mustered out with an honorable discharge in February 1947. He returned to his native Akron, Ohio, where trouble followed. He stole a car, probably not his first, but ditched it before lawmen could catch him and re-enlisted in the army, figuring that working for Uncle Sam was better than serving time for Uncle Sam.

Back in uniform, Sprenz ruined his chances for a second honorable discharge when he broke into the armory and stole a submachine gun and a pistol or two. He also "borrowed" a car to make good his escape. At the age of 17, his colorful life of crime was just beginning.

Authorities quickly nabbed him, and he was sent to the Ohio State Reformatory to get his mind right until he reached manhood. Records indicate he did reach manhood but his state of mind was still an open question. He managed to keep his nose somewhat clean (at least no records exist of his crimes during this period) until April 1958, when he went on trial for burglary and armed robbery. With the help of a prison trusty, and using a makeshift cell lock key made from a small metal slab from his bunk, Sprenz broke out of his cell and released four of his fellow inmates. Confronted by guards, Sprenz and his buddies used the only weapon available to them: hot coffee, which they sprayed all over the surprised screws. This gave them enough time to steal a shotgun, a couple of revolvers, and two county-owned cars.

In a scene Bonnie and Clyde would have admired, Sprenz and his pals crashed through a garage door and sped off into the night, with a platoon of Akron cops in hot pursuit. The ensuing shoot-out with the cops left one escapee dead and another captured. Sprenz and his remaining friends had better luck. They headed into the next county, where they boosted a car, one that wasn't as hot as the one they were driving, and hightailed it due south to Virginia. They were spotted by cops in Norfolk, who cornered the fugitives on a dead-end street. One was captured. Sprenz and Richard Hoskinson, the last two, wisely decided that he travels fastest who travels alone, and they split up.

It had been a long day, and Sprenz was tired, dirty, and ravenous. He broke into a house—no one was home, fortunately for them—and made himself right at home. He helped himself to everything in the icebox, took a bath, and stole some clothes. Then he dropped from sight.

With the G-men hot on his trail, Hoskinson quit running and gave himself up in Detroit a month later, in May 1958. Sprenz made the Most Wanted list on September 10, 1958. Over the next exhausting six months records show Sprenz heisted 30 cars and used almost 40 aliases in his cross-country flight from the law that zigzagged almost 25,000 miles. If Sprenz had one bad habit—other than being a chronic lawbreaker—it was thoughtfully sending birthday cards to his friends and relatives, which kept the Bureau boys hot on his trail.

Smarter than the average bear, Frenz liked to plan ahead. After he knocked over a bank in Hamilton,

Ohio, in March 1959, netting almost $30,000, he drove to nearby Middleton and stole an airplane. Like a criminal Indiana Jones, he barnstormed his way south to Raymondsville, Texas, where an airport manager recognized Frenz from his Wanted poster and alerted the law. Five days later, Frenz (now going by the name Harold Scali) was nabbed by Mexican cops in Cozumel. He was returned to the States, where he admitted to Feds why he'd fled to Mexico: "I just wanted to get to where there were no FBI men."

He got his wish. Sprenz was convicted on numerous counts of state and federal charges. After the judge tallied the numbers, Frank was handed a prison term of nearly two centuries.

INTERESTING FUGITIVE FACT:
According to his Wanted poster, Frank Sprenz "likes to wear Ivy League style clothing and is said to be studious and quiet spoken." Ample evidence of his courtly manners was witnessed during his robbery of the Hamilton, Ohio, bank. He graciously thanked the employees and customers for their cooperation as he made his hasty exit.

110. DAVID LYNN THURSTON, armed robber

LISTED: January 8, 1959
CAUGHT: February 6, 1959
DESCRIPTION: Born in 1928.

Dumb and Dumber. One almost had to feel pity for David Lynn Thurston—a five-time loser, he was one of the most inept criminals to ever make the Most Wanted list. More often than not, he always fled his crime scenes empty-handed. Serving in the U.S. Army, he went AWOL at the age of 18 and was quickly apprehended. A stint in the stockade at Fort Leavenworth followed, and he was dishonorably discharged in November 1947.

The next few years found Thurston busted for a host of small-potato crimes: vagrancy in California, car theft and burglary in Wyoming, and more burglary in Northern California—all before he turned 21. He was remanded to the California Youth Authority in late 1948 and was sent to a forestry camp in the summer of 1949. Davy bummed around for the next three years; he decided to try his luck in Los Angeles in late 1951, one criminal more or less was not apt to attract much attention in that city. He adopted the alias

James L. Moore, David Thurston being too familiar to the authorities.

In January 1952 Thurston got into a high-speed chase with cops after yet another botched robbery. To make matters worse, he smashed the getaway car into a police car. He was promptly cuffed and shoved into a patrol car by L.A.'s Finest. In an effort to piss off the LAPD even more, Thurston tried to grab a shotgun from the dashboard rack before cops beat him down. He was given a one-year sentence in the county lockup and five years' probation.

A smarter man might have called it quits on crime, but upon his release from jail David Thurston proved once more that stupidity always seeks its level. He went south to Long Beach, and in January 1954 he was popped again for trying to knock over a liquor store. Once in custody he went ballistic and tried to crash through a window to the street. When this failed, he flung himself to the floor and had a major tantrum, banging his head against the floor. He pleaded guilty to robbery and was handed a one-year to life sentence, serving his time in San Quentin.

He was paroled in late 1957 and quickly resumed his less than spectacular life of crime. With an accomplice he stole a bunch of cars and robbed his way up the coast to Portland, Oregon. They were picked up in January 1957.

Thurston escaped from custody in April 1958 and was named to the Most Wanted list on January 8, 1959. During this time deciding that the West Coast was too hot, he made his way east to New York City. Trouble followed in due course. He was nabbed by the NYPD after attempting to rob a Broadway restaurant—after a foot chase through theater crowds. He was shipped back to Oregon to face the music.

INTERESTING FUGITIVE FACT:
Thurston's accomplice in a Portland, Oregon, supermarket robbery proved every bit as inept as his friend. In the middle of the crime, the accomplice almost blew his genitals off when the pistol went off in his pocket.

111. JOHN THOMAS FREEMAN, armed robber

LISTED: February 17, 1959
CAUGHT: February 18, 1959

Dim Bulb. John Freeman was a specialist in armed robbery—banks, liquor stores, anywhere cash to be found. He was named to the Most Wanted list on February 17, 1959 after fleeing the state of Missouri

to avoid prosecution. He surfaced in Maryland, where agents caught up with him a day after his posting after a sharp-eyed citizen recognized his photo in a local newspaper.

112. EDWIN SANFORD GARRISON, murderer, robber

LISTED: March 4, 1959
CAUGHT: September 9, 1960
DESCRIPTION: Born March 25, 1900, in Newport, Kentucky. Five feet 9 1/2 inches tall, 137 to 143 pounds, with gray hair and blue eyes. Occupations: accountant, bookkeeper, auditor. Scars and marks: burn scar lower right leg, burn scar lower left leg. Wears false teeth, occasionally drinks to excess, reportedly can perform complicated arithmetical problems. Aliases: James Brown, George Coleman, James Gardner, Edwin Garretson, Edward Sanford Garrison, Gary Garrison, George E. Garrison, George E. Garry, George E. Martin, George Walker, George E. Williams, George Walter Williams, "Brownie," and others. Garrison reportedly will violently resist arrest. He has a record of several escapes from penal institutions and has been armed while arrested.

St. Louis Blues. Garrison was serving a life term in an Alabama lock-up when he broke out in August 1958. He made the Most Wanted list, for the second time, on March 4, 1959.

In the year and a half he was at large, Garrison made his way up to St. Louis, Missouri, where he had a number of criminal buddies. Reportedly a wizard at math, he easily found work as a bookkeeper. Suspecting that Garrison would flee to St. Louis, federal agents put some of his friends under surveillance. Their hunches paid off—one of them led the Feds straight to Garrison's apartment. He surrendered without incident, telling agents, "I'm glad it's over. I know the FBI. You can't fool the FBI for very long."

INTERESTING FUGITIVE FACT:
When he saw his mug on a Wanted poster after his arrest on a bulletin board, Garrison thoughtfully commented, "You can take my picture down now."

113. EMMETT BERNARD KERVAN, burglar, counterfeiter

LISTED: April 29, 1959
CAUGHT: May 13, 1959
DESCRIPTION: Kervan suffers from tuberculosis.

Gentleman Bandit. Emmett Kervan was already a seasoned, though not particularly successful, criminal by the time he walked into a Norwalk, Connecticut, bank in February 1959 and relieved a teller of some $30,000. It was easily his most successful score to date, made more impressive by the fact that he made it through a roadblock as he fled the scene.

It would have been a clean getaway had Kervan not sideswiped a trucker on the highway. The irate trucker phoned in a complaint to police, who quickly went into action. Kervan abandoned the car in Buffalo, New York, wisely removing the license plates. He neglected to take the registration slip, however, and authorities traced it straight back to Norwalk. Sketches were circulated, and workers at a local hospital ID'd Kervan, who'd worked there in between his criminal activities. He was named to the Most Wanted list on April 29, 1959.

"Nice gentleman" Emmett Bernard Kervan was arrested in El Paso, Texas.

Kervan journey south to El Paso, Texas, most likely for its easy proximity to Mexico should the need arise. Through diligence and hard work, FBI agents traced Kervan to El Paso and arrested him without incident on May 13, 1959, recovering $20,000 of the stolen bank money. Returned to Connecticut, Kervan pled guilty and was sentenced to prison.

INTERESTING FUGITIVE FACT:
Kervan's landlady in El Paso described him as "a nice gentleman."

114. RICHARD ALLEN HUNT, robber, kidnapper

LISTED: May 27, 1959
CAUGHT: June 2, 1959

Excitable Boy. Richard Hunt came from a bad home—drunken, abusive father and indifferent mother. To make matters even worse, local authorities placed him in an orphan's home run by the Women's Christian Temperance Union in Oregon, which was undoubtedly no picnic, either.

Hunt joined the army in 1950, the military being preferable to teetotaling Jesus freaks, but his problems with authority and his grudge against society made his life difficult. He ended up with the military police during the Korean conflict, but ended up spending more time in the brig than did the majority of men he was assigned to police.

Hunt was transferred stateside after the war, but trouble followed. He went AWOL and spent six months in an Oregon county jail for grand theft. He was released to the MPs but went AWOL. Finally, in October 1954, the army had had enough of Richard Hunt and booted him with a dishonorable discharge. At the same time he was handed an 18-month sentence for grand larceny. Never one to learn a lesson the easy way, Hunt escaped from the state prison in Deer Lodge, was recaptured the next day, and had another 18 months added to his sentence. He was paroled in late 1957, but he couldn't quite stay out of trouble.

He started passing bad checks in Idaho, stealing anything he could get his hands on (cars mostly), and drifted through Oregon, Nevada, and Wyoming. Then, in March 1958, Hunt, driving a stolen car, was pulled over for questioning by the police chief of Harrisburg, Oregon. Hunt kidnapped the cop at gunpoint and forced him into the trunk. Ten miles up the road, in Brownsville, Hunt was pulled over yet again by the police chief. Hunt bolted from the car and blasted the second cop, hitting him in the head. Hunt escaped, but in a scene straight out of a Warner Brothers crime movie, Hunt was pursued by a band of angry townspeople. Fortunately, Hunt knew the rugged terrain as well as his pursuers and vanished. The FBI issued a warrant for him in mid 1958.

Crazy Richard made the Most Wanted list on March 27, 1959. Ultimately, he ended up in Thermopolis, Wyoming, where he found work as a ranch hand. A week later, a local cop recognized Hunt's photo from his Most Wanted poster, arrested him, and turned him over to the Feds. He was extradited to Oregon, where he was tried for attempted murder and handed a life sentence.

INTERESTING FUGITIVE FACT:
After the cop shooting in Oregon, Richard Hunt gave the Feds a true run for their money. For over a year he was pursued through California, Arizona, Nevada, and New Mexico, with a side trip through Mexico.

115. WALTER BERNARD O'DONNELL, robber, heartbreaker

LISTED: June 17, 1959
CAUGHT: June 19, 1959

At Large. Walter Bernard O'Donnell was already a seasoned criminal by the time he hit on a most unusual and imaginative outlet for his talents. Wearing a fairly believable toupee and attending local dances, he would pick out the fattest (and usually most available) ladies on the premises and skillfully whirl them around the dance floor. O'Donnell would convince the portly lasses that he was a doctor and that he'd discovered a miracle pill that would help them shed dozens of unwanted pounds. Back at their homes he'd hand the unwitting ladies two barbiturate capsules that knocked them flat, often for hours and days at a time, leaving O'Donnell ample time to ransack the place for money, jewelry, and anything else that might fetch a few bucks. (One of his victims spent four days in a coma before recovering.)

Fluent in Spanish and fairly well educated—at least compared to the majority of pugs and mugs on the Most Wanted list—O'Donnell was wanted on fugitive warrants in California, Illinois, Pennsylva-

nia, Florida, and Washington, D.C. He made the Most Wanted list on June 17, 1959.

O'Donnell was going by the name of A. J. Rossi when agents nabbed him two days later in Norfolk, Virginia, where he was scheduled to address the local chapter of Alcoholics Anonymous. "I knew you'd get me eventually," he said to agents. "I'm glad it's over." He was given a 10-year sentence for transporting stolen goods over state lines, and an additional five years for an auto theft in Detroit.

INTERESTING FUGITIVE FACT:
During his days on the run O'Donnell was referred to as "the Sleeping Pill Bandit" by authorities.

116. BILLY OWENS WILLIAMS, kidnapper

LISTED: July 10, 1959
CAUGHT: March 4, 1960
DESCRIPTION: Born January 22, 1927, Tampa, Florida. Height: five feet 11 inches; weight: 164 to 175 pounds. Race: Negro. Occupations: laborer, stevedore, hotel bellboy, truck driver, baker, car washer, cook, kitchen helper. Scars and marks: small black moles on face; four-inch cut scar on inner side right forearm; burn scar on left forearm; several small scars inner side both elbows. Remarks: Williams has one gold upper tooth, occasionally wears a mustache. Aliases: Willie Anderson, Bill Williams, Gene Williams, Owen Williams, others.

For My Next Impression, Jesse Owens. Raised dirt poor in Tampa, Florida, Billy Owens Williams was first arrested at the age of 14 for chicken stealing. Like many aspiring thieves of the era, Williams was given a choice, serving his country or serving time. He opted for the former, and by 1947 he was serving with the U.S. Army in Korea. He burglarized the home of a Korean national, which earned him a dishonorable discharge and 10 years at hard labor. His sentence was remitted, however, and he was shipped stateside.

Back home Williams found that opportunities for uneducated black men were few. He worked the odd menial job—car washer, cook, kitchen helper, and baker—until he decided that maybe the military wasn't so bad after all. He re-enlisted in July 1947 and was sent to Japan. Billy couldn't seem to stay out of trouble, though, and in December 1947 he stole a car. Not so serious a crime in itself perhaps, but Williams also chose to lock the owner in the trunk, which was severely frowned upon. He was court-martialed a second time and sent stateside to serve 18 months of hard labor at the federal pen in Danbury, Connecticut. Prison doctors listed him as "delusional" and having major problems dealing with reality. Despite this, he was released in February 1951 and returned to his hometown of Tampa, where things went steadily downhill. He threatened his family with a knife on more than one occasion and was branded by Tampa officials as a menace to society (long before the term was regarded as a badge of honor by young gangstas).

Still, Williams managed to keep it together until June 9, 1954. With an accomplice he kidnapped a Tampa businessman and stashed the man in the trunk of his own car. The businessman promised to pay his abductors $1,000. No mental giants they, Williams and his friend actually believed the man and released him. The victim went straight to the cops. Williams's friend was picked up the next day and ultimately drew a life sentence. Williams wisely fled, stealing cars to make good his escape. Federal charges of unlawful flight to avoid prosecution were filed against him in Tampa.

He made his way to New York City, where one more crazy would hardly go noticed. On August 9 he heisted another car and was again stopped in New Jersey by police. This time he didn't escape. Lawmen promptly slapped him into a holding cell in Trenton to await transfer back to Florida.

Williams was not a model prisoner. He set fire to his cell and tried to hang himself with his belt. He claimed he was the real murderer in the infamous Sam Sheppard homicide case and tried to extort money from the family. The Trenton authorities were more than happy to send Williams back to Florida, where he was diagnosed as criminally insane and deposited in the state mental hospital in Chatta-hoochie in December 1954.

Williams bided his time and managed to escape from the TB ward in March 1958. He made the Most Wanted list on July 10, 1958. It took eight months, but the Feds finally caught up with Williams in New York City, where he was ratted out by a coworker. He offered no resistance.

INTERESTING FUGITIVE FACT:
On June 30, 1954, Williams was stopped by New Jersey cops on a routine traffic check. Before cops could check the license number, though, Williams bounded out of the stolen car like a hopped-up jackrabbit and escaped, leaving behind a pistol and 30 rounds of ammo.

Jenkins was arrested in a Buffalo, New York, motel after an informant tipped off the Bureau.

117. JAMES FRANCIS JENKINS, robber, con artist

LISTED: July 21, 1959
CAUGHT: August 12, 1959

If It's Tuesday, This Must Be Buffalo.   Jimmy Jenkins liked to play the ponies. To support his habit he spent the years between 1941 and 1949 plying his criminal trade, which included robbing banks, burglarizing homes and businesses, writing bad checks, and fencing stolen property. He spent the years between 1948 and 1958 in a number of prisons. Back in freeside he spent a year walking the narrow, but boredom set in. On March 4, 1959, along with an accomplice, Randall Nuss, Jenkins robbed a Broomail, Pennsylvania, bank of an impressive $18,000. The boys were nailed by FBI agents a week later in Providence, Rhode Island, and returned to Philadelphia to stand trial.

Jenkins had no intention of spending any more time in prison than was necessary. One smuggled screwdriver and four knotted-together bedsheets later, Jenkins and two others escaped from the Moyamensing County jail two weeks after landing there. Jenkins made his way to the home of a fellow con, Henry Kiter, who was free on bail and awaiting a trial for illegal possession of firearms. Kiter obviously felt his chances of acquittal were lousy, because he decided to join Jenkins and take it on the lam. Jenkins was named to the Most Wanted list on July 21, 1959.

They got as far as a cheap Buffalo, New York, motel when G-men descended on them three weeks later. Neither man put up a fight.

INTERESTING FUGITIVE FACT:
Jimmy Jenkins was not without a sense of humor. When his bail was set at $50,000 for escaping the Moyamensing County jail, he asked the bailiff, "Will you take a check?"

118. HARRY RAYMOND POPE, hired gun

LISTED: August 11, 1959
CAUGHT: August 25, 1959

Party Poper. Harry Pope was scourge of Dallas, Texas. Drug dealer, burglar, hired gun, no crime was too big or too small for Harry, who was dubbed "the walking arsenal" by local cops for the shotgun and three pistols he perpetually toted around. By the age of 30, he'd run up an impressive list of criminal credits. Known as a stand-up guy who'd shoot it out with cops rather than meekly surrender, Pope was a favorite of contract killers and Texas triggermen, who often used him on scores.

In November 1958 police in Phoenix, Arizona, closed in on Pope while he was robbing a drugstore. He bravely shot it out with cops, losing an eye to a bullet in the process. He escaped, but was nailed shortly thereafter and, miraculously, released on bond. He took it on the lam before his trial, and on August 11, 1959 he was named to the Most Wanted list.

Two weeks later, cops in Lubbock, Texas, received a tip that Pope was holed up in a local trailer park along with a Los Angeles couple with whom he was friendly, Clifton and Christine Thompson. On the afternoon of August 25, two federal agents, five Lubbock cops, and one Texas Ranger surrounded the trailer and took Pope and his friends without incident. For all his bravado and fearlessness, Pope knew lousy odds when he saw them, saying, "I knew I didn't have a chance. There were too many of them, and they were armed too heavily." If there had been only three, Pope reasoned, he might have shot it out with them. But eight was too many. "I'm not stupid," he said.

INTERESTING FUGITIVE FACT:
Harry Pope was apparently unaware that he had been named to the prestigious Most Wanted list until advised by the Feds.

Due to an FBI investigation, Pope was arrested in Lubbock, Texas, by the FBI and Texas Rangers.

119. JAMES FRANCIS DUFFY, robber

LISTED: August 26, 1959
CAUGHT: September 2, 1959
ALIASES: Allan Sullivan

I Ain't So Tough. Jimmy Duffy was already a hardened criminal who had served several prison terms (not to mention a stretch in a Pennsylvania nut house) by 1958. Unpredictable and given to irrational, violent outbursts, Duffy was one more James Cagney wannabe who often claimed he'd never be taken alive. "I'll fire all my bullets at the cops," he said, adding fatalistically, "except one, which I'm saving for myself." In March 1959, Duffy and two pals, identified as William McGee and the appropriately named Harry Shank, robbed an Upper Darby, Pennsylvania, roadhouse of $4,500. With cops in hot pursuit, Duffy and his companions managed to escape, but not before totaling their car. McGee and Shank were nabbed in due course, but Duffy managed to disappear.

Jimmy stayed lost for six months. Finally, federal agents traced him to Newark, New Jersey. Duffy's keen criminal instincts smelled the law on his tail, and he hightailed it back to his beloved Pennsylvania. He robbed a Philly drugstore on May 1, 1958. He was named to the Most Wanted list on August 26, 1959. Duffy adopted the alias Allan Sullivan when he checked into a hotel on September 2, where he was ultimately apprehended by federal agents.

INTERESTING FUGITIVE FACT:
Knowing full well of Duffy's claim of never being taken alive, the Feds surrounded the fleabag hotel and prepared to shoot it out with him. Ultimately, their precautions were for naught: Duffy was sitting alone in his room and surrendered without a struggle when agents burst in. "I knew you'd get me," he said forlornly as he was led away.

120. ROBERT GARFIELD BROWN JR., robber

LISTED: September 9, 1959
CAUGHT: January 11, 1960

Crime Pays, But Not for You. The term *dumbing down* may very well have been created expressly for Robert Garfield Brown Jr., a none-to-bright but still dangerous hard-ass from New Hampshire.

Orchard Beach, Maine, is one of those beachside resort towns that seem to be created for the express purpose of being instantly run down, sleazy, and often dangerous, along the lines of Coney Island and Asbury Park, New Jersey. On a hot July night in 1959, Canadian tourists Maurice and Lisa Couture were enjoying the rickety roller coaster and other low-rent attractions when they were bushwhacked by a pair of armed hoodlums. The attackers robbed the terrified couple, then shot Maurice Couture in the chest for good measure before escaping. The $190 they got in the robbery would buy Bobby Brown a lifetime of criminal screw-ups that ended in several long jail terms.

Shooting out-of-towners is considered poor form in seaside towns that rely on their tourist dollars for survival. Maine police set up roadblocks all over the Maine coast, but the gunners, Brown and his accomplice Kenneth Chenette, escaped. The cops caught a break when the fugitives' van was traced to a local repair shop. In the trunk police found burglary tools that were used in some local break-ins.

Brown and Chenette, in the meantime, hopped a Greyhound bus heading south and disappeared into the wilds of Boston. Brown was positively identified by Lisa Couture as one of the shooters. The law was well acquainted with Bobby Brown—he was already sporting convictions for burglary and B&E, not to mention being a habitual parole breaker.

Chenette was picked up in Westwood, Massachusetts, and identified by Lisa Couture as Brown's partner. Chenette confessed and was ultimately sentenced to 50 to 100 years in jail. Brown remained at large and graduated to the Most Wanted list on September 9, 1959. Federal agents tracked him to Cincinnati, Ohio, four months later and in January arrested him in a Salvation Army fleabag. Charged with the crimes of assault with intent to kill and two counts of armed robbery, a no-nonsense judge handed Brown a total of 100 years in the slammer.

Brown was paroled in 1974 and, once back in freeside, proved that experience is not always the best teacher. With a new playmate, one Terrill Jewett, Brown robbed a Portland, Maine, bank for $5,000 and an antitheft device the teller had dropped into their sack for good measure. The device exploded, spraying the getaway car with red dye and stinky smoke. The robbers dumped the car and were picked up a short time later. For his part in the caper Bobby pled guilty and was handed another 25 years in stir. Bobby Brown never could catch a break.

INTERESTING FUGITIVE FACT:
Bobby Brown wasn't all that hard to track down after the Orchard Beach shooting. He was easily identified by the Greyhound bus driver, who recalled Brown asking him about the best places to hop off a bus when being pursued by the law.

121. FREDERICK ANTHONY SENO, bank robber

LISTED: September 24, 1959
CAUGHT: September 24, 1959

À La Carte. Freddy Seno was a semiliterate Italian hood from Chicago whose culinary skills were far superior to his criminal ones. His criminal record dated as far back as 1926, when he was doing various chores for the Windy City syndicate. A Minnesota bank robbery, which netted him $20,000, sent him off to prison for five to 30 years. He was paroled in 1958 and immediately returned to a life of crime, robbing two supermarkets.

On December 11, 1958, Seno made a spectacular escape from the Cook County courtroom and vanished completely. He made the Most Wanted list on September 24, 1959. Agents acting on a tip arrested him the same day in Miami, Florida, where he was working successfully as a chef and a caterer. It was back to Chicago for Freddy Seno, who couldn't cough up the $10,000 bond.

INTERESTING FUGITIVE FACT:
Frederick Seno's services as a caterer took him into the homes of the some of Miami's richest residents, but he chose not to rob them. From all appearances he'd gone relatively straight—his culinary skills were quite in demand. It was a scenario Nat Hiken, creator of the TV hit *Sergeant Bilko*, borrowed for his follow-up series, *Car 54, Where Are You?*

122. SMITH GERALD HUDSON, murderer

LISTED: October 7, 1959
CAUGHT: July 31, 1960
DESCRIPTION: Born March 1, 1928, Westmoreland County, Pennsylvania. Height: five feet eight inches. Weight: 183 pounds. Occupations: coal miner, farmhand, laborer, truck driver. Scars and marks: half-inch scar outer left eyebrow, scar base of left thumb, scar at base of nail on right index finger; appendectomy scar. Remarks: Reportedly indulges heavily in intoxicating beverages and often becomes belligerent when drinking. Aliases: Smith Girard Hudson, "Pit" Hudson, Smith Hudson, Larry King, Calvin Rinehart, John Rhinehart, "Smitty."

Coal Miner's Slaughter. Smitty Hudson hailed from the hardscrabble coal mining country in and around Scranton, Pennsylvania. Like the rest of the miners in his small town, Smitty (or "Pit" as he was often called) worked hard and drank even harder. He had a few scrapes with the law, nothing considered too serious, or so official records indicated. His real troubles started when he was 23. Driving home drunk, Hudson killed his brother-in-law when he smashed his car into a stubborn tree. Hudson was charged with involuntary manslaughter. The county law set a low bond. In coal mining country, drunk driving fatalities were commonplace. Smitty went free.

It was either heavy drinking, continued light deprivation, or just plain guilt that made Smitty Hudson snap. One hot summer evening after a session of boozing Smitty picked up a shotgun and blasted his buddy John Ferguson into the next room. Not content to leave it at that, Hudson left a note for police to find, one in which he vowed to take out a few more unfortunates before killing himself.

He was nabbed four months later and sentenced to a term of 10 to 20 years. Whether he ever made good on his promise to slaughter others is lost to history. He escaped from the Pennsylvania state prison in 1957; it took the Feds more than a year to put him on the Most Wanted list, but make the list he did, on October 27, 1959. Smitty Hudson surfaced in Cozad, Nebraska. A storeowner there recognized Hudson (going by the name of Gerald Bennett and working as a ranch hand) from his Most Wanted poster. The Feds nabbed him on July 31, 1960.

INTERESTING FUGITIVE FACT:
As FBI agents were handcuffing him, Smitty Hudson muttered, in a stunning example of understatement, "I suddenly feel like a man who has no future."

123. JOSEPH LLOYD THOMAS, bank robber

LISTED: October 21, 1959
CAUGHT: December 16, 1959

A Double Life. Joseph Lloyd Thomas was first arrested for a series of small crimes—stealing a couple of autos and operating an illegal still, but by the 1950s he married, settled down, had a couple of kids, and owned a small restaurant in Terre Haute, Indiana. For all intents and purposes, Joey Thomas had gone straight.

Well, almost.

Once a criminal, always a criminal. He was reportedly one of three men who robbed a bank in Shreveport, Louisana, on February 13, 1958, making off with a hefty $35,000 in cash. His fellow bank robbers were caught quickly, but Thomas's luck was better—he made a clean getaway. Thomas was at large for almost two years when was named to the Most Wanted list on October 21, 1959.

He used his time wisely, resettling in the small South Carolina town of Pelzer, going by the name of George Ashley and using his share of the bank loot to open a used-car lot. His wife also adopted an alias, and their children were even enrolled in the local school. By all appearances the Ashleys were a solid, God-fearing American family.

It was Thomas's Wanted poster in the local post office that proved his undoing. Agents nailed him at a local gas station, and he surrendered without incident.

INTERESTING FUGITIVE FACT:
A smart fugitive is always prepared. When agents arrested Thomas on December 16, 1959, they found a gun hidden behind his car's radio, two hacksaw blades strapped to his leg, and $125 in cash stuffed into his shoe.

FUGITIVES
OF THE 1960s

Introduction

Call these "The Workhorse Years." There were more members of the Ten Most Wanted list in the 1960s than any other decade—a staggering 180 fugitives. (That's more than the 1980s and 1990s combined.) There were some banner years when it seemed that the FBI couldn't keep putting bad guys on the Top Ten fast enough. In 1960 there were 21 Top Tenners caught. In 1964 there were 18. The very next year 20 were caught. The year after that 16. And in 1968 the FBI enjoyed its all-time Top Ten record: 33 fugitives nabbed; seven of those were caught thanks to tips from the American public.

Maybe TV made a difference. During the 1960s Top Tenners had the dubious distinction of appearing on television on a regular basis, thanks to the Efrem Zimbalist Jr. drama *The FBI*. Before every episode Assistant Director Cartha D. DeLoach, on behalf of J. Edgar Hoover, introduced a new addition to the Top Ten list. "I would like to thank the American public for their splendid support in helping combat crime and subversion," DeLoach said during one broadcast in November 1965. "Only through such wholehearted cooperation can the security of our nation be maintained."

Notable fugitives in this decade include beer baron killer Joseph Corbett Jr. (#127); two-timer Ernest Tait (#23 and #133); bank robbery genius Al Nussbaum (#167) and his violent partner, Bobby Randall Wilcoxson (#168); long-time runner John William Clouser (#203); brothers Sam and Earl Veney (#206 and #207); Martin Luther King Jr. assassin James Earl Ray (#277); and Ruth Eisemann Schier (#293), the first woman to make the Top Ten.

124. KENNETH RAY LAWSON, burglar, drug dealer

LISTED: January 4, 1960
CAUGHT: March 17, 1960
DESCRIPTION: Born in Tennessee.

Red Streak. Kenneth Ray Lawson's criminal record stretches back more than half a century. His early career included a robbery at a Limestone, Tennessee, hardware store and, while that case was on appeal, a heist at a Greeneville, Tennessee, supermarket. He was also charged with felonious assault for throwing hams at the officers in pursuit. But his rookie days ended with a 12-to-30-year sentence at Brushy Mountain Prison. In his first escape attempt, January 31, 1958, Lawson scaled two prison walls, but was recaptured a few hours later in a stolen car. Two months later, he led a prison riot, and in April 22, 1959, attempted another escape with four other inmates, hiding behind a false partition in a railroad freight car parked inside the prison walls. His cohorts were captured, but Lawson remained at large. He was named the Most Wanted list on January 4, 1960.

Ten weeks later, he was arrested in Mexico City and returned to Tennessee to complete his sentence. Lawson's second criminal career started in 1965 in Marion, Ohio, when he was arrested for safe cracking and breaking and entering. He served several years for that crime and a subsequent parole violation. In 1990 he was arrested in Texas for fraud and sentenced to seven months in the pen. Upon his release he was charged with cocaine trafficking in Kentucky. But Lawson ran and stayed one step ahead of authorities for almost five years, dying his hair red and removing his tattoos. He was convicted of the drug charge in absentia and given 30 years. When he was captured in Beaufort, South Carolina in April 1996, a five-year failure-to-appear charge was tacked on. He's now serving his time in Kentucky.

INTERESTING FUGITIVE FACT:
Lawson did try to go straight. After an honorable discharge from the army and a dishonorable discharge from the air force—including two years in the disciplinary barracks—Lawson worked as a mechanic, a used-car salesman, a coal miner, and a dance instructor. "He's a very smart guy, very tough," Eastern District Kentucky Deputy Marshal Roger Daniel says. "He just didn't know how to use that intelligence on the outside."

125. TED JACOB RINEHART, robber

LISTED: January 25, 1960
CAUGHT: March 7, 1960
DESCRIPTION: Born January 21, 1927, in Poplar Bluff, Missouri. Fond of scotch and older women.

Better than Baby Face. Ted Jacob Rinehart once boasted that his criminal career made infamous bank robber "Baby Face" Nelson "look like a piker." The *Los Angeles Times* didn't agree, noting the 33-year-old burglar and jewel thief's March 7, 1960, capture with four paragraphs buried inside

Rinehart was arrested in Granada Hills, California, after a citizen recognized him from a Wanted flyer. Rinehart told agents he learned of his addition to the Top Ten list while watching television.

the paper. Law enforcement had been pursuing Rinehart from the age of 17, when he was arrested for breaking and entering. He improved his technique—his m.o. (modus operandi) was to move around, renting homes in a working-class area, and casing the wealthier neighbors—but the cops followed, charging Rinehart with grand larceny and armed robbery. He was jailed, finally, in Florida, sentenced to 10 years for jewel theft. Five and a half years later, he was paroled, but a parole violation had him running from the cops again, and the FBI named the fugitive to the Top Ten list on January 25, 1960. Six weeks later, Rinehart was apprehended by FBI agents as he drove through the Los Angeles neighborhood of Granada Hill. He surrendered without any resistance.

INTERESTING FUGITIVE FACT:
Rinehart grew a mustache and gained 40 pounds while he was on the run, but the disguise didn't fool the Feds—and probably slowed him down.

126. CHARLES CLYATT ROGERS, murderer

LISTED: March 18, 1960
CAUGHT: May 11, 1960
DESCRIPTION: Scar on neck, "Mother" tattoo on back of right hand. Alias: Charles Norris.

Dumbo's Last Flight. Rookie Minneapolis patrolman Donald M. Schilz spent his spare time studying the Most Wanted posters. His hobby was fugitive Charles Clyatt Rogers's downfall. Rogers's Most Wanted poster was printed March 18, 1960. It detailed the 31-year-old criminal's escape from a Chattahoochee, Florida, hospital for the criminally insane 11 months earlier. Rogers, serving a life sentence for first-degree murder, had been committed to the institution after an attempted suicide. He checked himself out of the institution on March 29, 1959, by climbing through a second-floor window on a ladder of bed sheets. Schilz memorized the fugitive's face—dark eyes, pointed chin, long forehead, and Dumbo ears. On the morning of May 11, 1960, while walking his beat on Marquette Avenue, Schilz saw that face again in the Minneapolis Salvation Army breakfast line.

INTERESTING FUGITIVE FACT:
Rogers should have stayed out of Schilz's way. The patrolman was known for his elephant memory and

eagle eyes. He'd captured an FBI fugitive the same way two years earlier.

127. JOSEPH CORBETT JR., kidnapper, murderer

LISTED: March 30, 1960
CAUGHT: October 29, 1960
DESCRIPTION: Born October 25, 1928, in Seattle, Washington. Six feet two inches, 160 to 170 pounds, with light brown hair. Corbett is nearsighted, and his two upper front teeth slant inward.

The Most Wanted Man Since Dillinger. On February 9, 1960, Adolph Coors, beer king of the West, left his ranch home, climbed into his family station wagon, and drove toward his office in Golden, Colorado. The burly 44-year-old never made it. By 10:45 A.M.—15 minutes into the weekly executive meeting, staff members became worried. William Coors called the ranch and learned that his brother had left hours before. A short while later, a milk truck driver named Daniel Crocker discovered an abandoned station wagon in the middle of his delivery route. The motor was still humming. Police arrived on the scene and found splotches of blood on a nearby bridge, and in the mud below it a tan baseball cap—just like the one Ad Coors was fond of wearing. A 100-man search party quickly formed, but no luck. Adolph Coors was missing, and it looked like a kidnapping. The FBI was called in to try to piece together what had happened.

The case was rough going. Coors had no enemies to speak of, and the FBI quickly ruled out Coors splitting on his wife and kids. (By all accounts, the beer king enjoyed a blissful family life.) There were no serious ransom demands, either—just a few crackpots sending notes, probably hoping to score some quick cash. Then one tip came in that started the case rolling. A Morrison, Colorado, resident remembered seeing a 1951 yellow sedan parked near the bridge that morning. Even better, the man remembered the license plate number: AT-62. A few days later, that car was found clear across the country in Atlantic City, New Jersey. The car, a yellow Mercury, had been torched, but the vehicle identification number was readable. The car belonged to one Walter Osbourne, from Denver, Colorado. Osbourne turned out to the alias of another man: Joseph Corbett Jr., a former con who had escaped from a Chino, California, prison where he was serving a term for second-degree murder. Although they didn't officially link Corbett to the Coors disappearance, he was named to the Ten Most Wanted list on March 30, 1960.

In the November 1960 issue of *Reader's Digest* was a detailed profile of Corbett along with the headline "THE FBI WANTS THIS MAN." The story detailed the Coors abduction, as well as Corbett's biography—a life marked by odd tragedy (his mother died when she fell off a roof that Corbett was supposed to have repaired) and false career starts (medical school, the military). The murder of Air Force Sgt. Alan Lee Reed in 1949—supposedly over a misunderstanding—led to Corbett's jail sentence. After his escape he cooked up the alias "Walter Osbourne" and settled in the Denver area. The *Reader's Digest* article was also full of amazing trivia that demonstrated how much the FBI researched their Top Tenners: "For several years, Corbett habitually bought $3 worth of gas each time he fueled his car. He is left-handed in most activities, but claims to be ambidextrous." The story ended with the plea: "If you see Joseph Corbett—in the library, the factory, at a restaurant or supermarket—go quietly to the telephone and call the FBI. The number is on the first page of the local telephone directories, or the operator will give it to you. Somebody, somewhere, knows this man. If you do, call the FBI at once."

The article worked.

Two issues later, *Reader's Digest* proudly ran the headline "HOW THE DIGEST HELPED CATCH KILLER CORBETT," and branded him the "most wanted killer in the United States since John Dillinger." As it turned out, Ad Coors's dead body was discovered in a mountain trash dump in September 1960, with evidence of two gunshots to the back. The day after the magazine hit newsstands on October 24, a tip came into the Toronto Police Department. "I worked with [Corbett] last summer at McPherson's Warehouse, but he didn't call himself Corbett," said the tipster. This led the FBI to a rooming house in Winnipeg, but as it turned out, they had just missed their quarry. They did, however, learn that Corbett had rented a red Pontiac, but never returned it. Word went out, and Vancouver police spotted the car on October 29, and eyewitnesses pinpointed a guy matching Corbett's description living in an apartment building nearby. A team of nine men—mostly Canadian police—were dispatched to the building. FBI Agent Al Gunn knocked on the door, and when the door popped open, Corbett's face was on the other side.

"I'm the man you're looking for," Corbett admitted. "I'm not armed."

Corbett was seized, then taken back to face trial for murder in Denver.

There's no official word on this, but it is presumed that J. Edgar Hoover renewed his *Reader's Digest* subscription that year.

INTERESTING FUGITIVE FACT:
Corbett insisted on drinking beer in a glass rather than right from the can or bottle.

128. WILLIAM MASON, murderer

LISTED: April 6, 1960
CAUGHT: April 27, 1960
DESCRIPTION: Born in Nashville, Tennessee. Described as a "dapper fellow."

Only a Matter of Time. FBI agents ran into murderer William Mason on the street on the way to his suspected Milwaukee hideout. "I knew it was only a matter of time until you got me," Mason told the agents. "I saw the posters you had out on me." Those posters fingered Mason for the murder and attempted murder of two men after a bar brawl in Detroit on March 10, 1959. Mason had been involved in a fistfight with two men, James Quinney, age 25, and Luther Johnson, age 27. The battle moved out of the tavern and into the street, and Mason slashed Quinney with a knife before fleeing the scene. That alone wouldn't have been enough to make the Top Ten list, but Mason, a former convict who'd served years for attempted murder and repeated parole violations, returned to the bar—where Quinney and Johnson were still drinking—a few hours later with a gun. He shot both men. Quinney died, but Johnson survived to finger Mason. Mason fled to Chicago and then to Milwaukee, where he lived for several months working as an arc welder, until he bumped into the FBI.

INTERESTING FUGITIVE FACT:
Though the FBI didn't mention it, apparently Mason loved to dance. His first conviction came after he tried to slit the throat of a constable who threatened to throw him out of a Tennessee dance hall.

129. EDWARD REILEY, bank robber

LISTED: May 10, 1960
CAUGHT: May 24, 1960
DESCRIPTION: Occupation: operator of an auto wrecking yard.

Life of Reiley. Thank God for used-car salesmen. A dealer in Rockford, Illinois, had stopped in to visit his local sheriff when he saw on the wall a photo he recognized. "That guy," he said. "That guy was pricing cars this morning." The photo was of Ed Reiley, a small-time burglar and car thief who had masterminded a series of successful bank heists in the fall of 1958—first a bank in Hamlet, Indiana ($3,390), one in Onarka, Illinois (total take unknown), and finally one in Logansport, Indiana ($19,827). Reiley was linked to these daylight robberies by his getaway car, which was brought in for repairs at an Illinois garage. (The mechanic became suspicious after he saw the shattered rear window and the burst of shotgun slugs along the body of the car.) On May 10, 1960, Reiley made the Top Ten, and just a few days later, he went shopping for a used car in Rockford.

The sheriff told his used-car-dealing buddy to keep his eyes peeled; if Reiley returned, give him a yell. On May 24 Reiley returned and plunked down a stack of green for a brand-new used car. The dealer took the money, watched Reiley drive away, then called his sheriff buddy with the make, model, and temporary license plate number of the car. Reiley was surrounded by Virginia farmboys with automatic pistols within minutes. Upon arrest he pleaded, "Don't shoot! I'm the guy you want."

INTERESTING FUGITIVE FACT:
Reiley was a father of four.

130. HAROLD EUGENE FIELDS, burglar, robber

LISTED: May 25, 1960
CAUGHT: September 5, 1960
DESCRIPTION: Born in Chicago, Illinois.

Sleeping in Cars with Dynamite. How do you make the Top Ten list? There are many ways, but violating parole and then jumping bail can certainly help the process. In 1958 Harold Fields robbed a Cicero, Illinois, nightclub while on parole for an earlier armed robbery conviction (he hit a Moose Club in Champaign, Illinois, back in 1952), and was given a sentence of 10 to 20 years. Fields posted $25,000 bail, then disappeared. This kind of unrepentant criminal behavior is just the thing that captures the attention of the FBI. On May 25, 1960, Fields was named to the Ten Most Wanted list. Meanwhile, Fields had been zigzagging his way across the Midwest, stealing

cars every so often and using them as temporary shelter. The only thing Fields brought along was a small bag of clothes and another bag full of burglary gear—including dynamite and a .38 revolver. Fields may have thought his lack of address would confuse the FBI, but in fact his habit of stealing cars only made it easy for them to track him down. Stolen cars are invariably reported, and when a pattern emerges, it's only a matter of time before the FBI catches up with you. This is how Fields was discovered in a Schereville, Indiana, restaurant on September 5, 1960. Parked outside was a car he had boosted a month before. "Once I made the list, I knew my days were numbered," he told arresting officers.

INTERESTING FUGITIVE FACT:
Fields had also been convicted of passing phony checks back in the 1940s.

131. RICHARD PETER WAGNER, robber

LISTED: June 23, 1960
CAUGHT: June 26, 1960
DESCRIPTION: Born in Ashland County, Wisconsin. Wagner is a confirmed thief who is said to be incapable of telling the truth.

Trouble Cooking. Richard Peter Wagner committed robberies in more than 15 midwest and western states; he was convicted of his crimes in seven of them, spending more of his adult life in jail than on the job. His specialty—besides getting caught by the cops—was burglarizing the homes of the wealthy, with an eye toward furs, jewelry, and expensive luggage, and he listed a Hollywood actor among his victims. Wagner finally gave cops the slip in Sandstone, Minnesota, where he had been serving time on the federal prison's wood-cutting detail for violating the Dyer Act. On December 17, 1959, with only 30 days left in his sentence, Wagner walked away from the detail toward New York City. He went from New York to Cleveland, from Cleveland to Pittsburgh, and from Pittsburgh back to Minnesota, settling first in Duluth and then in Ray, where he found work as a cook at the Chippewa Lodge. Although Wagner claimed to have 18 years of experience in the kitchen, his boss told authorities, "He cooked like he'd been in a lumber camp or a prison." The chef invariably made an impression on the lodge's guests, though not for the right reasons. Meals were often served an hour late or an hour early, and Wagner's attempts to earn money as a fishing guide were even less successful. On June 23, 1960, when Wagner was named to the Most Wanted list, attorney Phillip Lusk, who had visited the lodge a week earlier, remembered the lumber camp cook and tipped off the FBI.

INTERESTING FUGITIVE FACT:
Wagner didn't resist arrest when agents found him at the Chippewa Lodge. In fact, the fugitive greeted one agent who had arrested him previously with a smile.

132. JAMES JOHN WARJAC, burglar

LISTED: July 19, 1960
CAUGHT: July 22, 1960
DESCRIPTION: Born October 4, 1926, in Fort Wayne, Indiana. Five feet 11 inches, 170 pounds, with blond wavy hair and green-hazel eyes. Occupations: boilermaker, construction worker, dance instructor, laborer, oil field worker, salesman, steel worker. Scars and marks: two scars center of forehead, cut scar right cheek, small cut scar back of left thumb, small cut scar back of left index finger, small scar right elbow, two small cut scars left knee, small round cut scar below right knee. Remarks: Warjac is said to be a master of disguises, who may wear a mustache or dye his hair. He has been described as a very quiet-spoken but quick-tempered individual. Warjac reportedly is an excellent dancer and amateur artist. Caution: Warjac reportedly has carried firearms on his person and under the front seat of his automobile. He may have a small derringer pistol strapped to his leg and tear gas fountain pen on his person. Warjac should be considered extremely dangerous.

A Ph.D. in Fugitive Studies. Is there such a thing as higher learning for federal fugitives? If so, James Warjac could probably tell you a little about the course work. While on the lam from a Texas prison where he was serving a burglary sentence, Warjac reportedly took classes on makeup and disguise techniques, which he thought would help him elude authorities. Warjac had good reason to want to stay hidden: his rap sheet was ridiculously long, dating back 20 years and included such lowlights as juvenile delinquency beefs, auto theft, home invasions, burglaries, and gas station robberies. But the last straw was a burglary he pulled in Corpus Christi in 1955, which resulted in his most serious prison term yet: 12 years. Warjac didn't want to sit around for 12 years, so he took advantage of a nearby rodeo and managed to duck into the crowd after breaking out of the

county lockup. Five years passed; no sign of Warjac. Apparently those classes had paid off. He was named to the Ten Most Wanted list on July 19, 1960.

Sadly for Warjac, those classes didn't include tips on evading the FBI once you're one of the ten most hunted men in America. Warjac lasted only three days on the list, and thanks to an intensive FBI investigation, Warjac was discovered living in Los Angeles, California, the world capital of reinventing yourself.

INTERESTING FUGITIVE FACT:
Warjac's disguise techniques included changing his name: The fugitive's birth name was actually Dale Harold Cline.

133. ERNEST TAIT, burglar

LISTED: August 16, 1960
CAUGHT: September 10, 1960
DESCRIPTION: Born January 1, 1911, in Indianapolis, Indiana. Six feet and 1/2 inch tall, 163 pounds with dark brown hair and brown eyes. Education: eighth grade. Occupations: laborer, automobile mechanic. Scars and marks: several small moles on forearms, five vertical scars below left knee, vertical scar between nose and upper lip. Characteristics: Has high cheek bones and thick lips; reported to have impediment in speech. Aliases: Theodore Lawrence, Ted Malloy, Theodore Malloy, Ted Maloy, Emil Tait, Ernest Tate, Ernest Willhelm, George Wilson, Ted Wilson. Subject is believed to be armed and very dangerous. He has escaped several times, recently after a running gun battle with police officers.

Ernest Goes to Jail (Again). A run on the Top Ten list back in the early 1950s apparently didn't teach Ernest Tait a thing. (See #23.) After serving his five-year hitch, Tait soon fell back into his old routine, and police found him breaking into a bottling plant in Indiana with an idea to raid the safe. Tait jumped bail, and word got back to the FBI, who named him to the Ten Most Wanted list on August 16, 1960. As Yogi Berra once said, it must have been déjà vu all over again for Tait. The FBI pinned him down a few weeks later in dubious company: with a convicted murderer and recent prison escapee named Raymond Duvall. Once again Tait was arrested in the vicinity of an automobile—this time inside of one, instead of standing next to one. Tait was packing a loaded revolver in the glove compartment, but decided at the last minute that a shoot-out was probably not in his best interests. He surrendered to the FBI and was taken back to Indiana to face burglary charges.

134. CLARENCE LEON RABY, murderer

LISTED: August 19, 1960
CAUGHT: August 28, 1960
DESCRIPTION: Born September 2, 1932, in Claiborne County, Tennessee. Six feet, 150 pounds with brown wavy hair and blue eyes. Scars and marks: two-inch scar right cheek crossing over jawbone, one-inch scar between right finger and little finger, right hand; tattoos, six-inch dagger and snake left forearm, flowers on right forearm, scroll upper right arm, sailing ship on chest. Caution: Raby is wanted for brutal shotgun murder committed during a robbery and is also being sought for the cold-blooded murder of a deputy sheriff. He is believed to be armed with shotguns and revolvers, including a .357 magnum. Raby may be accompanied by Billy McCoy, FBI Identification order number 3391. Both should be considered extremely dangerous.

Rabid Raby. The moment Clarence Raby set foot off the Knox County, Tennessee, prison farm, things went from bad to worse, and then worse again. It was July 6, 1960. Along with another escapee Raby used a shotgun to knock over a sporting goods store in Andersonville the next day, taking $1,000 and the life of the elderly owner. Within days Raby's partner was arrested and named Raby as the triggerman; a manhunt ensued. Three weeks later, Union County sheriff's deputies spotted Raby speeding down a highway and offered pursuit. That led to a standoff in a nearby farm. Raby took a farmer named Fred Rutherford hostage inside his own pickup truck. One of the sheriff's deputies, Ben Devault, blocked the driveway, gun drawn. Raby didn't care about that, though—he opened fire, blasting the lawman off his feet, then sped away in the pickup truck. A few hours later, Raby took a couple hostage near Knoxville and forced them to drive him near his parents' home in Heiskel, Tennessee.

But Raby wasn't about to go home yet—he wanted to be near his folks, but not close enough to get picked up by the lawmen who were scouring the countryside, looking for the maniacal cop-killer. When Raby was named to the Ten Most Wanted list, he was living in the Tennessee woods, stealing food and trying to stay out of sight. He couldn't last forever, though. After all of the hostage taking and gunplay, Raby decided to surrender quietly to the FBI at

his parents' home. But that may have been just a tactic to let the heat die down a bit. While awaiting trial, Raby pulled his final jailbreak. Using a .357 pistol someone had smuggled in, Raby made it out of the prison and as far as the front lawn before sheriff's deputies nailed him in a hail of bullets. He was killed instantly, just like his victims.

INTERESTING FUGITIVE FACT:
Raby pulled his first crime—a purse-snatching—when he was 15 years old.

135. NATHANIEL BEANS, murderer

LISTED: September 12, 1960
CAUGHT: September 30, 1960
DESCRIPTION: Alias: Jim Hendley.

"It's All Over Now." The FBI described 39-year-old Nathaniel Beans as "mean and dangerous." Neighbors on the rough streets of Oakland Park, Florida, would have agreed. Beans, a petty criminal, was known for his violent temper even before March 5, 1960, when he ended a lover's quarrel with a gunshot. Such crimes were not unusual in Oakland Park, but Beans's escape was. Six months after Curley Raymond's death, with Beans still on the lam and the local cops without leads, the FBI named Beans to the Most Wanted list on September 12, 1960. The Most Wanted posters blanketed Oakland Park and Buffalo, New York, where Beans's two sisters and brother lived. On the evening of September 30, three Buffalo detectives tracked Beans to a second-floor apartment, where he was playing cards with three associates. The cops arrested Beans for possession of a knife and then confronted him with the Most Wanted poster. "It's all over now," Beans acknowledged.

INTERESTING FUGITIVE FACT:
Beans fled from Florida to New York in the hope that his siblings would help him. No such luck. According to one, Beans was "too mean to have anything to do with."

136. STANLEY WILLIAM FITZGERALD, murderer

LISTED: September 20, 1960
CAUGHT: September 22, 1960
DESCRIPTION: Born December 9, 1920, in Oakland, California. Five feet 10 inches, 190 pounds, reddish blond hair, bald on

top with blue-gray eyes. Occupations: bartender, carpenter, cement worker, dairy worker, heavy equipment operator, mechanic, painter, salesman, truck driver, welder. Remarks: Fitzgerald reportedly is an avid gambler and drinks alcoholic beverages to excess. Caution: Fitzgerald reportedly possesses a .22 caliber hi-standard automatic pistol. During the robbery he is alleged to have cold-bloodedly shot one victim five times, causing his death and shot the other victim in the arm and leg. He should be considered extremely dangerous. Aliases: Ray L. Fitzgerald, Stanley Fitzgerald, Stanley W. Fitzgerald, Clyde Herr, J. Vogel.

When Irish Eyes Are Running. When Stan Fitzgerald tossed back one too many pints, he couldn't help himself. He started leading bar patrons in Irish ballad sing-alongs, his deep, booming voice standing out from the crowd. It was a curious habit for a federal fugitive, and eventually it landed Fitz in hot water. A bad-check writer who decided to dabble in murder for money—he shot a drinking buddy and wounded another after a sloppy hold-up near San Francisco one drunken night—Fitzgerald made the Top Ten list on September 20, 1960. One day later, a Portland, Oregon, bar patron saw a man singing Irish ballads at the top of his lungs and thought he looked awfully familiar. Later, the patron looked at a copy of his local newspaper again, and that clinched it—the singer was a guy on the Top Ten list. FBI swooped down on Fitzgerald the next day in his motel. Oh, Stanny Boy.

INTERESTING FUGITIVE FACT:
After the arrest, FBI agents found a pistol in his briefcase.

137. DONALD LEROY PAYNE, sex offender

LISTED: October 6, 1960
PROCESS DISMISSED: November 26, 1965
DESCRIPTION: Born July 19, 1918. Five feet 10 inches, 140 pounds, brown hair with hazel eyes. Occupations: machinist, salesman, and tailor. Aliases: Roger Fielding, William Donald Johnson, William Charles Scott, Don Thompson, and Don Whitney.

The Rapist Goes Free. Nothing could stop Donald Payne from attacking women and children. Sadly, not even the Top Ten list. Payne was named to the list in October 1960 after he raped a dancer in Houston, Texas, and disappeared—but that was just the tip of his perverted iceberg. At the time of

that rape Payne had been on parole for the sexual assault of a nine-year-old girl and her 10-year-old brother in California in 1950, and even before that the assault and rape of a 15-year-old girl. If there ever was a fugitive who needed to be stopped, it was Payne. But sadly the system failed. Payne eluded authorities for over five years before prosecutors decided that the case was falling apart and dismissed federal process.

INTERESTING FUGITIVE FACT:
One year after escaping the clutches of the Ten Most Wanted list, Payne was arrested for molesting a child in Portland, Oregon. Seems that some fugitives who escape the list don't really escape after all.

138. CHARLES FRANCIS HIGGINS, robber

LISTED: October 10, 1960
CAUGHT: October 17, 1960
DESCRIPTION: Born in 1906. Medium height and build with brown eyes and brown-gray hair, a scar over his right eye and a tattooed heart with "C. H." on his right forearm.

"Okay, You've Got Your Man." Charles Francis Higgins's crime spree spanned four decades and four states. He was well known to Illinois cops from the age of 10, when he was arrested as a juvenile delinquent. At age 20 he was in jail for auto theft, carrying a concealed weapon, and assault with intent to kill, and by age 30 he was done serving time for that crime (a guilty plea let him escape with a five-year sentence) and back in the slammer for 20 to 25 years for the 1929 shooting of a Detroit cab driver and the theft of his cab—with three elderly fares in it. When he was paroled in May 1945, Higgins decided he'd overstayed his welcome in Illinois. He moved to Missouri. By 1946 he'd landed in a Jefferson City, Missouri, jail for his part in a St. Louis robbery. He was paroled a few years later, despite a failed escape attempt and tried his luck in Colorado. An aggravated robbery there earned him a 30 to 50-year stay—but Higgins's luck was improving. His next escape attempt on October 28, 1954, was a success, and Higgins was on the lam for six months—minus a short respite in a California cell for petty theft—before cops caught up with him in Florida. He was returned to Colorado, but escaped again on July 28, 1959. This time he had the FBI on his tail.

Ultimately newspapers, not law enforcement, were Higgins's downfall. When Higgins was named to the Top Ten list on October 10, 1960, the St. Louis *Globe-Democrat* printed the fugitive's picture. Two residents of Troy, Missouri, recognized the man, who had been living in a nearby cottage for two months. Higgins was on the run again. Less than a week later, a reprint of Higgins's picture in the *Globe-Democrat* spotted a vagrant stumbling down the street. The cop knew the drunk was Higgins, though the fugitive denied it until he was being fingerprinted.

"Okay, you've got your man," Higgins finally told 29-year-old Kirkwood, Missouri, patrolman Robert May. But Higgins wasn't ready to surrender. As May processed the arrest, Higgins pretended to lose his balance and attacked the officer. His fake was unsuccessful. Higgins ended up with a bump on his head and a return trip to the Colorado state pen.

INTERESTING FUGITIVE FACT:
Higgins's first escape attempt—from the Jefferson City, Missouri, prison—failed because, in their haste, Higgins and two fellow inmates tried to scale a homemade ladder to the top of the prison wall simultaneously. The ladder collapsed under the weight, dumping the would-be fugitives back into the prison yard.

139. ROBERT WILLIAM SCHULTZ JR., burglar

LISTED: October 12, 1960
CAUGHT: November 4, 1960
DESCRIPTION: "A revenge-crazed, jail-hardened bank robber and prison escapee who has allegedly threatened the lives of a United States Marshal, a Federal Judge and a former accomplice."

Threats. You have to wonder what goes through some prison officials' brains. Bob Schultz Jr. was a hotheaded burglar and would-be bank robber who threatened to kill cops and judges and U.S. marshals alike. Despite this, he was transferred from a high-security lockup—the U.S. penitentiary at Leavenworth, Kansas—to a low-security prison farm in Minnesota, just a year after making the aforementioned death threats. Schultz took advantage of the low security on September 6, 1960, when he was working alone on a road near the prison. Schultz bolted, and a little over a month later he made the Top Ten list. (Those death threats certainly helped the process.) Schultz's stay on the list was barely a

month, but it could have been a lot shorter. On October 22 the fugitive was arrested by Florida cops for not having a driver's license. Although Schultz readily admitted his true identity, the arresting officers had no idea they had a federal runner on their hands and allowed him to post $25 bail and split. Schultz had learned his lesson apparently. When FBI agents cornered him in Orlando a little over a week later, Schultz was living in a motel under the name "Frank Shelton."

INTERESTING FUGITIVE FACT:
Schultz, like many other Top Tenners of his time, had been convicted of deserting his military duty.

140. MERLE LYLE GALL, burglar

LISTED: October 17, 1960
CAUGHT: January 18, 1961
DESCRIPTION: Born March 21, 1923, in Cando, North Dakota. Five feet five inches, 135 pounds, with dark brown hair with hazel eyes. Scars and marks: scar right side of forehead, 3/4-inch scar under right eye, 3/4-inch scar left side of face, traces of pimple scars on face, scar under nose, little finger left hand deformed from injury. Remarks: Gall reportedly is soft-spoken, dresses neatly, preferring sport clothes and has a reputation of being a "ladies' man." Caution: Gall has engaged in gun fights and reportedly is armed with a pistol at all times. He has a violent temper and reportedly would not hesitate to kill anyone who gets in his way. Gall must be considered extremely dangerous. Aliases: John Conley, Clarence Gall, Merl Eyle Gall, Merl L. Gall, Leroy K. Knutson, William Francis McDermott, Berl J. Penrod, John W. Thomas, John W. Turner, and others.

Walking Gall. Some criminals walk the walk, while others merely talk the talk. Merle Gall was one of those in the latter category. While he repeatedly bragged to friends that he wouldn't die happy unless he managed to kill at least one cop during his time on Earth, Gall never managed to pull that off. An unrepentant burglar and phony-check writer, Gall was pinched in 1957 for stealing a wallet from a motel room in Great Falls, Montana, then later jumped his $15,000 bail and disappeared. Over three years later, Gall was named to the Ten Most Wanted list, and it didn't take long for the FBI to trace Gall to a roving crap game he and some associates had cooked up. When confronted by FBI agents in a Scottsdale, Arizona, parking lot in January 1961,

Gall apparently forgot all of his drunken boasts about bagging a law enforcement officer. He surrendered without even reaching for his pistol.

INTERESTING FUGITIVE FACT:
According to his FBI poster, Gall enjoyed "frequenting houses of prostitution."

141. JAMES GEORGE ECONOMOU, armed robber

LISTED: October 31, 1960
CAUGHT: March 22, 1961
DESCRIPTION: Born September 15, 1920, in Washington, D.C. Five feet eight inches, 150 pounds, brown hair with gray-green eyes. Scars and marks: scar under left eyebrow, scar over right eyebrow, small scar right side of chin, blotch scar inner left forearm, vaccination scar upper left arm, may have needle marks on arms from use of narcotics. Remarks: Economou reportedly is a heavy drinker and addicted to narcotics. He is reported to speak Spanish fluently and has been known to wear a mustache. Aliases: Jimmie Bruno, James E. Conomom, James J. Econom, Jimmie Econom, James G. Economos, James G. Economou, James Economow, "Jimmy the Greek," and others.

The First "Jimmy the Greek."   Some prison fights result in a trip to the infirmary. James Economou's fight resulted in his escape. He was slaving away with his prison work detail deep in a California forest when a bloody fight broke out; guards had to intervene and pounce on Economou with fists, batons, and handcuffs. The furry-browed fugitive was about to be transported to lockdown when he made a run for it in classic outdoor prison escape fashion: across a rushing creek and into the wild. Once the Feds received evidence that Economou— who routinely found himself colluding with L.A. gamblers, pimps, and drug dealers—had crossed the state line, he qualified for the Ten Most Wanted list and was named to it on Halloween 1960. But apparently Economou couldn't stay too far away from his favorite stomping grounds or the drugs he scored there. An informant told the FBI that Economou was holed up in an L.A. pad under the name "Louis Rasko," and he was surprised by a team of G-men and disarmed before he could offer resistance.

INTERESTING FUGITIVE FACT:
Economou was once arrested for evading railroad fare.

142. RAY DELANO TATE, bank robber

LISTED: November 18, 1960
CAUGHT: November 25, 1960

"Hello, *Mirror*?"   In June 1960 Ray Tate and two cohorts knocked over a bank in Newark, New Jersey, with a shotgun and a pistol. The take was a measly $2,704—not exactly the kind of haul an armed takeover team hopes for, and a crime that would barely make the headlines. Even worse, the dragnet spread over Newark in the days to follow managed to ensnare Tate's accomplices, who quickly sold their ringleader out. By late November 1960 Tate—a career robber with convictions dating back to his teenage years—was among the ten most hunted men in the United States. A week later, Tate was ready to crack; he felt eyes looking at him everywhere he turned, and his own eyes looking back at him from dozens of newspapers. So he called the editor of the *New York Daily Mirror*, told him who he was, and that he wanted to give himself up. The *Mirror* quickly dispatched a reporter and photographer to Vancouver, British Columbia, to meet their man, who consented to an interview and agreed to be handed over to the FBI right away. No word on whether or not the *Mirror* gave Tate a subscription to the newspaper to be delivered to his jail cell.

INTERESTING FUGITIVE FACT:
Tate once robbed a Trenton, New Jersey, clothing shop.

143. JOHN B. EVERHART, murderer

LISTED: November 22, 1960
CAUGHT: November 6, 1963
DESCRIPTION: Born June 24, 1922. Five feet six inches, 175 pounds, black hair with brown eyes. Occupations: cook, laborer, and truck driver. Aliases: John B. Eberhart, Harold Everhart, James B. Everhart, and "Slick."

Out of Trouble.   Walter Williams stood in the garage next to the San Francisco home, his brushes, cans, and roller at the ready. He was a freelance handyman, and this morning, November 6, 1963, he was steeling himself to tackle a house-painting gig. That's when a team of FBI agent showed up, looking to arrest him. Or, to be more precise, John B. Everhart, a Georgia man who once murdered someone in a fit of jealousy, tried to do the same thing to the police officer trying to arrest him, and later broke free of a prison work gang to make his escape. But Williams claimed he wasn't Everhart, he was Walter Williams. Fingerprints were taken, and finally Williams admitted the truth. "I've been here about five years," Everhart said. "I've stayed out of trouble to keep from coming in contact with the FBI." For the most part, staying out of trouble was a wise strategy—it kept the FBI at bay for nearly three years. But Everhart didn't count on the fact that the Top Ten program almost never gives up on its quarry.

INTERESTING FUGITIVE FACT:
Everhart was also wearing a favorite ring that had been mentioned in his FBI file. Tip to wannabe fugitives: Ditch your favorite jewelry.

144. HERBERT HOOVER HUFFMAN, murderer

LISTED: December 19, 1960
CAUGHT: February 29, 1960
DESCRIPTION: Born October 12, 1928, in White Oak, North Carolina. Five feet seven inches, 145 pounds, with dark brown hair, may be dyed, with gray eyes. Scars and marks: 1/4-inch scar left side of forehead, one-inch scar left temple. Remarks: Huffman has been described as a very antagonistic individual who has a vicious temper when drinking alcoholic beverages. Caution: Huffman is being sought for a savage and sadistic murder in which the victim was tortured and beaten to death. He is known to carry a gun on his person and in the glove compartment of his car. Huffman should be considered extremely dangerous. Aliases: Herbert Hoffman Jr., Herbert H. Hoffman, Herbert Junior Hoffman, Herbert J. Huffman, Hubert Huffman.

Burning Love. Herb Huffman wasn't exactly your dream husband. The stern-faced, square-jawed North Carolina native had racked up convictions for beating up women, abandoning his wife, and forgetting to send alimony payments. Then he pulled one of the most sadistic crimes in marital history in late June 1959. Huffman's common-law wife, Virginia Edwards, received an urgent telegram along with $100, saying that her man wanted her to drop everything and come to Chicago. Edwards did just that, little knowing that Huffman was planning on "teaching her a lesson." According to a friend, Huffman was racked with jealousy, convinced that Edwards was two-timing her. The Chicago trip was just a ruse. When Edwards arrived at the hotel room, Huffman beat her senseless, then proceeded to torture her with a lit cigarette and a crude torch made from a roll of paper. Her badly burned corpse was found by hotel employees on July 1, 1959, and over a year later, Huffman was named to the Ten Most Wanted list. Just 10 days later, a resident of Euclid, Ohio, saw Huffman's grim face on an FBI poster and immediately called the authorities. Huffman was arrested at his new job at a local warehouse and didn't attempt to duke it out with the arresting G-men. Apparently the wife-beater was all out of cigarettes.

INTERESTING FUGITIVE FACT:
Despite the presidential-sounding name, Huffman worked as a bus driver, truck driver, and warehouse worker.

145. KENNETH EUGENE CINDLE, armed robber

LISTED: December 23, 1960
CAUGHT: April 1, 1961
DESCRIPTION: Born in Oklahoma in April 1912.

A Near Miss. Ken Cindle's troubled life was a timeline of crime: forgery (1930), vagrancy (1932), booze violation (1932), armed hold-up (1935), parole violation (1949), drunk driving (1954 and 1955), theft (1957). Finally, in 1959, Cindle and a fellow crook knocked over a restaurant in Wichita, Kansas, stealing $236 and terrorizing the wait staff and customers with a sawed-off shotgun. He was arrested two days later—but on a minor charge, not the restaurant knockover. Before authorities realized who they had scooped up and let go, Cindle was on the run. By December 23, 1960, Cindle discovered that his long career in crime resulted in top (dis)honors in his industry: a nomination to the Top Ten list. The following spring the FBI discovered how Cindle had stayed on the lam—a farmer reported that he had picked up a hitchhiker who was skipping around the country, working odd jobs here and there. Later, that farmer saw Cindle's face on a television program. That led FBI agents to the ranch where the farmer had dropped off Cindle. They found the fugitive driving a tractor and claiming to be "William Merchant." A Social Security card backed up the story, but his fingerprints didn't.

INTERESTING FUGITIVE FACT:
Cindle enjoyed not one, but two near-misses with the law. On March 11, 1961, while still on the Top Ten list, Cindle was arrested after a Texas bar fight got

out of control. Cindle was claiming to be "Gus Anderson," but police didn't discover his true identity until long after the fact.

146. THOMAS VIOLA, murderer

LISTED: January 17, 1961
CAUGHT: March 27, 1961
DESCRIPTION: Born August 12, 1912, in Baltimore, Maryland. Five feet six inches, 168 pounds, with dark brown hair and brown eyes. Scars and marks: small scar right cheek, scar left side of lip, scar on chin, scar right index finger. Occupation: truck driver. Remarks: reportedly speaks in a low voice and has a sharp false lisp. Aliases: Vito Aicto, Frank Denoto, Tommy Donato, Thomas Puelo, Thomas Puleo, George Reni, Thomas P. Russo, Thomas Russow, Tommy Viola, and others.

One Last Run.   Fourteen years after landing in an Ohio prison for the gangland-style murders of a steak house owner and his nephew, Tom Viola got it in his head to escape. It was 1960, and Viola had spent most of his time behind bars, earning the trust of his jailers, eventually working his way to the honor bunks outside the prison walls. One day, September 22, Viola returned from his job in the prison's business office and took off without warning. The law had long stopped worrying about Viola—who had a reputation as a merciless enforcer for the Ohio mob. But now there was a potentially violent fugitive on the loose, many old scores to settle. Viola was named to the Top Ten list in January 1961. Viola was nabbed in Detroit, Michigan, after a resident saw his fretful mug in an article in *American Weekly*. A short while later, FBI agents swarmed on Viola, who was shacked up with a manicurist girlfriend, two guns, and $4,000 in cash. "The minute I knew the FBI had put me on the Top Ten, I knew my free time was up and those men would get me," Viola later told a reporter.

INTERESTING FUGITIVE FACT:
Killer Viola was diagnosed with lung cancer just a few years later and lived only a short while after his parole in March 1966.

147. WILLIAM CHESTER COLE, armed robber

LISTED: February 2, 1961
CAUGHT: February 6, 1961
DESCRIPTION: Born in Florida.

Turn Down the Heat.   A boyish-looking stickup man from Florida, William Cole never liked to stray too far from his relatives. That was a mistake. After skipping out on a prison camp hitch and robbing a series of innocent civilians and grocery stores in both Louisiana and Florida, Cole was named to the Top Ten list on February 2, 1961. Where did Cole flee? Right to his uncle, who lived in Gulf Breeze. His grandfather told the FBI where to find their man, and Cole was picked up without incident just four days after making the list. Perhaps he had sought the comfort of familiar faces. After his arrest Cole told his captors that the "heat" of the investigation had been too much for him to bear.

INTERESTING FUGITIVE FACT:
Cole always wore a stocking as a mask during his armed robberies.

148. WILLIE HUGHES, murderer

LISTED: March 15, 1961
CAUGHT: August 8, 1961
DESCRIPTION: According to the FBI, "a husky Negro" who typically sported a mustache.

Old J. Edgar Had a Farm.   Willie Hughes thought he had the FBI fooled. The fugitive, wanted in the June 12, 1960, beating and strangulation death of Russell Sharpe, had stayed one step ahead of the authorities—first Arizona, then Utah, Oregon, California, Colorado, Nebraska, Wyoming, and Idaho—for more than a year. In frustration the cops had named Hughes to the Top Ten list on March 15, 1961. Now he was in Pocatello, Idaho, working as a farm hand. He'd shaved off his mustache and changed jobs and names every couple of days to keep his identity and his record—with convictions for murder, manslaughter, assault with a deadly weapon, theft, and breaking and entering—a secret. As he walked to work on the morning of August 8, 1961, two fellow farm hands joined him. This time it was Willie Hughes who was fooled, as the "farm hands" cuffed Hughes's hands. "I was surprised those FBI men were dressed like that," the fugitive said. "If I had known they were federal men, I would have run for it. But before I found out who they were, they had me."

INTERESTING FUGITIVE FACT:
Willie Hughes wasn't a good friend to have. He counted Russell Sharpe—the man he murdered—among his closest friends.

149. WILLIAM TERRY NICHOLS, armed robber

LISTED: April 6, 1961
CAUGHT: April 30, 1962

Fish Story. It was a classic prison break: a team of four burly convicts overpowering their shotgun-carrying guard in a Seminole County, Georgia, prison camp. Three cons were quickly rounded up, but burglar and armed stickup man William Nichols managed to remain elusive. Then it became the classic FBI Ten Most Wanted story. After learning he was named to the list, Nichols decided to invent a new life for himself. He set up a commercial fishing business along Florida's southeastern coast, renamed himself "Luther Smith," and set about reeling in fresh bluefish and marlins for restaurants and fish shops. In classic Top Ten fashion the FBI reeled in their fugitive thanks to an unrelenting, painstaking search. Agents learned that Nichols had many former associates based on the southeastern Florida coast, and a thorough search turned up their fish on April 30, 1962.

INTERESTING FUGITIVE FACT:

Nicholas was once busted for his participation in an illegal commercial enterprise—importing whiskey from Canada without paying the proper taxes.

150. GEORGE MARTIN BRADLEY, bank robber

LISTED: April 10, 1961
CAUGHT: May 1, 1961

Fake. George Martin Bradley should have been nicknamed "Milton Bradley"—he was all about playing games. In 1950 Bradley bought a toy pistol, peeled it out of its plastic wrapping, then robbed a Cincinnati theater of its nightly earnings. Police were not amused, and Bradley found himself looking at a stretch in prison. Flash forward 11 years to the First Federal Savings and Loan Association in Davenport, Iowa. Bradley strolled in carrying a paper bag, then announced to the employees that he was holding a bomb. "Give me $60,000, or I let this go," he said. A quick-thinking employee decided to take a chance—after all, what bank robber would blow himself up?—snatching away the bag and throwing it across the room, just in case. Of course, there was no bomb. Bradley took off on foot and was soon pinned down by police in an alley. A fingerprint session revealed that Bradley had been

named to the Ten Most Wanted list barely a month before. Game over.

INTERESTING FUGITIVE FACT:

Bradley didn't always use imaginary bombs and toy pistols. He robbed a bank in Stuart, Florida, with a real shotgun (with bullets and everything) in January 1961, which put him on the Top Ten list.

151. PHILIP ALFRED LA NORMANDIN, robber

LISTED: April 17, 1961
CAUGHT: April 17, 1961
DESCRIPTION: A talented trumpeter. Aliases: Samuel Stewart, John Callan.

Just a Few Hours. Philip La Normandin had been on the run since a June 5, 1959, holdup in Reading, Massachusetts, when he was named to the Top Ten list on April 17, 1961, but his freedom lasted only a few hours. Though the fugitive was described as "desperado"—he engaged the cops in a gun battle as he and an accomplice fled, empty-handed, from the Massachusetts grocery robbery—he surrendered quietly to Newark, New Jersey, authorities operating on a tip. La Normandin had been living in Jersey City for six months, working as an oil burner service man, when the cops closed in. It was probably the longest period La Normandin had spent on the straight and narrow since his teenage days of truancy and auto theft. He was a familiar face at Massachusetts juvenile homes

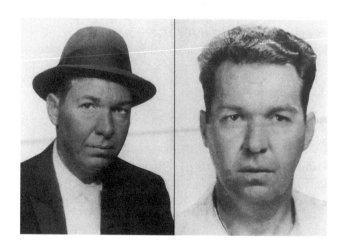

Bradley was arrested in Davenport, Iowa, by local police officers after an attempted bank robbery. He was identified after routine fingerprinting.

and landed in prison for the first time at the age of 17 for breaking and entering. He earned two more B & E convictions in the next half dozen years, then moved on to grand larceny in New York (a five-year stay at Sing Sing) and armed robbery in Pennsylvania (22 years in the slammer).

INTERESTING FUGITIVE FACT:
La Normandin got caught with his pants down—literally—during the June 5, 1959, robbery. Police caught up to the fleeing suspect while he was changing his clothes in the woods.

152. KENNETH HOLLECK SHARP, murderer

LISTED: May 1, 1961
CAUGHT: July 3, 1961

Stay Sharp.   Kenneth Sharp's stay on the Ten Most Wanted list may have been relatively short, but it was long in the making. Sharp was wanted for the unprovoked murder of a 75-year-old gas station attendant during a stickup in Illinois way back on September 11, 1952. A violent man with a hair-trigger temper, Sharp had also pulled a number of other robberies over the years. But nearly a decade of searching led law enforcement officials nowhere. After being named to the Top Ten, Sharp's bespectacled, slightly befuddled face appeared in the summer 1961 issue of *Master Detective* magazine, and an anonymous tipster directed FBI agents to a rooming house in Philadelphia. There Sharp was holed up as "Bryan Benton," and arrested without incident on July 3, 1961.

INTERESTING FUGITIVE FACT:
Sharp, oddly enough, was working as a gas station attendant when he was arrested by the FBI.

153. ANTHONY VINCENT FEDE, kidnapper

LISTED: May 22, 1961
CAUGHT: October 28, 1961
DESCRIPTION: Born in 1914, dapper criminal with a skill for sketching and barbering and a penchant for canaries and exotic dancers.

Fede to Black.   The FBI warned that Anthony Vincent Fede, wanted for the September 9, 1960, armed robbery of a Cleveland tavern—and the botched kidnapping of barmaid Phyllis Rose and manager

William Grouse, who escaped and armed himself forcing Fede to flee on foot—was "extremely dangerous." He'd been known to carry a hand grenade, but when the FBI caught up with him in Los Angeles on October 28, 1961, the only weapon Fede had in his possession was a toy pistol. Fede, a compulsive gambler, knew the big house was going to win this one. "I should have given myself up," he said. It was the gambling debts that made him commit the crime, which netted $1,500, Fede told authorities. It was a habit he probably picked up in prison; he'd been in and out of jail four times since his 15th birthday, twice for burglarizing candy stores, once for a June 1935 string of armed holdups, and later for larceny. With the cops on his tail again—and his May 1961 addition to the Top Ten list—Fede fled to sunny California. On a tip the Feds found him in a cheap hotel in Los Angeles and offered him long-term accommodations: 15 to 55 years in a Cleveland jail.

INTERESTING FUGITIVE FACT:
Also in Fede's possession at his arrest was a plastic detective's badge. He admitted he'd hoped to use it to bluff his way out of a confrontation with the law.

154. RICHARD LAURENCE MARQUETTE, murderer

LISTED: June 29, 1961
CAUGHT: June 30, 1961
DESCRIPTION: Born in Portland, Oregon.

The Pick-Up.   In early June random body parts were found scattered near Portland, Oregon. They belonged to a female. When the fingers were recovered, the prints matched those of a 23-year-old housewife who'd gone missing four days before, on June 4, 1961. Witnesses placed the housewife in the company of Richard Marquette, a floppy-eared, pug-nosed armed robber and occasional rapist. When investigators searched Marquette's house (their suspect had already flown the coop) they made another grisly discovery: the body part recovery effort wasn't finished. Marquette had kept some more parts in his refrigerator. Meanwhile, Marquette had raced down to Mexico, but realized that he didn't have enough money to live on. He sheepishly returned to the United States, settled in Santa Maria, California, found a job repairing furniture in a salvage shop, and grew a mustache to change his appearance. Maybe he should have considered a beard—the day after Marquette was named to the Top Ten list, a citizen recognized his face on a poster hanging in a credit bureau. "I knew the FBI would get me sooner or later," Marquette told the arresting agents. Marquette was convicted of first-degree murder and sentenced to life in prison.

INTERESTING FUGITIVE FACT:
Marquette became the very first "special addition"—those rare occasions when the FBI decides to add somebody to the Ten Most Wanted list even though there are no vacancies. In essence, Marquette's addition made it the "Eleven Most Wanted." (Special additions have stretched the list to include as many as 14 members.)

155. ROBERT WILLIAM SCHUETTE, armed robber

LISTED: July 19, 1961
CAUGHT: August 2, 1961
DESCRIPTION: Born May 2, 1922, in Baltimore, Maryland.

The Busiest Fugitive. Bob Schuette decided to end his 20-year sentence a bit early and broke out of the Maryland State Penitentiary on October 24, 1960. (He had served only three years.) Once free, Schuette put a lot of thought into staying free. The trick, he decided, was to stay on the move, so that cops or G-men wouldn't have the chance to get a fix on him. Thus began Schuette's amazing string of over 40 address changes and 25 different jobs . . . over a 10-month period.

Schuette hadn't ever been that busy—his criminal career was of the leisurely variety, with a dishonorable discharge from the U.S. Army for going AWOL one too many times, and a run of five armed stick-ups in the mid-1950s. But having experienced life behind bars, Schuette swore he'd do whatever it took to stay free, even if it meant he had to work for a living. But to no avail. The following July found Schuette on the Ten Most Wanted list, and just two weeks later, the FBI arrested him in Chicago. (Shuette had also been a resident of various cities and towns in Maine, Florida, Texas, and California.) "You fellows sure did a good job," Schuette told his captors. Schuette wasn't armed, but did have a clipping of a news story announcing him to the Top Ten list in his pants pocket.

INTERESTING FUGITIVE FACT:
Schuette also shaved his sideburns and mustache to avoid being recognized.

156. CHESTER ANDERSON MCGONIGAL, attempted murderer

LISTED: August 14, 1961
CAUGHT: August 17, 1961
DESCRIPTION: Born September 19, 1915, in Doniphan, Missouri. Five feet 10 inches, 200 pounds, with sandy, reddish blond receding hair and blue eyes. Scars and marks: two-inch scar center of forehead near hairline, one-inch scar right side of forehead, scar on right cheek; reportedly has tattoos on both arms, including "KAREN" inner side of left forearm. Caution: McGonigal has been armed with a rifle and with a knife in the past and has committed vicious assaults with these weapons. Considered extremely dangerous. Aliases: Chester Andison McGonigal, Chester Andy McGonigal, Chester Annison McGonigal, "Chick," and "Red."

Gall in the Family. Chester McGonigal was a burly, blowsy bear of a man with a passing resemblance to TV's Archie Bunker, but he was much harder on his family. Back in '48 he shot his own brother in the stomach and received a stretch in the cooler. In 1951 he stabbed his first wife and was slapped with another, longer stretch in prison. Flash forward to 1961, with McGonigal paroled and, apparently, in love again. After just four months as a newlywed, McGongigal again decided to use a knife on his bride, this time slashing his second wife across the throat and leaving her for dead in an Aspen, Colorado, bar.

Four months later, McGonigal was named to the Top Ten list, where he would remain for only three days before a citizen of Denver, Colorado, recognized the fugitive's face. The FBI staked out a local employment office—McGonigal had been traveling around, looking for odd jobs to support himself while on the lam—and pounced on him when he showed up the morning of August 17.

INTERESTING FUGITIVE FACT:
McGonigal was in such a hurry to flee after slicing up his second wife that he forgot his hat and coat.

157. HUGH BION MORSE, murderer

LISTED: August 29, 1961
CAUGHT: October 13, 1961
DESCRIPTION: Born in Kansas City in January 1930. Five feet 10 inches, and 130 pounds. Facial scarring. Diagnosed as a "aggressive sexual deviant." An avid motorcyclist and model car aficionado. Alias: Darwin Corman.

Morse's Code. When the FBI added 31-year-old murderer and rapist Hugh Morse to the Top Ten list on August 29, 1961, they didn't know just how many women around the country had been victimized by the fugitive. The FBI knew about 28-year-old Glorie Brie, raped and murdered in her Spokane, Washington, home on November 7, 1959, and 69-year-old Blanche Boggs, murdered on September 26, 1960. They knew about Beverly Myers, who survived Morse's brutal attack. And Mrs. Morse, the estranged wife Morse would have strangled and stabbed in her Reseda, California, home on October 28, 1960, had he not been interrupted by his screaming mother-in-law. But authorities didn't know, yet, about the two Atlanta, Georgia, women Morse raped in the spring of 1961, the two murders and an abduction in Spokane, the murder and the attempted murder in Alabama, or the string of rapes in St. Louis, Missouri.

Morse's abusive childhood at the hands of his maternal grandmother would be blamed for his violent tendencies—"I can't remember being happy at any time since I was born," he told police after his capture—and he had a long record of violence against women. His first arrest came in Wilmington, North Carolina, in May 1951 for indecent exposure and assault. After serving a six-month stint in a Los Angeles, California, jail for burglary, he was committed to a Fairfield, California, mental hospital for attempting to molest eight-year-old girls. He was released in January 1957. Morse was cured, doctors said.

After Morse was named to the Top Ten list, it took only six weeks to capture the fugitive, enough time for Morse to add another horrific crime to his rap sheet. Morse, who had relocated to St. Paul, Minnesota, stalked 34-year-old Carol Ronan, a single social worker, in his now usual method. He moved into a boardinghouse just four blocks from Ronan's apartment and spent several days casing the building. Twice he was chased away by the building caretaker for loitering. The third time he visited Ronan's home, September 19, 1961, Morse found the door unlocked. He hit her with a lock wrapped in a sock, bound her hands and raped her before strangling her with a silk stocking. Then he took her wristwatch and five dollars. When police located Morse three weeks later, they found the wristwatch—as well as a loaded .25 caliber automatic, a knife, and a straight razor. Morse, who was sleeping nude when the cops burst into the room at 6:40 P.M., did not resist arrest. He pled guilty to Ronan's murder and received a double life sentence.

INTERESTING FUGITIVE FACT:
Although he did not employ an elaborate disguise, Morse was not identified as a fugitive when he was arrested for voyeurism in the spring of 1961 in Atlanta, Georgia. Morse paid the $200 bail and walked past his Wanted poster on the way out of the police station.

158. JOHN GIBSON DILLON, dope dealer

LISTED: September 1, 1961
CAUGHT: March 2, 1964
DESCRIPTION: Born January 24, 1915, in Muskogee, Oklahoma. Five feet eight inches tall, 160 to 175 pounds, medium build with brown hair that is graying and balding, hazel eyes. Scars and marks: small scar right eyebrow, two large scars under chin, cut scar inside left wrist. Remarks: reportedly has partial dentures. Occupations: auto mechanic, carpenter, farmer, and sawmill operator. Caution: Dillon has been in possession of firearms in the past and allegedly attempted to run down a police officer with a car. He should be considered extremely dangerous. Aliases: John Gibson, Ray Larance Olson, Jerry Randall, Jerry Randolph, F. J. Vest.

That Ends Well. John Dillon—or "Matt," as he preferred to be called—had 30 years of criminal experience under his belt before making the Top Ten list in 1961. His rap sheet included convictions for auto theft, grand larceny, transporting a stolen car across state lines, burglary, fraud, and violations of narcotics laws. Once, in 1955, he even tried to run over an Oregon deputy sheriff who had the temerity to question him. But by 1961 the law had clamped down on Dillon, convicting him on a host of drug-dealing charges and preparing to smack him with a federal term of almost 200 years. That apparently was too much time in the freezer for Dillon's taste, so he ran. He was named to the Ten Most Wanted list, but nobody heard a peep out of Dillon until nearly three years later, when the FBI received an anonymous tip pointing them to a well on a farm in Chelsea, Oklahoma. His badly decomposed body was located at the bottom of a 15-foot water-filled well on a remote farm. It wasn't suicide; his feet and body were wired up to 400 pounds of oil well drilling equipment. A forensics team guessed that Dillon had been down that well for over a year.

INTERESTING FUGITIVE FACT:
John Gibson also used the alias "Matt Dillon," predating the *Outsiders* star by some 20 years.

159. JOHN ROBERT SAWYER, bank robber

LISTED: October 30, 1961
CAUGHT: November 3, 1961

Slumber Party. Many bank robbers have laid claim to the invention of the "sleepover heist"—a trick where the bandit visits the home of the target bank's manager the night before, holds his family hostage, then takes his unwilling hostage to the bank the next day and forces him to disable the alarm system and open the vault. John Sawyer and his accomplice John Moise probably weren't the first to pull a sleepover heist, but they helped perfect it. In August 1961 Sawyer and Moise invaded the home of a Omaha, Nebraska, bank manager, tied and gagged his family, then proceed to pistol-whip the manager until he spilled all of the security secrets of his bank. The next morning the bandits drove their bruised and weary hostages to the bank, where they were forced to help Sawyer and Moise steal $72,599. The only upside to the encounter? Sawyer and Moise let them live.

The heist was almost perfect, except that the bank manager and his wife were able to identify their captors from mug shots. Moise was picked up soon after in Manhattan, while Sawyer remained free. He was named to the Top Ten list the day before Halloween 1961. The lowdown on Sawyer was transmitted to every law enforcement agency in the country, including the Arizona Highway Patrol, which spotted the fugitive's license plates speeding past Wickendale, Arizona, just three days later. Sawyer was pulled over. In the passenger seat was Sawyer's girlfriend. In the back of the car was a loaded pistol. Sawyer didn't have time to reach for it and was arrested without incident. From there Sawyer could count on having many consecutive sleepovers in the state of Nebraska.

INTERESTING FUGITIVE FACT:
The $72,599 was never recovered, but Sawyer claimed to be flat broke. "I haven't got 30 cents in my pockets," he reportedly told the arraigning judge.

160. EDWARD WAYNE EDWARDS, armed robber

LISTED: November 10, 1961
CAUGHT: January 20, 1962

Dial-A-Breakout. Ed Edwards may have had a redundant name, but he was never one to overlook the obvious. When the armed robber and car thief was locked up in an Oregon prison in April 1961, he arranged for a buddy to call the prison posing as a probation officer. The friend demanded Edwards's immediate release, and damned if the prison officials didn't take the verbal request seriously. Edwards was instantly sprung and already running before the prison officials realized what they had done. Edwards made the Top Ten list the following November and seemed to celebrate his listing with a bank robbery in Akron, Ohio. Just three days later, however, a tipster in Atlanta, Georgia, alerted police about a suspicious character with a lot of money holed up nearby. On January 20 he was found in bed with a female friend, surrounded by a loaded gun, new clothes, and two grand in stolen bank loot. The next phone call Edwards made was probably to his lawyer.

INTERESTING FUGITIVE FACT:
According to his FBI memorandum, Edwards was an avid bowler and weight lifter.

161. FRANKLIN EUGENE ALLTOP, armed robber

LISTED: November 22, 1961
CAUGHT: February 2, 1962
DESCRIPTION: Born in Given, West Virginia, in 1933. Nicknames: "Top" and "Stub."

"I Know You're the FBI." Authorities were lining up to take a crack at Franklin Alltop, an Ohio-based stickup man. In 1954 Alltop pulled two shotgun robberies, one in Ohio and another in West Virginia. In October 1959, after serving four years of his sentence for the Ohio job, West Virginia came looking for a piece of the fugitive, too. Alltop had apparently decided he had forced down enough jailhouse chow. He hooked up with three other prisoners, and they worked together to saw through a set of steel bars, then used a makeshift rope made of tied blankets to lower themselves from a second-story window. Alltop was named to the Ten Most Wanted list in November, and less than three months later the FBI cornered him in Kansas City, Kansas. "I've been expecting you," said Alltop to the arresting Special Agents. "I know you're the FBI."

INTERESTING FUGITIVE FACT:
Alltop's name perfectly fit his mug shot. With close-cropped sides and a huge unruly nest of hair on top, the fugitive definitely looked like he was "all top."

162. FRANCIS LAVERNE BRANNAN, murderer

LISTED: December 27, 1961
CAUGHT: January 18, 1962
DESCRIPTION: Born in Frederick, Illinois, in 1925.

Laverne? Surely. Frank Brannan probably felt like a real tough customer while invading the home of a 72-year-old widow of a Presbyterian minister in Rushville, Illinois. She had most likely tried to fight back, and Brannan felt the need to pump a few bullets into her arm and back. But just three months later, with the FBI engaged in a nationwide manhunt to find him—a stolen car and a stolen shotgun had linked the 36-year-old drifter to the crime—Brannan snapped. He couldn't take life on the run anymore. He stepped out of his Miami, Florida, hideout, walked to a pay phone in a downtown gas station, pumped a dime in the box, and called the local FBI office. "Come and get me," he said. "I'm tired of running from the FBI."

INTERESTING FUGITIVE FACT:
Brannan had been convicted of "sexual perversion" on a California beach, public drunkenness, and drunk driving. A real party kind of guy.

163. DELBERT LINAWEAVER, burglar

LISTED: January 30, 1962
CAUGHT: February 5, 1962
DESCRIPTION: Born in 1932.

Farmer and the Del. In June 1960 Delbert Henry Linaweaver was sitting in a Salina, Kansas, sheriff's jail, awaiting transfer to the state penitentiary in Lansing. The 28-year-old had been pinched for burglary, the latest in a solid string of criminal offenses, and sentenced to five to 10 years. At some point, sitting on the cold hard bench, it must have occurred to Linaweaver that it would be easier to break out of

the two-bit prison rather than try the same thing at the state pen. He convinced two other prisoners to help, and then proceeded to overpower and beat both the guard, Martin C. Gellart, and Salina County sheriff Guy Lemmon with a sackful of broken glass. It was a bum deal for the two other prisoners; they were quickly rounded up. But Linaweaver got away.

Using an alias comprising nothing but first names—"John Edward Thomas"—Linaweaver hooked up with a migrant crew of farmers and worked his way through Nevada, Canada, and eventually settled in Floydada, Texas, where he'd found work as a farm laborer. The fugitive, now 30, even felt confident enough to marry a local girl. But planting roots was a big mistake. By early 1962 Linaweaver had been named to the Top Ten list, and days later a Floydada citizen recognized him from his Wanted poster hanging in a post office. Linaweaver was arrested without incident and shipped back to Kansas, where a judge held him on $25,000 bond—$15 large for the jail break and $10,000 extra for assaulting his jailers.

INTERESTING FUGITIVE FACT:
Linaweaver had four tattoos: "In God We Trust," "Mother," "Joy," and a flower—not exactly the stuff of a hardened criminal on the run.

164. WATSON YOUNG JR., murderer, rapist

LISTED: February 5, 1962
CAUGHT: February 13, 1962
DESCRIPTION: Born in Jefferson County, Kentucky, in June 1932. Five feet tall, 200 pounds. Diagnosed as a paranoid schizophrenic and a sexual deviant.

Some Kind of Nut. When the law caught up to Watson Young Jr. on February 13, 1962, he wasn't in hiding. He was driving up and down Main Street, Salina, Kansas, in a stolen ambulance with lights blazing and sirens blaring. "We thought he was some kind of nut," said police lieutenant Jack Richardson, who was pursuing the ambulance. "We sure didn't know who he was when we went up to him." But Young readily identified himself. He was a fugitive wanted for the December 1961 murders of an elderly Indianapolis couple and the rape of a housewife, and he had been named to the Top Ten list just one week earlier. Young had a lengthy record, which included forgery, car theft, impersonating a federal officer, and impersonating a mortician (he had spent some time in embalming school), but was repeatedly committed to mental institutions instead of incarcerated.

After stays in hospitals in Charleston, South Carolina, Philadelphia, Pennsylvania, Louisville, Kentucky, Dayton, Ohio, Kansas City, Missouri, and Marion, Indiana, he escaped from a Lakeland, Kentucky, hospital and headed for Indianapolis. When he was finally arrested, Young admitted to the crimes of murder and theft—"He said he killed [the Indianapolis couple] because the man tried to kill him," Salina police chief H. R. Salmans reported—but claimed to have "blacked out" during the rape of the housewife, remembering only "choking a woman and stealing some clothes." His confessions shook his landlord. "He was a nice young man, as friendly as can be. I was glad to rent him a room," Mrs. Nelson Sowell said. "But now I'm scared to death thinking about it."

INTERESTING FUGITIVE FACT:
Young's capture made the Salina jailhouse a little crowded. Top Ten fugitive DELBERT LINAWEAVER was already being held there, following his capture in Floydada, Texas, several days earlier. "They're both in solitary confinement and under maximum security," police chief H. R. Salmans said. "We're watching them mighty close because we don't want to have any more trouble around here."

165. LYNDAL RAY SMITH, robber

LISTED: February 14, 1962
CAUGHT: March 22, 1962
DESCRIPTION: Born March 31, 1924, in Drakesboro, Kentucky. Five feet 11 inches tall, 145 to 150 pounds, with brown hair and brown eyes. Scars and marks: small scar under left eye, scar near knuckle of left index finger; tattoos: blue and red crossed rifles and shield with "USA" and "1/9/39" left forearm, flying eagle, dagger, heart and ribbon with "Death Before Dishonor" on ribbon. Caution: Smith has been armed in the past with a .22 caliber revolver. He participated in a prison break in which a guard was bound and shackled. Consider very dangerous. Aliases: Vance Hudson, David Page, L. Roberts, Lyndall Ray Smith, Ray Lyndall Smith, Roy Lindall Smith, "Smitty," and others.

Smitty on the Run. Lyndal Smith—or "Smitty" as he preferred to be called—had racked up convic-

tions for petty larceny, transporting stolen automobiles, burglary, robbery, and even going AWOL from the U.S. Army by the time he lammed out of a California prison camp in February 1960. Smith overpowered one of his would-be captors, bound and shackled him, and then lifted $168 from the poor guy's wallet. Smith boosted a car and headed east, feeling good about himself. Flash forward two years to February 1962, when Smith was named to the Top Ten list. Suddenly, Smith didn't feel so good. He skipped around Milwaukee, Cleveland, and Chicago, but kept seeing his own skinny face and protruding ears looking back at himself from the local papers. In desperation Smith tried Baltimore, where he found work as a bartender. That didn't work, either. When Smitty saw his face in the Baltimore papers and on evening newscasts, he decided he'd had enough. Smitty hung it up and surrendered to the FBI on March 22.

INTERESTING FUGITIVE FACT:
Smith was the first Smith on the Top Ten list, and he would be the only Smith on the list until 1968. (Interestingly, the first Jones would make the list in 1968, too.)

166. HARRY ROBERT GROVE JR., armed robber

LISTED: February 19, 1962
CAUGHT: January 26, 1963
DESCRIPTION: Born December 1, 1927. Five feet eight inches, 140 to 152 pounds, light brown hair, gray and receding with blue-green eyes. Occupations: laborer, mechanic, musician, television repairman, typewriter repairman. Aliases: Harold Robert Kelley, George Gordon Marcus, and Jerry Miller.

Saving Trouble. Every man has his vices. For Harry Grove it was four-star restaurants, cocktails in swank nightclubs, and a good burlesque show. How did Grove bankroll these vices? By sticking up supermarkets, burglarizing shops, and printing his own funny money. But the 34-year-old swinger was pinched in December 1960 for robbing a Toledo, Ohio, meat market, and jumped bail. When Grove made the Top Ten list a little over a year later, the *Baltimore News-Post* ran the headline: "Veteran Ohio Criminal on 'Most Wanted' List: Fond of Night Life." The FBI had Grove pegged. (Remember: it always pays to "work the habits" of a fugitive on the run.) As it turned out,

Grove wasn't caught in a steak house or girlie show. A sharp-eyed resident of Uhrichsville, Ohio, noticed Grove and an accomplice casing the supermarket across the street from his home and called the police. Grove fled from the scene, but the Ohio State Highway Patrol scooped him up a short while later and discovered a bag full of burglary tools in his trunk. "I may as well save you some trouble," Grove told police. "I'm on the Ten Most Wanted list."

INTERESTING FUGITIVE FACT:
According to the FBI poster, Grove was known to carry a pistol hidden in the folds of a newspaper.

Wanted by FBI

IDENTIFICATION
ORDER NO. 3547
February 13, 1962

FBI No.
5,116,253

INTERSTATE FLIGHT – ARMED ROBBERY
HARRY ROBERT GROVE, JR.

ALIASES: HAROLD GROVE, HAROLD ROBERT KELLEY, HAROLD ROBERT KELLY, GEORGE GORDON MARCUS, JERRY MILLER

13 M 9 U IIO 12
M 1 U IIO

Photographs taken 1960

Harry Roberts Grove

DESCRIPTION
AGE: 34, born December 1, 1927, Toledo, Ohio
HEIGHT: 5'8"   RACE: white
WEIGHT: 140 to 152 pounds   NATIONALITY: American
BUILD: medium   OCCUPATIONS: laborer,
HAIR: light brown, greying   mechanic, musician, tele-
        and receding   vision repairman, typewriter
EYES: blue - green   repairman
COMPLEXION: fair
SCARS AND MARKS: scar back of left hand, 6" burn scar right leg

CRIMINAL RECORD
Grove has been convicted of theft of currency, unlawful possession of firearms, possession of burglary tools, burglary and larceny of a motor vehicle.

CAUTION
GROVE REPORTEDLY HAS BEEN ARMED WITH A LUGER PISTOL WHICH HE HAS CONCEALED INSIDE A NEWSPAPER OR UNDER THE SEAT OF HIS CAR. HE SHOULD BE CONSIDERED EXTREMELY DANGEROUS.

A Federal warrant was issued on May 9, 1961, at Toledo, Ohio, charging Grove with unlawful interstate flight to avoid prosecution for armed robbery (Title 18, U. S. Code, Section 1073). He is also wanted by U. S. Secret Service for having passed forged and counterfeit obligations in violation of Title 18, U. S. Code, Section 472.

IF YOU HAVE INFORMATION CONCERNING THIS PERSON, PLEASE NOTIFY ME OR CONTACT YOUR LOCAL FBI OFFICE. PHONE NUMBER IS LISTED BELOW. OTHER OFFICES ARE LISTED ON BACK.

IDENTIFICATION
ORDER NO. 3547

DIRECTOR
Federal Bureau of Investigation
Washington 25, D. C.

Grove was arrested in Uhrichsville, Ohio, by the Ohio State Highway Patrol after being observed loitering in a supermarket.

167. BOBBY WILCOXSON, bank robber

LISTED: February 23, 1962
CAUGHT: November 10, 1962
DESCRIPTION: Born July 10, 1929, in Duke, Oklahoma (not supported by birth records). Five feet eight inches, 150 to 160 pounds, with dark brown hair and brown eyes—

the right eye is artificial. Occupations: itinerant farm laborer, painter, produce worker, service station attendant, used-car salesman. Scars and marks: burn scar on left wrist, scar on right forearm. Caution: Wilcoxson is being sought for multiple bank robberies, in one of which a bank guard was slain and a police officer wounded. Wilcoxson is armed with a double-barreled,

IDENTIFICATION ORDER NO. 3549
February 15, 1962

Wanted by FBI

BANK ROBBERY
BOBBY RANDELL WILCOXSON

FBI No. 22,238 B

ALIASES: GLENN STEVEN DAVIS, BOB HURLEY, ROBERT RANDALL HUSLEY, BOB WILCOX, BOB R. WILCOXSON, ROBERT RANDELL WILCOXSON AND OTHERS

17 I 9 R 00I 17
M 18 U 00I

Photograph taken 1958

Photographs taken 1959

DESCRIPTION

AGE: 32, born July 10, 1929, Duke, Oklahoma (not supported by birth records)
HEIGHT: 5'8" to 5'9½"
WEIGHT: 150 to 160 pounds
BUILD: medium
HAIR: dark brown
EYES: brown, right eye artificial
COMPLEXION: ruddy
RACE: white
NATIONALITY: American
OCCUPATIONS: itinerant farm laborer, painter, produce worker, service station attendant, used car salesman
SCARS AND MARKS: burn scar on left wrist, scar right forearm

CRIMINAL RECORD

Wilcoxson has been convicted of interstate transportation of a stolen motor vehicle, issuing worthless checks, battery and disturbing the peace.

CAUTION

WILCOXSON IS BEING SOUGHT FOR MULTIPLE BANK ROBBERIES, IN ONE OF WHICH A BANK GUARD WAS SLAIN AND A POLICE OFFICER WOUNDED. WILCOXSON IS ARMED WITH A DOUBLE-BARRELED, SAWED-OFF, 12 GAUGE SHOTGUN; SUBMACHINE GUNS; HAND GRENADES; AND ANTITANK GUNS. WILCOXSON MAY BE ACCOMPANIED BY ALBERT FREDERICK NUSSBAUM, FBI IDENTIFICATION ORDER NUMBER 3548, WHO IS ALSO HEAVILY ARMED. WILCOXSON AND NUSSBAUM ARE CONSIDERED VERY DANGEROUS.

Federal warrants were issued on January 30, 1962, and February 12, 1962, at Buffalo, New York, and New York, New York, respectively, charging Wilcoxson with bank robbery (Title 18, U. S. Code, Section 2, 2113a, 2113d and 2113e).

IF YOU HAVE INFORMATION CONCERNING THIS PERSON, PLEASE NOTIFY ME OR CONTACT YOUR LOCAL FBI OFFICE. PHONE NUMBER IS LISTED BELOW. OTHER OFFICES ARE LISTED ON BACK.

IDENTIFICATION ORDER NO. 3549

DIRECTOR
Federal Bureau of Investigation
Washington 25, D. C.

Due to an FBI investigation, Wilcoxson was arrested in Baltimore, Maryland.

Bobby Randall Wilcoxson—bank robber

sawed-off, 12-gauge shotgun; submachine guns; hand grenades; and antitank guns. Aliases: Glenn Steven Davis, Bob Hurley, Robert Randall Husley, Bob Wilcox, Bob R. Wilcoxson, Robert Randell Wilcoxson, and others.

168. ALBERT NUSSBAUM, bank robber

LISTED: April 2, 1962
CAUGHT: November 4, 1962
DESCRIPTION: Born April 9, 1934, in Buffalo, New York (not supported by birth records). Five feet seven inches tall, 150 to 160 pounds, with light brown hair and blue eyes. Occupations: airplane mechanic, draftsman, electronics equipment repairman, gunsmith, locksmith, mechanic, salesman, welder. Scars and marks: tattoo of a snake entwined around dagger on upper left arm. Nussbaum may wear glasses and is an expert gun and locksmith and has ability to pilot and

repair airplanes. Aliases: Karl Kessler, Al Nest, Albert F. Nussbaum Jr.

Bobby and Al. Like so many great crime teams, Bobby Wilcoxson and Al Nussbaum met in prison—the federal reformatory in Chillicothe, Ohio, to be exact. Wilcoxson was serving a hitch for buying a car with a rubber check and then driving it across state lines; Nussbaum was in for possessing and transporting a Thompson machine gun.

The future partners couldn't have been more different. Wilcoxson was a tough, leathery thug who could barely read and had a glass right eye thanks to a childhood accident. Nussbaum was a bookworm who loved biographies and novels about bank robberies, as well as chemistry, firearms, and explosives textbooks. Wilcoxson liked betting on the ponies and flashing greenbacks at the track; Nussbaum was a master chess player and entered a correspondence tournament while in prison. Who knows how the two hit it off at Chillicothe, but they did, and agreed to go into business together upon their release. The business? The one Nussbaum loved reading about.

In mid-September 1960 the two met up at Nussbaum's Buffalo home to plot their first jobs. The first order of business was funding: Nussbaum told Wilcoxson it was important to have seed money to buy guns and rent cars so they could outshoot and outrun any pursuing cops. A few local burglaries later, the pair had enough of an operating budget to take their first bank.

Wilcoxson and Nussbaum, Inc. made their debut on December 5, 1960. They stormed into the First Federal Savings and Loan Association in Schiller Park, New York, with a handgun and a sawed-off shotgun. Nussbaum had the pistol and wore a gauze mask. Wilcoxson didn't bother with a disguise, and one witness later told the police that one of the gunmen had "something unusual about his right eye—it didn't focus." Wilcoxson and Nussbaum fled in a rented car with $18,979. On January 12, 1961, they struck again, this time at the Manufacturers and Traders Trust Company in Buffalo. Another witness commented on Wilcoxson's bum eye. The take: $87,288.

Then—precisely according to Nussbaum's plan—the partners separated, each of them setting up legitimate businesses with their ill-gotten gains. For Wilcoxson that meant buying a stake in a jewelry store, lettuce farm, and car dealership in Florida. For the gun-loving Nussbaum it meant opening up a weapons shop in Buffalo.

Nussbaum's true bank-robbing genius wouldn't be demonstrated until the following summer. In June 1961 the citizens of Washington, D.C., began to worry about a mad bomber who had been exploding city trash cans and mailboxes at random. Phone calls from a rabid white supremacist promised more explosions. Little did anyone know that the white supremacist was Nussbaum, and that the threats were merely meant to distract police from the real target: a bank. On June 30, while police were busy with a bomb found in an office building, Nussbaum and Wilcoxson raided the Bank of Commerce and stole $19,862.

Weeks later, Nussbaum and Wilcoxson hit the Trust Company in Rochester, New York, after an armored car made a delivery of fresh cash. The two walked away with $57,197—somehow missing an additional $81,700 that was behind a counter, already bagged. Meanwhile, an acquaintance from Chillicothe named Peter C. Curry had been released and put out the word that he was looking for work. Wilcoxson and Nussbaum welcomed Curry into the fold and prepared for their next knockover.

In mid-December 1962 Wilcoxson walked into the Lafayette National Bank in Brooklyn, New York, and joked to 53-year-old guard Henry Kraus that he was going to rob it. Kraus laughed. Wilcoxson then asked Kraus what he would do if someone *did* hold up the bank. Kraus's laughter died down, and he told Wilcoxson that if someone tried to knock over the bank then he guess he'd have to shoot it out.

Kraus should have given a different answer. Two weeks later, on December 15, Wilcoxson and Curry stormed the Lafayette National while Nussbaum sat outside in the getaway car. Curry leaped over the four-foot guard rail and shouted, "Everyone get down! Flat on the floor!" When Henry Kraus reached for his revolver—just as he said he would—Wilcoxson sprayed him with submachine-gun fire. Kraus took four bullets in the chest and only had time to cry "Oh!" before slumping to the floor.

"Don't move or I'll kill you!" shouted Curry, who started scooping up packs of money into his canvas bag. At each cage he would stop to press his revolver to the head of each employee and repeat: "Don't move, or you'll get what the guard got!"

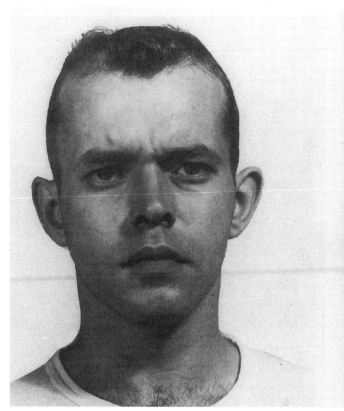
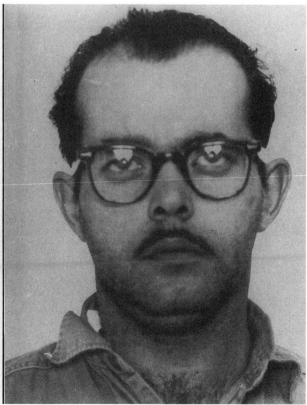

Albert Frederick Nussbaum—bank robber

In the confusion three customers managed to slip out of the bank. They summoned the first cop they saw—foot patrolman Salvatore Accardi. Nussbaum, outside in the getaway car, saw the cop approaching and calmly spoke into a radio unit, which carried his words to a receiver in Wilcoxson's ear. The machine

gunner spun around to see Accardi outside the bank doors, drawing his .38 service revolver. Wilcoxson blasted away through glass, and the bullets grazed Accardi's leg.

The cop fell to his knees, yet somehow kept his wits together and immediately returned fire. But

Nussbaum was arrested in Buffalo, New York, by the FBI after a 20-minute chase through downtown streets.

108

Accardi's .38 slugs couldn't penetrate the glass. Wilcoxson's submachine gun had no such problem. His bullets shattered the remaining glass and flung the cop back onto the sidewalk, knocking him out. Miraculously, the only bullet that hit the cop found his badge, saving him from death. One minute later, Nussbaum peeled away with Wilcoxson, Curry, and a sweet $32,763 score.

But the Lafayette heist was the turning point for the mad genius and the brutal killer. Their getaway car was soon discovered, as was the submachine gun used to kill Kraus. A trace of the serial numbers led FBI agents to Nussbaum's gun shop in Buffalo. When the FBI raided Nussbaum's joint, they found various machine guns with matching clips and magazines, 60 hand grenades, bulletproof vests, 14 automatic pistols, two Lahti antitank guns, and thousands upon thousands of rounds of ammunition. Making matters worse, one-time partner Pete Curry was captured by agents the day before Valentine's Day 1962 and immediately began to fink on his ex-partners.

In June the two robbed a Philadelphia savings and loan, but netted only $160. Next was a Pittsburgh bank that offered a bigger take—$4,373—but again, Nussbaum and Wilcoxson somehow missed over $10,000. The following month their faces were all over *Reader's Digest* in a feature article suggested by J. Edgar Hoover himself. The previous year an FBI Ten Most Wanted fugitive named JOSEPH CORBETT JR. had been captured thanks to eagle-eyed *Digest* readers, and Hoover thought lightning might strike twice with Wilcoxson and Nussbaum. The magazine even offered a $10,000 reward for information leading to their arrest.

The heat was starting to burn away the partnership. Nussbaum and Wilcoxson agreed to pull the proverbial "last job" together: the September 19, 1962, robbery of a Pennsylvania bank. But Nussbaum insisted on driving the getaway car, and nothing more. Wilcoxson couldn't believe it. After cracking the bank and bagging $28,901, Wilcoxson handed Nussbaum a paltry $500. "Your cut for driving," Wilcoxson explained. Nussbaum was furious beyond words and stormed away. Alone and on the run, Nussbaum—most likely in reaction to the *Reader's Digest* feature—sent taunting letters to J. Edgar Hoover. Years later, retired FBI agent Andrew Soltys paraphrased Nussbaum's letters to a reporter from APB News Online: "You dummy—you have all of these college-educated agents. Why can't you catch me?"

But those college-educated agents would catch Nussbaum, with help from the bank robber's own wife. Alicia Nussbaum was staying with her parents when her husband called her, desperate to see her and their 19-month-old daughter. When Alicia told her mother, Mrs. Macjchorowicz called the Feds. They set up an early morning sting at the Statler Hilton Hotel in downtown Buffalo, New York. On November 4, 1962, Nussbaum pulled up in his light blue 1962 Chevy sedan. Alicia waved from the front doors. It was a signal. Thirty unmarked cars full of FBI agents and Buffalo cops sprung into action.

Nussbaum saw what was happening, hammered the gas pedal, and squealed away. The law offered pursuit, but Nussbaum knew his hometown streets cold and was able to negotiate tight turns at 100 mph. No one could get a clear shot at his tires. About two miles away from the hotel a K-9 cop heard the sirens and steered his dog wagon out into the middle of the street to see what was going on. Nussbaum's Chevy smacked into the wagon, but still managed to squeeze past. A few blocks later, Nussbaum swerved to the side of the road, turned off the ignition, then flattened himself to the bottom of the car. He was hoping that the racing G-men would zoom right by and miss him.

They didn't. Seconds later, Nussbaum looked up and found himself staring at the barrel of an agent's rifle.

The arresting officers found two live hand grenades in the bank robber's jacket pockets and a .22 caliber rifle on the backseat. While Nussbaum declined to shoot it out—that was more Wilcoxson's style, anyway—he did swallow a handful of Seconal tablets in an attempt at suicide. The FBI rushed Nussbaum to nearby Columbus Hospital to have his stomach pumped. Afterward, Nussbaum remained silent, especially when asked about the whereabouts of his partner.

Ultimately, it didn't matter. Five days later, FBI agents surrounded Wilcoxson's hideout in Baltimore, waiting until he emerged from the house with his girl-friend Jacqueline Rose and carrying Rose's infant son, Kenny. Wilcoxson surrendered peacefully. The man that *Reader's Digest* had dubbed "The Most Wanted Criminal Since Dillinger" was in custody. Wilcoxson and Curry, with the blood of guard Henry Kraus on their hands, were sentenced to life in prison. Nussbaum received 40 years for his multiple bank robberies.

Years later, after winning parole, Nussbaum would find a legitimate outlet for his intellectual curiosity and love of planning capers: He became a mystery novelist. Nussbaum's works include *Gypsy* and *How to Be Sneaky, Underhanded, Vile and Contemptible for Fun and Profit,* along with dozens of short stories that appeared in digests such as *Alfred Hitchcock's Mystery Magazine*. Nussbaum died in 1995 after a lengthy illness, but his fiction lives on in the Internet. You can sample one of his short stories, "Collision," at Lady M's Mystery International website (www.mysteryinternational.com/manscrpts/AN/An1.htm).

INTERESTING FUGITIVE FACT:
In July 1962 writer Dan J. Marlowe opened up a fan letter from a guy named Carl Fischer, who praised Marlowe's novel *The Name of the Game is Death*. That book was about Earl Drake, an unrepentant bank robber who struggles to survive after a heist goes wrong. Fischer said he loved the book and asked Marlowe how he learned key pieces of information. Marlowe answered the letter, spelling out some of his research techniques.

Four months later, on November 6, two FBI agents showed up on Marlowe's doorstep, wanting to know more about this "Carl Fischer." As it turned out, Fischer was Al Nussbaum. According to an anecdote from the Mystery Writers of America website, Marlowe's letter to Nussbaum provided useful clues for helping the FBI track down Wilcoxson a few days later.

169. THOMAS WELTON HOLLAND, sex offender, robber

LISTED: May 11, 1962
CAUGHT: June 2, 1962
DESCRIPTION: Born November 26, 1931, in Baltimore, Maryland. Five feet 11 inches, 175 pounds, brown hair with hazel eyes. Scars and marks: small scar under chin, mole right side of throat, small scar back of right hand, appendectomy scar; numerous tattoos, including star upper left arm, "Blondie," "Mae," "Thelma," "212-28-0159" left forearm, "Bud" and dagger right forearm, "B. E." left side of chest. Caution: Holland has a history of vicious sex attacks on children. He has been armed with a gun and a knife in the past. Consider extremely dangerous. Aliases: Bob Mitchell, Robert Clay Mitchell, "Bud," "Tommy."

Bud Flight. Bespectacled and bookish-looking, Thomas Holland is probably the last guy you'd expect to have a long rap sheet. But you should never trust appearances. Starting at age 18, Holland—nicknamed "Bud"—started to rack up convictions for breaking and entering, larceny, auto theft, assault, robbery, and indecent exposure. Then, in his mid-

20s, Holland transmogrified into a full-blown sexual deviate, attempting to rape seemingly anybody who crossed his path—one young woman, two small boys, two underage girls—using whatever was handy, be it a lug wrench or a knife. Holland was convicted for these sex crimes, but somehow earned parole in 1960. When he bailed on his parole officer soon after, a warrant was issued on August 29, 1961 in Baltimore, charging him with unlawful interstate flight to avoid confinement after conviction. Holland made the Top Ten list nearly a year later and was arrested in La Harpe, Kansas, by a police officer who recognized the fugitive from his Wanted flyer.

INTERESTING FUGITIVE FACT:
Holland claimed he violated parole to go help the Cubans fight Fidel Castro.

170. EDWARD HOWARD MAPS, alleged arsonist, murderer

LISTED: June 15, 1962
PROCESS DISMISSED: December 1, 1967
DESCRIPTION: Born June 29, 1922. Five feet eight inches, 170 pounds, dark brown hair graying, with green eyes. Occupations: artist and sculptor. Aliases: Edward Maps, "Eddie."

Escape Maps. On January 21, 1962, a fire broke out in a home in Stroudsburg, Pennsylvania, leaving a four-month-old girl dead from smoke inhalation and her mother fighting for her life. But the fire wasn't to blame for the mother's injuries; somebody had caved in her skull with a heavy object. The same somebody had also set 10 separate fires throughout the home and popped open the gas oven to speed the process. That somebody, authorities believed, was the husband and father, Edward Maps. Barely a year before, the artist and self-styled bohemian was diagnosed with schizophrenia, and now it seemed that the condition had taken a grisly turn for the worse. Shortly after the blaze Mrs. Maps died, and in the weeks that followed, her Stroudsburg neighbors reported threatening calls from a man claiming to be Maps. By June Maps made the Top Ten. A little over five years later, Maps also made the Top Ten record books as one of the few to elude capture. Maps, a World War II vet, had appeared to vanish from the face of the Earth. In December 1967 the Stroudsburg district attorney's office decided that the case was too cold to ever be successfully prosecuted, and federal process was dismissed by local authorities in Scranton, Pennsylvania.

You can actually purchase a Edward Howard Maps painting; the missing man's work occasionally pops up in Internet art auctions. When the author last checked, the paintings "Forest," "The Light House," and "Delaware Water Gap" were available.

171. DAVID STANLEY JACUBANIS, bank robber

LISTED: November 21, 1962
CAUGHT: November 29, 1962
DESCRIPTION: Born July 10, 1910, in Baku, Russia. Five feet 10 inches, 165 to 175 pounds, medium build with gray hair and brown eyes. Occupation: barber. Aliases: Max George Bergen, Steve Cunningham, Lawrence Hurlbert, John Jacobson, Bob Jasson, John Nelson.

From Russia. In comic books the villains usually wore outlandish getups in garish colors; the idea was to make them distinctive, and to make the pages more vibrant. David Jacubanis, a Russian-born heister, seemed to take his fashion cues from the funny books. When he showed up at the Plaza Branch of the Dedham Institution for Savings in Massachusetts on March 27, 1962, Jacubanis was decked out in a bright red shirt, white leather gloves, and thick jaw clamped around a stubby cigar. Jacubanis pointed the business end of a .38 caliber revolver and instructed a teller to put all of the money in the paper sack. Just like in the comic books.

Jacubanis may have taken his cues from juvenile reading material, but he was no youngster. The 52-year-old man had a 37-year criminal record, which included convictions for carrying unlicensed weapons, breaking and entering, larceny, armed robbery, and of course, bank robbery. At the time of the Dedham heist he was out on parole after serving 10 years of a 25-year bank robbery hitch (part of which was served at Alcatraz). He also had the distinction of being stateless; born in Russia, Jacubanis resisted repeated attempts to deport him to Russia, Canada, England, or France. Comic book getup or not, it didn't take Superman to crack this case. Just eight days after being named to the Top Ten list, Jacubanis was arrested in Arlington, Vermont, and returned to Massachusetts to face a fresh set of charges.

INTERESTING FUGITIVE FACT:
According to an FBI memorandum, Jacubanis "is soft spoken with an extensive vocabulary, enjoys

Due to an FBI investigation, Jacubanis was arrested in Arlington, Vermont.

sport clothes, big cars, alcoholic beverages in moderation, cigars, cigarettes, good restaurants, steaks and betting on boxing and horse and dog racing."

172. JOHN KINCHLOE DEJARNETTE, bank robber

LISTED: November 30, 1962
CAUGHT: December 3, 1962
DESCRIPTION: Born September 15, 1921, in Kentucky. Five feet 10 inches, 135 to 150 pounds, medium build, with brown hair and eyes. Occupations: clerk, laborer, salesman, typewriter mechanic, and welder. Caution: DeJarnette is wanted for armed bank robberies in which a .38 caliber revolver was used. He is described as a vicious person who previously used explosives in an attempted escape from prison. Consider extremely dangerous. Aliases: John Carnett, John Conrad, J. S. Dalton, John Kenchloe Dejarnette, John D. Jarnett, John Marcum, and "John D."

Fast Money. Want to make almost $100,000 in 40 days? DeJarnette can tell you how: First walk into a Louisville, Kentucky, bank and demand $24,000 at gunpoint. Then do the same at another branch of the same bank, but netting $36,000 this time. Finally, fly up to Cincinnati and hit another bank for $37,000. Of course, the downside to this method is that you're certain to attract attention. DeJarnette did just that. On November 30, 1962, a little more than a month after the Cincinnati heist, DeJarnette was named to the Top Ten list.

DeJarnette, 41, had already been on parole for assault with intent to commit robbery and was famous for trying to break out of jail by digging tunnels, cutting bars, and once even lobbing a Molotov cocktail at a prison guard. The Top Ten memorandum on DeJarnette revealed that the heister was a skittish guy, hopping around the country in airplanes with his 28-year-old girlfriend, Doris Lee Nelson. It also described him as a highly intelligent yet nervous dope fiend who needed a "fix" before each job. (Ms. Nelson apparently had a monkey on her back as well; she was charged with obtaining narcotics by fraud and deceit.) The junk probably made the fugitive overconfident; DeJarnette swore not to be captured alive.

The FBI captured DeJarnette and Nelson just four days after the Top Ten announcement. An accomplice had been arrested on October 2 and revealed the location of DeJarnette's Hollywood apartment hideout. The drug-loving, bank-robbing couple was arrested by surprise. In front of them: stacks of Monopoly money, with game pieces and cards littering a table. Nearby, but out of reach: three loaded pistols. DeJarnette and Nelson did not pass Go.

INTERESTING FUGITIVE FACT:
In jail DeJarnette learned to read and speak Spanish, studied Plato, and took a Dale Carnegie personality course.

Bad Moon Rising. Michael O'Connor preferred to be called "Moon Mullins," which was his boxing name. But when the boxing gigs dried up and other honest jobs failed to produce the kind of bread he wanted, Moon Mullins turned into Mike O'Connor, stickup guy. A truck hijack here, a stickup there, followed by another cheap drink in a cheap bar. (For some reason the ex-pugilist preferred his drinks, meals, and lodging to be on the ultra-cheap side.) Clearly, Moon had seen better days. On August 27, 1962, O'Connor got into a blowsy argument with a drinking buddy named Michael "Knobby" Walsh, and the argument ended when O'Connor shot Walsh to death in a Jersey City dive. He was named to the Ten Most Wanted list a few months later.

A tip from O'Connor's wife led two FBI agents, John Waltos and Robert Kennedy, to stake out a cheap hotel in New York City. "We were freezing our [expletive] off, checking out every guy wearing a dark coat and horn-rimmed glasses," recalled Waltos to a reporter years later. "We must've braced 10 guys out there." The day only got colder and longer, so the two G-men decided to take a break and go for a bite. They hit a Bickford's cafeteria a few blocks away and as a result hit the jackpot. O'Connor was sitting at a table in the cafeteria, munching on a wedge of hot apple pie and sipping coffee.

"You're Moon Mullins the boxer, aren't you?" one agent asked.

"You remember me?" O'Connor replied.

They sure did. Upon his arrest O'Connor found out that one of the agents was named Robert Kennedy. According to Waltos, O'Connor joked: "It's quite an honor being arrested by Bobby Kennedy."

INTERESTING FUGITIVE FACT:
O'Connor used to obsessively pop Rolaids to ease chronic indigestion.

173. MICHAEL JOSEPH O'CONNOR, murderer

LISTED: December 13, 1962
CAUGHT: December 28, 1962
DESCRIPTION: Born February 11, 1906. Five feet 10 inches, 200 to 205 pounds, with brown hair and blue eyes. Occupations: longshoreman, salesman, truck driver. Aliases: Jimmy Delaney, Moon Mullins, Joseph Quinn, and John P. Stone.

174. JOHN LEE TAYLOR, robber, rapist

LISTED: December 14, 1962
CAUGHT: December 20, 1962
DESCRIPTION: Born December 7, 1933, in Tutwiler, Mississippi. Six feet one inch, 160 to 165 pounds, with black hair and brown eyes. Occupations: bakery helper, laborer. Aliases: Fred Boozer, Robert Smith, Jack Taylor, Lee Jack Taylor, and "Big John."

Lone Wolf. The tall stranger forced his way into the Champaign, Illinois, schoolteacher's apartment on July 8, 1961. After beating her unconscious, binding her hands, then raping her, the stranger then ransacked the apartment, stealing the middle-aged woman's cash and jewelry. That man, John Lee Taylor, left behind a broken life. But he also left behind his fingerprints.

A career criminal since he was 12 years old, Taylor's rap sheet was full of sex offenses and robberies—often both—and often preying on middle-aged or elderly women. This time, thanks to the telltale fingerprints, the brutal attack catapulted Taylor to the Ten Most Wanted list. Agents were told to look for a belligerent and brutal "lone wolf" predator who walked in a stooped position with his head down and, curiously, his right hand clenched tightly in a fist, as if the man were always poised to attack. With a description like that it wasn't difficult for the FBI to track Taylor down. Six days after he was named to the Ten Most Wanted list, G-men cornered the Lone Wolf in an apartment in Chicago, Illinois, and arrested him without incident.

INTERESTING FUGITIVE FACT:
Taylor "smokes Camel cigarettes, drinks beer moderately, dresses neatly, speaks softly, acts impulsively, and enjoys 'thrill' and 'sensational' movies," according to an FBI memorandum.

175. HAROLD THOMAS O'BRIEN, murderer

LISTED: January 4, 1963
REMOVED FROM THE LIST: January 14, 1965
DESCRIPTION: Born February 12, 1905, in Chicago. Five feet four inches tall, 165 pounds, with brown hair, partially bald, blue eyes, and a ruddy complexion. Occupations: bartender, chauffeur, and truck driver.

Reserve Heat. It was one of those sloppy bar arguments that got out of control. Harold O'Brien, a veteran armed robber in the 1930s who won parole and swore to live life on the straight and narrow, was boozed out of his mind in a tavern in Fox Lake, Illinois, on August 12, 1960. His equally drunk buddy wouldn't concede his point, so O'Brien decided to settle things the way he knew best. With a gun. O'Brien took a pistol and aimed it at his drinking pal. But a quick-thinking bartender managed to whip the gun out of O'Brien's hands, and everything seemed hunky-dory again. That is, until O'Brien

pulled a second gun out of his jacket pocket and pumped three bullets into his drunk buddy at close range. The man died. O'Brien, who'd tried to go straight, ran. He was named to the Ten Most Wanted list two and a half years later, after local authorities had no luck locating the violent drunk.

There would be no resolution to the federal government's quarrel with Harold O'Brien. After two years passed, Illinois prosecutors gave up the chase, thinking that too much time had gone by—too many tumblers of whiskey consumed—for witnesses to build a case against O'Brien. Federal process was dismissed by federal and local authorities in Lake City, Illinois.

INTERESTING FUGITIVE FACT:
O'Brien was serious about living the straight life. He repeatedly talked about opening a rooming house somewhere in California, Florida, or Arizona.

176. JERRY CLARENCE RUSH, bank robber

LISTED: January 14, 1963
CAUGHT: March 25, 1963

Rush to Judgment. The FBI's press release on heister Jerry Rush could double as the synopsis of a 1950s crime picture: "Jerry Clarence Rush, a trigger-happy gun-toting alleged bank robber, tattooed with the words 'Born to Lose' and believed using bank robbery loot to finance a big-spending honeymoon with his stripteaser bride, is one of the FBI's Ten Most Wanted fugitives." Guns. Money. A stripper wife. A fatalistic tattoo. What else do you need? But this wasn't a B-movie. Rush, a polished stickup artist, knocked over a Perth Amboy, New Jersey, bank for a cool $100,000 and burned the loot on a cross-country honeymoon. Due to an FBI investigation, Rush was arrested in Bay Harbor Islands, Florida, just as he was stepping out of a new luxury car.

INTERESTING FUGITIVE FACT:
Isn't the fact that Rush was blowing heist money on his stripper bride interesting enough?

177. MARSHALL FRANK CHRISMAN, bank robber

LISTED: February 7, 1963
CAUGHT: May 21, 1963
DESCRIPTION: Born August 22, 1925, in Denver, Colorado. Five feet nine inches, 190 to 200 pounds, brown hair

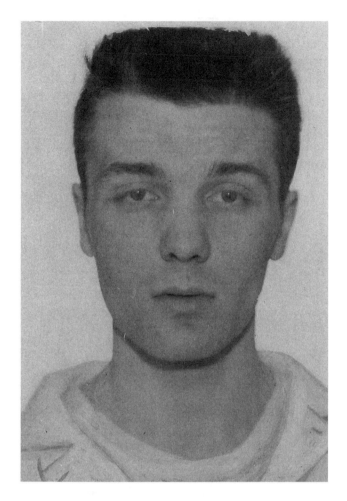

Due to an FBI investigation, Rush was arrested in Bay Harbor Islands, Florida.

tattoos that covered his flesh were inspired by a wartime hitch in the U.S. Navy, even though that branch of military booted Speedy out for "bad conduct." And robbing banks? That was just the natural evolution of Speedy's criminal career, which started at the tender age of 11 and included burglary, larceny, receiving stolen property, mail robbery, and assault.

In the summer of 1962 the National Bank of Toledo, Ohio, was hit for $12,264 by an odd crew of characters: three men, one of them with bright paint on his face and hair carrying a shotgun and revolver, and another guy with a revolver and an old-fashioned handkerchief mask wrapped around the lower half of his face. The guy in the handkerchief was Speedy Chrisman. Maybe it was a good luck charm—Speedy's three partners, including the weird guy in the face paint and a getaway driver, were rounded up and sentenced to the Ohio State Penitentiary. Speedy and his 15 tattoos remained at large and continued to pull stickups, even after he was named to the Top Ten list in February 1963. Like his corny tattoo of Betty Boop, it was a big mistake. In late May Speedy was arrested after knocking over a Los Angeles grocery store, and a routine fingerprint check revealed his identity—and his Most Wanted status.

INTERESTING FUGITIVE FACT:
According to an FBI memorandum, Chrisman was fond of both prostitutes and art—he considered himself a critic of the latter. (He also dug horse races, movies, and baseball games.)

with brown eyes. Scars and marks: scars over right and left eyes, circular scar right cheek, scar right side of neck, six-inch burn scar left shoulder blade, vaccination scar left arm, scars on left elbow, scar right hand; tattoos: ship, eagle, American flag, anchor, "Remember Pearl Harbor," "World War 2," left upper arm, "Betty Boop," "Hawaii," a hula girl left forearm, "U.S. Navy," a shield right upper arm, ship, hand, horse head, horseshoe, and "Good Luck" right forearm. Aliases: Jack Chase, Speed Chrismas, M. Christman, Johnny Lane, Johnny Love, Tommy Love, John Nelson, Johnnie Nelson, "Speedy," and others.

Drinkin', Inkin', and Sinkin'. Marshal Chrisman— "Speedy" to his friends—seemed to enjoy only three things: Seagram's Seven Crown whiskey, getting tattoos, and robbing banks. When Speedy tossed back the whiskeys, he became a loud-mouthed, belligerent drunk, capable of great violence. The multitude of

178. HOWARD JAY BARNARD, robber

LISTED: April 12, 1963
CAUGHT: April 6, 1964
DESCRIPTION: Born September 24, 1924. Five feet eight inches, 150 pounds, brown hair (may be dyed or bleached) with blue-green eyes. Occupations: farmer, judo instructor, salesman, truck driver. Aliases: Barney Anderson, James David Anderson, Howard Jay Bernard, James Craig, Roy Davis, and Jay Rodriques.

Strange Looks. Call Howard Barnard the Lon Chaney of federal fugitives. He went all out to distort his looks before an armed stickup—piling thick makeup on his face, shoving cotton balls up his nose and in his mouth Marlon Brando–style, and even using rubber bands to warp his ears a different way. (Lon Chaney employed similar face-stretching techniques in his horror movie career, most notably in *The Phantom of the Opera*.) Despite the efforts, Barnard got pinched every decade. In 1946 it was for a job in Memphis. In 1955, one in Huntington Beach, California. In 1962, Seattle. But this time, after the Seattle job, Barnard managed to break out of prisoner transport. On April 12, 1963, Barnard was named to the Top Ten list.

The FBI didn't hear from Barnard for almost a year, but that didn't mean he wasn't busy. Barnard robbed bars and supermarkets, still using his freaky disguise techniques. On April 6, 1964, Barnard used a disguise—two different sets of clothes to make him appear heavier, makeup, gold hair, and cotton in his nose and mouth—to stick up a motel in North

Sacramento for $1,000, but was shot by police during his getaway. Once police removed the glue from his hands so he could be fingerprinted, Barnard's Most Wanted status was revealed.

INTERESTING FUGITIVE FACT:
Barnard was discharged from the U.S. Army for "mental instability."

179. LEROY AMBROSIA FRAZIER, violent assaulter

LISTED: June 4, 1963
CAUGHT: September 12, 1963
DESCRIPTION: Born November 28, 1919, in Ocala, Florida. His black hair has been peroxided carrot red in the past, and he has worn a gold earring in his left ear.

Bad Boy Leroy.   Leroy Frazier, a violent white slaver and larcenist, would have done anything to get away from a cop. During one arrest in 1959 he bit a Washington, D.C., cop on the leg, then tried to shove him out a second-story window. His mouth also came in handy three years later, on January 14, 1962, when he broke out of the maximum security ward of St. Elizabeth's Hospital in D.C. with a lock pick made from the handle of a plastic toothbrush. He made the Top Ten list a year and a half later. Seems Frazier didn't like being locked up at all—his FBI poster warns that the man has "threatened to kill anyone attempting to return him to confinement." There was good reason to heed that warning. Frazier was "adept at hiding weapons on his person, habitually carries a gun or knife and is extremely strong."

The FBI found Frazier in Cleveland, where he tried to set up a contracting business under the name "Johnny Gray & Sons." (There was no Johnny Gray, and the two-fisting, hard-drinking pimp fugitive didn't have any sons, either.) Strangely enough, reports came in that Frazier was seen around town in women's clothing. Whether or not this was a clever disguise or fetish is unknown—although the FBI memorandum did classify Frazier as a "sex pervert." But it didn't matter. The FBI asked Cleveland papers to run Frazier's photograph, and the pressure led agents directly to Frazier's (or "Johnny Gray's") apartment door.

INTERESTING FUGITIVE FACT:
From the Top Ten memo: "Frazier is an excellent cement finisher . . . and has been a pimp." He also enjoyed scotch, vodka, and beer.

Chrisman was arrested in Los Angeles, California, by local authorities. Apprehended after robbing a grocery store, Chrisman was identified after a routine fingerprint check.

180. CARL CLOSE, bank robber

LISTED: September 25, 1963
CAUGHT: September 26, 1963
DESCRIPTION: Born 1915 in West Virginia. Five feet 10 inches, 190 pounds, black hair with brown eyes. Scars and marks: small mole left side of chin, small scar in center of right palm, appendectomy scar, hernia scar right side, scar on right thigh. Caution: Close has been armed in the past with a revolver and has been in possession of a submachine gun. He has made attempts to escape from custody. Consider extremely dangerous. Aliases: Carl Carter, Carl Closc, Robert Cramer, Carl Klosz, Carl Kloez, Carl Klos, Carl Klose, Roy Mann, Carl McCloskey, Paul Miller, James Scott, and Carl Stephens.

At Close Range. Carl Close's capture in Anderson, South Carolina, minutes after he robbed a local bank

Close was apprehended in Anderson, South Carolina, by local authorities after robbing a bank.

of over $28,000 was huge news—the story consumed countless column inches and included dozens of photos in the September 27, 1963, edition of the *Independent Anderson*. It was probably the biggest thing to hit Anderson in years. "One of U.S. Most Wanted Criminals Nabbed" was the headline of one photo spread and told the story of Close's foiled bank heist in a film noir–like sequence of pictures. The first photo: Close, with an embarrassing smirk on his face, as he's led away from the North Main Street branch of the First National Bank by the captain of the Anderson police force and another detective. The second photo: a close-up of the Berretta pistol Close had, along with a clip. Photo three: bank teller Mrs. Evelyn Jackson, who bravely faced the bank robber and complied with his demands. Photo four: exterior of the North Main Street branch itself. Photo five: the Cadillac that Close had procured from a used-car dealer in town, and which he planned to use to drive exactly two blocks. Photo six: the fin-tailed Buick that Close had parked two blocks away to make his getaway. A half-dozen photographs that perfectly captured a bank heist gone wrong.

Another story in the same edition quickly detailed Carl Close's criminal history. The reporters had the material easily on hand, because just the day before—September 25—they'd received a press release from the FBI naming Close to the Ten Most Wanted list. As it turned out, the newly minted fugitive was an old hand at bank stickups. Close and two of his brothers-in-law knocked over three banks in Maryland and West Virginia back in 1949 and were subsequently arrested in Tennessee, where police found them armed with two revolvers and a .45 caliber submachine gun. The trio tried to jackrabbit from their holding cells, but were quickly rounded up and sentenced to 35 years in prison each, plus a $15,001 fine. A few years later, Close tried to hatch a brazen plan to escape federal lockup in Atlanta, Georgia, by having a helicopter airlift them out, but prison snitches foiled the plan, and Close found himself transferred to Alcatraz. (*The Independent Anderson* highlighted this detail in the story headline: "Close Once Tried Escape from Prison by 'Copter.") In 1954 he was moved from The Rock to bank robbers' finishing school, a.k.a. the U.S. penitentiary at Leavenworth. By 1961 the prison board was convinced that Close had learned his lesson and granted him parole. Close resettled in Nokomis, Florida, living with his brother and making a run at the straight life by working sheet metal and refinishing furniture.

Apparently the straight life didn't work for Close. He remembered the easy money he and his brothers-in-law had made back in '49, and he convinced his brother Harold to take up the family business again. On March 18, 1963, the Close brothers hit the Edmondson Village branch of the Equitable Trust Company in Baltimore for $16,937. They would have scored more, but they dropped $4,141 while scrambling to their getaway car. (An honest citizen scooped up the money and promptly walked it back into the bank.) The brothers split up, and Harold got pinched in Roanoke, Virginia, on June 1. That didn't deter Carl, who robbed the Colonial American National Bank in the same town just three days later, netting $6,330. Two days later, a federal warrant was issued for Carl's arrest, and a little over three months later, he was named to the Top Ten.

The Anderson score would have been his biggest yet if it hadn't completely imploded at the end. First, Close visited McClellan's used-car lot, which was situated on a diagonal across from the bank. He explained to the dealer that he was interested in a 1955 Caddy with a white body and brown top that was sitting on the lot, and that he'd like to take it for a test spin. The dealer thought Close looked reputable enough, with his neat black trousers, white shirt, and thin black tie decorated with three white triangles at the top. He handed him the keys, and Close drove off. Fifteen minutes later, he returned, said he really liked the car, and would probably stop back. The dealer nodded and wasn't too surprised when Close returned a little over an hour later. Close explained that he wanted to show the car to his wife before forking over the money, and the dealer agreed. Close again drove off with the 1955 Caddy.

He drove directly to the First National Bank across and down the street. Close hopped out of the car, calmly walked into the bank—which had only one other customer inside—approached two tellers and an assistant manager, and instructed them to fill a paper shopping bag with money. Then he showed them his Beretta as a convincer. The tellers quickly complied, and Close stepped behind the teller counter to make sure they were putting every single buck in the bag. Then he turned to inspect an open safe on the floor. One of the tellers, Mrs. Katherine Erwin, took advantage of the distraction and pressed a silent alarm, which directly signaled the Anderson Police Department.

Close didn't know about that, nor about the scheduled delivery of cash from an armored car.

After the guard walked in, carrying two sacks full of money, Close disarmed him and told everybody to stay put until he was gone.

Outside, the armed guard's partner, Mason Evans, saw Close leave the bank, but thought little of it. "I could have picked the man off with a shotgun or rifle had I only known," he told a reporter. "At the time, Close appeared be just another customer leaving the bank."

But Evans didn't have to beat himself up too badly. Just one block down the street, Close found himself surrounded by Anderson police. Close smirked, dropped his shopping bag full of money, and raised his hands. "You fellows are on the ball," he said. Police disarmed him, taking the .38 Smith & Wesson that Close had taken from the guard, as well as the robber's own loaded Beretta.

"When you play this game, you can't win 'em all," Close said as he was led away. A newspaper photographer from the *Independent Anderson* snapped photos, capturing the quizzical, bemused look on Close's face.

INTERESTING FUGITIVE FACT:
According to an FBI bulletin, Close "drinks alcoholic beverages moderately, reportedly favoring beer and Seagram's V.O. whisky, enjoys home cooking, being particularly fond of chicken."

181. THOMAS ASBURY HADDER, thief, cop killer

LISTED: October 9, 1963
CAUGHT: January 13, 1964
DESCRIPTION: Born October 21, 1941, in Richmond, Virginia. Five feet nine inches, 170 pounds, reddish blond hair receding, blue eyes. Scars and marks: three-inch scar right thumb, appendectomy scar; tattoos: dolphin or shark on left biceps, "The South Will Rise Again" left forearm. Remarks: reportedly interested in weight lifting and judo. Caution: Hadder escaped from a mental institution while awaiting trial for killing a police officer. Consider extremely dangerous. Aliases: John Barker, Braxton Pate.

The Goodbye Song. Some journeys to the Ten Most Wanted list take years; in Thomas Hadder's case, it was only a matter of seconds. On May 2, 1963, he drove away from a gas station in Prince George's County, Maryland, without paying for a tire. A patrolman caught up with him and pulled Hadder's car over to the side of the road. Instead of handing over his license and registration, Hadder revealed a pistol and shot the officer in the chest at point-blank range.

It was apparently a spontaneous decision that Hadder came to regret, for the killer confessed the very next day and was arrested. Three months later, Hadder had yet another change of heart. Along with another inmate, Hadder broke through the second-floor window of the Clifton T. Perkins State Hospital in Maryland and escaped. A month later, he was named to the Ten Most Wanted list. Eagle-eyed citizens reported a man fitting Hadder's description in the Texas area; by mid-January 1964, he was pinpointed at a Salvation Army Center in Oklahoma City, Oklahoma, living under the name "Thomas Longstreet." When FBI agents arrived, Hadder was sitting back and listening to a group sing-along. It was the last song he would hear as a free man for a long, long time.

INTERESTING FUGITIVE FACT:

Hadder was a petty criminal from the beginning—the first entry on his criminal record was for "suspicion of purse snatching."

182. ALFRED OPONOWICZ, burglar, armed robber

LISTED: November 27, 1963
CAUGHT: December 23, 1964
DESCRIPTION: Born January 4, 1926, in Carnegie, Pennsylvania. Five feet 10 inches, 170 to 175 pounds, with brown hair, hazel eyes, and a ruddy complexion. Aliases: Albert Consolo, James Mallory, and Albert Opanowicz.

Breathless. No doubt about what Al Oponowicz was up to when the Cleveland police arrested him in the early morning hours of September 2, 1962. A quick search of his car—parked near a branch of the Cleveland Trust. Company—yielded burglary tools, two-way radios, a police radio, and a .38 caliber revolver. In his pocket: six .38 cartridges. It wasn't the first time Oponowicz was nabbed with a gun in his possession, either. The 37-year-old Pennsylvania native had burglary and armed robbery convictions dating back to when he was 14, and was often packing heat when arrested. Oponowicz used that heat back in 1947, when a Cleveland bank job turned sour and he had to shoot two citizens to make his getaway.

Oponowicz stood trial for the Cleveland burglary job on February 4, 1963 . . . for about an hour. He skipped court during recess, with his wife left hold-

ing his hat and coat. She'd be holding it for nearly two years. Oponowicz was named to the Top Ten list in November 1963 and was finally arrested a year later in Painesville, Ohio, by FBI agents and local authorities. You can't say Oponowicz didn't try hard. Cornered in a railroad switching yard, the burglar tried to fade into the background by lying completely submerged in a pool of brackish water while breathing through a reed. The air ran out, though, as did Oponowicz's luck.

INTERESTING FUGITIVE FACT:

Oponowicz was a baker, barber, salesman, and steel-worker.

183. ARTHUR WILLIAM COUTS, armed robber

LISTED: December 27, 1963
CAUGHT: January 30, 1964
DESCRIPTION: Born in Philadelphia, Pennsylvania. Five feet 10 inches tall, 169 to 176 pounds, with brown hair and hazel eyes. Occupations: automobile spray painter, business machine repairman, carpenter's helper, TV repairman, laborer, sheet metal worker, and painter. Scars and marks: tattoos on both arms and the center of his chest.

Oh, What a Night. Arthur Couts was a violent career criminal at the age of 32, racking up convictions of aggravated robbery, armed robbery, "atrocious" assault and battery, rape, carrying a concealed weapon, unlawful possession of firearms, possession of drugs, auto larceny, burglary, and good old-fashioned larceny. So the events of July 17, 1963, was merely more of the same. Couts, along with a fellow thug, strolled into a Philadelphia grocery, walked up to the guy working the check-cashing booth, leveled a revolver at him, and said, "Hand over the money or I'll blow your brains out." The grocer had more brains than Couts, however. He ducked behind a steel counter. This angered Couts, who started firing his gun anyway, causing grievous harm to the walls of the grocery store. Couts and his accomplice walked away empty-handed. It was a small-time crime that didn't earn Couts a penny, but it was enough of a career capper to land Couts on the Ten Most Wanted list in late December 1963. Couts lasted barely a month on the list. Even though he had grown a bushy mustache and dyed his hair, he stayed in his hometown of Philly, which made it easier for the G-men to track down their man.

INTERESTING FUGITIVE FACT:
Couts thought himself quite a ladies' man and enjoyed movies, dancing, TV, pool, and drinking beer in bars—"occasionally to excess," noted the FBI memorandum.

184. JESSE JAMES GILBERT, bank robber

LISTED: January 27, 1964
CAUGHT: February 26, 1964
DESCRIPTION: Alias: Donald Masters.

Gilbert was arrested in Philadelphia, Pennsylvania, by FBI agents. In order to hide his identity, he was wearing a wig, had on dark glasses, and had placed bandages over a tattoo on his left arm. After being apprehended by the agents, Gilbert remarked, "You men are real gentlemen, and if I had to be picked up I'm glad it was by the FBI."

Real Gentlemen. The first of two Jesse Jameses who would appear on the Ten Most Wanted list in the 1960s, Gilbert was wanted for crimes similar to that of his namesake. On January 3, 1964, Gilbert and an accomplice knocked over a savings and loan in Alhambra, California, to the tune of $11,500. The getaway was less than smooth; the duo used an innocent woman as a human shield, and ended up shooting an Alhambra police sergeant in the head. Plus, Gilbert lost his partner to a flurry of police bullets. More bad luck still: The brazen heist prompted his addition to the Ten Most Wanted list a few weeks later. Gilbert was arrested in Philadelphia by FBI agents. In order to hide his identity, he wore a wig, dark glasses, and had placed bandages over a tattoo on his left arm. After being apprehended by the agents, Gilbert remarked, "You men are real gentlemen, and if I had to be picked up I'm glad it was by the FBI."

INTERESTING FUGITIVE FACT:
During one prison term, Gilbert shanked another convict to death and had extra time added to his sentence.

185. SAMMIE EARL AMMONS, murderer

LISTED: September 10, 1963
CAUGHT: May 15, 1964
DESCRIPTION: Born December 7, 1934. Six feet two inches, 210 to 230 pounds, heavy build, with brown hair and blue eyes. Occupations: bus driver and truck driver. Aliases: Roger B. Bishop, Ralph Harrison, John Williams, John Williamson, "Big John." Caution: Ammons has allegedly impersonated law enforcement officers on several occasions and had been known to wear a special officer's badge and carry a .38 nickel-plated automatic pistol in a hip holster.

Babykiller. Sammie and his wife, Barbara Sue, started out forging payroll checks, but they soon descended into something far worse: the cold-blooded murder of two children. The Ammons family—Sammie, Barbara Sue, and their six children—were big on family trips through the South. They even let the babysitter tag along, as well as her two children, ages two and four. What happened next is still unclear; Ammons claimed that the babysitter's two children had died of medical complications—they were sickly, he explained, and that he merely did the humane thing of helping a grieving mother dispose of their bodies. But then why were both kids found, strangled to death, in an abandoned septic tank near Crossville, Tennessee?

Ammons was no angel. He had been wanted for passing forged checks in various southern states, and by February 8, 1963, the state of Tennessee was charging him with unlawful flight to avoid prosecution for forgery. However, it was the grisly discovery of the two strangled children in September 1963 that prompted Ammon's addition to the Ten Most Wanted list. Ammons was finally arrested in Cherokee, Alabama, by local police after attempting to pass a bad check in a Georgia store. A high-speed chase ensued, in which Ammons crashed through a roadblock, then attempted to hide in a nearby field when police shot out his back tires. His arrest, however, didn't do much to solve the mystery of the dead children. The babysitter repeatedly changed her story; in one version the kids were sick. In another Ammons was blamed for their deaths.

INTERESTING FUGITIVE FACT:
Ammons liked to visit roller-skating rinks. (Too bad he was rotting away in prison during the 1970s, when roller-skating was *really* popular.)

186. FRANK B. DUMONT, burglar

LISTED: March 10, 1964
CAUGHT: April 27, 1964
DESCRIPTION: Born May 19, 1921. Six feet tall, 175 to 200 pounds, brown hair that may be graying at the temples, hazel eyes. Occupations: blacksmith, cook, miner, truck driver, welder, and well driller. Aliases: John W. Bingham, Bud Beaumont, William Craig, Frank Guthrie, Bill Stacy, William Weston.

The Barefoot Cop. Frank Dumont, a Top Tenner who landed on the list after abducting, beating, and leaving a 14-year-old girl for dead, was pulling a breaking and entering job on an apartment in Tucson, Arizona. Little did he expect that nearby would be two men uniquely equipped to bring him down. The apartment building manager spotted Dumont and immediately called one of his tenants—an Arizona police officer named Richard Milne. The cop was off duty when the call came; in fact, he wasn't even wearing his shoes. But he set out right away to investigate the disturbance. When Dumont saw that he was spotted, he ran for it. The barefoot Milne gave pursuit, as did another tenant, Dennis Favero—who just so happened to be a champion wrestler from Notre Dame

University. Together, Milne and Favero subdued and arrested Dumont. (Actually, it was the cop who applied the law; the wrestler merely applied a strong hammerlock.) "Give me a break," muttered Dumont.

INTERESTING FUGITIVE FACT:
Dumont had dyed his brown hair and mustache red while on the lam.

187. WILLIAM BEVERLY HUGHES, armed robber

LISTED: March 18, 1964
CAUGHT: April 11, 1964
DESCRIPTION: Born September 16, 1929. Six feet two inches, 170 to 175 pounds, medium build, with dark brown hair and blue-green eyes. Occupations: auto mechanic, carpenter, and truck driver. Aliases: Willie B. Hug, W. J. Hughes, Willie B. Hughes, and "Sonny."

If I Was a Carpenter. Late in the summer of 1958 Hughes and a girlfriend stuck up a mom-and-pop beer store in Baldwin County, Alabama. He was pinched and was given 20 years in Alabama's Kilby Prison. But on June 3, 1961, only a few years into his sentence, Hughes escaped using a state-owned truck. The FBI had a tip that Hughes was working as a carpenter in the Bel Aire, Texas, area, but he had already split the scene before they arrived. A few weeks later, an Arizona highway patrolman spotted Hughes on Route 70, headed toward the San Carlos Indian reservation. The patrolman called reservation police, warning them that Hughes was going to be passing through, and two reservation cops forced him off the road near Bylas, Arizona. The cops discovered a man and a woman in the car, along with three children. The man claimed to be "Robert Holloway" from Houston, Texas, and showed them a draft card and driver's license to prove it. "Holloway" was taken into custody anyway, where he finally admitted to being Hughes.

INTERESTING FUGITIVE FACT:
The Top Ten memo reveals that Hughes liked "constant female companionship."

188. QUAY CLEON KILBURN, armed robber

LISTED: March 23, 1964
CAUGHT: June 25, 1964
DESCRIPTION: Born in Salt Lake City, Utah.

We Go Quay Back. After making the Top Ten list in 1958 (see #105), Quay Kilburn decided to make a return appearance just six years later. In the meantime Kilburn had served his days at Utah's state prison, winning parole on November 12, 1963. Kilburn had edited the inmate newspaper while in stir and became enraptured enough with his new role that he continued to refer to himself as "editor at large," even after winning his freedom. It didn't take long for the "at large" part of that moniker to take on a different, yet familiar, meaning. Settling back in Salt Lake City, Kilburn cashed a bunch of counterfeit checks and soon found himself back on the Ten Most Wanted list. Kilburn lasted a little longer during this run, but not by much. He never left the state of Utah, which made it relatively easy for FBI agents to nab him in Odgen, Utah, where he was found packing heat and most probably planning to get back into his old line of work. No, not editing.

INTERESTING FUGITIVE FACT:
Kilburn was the fourth man to make the Top Ten list twice.

189. JOSEPH FRANCIS BRYAN JR., child molester

LISTED: April 14, 1964
CAUGHT: April 28, 1964
DESCRIPTION: Born in 1939 in Camden, New Jersey. Caution: Bryan is a dangerous former mental patient.

"Tied Up and Screaming." Joe Bryan was a deeply troubled man. While in therapy as a teenager for molesting two other teenagers, Bryan admitted that he enjoyed "seeing small boys tied up and screaming." That was 1958. When he was later released from the psychiatric hospital, Bryan tried to find other ways to get his kicks—stealing cars, breaking into private homes—but those exploits only earned him more prison time. When he was paroled in January 1964, Bryan decided to go back to what he enjoyed best.

The first boy, a seven-year-old from Mount Pleasant, South Carolina, disappeared in late February. Another seven-year-old disappeared from St. Petersburg, Florida, almost a month later. A frantic search party turned up not that boy, but the remains of the missing boy from South Carolina. Evidence and eyewitness reports linked that boy with Joe Bryan, and he was named to the Ten Most Wanted list. On April 28, just 14 days after making the list, an FBI agent spotted Bryan driving in New Orleans in a stolen 1963 Cadillac. The G-man quickly signaled a partner, and the two pulled Byran over near a shopping mall. In the car with Bryan was an eight-year-old boy who had been reported missing from Humboldt, Tennessee, just a week before. Bryan tried to fight with the arresting agents, but to no avail. There was a happy ending for the Tennessee boy, but not the Florida boy who had been reported missing in late March. His remains were found in a palmetto grove by FBI agents who traced back Bryan's route from Tennessee.

INTERESTING FUGITIVE FACT:
Bryan's other major interest—aside from small boys tied up and screaming—was racetrack gambling.

190. JOHN ROBERT BAILEY, robber

LISTED: April 22, 1964
CAUGHT: May 4, 1964
DESCRIPTION: A "ladies' man." Alias: Charles Robert Carpenter.

The Plumber Beside Me. Charles Robert Carpenter, 44, was an upstanding citizen of Hayward, California, a hardworking plumber who had married a local widow and cared for her two daughters; John Robert Bailey, 44, was a robber and a rapist. It took almost two years for authorities to discover that Charles Robert was John Robert, a criminal the FBI had named to the Most Wanted list on April 22, 1964. Bailey's arrest record stretched back 24 years and included convictions for robbery, larceny, carnal abuse, and rape. He was sentenced to life in prison for the Arkansas rape, but was released on parole in November 1962. Three months later, the cops were after him again, this time for a February 22, 1960, holdup at a Hot Springs, Arkansas, motel. Bailey's three accomplices were captured, but he headed west, settling quietly in Hayward until May 4, 1964, when the FBI, acting on a tip, arrested him while he watched TV. Bailey was arrested in Hayward, California, where he had posed as a plumber for two years.

INTERESTING FUGITIVE FACT:
After his arrest Carpenter got no support from the widow he had married. "Death one can almost take," she said. "but this . . . I don't know what to think."

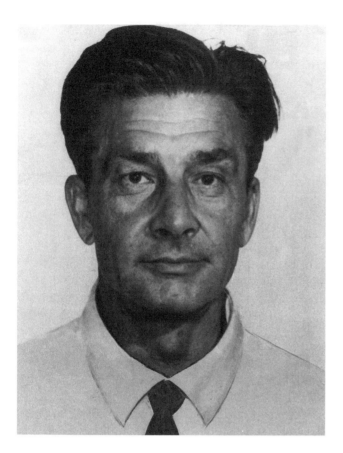

Zavada was arrested in San Jose, California, after a gun battle in which he was shot in the chest and rushed to a hospital in Santa Clara to undergo surgery.

191. GEORGE ZAVADA, bank robber

LISTED: May 6, 1964
CAUGHT: June 12, 1964
DESCRIPTION: Born January 16, 1916, in Cleveland, Ohio. Five feet five inches, 130 to 140 pounds, black hair with brown eyes. Scars and marks: scar left eyebrow, scar left cheekbone, scar lower lip, scar under chin, scars on right and left knees. Remarks: may wear glasses. Caution: Zavada has been armed in the past and reportedly possesses several .32 caliber automatic pistols. Consider dangerous. Aliases: R. Bond, George Drake, Gordon Drake, Angelo Libbyttie, George Zabada, George Zaneda, George Zavade, George Zavado, George Zawanda, and others.

Fall of the King. His robbery partners called him "the King." The nickname was appropriate, for in 1963 heister George Zavada charted more hits than Elvis Presley. First came a Whittier, California, super-

market raid in the spring ($2,633), followed by a Culver City savings and loan in June ($3,034), an L.A. company in July ($10,049), and another bank in Canoga Park just two weeks later ($33,771). During that last raid Zavada was becoming so confident he started to pull a stunt right out of the John Dillinger handbook for bank robbers. With a smile—and with his accomplices Howard Jensen and Clarence Kostich holding guns on the employees—the King leaped over the counter and helped himself to cash, just as Dillinger had 30 years before.

Such cockiness always comes back to bite you in the behind. In September Zavada's partners were arrested in a Hollywood motel, and a search of their apartment led authorities directly to Zavada, who was in his home base of San Francisco. A trial date was set for December 23, 1963, but by then Zavada had jumped bail and decided to try to beat his previous robbery record. He hooked up with two other ex-cons he knew from his time at Leavenworth in the 1950s and started fresh. A robbery attempt in Reno, Nevada, didn't quite work out—the manager refused to open the vault—but a late January heist in Los Angeles did, netting the King and his men $7,696. That was followed by a $4,478 bank job on March 13, and a $13,000 job on March 20. The FBI was sick of the King and slapped his mug on the Ten Most Wanted list on May 6.

Zavada's end came on the same day of his biggest score ever—the $73,000 robbery of a Sacramento bank. FBI agents spotted his car in front of a house in San Jose, and instead of surrendering peacefully as he did the previous year, Zavada ran out of the house, gun in hand. That didn't do the King any good. An FBI agent shot first, and Zavada was rushed to a hospital in Santa Clara to undergo surgery. He survived his wound and was slapped with a 25-year bank robbery sentence.

INTERESTING FUGITIVE FACT:
Zavada had his nickname, "the King," embroidered on his skivvies.

192. GEORGE PATRICK MCLAUGHLIN, hired killer

LISTED: May 8, 1964
CAUGHT: February 24, 1965
DESCRIPTION: Born July 9, 1927. Five feet six inches, 140 to 150 pounds, brown hair with brown eyes. Occupations: longshoreman and painter. Aliases: Edward Donovan, John Kelly, Charles Patrick McLaughlin, and John Ryan.

Bullet Shy. George McLaughlin, a slab of hired muscle for the tough Boston Irish mobs, didn't think twice about pumping a bullet into somebody. On March 15, 1964, a bank employee named William Sheridan was leaving a party when someone shot him in the face. Witnesses saw a car speeding away, and that car was traced to McLaughlin, whose criminal background made him a likely suspect and worthy for the FBI's Ten Most Wanted list. (To this day no one is sure if Sheridan's murder was a hit or a case of mistaken identity.) Close to a year later, McLaughlin was caught when a tipster directed FBI agents to an apartment house in Dorchester, Massachusetts. His chosen alias: "John O'Connor." McLaughlin had a number of loaded weapons at his disposal, but instead, meekly surrendered to the invading G-men. "Please don't shoot," he said.

INTERESTING FUGITIVE FACT:
McLaughlin allegedly fondled the girlfriend of a rival mob boss, sparking a blood-soaked war that left 40 gangsters dead.

193. CHESTER COLLINS, violent assaulter

LISTED: May 14, 1964
PROCESS DISMISSED: March 30, 1967
DESCRIPTION: Born December 1, 1913, in Dothan, Alabama. Five feet 8 1/2 inches, 176 pounds, black hair, graying, with dark brown eyes. Occupations: farm worker, laborer, and tractor driver. Alias: Chester Allen.

Roses Are Red, Collins Was Blue. Chester Collins was a whiskey poet—a heavy drinker who loved putting words together and living life to its passionate extremes. Sometimes these extremes turned violent. On December 8, 1956, the morning after an argument at a dance in Winter Haven, Florida, Collins appeared in his girlfriend's bedroom and used a hatchet to attack both her and her roommate. Both girls survived, but were left critically injured. Collins was arrested and had only two words to put together for the court: "I'm guilty." He was sentenced to 10 years in prison.

A half year later, Collins apparently lost his sense of remorse and escaped from his prison camp. Seven years later, with no leads, authorities decided to place Collins on the Ten Most Wanted list, in hopes that someone would have seen Collins somewhere. But those hopes were in vain. On March 30, 1967, federal process was dismissed in West Palm Beach, Florida. Collins was one of the few who got away.

INTERESTING FUGITIVE FACT:
Collins was an avid fan of dream interpretation. Maybe he thought the hatchet attack was simply a vivid nightmare.

194. EDWARD NEWTON NIVENS, armed robber

LISTED: May 28, 1964
CAUGHT: June 2, 1964
DESCRIPTION: Born September 2, 1921, in York, South Carolina. Five feet 10 1/2 inches, 155 to 165 pounds, black hair, graying and balding with blue eyes. Scars and marks: scars left eyebrow, right eyelid, under chin, right thumb. Remarks: reportedly an avid gambler. Occupations: salesman, and truck driver. Alias: Eddie Nivens.

The Way of the Gun. In early 1963 Edward Nivens was sprung from a federal penitentiary. Less than two months later, he decided to stick up a bar in Toledo, Ohio. (So much for being reformed.) He pointed a pearl-handled .22 caliber pistol at the bartender, who handed over $375. Nivens fled, but he didn't count on the bartender and a customer pursuing him. What that unlucky customer didn't know was that Nivens was a former firearms instructor in the army and an excellent pistol shot. Nivens fired a bullet into the customer's stomach, then commandeered a passing car. After a few blocks he dumped the driver. A few more blocks he dumped the car. That was the last anyone saw of Nivens for over a year.

The robbery and shooting was the capper to a life of crime that included armed robbery, interstate transportation of a stolen car, and forgery. The FBI named him to the Top Ten list in late May 1964. Nivens was arrested in Tampa, Florida, by the FBI after a citizen recognized him from a wanted flyer.

INTERESTING FUGITIVE FACT:
Nivens often made extra money donating blood.

195. LOUIS FREDERICK VASSELLI, armed robber

LISTED: June 15, 1964
CAUGHT: September 1, 1964
DESCRIPTION: Born in Chicago in August 1930.

Torture for $130. You can run from your criminal trial, but that doesn't mean a grand jury can't convict you all the same. This is what happened to Lou Vasselli, a Chicago-based hoodlum who participated in a violent home invasion in suburban Winnetka, Illinois. Vasselli and his thugs burst into the home of businessman G. Laury Botthoff on May 28, 1961, then proceeded to torture Botthoff, his wife, and two servants with punches and lit cigarettes until they told the invaders where they'd hidden cash and jewelry. Either the Botthoffs could handle their pain, or didn't have much in the way of cash and jewelry, because all that Vasselli and his boys made off with was a lousy $130 and some costume jewelry.

That lame haul landed Vasselli on the Top Ten list a few years later after he skipped bail and disappeared for a few years. There was a near capture when Vasselli was pinched for public drunkenness under the improbable alias "Theodopholus Riordan," but cops didn't get a hit on fingerprints until after Vasselli had paid his fine and moved on. Vasselli's luck ran out in September 1964, when an old classmate from Chicago recognized his face on a Wanted poster and directed the FBI to an apartment in Calumet City, Illinois. Vasselli, who was living there under the name "Tom Polito," was arrested without incident.

INTERESTING FUGITIVE FACT:
In 1959 Vasselli was accused of shooting two of his brothers-in-law, killing one, but was acquitted of the murder.

196. THOMAS EDWARD GALLOWAY, murderer

LISTED: June 24, 1964
CAUGHT: July 17, 1964
DESCRIPTION: Galloway is a woman-beater with a high I.Q. who lives luxuriously off the earnings of prostitutes.

Advice from Tom the Pimp. Violating the Mann Act means you've transported a woman across state lines for "immoral purposes." For Tom Galloway, the transporting of women for immoral purposes meant running a prostitution ring, which he was apparently did quite successfully. However, a life of running ladies of ill repute got Galloway in trouble with a St. Louis mobster named Paul J. Martorelli, and the latter was found shot to death in his car on January 29, 1963. Eyewitnesses put Galloway with Martorelli the night before, and the pimp was pinched. On October 28 Galloway jumped bail and

was named to the Ten Most Wanted list the following June.

Not even a month later, Galloway was arrested at a golf course in Danville, Virginia, by the FBI after a local resident recognized him from a newspaper article. Apparently Galloway liked running the show wherever he went. He was living under the alias "Roger McNally," often wandering a golf course in Danville and offering putting tips to whoever would listen.

INTERESTING FUGITIVE FACT:
Galloway was married nine times.

197. ALSON THOMAS WAHRLICH, child molester

LISTED: July 9, 1964
CAUGHT: October 28, 1967
DESCRIPTION: Born February 4, 1936, in Rensselaer County, New York. Five feet two inches, 135 to 140 pounds, brown hair with blue eyes. Occupations: dishwasher, hospital orderly, ranch worker, and truck driver. Wahrlich has poor eyesight, occasionally drinks beer and is "lost" without a car. Alias: Thomas Jefferson Clark III.

The Creep. Alson Wahrlich had a host of mental problems—blackouts, violent rants, an obsession with guns . . . and last but not least, compulsions to beat and rape elementary school girls. Wahrlich had been convicted of beating and molesting a five-year-old Phoenix, Arizona, girl in 1957, but was granted parole six years later. Jail was apparently the wrong answer for Wahrlich because just one year later, on April 16, 1964, he abducted a six-year-old girl from the streets of Tucson, choked her nearly to the point of death, beat her, molested her, then threw her out of a moving vehicle. Amazingly, the little girl survived and was able to identify her brutal attacker from hundreds of mug shot photos. The one she picked was the 1957 photo of Alson Wahrlich. He was named to the Top Ten list less than three months later.

Despite his mental defects, the kiddie rapist managed to elude the FBI for over three years. He was finally arrested in October 1967 in Treasure Island, Florida, after a citizen recognized Warhlich's description in *Argosy* magazine and passed the tip along to his cop brother-in-law. Turns out Warhlich had found work driving a truck for a seafood company. After the FBI brought Warhlich in, he explained the secret of his successful run: a story that ran in *Argosy* magazine a few years before. The story title? "81 Ways to Hide."

INTERESTING FUGITIVE FACT:
This might sound like a cliché, but Wahrlich actually once worked as the driver of an ice cream vending truck.

198. KENNETH MALCOLM CHRISTIANSEN, robber

LISTED: July 27, 1963
CAUGHT: September 8, 1964
DESCRIPTION: Born in 1931.

Drop the Cod—You're Under Arrest. The *Washington Post* called the September 8, 1964, capture of Kenneth Malcolm Christiansen—achieved with the help of several employees of a fast food restaurant, two office workers, three milkmen, and a police officer—"a Keystone Kops movie chase." In fact, the cops and the robber had been playing an absurd game of hide-and-seek for almost 15 years. In 1948, after being honorably discharged from the navy, Christiansen was charged with armed robbery and assault in a series of hotel robberies. Shortly after completing his two-year sentence, Christiansen was arrested again on two more counts of first-degree robbery. The scene repeated itself two more times, ending with a five-to-life sentence. But on Christmas Eve 1963 Christiansen and a fellow inmate escaped

from the California prison. His companion made it only to Seattle, but Christiansen took off on a spree of robbing jewelry stores, taverns, and supermarkets in the area. He was named to the Top Ten list on July 27, 1963.

Christiansen resurfaced in Silver Spring, Maryland, at the door of Captain Jerry's Seafood Restaurant. With a gun to the head of Captain Jerry's wife, Tina Kalivas, Christiansen tried to raid the restaurant's safe, but the arrival of the dishwasher distracted him. Kalivas ran into the parking lot, yelling, while the chef called the cops. Two employees of a nearby office raced after Christiansen, joined by three milkmen who had been in the parking lot. Christiansen was running toward the police station. Police officer Charles E. Kriss joined the pursuit and traded gunfire with the fugitive and finally cornered Christiansen, wresting two guns from his grip as he tried to steal a car. Still, the Keystone Kops caper wasn't over. Determined not to serve the 107 years awaiting him, Christiansen, with the help of a fellow inmate, pulled a gun on the guards while being transported from a court appearance. After handcuffing the guards, he made his getaway, abducting a motorist to drive him to Baltimore before shooting him. The motorist survived, Christiansen was recaptured, and the chase was finally over.

INTERESTING FUGITIVE FACT:
Christiansen always took time with his appearance—masks, theater makeup, and fake mustaches were all part of his robbery routine.

Christiansen was arrested in Silver Spring, Maryland, by local authorities after attempting to rob a seafood restaurant.

199. WILLIAM HUTTON COBLE, bank robber, burglar

LISTED: September 11, 1964
CAUGHT: March 1, 1965
DESCRIPTION: Born May 8, 1923. Five feet 10 inches, 160 to 170 pounds, brown hair with brown eyes. Occupations: baker, loom repairer, machinist, truck driver, and waiter. Aliases: John B. Bryant, Burtis Bee Covington, James Reed, James H. Sutton.

National Security. While hiding from the FBI, William Coble thought he had the perfect cover. He told his Charlotte, North Carolina, landlady that he was FBI Special Agent Marvin Ikard on an undercover assignment. Revealing his location, Coble warned her, would be violating national security.

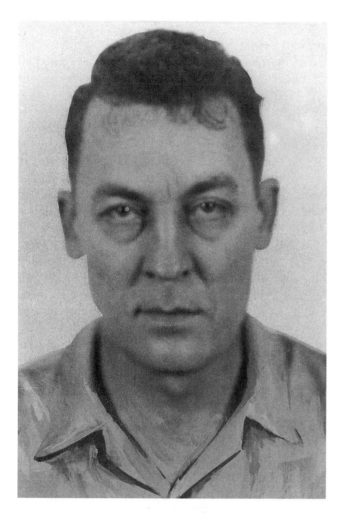

Coble was arrested in Charlotte, North Carolina, by Charlotte police after an unsuccessful attempt to rob a bank.

Truth was, Coble was a fugitive from the law following a May 15, 1964, jailbreak in Nashville, Tennessee, where he'd been serving a bank robbery hitch. His varied criminal background was enough to convince the FBI to put him on their Top Ten list on September 11, 1964, and just 19 days later, Coble hit another bank, netting $7,226. Clever as he was, Coble tripped himself up when he tried to rob a bank in Charlotte on March 1, 1965, and a cop on rounds took a peek into the windows and saw the robbery in progress. Coble bolted with $8,869, carjacked a woman and her two kids, and tried to make a high-speed getaway. That didn't work, either. Coble was quickly pinned down in an alley by pursuing cops and was talked into surrendering. Actually, the cops blasted four bullets into Coble's windshield, and that was all the convincing Coble needed.

INTERESTING FUGITIVE FACT:
Coble was only 12 when he had his first stay in reform school.

200. LLOYD DONALD GREESON JR., murderer

LISTED: September 18, 1964
CAUGHT: September 23, 1964
DESCRIPTION: Born August 30, 1924, in Baltimore, Maryland. Six feet one inch, 165 to 185 pounds, brown hair, graying, with blue eyes. Scars and marks: scars on chin, scar right shoulder, scar left elbow, scar left ankle and foot, appendectomy scar. Remarks: reportedly has crippled left leg; considers himself a ladies' man. Occupations: cab driver, carnival worker, chauffeur, chef, laborer, painter, steeple jack, and welder. Caution: Greeson may be armed. He is described as dangerous. Extreme caution should be used in approaching this individual. Aliases: Steven Anthony Coleman, Lloyd Davis Greeson Jr., Donald Francis Kelly, John M. Powell, Steven Anthony Randall, Steven Anthony Randell, Don Francis Merrow, and others.

The Ladies' Man. Was it love or money? For Lloyd Greeson perhaps it was a little of both. On the night of May 16, 1965, Greeson was seen canoodling with Lola Cotton, a 44-year-old Miami resident. On May 25 Cotton's naked body was discovered at home, traces of booze and drugs in her bloodstream. The odd thing was, Cotton was not a drug user. And one of her rings was missing. On June 13 Greeson was also spotted in the company of Margaret Ayoub, a 37-year-old Wilkes-Barre, Pennsylvania, woman. On June 16 Ayoub's body was found dead in a ditch near Bloomsburg. Greeson was on a roll. The FBI wanted desperately to put a stop to it, and named Greeson to the Ten Most Wanted list on September 18.

As it turned out, Greeson had fled clear across the country—either to scout for his next victim or elude authorities. A resident of Elsinore, California, saw Greeson's face in the local newspaper and recognized him as a guy who'd been painting houses in the area under the name "Don Francis Merrow." The local chief of police showed up and arrested Greeson without incident.

INTERESTING FUGITIVE FACT:
Greeson managed to receive dishonorable discharges from both the U.S. Army and the U.S. Marine Corps.

201. RAYMOND LAWRENCE WYNGAARD, armed robber

LISTED: October 5, 1964
CAUGHT: November 28, 1964
DESCRIPTION: Born in Wisconsin. Alias: Fred Rogers.

Mr. Rogers, Neighbor Hood. Ray Wyngaard probably thought he got away with it. After spending much of his adult life behind bars, Wyngaard was being transferred to a Detroit courtroom on July 24, 1961, when he and an accomplice escaped, embarking on a three-day crime spree. A supermarket, a gun shop, and an office building were robbed. A cop was shot. Three cars were stolen. Two Detroit citizens were abducted. When it was all over, Wyngaard was nowhere to be found. Three years later, still with no sign of the unrepentant crook, the FBI placed his name on the Most Wanted list.

As it turned out, Wyngaard had eventually returned to his home state of Wisconsin. By the time the FBI received a tip that he had settled in Madison under the alias "Fred Rogers," the fugitive was enrolled in a vocational school—apparently he had turned over a new leaf. "I've lived in Madison since August," he would later tell a reporter. "I went to the vocational school until they started broadcasting my description and put out the posters, and I sorta ducked out of sight." Wyngaard was captured thanks to a tip about a visiting girlfriend from Chicago, and a cooperative cab driver in Madison who agreed to allow FBI agents to tail his car and eventually surround it. The sting went down without a problem, and Wyngaard was returned to Detroit to face the music.

INTERESTING FUGITIVE FACT:
Later, when asked how it felt to be on the Top Ten list, Wyngaard said: "I felt sorta hemmed in."

202. NORMAN BELYEA GORHAM, bank robber

LISTED: December 10, 1964
CAUGHT: May 27, 1965
DESCRIPTION: Born February 1, 1919, in Boston, Massachusetts. Five feet 10 inches, 160 pounds, brown hair, graying and receding, with blue eyes. Scars and marks: small scar right side of face near nose, scar left cheek, scar under chin, vaccination scar left arm, scar left knee, right arm

deformed. Occupations: laborer, mechanic, and poultryman. Aliases: Norman Belyea, "Sam."

Norman Skips Out. A balding, Dumbo-eared stickup artist, Gorham was arrested in August 1964 after a $6,111 bank heist in Beverly, Massachusetts. The judge granted him $25,000 bail, which Gorham promptly posted—then promptly skipped town. When his November trial date came and went, Gorham found himself on the Ten Most Wanted list. He was arrested in Los Angeles after a local resident saw a TV program about his addition to the Top Ten.

INTERESTING FUGITIVE FACT:
Gorham once killed chickens for a living. Based on his grim, no-nonsense mug shot, some chickens may have died from fright before Gorham even laid a hand on them.

203. JOHN WILLIAM CLOUSER, robber, kidnapper

LISTED: January 7, 1965
PROCESS DISMISSED: August 1, 1972
DESCRIPTION: Born March 29, 1932, in Chicago, Illinois. Five feet nine inches, 175 to 200 pounds, blond hair (may be dyed black) with blue eyes. Scars and marks: tattoos: panther right shoulder, heart pierced by arrow left shoulder. Remarks: described as a weight lifter and has a knowledge of judo. Occupations: clerical worker and stock clerk. Aliases: Jack Clauster, John William Clauser, Jack W. Clouser, and Chuck A. Williams.

Nuts to You, Mr. Hoover. The Steven Spielberg film *Catch Me If You Can* was based on the life of con artist Frank W. Abagnale, but the same title could be applied to the movie version of Top Tenner John William Clouser's life. Clouser enjoyed one of the longest runs in Top Ten history—and by enjoyed, we mean enjoyed. Clouser loved to taunt the FBI, specifically J. Edgar Hoover, in a series of letters he sent to the Bureau. "Dear Mr. Hoover," read one. "Roses are red, violets are blue, your men aren't smart enough to catch me, so nuts to you." Another mash note read: "Boy, did I make fools of you guys in Los Angeles. You had me, man, and I got away from you. What a bunch of buffoons. What a bunch of phony bunglers."

Clouser might have been having fun, but he was also human. As he wrote years later in his memoir,

The Most Wanted Man in America, being on the Ten Most Wanted list was starting to get to him. "I wanted one peaceful night's sleep," he wrote. "I was constantly looking behind me . . . the wanted posters were the thing that bothered me most. I had to keep constantly changing my appearance, but there are basic things about the face that can't be changed." Clouser admits he felt anger, but also a weird kind of pride. He saw himself in the same league as John Dillinger and Jesse James. "In our own way, we were all romantic heroes."

Sort of, John Clouser was an allegedly crooked Florida cop who was linked to two kidnapping-for-money schemes in Orlando. That earned him a 30-year sentence at the Florida State Penitentiary, but some legal wrangling resulted in a new trial, which resulted in Clouser's skipping out of his court appearance. Two burglaries and two violent armed robberies later, Clouser was back and on trial, only this time the judge declared him legally insane, and he wound up in the state mental hospital. It was all an act on Clouser's part—he was as sane as the next guy. But it put him in a facility that had more security weaknesses than your average state pen. On April 2, 1964, Clouser and three other inmates broke out of the Florida State Hospital in Chattahoochee, using knives to overpower guards then using them as hostages to make their way out of the hospital grounds. The three other inmates were rounded up, but Clouser remained free. Ten months later, he was named to the Ten Most Wanted list.

Even though Clouser stayed free for nine years, he had a few close calls, all of them in 1965, when he was relatively new to the list. Clouser was living under the name "John Ripley" on the other side of the country, in Los Angeles, and was picked up in a city-wide dragnet of new faces. He was let go without fingerprinting or further questioning. Just days later, two FBI agents visited him at his job at a Goodyear factory, suspecting he was John Clouser. "We can settle it all very quickly with your fingerprints," said one agent. But Clouser, feeling the walls closing in, decided to fight the FBI with indignation. In short, he threw a fit. "Goddamn it! You ask me if I have any tattoos and I show you my tattoos. I could've said no, but I wanted to cooperate. I'm sick of this crap. If you have a charge, put it against me. Arrest me! Take me to jail! Take my toe prints! Look up my ass and check my piles! Do anything you want. But lemme tell you something, this is it. I've had it."

Amazingly, the FBI agents let him go. Clouser ran. (Later, the two agents received one-month suspensions without pay.)

Clouser eluded the FBI long enough to see his personal nemesis, J. Edgar Hoover, pass away on May 2, 1972. Shortly after, federal process was dismissed against him in Montgomery, Alabama. It was official. John Clouser had in fact beaten the Top Ten list with street smarts, bluster, and just a little bit of arrogance. His story would be one of the few exceptions in the history of the program.

But nobody stays free forever. Just because Clouser beat the Top Ten didn't mean the law wasn't still looking for him. Especially after one night in 1974, when a woman accused him of rape and California police picked him up. Once again, Clouser managed to split before fingerprints could be taken, but he suspected the end was near, that the FBI would be on his trail again. So working in collaboration with a crime writer named Dave Fisher—also famous for his "as-told-to" autobiographies of a Mafia killer named "Joey"—Clouser decided to turn himself in. A camera crew from NBC's *Today* show was there to record Clouser, giving himself up to the Florida police at the Tallahassee airport.

Oddly enough, Clouser looked back upon his life on the run with wistfulness. "I learned to cherish every day," he writes in his memoir. "I learned what freedom really means."

Is that a Hollywood ending, or what?

INTERESTING FUGITIVE FACT:
According to the FBI bulletin, Clouser was fond of wearing a wooden "tiki" doll on a rope around his neck. Who knows? Maybe that doll accounted for his stunning luck on the run.

204. WALTER LEE PARMAN, murderer

LISTED: January 15, 1965
CAUGHT: January 31, 1965
DESCRIPTION: Born in the Philippines.

Choke Hold. On January 9, 1965, the nude corpse of a 32-year-old woman was found in a Washington, D.C., alleyway. The suspect: Walt Parman, a married father of two who was spotted sipping cocktails with the same woman at a nightclub. Parman was quickly thrown on the Ten Most Wanted list and arrested two weeks later in Los Angeles, California, thanks to a tip from an eagle-eyed resident who'd recognized Parman from a newspaper article. Later, Parman—who had never before been convicted of a violent crime—admitted what had really gone down: The woman had rejected his crude attempts at a pass, and Parman had bitten and strangled her to death as punishment. He was sentenced to life in prison.

INTERESTING FUGITIVE FACT:
In 1972 Parman escaped from jail and reestablished himself as a manager at a San Francisco tech company. He remarried, made a comfortable $50,000 a year, and hid for 12 years before a tipster ratted him out. "These last 12 years of my life were the happiest I ever had, until this," he told a newspaper reporter. Pity Walter Parman.

205. GENE THOMAS WEBB, robber

LISTED: February 11, 1965
CAUGHT: February 12, 1965
DESCRIPTION: Born in Lemont, Illinois.

Shouldn't Have Stayed Home.   Gene Thomas Webb was a homebody. His childhood, his crime, and his capture all took place in Lemont, Illinois. On September 29, 1964, Webb and three accomplices raced into local Artel jewelry store, brandishing guns. They took more than $10,000 in cash, and when they met the cops during their getaway also took several hostages as human shields. Shots were fired, but Webb escaped unscathed. The FBI named him to the Top Ten list in February 1965 after two of Webb's three partners in crime were captured. A day after adding Webb's name to the list, the FBI was able to cross him off. FBI agents combing the city found Webb walking through Lemont.

INTERESTING FUGITIVE FACT:
The same day Webb was captured, his accomplice Frank R. Marcias—who didn't earn a spot on the Top Ten—was also arrested.

206. SAMUEL JEFFERSON VENEY, cop killer

LISTED: February 25, 1965
CAUGHT: March 11, 1965
DESCRIPTION: Born January 4, 1939. Six feet one inch, 185 pounds, black hair with brown eyes. Occupations: farm worker, laborer, and tractor driver. Scars and marks: curved scar near the center of his forehead, dark marks on the outside of both wrists, and a gold-crowned upper right tooth. Veney may be armed with a .32 caliber pistol and a sawed-off shotgun. Also known as "Sam."

207. EARL VENEY, armed robber

LISTED: March 5, 1965
CAUGHT: March 11, 1965
DESCRIPTION: Born February 14, 1933. Five feet nine inches, 165 to 170 pounds, black hair with brown eyes. Occupation: laborer. Aliases: James Brown, and "Pop."

The Flight Before Christmas.   The Baltimore liquor shop was open late on Christmas Eve 1964, mostly to accommodate customers who wanted to supply some last-minute holiday cheer at home. Sam and Earl Veney, along with two accomplices, took advantage of this fact and burst into the store, guns blazing. The clerk surrendered over two grand in cash, but also tripped a silent alarm. Within minutes a Baltimore police lieutenant was on the scene. Sam Veney saw only one way out: shoot the cop. Lieutenant Joseph Maskell was grievously injured, but not fatally, and the Veneys made their getaway. Sometime later, the Veneys encountered another cop, Sgt. Jack Cooper, who was investigating Maskell's shooting. Sam Veney again saw only one way out: shoot the cop. Cooper, however, wouldn't be so lucky as Maskell. The police sergeant's body was discovered in his squad car on Christmas morning. He had bullets in his chest and back. The caliber matched the slugs found in Maskell's body, and Sam Veney—who had a 10-year rap sheet that included convictions for assault, disorderly conduct, burglary, and escape—was identified as the triggerman.

Even though Sam looked like the shooter, his brother, Earl, was named to the Top Ten list within days of his younger brother. (Earl had to wait until a spot opened up.) The brothers pulled stickups; they decided to hide together, too. Sam and Earl found jobs under assumed names at a Garden City, New York, manufacturing plant. But just six days after Earl was named to the list, an undercover narc recognized the brothers from their Wanted posters. Conveniently, the Veney boys were arrested together, clearing two spots on the Ten Most Wanted list at once.

INTERESTING FUGITIVE FACT:
The Veneys were the first brothers to make the Top Ten list. (Ma Barker's boys probably would have made it first, had the list been around during the 1930s.)

208. DONALD STEWART HEIEN, murderer, armed robber

LISTED: March 11, 1965
CAUGHT: February 3, 1966
DESCRIPTION: Born June 23, 1937, in Minneapolis, Minnesota. Five feet seven inches, 140 to 150 pounds, with brown hair and blue eyes. Occupation: mason's helper. Scars and marks: A cross on his let forearm, a rose on the upper part of his left arm, the name "Don" on his left hand, a scroll with "Mom" on the upper part of his right arm, a pick and shovel plus "51" on the lower part of his right leg. Aliases: Donald Orville Heien, Donald Stewart, Donald Orville Stewart.

The Last Service Station. At age 18, Don Heien was hooked on heroin. On January 31, 1956, Heien reached a desperate low, and it seemed like the only way he could afford a fix was to knock over a gas station. He took a .22 caliber revolver and shot and killed the attendant at a Whittier, California, station. The attendant had a .38 caliber pistol, presumably for his personal protection, but Heien hadn't given him time to reach for it. Heien tossed his gun and took the .38, then over the next few months proceeded to rob more service stations, as well as several liquor stores. The spree came to a halt on March 12, 1956, when another gas station attendant managed to draw and fire his gun first, pumping a bullet into Heien's chest. The addict-murderer recovered, and was convicted of first-degree murder. The judge would have given him the chair, had Heien not been only 18 years old. Instead, the sentence was life in prison.

On May 4, 1964, the 27-year-old Don Heien decided he didn't like prison anymore and managed to escape from San Quentin Prison. He was named to the Top Ten list almost a year later. By this time, Heien had long kicked his heroin addiction and with a clear head decided to run as far away from Los Angeles as he possibly could. The FBI followed his trail anyway and arrested him in Newton Center, Massachusetts, thanks in part to a tip from a citizen who saw Heien's picture in the paper.

INTERESTING FUGITIVE FACT:
Heien had an I.Q. of 93, according to an FBI memorandum.

209. ARTHUR PIERCE JR., murderer

LISTED: March 24, 1965
CAUGHT: March 25, 1965
DESCRIPTION: Born in 1937.

Good-bye, Mrs. Robinson. In early 1964 Mabel Toney, 42, traded her jailbird husband for a recent parolee—Arthur Pierce, a 28-year-old burglar and car thief. She should have stuck with the first guy. On June 13, 1964, Indianapolis police found the bodies of Mabel and her 15-year-old daughter, naked and covered up to their necks with a blanket on Mabel's bed. Mabel had been strangled first, the forensics teams discovered, followed by the rape and strangulation of her daughter. It didn't take long before Pierce was identified as the killer, and he was named to the Top Ten list the following March. The very next day a citizen in Spring Valley, New York—near the Catskills—recognized Pierce in the newspaper as one of the local guys who did painting and wallpaper work. The tip was forwarded to the FBI, and within hours Pierce was in custody and sent back to Indianapolis to face murder charges.

INTERESTING FUGITIVE FACT:
While in hiding, Pierce traded in his dead 42-year-old girlfriend for a 20-year-old waitress. They married while Pierce was on the lam.

210. DONALD DEAN RAINEY, bank robber

LISTED: March 26, 1965
CAUGHT: June 20, 1965

Bank Robber and Son. In 1956 Donald Rainey robbed the Del Rey branch of the Bank of America in Fresno, California. The take: $5,147. Unfortunately for Rainey, he was captured soon after. The penalty: eight years in Leavenworth, the U.S. penitentiary that is the unofficial retirement home of America's most prolific bank robbers. Rainey, however, didn't appear to learn a thing from his roommates. In December 1964—eight months after winning parole—Rainey robbed the same Del Rey branch of the Bank of America in Fresno, California.

Due to an FBI investigation, Rainey was arrested in Nogales, Arizona.

The biggest difference this time around was that he'd brought along his 16-year-old son, who'd been only eight when dad had jacked this particular jug the first time. Dad gave the boy a sawed-off shotgun and a few rudimentary lessons in the art of bank robbery and equipped himself with a revolver. The take this time: $19,995. But the end result was much the same. Bank employees memorized the license plate on the getaway car. Apparently Dad Rainey had rented the getaway car under his Christian name. At least Dad could brag to his son three months later, when the old man made the Ten Most Wanted list. Still, even the cool job and sudden fame wasn't enough to impress the younger Rainey. When the FBI arrested him in Brownsville, Texas—curiously separated from his father—he quickly revealed his dad's whereabouts. Dad Rainey was arrested in Nogales, Arizona, with more than half of the Fresno loot in the car.

INTERESTING FUGITIVE FACT:
Both Raineys were wanted by the FBI, but only the elder Rainey was named to the Top Ten. To this date there has never been a father-son team on the Ten Most Wanted list.

211. LESLIE DOUGLAS ASHLEY, murderer

LISTED: April 6, 1965
CAUGHT: April 23, 1965
DESCRIPTION: Born in Houston, Texas.

Tears of a Clown. Carnival worker Jerry Auten noticed something strange in Bobo the Clown's trunk. There was a brunette wig and an FBI wanted poster. What the heck would Bobo be doing with something like that? The FBI was summoned, and the G-men found Bobo dozing—perhaps dreaming of cream pies or squeaky over-sized shoes. But this was no ordinary clown. Bobo was actually Leslie Ashley, a cross-dressing, blood-thirsty, Bible-quoting robber-murderer who had killed a Houston real estate broker and later feigned insanity to be placed in a Texas mental hospital. Of course it is much easier to break out of a mental hospital than a maximum security ward, and on October 6, 1964, Ashley escaped. (And presumably set off to find another wig—he made money doing female impersonations at gay clubs.) In early April he was named to the Top Ten list, and just two weeks later Bobo's sordid past was revealed. The next time somebody asks you why you hate clowns, you can tell them the story of Leslie Ashley.

INTERESTING FUGITIVE FACT:
Perhaps inspired by Leslie Ashley, *MAD* magazine once ran a spoof article titled, "The FBI's Most Wanted Renegade Clowns." The lineup included "Poppa Doppa, a.k.a. Trolla Bolla, Sam, Tim, wanted for attempting to pay debts with rubber chickens" and "Cleo the Clod, a.k.a. Carl Clod, Karl Clod, wanted for transporting plastic squirty flowers across state lines for immoral purposes."

212. CHARLES BRYAN HARRIS, gangster

LISTED: May 6, 1965
CAUGHT: June 17, 1965
DESCRIPTION: Born in 1896.

Grumpy Old Con. Charles "Black Charlie" Harris managed to survive multiple gang wars and run-ins with Prohibition squads in his 69 years, but in the end love would do him in. Black Charlie was in love with Betty Newton, a woman less than half his age. But Betty was embroiled in a passionate affair with a 27-year-old former serviceman named Jerry Merritt. On August 16, 1964, Harris discovered the two lovers inside a farmhouse a short distance from Merritt's home in Fairfield, Illinois, doing what lovers do. Harris couldn't stand it. He took a shotgun, blasted Newton and Merritt to death, then set fire to the farmhouse to cover his trail. The former gangster was named to the Ten Most Wanted list the following May. As it turned out, the FBI needn't have looked very far. Harris was holed up inside another farmhouse right outside of Fairfield. (A neighbor had tipped off the G-men.) "I'm your man," Harris said when he peacefully surrendered to a squad of heavily armed agents. Later, at his trial, the trim and dapper ex-gangster calmly told a reporter: "Well, this is just one of those things. I'm just riding out the storm." As it turned out, Harris would ride out this particular storm until his death: the 69-year-old killer was given a 60-year prison term for double murder and arson.

INTERESTING FUGITIVE FACT:
At the time, Harris was the oldest man to be named to the Ten Most Wanted list.

213. WILLIAM ALBERT AUTUR TAHL, murderer, robber

LISTED: June 10, 1965
CAUGHT: November 5, 1965
DESCRIPTION: Born July 1, 1938, Alaska. Five feet 11 inches, 170 to 175 pounds, black hair with brown eyes. Scars and marks: vaccination scar left arm, scar left index finger, scar upper right arm, scar right little finger, birthmark left side of abdomen; tattoos: "Art" left forearm, flying eyeball left chest, snake's head with wings upper right arm. Occupations: laborer, maintenance man, plumber's helper. Aliases: B.T. Conway, Bill Tahl Conway, Arthur Spencer, Art Tahl, Bill Tahl, William Albert Arthur Tahl, and others.

Invading Spaces. You didn't want to include Bill Tahl in your circle of friends. By the time he was named to the Ten Most Wanted list, Tahl had shot and robbed his own employers—the husband and wife owners of a yacht club in San Diego, California—and stripped, stabbed, and robbed a 24-year-old man he'd befriended in Dallas, Texas. After making the list, Tahl changed his identity to "J. D. Baxter" and made yet another friend, a St. Louis teacher named Marvin Thomas, who he treated to a brutal beating with a sock full of buckshot on November 5, 1965. Tahl also forced Thomas to sign over $400 in checks to "Baxter" and left the apartment. By the time he returned, perhaps to administer another beating, Tahl encountered an apartment full of St. Louis's finest. Tahl was arrested, but begged for the chance to go to the bathroom before being hauled away. The wish was granted, and it was a mistake—Tahl had a pistol hidden in the john. Instead of blasting away at the cops, Tahl pointed the weapon at his own head and confessed his Ten Most Wanted identity, as well as his many grisly accomplishments over the past year. The cops waited him out, and Tahl eventually surrendered without killing himself.

INTERESTING FUGITIVE FACT:
Reportedly, Tahl was first caught stealing at the tender age of three.

214. DUANE EARL POPE, bank robber, murderer

LISTED: June 11, 1965
CAUGHT: June 11, 1965
DESCRIPTION: A brawny campus athlete and gun enthusiast, as well as an accomplished athlete and co-captain of the football team at McPherson College.

Pope Gives Up. The Ten Most Wanted list was designed to encourage citizens to pass along tips about wanted fugitives. Sometimes the list has the odd effect of encouraging the fugitives themselves to give up. Such was the case with Duane Pope, a college football star who, oddly enough, was the gunman in one of the bloodiest bank robberies in U.S. history. On June 4, 1965, Pope walked into a bank in Big Springs, Nebraska, ostensibly to inquire about a loan. Instead, he ordered four employees—Andreas Kjeldgaard, 77; Glen Hendricks, 59; Lois Ann Hothan, 35; and a 25-year-old assistant cashier—to lie facedown on the floor. Then Pope did what very few bank robbers would ever do: He shot his hostages. All of them, with a .22 caliber automatic pistol at point-blank range. Pope took $1,598 from the teller's cages and fled. Only a week before, Pope had graduated from McPherson College.

The only survivor of the bloody heist, the 25-year-old cashier, managed to summon police. The getaway car was later linked to Pope, and just six days later the violent stickup man with the newly minted college degree found himself on the FBI's Ten Most Wanted list. Former classmates were perplexed, as was the president of McPherson College. What would possess their football star to murder three people for a lousy thousand bucks? The president, Desmond Bittinger, pleaded with Pope through the media to turn himself in. Oddly enough, Pope listened. "I heard your plea for me to give myself up, and I decided this is the thing to do." Pope dutifully called the Kansas City police, who quickly arrived to

arrest him. "I'm tired of running," Pope told them. "Come and get me."

INTERESTING FUGITIVE FACT:
Pope was originally sentenced to death, but thanks to a technicality, his punishment was changed to life in prison.

215. ALLEN WADE HAUGSTED, murderer

LISTED: June 24, 1965
CAUGHT: December 23, 1965
DESCRIPTION: Born January 13, 1931, in Minneapolis, Minnesota. Five feet 10 inches, 200 pounds, brown hair with blue eyes. Occupations: baker, cook, handyman, janitor, motion picture projectionist. Aliases: Allen Wade Haugstad, George C. Lake, and Paul Urban.

A Real Family Man. We've all wanted to throttle our mother-in-law at some point or another, but successful baker Allen Haugsted took that urge to a horrifying extreme. On February 19, 1965, Haugsted broke into his mother-in-law's house, where his ex-wife and seven-year-old daughter were staying in the wake of a messy split-up. The ex-wife was promptly shot to death. His mother-in-law was beaten and shot. Then Haugsted—clearly crazed beyond logical thought—shot his own daughter in the head. The FBI shined the hot lights on the baker-slayer on June 24, 1965, and six months later a reader of the *Houston Chronicle* recognized Haugsted as the guy who had set up shop as a baker at a local shopping mall. He was arrested without incident and sent back to Minnesota. Presumably to fry, not bake.

INTERESTING FUGITIVE FACT:
Haugsted had grown up a juvenile delinquent, but seemed to have turned over a new leaf when he found joy in his career as a baker.

Pope surrendered to local police in Kansas City, Missouri, shortly after he was added to the "Top Ten" list.

216. THEODORE MATTHEW BRECHTEL, armed robber

LISTED: June 30, 1965
CAUGHT: August 16, 1965
DESCRIPTION: Born July 2, 1938, in New Orleans. Five feet 10 1/2 inches, 145 pounds, light brown hair, may be dyed black, with blue eyes. Occupations: body and fender repairman, salesman, typist. Aliases: J. Schuler, George Strends, Fredrick Walhoim, and "Ted" Brechtel.

"I Know What You Want." Like many Ten Most Wanted fugitives before him, Ted Brechtel vowed not to be taken alive. Like many fugitives who have made that claim, Brechtel wimped out in the end. When FBI agents approached the Chicago shop where he was working as a painter under an alias, Brechtel confessed to his identity quickly. "I know what you want," he said. "I'm it." He had been responsible for a series of armed stickups and bank robberies, often in the company of his girlfriend. Brechtel made the list after he jumped out of the second-story bathroom window of the U.S. Public Health Service Hospital in New Orleans, where he had been taken to receive treatment as a federal prisoner on May 7, 1964. While on the run, Brechtel racked up as many additional robberies as he could by day, and slept with a pistol under his bed by night, swearing to kill any John Q. Laws who tried to take him in. That habit didn't do him any good on August 16, 1965, when he was taken alive, after all. Maybe he should have tried stashing the piece in a gallon of paint.

INTERESTING FUGITIVE FACT:
Brechtel was a sports nut. While incarcerated, he was active in the prison track and field events. He was—and this should come as no surprise—a swift runner.

217. ROBERT ALLEN WOODFORD, armed robber

LISTED: July 2, 1965
CAUGHT: August 5, 1965
DESCRIPTION: Born March 4, 1939, in Warrenton, Oregon. Five feet eight or nine inches tall, 140 to 150 pounds, with brown hair and hazel eyes. Occupations: factory worker, farm worker, truck driver.

They Let Him Get Away. Bob Woodford got lucky. The 25-year-old armed robber was cooling his heels in the California Medical Facility in Vacaville, serving a five-years-to-life hitch for robbing a San Jose market. (Why a medical facility? Woodford had an awfully violent temper and had received treatment at mental hospitals in the past.) Then, in August 1964, he was indicted by a federal grand jury for a small-time bank heist he'd pulled earlier in the year. It was the best thing that could have happened to Woodford. On December 14 he was brought to San Francisco, where the bank robbery charge was dismissed, since he was already serving time for the market robbery. Then, through some

weird misunderstanding, Woodford was set free. It was a classic "Get Out of Jail Free" card, all because Woodford had pulled two armed robberies instead of one. Three days later, prosecutors realized their mistake, and Woodford was charged with unlawful interstate flight to avoid confinement after conviction for robbery. But by then Woodford was long gone. And 14 days later, Woodford robbed the Market-Geary branch of the Bank of America in San Francisco, netting $2,280.

The FBI, seeking to fix the mistake, named Woodford to the Ten Most Wanted list the following July. Woodford had been hiding in Seattle, but a local resident recognized his face as matching one on a Wanted poster he'd seen. The formerly lucky robber was arrested in his Seattle hotel room and even seemed grateful to be taken in by the FBI. "You're such nice guys," he reportedly said.

INTERESTING FUGITIVE FACT:
Woodford often took manual labor jobs, but reportedly hated strenuous work and getting dirty. An FBI memorandum also adds that he "drinks beer, wine and vodka moderately, likes spaghetti and Spanish foods, dresses neatly, favoring expensive sport clothes, frequents bowling alleys, regularly exercises with weights, likes gymnastics and has a reputation of molesting young girls." He sounded like a decent guy, until that last bit.

218. WARREN CLEVELAND OSBOURNE, murderer

LISTED: August 12, 1965
KILLED: September 9, 1965
DESCRIPTION: Born September 7, 1920, in Nashville, Tennessee. Five feet 8 1/2 inches, 155 to 160 inches, brown hair with brown eyes. Scars and marks: circular scar left forearm, right arm crooked at wrist. Remarks: right arm reportedly shorter than left arm. Caution: Osbourne allegedly killed one individual and wounded another with a .38 caliber revolver. He reportedly has suicidal tendencies. Consider extremely dangerous. Occupations: barber, sheet metal worker, truck driver. Aliases: Warren Cleveland Orborne, William Cecil O'Reilley, Warner Osbourne, Imando Riley, Anthony Sherg, and "Pee Wee."

The Other Osbournes. Warren Osbourne was a jealous man. In July 1964 he followed his ex-wife into a Nashville, Tennessee, beauty parlor, intent to show her how upset he was. In his hand was a gun. The owner of the shop, Anna Corlew, tried to stop him, and she received a bullet for her trouble. As did a passing cab driver, who slowed down to see what the hell was going on. (Corlew died on the scene; the cabbie lived.) Osbourne fled the scene and found himself on the Top Ten list the following summer. Barely a month later, Osbourne was spotted driving 115 MPH by a Kentucky cop, and a chase ensued. Osbourne probably thought that the G-men were finally on to him and kept his foot firmly pressed against the accelerator. It would be a fatal mistake. His car flipped and rolled, killing the fugitive instantly. Osbourne would never know that he was being pursued only for speeding, not murder.

INTERESTING FUGITIVE FACT:
An unsolved mystery cropped up in the wake of . . . well, Osbourne's untimely death. In his car was $22,000, divided into four stacks of $100 bills. To this day nobody knows where the money came from; no one has ever reported it stolen or missing.

219. HOLICE PAUL BLACK, murderer, armed robber

LISTED: August 25, 1965
CAUGHT: December 15, 1965
DESCRIPTION: Born in Chicago, 1944.

Look After Your Brother. On August 4, 1965, Holice Black burst out of a Chicago supermarket, feeling good about himself. In his hands were $3,500 in proceeds from the robbery he'd just pulled—a damned nice haul for a market. Then he saw his brother—and robbery partner—Richard, being searched by Chicago police sergeant Charles Eichorst, who'd responded to the supermarket's silent alarm. Holice hoisted his pistol, took quick aim, then shot Eichorst through the head, killing him. Holice and Richard hopped in their car and hightailed it to Gary, Indiana. Just a few weeks later, Eichorst's execution was enough to vault small-time hood Holice Black to the Ten Most Wanted list. (Previously, Black had small-time convictions for auto theft, criminal trespass, and battery.)

The brothers soon separated, and Holice Black took off to Miami, where he grew a mustache and goatee to hide his normally clean-cut face. A tipster

directed FBI agents to the broken-down boardinghouse where Black was hiding under the alias "Fred Perkins." "He wasn't expecting it," said one arresting FBI agent. "None of them are. He was quite surprised we had found him." Surprised yes, but also grateful. "I'm quite relieved," said Black after the arrest. "I was tired of looking over my shoulder."

INTERESTING FUGITIVE FACT:
Black was known as a "ladies' man" who, according to the FBI, was "frequently romantically involved with several women at the same time."

220. EDWARD OWENS WATKINS, bank robber

LISTED: September 21, 1965
CAUGHT: December 2, 1966
DESCRIPTION: Born in Pittsburgh, 1919. Five feet 10 inches tall, 190 pounds, with black, graying hair and brown eyes. Believed heavily armed with revolvers, Watkins is probably accompanied by a 22-year-old striptease dancer and model named Kathleen Marie Rosen, also wanted for a bank robbery violation. Watkins is extremely dangerous. No private citizen should attempt to apprehend him.

Fast Eddie. Ed Watkins made just over a cool hundred grand ($103,000) robbing a series of Ohio banks in 1965. That was what helped Watkins make the Top Ten list, but it was just the tip of a deep criminal iceberg for the prolific bank robber, who would rack up more than 61 bank heists over his career. Watkin's method, which earned him the nickname "Fast Eddie," almost never changed: Show a gun or bomb, scoop the money out of the drawers, and split. By the 1960s Watkins was bringing along his young wife for robberies, à la Bonnie and Clyde. The couple lived as "Robert and Dee Johnson" in Montana and made special trips to other cities to pull their jobs. Watkins was arrested in Florence, Montana, thanks to his strange love of all things western. (Boots, hat, fringe, the whole nine.) FBI agents displayed photos of Watkins to stores selling western clothing in the Montana area, and a salesman recognized him.

INTERESTING FUGITIVE FACT:
In 1980 Watkins—by then 59 years old—broke out of an Atlanta prison and staged a comeback, knocking over seven banks and catching a bullet before he was captured and sent back to jail.

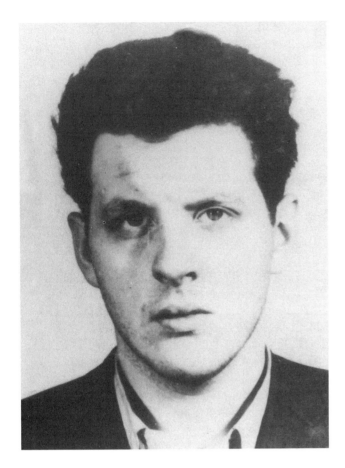

Singer was apprehended in Montreal, Quebec, by Montreal police. He had been the object of an intensive joint investigation by the FBI and Canadian authorities.

221. JOEL SINGER, burglar

LISTED: November 19, 1965
CAUGHT: December 1, 1965
DESCRIPTION: Born April 13, 1943, in Montreal, Quebec, Canada. Six feet one inch, 190 to 210 pounds, with brown hair and blue deep set eyes. Occupation: salesman. Remarks: Singer may wear glasses; reportedly speaks French fluently. Aliases: Joel Fisher, G. Harris.

The Big Gun. Joel Singer was a two-bit burglar with big plans—and even bigger firearms. Along with his uncle, Singer schemed to open a Brink's vault in Syracuse, New York, with torches, drills, nitroglycerin . . . and a 20mm Finnish antitank gun. Early on the morning of October 25, 1965, Singer and his uncle successfully used their smuggled antitank gun to blast apart the 18-inch walls

of the vault and help themselves to $423,421 inside. The burglars then drove and dumped their gun into the waters off Jones Beach, New York. (Apparently the nearly half a million was enough to hold them for a while; they wouldn't need the gun again in the near future.) But by November 1 the uncle was in custody and coughing up details of the scheme, including how he purchased the gun from a manufacturer in Virginia. FBI agents were chagrined to learn that they had actually been tracking that antitank gun up the East Coast, from Alexandria, Virginia, to Plattsburgh, New York, and finally to Montreal, thinking it was part of a terrorist plot. Singer knew the gun was being watched, so he arranged to steal it from himself as it sat in the Montreal warehouse. Once Singer's uncle fingered him, it would only be a few weeks before he was named to the Top Ten list and became the target of an international manhunt. Singer was arrested 11 days later in Montreal by a joint team of FBI agents and Royal Canadian Mounted Police. Apparently Singer was plotting another job or a grisly escape plot since authorities found a vial of nitroglycerin in his car. Only $188 of the Brink's money was recovered, making the crime one of the most unusual—and lucrative—heists of the 1960s.

INTERESTING FUGITIVE FACT:
In February 1973 Singer was found dead, apparently a suicide.

222. JAMES EDWARD KENNEDY, bank robber

LISTED: December 8, 1965
CAUGHT: December 23, 1965
DESCRIPTION: Born November 16, 1937, in Worcester, Massachusetts. Five feet seven inches tall, 160 pounds, with brown hair and eyes and a ruddy complexion. Occupations: construction worker, laborer, operating room technician, truck driver. Scars and marks: "LOVE" is tattooed on the web of his left hand; an eagle and "J.E.K." is tattooed on the upper part of his left arm.

The Bedsheet Rope. On the night of November 10, 1964, a rope made of bedsheets dropped from a window on the fourth floor of the Cuyahoga County Jail in Cleveland, Ohio. Five prisoners shimmied their way down the makeshift rope, with hacksaw blades they'd used to remove the steel bars still in their pockets. One of those prisoners was James Edward

Kennedy, a career robber with nine years of heisting experience under his belt. Since 1963 he'd been spending most of his nights at the federal lockup in Marion, Illinois, but Cleveland wanted a word with him as well, due to a bank job he'd pulled there. Kennedy took advantage of the relatively low-security facility to make his escape with four accomplices. Everyone was quickly rounded up after the escape, save Kennedy, who fled to his home state of Massachusetts. He was placed on the Top Ten list a little over a year later. One of his fellow Massachusetts residents recognized Kennedy's photo in the newspaper a short while later, and the FBI used the tip to throw up a series of stakeout points along the major roadways surrounding Kennedy's hometown of Worcester. On December 23 one of the agents recognized Kennedy and gave pursuit. The bank robber tried to outrace the G-men, but ended up crashing into a road overpass. Then he tried to shoot his way out, but received a gunshot wound in return and quickly surrendered.

INTERESTING FUGITIVE FACT:
According to an FBI memorandum, Kennedy was fond of "low-class bars and night clubs where he drinks Seagram's V.O. and 7-Up and likes drive-in restaurants where he favors hamburgers and milk shakes. He is also known as a generous tipper and avid baseball fan, particularly fond of the Boston Red Sox. He boasts of his athletic prowess, and has boxed and played football and baseball while in prison."

223. LAWRENCE JOHN HIGGINS, bank robber

LISTED: December 14, 1965
CAUGHT: January 3, 1966
DESCRIPTION: "An excellent chef who frequently carries with him a book of his favorite recipes" and an accomplished trumpet player who disguised himself with horn-rimmed glasses and a mustache.

Recipe for Trouble. If Lawrence John Higgins had stayed on the wagon, he might have stayed out of prison. The 52-year-old fugitive, a chef at a Sacramento rest home, was driving to nearby Snow Country with two friends. Along the way the trio stopped for a drink—or two, or three— then swerved back onto the road with Higgins behind the wheel. At twilight during a heavy snow fall patrolman L. J. Williams spotted the 1958

Cadillac weaving down Interstate 80 near Emigrant Gap. Williams pulled the Cadillac over and arrested Higgins and one of the passengers, Teddy Smith Matlock, for drunkenness, leaving the less intoxicated "Curly" to drive the car. The officer processed the arrests, entering the men's names and descriptions in a State Department of Motor Vehicles database in search of prior drunken driving offenses. Higgins's record was clear, except for the note that he was named on the FBI's Top Ten list.

Higgins was wanted for the armed robbery of Crocker-Citizens National Bank in Covina, California, in February 1965. The robbery had occurred just 18 days after Higgins completed a five-year stay in an Arkansas prison on burglary and grand larceny charges. That wasn't the giveaway, though. In fact, Higgins spent much of his adult life in prison for charges such as the interstate transportation of a stolen car, burglary, grand theft, and assaulting an officer. His record went back more than 30 years. Higgins was the prime suspect in the $774 Covina armed robbery because he had used a relative's car in his getaway.

INTERESTING FUGITIVE FACT:
Higgins, Matlock, and Curly were members of the same club—the Sacramento Chapter of Alcoholics Anonymous.

224. HOYT BUD COBB, murderer

LISTED: January 6, 1966
CAUGHT: June 6, 1966
DESCRIPTION: Born May 27, 1931, in Toccoa, Georgia. Five feet 10 inches, 165 to 175 pounds, with brown balding hair and blue eyes. Occupations: car salesman, construction worker, heavy equipment operator, laborer, salesman, welder. Scars and marks: mole on right cheek. Cobb is an excessive drinker of alcoholic beverages and uses narcotics. Aliases: William Cawthon, Garfield Cobb, Robert Johnson, and Joe Pless.

Unlucky Sixes. June 6, 1966, was a day feared by many superstitious people around the world. After all, the date spelled 6/6/66, and the number "666" is considered to have evil connotations. As it turned out, the only person who really should have feared sixes was Hoyt Cobb. The FBI named him to the list on January 6 and ended up nabbing him on June 6. Cobb was an escapee from a Georgia state prison who carjacked a 58-year-old makeup saleswoman named Frances Johnson and shoved her bleeding, dead body into the trunk. A gas station attendant noticed a fluid dripping from the back of the car, and it sure wasn't oil. He memorized the plates, and later the car—and Cobb's fingerprints—were found abandoned. Johnson's rotted corpse wouldn't be found for another couple of months; soon after, Cobb was named to the Top Ten list. Cobb was arrested in Hialeah, Florida, by the FBI after a citizen recognized him from a *Front Page Detective* magazine article.

INTERESTING FUGITIVE FACT:
Frances Johnson wasn't Cobb's first murder victim. The Top Tenner was also convicted of beating to death another robbery victim in the early 1960s.

225. JAMES ROBERT BISHOP, armed robber

LISTED: January 10, 1966
CAUGHT: January 21, 1966
DESCRIPTION: Born February 21, 1918, in Greenville, South Carolina. Five feet 11 1/2 inches tall, 150 to 160 pounds, with brown hair and hazel eyes. Occupations: laborer, machinist, miner, painter, rigger, steeplejack.

Bagging Bishop. Jim Bishop had an unusual—albeit low-rent—stickup method. He'd stick one paw in a brown bag, then hold a brown bag in the other. Then he'd walk into his target store and tell the clerk that he had a gun in one bag, and that if he knew what was good for him, he'd fill the other one with money. Now if you were to sidle up next to Bishop in a bar and ask him about his criminal history, he'd brag about passing phony checks worth thousands of dollars all across the United States. But it was his two-bag stickup of a Phoenix Safeway market on September 28, 1963, that eventually led to Bishop's promotion to the Ten Most Wanted list two and a half years later. Right after Bishop discovered he made the list, he packed his bags—literally—and fled to Aspen, Colorado, where he tried to fade into the background as a kitchen helper. But fellow employees recognized his picture from the newspapers, and the FBI was summoned. Bishop threw in the bag without resistance.

INTERESTING FUGITIVE FACT:
Bishop is the only former steeplejack to make the Ten Most Wanted list.

226. ROBERT VAN LEWING, bank robber

LISTED: January 12, 1966
CAUGHT: February 6, 1967
DESCRIPTION: Born March 27, 1921. Six feet tall, 140 to 145 pounds, with blond graying hair and blue eyes. Occupations: chauffeur, cook, painter, seaman, welder. Van Lewing is believed armed with a .22 caliber automatic and a .22 caliber revolver and has reportedly vowed not to be taken alive.

The Left Arm of Crime. On October 28, 1965, Robert Van Lewing and an accomplice knocked over the Northeast National Bank in Houston, Texas, stuffing $31,493 into a bag and warning the bank employees not to sound any alarms. It was just the latest heist in Van Lewing's 25-year criminal career. He'd been convicted of robbery, robbery by assault, embezzlement, and violation of the White Slave Traffic Act. (In other words, Van Lewing had spent some time pimping.) After abandoning their stolen getaway car, Van Lewing and his partner disappeared. Authorities believed that Van Lewing had made his way to Los Angeles with an 18-year-old Texas girlfriend, but that's where the trail went cold. He was named to the Top Ten list on January 12, 1966.

Van Lewing wouldn't seem hard to spot, since his left hand and arm were partially deformed, and he was missing the tip of his middle left finger. Perhaps because of this, he tried to beautify his right arm with the tattoo of a woman's head and flowers on the inside of his forearm. According to the FBI, their fugitive "lives quietly and modestly, drinks beer moderately, usually dresses in work or sport clothes and keeps company with younger women." Still, he remained at large for over a year and robbed another bank in St. Louis before a tipster saw Van Lewing's face in a feature story in *This Week* magazine. This led the FBI to his hideout in Kansas City, Missouri, where he surrendered without a fight.

INTERESTING FUGITIVE FACT:
Van Lewing was a member of the Brotherhood of Painters, Decorators and Paper Hangers of America.

227. EARL ELLERY WRIGHT, bank robber

LISTED: January 14, 1966
CAUGHT: June 20, 1966

DESCRIPTION: Born July 16, 1929, in Kentucky. Five feet nine or 10 inches tall, 160 to 180 pounds, with light brown hair and blue eyes. Occupations: construction worker, farmer, office clerk, truck driver. Aliases: Don A. Angel, Bill C. Bullock, Frank F. Kinders, Lenny C. Price, Carl L. Prichard.

The Finer Things. Earl Wright was particular about his things. He only stayed at Holiday Inns, preferred Oldsmobiles to other models of cars, only smoked King Edward filter tip cigars, and thought the best form of evening entertainment was a go-go bar. Wright liked hobnobbing with the upper crust, but also preferred to pick up women in Greyhound bus stations. And he preferred stealing things to earning them. Wright pulled his first crime—bike theft—at age 14, and followed it up years later with a series of bank robberies. The two that earned the attention of the FBI came in 1965. On June 21 Wright hit the Coral Hills, Maryland, office of the Suburban Trust Company for $61,203, and five months later knocked over the Ashville Bank in Ashville, Ohio, for $49,289. Both times he threatened to wipe the employees off the face of the Earth if they gave him any trouble. He made the Top Ten list the following January. Even though the FBI believed that Wright had an I.Q. of 128, he wasn't terribly hard to trace. Eventually, he was arrested in Cleveland, Ohio, without a fight, and sentenced to 35 years in prison. No Holiday Inns, no King Edward filter tips, no go-go bars.

INTERESTING FUGITIVE FACT:
Wright was paroled in 1978 and apparently missed the finer things so much he starting robbing banks again before being recaptured in 1980 and given another prison sentence—this time 50 years.

228. JESSIE JAMES ROBERTS, bank robber

LISTED: February 3, 1966
CAUGHT: February 8, 1966
DESCRIPTION: Born November 13, 1920, in Sylvester, Georgia. Six feet three or four inches tall, 240 to 265 pounds, with graying dark brown hair and blue eyes. Occupations: auto body worker, car salesman, carpenter, truck driver. Aliases: Chester Robert Carter Jr., Charles C. Collins, Robert E. Griffin, Charles Boyd Powell, James J. Roberts.

Another Jesse. On September 7, 1876, the Jesse James gang tried to pull off the holy grail of bank heists: two robberies in the same day. They failed.

On January 10, 1966, namesake Jessie James Roberts tried to pull the same thing. First he hit the Bank of Lenox in Lenox, Georgia, for $38,322. Then he hopped in his getaway car, drove 20 miles, and tried to do the same thing at the Bank of Alapaha in Alapaha, Georgia. But Roberts failed, too, when a bank employee grabbed at the bandit's gun, forcing him to flee early without any cash. The bank vice president was obviously upset and fired shots at Roberts's speeding getaway car. This, in turn, upset Roberts, who returned fire, slightly wounding the banker. The double heist had turned ugly, just as it had for the James Gang 90 years before.

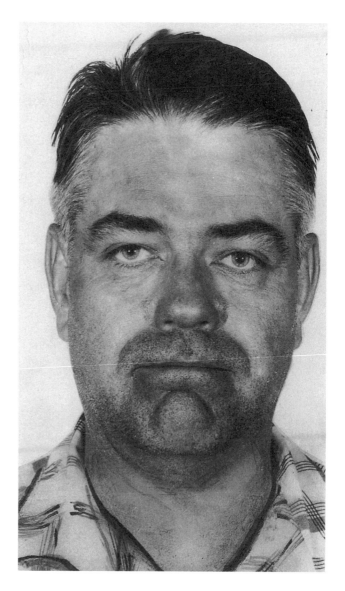

Jessie James Roberts, the second "Jesse James" to make the list.

139

But these robberies, along with another bank heist in Quapaw, Oklahoma, and two post office burglaries, helped lend Roberts a bit of the James Gang infamy. In early February 1966 Roberts was named to the Ten Most Wanted list, a dishonor roll that Jesse and Frank James certainly would have made had it been around back in the 1870s. The FBI memorandum on Roberts reported that although the fugitive was a high school honor student, he also had spent most of his adult life in lockup. "He may employ disguises, dresses neatly and conservatively, has a congenial personality, speaks Spanish, flies an airplane, gambles extensively, sometimes frequents nightclubs but does not drink, although [he is] very experienced in making illegal moonshine liquor," read a mini bio of Roberts.

The infamous Jesse James would enjoy a long heisting career before being shot in the back by a traitor; Jessie James Roberts lasted only five days at the top of the criminal charts. Thanks to a speedy FBI investigation, Roberts was arrested in Laredo, Texas, without incident.

INTERESTING FUGITIVE FACT:
Roberts was the second "Jesse James" to grace the Top Ten list in two years. See also JESSE JAMES GILBERT (#184).

229. CHARLES LORIN GOVE, bank robber

LISTED: February 16, 1966
CAUGHT: February 16, 1966

230. RALPH DWAYNE OWEN, bank robber

LISTED: February 16, 1966
CAUGHT: March 11, 1966
DESCRIPTION: An avid hot-rod racer, with long hair. Often used the alias Tommy Harthun.

This Side of Peculiar. The honeymoon didn't last very long for Mrs. Tommy Harthun. On March 11, 1966, one week after the wedding, federal agents invaded the Harthuns' Kansas City duplex to arrest "Tommy," a serial bank robber and prison escapee better known as Ralph Dwayne Owen. Owen had been on the lam since Halloween 1965, when he and sometime-accomplice Charles Lorin Gove escaped from a California medical prison by prying open a

steel-framed window, cutting through three chain link fences, and disarming two deputies. He had been serving five years to life for a Sacramento robbery. For months Owen and Gove were hiding in plain view, wreaking havoc on a cross-country trip—robbing a Napa County ranch while holding the residents at gun point on November 5; the Bank of Alexandria at Cold Springs-Highland Heights, Kentucky, on November 25 and the same bank three weeks later on December 13. The pair then parted ways. Gove went to New Orleans, where he robbed the Whitney National Bank on February 10, and Owen went to Missouri, where he knocked over the Cass County Bank in Peculiar on January 3. On February 16 both fugitives were added to the Top Ten list. Gove fell first, arrested on February 16 on Bourbon Street during Mardi Gras. He took Owen down, telling FBI agents where to find his partner in crime.

INTERESTING FUGITIVE FACT:
Owen often wore women's clothes as a disguise during his heists. But the dresses didn't stop the Case County Bank president from picking him out of a lineup.

231. JIMMY LEWIS PARKER, murderer

LISTED: February 25, 1966
CAUGHT: March 4, 1966
DESCRIPTION: Born April 24, 1935, in Iredell County, North Carolina. Five feet 11 inches tall, 148 pounds, with blue eyes and brown hair, which may be dyed blond or red. Tattoos: dice on his left arm, as well as "June"; "Jim" on his right arm. He reportedly keeps constant company with women, drinks large amounts of milk for stomach ulcers, smokes cigars and cigarettes, drinks beer and whiskey, likes television, and is skilled at pencil sketching.

The Outlaw and the In-Laws. Jimmy Parker wasn't fond of his estranged wife . . . but he clearly had a bone to pick with her parents. He shot them to death in April 1961, was sentenced to life in prison, and received an additional 20 to 25 years on top of that for kidnapping a family of four to make his getaway. The state wanted Jimmy Parker behind bars for the remainder of his life. Parker didn't see it that way. In December 1964, while being transferred to another prison, the murderer sawed through bars on the bus and ran away from his captors. He stayed free for more than a year before the FBI decided to place him on the Ten Most Wanted list. Very quickly a tip came in that Parker was living in Detroit as "Joe Lee Young" and reupholstering furniture. A squad of G-men burst in on March 4, 1966, and Parker was returned to finish his sentence.

INTERESTING FUGITIVE FACT:
According to the FBI release, Parker played the guitar . . . "poorly."

232. JACK DANIEL SAYADOFF, bank robber, kidnapper

LISTED: March 17, 1966
CAUGHT: March 24, 1966
DESCRIPTION: Sayadoff has a tattoo on his right forearm that reads: "Born to Love."

Two Kinds of Custody. It was an unusual deal. Jack Sayadoff, a lone-wolf bandit, thought he needed a bank-robbing partner to steal the big money. Patsy Janakos had lost a custody battle and badly needed

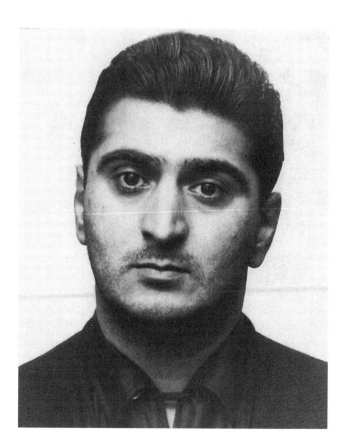

Jack Daniel Sayadoff, a bank robber and kidnapper

her three-year-old daughter back. So Patsy agreed to help Jack if Jack could get Patsy's daughter back. A deal was struck. In late 1965 the pair burst into a Newark, California, home, bound and gagged an elderly babysitter, and took back Patsy's daughter. Now it was Patsy's turn to help. From December 8, 1965, to March 14, 1966, the duo robbed three banks: a San Francisco bank ($3,131), a Lakewood savings and loan ($2,186), and a bank way out in Hampton Township, Pennsylvania, ($11,113). By that time Jack and Patsy had been living together as "Mr. and Mrs. Jack F. Delano" in Indianapolis, and the FBI had placed Jack on the Top Ten list. Within days, a tip came in that pinpointed the happy couple's new location. Jack was nabbed at the mall; Patsy at home. And Patsy's young daughter received the worst deal of all— she was immediately placed in a children's shelter.

INTERESTING FUGITIVE FACT:
Sayadoff had robbed banks in California and Georgia before hooking up with Patsy Janakos.

233. ROBERT CLAYTON BUICK, bank robber

LISTED: March 24, 1966
CAUGHT: March 29, 1966
DESCRIPTION: Born in Pennsylvania.

As Seen on TV. Bob Buick once watched a TV special on the FBI's Ten Most Wanted list and thought it was pretty awful, all that attention from every part of the country. Not long after Buick, a prolific California-based bank robber—he hit 18 banks in all, some of them more than once—found himself at the center of all that unwanted attention. Seemingly every personal detail was publicized, including such details as Buick "drinks expensive wines and liquors, frequents good restaurants, nightclubs and beach resorts . . . likes swimming, boating, dancing, television and jazz music . . . is said to dress neatly and conservatively, to travel by air and private automobile, usually exceeding the speed limit, and to wear a diamond ring, a gold identification wrist bracelet and a gold religious neck medal . . . reportedly smokes cigarettes, is especially fond of Italian and Mexican food and is fairly fluent in the Spanish language." The only thing the FBI left out of the description was Buick's underwear size. Buick lasted only five days on the run before he was arrested in Pecos, Texas, by a police officer who recognized him from a Wanted poster.

INTERESTING FUGITIVE FACT:
Buick was a part-time bullfighter.

234. JAMES VERNON TAYLOR, alleged murderer

LISTED: April 4, 1966
FOUND DEAD: April 4, 1966
DESCRIPTION: Born November 10, 1922, in Baltimore, Maryland. Five feet nine or 10 inches tall, 160 to 165 pounds, with black hair and brown eyes. Occupations: baker's helper, bellhop, bus boy, dishwasher, doorman, gardener, hospital orderly, laborer, truck loader. Scars and marks: Scar on left elbow, appendectomy scar, scar on left knee, scars on both legs. Tattoos of heart, ribbon, arrow, and "Clarice" on left upper arm, heart, ribbon, and "True Love" and "Teensy" on right forearm. Aliases: James Vernon Taylor-El, "Stoney Brook," "Stony."

Dead in the Water. On April 4, 1966, two separate law enforcement teams were working on the same case, although they didn't know it at the time. While the FBI's Fugitive Task Force was announcing new Top Tenner James Vernon Taylor, who was wanted for the vicious stabbing and throat-slicing murder of his own wife and three children (aged five, three, and 18 months) on January 22, 1966, forensics specialists with the Baltimore police department were trying to ID a John Doe found floating in the harbor. A few hours later, that John Doe turned out to be "Stony" Taylor.

INTERESTING FUGITIVE FACT:
Taylor was a former mental patient.

235. LYNWOOD IRWIN MEARS, burglar

LISTED: April 11, 1966
CAUGHT: May 2, 1967
DESCRIPTION: Born June 8, 1913. Six feet two inches tall, 190 to 200 pounds, with brown hair and blue eyes. Occupations: elevator construction worker, laborer, grocery store manager, salesman. Aliases: Irwin Linwood Mears, Linwood Irvin Mears, Lynn Mears, "Moose."

Moosehead. Lynwood Mears preferred the nickname "The Old Master," but most of his buddies called him "Moose," a creature that he resembled, if you squinted just right. Mears thought he deserved the more distinctive moniker because of his storied career as a B&E artist, safecracker, and larcenist.

However, the Old Master got pinched in 1952 and spent the next 11 years in stir, serving the various prison sentences that accompanied his great accomplishments. In January 1963, just a year before Mears was up for parole, he escaped from a North Carolina prison. Time passed, and no sign of the Old Master. He was named to the Ten Most Wanted list in April 1966, an accomplishment that was surely noted with a great swell of pride in Mears's diary and scrapbook. The publicity, however, did him in. Mears was arrested in Winston Salem, North Carolina, by the FBI after a neighbor recognized him from an article in the *Twin City Sentinel* newspaper.

INTERESTING FUGITIVE FACT:
Mears—or, "Howard Jackson," as he'd been known—had been so well liked in his community of Walburg, North Carolina, that his neighbors petitioned to have him released early. And he was, serving only 178 days before returning to the life he lived while on the lam.

236. JAMES ROBERT RINGROSE, robber

LISTED: April 15, 1966
CAUGHT: March 29, 1967
DESCRIPTION: Born April 19, 1942. Six feet one inch, 140 to 160 pounds, with brown hair and blue eyes. Occupations: auto mechanic, service station attendant. Aliases: Robert Anderson, John David Baldwin, John J. Baxter, John J. Lewis, Philip George Riley.

What a Card. Writing bad checks was Jim Ringrose's racket, and he and his gang were responsible for the passage of a stack of bad checks across the United States. They used the classic bank con artist's technique of opening phony bank accounts, then using those accounts to write bad checks to open even more phony accounts—scammers call this technique "the float," referring to the waiting period between the time a check is presented and when it is cashed. Ringrose also forged cashier's checks, which he traded in for traveler's checks.

Traveler's checks would come in handy for Ringrose. After he was named to the Top Ten list, the fraudster hightailed clear around the world and settled in Osaka, Japan. But the prolific check writer couldn't help himself, and he was nabbed by Japanese police almost a year later trying to pass more rubber checks. The Japanese cops asked Ringrose why he pursued this line of work, and the fugitive answered with self-justification: "Banks are insured and insurance companies are making huge profits. So who's getting hurt? I am helping retails by spending the money." He was arrested in Hawaii after his extradition to the United States from Japan. There he smirked and told the FBI agents he had been saving an item for several years and now he needed it. He then presented them with the Monopoly game card, "Get out of jail free."

INTERESTING FUGITIVE FACT:
According to an FBI bulletin, Ringrose favored "Ivy League" garments and huge cigars.

237. WALTER LEONARD LESCZYNSKI, armed robber

LISTED: June 16, 1966
CAUGHT: September 9, 1966
DESCRIPTION: Born May 12, 1930, in Chicago, Illinois. Five feet 11 inches, 175 to 185 pounds, with dark brown hair, receding, and hazel eyes. Occupations: machine operator, machinist.

The Mighty Lesczynski. This Chicago-born Polish bandit might have looked like an accountant, but he boasted convictions for bank robbery, armed robbery, and petty larceny. On August 20, 1965, Lesczynski perpetrated his most heinous crime yet: the $20,000 robbery of a kid's amusement park in his hometown. Cops arrived just in time though and pumped the bandit with nine bullets before he finally surrendered. Ordinarily, this would have been the end of the story, and Lesczynski wouldn't have lived long enough to make the Ten Most Wanted list. However, the robber survived his wounds and surprised his captors by escaping from Cook County Hospital four months later, using only his wits and a ballpoint pen, which he used to pick his handcuffs and leg irons. When Lesczynski was named to the Top Ten list, the FBI took great care to detail the astounding number of gunshot wounds on the fugitive's body. Just a few months later, the FBI traced Lesczynski all the way to . . . well, Chicago, Illinois, where he was arrested without incident or gunplay.

INTERESTING FUGITIVE FACT:
After the failed amusement park heist, Lesczynski refused to name his accomplice, who escaped.

238. DONALD ROGERS SMELLEY, armed robber

LISTED: June 30, 1966
CAUGHT: November 8, 1966
DESCRIPTION: Born September 29, 1930, in Oklahoma City. Six feet two or three inches tall, 200 to 210 pounds, with brown hair, receding, and blue eyes. Occupations: baker's helper, bartender, cook, laborer, laundryman, plasterer. Scars and marks: a tattooed heart with "Don" and "Billie" on his right forearm, a hypodermic syringe on his left forearm, twin pigs on his lower left leg, a paratrooper insignia on his right arm, a nude woman on his lower right leg, and needle marks on his left arm. Aliases: John Dennis Fuchs, Bill Mason, Roger Miller, Will Westfall, John White.

Picking Up the Scent. Maybe pug-faced Don Smelley really liked that particular market in Albuquerque. He must have, to have robbed it two months in a row—February and March 1964. The second time, Smelley punctuated the holdup by taking a shot at a store employee before fleeing the scene. Thankfully, he missed. He was later pinched for both robberies, but failed to show up at court in March 1965 to face trial. That, plus an armed robbery and burglary rap sheet that dated all the way back to 1945, eased Smelley's nomination process to the Ten Most Wanted list. Once on the list it wasn't hard to pick up the fugitive's scent. Smelley was arrested in a restaurant in Hollywood, California. "I'm glad it's over," he told the arresting G-men with a gap-toothed smile. "You guys are too hot for me."

INTERESTING FUGITIVE FACT:
According to the FBI memorandum, Smelley was "a sexual pervert who associates with both female prostitutes and male homosexuals. He dresses neatly, drinks heavily, frequents bars and is known as a boisterous 'loud mouth.'"

239. GEORGE BEN EDMONSON, armed robber

LISTED: September 21, 1966
CAUGHT: June 28, 1967
DESCRIPTION: Edmonson is said to have a high IQ and is a skilled computer operator, thanks to prison data-processing courses.

Exposure. Sometimes it takes being on the Ten Most Wanted list to teach a fugitive a valuable life lesson. George Edmonson had knocked over a bank in 1955 and a department store in 1961, broke out of a Missouri state prison, and then years later found himself on the FBI's hot list. Edmonson hightailed it to Quebec and apparently decided to make a run at the straight life. He married a schoolteacher, had a baby, hung out a shingle as an engineer, then landed a plum gig designing a pavilion for Germany in the 1967 World Expo, which happened to be located in Quebec that year. But living in Canada as "Alex Peter Bormann" turned out to be a mistake. Edmonson was arrested in Campbells Bay, Quebec, Canada, by the Mounties after a Canadian citizen recognized "Bormann" in an American magazine roundup of FBI fugitives. He was arrested without incident.

INTERESTING FUGITIVE FACT:
Edmonson robbed that bank (for just over $4,000) when he was only 17 and a new navy recruit.

240. EVERETT LEROY BIGGS, bank robber

LISTED: November 21, 1966
CAUGHT: December 1, 1966
DESCRIPTION: Born March 8, 1936, in Peoria, Illinois. Five feet 11 inches tall, 200 to 210 pounds, with brown hair and blue eyes. Occupations: bartender, truck driver. Scars and marks: scar over left eye, appendectomy scar. Biggs may be in possession of a snub-nosed revolver and reportedly has stated that he will resist arrest. Consider very dangerous. Alias: Everett Leroy Biggs Jr.

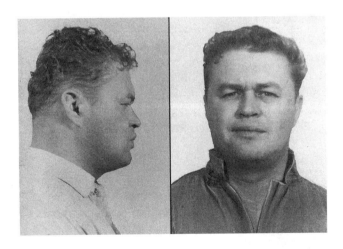

Bank robber Everett Biggs was arrested in Broomfield, Colorado.

Playing in Peoria. A series of Montana and Illinois bank heists—one of them which almost devolved into a Three Stooges comedy when Everett Biggs accidentally discharged his gun—earned this thick-faced bandit a spot on the Top Ten list in November 1966. (Reportedly, Biggs was all apologies to the bank staff about the stray bullet.) Witnesses easily identified Biggs's face from mug shots. With a tuft of hair like steel wool, squinty dark eyes, a flattened nose, a square jaw that could take a punch, and a neck thick enough to withstand the first axe blow, the bank robber was hard to miss. The FBI traced Biggs first through one of his accomplices, John Larson, who was hiding with guns and money in a rented Denver, Colorado, house. Biggs wasn't too far away in another rented hideout, and he had even more guns and money socked away. Both were arrested on December 1, 1966.

INTERESTING FUGITIVE FACT:
The Big Guy had a soft spot for his parents: "Mom & Dad" were tattooed on his right forearm.

241. GENE ROBERT JENNINGS, armed robber, kidnapper

LISTED: December 15, 1966
CAUGHT: February 14, 1967
DESCRIPTION: Born 1927 in Penns Grove, New Jersey. Alias: Joseph Cook.

Fix It with Duct Tape. Gene Jennings had a knack for prison escape and a knack for taking car-driving hostages at gun or knifepoint while doing so. During his fourth breakout from a Kentucky lockup on September 4, 1966, Jennings commandeered a car with one adult driver and five kids. He ditched the passengers—maybe they were singing too many road songs for his liking—but not before stealing the driver's shirt and wallet. Two months after Jennings was named to the Ten Most Wanted list, he was arrested in Atlantic City, New Jersey, by the FBI after a gambler recognized him from an article in *This Week* magazine. Jennings had tried to wear extra socks to seem taller and wrapped one of his tattoos with tape to hide it, but neither trick worked.

INTERESTING FUGITIVE FACT:
Penns Grove is also the birthplace of Bruce Willis, and in some ways Jennings's face resembled Willis's.

242. CLARENCE WILBERT MCFARLAND, armed robber

LISTED: December 22, 1966
CAUGHT: April 4, 1967
DESCRIPTION: Born in Washington, D.C.

Bad Money. Type "unrepentant criminal" in an Internet search engine, and Clarence McFarland's mug shot might pop up. On March 13, 1966, McFarland and an accomplice hit a Washington, D.C., bank and stole $5,900 in old cash that was destined for the incinerator. The getaway was a fumbling, bullet-punctuated affair that ended one crashed car and one home invasion later. While free on bail, McFarland was caught (and shot) during an attempted burglary. When he was finally convicted of the bank heist—but still free on bail until his sentence was handed down—McFarland was caught buying a gun. After he was finally placed behind bars in Rockville, Maryland, McFarland sawed off one of his cell bars, used it to pry open a wire mesh window, then scaled a 12-foot wall. He was placed on the Ten Most Wanted list shortly after. How was McFarland apprehended? Three guesses. That's right—McFarland was caught by Baltimore police, trying to pull yet another burglary. Fingerprints revealed his "Most Wanted" status, and he was returned to prison.

INTERESTING FUGITIVE FACT:
McFarland considered pleading insanity on the bank robbery charges, but later changed his mind.

243. MONROE HICKSON, murderer

LISTED: February 17, 1967
FOUND DEAD: January 30, 1968
DESCRIPTION: Born July 8, 1908, in Aiken County, South Carolina. Five feet 10 inches tall, 162 pounds, with black hair and brown eyes. Occupations: construction worker, farmer, laborer. Scars and marks: operation scar on right side of stomach. Remarks: Hickson may wear small mustache; usually wears silver-rimmed glasses; reportedly has three upper gold teeth and one tooth with gold rim. Aliases: "Blue" and "Bluecorns."

Run Down. Hickson was another Top Tenner who was nabbed by the Grim Reaper before J. Edgar Hoover could get his hands on him. The FBI threw him on the Most Wanted list in February 1967 after he escaped a life sentence for a series of grisly robbery-murders in 1946. (One murder involved an axe, another a club, and two more a pistol. He also assaulted two women shopkeepers with a brick. At least Hickson varied his technique.) Nearly a year later, in Chapel Hill, North Carolina, a couple recognized Hickson's photograph in a Top Ten display and identified him as a migrant worker who had died of natural causes. Positive identification was made by fingerprints.

INTERESTING FUGITIVE FACT:
The FBI memo called Hickson a "mean, ruthless, intelligent and cunning" fugitive.

244. CLYDE LAWS, armed robber

LISTED: February 28, 1967
CAUGHT: May 18, 1967
DESCRIPTION: Born in Crocker, Missouri, in 1927.

Laws Breaker. The rap sheet was impressive. Theft in Nebraska at age 18, forgery beefs in Missouri and Kansas, and parole violation. But the crime that vaulted Clyde Edward Laws and his accomplice, THOMAS FRANKLIN DORMAN (#247) was a simple $1,500 supermarket stickup in Wheaton, Maryland, that devolved into a messy shoot-out with police on February 8, 1967. A cop was left fighting for his life with a bullet in his gut, while Laws and Dorman carjacked a passing motorist to make their getaway. Twenty days later, Laws was placed on the Ten Most Wanted list. (Dorman would have to wait nearly two months for a spot to open up for him.) Laws had returned to his home state to hide out, but a relative snitched on him, telling the FBI about his hideout in Raytown. When confronted on May 18, Laws yet again engaged in a shoot-out with law enforcement, but the result was much different this time. A bullet grazed Laws's skin, and he was forced to submit to arrest.

INTERESTING FUGITIVE FACT:
Laws had his prosecution for his first theft deferred by joining the U.S. Army for a hitch.

245. CHARLES EDWARD ERVIN, robber

LISTED: April 13, 1967
CAUGHT: July 25, 1967
DESCRIPTION: Scars indicative of plastic surgery.

246. GORDON DALE ERVIN, robber

LISTED: April 13, 1967
CAUGHT: June 7, 1969
DESCRIPTION: "Bespectacled and clean-cut," according to a landlady; "withdrawn, almost shy," according to a neighbor. Alias: David Anderson.

The Ervin Boys. The criminal records of twins Charles Edward Ervin and Gordon Dale Ervin weren't identical; Gordon got a head start, with four convictions for larceny and breaking and entering starting in 1949. By 1954 Charles was imitating his brother. The Ervin twins held up a Michigan supermarket together were arrested together, and were convicted together. They also tried to escape from the courthouse together; they failed together, with Gordon wounded in the shoulder by a police officer and Charles injured in a 40-foot fall. The next day they were convicted together, to 50 to 60 years in the state pen. In jail the twins were the model citizens they had never been on the outside. Their good behavior earned them a host of privileges, including the right to work outside prison walls. On October 8, 1965, the twins disappeared together and headed for Canada. But then the two split up. Again, Charles's criminal talents lagged behind his brother's. Charles was captured on July 25, 1967, by the Royal Canadian Mounted Police in Hawkesbury, Ontario. He was returned to Michigan. Gordon evaded the Mounties for almost two more years. Eventually though, the authorities discovered him in a rooming house in Winnipeg, Manitoba. His landlady called him "an honest man" who always paid his rent on time, but the Mounties called him a dangerous criminal. Entering the rooming house while Gordon was sleeping, the Mounties arrested the fugitive without struggle. "He'll never see the outside again," a Michigan prison official promised.

INTERESTING FUGITIVE FACT:
The Michigan cops had learned their lesson with the Ervin twins. When the escaped convicts were returned to the state pen, they were separated, Charles in Jackson, Michigan, and Gordon in Marquette, Michigan.

247. THOMAS FRANKLIN DORMAN, armed robber

LISTED: April 20, 1967
CAUGHT: May 20, 1967
DESCRIPTION: Born in Indiana in 1931.

Partner in Laws. Dorman was along for that $1,500 supermarket stickup in Wheaton, Maryland, with CLYDE LAWS (see #244), but had to wait for his own Top Ten spot to open up on April 20. Just a few days after Laws went down in Raytown, Missouri, Dorman's gig was up, too. He was arrested without incident in Grantsburg, Indiana, by the FBI, which was given a helping hand by local and state police.

INTERESTING FUGITIVE FACT:
Dorman had a tattoo on his left arm that was eerily prophetic. It read: "Born to lose."

248. JERRY LYNN YOUNG, bank robber

LISTED: May 12, 1967
CAUGHT: June 15, 1967
DESCRIPTION: Born in Russellville, Alabama, in October 1942.

Young Talk. "I'll never be taken alive," Jerry Lynn Young would boast to bank-robbing buddies like William J. Webb, but Young was all talk. When the cops came for him in an Akron, Ohio, hotel, Young reached for his pistol—after all he'd had no problem using a gun in his recent holdups—but never fired a shot. The FBI was after Young for three bank robberies. Young had served time for the 1961 Richlands, North Carolina, heist, which netted $4,359, but violated his August 1963 parole the day after his release when he entered an Asheville, North Carolina, bank, with a shotgun and left with $13,671, stealing a car and firing at a bank employee in pursuit. On April 14, 1967, Young tried the same trick in Olive Branch, Mississippi, walking away with $14,919 and a spot on the Top Ten list. He held that honor for a month before a tip led the Feds to Young's door.

INTERESTING FUGITIVE FACT:
Young's bank-robbing hobby got in the way of his day job as a U.S. Marine. His first bank job also scored him a dishonorable discharge from the corps.

249. JOSEPH LEROY NEWMAN, robber

LISTED: June 2, 1967
CAUGHT: June 29, 1967
DESCRIPTION: "A Negro of medium complexion, about 5 feet 6 and 135 pounds with curly, 'processed' hair and two scars on his face." Alias: James Fields.

which included unlawful flight to avoid confinement and violations of the Dyer Act. Newman was added to the Most Wanted list on June 2, 1967. Within a month the FBI found Newman window-shopping in Journal Square, Jersey City, New Jersey. He was arrested without incident, and obligingly confessed to numerous unsolved robberies in the D.C. area.

INTERESTING FUGITIVE FACT:
The method of Newman's escape from Lorton baffled prison officials who had not allowed an escape in almost a decade. All six fugitives were assigned to different prison detachments, and there were no footprints in the snow leading from the cells.

250. CARMEN RAYMOND GAGLIARDI, murderer

LISTED: June 9, 1967
CAUGHT: December 23, 1968
DESCRIPTION: Considered "dangerous" and "troublesome." Disguised himself by gaining 40 pounds, growing a beard, and wearing sunglasses.

Big Carmen. Carmen Raymond Gagliardi ran a red light. That's why the cops pursued his rented car through the streets of Boston just before 4 A.M. on the morning of April 18, 1967. Propped up in the front seat of the car was the body of Joseph F. Lanzi, a North End bartender and gangster groupie. He had been shot four times, three times in the chest and once in the back of the head. Gagliardi and two others ran from the car into the night, leaving behind the body, a baseball bat, a .38 revolver, and a double-barreled Derringer. That's why cops pursued Gagliardi for the next 20 months, finally capturing the Boston mobster two days before Christmas 1968. His accomplices, Frank P. Oreto, who was captured immediately, and Benjamin De Christoforo, who remained on the lam for 19 months, were also charged with the murder. Lanzi's death was the 45th gangland-style murder in Beantown in a 37-month spree, and Gagliardi was prime suspect in several of the murders, although no arrests had been made. This time he'd given police the evidence they needed, renting the now-bloodied car in his own name and parking it in front of his Fifth Street home. The FBI named the suspected trigger man to the Top Ten list on June 9, 1967. The loan-sharking, gun-running extortionist didn't let the manhunt push him from his turf, he was

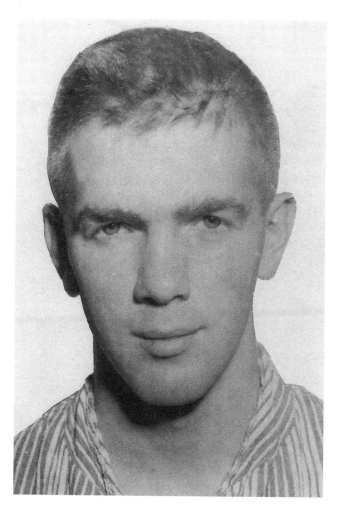

Young was arrested in Akron, Ohio, by the FBI and local authorities.

Mysterious Escape. Joseph Leroy Newman was just a small-time thief, with a long record of minor burglaries and robberies. At age 30 he was serving two to six at Washington, D.C.'s, Lorton Reformatory for breaking and entering. So Newman decided to try his hand at breaking and *exiting*. Newman and five fellow inmates escaped from the medium security prison on the morning of February 11, 1967, in a prison laundry van driven by an inmate in a stolen guard uniform. On the run from authorities, this small-time thief became a Most Wanted man when he shot an off-duty police officer who appeared to recognize him on May 13, 1967. The officer survived the four .25 caliber shots to the torso, a tumble down two flights of stairs, and four hours of surgery. An assault with intent to kill charge was added to the thief's growing rap sheet, arrested at his mother's Medford, Massachusetts, home.

INTERESTING FUGITIVE FACT:
Gagliardi was well known to area police, in part because his brother was a Medford police officer.

251. DONALD RICHARD BUSSMEYER, bank robber

LISTED: June 28, 1967
CAUGHT: August 24, 1967
DESCRIPTION: A hulking and heavily tattooed bank robber. Tattoos include "Easy to Hate," "Don," a boy, a heart with an arrow, "Mom," a sailboat, and a cross on his right arm. An ace of hearts, an ace of spades, a cross, a bird, "Cool Man," a dagger, a ship, two dice, "Born," "Win," "Joyce," a star, and a tiger are tattooed on his left arm. On the back of his left hand he has the tattoos "Born to Win," and a set of dice. On his chest he bears the tattoos "Don Bussmeyer Loves Joyce," a heart, "Rum," and "Coke." Tattoos of a woman appear on each shoulder blade.

Why Don't You Take Out an Ad? If you're wanted by every law enforcement officer in the country, what's the last thing you want? How about a tattoo on your chest, proclaiming your full name? Don Bussmeyer must have rued the day he decided to have the wordy declaration of love "Don Bussmeyer Loves Joyce" inked on his beefy, hairy chest when he was named to the Top Ten list. Hell, arresting officers wouldn't even have to bother with fingerprints. And in fact, when FBI agents stormed Bussmeyer's hideout, the fugitive was sitting there, shirtless.

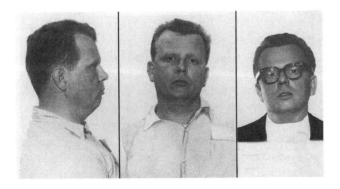

Bussmeyer was arrested in Upland, California, clad only in shorts. A tattoo on his chest, "Don Bussmeyer Loves Joyce," gave away his identity.

In fact, Bussmeyer's blazing stupidity almost overshadows the fact that he and two accomplices pulled off a fairly lucrative heist—$75,000 from a bank in Los Angeles (the bank robbery capital of the United States) on March 2, 1967. Bussmeyer's accomplices were rounded up quickly in days after their heist, but Bussmeyer, along with his fat $45,000 cut of the loot, remained missing. That is, until tips came in to the FBI, placing Bussmeyer in an apartment in Upland, California.

INTERESTING FUGITIVE FACT:
Even more bizarre is that Don Bussmeyer's wife—who reportedly was very skilled with a pistol and could shoot the flames off candles from dozens of yards—was named "Hallie."

252. FLORENCIO LOPEZ MATIONG, murderer

LISTED: July 1, 1967
CAUGHT: July 16, 1967

253. VICTOR JERALD BONO, murderer

LISTED: July 1, 1967
CAUGHT: July 16, 1967

Traffic Jammed. On June 16, 1967, two INS border patrol officers failed to reach their daily checkpoint. Patrolmen Theodore Newton and George Azrak were found three days later in a mountain cabin near Anza, California. Both were handcuffed to an old stove, and both had bullets in their brains. Fingerprints and tracks left in the mud led investigating FBI agents to the names of Florencio Mationg and Victor Bono, two of the most notorious drug smugglers along the California-Mexico border. They were both named to the Ten Most Wanted list on the same day and captured a little over two weeks later, when FBI agents stormed their L.A. apartment hideout. Mationg and Bono were sleeping when agents lobbed tear gas inside. Mationg came stumbling out and was arrested; Bono put up a small fight, but was taken into custody just the same. When the smoke cleared, agents found enough marijuana ($150,000 street value) and weapons (seven rifles, four shotguns, three submachine guns, a pistol, buckets full of ammo) to fuel a serious gun battle. Thankfully, it hadn't come to that.

INTERESTING FUGITIVE FACT:
Bono, also known as the "King of Smugglers," was already a federal fugitive before he was linked to Newton and Azrak's murders.

254. ALFRED JOHNSON COOPER JR., armed robber

LISTED: July 27, 1967
CAUGHT: September 8, 1967
DESCRIPTION: Born in Camden, New Jersey.

Criminal Display. Al Cooper will forever be known as the Ten Most Wanted fugitive who was caught thanks to a visitor taking the FBI tour in Washington, D.C. There's a special display of the Top Ten along the tour, which includes the current roster. In late summer 1967 an individual was taking the tour and was stunned to realize that he knew one of the men on the list. The tip enabled the FBI to pin down Cooper—who was using the alias "Joe Brady"—on a downtown Boston street corner. Cooper had been wanted for a host of crimes, including robbery, assault, kidnapping, and a violent 1966 gas station stickup in Cinnaminson, New Jersey, in which a local cop was shot and lost sight in one eye.

INTERESTING FUGITIVE FACT:
Sometimes you have to pause your flight for a quick chance to fight. While on the run, Cooper competed in the Holyoke Golden Gloves boxing tournament under his alias, "Joe Brady."

255. JOHN D. SLATON, bad check writer

LISTED: August 2, 1967
CAUGHT: December 1, 1967

Resisting Arrest. John D. Slaton would have been ignored by the Ten Most Wanted list if he'd just stuck to passing bad checks and other petty cons. But on the day before Halloween 1965, police in Oroville, Washington, showed up at Slaton's trailer to ask him about a bad check he'd passed. Slaton freaked and tried to drive his way out of the situation. The cops cornered him, and Slaton believed he had only one option left to him: shooting it out. He grabbed a rifle, pumped a few shots at his pursuers, then escaped on foot. Nearly two years later, Slaton was named to the Top Ten, and thanks to dogged FBI investigation, Slaton was arrested at a labor camp in Harquahala Valley, Arizona.

INTERESTING FUGITIVE FACT:
Slaton didn't try to resist arrest a second time. He admitted his true identity at once.

256. JERRY RAY JAMES, burglar, robber

LISTED: August 16, 1967
CAUGHT: January 24, 1968
DESCRIPTION: Born in Electra, Texas.

The Other James Gang. Jerry James was arrested in Tucson, Arizona, by FBI agents and local police. His partner, DONALD E. SPARKS (see #259), was arrested with him.

INTERESTING FUGITIVE FACT:
James, in his post–Most Wanted career, turned into a government snitch. At Leavenworth James became friends with Jamiel "Jimmy" Chagra, a notorious drug dealer who was accused of killing a federal judge. James allegedly heard Chagra bragging about this in jail and agreed to testify in exchange for his freedom. In this case the snitch lost out. Chagra was acquitted, and James stayed right where he was.

257. RICHARD PAUL ANDERSON, murderer, kidnapper

LISTED: September 7, 1967
CAUGHT: January 19, 1968
DESCRIPTION: "A dapper, handsome man," according to newspaper accounts.

Obsessed. Richard Paul Anderson thought he was safe in Canada. On the run from the FBI, which had named him to the Most Wanted list two months earlier, on September 7, 1967, Anderson, 27, had settled in Toronto, posing as a business executive. His ruse was convincing, until his business became robbery. Anderson had quite the résumé for that line of work, with numerous robbery arrests in New York and Missouri. Most of the charges were dropped for insufficient evidence. It was murder and kidnapping that had the FBI on his tail. He had shot the parents of a Missouri girl he was infatuated with on July 15, 1967, kidnapped a Mississippi gas station attendant three days later, robbed him and left him handcuffed to a tree, and then fled to California, where he assaulted a Long Beach man. Now he needed money. Anderson hit a department store on November 24, netting $10,000, and pulled a $2,400 bank job three weeks later. Less than a month later, he'd gotten into the kidnapping game again. His first target, 19-year-old hockey player Sam Kimberely, thwarted Anderson's attempts by throwing ice skates at the kidnapper. The second victim, a 60-year-old salesman, gained his freedom with a $50 withdrawal from his savings account. But the crimes alerted authorities to Anderson's whereabouts. He was arrested in his Millwood Road duplex while he slept. Canada had first crack at the hardened criminal, imprisoning him for nine years for robbery and kidnapping. Then it was Missouri's turn to put Anderson away. He was sentenced to 60 years for the double murder. On parole in November 1972, Anderson earned himself another 12-year stay for his part—two counts of attempted murder and possession of a dangerous weapon—in a bar brawl.

INTERESTING FUGITIVE FACT:
If Anderson could have just stayed out of trouble in that 1972 bar brawl, he would have gained his freedom. The double murder conviction was overturned in 1974.

258. HENRY THEODORE YOUNG, murderer, robber

LISTED: September 21, 1967
CAUGHT: January 9, 1968
DESCRIPTION: Born June 20, 1911, in Kansas City, Missouri. Five feet eight inches tall, 135 to 140 pounds, with brown hair and eyes. Occupations: cement finisher, farm laborer, mechanic, structural site worker. Scars and marks: scars left side of forehead, right cheek, left leg, vaccination scar left arm. Tattoos: Kewpie doll, "D.P.," "Little Henry," and "W" on left forearm; donkey right arm; winged head and dagger right forearm; dagger upper right leg. Young should be considered armed and very dangerous. He may have suicidal tendencies. Aliases: Donald Theodore Patton, Eugene Taylor, Henri J. Young, Howard James Young.

Forever Young. Henry Young was a 1930s burglar and bank robber who ended up in Alcatraz—a.k.a. "The Rock"—at the same time as Arthur "Dock" Barker, eldest of the notorious Barker boys. (Ma and brother Freddie had been shredded by G-man bullets back in January 1935, during one of the bloodiest years in American outlaw history.) On January 13, 1939, Young hooked up with Barker in a classic prison breakout, complete with swirling searchlights and machine-gun fire chopping up the surrounding waters. Barker was struck by bullets while trying to swim to freedom and died a short while later. Young and his three other accomplices were recaptured. Flash forward 30 years later: Young had grown old, but apparently never stopped trying to break out and resume his Depression-era profession. On June 8, 1967, Young broke out of the prison at Walla Walla in Washington State; he had been finishing up still another sentence there after winning parole from Alcatraz in 1955. A few months later, Young found himself at the top of the outlaw charts. The 56-year-old Young was arrested in Kansas City, Missouri, after a local resident recognized his grizzled mug in an *Inside Detective* magazine article.

INTERESTING FUGITIVE FACT:
While at Alcatraz in 1940, Young admitted to killing a baker during a robbery and had a life sentence tacked on for his trouble.

259. DONALD E. SPARKS, robber

LISTED: November 13, 1967
CAUGHT: January 24, 1968
DESCRIPTION: Born in Corpus Christi, Texas. Aliases included David Eugene Sparks, Delbert Sharp and Donald C. Chapman.

The Surprise Next Door. FBI agents were after Top Ten fugitive JERRY RAY JAMES when they set up a stakeout near a home on Tucson's East Side on January 24, 1968. Neighbors had reported suspicious activity, and cops had pursued James's 1967 Cadillac through the city earlier that day. (He escaped on foot before a cruiser rammed his car, leaving an associate to face the charge of harboring a fugitive.) The agents outside the 29th Street home expected a gun fight—and they didn't expect Donald E. Sparks, a Top Tenner for his part in three armed robberies in Collinsville, Florida, and Ft. Payne, Alabama. When the house was raided at 5 P.M., the fugitives were watching TV and surrendered peacefully. The agents' concern was not unfounded: a .30 caliber carbine, .357 magnum revolver, two .22 caliber pistols, and "a considerable amount" of ammunition was confiscated from the house. "There would have been some shooting," Sparks told agents. "If the wife and kid had not been here, it would not have been so easy."

Sparks's wife, Nelda, and seven-month-old child were in the house at the time of the raid. They'd been living in Tucson as the Chapman family for 10 months.

260. ZELMA LAVONE KING, murderer

LISTED: December 14, 1967
CAUGHT: January 30, 1968
DESCRIPTION: According to the FBI, "a Black Muslim with a violent hatred for whites." Alias: Charles M. Bracey.

A Cold Case. Zelma Lavone King was one cool criminal. The 25-year-old murdered three people during an argument over the sale of a refrigerator. The May 5, 1967, Chicago murders put authorities in hot pursuit of King. When he hadn't surfaced in six months, the FBI added King to the Top Ten list on December 14, 1967. Six weeks later, four agents surprised King at his job as a porter for Phoenix, Arizona's, McGraw-Edison International Metal Products. "Charles M. Bracey" confessed his true identity immediately.

INTERESTING FUGITIVE FACT:
Phoenix agents were busy that winter. King was the fourth Top Ten fugitive arrested in as many months.

261. JERRY REECE PEACOCK, armed robber, murderer

LISTED: December 14, 1967
CAUGHT: March 5, 1968
ALIAS: Randy Kastor.

Mr. Potato Head. Jerry Peacock was a guest of the California State Prison at Soledad in the mid-1960s, thanks to his robbery of an armored car full of cash in Santa Ana. On October 23, 1966, Peacock and a fellow con used a slightly offbeat escape plan: First, they made their way to the prison boiler room, then overpowered the janitor. Next, they stole one of the janitor's ladders and used it to scale the fence. Finally—and this is where sheer luck enters the picture—Peacock and his accomplice ran to the nearest road and hopped on a potato truck that just happened to be traveling past the prison at a low speed. Once free, Peacock demonstrated that he hadn't been reformed one iota. He pulled another heist, a kidnapping, and then beat a man to death in Hollywood, California. The efforts propped Peacock up on the Ten Most Wanted list, and three months later, FBI agents tracked their bird to a ranch in Mesquite, Nevada.

INTERESTING FUGITIVE FACT:
Peacock had grown a beard and lost weight to fool his pursuers. It didn't work, but it most likely improved his looks. In Peacock's FBI mug shot, the man is somewhat of a thick-necked dough boy.

262. RONALD EUGENE STORCK, burglar, murderer

LISTED: January 19, 1968
CAUGHT: February 29, 1968
DESCRIPTION: Born in Bucks County, Pennsylvania. Alias: Robert Berk.

Sail Away. It was no mystery who had murdered the elderly Brickajliks and their 11-year-old grandson in the couple's Bucks County home. Ronald Eugene Storck, a paroled burglar, had been seen walking toward the house on November 22, 1967, one day before Thanksgiving when visiting relatives discovered the shotgunned bodies. Later that same day, Storck was seen driving away from the house in the Brickajliks's pickup truck, found abandoned at the Philadelphia airport. The only mystery was where the fugitive had gone with the $6,000 he had stolen from the family. Charged with three counts of murder on November 28, 1968, Storck was added to the Most Wanted list on January 19, 1968. Six weeks later, the money led agents to Storck, living under the name Robert Berk in Honolulu, Hawaii. Storck had purchased an ostentatious 30-foot yacht. He had also purchased a .22 rifle and two automatic pistols, but did not resist arrest.

INTERESTING FUGITIVE FACT:
Despite the yacht purchase, Storck was a frugal thief. When agents cuffed him, three months after the murders, he still had $3,800 from the robbery.

263. ROBERT LEON MCCAIN, bank robber, murderer

LISTED: January 31, 1968
CAUGHT: February 23, 1968
DESCRIPTION: Born in Texas. Alias: Anthony Taylor.

Sometimes You Hit the Bottle, Sometimes the Bottle Hits You. When the FBI added Robert Leon McCain to the Most Wanted list on January 31, 1968, the agency declared he was responsible for "hundreds of armed robberies in the Texas area." Quite an accomplishment for someone who was only 26. For McCain armed robbery was a lucrative—and thus far, low-risk—way to make a living. But his good luck ran out during an August 8, 1967, bank robbery in Dallas, when he shot and killed a bank customer. He and his gang got away with the loot, but the FBI was on his tail. Six months later, McCain made another mistake during a supermarket holdup in Gulfport, Florida. This time McCain, wearing a Halloween mask, shot himself when a customer attempted to pin him down. As McCain limped away, another customer knocked him out with a soda bottle. McCain came to as police arrived.

INTERESTING FUGITIVE FACT:
McCain refused to admit to his identity, but his fingerprints eventually gave him away.

264. WILLIAM GARRIN ALLEN II, murderer

LISTED: February 9, 1968
CAUGHT: March 23, 1968
DESCRIPTION: Born in Nashville, Tennessee. African American.

265. CHARLES LEE HERRON, murderer

LISTED: February 9, 1968
CAUGHT: June 18, 1986
DESCRIPTION: African American. Alias: William Spencer.

Short and Long. William Garrin Allen II and Charles Lee Herron were known to Nashville, Tennessee, and Cincinnati, Ohio, police for their support of the "black power movement." Allen had been in trouble before, with arrests for marijuana possession and disorderly conduct during a riot, and Herron was on his way to being in trouble—police wanted to question him for arson. However, it was not political activism but forged money orders that started a chain reaction that placed the pair on the Most Wanted list. On January 16, 1968, William Garrin Allen II, Charles Lee Herron, and three acquaintances—John Alexander, Steve Parker, and Ralph Canady—purchased liquor at a

Nashville store with the forged money orders. The proprietor called the police, and the suspects' car was located quickly. As two cops—Thomas Johnson and Charles Thomasson—approached, however, its occupants opened fire. Johnson was killed; Thomasson was wounded. He survived to testify at trial against Parker (surrendered a few days after the shooting), Canady (captured a couple of days later), and Allen (added to the Most Wanted list, but captured in Brooklyn in late March). Each man was sentenced to 99 years in the state pen. John Alexander would be captured in 1971 and sentenced to just 10 years for manslaughter. Herron was still on the loose.

He was still on the loose in 1974, when the four other men gained their freedom. Alexander was granted parole; the other three murderers seized their own parole, walking away from the Nashville prison. It would be a dozen years before the men resurfaced. In April 1986 Canady was captured in

Due to an FBI investigation, Herron was arrested in Jacksonville, Florida.

Baltimore, but he hanged himself before cops could question him. In May 1986 William Allen applied for a Jacksonville, Florida, driver's license under the name "William Spencer." Cops sought him for fraud. When they knocked on his door, Herron, missing for more than 18 years, opened it. Cops didn't recognize the aged fugitive immediately, but he was still there when they returned with a SWAT team.

INTERESTING FUGITIVE FACT:
Charles Lee Herron has the distinction of being on the Most Wanted list for longer than any other fugitive—18 years, nine months, and four days.

266. LEONARD DANIEL SPEARS, robber and murderer

LISTED: February 13, 1968
CAUGHT: March 2, 1968
DESCRIPTION: Born in Arkansas in 1935. Often used the alias Billy Smith.

What $3,000 Buys You. Eighteen days after he earned a spot on the Top Ten list, Leonard Daniel Spears was in custody for the slaying of a Louisville, Kentucky, police officer. Officer William Meyers Sr. was in pursuit of Spears and three accomplices as they sped away from a grocery store in a rented getaway car with $3,000. One of the bandits shot and killed Meyers, but eventually all four men would face jail time for the crimes. Getaway car driver Leonard Thomas Pope was arrested one day after the holdup, on September 2, 1967, at an Indiana gas station with $272 in coins from the supermarket. The rented car was found abandoned nearby, with the fingerprints of Carl Sims Pinsky and Verser Joseph Swaite, both arrested soon after, and Spears. Spears successfully evaded the law for almost six months before he was targeted by the FBI, which quickly located him in a Tampa apartment. Spears surrendered immediately, but denied his identity, claiming to be Billy Smith, until an officer produced the Top Ten poster. Spears was returned to Kentucky and convicted of robbery, murder, and fleeing from prosecution.

INTERESTING FUGITIVE FACT:
The local cops lucked out, finding burglar Paul Clifford Hill III, who was wanted in Illinois, in the same Tampa apartment.

267. WILLIAM HOWARD BORNMAN, robber, murderer

LISTED: February 13, 1968
CAUGHT: February 13, 1968
DESCRIPTION: Born May 31, 1928, in New Haven, Connecticut. Five foot five, 130 pounds with multiple tattoos. Aliases: Richard H. Borman, William H. Borman, Richard Howard Bornmans, Albert W. Riley, Robert Hanley, William John Shanley, James Howard Tillman, William Howard Tillmen, Billy the Kid, and others.

Arsenic and Old Race. William Howard Bornman was a man of many names and many faces. His FBI identification order lists more than 10 aliases and three hair colors (dark brown was his natural color). It also includes a litany of Bornman's crimes: statutory burglary, breaking and entering, grand larceny, theft, receiving stolen goods, armed robbery, interstate flight to avoid prosecution, shooting with intent to kill, and interstate transportation of a stolen motor vehicle. It wasn't that the authorities couldn't catch up with him—by the time he was added to the Top Ten list in February 1968, Bornman had served seven prison sentences—it was that they couldn't hold onto him. He attempted suicide while in custody in 1964, then escaped twice from a Connecticut mental hospital in 1965. Recaptured in Baltimore in 1967 after shooting an Ohio police officer during a bungled tavern robbery, Bornman swallowed arsenic tablets, then escaped from the hospital where he was being treated. Re-recaptured the following day, Bornman attempted suicide again, then, although he was handcuffed to his hospital bed, escaped again. Arrested for shoplifting in Rhode Island in late September 1967, Bornman was released before he was identified as a fugitive. But when the FBI turned its attention to Bornman, his run was over. The FBI caught up to—and held onto—the criminal in Kentucky the same day he was added to the Most Wanted list.

INTERESTING FUGITIVE FACT:
Bornman was a master at hiding weapons and escape tools on his body. He had been known to carry hidden handcuff keys, poison, razor blades, and even a pistol.

268. JOHN CONWAY PATTERSON, robber, murderer

LISTED: February 26, 1968
CAUGHT: March 17, 1968

Left Behind. If John Conway Patterson hadn't left behind his partner in crime, LaCarettle Jones, as he fled from a bloody liquor store robbery in St. Louis, Illinois, he might never have served time for the heist. But Jones, just before being sentenced to 99 years in prison for the robbery and the shooting death of one officer who responded to the store's burglar alarm, fingered Patterson for the July 30, 1966, crime. Patterson remained at large for a year and a half—he was added to the Most Wanted list on February 26, 1968—before being apprehended by Milwaukee cops while casing a house. He tried to run again, but wasn't as successful.

INTERESTING FUGITIVE FACT:

Patterson wasn't exactly on the run from the cops after the burglary. He was living with his wife and four children in a Milwaukee tenement.

269. TROY DENVER MARTIN, murderer and kidnapper

LISTED: March 8, 1968
CAUGHT: March 19, 1968
DESCRIPTION: Born in Wheelwright, Kentucky, in January 1927. Often used the alias Bruce Collins.

The Corpse in Back. Troy Denver Martin had a fiery temper and a lengthy rap sheet for forgery. This time his rage was targeted at one of his in-laws, Julius E. Spivey. Martin shot the man in the back, put his body facedown in the back of his own pickup truck and sped off through the Michigan winter. Martin's case might have ended with the murder, but Martin swerved off the icy road into a farmyard. He abandoned the truck and the corpse and kidnapped a farmer at gunpoint, forcing him to drive to Toledo. The farmer was released unharmed at the end of the line and immediately informed authorities about the dead body he'd seen in the pickup truck. A warrant was issued for Martin's arrested on January 29, and he was added to the Top Ten list on March 8. Eleven days later, Martin was nabbed in downtown Seattle, where he had been working for a week as a day laborer under the name Bruce Collins.

INTERESTING FUGITIVE FACT:

Martin's legendary anger made him something of a loner. His friends kept their distance after several incidents when he lashed out with knives and guns.

270. GEORGE BENJAMIN WILLIAMS, bank robber

LISTED: March 18, 1968
FOUND DEAD: May 26, 1968
DESCRIPTION: Born June 15, 1911, in Malheur County, Oregon. Five foot six, with blue eyes and balding brown-gray hair. Tip of the ring finger of his right hand missing. Aliases: Allen Benjamin Colby, Ben Jackson, George Benjamin William.

Career Capper. The first time George Benjamin Williams robbed a Newcastle, California, bank in 1946, he didn't make the Most Wanted list. So he did it again in 1968. This time the well-known bank robber, who had spent more than 35 years

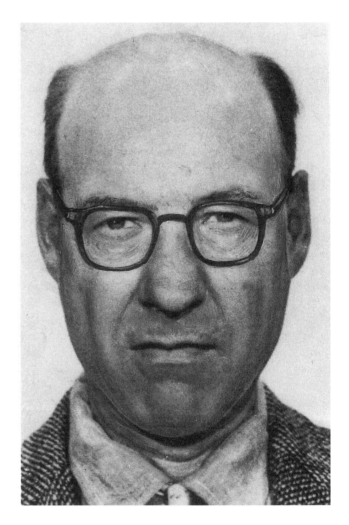

Williams's skeletal remains were found by prospectors near a mine in Nevada. Three bullet holes were in his skull. Williams had been dead for six months.

robbing banks and serving time, scored $19,534 and a spot on the FBI's list. Someone else got him first, though. Two months later, on May 26, 1968, prospectors discovered Williams's skeletal remains near a Nevada mine. There were three bullet holes in the skull.

INTERESTING FUGITIVE FACT:
It wouldn't be unusual to find Williams alone in the woods; he was described by the FBI as a loner and camping enthusiast. The bullet holes, though, were new.

271. MICHAEL JOHN SANDERS, robber

LISTED: March 21, 1968
CAUGHT: April 8, 1968
DESCRIPTION: Born July 19, 1940, in Reno, Nevada. A slender man, five foot 10, 145 pounds, with a dimpled chin and a penchant for motorcycles. Aliases: Kenneth Metzler, John Sanders.

Born to Be Wild. Michael John Sanders wanted to be known as an outlaw. He was a member of a motorcycle gang and boasted of his bad-boy antics— dishonorable discharge from the army, an armed robbery conviction in Tennessee, and escape from court-ordered psychiatric treatment. With bleached blond hair, clipped eyebrows, a goatee, and several tattoos and scars, Sanders looked the part of a criminal. But it wasn't until a Santa Cruz County shopkeeper called the cops on Sanders and some associates who were loitering in front of his store on February 7, 1964, that Sanders became a Most Wanted fugitive. When the police arrived, Sanders and the others assaulted the officers and fled in a volley of gunfire. Sanders stayed on the run for four years before being named to the infamous list in 1968. He was captured 18 days later in New York City.

INTERESTING FUGITIVE FACT:
The self-proclaimed outlaw also spent time working as a doorman, grape picker, and theater manager.

272. HOWARD CALLENS JOHNSON, murderer

LISTED: March 21, 1968
CAUGHT: April 24, 1968
DESCRIPTION: Born in Dallas County, Alabama, in April 1916. Described by the FBI as a "lone wolf."

"Some Member of This Family Will Get Sick and Die." Starting in 1935 at the age of 19, Howard Callens Johnson worked his way up from petty state liquor violations to assault and arson before his role in the 1952 fire at his estranged wife's home put him in jail for almost a decade. Released in 1961, Johnson picked up where he left off, moving from arson to murder. On May 3, 1966, Johnson quarreled with a female acquaintance in her Summerfield, Alabama, home. As he stormed away from the property, Johnson was heard yelling, "Sometime during the night, some member of this family will get sick and die." Two hours later, the woman's 18-year-old son was gunned down in the front yard. Johnson was charged with the murder, but he was nowhere to be found. After almost two years without success, the FBI named the fugitive to the Most Wanted list on March 21, 1968. One month later, the agency arrested Johnson at 5:30 A.M. on April 24, 1968, while he worked as a maintenance man at the University of Louisville.

INTERESTING FUGITIVE FACT:
When he was arrested, Johnson had been employed at the University of Louisville—under his real name—for six months.

273. GEORGE EDWARD WELLS, robber, murderer

LISTED: March 28, 1968
CAUGHT: May 27, 1969
DESCRIPTION: Born in Belmont County, Ohio. According to the FBI, "a vicious and sadistic killer."

An Afterlife of Crime. Ohio authorities never expected to be pursuing George Edward Wells again. He had been sentenced to death for the shooting death of an Akron tavern owner. But 12 hours before the execution in 1938, the Ohio governor commuted his sentence to life imprisonment. Twenty-three years later, the sentence was commuted again, from first- to second-degree murder, and Wells was paroled. Despite the prison sentence, Wells was still a menace. In 1967 he was linked to the robbery and beating of an Ohio coin collector and a jewelry store robbery near Cleveland. He was named to the Most Wanted list on March 28, 1968, and captured outside a motel in South Point, Ohio, 14 months later.

INTERESTING FUGITIVE FACT:
Wells was convicted of the 1967 robberies and

sentenced to nine years in jail. The governor didn't commute the sentence this time.

274. DAVID EVANS, bank robber

LISTED: April 3, 1968
CAUGHT: April 26, 1968
DESCRIPTION: Born October 11, 1944, in York, Pennsylvania. A five-foot-eight, 150-pound black man with the nickname Pee Wee.

Auld Lang Crime. It wouldn't be a happy new year for David Evans, the bank robber who held up the First National Bank and Trust Company in Bethlehem, Pennsylvania, on December 28, 1967. Clad in a ski mask and brandishing a semiautomatic, Evans yelled "Happy New Year!" to the bank employees before fleeing with $26,000. The year 1967 had been good for the bank robber, with a successful string of robberies, but 1968 would mark the end of his life of crime. Evans was added to the Most Wanted list on April 3, 1968, and was shot and captured by Philadelphia police responding to a burglar alarm 23 days later.

INTERESTING FUGITIVE FACT:
Evans had served time before getting tagged with the bank robberies. He had been convicted of assault and battery for throwing a young boy from a York, Pennsylvania, bridge. Evans's defense: He just "felt like killing someone."

275. FRANKLIN ALLEN PARIS, robber

LISTED: April 9, 1968
CAUGHT: May 21, 1968

Paris in the Spring. For the early part of his criminal career Franklin Allen Paris was a safecracker, but after he was arrested twice for his work in Shasta County, California, Paris jumped bail and changed his M.O. Now he targeted supermarkets—specifically the families of supermarket managers. From Santa Cruz in January 1967 to San Jose and Santa Clara in November of that year, Paris perfected his approach, kidnapping family members and demanding ransoms from the supermarket safes. Paris was named to the Most Wanted list on April 9, 1968, and authorities, operating on a tip, attempted to capture him in a roadblock in North-

ern California. True to form, Paris fled from the trap into a Lakehead, California, grocery store, where he kidnapped a bystander. In the ensuing shoot-out the criminal was badly wounded. He survived the gunshots, but not the charges. He was convicted of unlawful flight as well as 29 felony counts for crimes from robbery to assault with a deadly weapon.

INTERESTING FUGITIVE FACT:
Being a victim would have been more profitable than being a criminal, Paris learned in his last kidnapping. The human shield he abducted from the Lakehead, California, grocery store was severely wounded in the shoot-out. The victim settled a lawsuit against the criminal and the cops for $50,000.

276. DAVID STUART NEFF, bank robber

LISTED: April 18, 1968
CAUGHT: April 25, 1968
DESCRIPTION: Born in Boston, Massachusetts.

'Neff Said. On April 25, 1968, FBI agents Andy Rearick and Bill Quinn waited patiently outside an apartment building in Brooklyn. The Boston-based agents had information that David Stuart Neff, a Boston bank robber who had been named to the FBI Ten Most Wanted list a week earlier, was inside. Rearick and Quinn were cautious. "He was considered armed and dangerous," Rearick recalls. Neff, an accomplished car thief, had convictions for forgery, breaking and entering, larceny, and possession of firearms; he always carried a .45-caliber automatic pistol. He had brandished the weapon in a Lynn, Massachusetts, bank during an October 4, 1967, holdup, scoring $23,851, and during a March 27, 1968, holdup at a Beverly, Massachusetts, bank, which netted $28,500. Suddenly, Rearick and Quinn spotted the 32-year-old Neff. "Well, we saw him coming toward us and he just kept walking casually. When he crossed the street, I got out of the car in front of him and Bill came up behind him and I said 'FBI! You're under arrest!' And Bill grabbed him." Neff gave up without a fight.

INTERESTING FUGITIVE FACT:
Neff was also sought by the U.S. Secret Service for forging U.S. war bonds.

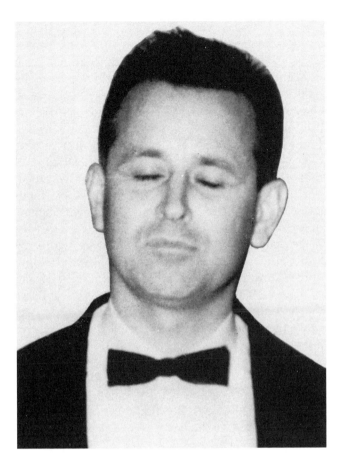

Ray was apprehended in London, England, by British authorities.

277. JAMES EARL RAY, assassin

LISTED: April 20, 1968
CAUGHT: June 8, 1968
DESCRIPTION: Born March 18, 1928, in Alton, Illinois. Five foot 10 and 170 pounds, with blue eyes and brown hair. Described as a "lone wolf" with a "noticeable protruding left ear" and small scars on his forehead and right palm. Known to have attended dance instruction and bartending courses. Aliases: Eric Starvo Galt, W. C. Herron, Harvey Lowmyer, James McBride, James O'Conner, James Walton, James Waylon, John Willard, Ramon George Sneyd.

Infamous. James Earl Ray was a petty criminal: drunkenness on a U.S. Army base in Germany (leading to his discharge from the service); burglary at a Los Angeles cafeteria (he was released early from a 90-day sentence with the stipulation he leave California); vagrancy in Cedar Rapids, Iowa, and Quincy,

Illinois; robbery of a Chicago cab driver (he served one year of a two-year sentence); and a string of burglaries, skipped bail, stolen money orders, and more burglaries before his 20-year conviction in Missouri.

Things changed after Ray escaped from the Jefferson City prison in a bread truck on April 23, 1967. Ray became Eric Stavro Galt, the man who would assassinate Martin Luther King Jr. At 6:01 P.M. on April 4, 1968, King was felled by a single bullet. Ray fled the scene in a white Ford Mustang registered under the name Galt. The rifle, too, had been purchased under that name. But fingerprints on record from Ray's past crimes betrayed him, and his name, not the alias Galt, was added to the Most Wanted list 16 days after the murder. Authorities traced Ray—now using the name Ramon George Sneyd—to Toronto and then London. He was arrested by English law enforcement after six weeks on the lam and returned to the United States to face a 99-year sentence. He would die in jail, despite protestations of innocence.

INTERESTING FUGITIVE FACT:
A House of Representatives committee investigating the assassination concluded—and many conspiracy theorists agree—that King was "probably" the target of a larger plot, but no other suspects were ever uncovered.

278. JOHN WESLEY SHANNON, bank robber

LISTED: May 7, 1968
CAUGHT: June 5, 1968
DESCRIPTION: Born in Pleasantville, New Jersey, on July 9, 1936. Five-foot-10, 150-pound African American with black hair and brown eyes. Scars on both temples and a burn scar on his left arm. Casual dresser with an affinity for gambling and pool.

Tiny Take, Quiet Takedown. According to the FBI, John Wesley Shannon was the "brains" behind a May 26, 1967, heist at the Collective Federal Savings and Loan Association in Northfield, New Jersey. Unfortunately, his plan wasn't fully thought out. When divided among Shannon and his four accomplices, the $8,881 take wasn't worth the jail time. Three of the men were arrested almost immediately and convicted of the crime. (The fourth was arrested, but jumped bail). Shannon, a veteran criminal with a record, including larceny, robbery, possession of a weapon, and sodomy, dating back to 1957, outwitted the cops for a longer time by living a normal life.

He had practice at that. Over the years he'd made a decent living as a caddy, a dishwasher, and a hospital orderly. But he'd never made quite enough to support his gambling and drug habits. Almost a year after the robbery, Shannon was named to the Top Ten list. On June 5, 1968, he was apprehended on his way to work at a Marlton, New Jersey, construction site.

INTERESTING FUGITIVE FACT:
Shannon was reputed to have a violent temper, but his quick passion also made him a successful prize-fighter.

279. TAYLOR MORRIS TEAFORD, alleged murderer

LISTED: May 10, 1968
PROCESS DISMISSED: May 25, 1972

Are You Reading This, Taylor? The Oakland, California, police department is still looking for Taylor Morris Teaford (aka Melvin Teaford), even though the FBI took the alleged murderer off the Ten Most Wanted list 30 years ago. According to the Oakland P.D., in 1969 Teaford murdered an unidentified woman in room 15 of the St. Louis Hotel, near the North Alameda County jail, beating her beyond recognition and strangling her with her own clothing. And that's not even why the FBI was after Teaford. Teaford, born on June 18, 1935, started his criminal career in 1954 at the age of 18, burglarizing cabins near a California lake. He was convicted and imprisoned for two years. In 1957 he raped a 15-year-old girl. He was convicted and imprisoned for 10 years. In 1967 he allegedly shot and killed his grandmother, wounded his sister, and shot a Madera County deputy sheriff. Finally, Teaford had earned himself a place on the Ten Most Wanted list. Four years later, the Madera County prosecutor asked the FBI to end the manhunt. The passage of time had faded hopes for a conviction, but the Oakland cops haven't given up. An age-enhanced photo shows the six-foot, 185-pound Teaford as a distinguished 60-year-old with squinting brown eyes and graying brown hair, a grandfatherly figure with a murder warrant.

280. PHILLIP MORRIS JONES, bank robber

LISTED: June 5, 1968
CAUGHT: June 26, 1968
DESCRIPTION: Born in Florida. An avid gambler with a penchant for blackjack, poker, and marking cards.

The Other Phillip Morris. In Phillip Morris Jones's strangest caper on April 8, 1968, the bank robber scored $79,874 from the American National Bank in Winter Haven, Florida, locked eight people in the bank's vault, and raced back to his motel—where he changed into his bathing suit for some sunbathing poolside. When a police car approached the motel, Jones fled on foot, stole a car, drove it into a lake, then swam to safety on the other side. Despite all that, the robbery wasn't a success. Jones escaped, but the cops recovered $76,597 of the loot. Jones just wasn't very good at this bank-robbing thing; his first robbery in Bakersfield, California, on February 28 netted him $5,637, but he got away with only $500. Jones did improve, earning—and holding onto—almost $12,000 from bank robberies in Wheaton, Maryland, and Phoenix, Arizona, later that month. On June 25, 1968, Jones faced a new challenge: learning how to be a Top Ten fugitive pursued by the FBI. He held out for three weeks, before deciding he wasn't going to be good at that either. Jones walked into the FBI office in San Mateo, California, and handed a paper bag to FBI agent John "Rocky" Breslin. "You people want me," Jones said. In the bag was a loaded 9 mm automatic pistol.

INTERESTING FUGITIVE FACT:
When he surrendered, Jones was also carrying a paperback novel titled *The Plot*. Perhaps he was studying up.

281. JOHNNY RAY SMITH, robber

LISTED: June 20, 1968
CAUGHT: June 24, 1968
DESCRIPTION: Born in Monroe County, Alabama. Described by the FBI as a "trigger-happy escapee from a Florida jail with a notorious record for prior prison breaks."

The Ugly Underneath. "I'm tired of running," 45-year-old Johnny Ray Smith told the Ocean Springs, Mississippi, police who arrested the Top Ten fugitive on a tip from a waitress in a neighboring Alabama town. No wonder he was tired—Smith's April 16, 1968, prison break was the criminal's fourth sprint to freedom in 14 years. The first was a successful escape from a Florida federal prison in 1944 where he was serving time for auto theft and armed robbery; the second was a daring shoot-out departure from a Panama City, Florida, prison in 1949 that sparked a statewide manhunt in Smith's home state of Alabama. Six days after the escape Smith and hostage Alan Spearman Jr. were discovered at a hotel in Geneva, Alabama. Spearman was released unharmed, and Smith was sentenced to 30 more years for kidnapping. (The conviction was later overturned by the U.S. Supreme Court on procedural grounds.)

In 1961 Smith attempted to disappear from a Florida prison camp, but was shot for his efforts. His escape plans foiled, Smith had to wait to be released from prison to get back into the armed robbery racket. The cops caught up to Smith again in Pensacola, Florida, on February 4, 1968—with a stolen car from Houston, Texas, and money orders taken in a Pensacola holdup—and put him back in jail. Two months later, he was on the run again, in a 1963 automobile with Arkansas tags, the tipster waitress told cops. Smith's marathon, which earned him a spot on the Top Ten list, finally ended at 8:14 A.M. on June 24, 1968.

INTERESTING FUGITIVE FACT:
Smith wasn't discovered hiding *out* at that hotel in Geneva, Alabama. He was discovered hiding *under* it. The spider sense of one local cop, who knew Smith was a former exterminator who had treated the building, was the fugitive's downfall.

282. BYRON JAMES RICE, robber

LISTED: July 5, 1968
CAUGHT: October 2, 1972
DESCRIPTION: Born 1936.

Bored Byron. Byron James Rice seemed to enjoy his life of crime, racking up a long list of robberies and convictions before a February 21, 1966, armored car holdup that went awry. Rice and two accomplices had their eyes on the $30,000 prize when they stopped the armored car in Mountain View, California. Rice got the money, his accomplices got caught, and one of the guards was shot to death. Rice was named to the Most Wanted list on July 5, 1968, and tried to go straight to avoid detection. He moved from city to city, working odd jobs. But he didn't like that life. He turned himself in to Chicago agents on October 2, 1972.

INTERESTING FUGITIVE FACT:
Rice, a lifelong robber, spent some time while on the lam working as a security guard.

283. ROBERT LEROY LINDBLAD, murderer

LISTED: July 11, 1968
CAUGHT: October 7, 1968
DESCRIPTION: Born in San Francisco, California, in 1933. An expert in judo and karate, a ski buff, and the author of a book on wilderness survival.

Survival of the Sickest. Before becoming a Most Wanted fugitive, Robert Leroy Lindblad was an air force instructor, teaching recruits how to survive in the wilderness. He even wrote a book on the subject, but in the end Lindblad would become best known for teaching two Wyoming businessmen how to die in the wilderness. The men, two of three partners in a Jackson Hole, Wyoming, hotel that burned under suspicious circumstances, had been missing for three months when they were discovered shot and stripped in a shallow grave in Lyon County, Nevada. Authorities charged the third business partner and two conspirators with planning the double murder, but targeted Lindblad, who had been unsuccessful at leading the life of a law-abiding civilian, as the hitman. Lindblad was named to the Most Wanted list on July 11, 1968, and surrendered to authorities in Yerrington, Nevada, on October 7, 1968.

INTERESTING FUGITIVE FACT:
Lindblad, described by the FBI as a judo expert, was supposed to have killed the two men with a swift chop to the throat. His skills failed him, and he had to resort to a gun.

284. JAMES JOSEPH SCULLY, bank robber

LISTED: July 15, 1968
CAUGHT: July 23, 1968
DESCRIPTION: Born in Blackstone, Massachusetts, in August 1920.

The Paperboy Gets It. James Joseph Scully was known to harbor suicidal tendencies. When he was angry, which was often, he was also known to harbor homicidal tendencies. Although he never killed anyone, he shot and critically wounded a Santa Rosa, California, newspaper delivery man who walked into a robbery. Apparently Scully was enraged that the bank holdup, his fifth in the area in less than four months, had netted so little. He scored less than $10,000 total in the five heists. Scully, already on parole for an earlier bank robbery, was named to the Most Wanted list on July 15, 1968. Eight days later, authorities cornered him in Arcadia, California.

INTERESTING FUGITIVE FACT:
Despite his violent tendencies, Scully surrendered peacefully to authorities.

285. BILLY RAY WHITE, robber, murderer

LISTED: August 13, 1968
CAUGHT: August 17, 1968

A Show of Mercy. By the time drifter Billy Ray White met Aurora "Flossie" Rice in the back room

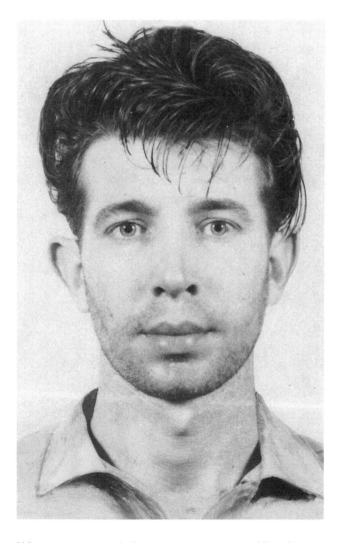

White was arrested after a citizen recognized him from an article in the St. Louis Globe-Democrat.

of the New Mexico trading post he was robbing, he was wanted for stealing $4,000 worth of diamonds from a Metairie, Louisiana, jewelry shop and more than $1,600 from an Albuquerque savings and loan. On the night of November 18, 1967, White had drifted into the small town of Budville, New Mexico, with an accomplice and a pistol and held up 54-year-old Bud Rice and his 81-year-old clerk Blanche Brown. There was only $300 in the till. In a rage White killed both Rice and Brown. A moment later, White discovered Flossie in a back room. He tied her up, taped her mouth, and pointed a gun at her head. He didn't pull the trigger—and that was his downfall.

On August 13, 1968, White, still on the run from his multiple armed robbery and murder charges, was named to the Ten Most Wanted list. He stayed on the lam only four more days, when federal agents discovered him hiding in the closet of a Wood River, Illinois, home. The agents also found a map of Illinois with 70 towns circled, each marking the site of a successful or planned robbery. White was extradited to New Mexico, where, despite testimony by Flossie Rice, a jury found White innocent of the murders of Bud Rice and Blanche Brown. "I think justice has been done," he told applauding spectators.

But later, in the Louisiana State Penitentiary where he was serving time for the jewelry shop heist, White confessed to the murders. Then "one of the most fearless and dangerous men ever to hit this place," in the words of fellow inmate Billy Sinclair, slashed his wrists with a razor blade. "He literally chewed the veins out of his arm, spitting a mouthful of tissue, sinew, and blood into the toilet," Sinclair wrote in his award-winning prison magazine *The Angolite*. "He didn't even flinch."

INTERESTING FUGITIVE FACT:
White had claimed to be a traveling insurance salesman, which was his attempt to explain away the robbery maps.

286. FREDERICK RUDOLPH YOKOM, robber

LISTED: August 21, 1968
CAUGHT: September 6, 1968
DESCRIPTION: Born in New York in February 1946. Alias: Alfredo Rivas Loya.

Soft Touch. Ike and Mary Belle Macy were used to being robbed. That was Ike's fault. The retired tennis pro and prominent Miami socialite often bragged of the large sums of money he kept in the couple's $50,000 southwest Miami home. Frederick Rudolph Yokom was used to robbing. Armed robbery was, Yokom told acquaintances, his occupation. The head of the "Yokom Gang," a ragtag crew of Florida jewel thieves, had been arrested several times in the course of his work. At 8:30 P.M. on January 7, 1968, the Yokom Gang made an "appointment" with the Macys, bursting into their home with a gun while the couple watched television. The intruders shot 52-year-old Mary Belle (she would survive) and then gunned down her 65-year-old husband before fleeing, one on foot and the other two in separate getaway cars. Cops and neighbor Clarence Vicklund, who had heard the gun shots, identified Yokom as the culprit. Yokom, who had been scheduled to appear in court on burglary, robbery, and assault charges, and who was wanted in a January 4, 1968, robbery at a Miami jeweler's home, had skipped town. He was named to the Top Ten list on August 21, 1968, and remained on the lam for 16 days. The FBI collared 22-year-old Yokom—using the name Alfredo Rivas Loya—at a Los Angeles restaurant on September 6, 1968. Convicted of murder, Yokom was sentenced to 99 years in prison.

INTERESTING FUGITIVE FACT:
Despite the 99-year sentence, Yokom only served 15 years. Then he went back to his "job." In 1998 he was sentenced for stealing $308,000 in fine jewelry in a 1991 heist. This time he was sentenced to 12 years.

287. HAROLD JAMES EVANS, robber

LISTED: September 19, 1968
CAUGHT: January 2, 1969
DESCRIPTION: Born on January 13, 1945, in Chicago, Illinois. Five foot 11 and 175 to 210 pounds with blue eyes, brown hair, and a tattoo reading "Annette" on his left forearm. Aliases: James Harold Evans, James Herold Evans, Jim Evans, Gary Dave Ricketsen, Jimmy, Big Jim, Big Bob, Big Ed.

Handcuffed to a Corpse. Before Harold James Evans made the Most Wanted list, he had racked up arrests in four states on two coasts and Canada. His last was in Norristown, Pennsylvania, where he was convicted of, among other things, burglary, armed robbery, assault and battery, rape, conspiracy, and carrying a deadly weapon. On June 23, 1967, he added unlawful flight to the list, escaping in transit from a courtroom to his jail cell. Evans took a fellow prisoner with him; they were handcuffed together. That partnership didn't last long after the pair darted away from guards into traffic. Evans's companion was found dead in the Schuylkill River two days later, an apparently accidental death. Evans was already on his way home, Chicago. That's where FBI agents found the Most Wanted criminal in early January 1969, less than four months after adding his name to the list. Evans was returned—well guarded—to Pennsylvania to serve his time in a maximum-security prison.

INTERESTING FUGITIVE FACT:
Evans's résumé included nightclub proprietor, painter, service station attendant, tile setter, truck driver, and member of a notorious burglary gang.

288. ROBERT LEE CARR, robber

LISTED: October 16, 1968
CAUGHT: November 4, 1968
DESCRIPTION: Born in Sunbury, Pennsylvania, on May 5, 1946. Tattoo "LOVE" on knuckles of his left hand. Alias: Robert Daniels.

The Man Who Loved to Rob. Robert Lee Carr had "Love" tattooed on the knuckles of his left hand, but the only thing he seemed to love was the rush of a robbery. He got addicted to that thrill early, racking up juvenile offenses for burglary and auto theft. As an adult he kept looking for that fix between jail sentences, parole violations, and the occasional, legal construction job. In September 1968 Carr was in jail again, awaiting trial on robbery charges. But Carr saw a chance to break the cycle of his life. With the help of several fellow inmates Carr escaped from the Northumberland County jail by locking the prison guards in a cell. Free to rob, Carr started his spree in a Millersburg, Pennsylvania, home, scoring a rifle and $6,000 in cash. Over the next several days authorities credited Carr with numerous robberies in the area. Carr was named to the Most Wanted list one month after his prison break. By the time the FBI caught up with him in South Gate, California, on November 4, 1968, Carr was trying to go straight again, working as a gas station attendant.

INTERESTING FUGITIVE FACT:
Michael Clark, an Northumberland County inmate who escaped with Carr, also worked at the gas station where the FBI captured Carr. Although Clark was not on the payroll when agents arrived, Clark was at the gas station and was also arrested.

289. LEVI WASHINGTON, bank robber

LISTED: November 15, 1968
CAUGHT: December 9, 1968
DESCRIPTION: Born in Alligator, Mississippi.

Alias: Paul Carter. Everybody was looking for Levi Washington in 1968. He was on parole for a narcotics conviction in Mississippi; he was charged

Washington was arrested in Jackson, Michigan, for a local bank robbery. A fingerprint comparison revealed his true identity.

with three 1967 bank robberies in Louisiana; and he was wanted by the FBI for robbing a Chicago church. The FBI pulled rank, and Washington was transported to the Cook County jail to await trial. But Washington didn't wait very long. On August 16, 1968, he gave all of his pursuers the slip, escaping from the Illinois lockup with several fellow inmates. The Most Wanted fugitive resurfaced with a mask, a gun, and a canister of riot gas in a Jackson, Michigan, bank on December 5, 1968, though the cops didn't realize it for several days. Authorities arrested Paul Carter and Allen Rose for the $37,000 heist and were surprised to learn through fingerprint comparisons that Paul Carter was Levi Washington and Allen Rose was Washington's Cook County cell mate, Louis Carr. (A third escaped fugitive, Delbert Beard, ended up back behind bars when he tried to visit the pair in jail.) Still, Washington wasn't done. On July 23, 1968, the morning of his federal trial, Washington attempted to flee from the courthouse. He was recaptured in the basement and finally stood trial for his crimes.

INTERESTING FUGITIVE FACT:
Washington was also charged with planting the bomb that exploded at the Jackson, Michigan, city hall at midnight on December 5. Authorities speculate that it was designed as a diversion during the bank robbery, but malfunctioned.

290. RICHARD LEE TINGLER, murderer

LISTED: December 20, 1968
CAUGHT: May 19, 1969
DESCRIPTION: Claimed to have been born on December 2, 1940, in Portsmouth, Ohio. Five foot eight and 145 pounds with blond hair and blue eyes, the sometimes electrician and mechanic was also thought to be a female impersonator. Aliases: Don Williams, Dick Tingler, "Junior."

Wild Ting. Richard Lee Tingler had his first run-in with police in June 1959, at the age of 18, when he and a friend went AWOL from their Alaska Air Force station and committed several robberies in Anchorage. He had his last run-in with authorities on May 19, 1969, when he was arrested in Dill City, Oklahoma, for six murders. He was sentenced to death for the crimes: the deaths of a Cleveland, Ohio, tavern owner; two bartenders and a prostitute taken hostage during a robbery and discovered by joggers in the city's Rockefeller Park; and the murder of two teenage employees of a Columbus, Ohio, dairy bar. The dairy bar owner had survived Tingler's attempts to strangle her with a wire coat hanger and identified the well-known robber and murderer. Before cops caught up with him, Tingler would shoot one more person in the head, an unsuspecting acquaintance from whom Tingler stole cash and a car. Tingler was running scared, having seen himself on the television show *The FBI*. Still, it wasn't the show, but his increasingly erratic behavior—he killed a neighbor's dog and liked to take target practice shooting at high tension wires along the highway—that led to his arrest.

INTERESTING FUGITIVE FACT:
Police actually visited the increasingly unpredictable Tingler twice at the Dill City farm where he was working under the name Don Williams, before realizing his resemblance to the Wanted fugitive.

291. GEORGE MICHAEL GENTILE, robber

LISTED: June 20, 1968
CAUGHT: June 24, 1968
DESCRIPTION: Born in New York in April 1902.

Do Not Go Gentile into the Night. George Michael Gentile was a drifter with a lengthy list of convictions—everything from extortion to murder—and just as lengthy a list of parole violations and a hobby of impersonating the very cops he was always trying to avoid. His signature crime was posing as a police officer to extort money from homosexuals afraid of arrest or exposure. It worked in Texas, where Gentile earned $2,500 in February 1965, and it worked one month later in Alexandria, Virginia, where Gentile earned another $1,000 and a spot on the Most Wanted list. But Gentile's cop impersonation wasn't good enough to fool 32-year-old New York City detective Warren Taylor. Taylor spotted the Most Wanted fugitive—with seven outstanding indictments for grand larceny and extortion—on Eighth Avenue, waiting to cross the street. Gentile tried to flee, but Taylor subdued him.

INTERESTING FUGITIVE FACT:
Detective Warren Taylor was part of a detail assigned to protect then president-elect Richard Nixon during an appearance when he spotted Gentile.

292. GARY STEVEN KRIST, kidnapper

LISTED: December 20, 1968
CAUGHT: December 22, 1968
DESCRIPTION: Habitual criminal.

293. RUTH EISEMANN SCHIER, kidnapper

LISTED: December 28, 1968
CAUGHT: March 5, 1969
DESCRIPTION: Born in Honduras. Alias: Donna Sue Wills.

A Couple of Kidnappers. Ruth Eisemann Schier was a biology researcher. Gary Steven Krist was a smooth-talking criminal. And 20-year-old Barbara Jane Mackle was the wealthy kidnapping victim who was to be the pair's big score. On December 17, 1968, Krist and Schier abducted Mackle from a suburban Georgia motel, where she was staying with her mother while recovering from the flu. Mackle, the daughter of a millionaire land developer, was buried alive 20 miles away in a box fitted with an air pump. The ransom note—demanding $500,000 in old $20 bills—was buried in the front yard of the Mackles' Coral Gables, Florida, home. The distraught parents followed the kidnappers' directions to a T, until Robert Mackle got lost on the way to the Fair Isle drop-off point on December 19. He arrived an hour late, but a greedy Krist was still waiting. That was his mistake. As Krist retrieved the ransom, a police officer mistook him for a robber and gave chase. Krist fled on foot, leaving his car and its clues.

The following day an anonymous phone call led officers to Barbara Mackle, who was unharmed, despite 83 hours underground. The purchase of a boat led authorities to Krist. A Coast Guard copter spotted him in Charleston Harbor. He was arrested on December 22, two days after being named to the Most Wanted list. (He was held on $500,000 bail. Too bad he'd spent the ransom money on the boat). Schier, inexperienced at being on the lam, avoided cops until March 5, 1969, when she interviewed at a nursing home under the name Donna Sue Wills. A routine fingerprint check revealed her true identity. Krist, with several robberies, a prison escape, and—much to the surprise of his jailors—detailed confessions to three murders in two states, was sentenced to life in prison for the kidnapping. Schier confessed. She was sentenced to seven years with a scheduled deportation to Honduras on her release.

With Krist's help, Schier became the first woman named to the Most Wanted list.

294. BALTAZAR GARCIA ESTOLAS, murderer

LISTED: January 3, 1969
CAUGHT: September 3, 1969
DESCRIPTION: Of Filipino descent. Alias: Tomy Isuki Hwamei.

The Likeable Killer. "He is a very likeable boy. We all thought the world of him," Langtry, Texas, postmistress Pearl Dodd Nicholson said after FBI agents arrested the man she knew as Tomy Isuki Hwamei. Estolas had worked under that alias at Nicholson's post office/dairy bar, Jersey Lilly Dairy Bar, as a cook and handyman for two months before an anonymous tip ended his 15 months on the lam. Estolas, it turned out, was not a very likeable boy, but a robber, kidnapper, and murderer. He earned a spot on the FBI's Top Ten list following a May 31, 1968, robbery in Stockton, California. After robbing a clothing store of $2,203, he shot two of the store's employees in the head at close range. As he fled the scene, he wounded two bystanders in a shoot-out with a nearby storekeeper before commandeering a car and taking its two young female occupants hostage. The girls were released several hours later in San Francisco, and Estolas disappeared. He resurfaced at the Texas border, and a local resident recognized him when a San Antonio TV station broadcast Estolas's picture. When agents approached him at the dairy bar, he did not resist arrest, but would not admit to being the Wanted man. Fingerprint comparisons identified him.

INTERESTING FUGITIVE FACT:
Estolas did not use a disguise, but he did tell people he was Hawaiian, not Filipino.

295. BILLIE AUSTIN BRYANT, bank robber

LISTED: January 8, 1969
CAUGHT: January 8, 1969
DESCRIPTION: Born in North Carolina in 1939.

Hello, Bang Bang. Billie Austin Bryant was an upstanding citizen for the first 27 years of his life. He was a family man and a hardworking auto mechanic. Then, in 1966, he was arrested for simple assault during an argument with a business partner. The first arrest was followed by a second arrest the following year. This time Bryant was charged with three armed robberies and sentenced to 18 to 54 years in a Virginia reformatory. His auto shop experience was his ticket out of the pen; he worked as the prison mechanic and used a government car to barrel out of lockup on August 23, 1968. He went right back to bank robbery, holding up a Prince George's County, Maryland, bank on January 8, 1969. He scored $1,800, but was recognized by a teller as a former law-abiding customer. A half hour after the robbery police officers visited the home of Bryant's wife. The fugitive answered the door and opened fire, killing two cops and immediately earning a spot on the Most Wanted list. Later that evening a neighbor alerted police to strange noises coming from the attic of his apartment building. What officers thought was a routine prowler investigation was the collar of a cop-killing criminal. Bryant was arrested in the attic and sentenced to 20 years for his prison break and subsequent bank heist and then sentenced to two consecutive life sentences for the murders. He also had to serve the 17 to 53 years he thought he'd escaped from.

INTERESTING FUGITIVE FACT:
Bryant was not looking for a second chance to escape jail time. Addressing the court before he was sentenced on the murder convictions, Bryant said: "I can't say I'm sorry for what happened to the two men. I feel they brought their death on their own self . . . If killing a man means surviving, I'm afraid I'd have to do it over."

296. BILLY LEN SCHALES, rapist

LISTED: January 27, 1969
CAUGHT: January 30, 1969
DESCRIPTION: Diagnosed as a sexual deviate. Alias: Bill Miller.

Wanted Ad. Billy Len Schales was, by doctors' diagnosis and criminal conviction, a sexual deviate. Previously imprisoned for molesting a young girl, Schales tried to rape a second woman in Houston, Texas, on April 4, 1967. Using the name Bill Miller, Schales answered an apartment rental ad. While touring the building, he attacked the owner, inflicting superficial knife wounds before the woman fought back, cutting Schales. He fled, but his victim identified him, and Schales was named to the Most Wanted list on January 27, 1969. Three days later, Schales was arrested in Bossier City, Louisiana, after a citizen recognized him from a newspaper article in the *Shreveport Times*.

INTERESTING FUGITIVE FACT:
Schales didn't surrender until detectives threatened him with tear gas.

297. THOMAS JAMES LUCAS, bank robbery

LISTED: February 13, 1969
CAUGHT: February 26, 1969
DESCRIPTION: Born in Durham, North Carolina. Alias: Anthony Lee.

Check, Please. Thomas James Lucas joined up with two other gunmen for a West Baltimore, Maryland, bank heist in February 1968. The robbery went smoothly, with the trio netting $22,398, and Lucas went on to hit several more area banks, cooling his heels between holdups with a job as a waiter at a private Washington, D.C., club under the name Anthony Lane. He was named to the Most Wanted list on February 13, 1969, and arrested less than two weeks later, when a citizen spotted him walking in Northwest Washington.

INTERESTING FUGITIVE FACT:
Lucas had committed more violent crimes than bank robbery—he'd served a stretch for murder—but the West Baltimore holdup was the first time he'd crossed the Feds.

298. WARREN DAVID REDDOCK, murderer

LISTED: March 11, 1969
CAUGHT: April 11, 1971
DESCRIPTION: Born in Texas. Alias: Walter P. Thompson.

King Con. Warren David Reddock had been a con man for years. He had 15 felony arrests and five convictions to prove it, but this was his biggest scheme yet. His victim was Chicago accountant Harvey Rosenzwig, who had answered a newspaper ad seeking investment partners for European Arms Corporation, a nonexistent real estate venture. Rosenzwig was an easy mark. He agreed to front the necessary money and quit his job, joining Reddock

on August 14, 1968, for a tour of 1,050 undeveloped acres of land that would become the European Arms Corporation's multimillion-dollar recreation center. All that was necessary to seal the $1.5 million deal was a trip to Monaco to meet the European Arms Corporation CEO. Rosenzwig never made it to Monaco; he got as far as rural Lack County, Illinois, where his decomposed body was found on September 26, 1969.

Reddock didn't make it to Monaco either, but he did use Rosenzwig's credit cards to get to New York, Paris, New Delhi, Hong Kong, and Mexico City before returning to Los Angeles. He continued to hopscotch around the continent—Canada, Mexico, Jamaica—before dropping out of site completely about the time the FBI added his name to the Most Wanted list. It took a *Life* article to smoke him out. A tip to the FBI's San Francisco office led agents to a Pacifica, California, ranch where Reddock, 44, had been working since being named a Most Wanted fugitive.

INTERESTING FUGITIVE FACT:
After running from cops on three continents, Reddock quietly accepted punishment for his crimes, waiving a jury trial. He was convicted of murder by the judge and sentenced to 30 to 50 years.

299. GEORGE EDWARD BLUE, bank robber

LISTED: March 20, 1969
CAUGHT: March 28, 1969

Get a Clue, Blue. George Edward Blue wasn't very good at being a bank robber; he never got much cash and always seemed to get caught. In July 1968, just on parole from one bank robbery conviction, Blue held up an Evansville, Indiana, bank for $5,670. That time he didn't get nabbed right away, and he held up an Atwood, Indiana, bank for another small take in November of that year. The two charges, plus the parole violation earned him a place on the Most Wanted list . . . for exactly eight days. Blue was captured at a Chicago Greyhound bus terminal. When you gotta go to the federal pokey, go Greyhound.

INTERESTING FUGITIVE FACT:
Blue made it easy for authorities. When he was apprehended, Blue was traveling with Mary Ann Downs, a material witness in the Atwood heist.

300. CAMERON DAVID BISHOP, radical

LISTED: April 15, 1969
CAUGHT: March 12, 1975
DESCRIPTION: A member of Students for a Democratic
  Society.

Bishop Takes Fall. Cameron David Bishop first
came to the attention of authorities during the 1968
occupation of a Colorado State University building.
Bishop was charged with burglary for his part in
the protest. A year later, he became the second
American citizen indicted under World War II sabotage laws, for the bombing of four utility towers
providing electric power to Colorado defense
plants. His name and face on the Most Wanted list,
Bishop went underground, surfacing almost six
years later in the parking lot of an East Greenwich,
Rhode Island, bank. An anonymous phone call told
local police to be on the lookout for four armed
men in a car near a bank. Two days later, police
located the car and arrested the men; Bishop was
one of them. He was convicted for three of the four
utility tower bombings, but sentenced to only two
concurrent seven-year prison terms of the possible
120-year punishment.

INTERESTING FUGITIVE FACT:
Bishop was the first radical named to the Most
Wanted list.

301. MARIE DEAN ARRINGTON, murderer

LISTED: May 29, 1969
CAUGHT: December 22, 1971
DESCRIPTION: Described by Florida prosecutors as "a wild,
  cunning animal who will kill and laugh about it." Alias:
  Lola Nero.

The Kind You Don't Bring Home to Mother.
Murder and mayhem was a family business for the
Arringtons. While mom Marie was serving a 20-
year sentence for the July 1964 shooting death of
her husband, her daughter was doing two years
for forgery, and her son, Lloyd, was in for life on
an armed robbery charge. Like any good mother,
Arrington wanted to see her children happy. The
habitual criminal—her record included assault and
battery, robbery, grand larceny, and unlawful
flight—devised a plan to get her children out of
the slammer. She kidnapped a legal secretary from

the Lake County, Florida, public defender's office
and threatened to return the woman "piece by
piece" unless her children were freed. Her
demands were not met. The secretary was found
shot and repeatedly run over in a citrus grove;
Arrington was sentenced to death for the murder.
Following her escape from death row in March
1969 (she used a book of matches to burn the
screen on her cell window), Arrington was named
to the Most Wanted list. She was apprehended two
and a half years later in the New Orleans drug
store she worked at under the name Lola Nero.
She denied her identity, but fingerprint evidence
sent her back to the slammer and she was returned
to death row.

INTERESTING FUGITIVE FACT:
While on the lam in the Big Easy, Arrington picked
up some of the local superstitions. She sent a voodoo
doll with a pin through its chest to the judge who
had sentenced her to death.

302. BENJAMIN HOSKIN PADDOCK, bank robber

LISTED: June 6, 1969
REMOVED FROM LIST: May 5, 1977
DESCRIPTION: Born in Wisconsin. Bald, with nicknames
  including "Big Daddy," "Chrome Dome," and "Old Baldy."
  Alias: Bruce Ericksen.

No Escape. Benjamin Hoskin Paddock spent
eight years on the Most Wanted list for his December 31, 1968, escape from the federal penitentiary
in La Tuna, Texas, where he had been serving 20
years for a bank robbery. His name was removed
from the list in May 1977 not because he was captured, but because the FBI no longer wanted Paddock quite so much, needing room on the list for
other, more dangerous criminals. But authorities
never stopped looking for the fugitive. In early September 1978 FBI agents, acting on a tip, staked out
the Bingo Center in Springfield, Oregon. Bingo
Center owner Bruce Eriksen was lured outside by a
G-man playing the part of an irate customer. Eriksen, it turned out, was just another alias of Paddock's.

INTERESTING FUGITIVE FACT:
Paddock was hiding in plain sight, promoting himself—under the name Ericksen—as the "Bingo King
of the State."

303. FRANCIS LEROY HOHIMER, robber

LISTED: June 20, 1969
CAUGHT: December 21, 1969
DESCRIPTION: Born 1928. Sporting numerous scars and tattoos. Often used the alias John P. Reynolds.

IHOP Away from the FBI.   On September 8, 1967, Francis Leroy Hohimer was arrested in Alton, Illinois, for the possession of burglar's tools and an illegal firearm. He skipped bail in December and was named to the Top Ten list a year and a half later. It wasn't the minor charges that had the FBI after Hohimer. It was where he might have used those tools of the trade—to score $84,000 in jewelry, cash, and traveler's checks in an August 17, 1967, holdup at the Denver home of architect Temple Buell. That take wasn't enough to live a life of leisure. While he ran from the law, moving from his family home in the Midwest to the East Coast, Hohimer held a series of bartending and short order chef jobs. The jobs were good training for his new job in Connecticut, as the owner of an International House of Pancakes (IHOP) in Greenwich. The jobs were also a good trail for the authorities who tracked down "John P. Reynolds," his wife, and their baby daughter two months after the restaurant opened. Hohimer denied his identify until confronted with pictures. "I'm tired of running away," he said.

INTERESTING FUGITIVE FACT:
Hohimer was a family man. He was also supporting four more children living with his parents in the Midwest.

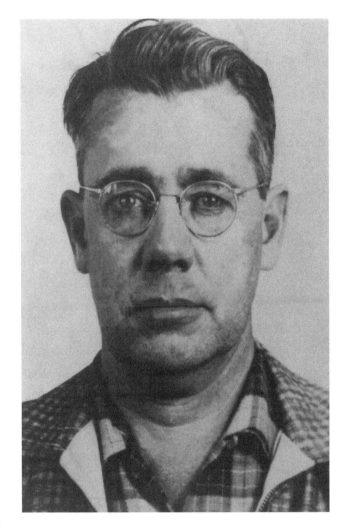

Due to an FBI investigation, Thomas was arrested in Peoria, Illinois.

304. JOSEPH LLOYD THOMAS, bank robber

LISTED: September 2, 1969
CAUGHT: March 8, 1970
DESCRIPTION: Born in Terre Haute, Indiana. Aliases: George Ashley, James Senior.

Second Verse, Same as the First.   Serial bank robber Joseph Lloyd Thomas was named to the Most Wanted list for a second time on September 2, 1969. The first time he'd been so honored, following a Louisiana bank robbery, he'd stayed one step ahead of authorities for just two months and ended up with an eight-year prison stay. This time he was more successful. He'd robbed a Terre Haute, Indiana, bank in February 1969, making off with $22,072, and here he was, more than a year later, sitting in a Mr. Donut in Peoria, Illinois, drinking coffee. The FBI never revealed who tipped them off to Thomas's whereabouts (perhaps Thomas should have picked a better hiding place than a donut shop), but agents Elias Williams, Jerome Di Franco, and John F. Leuck were lying in wait when Thomas left the shop. Thomas was stripped of his snub-nosed revolver and taken into custody.

INTERESTING FUGITIVE FACT:
The same three agents who arrested Thomas would also be responsible for the capture of Most Wanted fugitive WILLIAM HERRON (#333) in Peoria, Illinois, five years later.

FUGITIVES
OF THE 1970s

Introduction

At the beginning of the 1970s, the FBI's Top Ten list was starting to look like a college yearbook. That's because the FBI, at the tail end of the 1960s, started turning its attention to political revolutionaries who, in protest of the Vietnam War and other perceived injustices, started bombing and robbing and inciting riots. The only problem: Young political dissenters weren't easy to catch. Revolutionaries had a network of underground supporters who would gladly hide a brother or sister protester and wouldn't talk to an FBI agent if their lives depended on it. "In the new fugitive subculture," wrote J. Anthony Lukas in *The New York Times Magazine* in 1970, "a wanted poster in your local post office is a status symbol. But the ultimate accolade, of course, is a place on the '10 most wanted' list."

In the early 1970s, the Ten Most Wanted list was populated by the kinds of criminals that would continue to populate the list for decades to come: serial killers, drug traffickers, and terrorists. The crimes (and times) had become more serious. While a series of car thefts could have propelled you to the Ten Most Wanted list back in the 1950s, in the 1970s you had to hijack a plane, run a drug ring, or kill a bunch of strangers to even be considered. "We're after the best fugitives," Raymond A. Connolly, head of the FBI's fugitive unit in the late 1970s, told the Associated Press in 1979. "We select the ones who are most violent prone [sic] and who have demonstrated high mobility."

Notable fugitives in this decade include political revolutionaries Larry Plamondon (#307), Rap Brown (#308), Angela Davis (#309), Bernardine Dohrn (#314), Katherine Ann Power (#315) and Susan Saxe (#316); Leonard Peltier (#335); radical bomber Carlos Alberto Torres (#356); and serial killer Ted Bundy (#360).

305. JAMES JOHN BYRNES, armed robber

LISTED: January 6, 1970
CAUGHT: April 17, 1970
DESCRIPTION: Born February 1928 in Los Angeles, California.

Flight Risk. Jim Byrnes had two useful talents: He knew how to play jazz riffs on a tenor saxophone, and he knew how to fly a plane. He used the former talent to make some money between robberies; he used the latter to flee from the law when his armed stickups went awry. Byrnes was in and out of lockups in Iowa, Oklahoma, and Kansas over the years, and it finally came to a head on January 26, 1969. That's when a Kansas cop pulled over Brynes's car, wanting to question Byrnes and his companion about a supermarket heist in Wichita the previous day. Byrnes knew he had probably logged one parole violation too many. He and his accomplice smacked the cop around, threw him in the trunk, then drove to an airport in Stafford, Kansas, where Byrnes commandeered a small airplane and made his escape.

Smart escape trick. Unfortunately for Byrnes, the police were waiting for him when he landed in El Reno, Oklahoma. The stunt earned him a 15-year jail term.

With nothing to lose, Byrnes decided to pull the same trick again. On September 26, 1969, he and an inmate named Ronald Archer got the drop on the warden at the St. John, Kansas, county jail. One stolen car and one kidnapping victim later, Byrnes found himself at an airport in West Plains, Missouri, where he stole yet another plane. This time the trick worked. Authorities found the stolen plane in Des Moines, but no Byrnes. He was named to the Top Ten list the following January, becoming the first most wanted fugitive of the 1970s. Thanks to a speedy FBI investigation, Byrnes was arrested in Huntington Beach, California. He returned to face charges of robbery, kidnapping, grand theft auto, and a charge not exactly common among Top Tenners—interstate transportation of stolen airplanes.

INTERESTING FUGITIVE FACT:
Byrnes wasn't just messing around with his horn. He was considered an accomplished jazz musician.

306. EDMUND JAMES DEVLIN, bank robber

LISTED: March 20, 1970
CAUGHT: August 15, 1970
DESCRIPTION: Born in Connecticut.

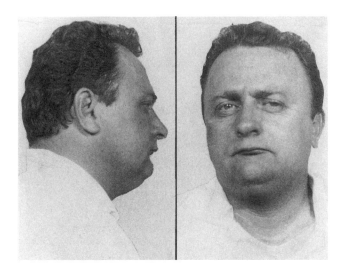

Due to an FBI investigation, Devlin was arrested in Manchester, New Hampshire.

The $105,816 Ticket. Ed Devlin was the leader of a gang of Irish bank robbers who worked the Connecticut area during the late 1960s, their biggest heist grabbing New England headlines in early January 1969. That's when Devlin, along with gang members Edward Reed and Ralph Masselli, walked into a Fairfield County Trust Company branch, waved guns around, and walked back out with $105,816—an extremely impressive amount for a small takeover team. The FBI managed to trace the getaway car back to Devlin, however, and the heist landed him on the Top Ten list in late March 1970. (Reed and Masselli was arrested soon after the car was discovered.) Five months later, Devlin were arrested in downtown Manchester, New Hampshire. He was unarmed and surrendered without a fight.

INTERESTING FUGITIVE FACT:
In 1977 Devlin keeled over and died during a prison basketball game.

307. LAWRENCE ROBERT PLAMONDON, radical bomber

LISTED: May 5, 1970
CAUGHT: July 23, 1970
DESCRIPTION: Born in Traverse City, Michigan, in 1946. Plamondon has reportedly been active in a "hippie" commune known as "Trans-Love Energies" in Ann Arbor, Michigan, said to be a source of narcotics traffic. Acquaintances

describe his normal appearance as dirty and unkempt and his living, eating, and hygienic habits as poor. He reportedly usually dressed in "hippie" style, but may adopt neater dressing habits to evade capture. He is said to enjoy living in a communal manner and to have a pronounced persecution complex. Plamondon reportedly possesses a rifle and shotgun, has allegedly used dynamite for a crime for which he is sought, and should be considered very dangerous.

An Unfortunate Can of Beer. In the summer of 1970 Larry "Pun" Plamondon was happy and relaxed. Sure, he had been named to the Ten Most Wanted list in May, but the G-men had been after him for eight months, and they still hadn't caught up with him. Plamondon was the Defense Minister of the White Panther Party and had pulled off the brazen bombing of a CIA office in Ann Arbor, Michigan. This was in addition to at least seven other bombings of government buildings since 1968. To the burgeoning underground movement Plamondon was a revolutionary hero, and his star only rose after he was named to the Top Ten. So he and two other Panther officials, speeding in a Volkswagen bus through Mackinac County, Michigan, decided to do a little celebrating. They picked up a six pack of beer and started to drain them as they drove, whipping the empties out of the window.

Bad move. A state trooper noticed the airborne can and promptly pulled Plamondon over. He asked for papers, and Plamondon and his crew produced fakes. The trooper, however, let them go with a warning. A short while later, the trooper realized he had a made a mistake; an alert was sent over the national police network, saying that Plamondon had been seen in the general area. The trooper radioed ahead to the next town, St. Ignace, and told them he had stopped "two suspicious-looking hippies and another guy." That other guy was Plamondon. Though his Wanted poster featured him with a bushy mop of hair and thick beard, he had had his hair trimmed and beard shaved after making the Top Ten.

Plamondon was caught driving on U.S. Route 2 minutes after that state trooper called ahead. Plamondon had reportedly told his friends: "I'm not going to be apprehended. The press release that the FBI is sending out about me being a crazed criminal is just setting it up so they can be justified in killing me when they find me." But that's not what happened. Even though he had a loaded gun and rifle in the car, he offered no resistance and was taken in peacefully.

308. HUBERT GEROID BROWN, revolutionary

LISTED: May 6, 1970
CAUGHT: October 16, 1971
DESCRIPTION: Born October 1943 in Baton Rouge, Louisiana. Six feet three inches tall, 180 to 185 pounds, with brown eyes and black hair. At times he has worn glasses.

Rap Brown Goes Down. "Get yourself some guns," Hubert Brown told his audience, "and burn this town down." It was July 24, 1967, and Brown—better known as Rap Brown, a famous spokesperson for a militant fringe of the late 1960s Black Power movement—was making a speech to black residents of Cambridge, Maryland. "We must wage guerrilla war on the honkie white man." Then he mentioned a local elementary school and told his listeners that they should have "burned it down long ago."

Apparently some of Brown's listeners took his advice to heart. By dawn the next morning, the school was ablaze. The fire spread throughout two city blocks, destroying much of the black section of town. That event sparked a series of ugly confrontations with law enforcement. Brown was charged with inciting a riot and arson and three years later failed to appear for his trial in Ellicott City, Maryland, after being freed on bail. In the meantime, Brown had also racked up indictments for illegally transporting a gun and "intimidating an agent of the FBI." By May 1970 the former chairman of the Student Nonviolent Coordinating Committee (SNCC) found himself as a special addition to the Ten Most Wanted list. In special cases the FBI felt it necessary to expand the list, which is how Rap Brown became number 11 on the Top Ten list. This wasn't the only thing that made Brown a special member of the list. The majority of Most Wanted fugitives are unknown to the general public—the idea being that famous criminals will already have the eyes of the nation on the lookout for them. But the FBI apparently felt that Brown was such a threat, they needed to use any means at their disposal to bring him in.

Upon his announcement, rumors abounded about Brown. Some said that he split the United States and defected to Cuba, where he was holed up with Communist groups. Other said he lammed it to Canada or Algeria. Another popular theory had it that Brown was killed in a car bomb explosion that took the lives of two fellow revolutionaries in Bel Air, Maryland, on March 9, 1970. But the real answer came at 2 A.M. on October 16, 1971, more than 15 months after Brown made the Top Ten. A telephone tipster told the NYPD that someone was sticking up a saloon, the Red Carpet Lounge, on West 85th Street. The cops arrived to find four armed robbers running out of the bar. The bullets started flying, and two patrolmen caught bullets. The four gunmen raced across the street and into an apartment building. The police gave pursuit and managed to subdue three of the robbers on a staircase. The fourth made it to the roof and hid on top of a shanty that housed the apartment's elevator. Patrolman Ralph Mannetta ran up to the roof, but didn't see anybody at first. He then made a running leap over an air-conditioning duct and quickly scanned the area. That's when he spotted the fourth gunman hiding on top of the shanty. Mannetta fired three bullets from his service revolver and struck the hiding robber in the liver and abdomen. The wounded man rolled off the shanty and was subsequently rushed into emergency surgery, and only then was his identity revealed. It was Rap Brown, federal fugitive.

Brown received five to 15 years for charges relating to the gunfight. He was paroled in October 1976, then in 1983 changed his name to Jamil Abdullah al-Amin, converting to Islam and disavowing all of his previous violent acts.

INTERESTING FUGITIVE FACT:
Nearly 30 years after making the Top Ten list, Brown—now al-Amin—was accused of murder. Brown allegedly shot an Atlanta sheriff's deputy three times after he tried to serve Brown with a warrant for receiving stolen property and impersonating a police officer. Brown's defense lawyer claimed it was a case of mistaken identity, and Brown complained that the charge was merely the latest in a life-long government conspiracy against him. In March 2002 Brown was convicted of murder and faces the death penalty.

309. ANGELA YVONNE DAVIS, revolutionary

LISTED: August 18, 1970
CAUGHT: October 13, 1970
DESCRIPTION: Born January 26, 1944, in Birmingham,

Alabama. Five feet eight inches tall, 145 pounds, with brown eyes and black hair. Scars and marks: a small scar on both knees. She occasionally wears "granny-type" glasses and styles her hair in a natural "Afro" fashion and has been known by the nickname "Tamu."

In Contempt. James McClain, a black convict accused of stabbing a prison guard at San Quentin, stood trial on August 7, 1970. Also on the second floor of the Marin County Hall of Justice were Ruchell Magee and William Christmas, two convict witnesses. Magee was on the stand, testifying, when suddenly a 17-year-old high school student from Pasadena stood up and pointed a .38 at Judge Harold Haley. "This is it," said Jonathan Jackson. "Everybody freeze." Jackson tossed a pistol to McClain, and then another gun to Magee, who ran another gun out to Christmas, who was out in the hallway. It was the start of a brazen jailbreak, and it was moments away from turning bloody.

"Call off your dogs, pig, or we'll kill everybody in the room," threatened McClain over the phone to the Marin County sheriff. Five hostages—Judge Haley, A.D.A. Gary Thomas, and three female jurors—were selected and ushered outside, guns to their heads. Judge Haley had a sawed-off 12-gauge shotgun pressed up against his neck and held in place with tape. The party of nine made it to a getaway van in the parking lot then started to drive away. John Matthews, a guard at San Quentin, stood in the van's path, armed with a rifle. What followed was a grisly, bullet-punctuated gunfight, both inside and outside the van. Someone from the front seat of the van fired first, and Matthews returned fire. The van stopped. Inside, A.D.A. Thomas took advantage of the situation, wrestling a gun away from his captors and starting to shoot them. Bullets ricocheted inside the van as the escapees returned fire. When police finally surrounded the van and opened the back doors, there were bodies everywhere. Jackson, McClain, and Christmas were dead. Judge Haley was also dead, apparently due to a blast from the shotgun taped to his neck. Escapee Magee and Thomas were seriously wounded, and one of the female jurors suffered a bullet wound in her upper arm. Only two out of the nine walked out of the van without a scratch. It was a blood-soaked escape attempt, one of the bloodiest in U.S. history.

So what did it have to do with Angela Davis, a black intellectual and former UCLA philosophy instructor?

Davis, only 26, was an avowed Communist and vocal supporter of Black Power who grew up watching African Americans suffer at the brutal hands of racism. One of her childhood friends was among the four girls who died when the Ku Klux Klan bombed a black church in 1963. Her beliefs eventually led to her dismissal from UCLA in 1969 and an empassioned love affair—through correspondence only—with George Jackson, a black radical and convict at San Quentin. Jackson's younger brother, Jonathan, became Davis's "bodyguard." After the bloody break from the Marin County Hall of Justice, the weapons smuggled in by the younger Jackson were traced back to Angela Davis, who according to the FBI, had purchased them slowly over a two-and-a-half year period. On August 18, 1970, Davis was named to the Top Ten list, an announcement that shocked much of the country, but also signaled that the FBI was indeed chasing a very different kind of fugitive in the new decade. Car thieves and bank robbers were being cleared in favor of radicals and revolutionaries—and, apparently, scholars and thinkers. Meanwhile, signs started appearing in homes and businesses across the country: "Angela, sister, you are welcome in this house."

Meanwhile, Davis hid underground with various radical groups, planning to make her eventual escape to Cuba. But the FBI traced her movements, and Davis was arrested at a motel room in New York City. After 16 months in prison, an all-white jury found her not guilty of all charges, and Davis later wrote about her Top Ten experience in her autobiography. Today Davis is a tenured professor at the University of California at Santa Cruz and author of many books on prison reform.

INTERESTING FUGITIVE FACT:
Radical views aside, Davis was noted at the time for being the most attractive Top Tenner in the program's history. "I'll wager," said one anonymous FBI agent to *Newsweek* magazine in 1970, "that half of the tall, good-looking girls with Afros from Maine to California will be under some kind of surveillance by law officers in the next few weeks."

310. DWIGHT ALLEN ARMSTRONG, radical bomber

LISTED: September 4, 1970
REMOVED FROM LIST: April 1, 1976
DESCRIPTION: Born in 1950 in Madison, Wisconsin.

311. KARLETON LEWIS ARMSTRONG, radical bomber

LISTED: September 4, 1970
CAUGHT: February 16, 1972
DESCRIPTION: Born in 1948 in Madison, Wisconsin.

312. DAVID SYLVAN FINE, radical bomber

LISTED: September 4, 1970
CAUGHT: January 8, 1976
DESCRIPTION: Born in 1951 in Wilmington, Delaware.

313. LEO FREDERICK BURT, radical bomber

LISTED: September 4, 1970
REMOVED FROM LIST: April 7, 1976
DESCRIPTION: Born April 18, 1948, in Darby, Pennsylvania. Five feet 11 inches, 185 pounds, with hazel eyes and brown hair. Occupations: laborer, watchman. Remarks: reportedly wears mustache and beard, hair worn long in back.

The New Year's Gang. Sterling Hall at the University of Wisconsin was the home of the physics department and the U.S. Army's Mathematics Research Center. To the white radical left of the late 1960s it was an extremely desirable target. "If the military suppresses life and freedom," the radical saying went, "then we must suppress the military." At 3:40 A.M. on the morning of August 24, 1970, an anonymous phone call was placed to Madison, Wisconsin, police. Sterling Hall was going to be destroyed, the voice said. Two minutes later, it was. A van packed with fertilizer and fuel oil was detonated, and the resulting explosion completely gutted the $8 million research building. Inside the building was a 33-year-old postgraduate researcher named Robert Fassnacht, whose body was found floating in a submerged basement room. (A handful of others suffered minor injuries.) The blast was so intense, pieces of the van were found three blocks away—on top of an eight-story building. The explosion happened only four months after the National Guard killed four students at Kent State University in Ohio. Suddenly America's college campuses were beginning to resemble battlegrounds.

Within a few weeks of intensive investigating, the FBI had the names of university students who were both avowed leftists and who had suddenly disappeared in the days following the bombing. There were four: university student Karleton Armstrong, 22; his brother Dwight, 19, a high school dropout; David Sylvan Fine, 18, an editor at the school paper; and Leo Burt, 22, a writer for the school paper. A letter was discovered, allegedly from two of the suspects, that said the bombing was "a conscious action taken in solidarity with the Viet Cong, the Tupamaros, the Cuban people, and all other heroic figures against U.S. imperialism." It would later be discovered that these four called themselves the "New Year's Gang," and were responsible for at least three other minor bombing incidents on campus. J. Edgar Hoover

Burt was removed from the list when it was felt he no longer fit the Top Ten criteria.

personally named the four students to the Top Ten list as "special additions" on September 4, 1970, and the Top Ten list swelled to 14 fugitives.

The hunt for the New Year's Gang ended in mixed results. Karleton Armstrong was arrested by the Royal Canadian Mounted Police in Toronto a year and a half later, and was sent back to Wisconsin to face a 14-year sentence for arson and second-degree murder. Much of what is known about the plot is thanks to prison interviews with Karelton, who was happy to talk about why they set the bomb, but careful not to reveal the locations of his brother or other members of the gang. "Army Math was always the ultimate target in Madison," he explained. "For two years, ever since its relationship to secret projects like the electronic battlefield and the air war in Vietnam was exposed, every demonstration was directed at removing Army Math."

David Fine stayed on the lam until January 8, 1976, when he was finally arrested in San Rafael, California. He was sentenced to seven years for third-degree murder, but ended up serving only three. He earned a law degree in 1984 and today lives somewhere in the Pacific Northwest.

The other two members of the New Year's Gang managed to escape the clutches of the Top Ten list entirely. The moment that David Fine easily made bail, the FBI decided that Dwight Armstrong and Leo Burt really didn't belong on the list any longer. They were still very much fugitives, just not Ten Most Wanted fugitives. Dwight was arrested in Canada not long after his dismissal from the list and ended up serving seven years. Leo Burt had promptly disappeared on September 4, 1970, and hasn't been seen since. With the 2002 roundup of the last remaining Symbionese Liberation Army members in hiding, Burt became pretty much the last revolutionary fugitive still at large. If anybody sees Leo, be sure to tell him it's okay to come out now.

INTERESTING FUGITIVE FACT:
Today Karl Armstrong operates a campus juice stand a few blocks away from Sterling Hall at the University of Wisconsin; his brother Dwight drives a cab in the area.

314. BERNARDINE RAE DOHRN, revolutionary

LISTED: October 14, 1970
REMOVED FROM LIST: December 7, 1973
DESCRIPTION: Born January 12, 1942, in Chicago, Illinois. Five feet five inches tall, 125 pounds, with brown hair and brown eyes. Dohrn may resist arrest. She has been associated with persons who advocate the use of explosives, and she may have acquired firearms. She should be considered very dangerous.

Weatherwoman. "We were in an airplane, and we went up and down the aisle 'borrowing' food from people's plates," said Bernardine Dohrn at one Weathermen meeting in Flint, Michigan, in 1969. "They didn't know we were Weathermen; they just knew we were crazy. That's what we're about, being crazy motherfuckers and scaring the shit out of honky America." Clearly it was working. By late 1970 the FBI had directed a serious amount of its investigative efforts toward breaking up radical groups like the Weathermen, a militant revolutionary group that split from the Students for a Democratic Society (SDS) in the late 1960s and staged riots to protest the Vietnam War, most notably the infamous riot that disrupted the 1968 Democratic Convention in Chicago. Dorhn was an outspoken member of the Weathermen who came to the table with a law degree and a forceful yet eloquent way of imparting her group's views; by 1970 she would become their de facto leader.

On April 2, 1970, Dohrn and 11 fellow Weatherpeople were indicted on charges of crossing state lines to incite riots. Dohrn immediately went into hiding, and the indictments kept piling up: unlawful possession of firearms, conspiracy to transport explosives across state lines, and unlawful flight to avoid prosecution. That last one qualified her for the Top Ten list, and she was named to it on October 14, 1970, becoming only the fourth woman on the list in its 20-year history. Dohrn responded by declaring war on the American government. It wasn't the usual response from a federal fugitive, but then again, Bernardine Dohrn wasn't your usual federal fugitive.

In the end, though, Dohrn would be removed from the list when the bombing conspiracy case against the Weathermen fell apart—but not in the way you might think. According to one U.S. attorney, successfully prosecuting the Weathermen would have meant that the FBI would have to reveal certain investigative techniques, which would jeopardize national security. Even though Dohrn was taken off the list on December 7, 1973, she stayed hidden until 1982. Today she is the director of the Children and Family Justice Center at the Northwestern School of Law.

INTERESTING FUGITIVE FACT:
According to a profile in *Esquire* magazine, in eighth grade Dohrn had a huge crush on Elvis Presley and plastered her bedroom wall with his photos.

315. KATHERINE ANN POWER, revolutionary, bank robber

LISTED: October 17, 1970
REMOVED FROM LIST: June 15, 1984
DESCRIPTION: Born January 25, 1949, in Denver, Colorado. Five feet 140 to 150 pounds, with light brown hair (may be dyed black) and hazel eyes. Alias: "Helen."

316. SUSAN EDITH SAXE, revolutionary, bank robber

LISTED: October 17, 1970
CAUGHT: March 27, 1975
DESCRIPTION: Born January 18, 1949, in Albany, New York. Five feet five inches tall, 160 pounds, with brown hair and hazel eyes. Alias: "Susie."

Saxe and Power. It was like Bonnie and Clyde—two young lovers meet and decide to rob banks—only updated for the 1960s. In this case the lovers were radical lesbians, and the bank loot was meant to fund revolutionary operations. Susan Saxe, an English major, met sociology major Katherine Ann Power at Brandeis University, fell in love, and soon joined various leftist groups such as Women's Liberation and the Students for a Democratic Society (SDS). After spring 1970, when President Nixon ordered the invasion of Cambodia, talk turned into serious action. In August 1970 Power and Saxe raided an arsenal in Massachusetts and stole a cache of automatic weapons; on September 1 Saxe was linked to a $6,240 bank robbery in Philadelphia. The plan was to steal enough money to buy explosives, and the explosives would be used to melt the wheels of trains carrying weapons to the U.S. Army. Then the weapons would be given to the Black Panthers, and a major victory against the "imperialist U.S." would be theirs.

On September 23, 1970, Power, Saxe, and three ex-convicts they'd befriended—they were at Brandeis as part of an inmate education program—pulled a bloody robbery at the State Street Bank and Trust Company in Brighton, Massachusetts, stealing

$26,000 from the frightened employees. During the getaway 42-year-old Boston cop Walter A. Schroeder, a father of nine, tried to stop the fleeing radicals and received a burst of automatic gunfire across his chest. Schroeder died 24 hours later. By that time cops had captured the image of one of the robbers on the bank's closed-circuit cameras. By nightfall all three of the male bandits were under arrest, and Saxe and Power were on the run. They were named to the Top Ten on October 17, 1970. With their additions, the Ten Most Wanted list swelled to an all-time high of 16 fugitives—half of them being young radicals.

Both women stayed free for abnormally long periods of time. Saxe lasted five years before she was arrested at the corner of 12th and Chestnut Streets in downtown Philadelphia. A police officer recognized her from a photo distributed by the FBI the same day—the FBI had received a tip that Saxe was in the

Saxe was arrested in Philadelphia, Pennsylvania, after a Philadelphia officer recognized her from a photo distributed by the FBI the same day.

area. She was eventually convicted of bank robbery and manslaughter and was released from prison in 1982. Today she works at a Jewish charity in the Philadelphia area.

Power was removed from the list when it was felt she no longer fit the Top Ten criteria and remained hidden until 1993, when she finally turned herself in, astonishing many—including Power's new husband. Finally the world learned where Power had hidden all of those years. First she spent almost a decade in various feminist communes—not exactly the easiest group for the FBI to penetrate—then reinvented herself as "Alice Metzinger" and settled in Oregon as a gourmet chef. But the past ate away at her, and finally, after 24 years on the run, Power gave herself up. She apologized to the family of the slain Boston cop and was sent to prison on charges of bank robbery and manslaughter.

INTERESTING FUGITIVE FACT:
Power was the winner of a Betty Crocker Homemaker award in high school, and Saxe was an honor student at Brandeis.

317. MACE BROWN, professional killer

LISTED: October 20, 1972
KILLED: April 18, 1973
DESCRIPTION: Born February 21, 1943, in Birmingham, Alabama. Six feet one inch tall, 165 pounds, with black hair, brown eyes, a slender build, and medium complexion. Occupations: clerk, cook, salesman. Scars and marks: scar on left forearm, hernia scars, scar on right thigh. Reportedly well-spoken and very neat in appearance. Aliases: Macee Brown Jr., Mace Brown Jr. Macedo Brown, Macy Brown, Marc Brown, Philip M. Brown, Maurice Jackson, Vernell Pete Reed.

The Real Super Fly. Mace Brown carried an attaché case full of African-styled dashikis, but he wasn't the natty fashion salesman from Harlem he claimed to be. When he stayed at the Charter House Motel in Washington, D.C., in late October 1970, it wasn't because he was planning to ply his wares at area shops. He was in that $17-a-night room waiting to kill someone. That someone was Charles "Popeye" Hailes, star witness in a headline-grabbing trial that threatened to bring down a 55-member, multimillion-dollar heroin operation. Brown was handed a shoebox full of money, and in return his employers wanted "Popeye" Hailes in a box in the ground.

On the morning of October 21 Hailes left his apartment building on the 2300 block of Lincoln Drive to take his wife to work. Brown walked up behind him, pressed a .32 caliber gun to the back of Hailes's head, then pulled the trigger. Hailes's wife screamed in terror, which got the attention of a plainclothes cop who was walking down the street. Brown hopped into his rented green Javelin and sped away. The make and model of the car hit police radio, and Mace Brown was in cuffs within 20 minutes. Brown refused to identify his employers, but it became known that whoever had hired Brown also gave him two more names to put on his "People I Must Kill" list: the head prosecutor and judge in the heroin trial. Brown was tried, then sentenced to death in the electric chair on March 24, 1971.

Brown didn't seem particularly worried about it, though. Maybe that's because he knew help was on the way. On October 2, 1972, while guards were watching *Monday Night Football,* Brown and seven other inmates used smuggled saws to make their way out of their cells, climbing up to the roof to wait for reinforcements. Two cars pulled up outside the jail. Brown and his men used a fire hose to lower themselves to ground level, then hopped into the car. A trained killer who had threatened to snuff a U.S. attorney and judge was now free on the streets. The professional killer—who was considered an urban folk hero to some hoodlum wannabes—disappeared. Eighteen days later, the FBI put him on the Top Ten list. The following April, Mace Brown suddenly resurfaced. But it wasn't due to the investigative efforts of the FBI. Brown, along with two accomplices, decided to knock over a Chase Manhattan Bank branch in New York. The heist turned ugly. Shortly after police arrived, Brown decided to take hostages and shoot his way out. The gun battle didn't turn out the way Brown had expected. He was shot dead by the NYPD.

INTERESTING FUGITIVE FACT:
Brown racked up his first convictions at age 13, when he stole a car, then a few weeks later stabbed a kid with an ice pick.

318. HERMAN BELL, cop killer

LISTED: May 9, 1973
CAUGHT: September 2, 1973
DESCRIPTION: Born in Mississippi in 1958.

Scoping Pigs. The Black Panthers were never afraid to take it up a notch when confronting police officers. But a Panther offshoot called the Black Liberation Army allegedly took it one step further. According to some law enforcement officials, the BLA didn't want to wait to be confronted by police. They advocated provoking fights with police—in fact, they advocated going out and assassinating police officers at random. The practice was known as "scoping pigs." On the night of May 21, 1971, New York police officers Joseph Piagentini and Waverly Jones rushed to answer a distress call at a Harlem housing project and received a volley of bullets in their back. Their assailants continued to fire, even after the cops hit the sidewalk. The police-issue revolvers were taken from the dying officers, and then three gunmen ran away into the night.

Officer Jones's stolen .38 caliber revolver surfaced a few months later in San Francisco. It was one of three guns found in the car of Anthony Bottom and Albert Washington, who tried to kill a San Francisco patrolman, then were caught after a violent crash and gun battle. It didn't take long to connect Bottom and Washington with the slayings of Piagentini and Jones, and further investigations revealed the identity of the third gunman: Herman Bell, a high-ranking member of the BLA. Six months later, it happened again in New York. Two cops named Gregory Foster and Rocco Laurie were shot to death by three black gunmen in Manhattan. And Bell again was thought to be among the cop killers. Bell was indicted on murder charges, but managed to elude the law. (Bell only seemed to come in contact with the police when he planned to kill one of its members.) On May 9, 1973, Bell was named to the Top Ten, the first addition to the list that year.

Like Mace Brown the year before, it would be a bank robbery that would end Bell's run from the law. But not one that Bell perpetrated. New Orleans cops investigating a bank heist came across a witness who described a man fitting Herman Bell's description hanging out at a local BLA office. Bell's movements were tracked, and on September 2 he was surrounded by FBI agents and New Orleans police officers while stopped at a traffic light. Bell, the suspect cop slayer, surrendered without a fight. He was later sentenced to two consecutive terms of 25 to life for the murders of Piagentini and Jones.

INTERESTING FUGITIVE FACT:
In 1989 Bell—one of the so-called New York Three—filed a lawsuit claiming that he, Bottoms, and Washington were innocent of the cop killings. Their lawyers claimed that ballistics evidence was wrong, and that guns seized in the San Francisco shoot-out could not be linked with guns used in the murders of Piagentini and Jones. The challenge was shot down by the New York County Supreme Court in 1998.

319. TWYMON FORD MYERS, armed robber, cop killer

LISTED: September 28, 1973
KILLED: November 14, 1973
DESCRIPTION: Born November 27, 1950, in the Bronx, New York. Five feet seven inches to five feet eight inches tall, 170 to 180 pounds, with black hair and brown eyes. Myers allegedly has been in possession of firearms in the past. He reportedly is closely associated with persons who are heavily armed with explosives and a variety of guns. Consider extremely dangerous. Aliases: Earl Coleman, Twyman Ford Meyers, Earl Myers, Miles Twyman, "Twine."

A Fatal Fare. Twymon Myers was another professed member of the Black Liberation Army (BLA; see #318, HERMAN BELL) who was accused of at least three bank robberies and one murder during the early 1970s. The FBI's bulletin on Myers wasn't shy about making connections: "[Myers] has been intimately associated with others who have been involved in assaults upon police, killings of police officers and bank robberies." The first in the series of crimes that would ultimately plant Myers on the Top Ten list was the August 4, 1971, heist of a social club in New York City. Myers and his accomplices didn't think to bring along a getaway car; instead, after knocking over the club, the bandits commandeered a passing taxi. Police gave pursuit, and a gun battle broke out, resulting in the death of the innocent cab driver. The following March Myers was connected with a bank job at the Bankers Trust Company in the Bronx, which resulted in yet another gun battle with the NYPD. The follow year the armed robbery of a Queens savings and loan (on April 10) and a Bronx bank (July 18) were also thought to be the handiwork of Myers and his band of BLA cronies. Myers was named to the Top Ten in late September.

A month and a half later, the FBI and NYPD had Myers cornered in an apartment building believed to be a popular hiding spot of BLA members. Once Myers saw he was surrounded, he whipped out a 9 mm pistol and started blasting away. Two police officers were wounded, but so was Myers—fatally. He died at the scene.

INTERESTING FUGITIVE FACT:
Before he started shooting at cops and robbing banks, Myers toiled as a laborer and garment worker.

320. RONALD HARVEY, murderer

LISTED: December 7, 1973
CAUGHT: March 27, 1974
DESCRIPTION: Born July 1, 1940, in Philadelphia, Pennsylvania. Five feet 11 inches tall, 195 to 210 pounds, with black hair and brown eyes. Occupations: baker, butcher, delivery man. Aliases; Harry Harvey, Clifford Jeffries, Ronald Woods, Ronnie Woods, Ronald 14X, Ronald 13X.

321. SAMUEL RICHARD CHRISTIAN, drug dealer, murderer

LISTED: December 7, 1973
CAUGHT: December 12, 1973
DESCRIPTION: Born March 20, 1938, in Philadelphia, Pennsylvania. Five feet 10 inches, 184 ponds, with black hair and brown eyes. May have Afro haircut, long sideburns, and a mustache. Occupations: baker, salesman. Aliases: Samuel Bay, Sam Bazahad, Richard Bey, Samuel Bey, Sulieman Bey, Richard Carter, Sam Christie, Dave Chenault, Benjamin Kyler, Samuel 6X.

The Black Mafia. At its most powerful, Philadelphia's so-called Black Mafia controlled 80 percent of the drug trafficking in that beleaguered city. It was founded out of the remnants of black South Philly drug gangs in 1968 by Samuel Christian, along with Ronald Harvey and others. Over the next decade, police say, the Black Mafia—originally called "Black, Inc." by its members—orchestrated drug deals, murders, prostitution, numbers games, and extortion schemes, all of which resulted in the deaths of at least 50 people. (In the 1980s the sons of the Black Mafia formed the Junior Black Mafia, repeating their fathers' crimes and schemes, but in an even more bloodthirsty manner.)

Over the years both men were linked to a host of crimes: armed robberies, shoot-outs with police officers, and even outright assassinations of gangland rivals. What finally brought Christian and Harvey to the attention of the FBI's Ten Most Wanted list? According to his FBI rap sheet, Christian was allegedly responsible for a) a 1971 New Jersey armed robbery that ended in a high-speed chase and a shoot-out with police, b) a 1971 record store robbery that ended with one dead New York police officer, and finally, c) the gangland hit of drug dealer Tyron Palmer, who was partying at Club Harlem in Atlantic City at the time. Five people died during that last shooting spree—including Palmer—and four others were hospitalized.

Meanwhile, his business associate, Ronald Harvey, was just as busy. The Black Mafia was ostensibly connected with the Nation of Islam, but Orthodox (Traditional) Muslims were upset that Christian and Harvey were corrupting the church with smack, scams, and slayings. Among the most vocal critics were the Hanafi Muslim sect, based in Washington, D.C. Harvey responded to the critiques by taking a posse of gunmen down to D.C. and killing seven members of the Hanafi sect—including four children, who were drowned, and a nine-year-old, who was executed at point-blank range. (The other victims were adults.) At the time it was the largest mass murder in D.C.'s history, and D.C. is widely acknowledged by law enforcement officials as the murder capital of the world.

As if the blood washing over the streets of Philly, D.C., and New York weren't enough, Christian and Harvey were also linked to the June 8, 1973, murder of Major Coxson, an alleged South Jersey gang lord, onetime candidate for mayor of Camden, New Jersey, and friend of boxing titan Muhammad Ali. Coxson, along with his common-law wife and her daughter, died in the attack. A few months later, Christian and Harvey were named to the FBI's Top Ten list.

Fortunately, their collective stays on the list were relatively short. Christian was picked up in Detroit, Michigan, after just five days, and Harvey was nabbed four months later in the company of Black Muslims in Chicago, Illinois. "Running is a bitch," said Harvey to his captors. Christian was finally convicted of the 1971 record store murder and received a 15-year to life sentence. Harvey's trial was another matter. The trial of the grisliest mass murder in D.C. made headlines for weeks, and eventually Harvey was given a sentence as serious as the crime: 140 years.

INTERESTING FUGITIVE FACT:
Nearly 30 years later, Christian was again sought by

the FBI, this time for violating his parole. But when the FBI and Philly PD picked up the former godfather of black crime, Christian was described by one FBI agent as "a shadow of his former self." At 62 years of age Christian was hooked on smack and looked bedraggled, with unkempt gray hair and a mangy beard. Still, noted the *Philadelphia Daily News,* he was still a suspect in a pile of unsolved murders in the city.

322. RUDOLPH ALONZA TURNER, kidnapper

LISTED: January 10, 1974
CAUGHT: October 1, 1974
DESCRIPTION: Born August 30, 1941, in Jacksonville, Florida. Five feet eight inches tall, 140 pounds, with black hair and brown eyes. (Left eye is reportedly artificial.) Occupations: laborer, restaurant worker. Tattoos and marks: "Rudy" tattooed on his left forearm, and "Bernice and Rudy" tattooed on his chest. Aliases: Rudolph Alonso Turner, "Rudy," and "Ruddy."

"I Knew You'd Get Me Sooner or Later." Rudy Turner had a potentially lucrative kidnapping plot in mind. He and some buddies targeted two businessmen in Moultrie, Georgia, then kidnapped one of their fathers-in-law. The ransom demand: $23,000. When the payout was made, local police converged on the scene and encountered Turner, who decided to try to shoot his way out. Unfortunately for Turner, his pistol misfired. A Georgia police lieutenant returned fire with a shotgun, striking Turner, while one of Turner's accomplices fired back, blasting the cop in the chest at point-blank range. The lieutenant died as a result, and Turner managed to get away.

Turner's accomplices weren't so lucky. They were quickly rounded up. Meanwhile, Turner was charged with armed robbery, kidnapping, and the murder of a police officer. This was on top of a long rap sheet that dated back to 1959, and included convictions for breaking and entering, assault and battery on a police officer, packing a concealed weapon, escape, and auto theft. He was named to the Top Ten list in early January 1974. Eight months later, the FBI found Turner hiding in his hometown of Jacksonville, Florida. He reportedly told arresting agents, "I knew you'd get me sooner or later."

INTERESTING FUGITIVE FACT:
According to his FBI Bulletin, Turner was "unable to straighten his left little finger because of an injury."

323. LARRY GENE COLE, kidnapper

LISTED: April 2, 1974
CAUGHT: April 3, 1974
DESCRIPTION: Born in 1947 in West Virginia.

Couple of Kidnappers. "She was the hardest female I'd ever seen," recalled kidnapping victim Betty Van Balen, nearly 30 years after her abduction. "You could have hit her with a hammer, and it would have broken the hammer." Van Balen was referring to Bonnie Cole, the 23-year-old wife of Larry Gene Cole. On March 6, 1974, the Coles abducted Van Balen, luring her out of her real estate office with a phony request to see property. Bonnie Cole pretended to be "Mary Bryan," and asked to see some properties up in the southwestern Virginia mountains. Van Balen didn't think anything of the request and drove "Bryan" toward Smith Mountain Lake. Halfway through the drive, a beat-up car cut them off, and a strange-looking man popped out.

"Lock your door," Van Balen told her potential customer.

But instead of panicking or locking her door, Bryan took a pistol from her purse and aimed it at Van Balen.

"Unlock the doors, Mrs. Van Balen."

The strange man, of course, was 27-year-old Larry Cole. Together, the Coles taped Van Balen's hands behind her back, bound her ankles, then silenced her with a final piece of tape across her mouth. They told her that her husband, Frank Van Balen, would have to cough up $25,000 if they ever wanted to see her alive again. Then Van Balen was forced into the trunk of her own car. Later, Frank Van Balen was called, and the demands were issued—no cops, no tricks, just the money. Cole then drove Betty to an abandoned railroad station, sat her down, then hid behind an abandoned bus, his gun pointed at her the entire time, just in case Frank were to try anything stupid.

A little past midnight on March 7, Frank arrived. He dropped the bag of money, and Cole issued one last warning. "You didn't call the cops, did you?"

"I did not," Frank said, calmly.

Cole told the Van Balens to follow the railroad track into the woods, which would lead them back to a main road. As they walked nervously along the wet tracks, Frank whispered to his wife, "Betty. Run like hell—I did call the police."

But Cole was already gone, having hopped into Frank Van Balen's car and sped off into he night. FBI agents met the Van Balens in the woods, and a few weeks later, they put Larry Cole on the Ten Most Wanted list.

As it turned out, Larry Cole had worked for Frank Van Balen's fiberglass plant a year before, and somewhere along the line hatched his kidnapping plot and brought his young bride in on the action. As smart as Cole might have been about the kidnapping, he didn't know the first thing about being a fugitive. A New York state trooper spotted the Coles in their brand-new Jaguar, driving toward Buffalo. (Fugitive Rule #1: Stay inconspicuous.) When approached, Cole tried to bluff his way out of the situation by claiming to be a member of the U.S. Department of Justice. (Fugitive Rule #2: Never claim to be a member of law enforcement.) The Coles were cuffed. Larry received 25 years, while Bonnie received 18.

INTERESTING FUGITIVE FACT:
In 1999 Cole—who had been paroled from prison in 1982 after only eight years—was charged with the abduction and brutal shooting murder of an Oregon park ranger. On April 25, 2001, he was found guilty of aggravated murder, aggravated attempted murder, robbery, burglary, theft, and felon in possession of a firearm. He was sentenced to life in prison. Betty Van Balen couldn't believe the news when she heard it. "Is that the same one that kidnapped me? No kidding? Lord."

324. JAMES ELLSWORTH JONES, kidnapper, murderer

LISTED: April 16, 1974
CAUGHT: June 15, 1974

The Fugitive Special. Florida cop Steve Fuller liked to study faces—the ones he found on the posters tacked up at work. The FBI's Top Ten, especially. Every day he'd take a few minutes and scan them, trying to get to know them, as if he were trying to remember guests at a cocktail party. On June 15 Fuller was off-duty and kicking back with some friends in a Coral Gables restaurant. A young couple entered the restaurant, almost took the booth next to Fuller, but then changed their minds and headed for the counter. Something clicked in Fuller's head. The guy—he looked familiar. Then it hit him. The names popped into his head, all three of them, in an instant. James Ellsworth Jones. Fuller managed to sneak away to call the FBI, and they converged on the scene within the half hour.

Jones was a prison escapee who had been sent up for the brutal kidnapping and claw-hammer murder of a gas station jockey in Virginia. He'd been on the lam since the previous October and had been named to the Top Ten list just two months before Fuller encountered him in that restaurant. At first Jones tried to pretend he was somebody else. Perhaps he thought the mustache he grew was disguise enough. But fingerprints bore out the truth, and he was arrested and sent back to prison.

INTERESTING FUGITIVE FACT:
When confronted, Jones claimed to be a health food salesman.

325. LENDELL HUNTER, rapist, kidnapper, burglar

LISTED: June 7, 1974
CAUGHT: July 31, 1974
DESCRIPTION: Born in 1953 in Augusta, Georgia.

Nights of the Hunter. By the time he was 18 years old, Lendell Hunter had been convicted of 15 different felonies, including a shocking series of violent rapes in Augusta, Georgia, in the early 1970s. One victim was a 31-year-old woman who had been sleeping in the home of her wealthy parents. Hunter broke in, then used a table leg to beat the woman into unconsciousness. (She would temporarily lose her vision from the assault.) Another time, Hunter kidnapped a woman during a home invasion, led her outside at knifepoint, then raped her before letting her go. These assaults earned Hunter a hitch at Alto Prison in Georgia, but he escaped in December 1974, and the following February he was at it again in Augusta—this time robbing and beating to death a 78-year-old woman in her own home. Her 12-year-old grandson was sleeping over at the time. Hunter didn't give the boy a chance to wake up and defend himself—he started beating the child while he was still asleep, pummeling him near death. Fingerprints gave Hunter away, and the FBI put the kill-crazy rapist on their Ten Most Wanted list on June 7, 1974.

Nearly two months later, they found Hunter staying at a Des Moines, Iowa, YMCA under the alias "Carey Baker." Hunter was sent to prison, but that apparently didn't cure him of his bloodlust. In 1983 he stabbed two prison guards, and as a result was kept in isolation most of the time. In 1997 an *Atlanta*

Journal and Constitution story noted that Hunter was the "longest-serving inmate in isolation," having at that point spent 21 years in the "hole."

INTERESTING FUGITIVE FACT:
Hunter is only one of four Top Ten fugitives who chose to hide in Iowa. "People in Iowa tend to bring you over a casserole and ask for your life story when you move in," explained Kevin Curran, an FBI spokesman in Des Moines. "People here are so darn friendly that they will seek you out, and that makes fugitives real uncomfortable."

326. JOHN EDWARD COPELAND, rapist

LISTED: August 15, 1974
CAUGHT: July 23, 1975
DESCRIPTION: Born April 3, 1944, in Newport News, Virginia. Five feet 11 inches, 200 pounds, with black hair and brown eyes. Aliases: "Cope," "Ed," "Eddie," and "Johnny O."

The Rapist Who Talked Too Much. Described by the FBI as a "paunchy accused sex deviate," Copeland had an unusual M.O.: He'd take his victims at gunpoint to a secluded place, rape them repeatedly, and regale them with his brilliant blackmail and hijacking schemes. Copeland usually worked with an accomplice, and once they kidnapped a hitchhiking couple. The woman was raped; the man was forced to take the twin barrels of a shotgun into his mouth. Copeland then allegedly pulled the trigger, but by some miracle the shotgun didn't fire. Copeland's partner was eventually arrested, but Copeland avoided the law until he was placed on the FBI's Top Ten list in August 1974. Upon making the list, he lammed out to Boston, but thanks to a tip from a citizen, Copeland was apprehended on July 23, 1975, in Dorchester, Massachusetts, after riding his bicycle home one evening.

INTERESTING FUGITIVE FACT:
Copeland had a wheezy, high-pitched voice, which made the violent rapist sound a bit like Mickey Mouse.

327. MELVIN DALE WALKER, bank robber

LISTED: October 16, 1974
CAUGHT: November 9, 1974

DESCRIPTION: Born February 3, 1939, in Scott County, Missouri. Five feet eight inches tall, 174 pounds, with receding dark brown hair and blue eyes. Occupations: construction worker, laborer, salesman, trucker. Walker has engaged in gunfights with police officers to avoid arrest in the past. Alias: Melvin Dalle Walker.

One Last Time Around the Block. Melvin Dale Walker was an old-school heister: unrepentant and seemingly unstoppable. On August 10, 1974, Walker and a crew of prison buddies broke out of a federal prison near Lewisburg, Pennsylvania, by smashing a garbage truck through a rear gate. It was a dangerous gang of four. Walker had nearly 20 years of burglary, bank robbery, and safe-cracking behind him. Richard Floyd McCoy was a former Green Beret, famous for hijacking a commercial airliner in 1972 and bailing out over Utah with a cool half-million in ransom money. (He was caught two days later after a citizen called to report that a guy he knew was bragging about a "foolproof" method of hijacking a plane. Some even suspect that McCoy was actually the infamous D. B. Cooper, who had pulled a similar stunt in 1971 and was never seen again.) The two others, Philadelphian Joseph Havel and Iowan Larry Bagley, were both serving 10 and 20 years in the federal pokey, respectively.

Within hours the gang had committed their first crime as fugitives: breaking into a home near Forest Hill, Pennsylvania, tying up a married couple and stealing their car. A few days later, the group allegedly knocked over a Pollocksville, North Carolina, bank for $16,000. But it was a costly heist: During a half-hour gun battle with police, both Bagley and Havel surrendered and were nabbed by the cops. Walker and McCoy slipped through a dragnet and remained at large. Walker was named to the Ten Most Wanted list a few months later.

A few weeks later, the FBI came up with a hideout address for Walker and McCoy, located in a quiet area of Virginia Beach. Agents watched the house for two days before their fugitives left. But instead of pouncing on them right away, the decision was made to get the drop on the men from inside the house. When Walker and McCoy returned, McCoy was first to walk to the front door. Walker, meanwhile, kept driving, perhaps to keep a lookout for anything suspicious. McCoy certainly saw something suspicious when he turned the key and stepped inside: three G-men, guns drawn, ordering him to freeze. McCoy went for his gun and fired, missing his targets. The

FBI's aim was much better, and McCoy died at the scene.

Walker, meanwhile, heard the shots and decided it might be a good idea to keep on truckin'—fast. But another team of G-men saw him take off, but had him surrounded within a few blocks. Walker had two loaded pistols in the car, but declined from going the way of his partner. He surrendered without incident and was shipped back to Lewisburg.

INTERESTING FUGITIVE FACT:
In an FBI brief, Walker was described as an individual "who would kill at the drop of a hat."

328. THOMAS OTIS KNIGHT, murderer

LISTED: December 12, 1974
CAUGHT: December 31, 1974
DESCRIPTION: Born February 4, 1951, in Fort Pierce, Florida.

Trouble Comes Calling. Miami millionaire Sydney Gans and his wife came to work on the morning of July 17, 1974, and stared Trouble right in the face. The word was printed on both sides of a M-1 carbine pistol, and it was held by one of Gans's employees, Thomas Otis Knight. Knight wanted $50,000 from them, or else they were going to have a very bad day. Shaken, Gans and his wife agreed to take Knight to their Miami bank and paid him his money. But instead of letting the Ganses go, he escorted them to a construction site in Dade County and shot them both to death with the M-1. Somewhere along the way, Knight must have missed the finer points of "pay and release" when he studied the art of kidnapping.

Knight also missed the part about fleeing the scene of a crime, because cops swarmed the area and found him—gun and money still on his person—and arrested him for the double murder. Two months later, Knight joined up with 10 other prisoners and smashed through a stone wall in the Dade County jail. All of the 10 escapees were captured right away, but not Knight. He stayed on the run long enough to plan his next score, a liquor shop knockover in Cordele, Georgia, on October 21. Once again, Knight murdered two people in cold blood, this time the shop's employees. That kind of behavior is an easy way to speed your passage to the Ten Most Wanted list. Knight was named on December 12. On New Year's Eve 1974 Knight was traced to a rooming house in New Smyrna Beach, Florida. At some

point Knight must have decided to shoot it out, as he was heavily armed and barricaded behind a door. But when he saw the FBI Swat Team swarming about, he decided to lay down Trouble and give up without a fight.

INTERESTING FUGITIVE FACT:
Knight grew up dirt poor; according to court documents, he and his eight siblings had to share two beds.

329. BILLY DEAN ANDERSON, armed robber

LISTED: January 21, 1975
KILLED: July 7, 1979
DESCRIPTION: Born July 12, 1934, in Fentress County, Tennessee. Five feet eight inches tall, 160 to 170 pounds, with blue or green eyes and brown hair. Occupations: artist, mechanic, laborer, tree surgeon, farmhand. Scars: scar across nose, scar on the left side of forehead, a surgical scar on the ride side of stomach, and another on the lower spine. Reportedly wears braces on both legs, suffers from atrophied legs. May be wearing long hair and beard. Aliases: Bill Dean Anderson, Billie Dean Anderson, James Forster, William David Upchurch.

Collecting Tin Badges. Billy Anderson tried very hard to be a cop killer, but never quite succeeded. The first attempt: October 26, 1962. Anderson, then in his late 20s and with a criminal record dating back to 1957, saw a state trooper's vehicle and hammered the gas pedal, almost as if to tease him. Trooper Steve Webb and his partner gave pursuit, and soon Anderson pulled to a screeching halt. But he wasn't about to wait for a ticket or a lecture. Anderson popped out of his car and started blasting away with a gun. Trooper Webb was seriously wounded, but his partner managed to return fire, lodging a bullet in Anderson's spine. When Anderson hobbled into court on braces a few months later, he was convicted of assault with intent to commit first-degree murder and sentenced to 10 years in jail.

Attempt number two came just five years later. Anderson was sprung from jail early, and he again took a shot at a law officer, Irvin Jones, this time in his native Fentress County, Tennessee. Third time was 1973, when Anderson, again sprung early, convinced his wife to help him rob a nightclub near Jamestown, Tennessee. The heist was spoiled when a Fentress County deputy sheriff surprised him mid-act, and Anderson blasted away at the man. The cop was seriously wounded, and this time Anderson was going away for a long, long time.

Or was he? On August 6, 1974, Anderson and a prison pal popped out of the Morgan County jail in Wartburg, Tennessee. Two days later, a federal warrant was issued in Knoxville, charging Anderson with unlawful flight to avoid prosecution for assault with intent to commit first-degree murder, use of a deadly weapon in commission of a felony, and a host of other crimes. His name slid onto the Ten Most Wanted list the following January.

Anderson hid well, and he hid for over four years. That's because he was an accomplished outdoorsman and able to hide in caves around the Cumberland Mountains of Tennessee. Friends and sympathizers probably kept him in food and supplies during his exile. But what tripped him up in the end was the need to visit his mother, who lived in Pall Mall, Tennessee. Over the Fourth of July weekend in 1979, Anderson took a chance and came home for the holiday. A tipster had told the FBI about this planned reunion, and 13 agents had the house under heavy surveillance. When Anderson showed, the agents emerged, guns in hand. Anderson decided to do what he did best and pointed his weapon at the law enforcement agents who had gathered around him.

Only this time the agents dropped him before he could pull the trigger.

INTERESTING FUGITIVE FACT:
Before following the way of the gun, Anderson studied art and even preached in churches for a while. "He was one of the finest and most unique persons I've ever known when he was preaching at the Wolf River Methodist Church," said Buster Stockton, a former Fentress County sheriff. "Looking back, I still can't figure out what happened to the boy to make him turn into the man he was."

330. ROBERT GERALD DAVIS, drug dealer, cop killer

LISTED: April 4, 1975
CAUGHT: August 5, 1977
DESCRIPTION: Born November 1947 in Camden, New Jersey.

Three Bad Days. Robert Davis was a small-time hood planning a small-time heist that quickly spiraled into big-time trouble. On July 1, 1974, Davis and three accomplices robbed a Camden grocery

store of $10,000, but didn't get away clean—they shot a 13-year-old boy and five other innocent bystanders to make their getaway. Everyone survived the assault except for the boy, tragically enough. Apparently Davis wasn't too broken up about the murder, for two days later he was driving around Pittsburgh, looking for action and trying to stay as far away from Camden as possible. When a friend got pinched for dealing that same day, Davis and an accomplice swerved to a stop, allowed their handcuffed buddy to jump in the car, then shot it out with Pittsburgh police officers. One of the two arresting officers died in the street. Davis and friends sped away and this time managed to stay hidden. On April 4, 1975, he was named to the Top Ten list.

It took two years of hard legwork, but the FBI finally got a lead on their cop killer. He was holed up in Venice, California, and seemed genuinely stunned when FBI agents came bursting into his apartment. Davis surrendered without a fight and was later given a sentence of life plus 45 years.

INTERESTING FUGITIVE FACT:
Davis's mug shot does fit the crime—the convicted drug dealer's eyes are half shut, as if he was almost too tired to pose for the police photographer.

331. RICHARD DEAN HOLTAN, bank robber, murderer

LISTED: April 18, 1975
CAUGHT: July 12, 1975
DESCRIPTION: Born February 24, 1935, in Watertown, South Dakota. Five feet five inches tall, 140 pounds, with brown hair and brown eyes. Occupations: shipping clerk, upholsterer. Aliases: Dick Holtan, Richard Dean Holten, Richard D. Holton, Dick Martinson.

Hawaii 5-0 Hangs Tenner. Richard Holtan had a criminal record dating back to 1952, but he hadn't learned much in 20 years. In November 1973 he knocked over a Seattle bank for a measly $1,000. The minor league heist landed him in a special Resident Release Program—a kind of halfway house setup—for a year. A year was too long, Holtan decided, and escaped soon after arriving. He made his way to Omaha, Nebraska, where he skipped the banks and instead decided to rob a tavern. On November 1, 1974, he burst into a bar with a pistol and ended up blasting away "without provocation,"

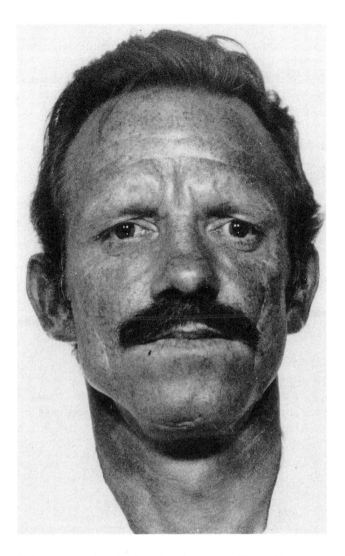

Holtan surrendered to local authorities in Kauai, Hawaii.

according to the FBI. When the gun smoke cleared, the bartender was dead, and two patrons were wounded.

Holtan fled, and a few weeks later a federal warrant was issued charging him with unlawful interstate flight to avoid prosecution for murder. By the following March Holtan was charged with bond default. By April he was named to FBI's Ten Most Wanted list. The fugitive fled the farthest he could without leaving American soil—Hawaii. But the national spotlight was much too bright for the small-time stickup man. He surrendered to local authorities in Kauai, Hawaii, just short of three months after making the list. Holtan was shipped back to Nebraska to face murder charges and was later sentenced to death.

INTERESTING FUGITIVE FACT:
Holtan had a rather prophetic set of tattoos on his left wrist and forearm. Both read: BORN TO LOSE.

332. RICHARD BERNARD LINDHORST JR., murderer

LISTED: August 4, 1975
CAUGHT: August 7, 1975
DESCRIPTION: Born in Missouri in March 1942.

Double Trouble. It was December 20, 1974, and Richard Lindhorst had a lot going on. He had recently murdered a couple in Hunstville, Alabama—word was, it was a contract killing—and now found himself robbing a bank of $20,000 in Wever, Iowa. On the way out, Lindhorst and his two compatriots decided to burn a barn to distract the cops. Murder, robbery, arson—just the kind of felonies that could land an average street criminal on the FBI's Ten Most Wanted list. The following August this came to pass. But Lindhorst lasted merely three days at the top of the criminal charts. FBI agents and local cops pinned him down in Pensacola, Florida, and he was swiftly returned to Alabama to face the music on those contract killings. The robbery and arson beefs would just have to wait.

INTERESTING FUGITIVE FACT:
Lindhorst had a dragon tattooed on his chest.

333. WILLIAM HERRON JR., cop killer

LISTED: August 15, 1975
CAUGHT: October 30, 1975
DESCRIPTION: Born in Paducah, Kentucky. "A vicious, cunning, professional killer."

Thanks for Nothing, Buddy. On April 11, 1975, William Herron and a fellow convict at the Kentucky State Prison were riding in a prison vehicle, on their way to a medical clinic for the treatment of various ailments. In Herron's case, however, the ailments were imaginary. Herron had a plan, and he had a .38 caliber revolver secretly stashed away. On the way back from the clinic, Herron pulled the pistol on the prison guard and forced him to drive to a desolate stretch of Kentucky wilderness. Herron took the guard's weapon, then attempted to recruit his fellow convict to help aid in his escape. The convict—perhaps seeing the wild gleam in Herron's eyes—refused to take part. That was fine with Herron. Instead of one man shackled to a nearby tree, there would be two, the guard and the convict. Herron drove away, and right onto the Ten Most Wanted list four months later. The latest addition to the Top Ten was the very type of fugitive that the FBI enjoyed putting away: an alleged professional hit man and convicted cop-killer. Herron had been sentenced to Kentucky State Prison the year before for shooting a cop during a routine traffic stop in Peoria, Illinois. On October 30 Herron had an altogether different kind of traffic stop: one orchestrated by the FBI, and one that resulted in his capture and return to prison to complete his sentence.

INTERESTING FUGITIVE FACT:
Special Agents Elias Williams, Jerome DiFranco, and John Leuck, the same FBI agents who arrested Herron, also arrested another Top Ten fugitive— JOSEPH LLOYD THOMAS (#304)—back in March 1970.

334. JAMES WINSTON SMALLWOOD, bank robber

LISTED: August 29, 1975
CAUGHT: December 5, 1975
DESCRIPTION: Born December 11, 1949, in Washington D.C.

A Gun to the Head.   In December 1974 convicted bank robber James Smallwood was riding in a government vehicle, on the way to a Washington, D.C., courtroom for a scheduled appearance. Somewhere along the line he had gotten his hands on a .32 caliber revolver and successfully hid it somewhere in his prison clothes. When the time was right, he produced the weapon and pressed it to the temple of his escort, a U.S. marshal. Smallwood forced the marshal to pull over to the side of the road, then took his gun and left the car—but not before firing a shot at his captor. The marshal wasn't injured, but the message was clear: Follow me, and you'll get a bullet. Smallwood had just started a 30-year sentence for bank robbery; it was too soon to let this bird out of his cage. After a D.C.-manhunt failed to catch him, Smallwood was named to the Ten Most Wanted list in August 1975 (the third fugitive added that month). He lasted four months on the list, but might have made it longer if he hadn't decided to pull another bank job. On December 5 he robbed a small bank in suburban Maryland, but by the time he popped out of the front doors, local police were already on the case. Smallwood got the idea to speed away from the scene of the crime, pull over, then hide in the trunk. It worked . . . for a few minutes. Police popped the trunk, and eventually Smallwood found himself back in D.C. to complete that 30-year sentence.

INTERESTING FUGITIVE FACT:
Most bank robbers try to ply their trade far from home, but Smallwood always worked in or around his hometown: Washington, D.C.

335. LEONARD JAMES PELTIER, murderer

LISTED: December 22, 1975
CAUGHT: February 6, 1976
DESCRIPTION: Born September 12, 1944, in Grand Forks, North Dakota.

The FBI's Least Favorite Fugitive.   On the morning of June 26, 1975, two FBI agents named Jack R. Coler and Ronald A. Williams were driving in separate cars toward the Pine Ridge Indian Reservation, tucked away in the southwest corner of South Dakota. They were looking for a red-and-white vehicle that belonged to James "Jimmy" Eagle, wanted along with two others for a robbery on the reservation. At 11:50 A.M. Williams radioed back to headquarters, saying that he had spotted the vehicle, and that he and Coler were going to check it out. A short while later, shooting broke out. Coler and Williams came under heavy fire, both cars absorbing over 125 bullets. The agents' own weapons—service revolvers and a shotgun—were pretty much useless, as their attackers were hunkered down 250 feet away and using long-range assault rifles. Williams radioed for backup, but the nearest agent was 12 miles away. Both agents hid behind their vehicles and prayed for an escape.

None came. Williams was struck in his left arm, and then Coler got a bullet in his arm, nearly severing it from his torso. He flopped back to the ground. Williams scrambled over, ripped off his shirt, and tried to apply it as a tourniquet. The firing stopped, and at least one of their attackers approached the bleeding agents. According to the FBI, one lone gunman approached with an AR-15 assault rifle. Williams reached up and touched the barrel of the AR-15. The gunman pulled the trigger, blasting away three of Williams's fingers and part of his face. Then the gunman turned to Coler and finished him off with a bullet to the head, then the throat.

When FBI backup finally arrived four hours later—there were more bullets exchanged between the FBI and the gunmen throughout the afternoon—they found the bodies of Coler and Williams next to one of the cars. According to a story by Scott Anderson in *Outside Magazine,* two vital clues were left behind. A fingerprint on one of the agents' cars turned out to be that of Leonard Peltier, a member of the American Indian Movement (AIM), a militant radical group whose goal was to create a unified American Indian nation through whatever means necessary. And Coler's and Williams's weapons were missing from the scene. Later, a September 1975 raid on an AIM camp uncovered the agents' missing weapons, along with the murder weapon, that AR-15. With this evidence in hand, Peltier was named to the FBI's Most Wanted list on December 22, 1975.

Peltier fled to Canada, but was soon arrested in Hinton, Alberta, Canada, by Royal Canadian Mounted Police. After a 10-month battle over extradition, Peltier was returned to the United States to stand trial. During the trial one of the Canadian Mounties testified that Peltier had admitted to being part of the shooting. "[The agents] were shot," Peltier allegedly said, "when they came to a house to serve a warrant on me." As it turned out, Peltier had already been wanted in Milwaukee in connection with an attack on a police officer. This did not endear the jury to Leonard Peltier. He was found guilty on two counts of first-degree murder.

Peltier eventually became the Ten Most Wanted list's most controversial member—not because of the incident, or his listing, but because so many people have been convinced that Peltier is innocent of the charges. Celebrities such as Robert Redford and Nelson Mandela continually lobby for Peltier's release from prison. *Incident at Oglala,* a documentary produced by Robert Redford and directed by Michael Apted, presents a decidedly pro-Peltier version of the events of June 26, 1975. There was even the appearance of a "Mr. X"—a man who claimed to be the man who really killed Coler and Williams—in Peter Matthiessen's pro-Peltier *In the Spirit of Crazy Horse,* and a follow-up segment that aired on *60 Minutes* in 1991. ("Mr. X" was hidden behind sunglasses and olive-drab bandages and claimed he killed both agents in self-defense.) Momentum grew. At the end of his second term

President Bill Clinton faced the ire of many FBI agents when he said he would consider giving clemency to Peltier. "I hear nothing but abhorrence," said former FBI director Louis Freeh, "that there is a possibility, let alone a probability, that Peltier could be released despite his repeated and open expression of willingness to murder law enforcement officers, and, in the case of agents Coler and Williams, doing so without hesitation."

In late 2000 Peltier again proclaimed his innocence, this time in an interview with the *Seattle Times.* "I didn't kill those people," he said.

INTERESTING FUGITIVE FACT:
In prison Peltier started oil painting; his works now sell for at least $5,000 apiece to "Hollywood cognoscenti," according to *Outside Magazine.*

336. PATRICK JAMES HUSTON, bank robber

LISTED: March 3, 1976
CAUGHT: December 7, 1977
DESCRIPTION: Born in 1930. Tattoos and marks: "In Memory of Mom" on his upper right arm.

The Old Prison. By 1974 the old West Street jail in Manhattan—technically, the Federal Detention Headquarters—was in dire need of replacement. The facility had been built in 1915 and in recent years had become something of a joke among convicts. Nine men had escaped in three separate jailbreaks in

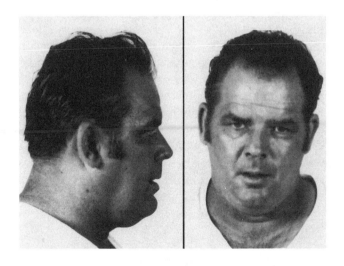

Bank robber and fugitive Huston was arrested in Fort Lauderdale, Florida.

the past year alone. Finally, a new detention center was built at Foley Square, and by early 1975 the prison officials were preparing to move equipment, telephones, and prisoners to the new facility. However, one last team of convicts managed to rack up one last jailbreak.

On March 16, 1975, Patrick Huston—a convicted bank robber who stole $31,000 from the First National City Bank in Jackson Heights, Queens, then used a politician's campaign car as a getaway vehicle—helped orchestrate a breakout from West Street. All of the escapees were bank robbers, but not all of them had worked together before. They were simply united in their need for freedom. Huston, along with Emmett Ivers, Steven Wechsler (both his partners during the Jackson Heights heist), Robert E. Foss, Jeremiah Geaney, and Edward McConnell cut their way through three wire-mesh screen doors, smashed through a skylight, then lowered themselves to a sidewalk with a "ladder" made of bedsheets and tight knots. The break was merely the latest embarrassment in a long string of embarrassments for the West Street jail. "It was never designed to be a jail," explained the prison's warden in *The New York Times* the next day. "The fact that we do not have tool-resistant steel makes it pretty hard to supervise as many people as we have here. We have 383 inmates at the facility—minus six at this point." The jail was originally designed to hold 125 men.

After a year of no leads, Huston was finally named to the Top Ten list. Huston enjoyed a nice run—over two years since the jailbreak—before the FBI finally located him in Fort Lauderdale, Florida. It happened by chance, as briefly mentioned in Philip Gourevitch's *A Cold Case,* the crisp, lean tale of a New York City cop haunted by a 30-year-old homicide. During the course of that investigation New York City cops managed to arrest a professional hit man who, in turn, was in contact with a certain bank robber from Queens. The exact details aren't clear, but somehow the NYPD forwarded Huston's new address to the FBI. Huston was taken completely by surprise. The fugitive was riding his bicycle along the streets of Fort Lauderdale when FBI agents surrounded him. He was not armed and didn't attempt to pedal himself to freedom.

INTERESTING FUGITIVE FACT:
Huston's rap sheet began back in 1946, with a pinch for armed robbery.

337. THOMAS EDWARD BETHEA, bank robber, kidnapper

LISTED: March 5, 1976
CAUGHT: May 5, 1976
DESCRIPTION: Born November 25, 1937, in McColl, South Carolina.

A Bahamas Getaway. Tom Bethea had the ultimate getaway planned—literally. After taking part in the 1976 kidnapping of a wealthy trucking magnate from Miami named Alan Bortnick—which resulted in a $250,000 ransom payday for Bethea and his partners—Bethea split the country. His destination: Nassau, in the Bahamas. Bethea was an African-American man flush with cash, and he reasoned that he'd be practically hailed a hero down in the Bahamas. Not quite. After Bethea was named to the Top Ten list, he was arrested, deemed an "undesirable alien," and sent back to Miami, where FBI agents were waiting to greet him.

INTERESTING FUGITIVE FACT:
Before trying his hand at the kidnapping trade, Bethea robbed banks and was on parole for his most recent heist when he took part in the Bortnick snatch.

338. ANTHONY MICHAEL JULIANO, bank robber

LISTED: March 15, 1976
CAUGHT: March 22, 1976
DESCRIPTION: Born in Highlands, New Jersey. Five feet two inches tall.

Mutt and Jeff. Thirty-eight bank robberies in two and a half years, with over $1 million stolen. It was an impressive run by any heister's standard, and it was beginning to earn the perpetrators the grudging respect of both the NYPD and the FBI. "Willie Sutton was an amateur compared to these people—he could have learned from them," said the NYPD's Daniel McMahon, then head of the department's Special Investigations Division. The pair of robbers hit banks mostly in Queens and Brooklyn, with a few in Nassau County as well. But they always used a late-model GM car to make their getaways. And that was the one detail that eventually helped the police—who toward the end had assigned 70 men to the case—break up the robbery gang.

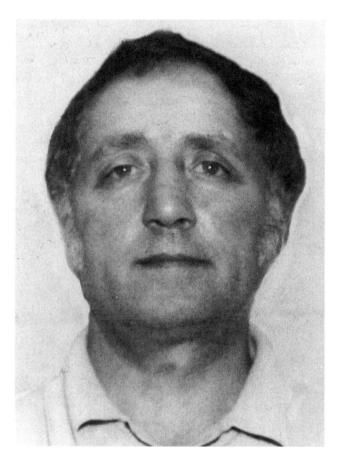

Juliano was arrested in Mecklenburg County, Virginia, after a meter maid recognized him in a parked car.

The word went out to the rank and file: You spot any stolen late-model GM cars on the street during your shift, don't tow 'em. Watch 'em. One such observation on November 4, 1975, led police to the Flushing, Queens, home of Marshall Kenneth Schreter, where arresting officers and agents found $9,500 in $100 bills, $100,000 in savings bonds, and a host of deadly weapons—10 handguns, two shotguns, an M-1 army carbine, and boxes of ammo. Schreter was arrested, which led police to seek out another man: his alleged partner, Anthony Juliano, who had already been sentenced to 15 years in prison for five other bank heists. A manhunt failed to unearth Juliano, so he was placed on the Ten Most Wanted list the following March. Just one week later, a meter maid working Mecklenburg County, Virginia, recognized Juliano's face as one she'd seen on a Wanted poster. She called it in to the local sheriff, and within minutes Juliano was scooped up off the highway and arrested.

INTERESTING FUGITIVE FACT:
Apparently Juliano wasn't happy with making just the Ten Most Wanted list. In 1988—nearly a decade later—Juliano made the U.S. Marshal's Most Wanted list for a weapons violation. That time he stayed at large until December 7, 1993, when he was arrested at his grandson's first birthday party.

339. JOSEPH MAURICE MCDONALD, gangster

LISTED: April 1, 1976
CAUGHT: September 15, 1982
DESCRIPTION: Born in Medford, Massachusetts, in 1917. Occupation: truck driver.

"Hey Fellas, I'm Wanted by the FBI." Sometimes you go after a gangster with anything you've got. Eliot Ness used tax evasion to pin down Al Capone during the 1930s. When the FBI wanted Joseph Maurice McDonald—allegedly a high-ranking member of the Boston syndicate—they turned to stamps. Specifically, the heist of a stamp collection worth $50,000. Not a minor crime, by any stretch, but it was certainly minor compared to the rap sheets of most Top Tenners. And minor compared to what McDonald was believed to be involved in, namely loan sharking, illegal gambling, conspiracy, and murder.

McDonald's rap sheet stretched back to 1961, when he was sentenced to 12 to 18 years for armed robbery. He broke out of a prison camp two years later. Then in 1966 he was arrested after trading bullets with some Boston cops. He was released from prison in 1969. In 1971 came the stamp robbery, in which McDonald and James L. Sims, another alleged member of the Boston syndicate, allegedly took $50,000 in stamps at gunpoint from Jack E. Molesworth, a former Massachusetts politician. Sims was arrested, and the FBI lined up a stamp dealer named Raymond A. Lundgren to testify against both crooks. In 1976, however, Lundgren was found shot to death before he could testify. A short while later, McDonald was named to the Ten Most Wanted list.

The well-connected Irish mobster managed to avoid the Feds for over six years, but when the end came, it came hard and fast. On September 15, 1982, a Hollywood, Florida, cop watched a man board a train. Something didn't seem right about the guy, so he asked the stranger to open his luggage. The cop was thinking drug bust. The stranger refused to open his bag, and the Hollywood cop found himself without probable cause, so he had to let the man go. But the cop wasn't about to give up. He phoned the NYPD and told them what he'd seen. Several hours later, officers stopped the stranger as he disembarked from his train at Penn Station. Two U.S. Customs dogs were on the scene, too—one to sniff for drugs, the other to sniff for gunpowder. The dogs jumped all over the place. Bingo. Probable cause.

The stranger said his name was "Jack Kelly," and that he was a businessman from Fort Lauderdale, but nothing doing. The police found three semiautomatic pistols, three silencers, and boxes of bullets. After eight hours of interrogation, the stranger finally gave up. "Hey, fellas," he said, "I'm wanted by the FBI." The man, of course, was Joseph McDonald. "There comes a time when you realize your bluff isn't going to work," noted arresting officer Capt. Thomas Jennings, then head of the NYPD's narcotics squad, to the *Boston Globe*. "He fit the mold of a guy who's done heavy time. If I stopped you or somebody stopped my wife, you'd get a little upset. But he didn't. He played it cool. I said, we've got a big time here."

INTERESTING FUGITIVE FACT:
Boston Herald columnist Howie Carr claims that the tipster who turned McDonald was not that Hollywood, Florida, cop, but a man who would later become a Top Tenner himself—JAMES J. BULGER (#458).

340. JAMES RAY RENTON, cop killer

LISTED: April 7, 1976
CAUGHT: May 9, 1977
DESCRIPTION: Born on December 13, 1937, in St. Louis, Missouri. Five feet, eight inches, 150 pounds, with red hair and blue eyes. His left forearm is tattooed with a wreath of flowers and his army serial numbers. His right arm is tattooed with the nickname, "Smiley." Aliases: James R. Benton, Gene Chapman, Harold Grayson, H. E. Hughes, Joe William Knock, Ken Saxon, Anthony Speck, Billy Wakens, and Billy Warren.

Smiling Death. James Renton's criminal career spanned nearly 40 years, beginning with an arrest at age 14 and a conviction by the time he was 18. Throughout the 1950s and 1960s Renton was convicted for post office burglary, drug possession, forgery, counterfeiting, and parole violation. Renton, a one-time printer and advertising director, loved working with paper and the multitude of ways paper could be manipulated for criminal purposes. But crisp paper was no substitute for cold steel, and that's what would prompt the addition of Renton's name to the Top Ten list.

On December 22, 1975, Renton and buddies were stopped by a 23-year-old rookie cop named John Hussey near Springvale, Arkansas. Renton—who went by the nickname "Smiley"—knew he was wanted for parole violation. So he reached for his gun, forcing Hussey to his knees before handcuffing him to a tree. Using the cop's own .357 Magnum, Renton blasted at Hussey's head three times, execution-style. A little more than four months later, Renton was a Ten Most Wanted fugitive. He stayed on the lam for 13 months before FBI agents cornered him in Denver. Renton was convicted of murder and slapped with a life sentence.

Even though Renton's Top Ten story ended there, the most interesting part of his criminal career was yet to come. On July 11, 1988, Renton and three other inmates broke out of the Maximum Security Unit of the Arkansas State Penitentiary. It was a classic jailbreak: Renton used a dummy stuffed in his bed to fool cell guards, followed by a climb down a 25-foot wall with bedsheets tied into a rope, followed by the cutting of a chain link fence. Renton's three companions were rounded up within days, but the cop killer remained at large, bringing him to the attention of the FBI once again. An article in the *Arkansas Democrat-Gazette* on July 22 reported that Renton was a likely re-addition to the Ten Most Wanted list. (He had already made the U.S. Marshal Service's "Top 15" list.) "We're trying to communicate to officers that he is extremely dangerous," said Bill Baugh, an FBI agent with the Little Rock office who said he planned to ask Washington to add Renton to the Top Ten. His new fugitive poster added that Renton "possesses an extreme hatred for police officers." Baugh told the *Democrat-Gazette*, "That's about as harsh a statement as I've seen in my career."

But Renton never made it back to the Top Ten list. You see, the world had changed since Renton had been put away; now, in the late 1980s, there was a television show called *America's Most Wanted*. (See Fugitives of the 1980s.) The show received more than 200 tips when it aired its feature on Renton, and one of the tips led police to a Salvation Army in Austin, Texas. On September 6, cops searched bed by bed until they found Renton, who had been packing a 12-gauge shotgun, a flare gun jerry-rigged to shoot bullets, a knife, burglary tools, and a makeup kit. One of the officers tapped Renton on the shoulder; he surrendered without a fight.

INTERESTING FUGITIVE FACT:
After his 1988 escape Renton went through drastic measures to disguise his appearance, including shaving part of his head to fake baldness, covering his tattoos in gauze, and popping out four of his own front teeth.

341. NATHANIEL DOYLE JR., bank robber

LISTED: April 29, 1976
KILLED: July 15, 1976
DESCRIPTION: Born November 24, 1945, in Springfield, Ohio. Five feet 11 inches, 195 to 220 pounds, with black hair

Doyle was killed in a gun battle with local police in Seattle, Washington.

and brown eyes. Occupations: auto mechanic, waiter. Scars: hyperpigmentation in center of face, a scar on his upper lip, burn scars on his left forearm, right forearm, and index finger. Aliases: Nat Johnson, Nate Johnson, Nathan Daniel Johnson, Sonny Johnson, James Lewis Griffin, James Louis Griffin, Johnny DeWayne Mitchell, Johnny Duane Mitchell, James Watson, and others.

Nightmare Rental. If you're going to rent a vehicle to use as the getaway car, don't bother bringing the thing back to Avis after you've pulled the heist. And don't give your real name and address to the friendly Avis people in the first place. But that's what Barbara Brinkley—accomplice of Nathaniel Doyle, a member of the Ten Most Wanted list—did on July 15, 1976, after helping Doyle pull a bank job in Bellevue, Washington.

Throughout the previous year the dapper Doyle had been frustrating G-men with a series of bold bank jobs—one in Columbus, Ohio, another in South Bend, Indiana, and a particularly violent heist in Fresno, California, which ended in a shoot-out with the California Highway Patrol. Doyle escaped every time. Enough was enough. Doyle was named to the list on April 29, 1976. Shortly after the Bicentennial Doyle and his girlfriend stuck up that bank in Bellevue, and Brinkley made the dumb move of returning the rental car after the heist. Seattle police nabbed her and found the address of an apartment on the rental contract. When the cops stormed the tiny apartment, they found Doyle hiding there, along with Brinkley's teenage son. The presence of a minor, however, didn't prevent Doyle from blasting away at the police. Officer Owen McKenna was wounded in the exchange, and Doyle himself never made it out of the apartment alive.

INTERESTING FUGITIVE FACT:
Doyle was fond of telling people he used to be a professional football player.

342. MORRIS LYNN JOHNSON, bank robber

LISTED: May 25, 1976
CAUGHT: June 26, 1976
DESCRIPTION: Born in Kentucky.

The Fugitive Who Stole Christmas. Together, Morris Johnson and his brother, Leon, were part of the famous Midwest gang of thieves known as Robbery, Inc. Police have estimated that the Johnson boys' gang pulled off more than 3,000 robberies—including more bank jobs than John Dillinger "ever dreamed of," noted one Indianapolis newspaper. Daylight heists, nighttime burglaries, it didn't matter. (Leon Johnson became so notorious, Indianapolis police used to search his trunk whenever they saw him, just in case.) Their criminal exploits earned Morris a spot on the FBI's Top Ten list in late May 1976.

Johnson was nabbed in New Orleans, Louisiana, after trying to flee along a canal bank. He was thrown in prison, but managed to escape yet again on November 6. Johnson had promised that he would send Christmas cards if he ever managed to free himself. True to his word, cards from Johnson appeared in the mailboxes of a federal judge, a federal prosecutor, and Charles Draper, the FBI agent who helped nail him. The card to Draper read: "I do my thing and you do your thing. If we should ever meet again, it's beautiful."

Johnson and the FBI did meet again a few months later, but it wasn't so beautiful for the bank robber. He ended up in a maximum-security prison and as of this writing hasn't managed to escape. Or send any more Christmas cards, for that matter.

INTERESTING FUGITIVE FACT:
Johnson's brother Leon missed making the Top Ten list by a day—he was arrested before he could be named.

343. RICHARD JOSEPH PICARIELLO, radical bomber

LISTED: July 29, 1976
CAUGHT: October 21, 1976

344. EDWARD PATRICK GULLION, radical bomber

LISTED: August 13, 1976
CAUGHT: October 22, 1976

The Fred Hampton Unit. You want to get somebody's attention? Blow something up. That's the strange lesson we learn from over-the-top action movies and modern-day suicide bombers, and it was the same lesson radicals learned back in the 1960s and 1970s. Richard Picariello obviously believed that explosions were the only way to make a point. Picariello was a member of the fist-pumping Fred Hampton Unit of the People's Army, a supposed prison reform group named after a slain Chicago

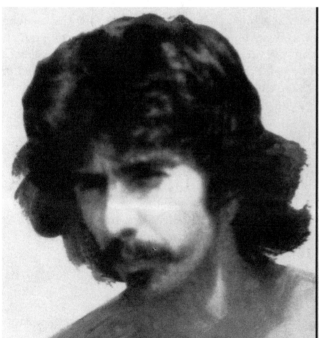

Due to an FBI investigation, Picariello was arrested in Fall River, Massachusetts.

Due to an FBI investigation, Gullion was arrested in Providence, Rhode Island, where he was employed at a jewelry store.

Black Panther. The only way to achieve better conditions in prison, reasoned the Fred Hampton Unit, was to set off bombs at the very heart of American capitalism. With Picariello's help the Unit bombed a plane at Boston's Logan Airport, blasted two National Guard trucks at an armory in Dorchester, and set off explosions at the Suffolk County Courthouse in Boston and the Essex Superior Courthouse in Newburyport. The Unit also hit the Polaroid Company in Cambridge, A&P's headquarters in Boston, and a post office in Seabrook, New Hampshire. Dozens of people were injured, but the Unit thought the violence entirely justified. U.S. imperialism needed to be taught a lesson.

In early July, after the National Guard truck blasts, the United States fought back, rounding up two Fred Hampton Unit members named Joseph Aceto and Everett Carlson. The two radical bombers, facing severe jail time, coughed up two names to the authorities: Picariello and another member named Edward Gullion, who had a string of robbery and breaking and entering convictions. (Oddly enough, Aceto and Carlson snitched on July 4, 1976.) Ten days later, Picariello and Gullion were indicted,

charged with bombing buildings and transporting explosives across state lines. By summer's end both bombing suspects had been named to the Top Ten list.

Even though Picariello and Gullion were named two weeks apart, they were both captured within hours of each other. In late October of that same year, the FBI discovered that the radical pair had holed up in Fall River, Massachusetts, where they both worked at a jewelry store. Picariello was nabbed first and fought his arrest with all of his might, sustaining an injury in the mêlée. Meanwhile, Gullion had split across state lines, but was picked up a few hours later in Providence, Rhode Island. Both were later sentenced to prison for the bombings. Now the only way the Fred Hampton Unit could work on prison reform was to do it from the inside.

INTERESTING FUGITIVE FACT:
Years later, after Picariello was released from prison, he took up the role of political activist once again. His target this time: M.I.T. In July 1997 Picariello was arrested for trespassing inside the M.I.T. student center, and like his Top Ten arrest two decades before, the arrest turned ugly. According to the *Boston Globe*, Picariello cursed at the campus cop, then kicked him in the chest, and wrestled him to the ground. (Picariello maintains he was simply sitting on a couch, waiting to attend a pro-Cuba political meeting, and the cops started messing with him.) When Picariello was booked, he refused to give his occupation. "I'm a political activist," he said.

345. GERHARDT JULIUS SCHWARTZ, armed robber

LISTED: November 18, 1976
CAUGHT: November 22, 1976
DESCRIPTION: Born May 20, 1929, in New York City. Five feet 10 inches tall, 170 to 180 pounds with graying black hair and brown eyes. Tattoos: Schwartz's upper arm has two hearts emblazoned with: "True Love, Mom and Dad, 1946," and his right forearm has one with a heart and "Mother" as well as a dagger. Aliases: Bill Lally, William Lally, Al Schwartz, Jerry Schwartz, "Blackie."

A Turn of the Knife. Gerhardt Schwartz clearly loved his parents, and the tattoos on his arms reminded him of the love his parents shared. However, his parents forgot to impart one important lesson to their little boy: If you're going pull a stickup with a group of thugs, don't try to double-cross them. Paybacks can cut deeper than a knife.

Schwartz had a compulsive gambling problem, and he depended on armed robberies to feed that compulsion. On April 9, 1976, he and a bunch of other professional robbers hit a Rochester, New York, savings and loan, armed with sawed-off shotguns. The heist was so successful, Schwartz decided to do it again—same town, same crew, only this time the target was a supermarket. That hit, too, was successful, but things went a little haywire afterward. Something angered Schwartz, and he took a knife and brutally hacked away at one of his own gang members, leaving him for dead. Police later scooped up other members, who were all too happy to finger Schwartz as their leader. On July 29, 1976, a federal warrant was issued, charging Schwartz with bank robbery, conspiracy, and attempted murder. Schwartz stayed elusive for close to four months before he was kicked up to the FBI's Top Ten list. There he lasted a mere four days. A telephone tipster clued cops to his Bronx hideaway, and there he was arrested without incident. At least Mom and Dad could be proud that their son surrendered peacefully.

INTERESTING FUGITIVE FACT:
When he wasn't sticking up banks and supermarkets, Schwartz occasionally earned an honest buck as a painter.

346. FRANCIS JOHN MARTIN, rapist

LISTED: December 17, 1976
CAUGHT: February 17, 1977
DESCRIPTION: Born December 8, 1946, in Wilmington, Delaware.

Two Times Lucky. Francis Martin beat the odds twice. The first time was when he was charged with a string of kidnappings and rapes in Delaware, and one of his victims ended up dead. Martin got lucky when the prosecution was unable to find physical evidence linking the sexual sadist to his dead victim. He was packed up and shipped off to the Delaware Correctional Center at Smyrna, where Martin had his second lucky break. A prison break, to be exact. On August 21, 1976, Martin and three other prisoners used smuggled pistols and makeshift knives to claw their way out of the slammer and flee into the surrounding area. Every single escapee was picked up—with the lone exception of

Francis Martin, who left Delaware and ran clear across to the other side of the country. By December Martin had made the Ten Most Wanted list, which is enough to ruin anybody's luck. He lasted exactly two months before a telephone tipster told the FBI he was staying in Newport Beach, California. Martin surrendered peacefully and was shipped back to Smyrna to complete his sentence.

INTERESTING FUGITIVE FACT:
Martin was a well-rounded criminal, dabbling in auto theft and small-time burglary in addition to his main pursuits of kidnapping and raping innocent women.

347. BENJAMIN GEORGE PAVAN, armed robber

LISTED: January 12, 1977
CAUGHT: February 17, 1977
DESCRIPTION: Born December 1939 in San Francisco. Aliases: Joseph Benjamin Costa, J. Costini, Louis Landerini, Ben Panalli, Benjamin Louis Pavan, Benny Pavan, Lou Pavan, Louis Benjamin Pavan, and Joseph Spinelli.

Homeboy. Professional criminals never like to work where they live, but nobody gave Benjamin Pavan that bit of wisdom. Pavan was a San Francisco native, and he enjoyed pulling armed robberies in his very own backyard of Northern California. By 1974 law enforcement was eager to nab this homegrown talent. Pavan had racked up indictments charging him with five armed robberies, three safe burglaries, and one count of grand theft auto and another count of receiving stolen property. Pavan didn't seem to care that his chances of being spotted were greatly increased by working where he lived, but then again, perhaps that didn't matter to him. After all, he stayed free for two and a half years after those 1974 indictments.

The national spotlight fell on Pavan when he made the FBI's Top Ten list on January 12, 1977. Suddenly, all of Northern California was too small to hide in. The fugitive holed up in Seattle, but someone ratted him out a little over a month later, and a team of FBI agents swooped down to arrest him. As it turned out, Pavan would be spending a lot of time in his home state. In fact, he would be a guest of the state for quite a few years.

INTERESTING FUGITIVE FACT:
February 17, 1977, was a good day for the G-men.

Two consecutive Top Tenners—Martin (#346) and Pavan (#347)—were both nabbed at approximately the same time, in different parts of the West Coast.

348. LARRY GENE CAMPBELL, murderer

LISTED: March 18, 1977
CAUGHT: September 6, 1977
DESCRIPTION: Born in 1943.

Wild in Buffalo. Larry Campbell could have been a poster child for paroles gone wrong. In 1976 Campbell was a 33-year-old former convict fresh out of the slammer, attending New York State University at Buffalo under a "disadvantaged student" program. Apparently this program didn't give him much in the way of drug money, which is why police think Campbell decided to break into an off-campus apartment on the night of June 8. But no one can explain the three-hour torture-murder session that followed.

Earlier that night, four roommates—Rhona Eiseman, Teresa Beynart, Thomas Tunney, and Michael Schostick—had decided to go out for pizza. When they returned, Beynart and Tunney hit the laundry room to catch up on some wash, while Eiseman and Schostick keyed into their apartment. They were surprised by Campbell, a student they knew from around campus, who'd even been to their apartment a few times. But this was no social call. Campbell grabbed Eiseman and put a knife to her throat. After demanding money, the former con tied up the two students with their own bedsheets in Eiseman's bedroom. Soon after, Beynart and Tunney returned to the apartment and were subdued in the same way.

That's when Campbell started choking Schostick. His three roommates cried out for him to stop, and Campbell did. But then he calmly, methodically

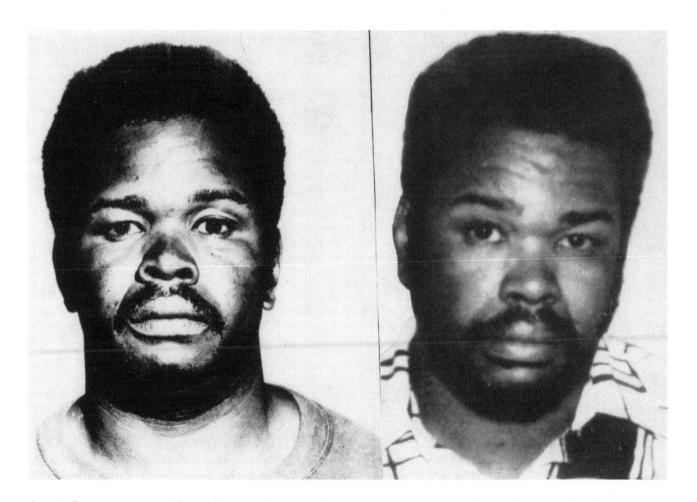

Campbell was arrested in Atlanta, Georgia, after a neighbor recognized him from a Wanted flyer in the local post office.

strangled the life out of Tunney, an early education major. The others could only watch in horror. Nothing made sense. Why was Campbell doing this? It couldn't just be for the $100 he'd stolen already.

"Please don't kill me," said Eiseman, a 21-year-old human development major. "I have a car. Take my car. We'll do anything for you."

Campbell didn't want Eiseman's car, however. He proceeded to rape and sodomize Eiseman, then strangled her as well. Next, Campbell picked up Beynart and carried her out of the bedroom—to this day no one knows why—then took his knife and returned to stab Schostick in the face, cheek, and tongue. With blood running down his cheeks, Schostick finally asked, "Why don't you just cut my throat so we can do this thing quick and it will be done?" Campbell's reply: two sharp knife thrusts to Schostick's back. Then the madman stood up and went to his last victim.

But Beynart had already managed to slip out of her bedsheets and started running for her life. Campbell tore after her. Meanwhile, Schostick, somehow still alive, managed to hop away to find help. The three-hour ordeal was over, and Schostick and Beynart lived to identify their attacker. But Campbell eluded police for months before he was named to the Ten Most Wanted list in March 1977.

Six months later, someone saw Campbell's face at a post office in Atlanta and promptly called the police, saying that the Most Wanted guy looked a lot like a new neighbor of his. At the prompting of the FBI, that same informant called back a number of times, each time giving better and better descriptions of Campbell—and more important, his vehicle. Agents scoured a poor section of Atlanta until the car was finally identified and staked out. Campbell was arrested returning to it hours later.

Campbell tried to fight his extradition to Buffalo and tried to fight prison itself by refusing to eat. But it didn't matter; in 1978 he received 87 years to life in Sing Sing Correctional Facility for his brutal crimes—crimes that Campbell swears he doesn't remember committing.

INTERESTING FUGITIVE FACT:

In spring 1999 when Campbell was up for parole due to a quirk of sentencing laws, his prosecutor told the *Buffalo News:* "Are they crazy? If we could pick one person out of the 70,000 that are incarcerated in this state and let the other 69,999 go, he's the one who should stay."

349. ROY ELLSWORTH SMITH, child killer

LISTED: March 18, 1977
FOUND DEAD: June 2, 1977
DESCRIPTION: Born November 30, 1949, in Painesville, Ohio. Five feet 11 inches tall, 150 to 160 pounds, with brown hair and blue eyes. Scars and marks: scar on left shoulder, appendectomy scar. Occupations: clerk, custodian, dishwasher, handyman, plasterer's helper. May be wearing mustache and/or goatee, and reportedly is a frequent user of alcohol. Aliases: Roy Ellsworth Smith Jr., Roy E. Smith.

The Hammer. Roy Smith had a drug-and-booze-fueled adolescence and a chip on his shoulder the size of Rhode Island. By the time he turned 20, he'd already been in and out of psychiatric institutions and finally the Ohio State Penitentiary for a statutory rape conviction. Things seemed to brighten a bit by 1976, when Smith became serious with a girl named Sandra Bracken. But then the relationship soured, which sent Smith into a familiar downward spiral of rage and spite. Then on one horrible, bloody night in May 1976, Smith took his revenge upon the world. And Sandra Bracken, in particular.

Bracken was off in Las Vegas for a little breather. Her two children, however—a 14-year-old girl and a 12-year-old boy—were still at her home in Kirtland, Ohio. Police say that at some point on the night of May 10, Smith slipped into the house, took a ball peen hammer, and viciously bludgeoned both children to death. The hammer, bloodied and covered with Smith's fingerprints, was left at the scene. One of Smith's relatives spied him trying to break into the home of his sister-in-law later that night, and that was the last time anyone saw him alive. After murder indictments and close to a year of searching, Smith was named to the Top Ten list on March 18, 1977. There he remained for a few months, but it wasn't the FBI who would bring him down. It was Smith himself.

Apparently there was a glimmer of humanity left in Smith, after all. A hiker found his skeletal remains in Perry Township, Ohio. The Lake County Sheriff's Department of Painesville, Ohio, determined that he had committed suicide by hanging.

INTERESTING FUGITIVE FACT:

Mother Nature exacted a bit of grisly revenge on Smith's dead body. According to a forensics exam, wild predators appeared to have ripped his corpse to shreds.

350. RAYMOND LUC LEVASSEUR, radical bomber

LISTED: May 5, 1977
CAUGHT: November 4, 1984
DESCRIPTION: Born October 1946 in Sanford, Maine. Tattoos: a panther head and "Liberation" on one arm.

Wanted, with Children. The People's Army, a radical "prison reform" group, chose to make their points with bombs, not words. Fellow Top Ten criminals JOSEPH PICARIELLO and ED GULLION (#343 and #344, respectively), represented the Fred Hampton Unit of the group with their run of bombings in the Boston area. Raymond Levasseur's branch of the People's Forces, the "Sam Melville-Jonathan Jackson Unit," was arguably more dangerous. They continued their campaign of terror well into the 1980s, a time when very few 1970s-era radical bombers were still roaming free. Levasseur and his colleagues—which included fellow radical and Top Tenner THOMAS WILLIAM MANNING (#378)—were believed to be responsible for at least seven bombings in New England and a handful of bank robberies. This resulted in Levasseur being named to the Ten Most Wanted list on May 5, 1977.

But by that time Levasseur was simply getting warmed up. On the night of December 21, 1981, Levasseur, Manning, and a fellow radical named Richard Williams were caught speeding in Warren County, New Jersey, by a state trooper named Philip Lamonaco. Lamonaco had discovered that the group had weapons in the car and began to arrest them when Williams started shooting, leaving the state trooper with eight bullets in his body. The trio peeled away. (Manning's bloody fingerprint was found in an abandoned car just three miles from where Lamonaco died.) After that grisly encounter Levasseur and his group turned their full attention to fund-raising, knocking over banks all over New England, and netting more than $500,000 for the People's Forces—which was now calling itself the United Freedom Front. The FBI was more intent than ever to lay their hands on Levasseur and his band of radical 1970s leftovers.

Their chance came on November 4, 1984, when agents—after spending seven years tracking Levasseur—surrounded the fugitive, his common-law wife, and their three children as they were driving near Deerfield, Ohio. FBI agent Charles S. Prouty led the team that wrestled Levasseur to the ground and relieved him of the 9 mm handgun he was carrying. "We got the fun part," said Prouty to *Boston*

Magazine. "The hard part was tracking him down." (Today Prouty is the special agent in charge of the FBI's Boston office.)

For all of the bombings and robberies and killing, however, the most shocking thing about Levasseur's life came to light only after his arrest. When he wasn't being radical, he was living a fairly normal American life. Levasseur's family lived in Deerfield, where the fugitive posed as a sales manager for a cash register company. His daughters were noted as being extremely well behaved and attentive students and enjoyed a backyard full of playground gear, including a sandbox and swings. Scratching beneath the suburban surface, however, investigators found a virtual arsenal full of automatic weapons, bomb-making guides, and a list of potential targets, which included office buildings in New York City. The old 1970s radical was never far from home, after all.

INTERESTING FUGITIVE FACT:
Levasseur had been on the scene for the arrest of another Top Ten fugitive, CAMERON DAVID BISHOP, in early 1975. Both men were caught in front of a Providence, Rhode Island, bank with a car full of weapons. Bishop was handed over to the Feds, but Levasseur was freed on bail . . . and free to enter the infamous list himself two years later.

351. JAMES EARL RAY, assassin

LISTED (AGAIN): June 11, 1977
CAUGHT (AGAIN): June 13, 1977
DESCRIPTION: See Ray's 1960s listing (#277).

Leaf Me Alone. In the 1970s James Earl Ray was perhaps the world's most notorious living assassin. So it shouldn't come as a big surprise that if Ray were to have so much as left his prison bed unmade—let alone break out of jail—he was almost guaranteed to make headlines. But break out Ray did, and the nationwide attention was crushing. So much so that he barely lasted two days on the run. (On his first time on the Top Ten list Ray managed to stay hidden for a month and a half. For more, see entry #277.)

Ray had been sentenced to 99 years in prison after confessing to the murder of Martin Luther King Jr. and was shipped off to the state prison in Brushy Mountain, Tennessee. He tried to escape once, but the attempt was foiled. Ray was more successful on June 10, 1977, however. Accomplices in the exercise yard staged a fake fight, giving Ray and a half dozen other prisoners the opportunity to race to a wall, put together a makeshift ladder made of pipes, and proceed to scale the wall one by one. Six, including Ray, made it. The seventh man, Jerry Ward, received a bullet and was dragged back down into the prison.

When the prison administration realized exactly who had escaped, the alarm bells went off. In an unprecedented move Ray was named to the Top Ten list the very next day. (Usually it takes weeks, if not months, of waiting and case-pleading for a fugitive to make the list.) The FBI was not about to let MLK's assassin escape into the countryside. But for all of the furor, Ray's recapture was a bit on the lame side. He was found not too far away from the prison walls, trying to hide beneath a pile of leaves. Bloodhounds sniffed him out in moments, and he returned to prison without a fight.

INTERESTING FUGITIVE FACT:
Ray is only one of six fugitives to have made the Ten Most Wanted List twice. (Nobody has ever made it three times.)

352. WILLIE FOSTER SELLERS, bank robber

LISTED: June 14, 1977
CAUGHT: June 20, 1979
DESCRIPTION: Born in 1934. Six feet two inches, 221 pounds, with reddish brown hair and hazel eyes. Reportedly, Sellers is in need of root canal surgery and requires a daily dose of Orinase, an antidiabetic drug. Sellers had been seen driving a 1975 metallic brown Ford Grenada and a brown late model Buick or Oldsmobile with a light tan or white roof. One vehicle may be pulling a U-Haul trailer with a Mississippi license plate.

Flashback. You can't say that the notorious Deep South criminal team, the so-called Dawson Gang, didn't care about its members. After 43-year-old Willie Foster Sellers got sent up on federal bank robbery charges, the Dawson crew arranged to have a bundle of shiny new hacksaw blades sent to Sellers in an Atlanta prison. The prison screws intercepted that care package, so the Dawson guys sent another one . . . this time via special delivery.

On March 17, 1977, three unknown armed men used extremely sharp clippers to bite through the chain link surrounding Sellers's cell block window. Then they passed Sellers an acetylene blowtorch, which he used to burn through bars to free himself

and fellow Dawson member Charles Calvin Gary. (There were 16 other convicts in that cell block, but only the Dawson boys escaped.) From there Gary and Sellers hooked up with other members of Dawson Gang—named for the first bank they allegedly hit in Dawson County, Georgia—and established a safe house near Virginia Beach. Apparently Sellers was a valuable member of the team worth springing; he was later linked to bank heists in four states that netted close to a half million dollars. And not long after their escape Gary and Sellers were also sought in connection with the slaying of an Arlington County, Virginia, cop named John W. Buckley after a heist at the Virginia National Bank in April 1977. "Apprehension of the suspects doesn't sound too promising," admitted Arlington sergeant Raymond King in the *Washington Post* a few days after the killing of the 26-year-old cop. Gary would be arrested in Louisiana not long after; but Sellers remained at large, making the Ten Most Wanted list in June.

When Sellers was finally nabbed two years later by agents who had tracked him to Hartsell Airport in Atlanta, he was charged with multiple bank robberies, although not the Arlington heist that resulted in Buckley's death. He was sent back to prison, and this time there would be no care packages of blades or torches or wire cutters.

However, there is a surprise ending. Flash forward 23 years: Buckley's case is reopened by the FBI and an Arlington County police squad specializing in cold cases, and in 2000 new evidence is found linking Sellers, Gary, and fellow Dawson member Larry Hacker to the murder of James Michael Miller. Allegedly, the trio had planned a heist with Miller, but then changed their minds and iced him in Virginia Beach on April 12, 1977. Three days later, the Virginia National job was pulled, and Buckley was shot as three masked men burst out of the bank's front doors. Investigators now believe that Gary, Sellers, and Hacker may have been those men. All three were indicted for murder in March 2001. This time authorities wouldn't have to search the country for Sellers; he was still in prison serving time for his original robberies. The investigation continues as of this printing.

INTERESTING FUGITIVE FACT:
For Sellers life on the run was a family affair. While a Top Ten fugitive, Sellers traveled with his wife, Barbara, and their four children—the youngest of whom was born on the lam.

353. LARRY SMITH, professional killer

LISTED: July 15, 1977
CAUGHT: August 20, 1977
DESCRIPTION: Smith bears several bullet-wound scars as a result of his lifestyle and has been described by individuals as a "trigger man" responsible for several homicides. He has many associates in the Detroit metropolitan area and in the past has maintained contact with several of them. Smith normally wears a hat and has been employed in the past as a janitor, carpenter, and laborer.

A Streetcar Named "Capture." $1,500. That's all it would cost you to hire Detroit trigger man Larry Smith to shoot somebody. In 1977 Smith was serving a life sentence for armed robbery and assault with intent to kill in Huntsville, Texas, when the contract killing charge came up, forcing Smith to be shipped back to Detroit to face the new charges. That's when he had the brainstorm to complain about a supposed finger injury, which earned him a trip to a nearby hospital on May 16, 1977. Smith quickly managed to escape. He was slapped with charges of unlawful flight to avoid prosecution for murder, and made the Top Ten list just two months later.

But just as quick as Smith made the list, the list caught up with him. The killer-for-hire was nabbed in Toronto, Canada, by that city's police force. Smith made the mistake of driving past the open door of a city streetcar—a big no-no in Toronto. The Canadian cops pulled him over and found a concealed weapon and some marijuana. After a fingerprint check Smith was revealed to be a Top Tenner and was quickly sent back to the United States to face trial for murder and conspiracy to attempt murder.

INTERESTING FUGITIVE FACT:
According to his FBI bulletin, Smith had the unusual habit of walking "very erect, with his head back."

354. RALPH ROBERT COZZOLINO, robber, cop killer

LISTED: October 19, 1977
CAUGHT: January 6, 1978
DESCRIPTION: Born in Tennessee.

The Jackrabbit's Last Jump. Ralph Cozzolino really, *really* didn't like spending time behind bars. A career stickup man, Cozzolino bolted his first prison—the state lockup in Nashville—in September

1956. This was followed by another robbery arrest in 1958, and yet another prison break two months later, this time from an Alabama prison. Then came even more robberies, another arrest, and still another pair of jailbreaks in 1968. Cozzolino seriously did not want to be kept locked up in a cage.

This might account for Cozzolino's violent actions in an otherwise ordinary grocery store stickup in Chattanooga, Tennessee, in August 1977. Along with another crook named Clarence Parker, Cozzolino was going about his robbery when he spied every crook's worst nightmare: a uniformed police officer, right there in the store. Perhaps motivated by the specter of another jail term, Cozzolino shot the cop in the face then pumped more bullets into the fallen officer's back. Officer Charles Hambler died at the scene. Meanwhile, the grocery store owner seized the opportunity to grab his own pistol and blasted away at Parker, wounding him. Cozzolino chose not to return fire and ran. He was indicted for murder in September and joined the ranks of the Ten Most Wanted in October. Jackrabbit escapees always have an easier time making the list than other criminals, and a cop killing only made Cozzolino's case more urgent.

After a dogged FBI investigation, Cozzolino was arrested near a gas station in Jonesboro, Georgia. His bail was immediately set at $1 million. Apparently nobody wanted Cozzolino jumping off again.

INTERESTING FUGITIVE FACT:
Cozzolino once served a hitch at Alcatraz—a.k.a. The Rock—but never managed to escape. He saved his disappearing acts for smaller, southern prisons.

355. MILLARD OSCAR HUBBARD, bank robber

LISTED: October 19, 1977
CAUGHT: October 21, 1977
DESCRIPTION: Born August 15, 1928, in Whitley County, Kentucky. Five feet eight inches, 145 to 150 pounds, with graying black hair and brown eyes. Occupations: carpenter, construction worker, concrete worker, truck driver. Reportedly an avid fisherman and hunter. May wear wig and glasses. Lower teeth false. Aliases: Dick Bedillion, Bill Campbell, Harry Cox, Jim Lovelace, John Lovelace, Wayne Lycans, Ralph Moore, "Dillinger," and "Hubb."

Violent Endings. Millard Hubbard had been causing trouble since the 1950s, but by the 1970s he had become a swift and efficient bank robber. He even had his M.O. down pat: Strike swiftly, incapacitate the crowds, and if all else fails, grab your trusty M-16 rifle and start spraying. By 1976 Hubbard had pulled off four big-time bank heists, including one $105,000 job at a bank in Tazewell, Tennessee, during which he tied bank employees to furniture and traded bullets with cops during the getaway. (He was also charged with sticking up banks in Steubenville, Ohio, St. Clairsville, Ohio, and Washington, Pennsylvania.) His violent, trigger-happy ways certainly eased his path to the Top Ten list, to which he was named in mid October 1977. The spotlight was the worst thing that could have happened to Hubbard. Two days later, the FBI had Hubbard pinned down in Lexington, Kentucky, thanks to a tip from locals. True to form, Hubbard reached for his M-16 and pointed it at arresting agents. The FBI, however, was quicker on the draw. Agents pumped two bullets into Hubbard and then took away his M-16 for the very last time. He survived his wounds and was sentenced to 37 years in prison for a host of robbery, assault, and firearms charges.

INTERESTING FUGITIVE FACT:
Even though Hubbard survived his gun fight with the G-men, he wouldn't survive prison. On April 29, 1984, a fellow inmate beat Hubbard to death after an argument.

356. CARLOS TORRES, radical bomber

LISTED: October 19, 1977
CAUGHT: April 4, 1980
DESCRIPTION: Born September 19, 1952. Five feet five or six inches tall, 160 pounds, with brown hair and brown eyes. Sometimes wears glasses.

Dude May Look Like a Lady.   In November 1976 a drug addict broke into a Chicago apartment, looking for something to steal. What he found was much better than a TV or stereo—it was a mother lode of dynamite and explosives gear. The addict gathered up as much as he could, then started selling it on the streets. Word got out to the Chicago PD, who arranged an undercover buy. Once the addict was in handcuffs, he admitted he had stolen the explosives from an apartment and gave them the address. It turned out that the apartment was rented to one Carlos Alberto Torres.

Torres was a young member of the Episcopal Church's Hispanic commission. But he was involved in much more than religious texts and hymn books.

He was also a member of Fuerzas Armadas de Liberacion Nacional (FALN), or the Armed Forces of National Liberation. And his apartment was a virtual "bomb factory," in the words of one investigator. FALN needed a bomb factory because between August 1974 and March 1977 the radical organization set off more than 50 explosions, all in the name of "dramatizing the strangulation of the Puerto Rican people in the island as well as in the U.S. by the yoke of Yanki imperialism." The worst blast of the series: the January 24, 1975, bombing of Fraunces Tavern near Wall Street, which left at least four dead and more than 50 injured.

Thanks to that drugged-out burglar, investigators finally had a lead on one of the men behind the deadly blasts. Torres was named a federal fugitive, and his name made it to the Top Ten list in October 1977. The notes on Torres included an interesting tidbit: Police believed that Torres might disguise himself as a woman to elude capture.

FALN's activities continued, even with Torres on the lam, although the explosions tapered off, no doubt thanks to the dismantling of one of their "bomb factories." In 1980 the group raided campaign headquarters for then-president Jimmy Carter in Chicago and Republican vice-presidential candidate George H. W. Bush in New York. Staff members were taken hostage and slogans were slapped on walls, but both incidents were over briefly, with no injuries reported. Then in April 1980 Evanston police received a report about a suspicious van parked on a residential street. When law enforcement officials arrived on the scene, they discovered Torres and 10 other FALN members, who had holed up in a nearby house with shotguns and pistols, but no explosives. Torres was taken into custody dressed as a man.

INTERESTING FUGITIVE FACT:
Another FALN member, William Morales, was captured in 1978 after an experiment with explosives in his Queens home went awry. Morales lost both hands in the blast.

357. ENRIQUE ESTRADA, robber, murderer

LISTED: December 5, 1977
CAUGHT: December 8, 1977
DESCRIPTION: Born in 1941. Alias: Hank Estrada.

The Thug Had a Familiar Face.   Criminals who target senior citizens are usually a craven lot, small-time hoods who lack the strength to pick on people their own age. Enrique Estrada liked elderly targets, but took the assault to a psychotic level. In two separate instances he broke into the home of an older woman, threatened and robbed her at knifepoint, then bound her and proceeded to viciously beat her to death. Both murders took place in Los Angeles in Fall 1976; after a year of searching, Estrada was finally named to the Ten Most Wanted list.

If there is a textbook example of how the Top Ten list—nearly 30 years after its creation—still had the power to catch the country's most vicious criminals, it's Estrada. Just three days after he was named to the list, narcotics officers in Kern County took special notice of the Top Ten bulletin issued by the FBI. The face on the poster looked just like Hank Estrada, a drug abuser who'd they been tracking for some time. The narcotics officers trailed Estrada to a gas station in Bakersfield, California, then arrested him without incident. He was shipped back to Los Angeles to face charges of murder, robbery, and unlawful flight to avoid prosecution.

INTERESTING FUGITIVE FACT:
Estrada was into more than robbery-murders. His 32 felony arrests included larceny, property damage, and drug possession.

358. WILLIAM DAVID SMITH, bank robber, murderer

LISTED: February 10, 1978
CAUGHT: October 27, 1978
DESCRIPTION: Born in 1943 in Michigan.

Burn Rate. William Smith was a habitual bank robber, in and out of jail and violating parole after parole. This alone wasn't something that automatically earned a place on the Ten Most Wanted list. Murdering his ex-wife's new husband and burning his corpse, however, was what it took to do the trick. This is the crime Smith was accused of in April 1977 in Flint, Michigan, and it was enough to earn him a Top Ten spot nearly a year later. Smith managed to hide out in Chicago until a telephone tipster led FBI agents to him. He was arrested without a fight on October 27, 1978.

INTERESTING FUGITIVE FACT:
Smith made the Top Ten list with two other fugitives. The second, like Smith, would be largely forgotten.

The third, however, would live in infamy. His name: TED BUNDY (#360).

359. GARY RONALD WARREN, bank robber

LISTED: February 10, 1978
CAUGHT: May 12, 1978
DESCRIPTION: Born in San Pedro, California.

Top 40. A man in a curly brown wig walked into the Maryland National Bank in Towson, Maryland, and told a teller that he had a suitcase equipped with a bomb. The teller immediately handed over a pile of cash—certainly nothing to retire on—which the robber stuffed under his shirt. Then he plopped the suitcase on top of the counter and fled the bank. Two hours later, a local bomb squad technician finally opened the case and found six flares and a transistor radio.

It was just another workday for Gary Warren, professional bank robber. By the summer of 1977 Warren—then 32—had more than 40 bank heists to his credit, in addition to burglary, rape, and grand theft auto charges. Warren had been caught years before and slapped with a 40-year sentence in a Florida prison, but he managed to escape in March 1977 to get back into the business he knew best: liberating cash from banks. After the jailbreak the FBI began connecting Warren and his weird wigs (brown one heist, blond the next) with armed heists in Florida, West Virginia, Missouri, and California. It was time to stop Warren before he hit 50. On February 10, 1978, Warren was named to the Ten Most Wanted list. Three months later, the FBI and local police cornered Warren in Cumberland, Maryland, where he'd been hiding out.

INTERESTING FUGITIVE FACT:
Warren was named to the Most Wanted list the same day as TED BUNDY.

360. TED BUNDY, serial killer

LISTED: February 10, 1978
CAUGHT: February 15, 1978
DESCRIPTION: Born November 24, 1946, in Burlington, Vermont. Six feet tall, 175 pounds, with blue eyes and brown hair.

The Perfect Psycho. Theodore Robert Bundy is by far the most famous member of the Ten Most

Wanted list, which seems to fly in the face of the purpose of the list: to shine a spotlight on those crooks who have managed to stay hidden for a long time, using publicity as a tool. When he was named to the Top Ten on February 10, 1978, Ted Bundy wasn't the household name he is today. All the public knew was this relatively innocent-looking guy was being accused of a slightly unbelievable series of grisly crimes. The legend would come later.

Countless books and magazine articles have been written about Bundy, perhaps the most famous being Ann Rule's *The Stranger Beside Me,* a harrowing account of how Rule—now a wildly successful true crime writer—once worked with Bundy at a counseling center back in 1971. Let's focus however, on Bundy as a Top Ten fugitive, which technically began on June 9, 1977, when he escaped from a courtroom during a recess in Aspen, Colorado. ("The sheriff's department was patently naive, bordering on criminally stupid, to leave Bundy in the courtroom alone," complained one city employee in Aspen.) Bundy was in Aspen, awaiting trial for the murder of Caryn Campbell, a nurse from Michigan who was found raped and murdered after vacationing in Aspen in 1975. But this wasn't Bundy's first brush with the law. The handsome, clean-cut former Boy Scout was in Aspen on loan from Utah State Prison, where he had been convicted of aggravated kidnapping and had served a year of his one- to 15-year sentence.

Ted Bundy, on the loose in Aspen, created a minor panic in town. Schools were closed, search dogs were unleashed, and area residents were warned to stay inside and lock their doors. Fortunately, Bundy was captured eight days later and returned to prison. Bundy spent the next six months losing 30 pounds, and on New Year's Eve 1975 he managed to squeeze out of a one-foot hole in a maximum security prison in Colorado.

After Bundy escaped for the second time, police really began connecting the dots, and it soon became shockingly clear that Bundy—"the kind of guy you'd want your daughter to bring home," in the words of one investigator—might be responsible for the strangulation murders of at least 36 women. In early 1978 it became clear that Bundy was killing again. An unknown man entered a sorority house at Florida State University in Tallahassee on January 15, then beat and strangled two sleeping students. One of them was raped. Three other students were beaten with a tree limb. Then, on February 9, a 12-year-old girl named Kimberly Leach disappeared from a schoolyard in Jacksonville; a stolen credit card statement put Bundy in that exact area at the same time. With frightening evidence mounting, Bundy was named to the Ten Most Wanted list the very next day.

Eventually, Ted Bundy would be linked to 36 sex murders over a seven-year span and would confess to at least 28 of them by the end of his legal process. They were stealthy crimes committed by a man who thought he was above reproach—a friendly, handsome guy with a degree in psychology who was studying law at various institutions in the western United States. Bundy might have been the perfect psycho, but he was a pretty lousy fugitive. Just five days after making the list, Bundy was stopped in Pensacola by a local cop who caught him speeding. The officer called in the license plate and learned it was stolen. Bundy tried to run for it, but was subdued by pursuing officers. Forensic evidence—most notably, teeth marks—linked Bundy to the sorority slayings at Florida State, and he was convicted of those murders in June 1979. Bundy died in the electric chair at 7:16 A.M. on January 24, 1989, just over 11 years after those murders.

INTERESTING FUGITIVE FACT:
According to a 2000 update of Ann Rule's classic *The Stranger Beside Me,* Ted Bundy traded letters with David Berkowitz (the Son of Sam killer) and John Hinckley (the man who shot Ronald Reagan) while in prison.

361. ANDREW EVAN GIPSON, bank robber

LISTED: March 27, 1978
CAUGHT: May 24, 1978
DESCRIPTION: Born May 29, 1936. Alias: Phillip Daigls.

"A Damn Good Worker."   On January 19, 1968, a stick of dynamite was shoved into an air conditioner at Overland Park City Hall, then detonated. "My first thought was that a jet had just broken the sound barrier," recalled Police Chief Myron Scafe to the *Kansas City Star.* Then Scafe saw dust and debris and realized that it was no jet. A short while later, word came that the Metcalf State Bank across town was being robbed. "It didn't take us long to figure out this was a diversion," Scafe said. "We immediately dispatched officers to the vicinity of the bank."

Setting off a diversionary bomb to aid a bank robbery is a time-honored stunt; in fact, Top Tenners BOBBY WILCOXSON and ALBERT NUSSBAUM (#167 and

#168) had mastered the technique back in the early 1960s. Too bad for Andrew Evan Gipson and his partner, Henry Floyd Brown, two self-styled revolutionaries, that the Overland Park Police were wise to the trick. Gipson and Brown actually made it out of the bank with $13,000 shoved into a pillowcase, but eagle-eyed employees of the Kentucky Fried Chicken next door saw the whole heist go down and even hopped into a car to give pursuit. The KFC posse didn't manage to stop Gipson and Brown or even get a license plate. But they passed along the make and model of the getaway car—along with a general heading—to the police. The info was broadcast on police frequencies, and the hunt was on.

Gipson and Brown were nearly caught when motorcycle patrolman Chester Sundbye gave pursuit. Gipson steered while Brown blasted away at his pursuer through the rear window. Sundby was shot in the face, but miraculously, the bullet simply passed through his left cheek and exited his open mouth. Other bullets shattered his police radio. Gipson and Brown raced away, leaving Sundbye on the asphalt, counting his blessings.

Unsure if their getaway car had been identified, Gipson and Brown commandeered a car from a woman and her 13-year-old son. An hour later, a car matching that description was seen pulling into the Heatherwood Apartments in Overland Park. "I'm here in my apartment," said the phone tipster, "I'm listening to the radio, and I just saw that car back in."

Authorities in and around Overland Park clearly took the bomb and bullets personally. More than 150 law enforcement officials surrounded the Heatherwood. "We had officers show up we didn't even call for," recalled Scafe to the *Star*. Police started searching apartments one by one, until bingo—Brown. But Brown was holding a shotgun in one hand and an M-1 rifle in the other. He opened fire. In the dizzying gun battle that followed, one bullet Brown fired shattered through the windshield of Highway Patrol sergeant Eldon Miller and hit him directly between the eyes, knocking him into the backseat. Gunfire was returned; tear gas was lobbed. After a few violent minutes police found Brown on the floor of one of the apartments, wounded in the stomach, right arm, and legs. Gipson, however, was gone.

As it turned out, Gipson had already split with the heist's two silent partners—the girlfriends of the would-be revolutionaries. Brown's girl went her own separate way and was arrested in Cedar Rapids, Iowa, but Gipson and his girlfriend survived at large

for 10 days before the heat of a manhunt proved too intense, and they surrendered to authorities.

Gipson had racked up quite an impressive set of charges—assault with intent to kill, bank robbery, grand larceny, firearm possession—to go along with the charges he'd already racked up as a journeyman criminal. He received a sentence of 40 to 90 years in prison, but served only nine of them before escaping the state penitentiary at Lansing in July 1977. Nine months later, law enforcement decided enough was enough. Gipson was named to the Ten Most Wanted list.

Apparently any revolutionary ideas Gipson may have had were smothered during his time in the slammer. Barely two months after he made the list, G-men found Gipson living as a construction worker in Albuquerque, New Mexico. In fact, he'd just been promoted to foreman. "He was a damn good worker," said one fellow employee, who was stunned to hear that he'd been hoisting tools with an escaped felon. Gipson surrendered without a fight and was sent back to prison.

INTERESTING FUGITIVE FACT:
Like so many great partners, Gipson and Brown met in prison, at the U.S. penitentiary at Leavenworth.

362. ANTHONY DOMINIC LIBERATORE, gangster

LISTED: May 24, 1978
CAUGHT: April 1, 1979
DESCRIPTION: Born in 1922 in Cleveland, Ohio.

Running in the Underworld. Tony Liberatore worked as a member of the regional sewer commission and was an official of the Laborers Union Local 860 in Cleveland. He was also up to his neck in organized crime, which made him a rarity among his fellow Top Tenners. For years J. Edgar Hoover himself dismissed the very idea of an organized crime family, thus very few members were ever named to the FBI's Most Wanted list.

Before he got involved in the union rackets, Liberatore worked as hired muscle for the Cleveland mob, and at the tender age of 16—this was back in 1938—was convicted of helping to kill two police officers. He was sentenced to life behind bars. But in 1957 Liberatore caught a lucky break. His sentence was commuted by Governor John Brown, an interim officeholder who filled an 11-day vacancy. Once sprung, Liberatore ran right back into the arms of the mob, this time ensconcing himself in the local unions, ingratiating himself with the area politicians, and rising in the ranks of the underworld. After a while the Cleveland residents didn't see Liberatore the gangster; they saw Liberatore the union official, Liberatore the friend of the mayor, and even Liberatore the frequent lecturer on penal reform.

But the ugly face behind the public mask soon revealed itself. In March 1978 Liberatore was indicted on charges of conspiring to kill a fellow mobster and former partner, Daniel J. Greene, who was literally blown to bits after visiting his dentist. Apparently Liberatore and Greene were grappling over running the local syndicate; Greene wanted his Irish gang to run the show, while Liberatore was favoring the Italian group, the Jack White Organization. Liberatore disappeared the day before the indictment and was named to the Top Ten list just two months later.

Liberatore was not going to be easy to catch—he had money and connections and could afford to stay hidden away for a long time. Life on the run wouldn't be too hard on him, either. "He's the type of guy who's going to stay in a Ramada and not in a sleazy motel," said a spokesman in the FBI's Cleveland office.

Or at the home of a fellow gangster. G-men traced Liberatore to the home of a mob associate in Eastlake, Ohio, and pounced on him on April Fool's Day. The home had been considered safe by the syndicate. They were wrong.

INTERESTING FUGITIVE FACT:
Liberatore enjoyed deep-sea diving and private planes, which led some agents to believe that the gangster may have fled the country. As it turned out, Liberatore hadn't strayed too far at all.

363. MICHAEL GEORGE THEVIS, pornographer

LISTED: July 10, 1978
CAUGHT: November 9, 1978
DESCRIPTION: Born February 25, 1932, in Raleigh, North
    Carolina.

$31,000 Ticket Out. The man who would be dubbed the "Sultan of Smut" started small, with just one newsstand in Atlanta in the late 1960s. Over the next 15 years Michael Thevis built an empire of 200 businesses worth an estimated $100 million dollars. His game? Porn—peep shows, book and magazine

shops, and films with titles such as *Beat Me, Baby, Violent Vixens,* and *Dirty Sex Dreams of Uptight Men.* Thevis walked a fine line. Some only saw his public, generous side, applauding as the southern porn lord offered his $3 million mansion as a home for gifted children and tried to invest in nonporn enterprises. "I could be this city's best goodwill ambassador, if they only knew it," said Thevis, who wouldn't even keep a copy of *Playboy* in his home, lest his kids discover it. However, other people—mostly competitors—saw his secret side. The side that wouldn't hesitate to kill or destroy to get rid of any perceived threat to his flesh-peddling fiefdom.

Thevis was no stranger to run-ins with the law; in fact, he used to brag about his nearly 100 arrests for distribution of pornography. Then the charges became increasingly serious. In 1974 he was ordered to jail after a federal appeals court review of a conviction for transportation of obscene materials.

Thevis, called "The King of Pornography," was arrested in Bloomfield, Connecticut, by FBI agents and local police.

Thevis was first imprisoned in Terre Haute, Indiana, but thanks to greasing the palms of Georgia politicians (about $400,000 worth of grease, in campaign contributions), the porn lord was moved to a cozier prison hospital in Lexington, Kentucky, where he enjoyed the use of a telephone and frequent conjugal visits.

But jail didn't stop the mounting charges. In 1977 a jury ordered Thevis to pay $667,000 after a jury linked him to an arson fire that destroyed a competing porn shop. A year later, a federal grand jury in Atlanta charged Thevis with arson, extortion, racketeering, and murder, all in the name of controlling the Georgia porn industry. The murder charge stemmed from two corpses: one being the body of a Thevis business associate that was found stuffed in the trunk of a Cadillac, and other the remains of a porn shop manager who rocketed through the roof of his van thanks to a dynamite explosion.

Thevis was starting to get jumpy, waiting for the federal axe to fall. By that time he was at a local jail in New Albany, Indiana. On April 28 Thevis went to make a phone call and was left alone by the guards. When the guards returned, Thevis was gone. Close to three months later, Thevis was named to the Ten Most Wanted list.

Any fugitive who is named to the Top Ten becomes a priority for the FBI. While on the lam, Thevis managed to up the stakes even further. On October 25, an unidentified gunman shot Roger Underhill, 50, who was the key witness in the government's 14-count racketeering case against Thevis. "It was a clean professional hit," a police spokesperson told the *Washington Post*. The government's case was suddenly weakened, and other witnesses were spooked. One witness reportedly called the *Atlanta Constitution* and said: "Get a message to Mike. I want Mike to accept my apology. Tell Mike, leave me alone. Forget it, I'll leave you alone. I don't want to be like Roger." The FBI wanted Thevis caught more than ever.

Meanwhile, Thevis had shaved his goatee and started wearing a toupee. But he drew attention to himself on October 13, when he deposited a $30,000 check at the Bloomfield State Bank in Connecticut under the name "A. J. Evans." The fat deposit raised the eyebrows of one bookkeeper, who reported it to bank officials. They watched the check—drawn on a bank in South Carolina—clear, but it still seemed fishy. The bank president called local police. A few weeks later, "Evans" called the bank and told them that he'd be stopping by to withdraw $31,000. The

bank again alerted the police, who were waiting for Thevis when he arrived.

Thevis said there must be some kind of mistake—he was just a contractor from Meban, North Carolina. Police put Thevis on the phone with people who knew the real A. J. Evans (he turned out to be a brother of one of Thevis's friends), and was asked personal questions that Thevis couldn't possibly answer. Fingerprints were taken; another FBI Top Tenner was under arrest. "We had no idea who we had at the time," said Bloomfield police chief Harold Jackson to the *Washington Post*, "but we knew it was somebody."

Thevis told the police: "Well, I knew it had to happen sooner or later. I knew they were after me."

INTERESTING FUGITIVE FACT:
Thevis once studied to be a Greek Orthodox priest.

364. CHARLES EVERETT HUGHES, drug dealer

LISTED: November 18, 1978
CAUGHT: April 29, 1981
DESCRIPTION: Born 1945. Hughes is an avid motorcyclist, with a fondness for Harley Davidsons and is skilled at auto repair. He has been heavily involved in the drug scene, and is known to carry firearms on his person at all times.

The Sandy Creek Murders. In late summer 1977 a group of students from the University of Florida packed up their skin-diving gear and plunged into the murky depths of a Gulf Coast sinkhole, hoping to uncover Indian artifacts. But they didn't find peace pipes. Instead, the students found four skeletons, which had been tied, gagged, and sunk with cement blocks.

The corpses were later identified as Harold Sims, 39, Douglas Glen Hood, 21, Sandy McAdams, 16, and Sheila McAdams, 14. Seven months before, on January 23, Sims and Hood had been cruising for chicks at a nightclub in Panama City in northern Florida. They met the underaged McAdams girls and talked them into a midnight drive to a quiet stretch of the Gulf coastline known as Sandy Creek. Unfortunately, they stumbled into a $1.2 million marijuana shipment—an estimated 35 tons of pot—fresh from South America on a shrimp trawler named *Gunsmoke*.

The band of smugglers were not happy. Sims was shot first, and his three companions were bound and gagged. Then all four were driven 125 miles away to a secluded location in Taylor County. Hood and McAdams were shot in the head, execution-style, then weighted down and dropped into the sinkhole. They might have gone undiscovered, if not for the University of Florida diving expedition. Four names quickly emerged in the subsequent investigation, and among them: Charles Hughes. While two of his partners were charged with the actual murder, Hughes was believed to have helped, providing the rope to tie the victims and the van that would transport them to their watery graves. A warrant was issued for Hughes's arrest in January 1978, and he was named to the Top Ten list the following November.

It took nearly three years, but the FBI finally found Hughes in Myrtle, Mississippi, where he was hiding out under the name "George Hacker" and working as an auto mechanic. He was extradited to Panama City to face up to his part in the Sandy Creek murders. But the town of Myrtle, population 300, had grown to love the fugitive. Residents subsequently raised $2,000 for Hughes's defense fund and printed up T-shirts with Hughes's picture and the slogan "We're Still With You." As part of the fund-raising efforts, Myrtle held a bake sale, rummage sale, and pool tournament. Children even mowed extra lawns and donated portions of their allowances to help with Hughes's legal bills. "I don't think he was capable of the things they said he did," said resident Opal Hudson, a café owner. "We knew George Hacker—this Charles Hughes is somebody I don't know."

Despite the milk money from Myrtle, Hughes was sentenced to 15 years in prison. He was released after serving five of them.

INTERESTING FUGITIVE FACT:
According to friends of "George Hacker" in Myrtle, the fugitive never ate a meal without saying grace first.

365. RONALD LEE LYONS, armed robber

LISTED: December 17, 1978
CAUGHT: September 10, 1979
DESCRIPTION: Born in 1946 in Cincinnati, Ohio.

The Great Escape. You've got a prison full of bored inmates who need some R&R. What do you do? If you're in Tennessee, you take them bowling.

That's where Ronald Lee Lyons found himself on September 13, 1977—a bowling alley in Dickson, Tennessee. Lyons was there with other inmates and guards (of course), looking for strikes and trying to stay out of the gutter. Lyons, however, also had another score in mind: the two sawed-off shotguns hidden in the drop ceiling of the men's room.

Lyons, along with three other cons—Larry Chism, Floyd Brewer, and George Bonds—all had the urge to hit the men's room at the same time. When they came back with the weapons, the foursome quickly took control of the bowling alley. Prison guards opened fire, but one of the men grabbed a young snack bar employee named Carolyn Barnette, and the guards were forced to surrender their weapons. The four convicts, along with their hostage, took off in a stolen car.

They were headed to the Dickson airport with an escape plan firmly in mind. As would later be revealed, Lyons and his buddies had been plotting this for a while. (Prison authorities had even picked up on some vague references to a jailbreak when monitoring Lyons's phone calls, but dismissed it as idle chatter.) The next part of the plan: Kidnap an airport employee and force him to fly to Arkansas. Airport manager Mel Romine had no choice but to obey, but was forced to crash-land in Lee County, Arkansas, after running out of fuel. Romine was freed, and the convicts invaded the home of an elderly couple, Mr. and Mrs. John King of Woodlawn, Arkansas. In the morning the fugitives split up. Brewer and Bonds took the Kings' pickup truck in one direction, while Lyons and Chism took the Kings and their car in another.

From there the great escape began to unravel. Law enforcement officials snared Bonds and Brewer in a roadblock, arresting them without incident. Meanwhile, Lyons forced the Kings to drive him to Covington, Kentucky, where he asked to borrow $2, and then walked across an Ohio River bridge into Cincinnati, Lyons's hometown. (Chism had gone his own way earlier and was soon arrested.) The Kings—like every other hostage abducted during the two-day escape spree—were released unharmed. More than a year later, Lyons was still at large, and law enforcement officials were eager to have a little chat with him. He was named to the Ten Most Wanted list in December 1978, charged with kidnapping, conspiracy, and a rather unusual charge for a Top Tenner, air piracy.

The following September, Lyons was arrested in Hungry Valley, Nevada—a small town near Reno—

by FBI agents and the Washoe County sheriff's department. Thirty years was added to Lyons's original 50-year sentence, and this time there would be no more bowling trips.

INTERESTING FUGITIVE FACT:
Lyons had originally been in jail for the armed robbery of two Moose Lodges in Tennessee.

366. LEO JOSEPH KOURY, murderer, extortionist

LISTED: April 20, 1979
FOUND DEAD: June 16, 1991
DESCRIPTION: Born July 14, 1934, in Pittsburgh, Pennsylvania. Five feet 11 inches tall, 240 pounds with brown eyes and black hair. Koury is reported to be a diabetic requiring insulin shots. He may speak Spanish and has worked as a restaurant operator and baseball umpire. He frequents Lebanese restaurants whenever possible. Known to carry a

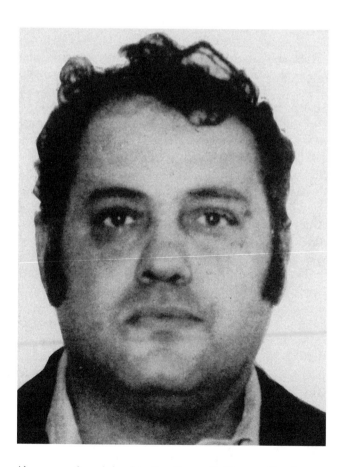

Koury was found dead in San Diego, California. Death was due to massive cerebral vascular hypertension.

revolver in an ankle holster, Koury is considered armed and dangerous.

"An Eggshell with Nothing Inside." Koury owned several gay bars in Richmond, Virginia, but he wasn't satisfied with that. He wanted to control them all, especially the new upstarts that in the mid-1970s had set up shop in town, muscling into his monopoly. So Koury decided to muscle back the hard way.

A rival bar's bouncer was the first target; in March 1975 he was found in a nearby river, tied down with weights. He had been shot to death, a killing allegedly ordered by Koury. Later that same year Koury was believed to have started planning a high-paying kidnapping scheme, in which they would snatch Richmond millionaire E. Claiborne Robbins and demand a cool $500,000 for ransom. (The plot blew up when G-men nabbed one of Koury's kidnapping team members for another crime.) In January 1977 another Koury-engineered shooting took the lives of three people at yet another rival bar. These three incidents were just the highlights of a long criminal career that included insurance fraud, racketeering, arson (torching his own cars and boat), armed robbery, loan sharking, threatening a grand jury witness, and obstructing justice. The heat finally caught up with Koury, and Richmond's would-be criminal kingpin was indicted by a federal grand jury the day before Halloween 1978.

However, the day before that, Koury disappeared. Six months later, he was named to the Most Wanted list. But unlike most people named to the Top Ten, Koury managed to stay on the lam for an astounding 13 years, one of the longest Top Ten runs. He might have remained undiscovered—after years of wanted posters, billboards, and three *America's Most Wanted* appearances—if not for one enterprising county employee.

In June 1991, clear across the country from Virginia, a man named William Franklin Biddle died from a cerebral hemorrhage. He was a slightly overweight guy who worked at a San Diego convenience store and whom everyone liked, but no one knew all that well. Biddle's boss and friend, Souhel "Sam" Houshan, recalled that he'd been to Biddle's apartment only once or twice. But according to Houshan, you couldn't find a better guy. "He's the nicest man I ever met," Houshan said in an interview. "Very honest, very straight, never cussed." Biddle had always claimed to be an orphan and Vietnam vet who lived on a humble pension given to him by the International Red Cross, where he'd worked most of his adult life. The convenience store gig was just a way to pass the time, shooting the breeze with customers and sipping coffee.

When Biddle dropped dead, his case file landed on the desk of Susan Graves, a deputy public administrator who looked into pauper deaths when no one showed up to claim the body. Graves's investigation began with Houshan, who told her that Biddle also used to run grocery errands for local seniors and would routinely loan friends large sums of money, no questions asked. Biddle didn't own a car, but didn't really seem to need one, since he only left his apartment to attend Saturday evening Mass or to report to the convenience store for work.

But when Graves started digging deeper, things got sticky. The U.S. Army had no records of any Biddle serving in Vietnam—in fact, no William Franklin Biddle, period. Ditto with the Red Cross. Also weird was the fact that some friends thought Biddle was Hispanic, since he lapsed into Spanish every so often, while other friends heard him lapse into Arabic.

Then came a creepy phone call: Graves was warned not to visit Biddle's apartment.

But Graves wasn't about to quit. She made her way to Biddle's pad in East San Diego and inside found something even stranger: evidence of a blank life. No pictures on the walls. No scrapbooks. No letters. In fact, no paper trail of any kind, aside from a birth certificate, driver's license, Social Security card, and video rental card. "It was clear there was something not right," Graves later told a reporter. "His life seemed like an eggshell with nothing inside it." Graves popped open a bank security deposit box under Biddle's name and found $25,000, all in hundreds.

Finally, a phone call would solve the mystery. A man named Barrett Rossi was looking for information about his uncle, Leo Koury, who had died recently. As the conversation went on, and Rossi said that Uncle Leo had been known to speak a little Arabic, alarm bells went off in Graves's head. She called the FBI, and with a fingerprint check of the corpse a 13-year-old manhunt that had cost the government well over $1 million—and filled 48 volumes of paper at FBI headquarters—was over. Biddle was Koury.

"Over the years we have interviewed thousands of people," said Special Agent Henry O. Handy Jr. after the news broke in July 1991. "Some of them were such lookalikes that the only way we could eliminate them was through fingerprints."

Koury was one of the rare Top Tenners who figured out a way to beat the system, avoiding a flashy life, or even the luxury of a car, to stay well under radar. (It's hard to get nabbed by a police checkpoint if you don't drive.) No one will ever know what compelled Koury to trade his freewheeling, blood-soaked life of crime for a Walter Mitty existence thousands of miles away, but for 13 years, the trade-off worked.

INTERESTING FUGITIVE FACT:
Koury was the first federal fugitive whose face was slapped on billboards—11 of them, scattered throughout the city of Richmond, Virginia, in September 1982. "It's like putting a couple of thousand agents in the field," a billboard company representative told an AP reporter.

367. JOHN WILLIAM SHERMAN, bank robber, terrorist

LISTED: August 3, 1979
CAUGHT: December 17, 1981
DESCRIPTION: Sherman is a known bomb specialist, and a master of disguise. Alias: James Morgan.

"A Real Bad Apple." It's hard to say what John Sherman was better at—robbing banks or blowing up stuff. By the time he was taken down for good, Sherman had scored 14 bank heists and 11 bombings, all in the Pacific Northwest, and all in the name of the revolution. Sherman was another one of those 1970s-era radical terrorists, the "George Jackson Brigade" in particular. (Jackson was the name of a radical prisoner killed by San Quentin prison guards in 1971.) "I'm dedicated to the destruction of the evil American system," Sherman once said in court. "He's what we call a real bad apple," said one FBI special agent.

The Jackson Brigade began their assaults on New Year's Day 1976, when a Seattle power substation was blown up. That was followed by bomb blasts at banks, government buildings, and even car dealerships. (Fortunately, no people were injured in these blasts.) Bank raids funded the group's bombing campaign, and after one early heist in Seattle, Sherman was shot and arrested by police. But that wasn't a problem—not when Sherman had a band of devoted brigade members willing to come to his rescue. While Sherman was being led by a guard from the hospital, a fellow revolutionary disguised as a medical assistant shot the guard and helped Sherman flee the scene. More bombs and bank robberies followed.

When FBI agents finally pinned Sherman down in March 1978 outside of a Tacoma, Washington, drive-in, the revolutionary leader was disguised as a priest. Father Sherman, however, was accompanied by two women, one of them carrying a 9 mm pistol. All three were arrested, and Sherman was slapped with a 35-year sentence at a federal prison in Lompoc, California, for bank robbery and escape.

Sherman was out of commission for only a year, though. In April 1979 he was taken to downtown Lompoc to receive treatment from an ophthalmologist. Sherman had somehow gotten word of this visit to his wife, who managed to hide a gun in the ophthalmologist's bathroom. Sherman excused himself to powder his nose, and then excused himself from the custody of the state. His wife was waiting outside in a getaway car, and once again, the leader of the George Jackson Brigade was free. His name was added to the Ten Most Wanted list in late summer 1979.

The "master of disguise" did manage to stay hidden for quite a while, but after a dogged investigation the FBI tracked him to a hideout in Golden, Colorado. Strangely, Sherman hadn't kept quiet during his time in Colorado—he tried to help organize machinists into a union. When he was fired, the National Labor Relations Board sued on his behalf and won him a settlement of $7,200. (Fugitives usually keep a slightly lower profile.) Months later, the FBI fixed on his location, and Sherman was arrested climbing into his car. He was taken into custody along with his wife, Marianne, and another female friend, the two women charged with harboring a fugitive. No Brigade members swept in to save them; there was no chance for hidden guns, either. Five years were added to Sherman's sentence, and he was returned to prison.

INTERESTING FUGITIVE FACT:
Sherman's escape from Lompoc was supposedly inspired by a similar prison break in *The Godfather.*

368. MELVIN BAY GUYON, armed robber, rapist, murderer

LISTED: August 9, 1979
CAUGHT: August 16, 1979
DESCRIPTION: Born in 1960. Alias: Tyrone Little.

Two Gunfights. Six G-men entered the crumbling Cleveland housing project early Thursday morning, August 9, 1979. They were seeking Melvin Guyon—a 19-year-old suspect in at least 10 rapes of teenage girls in Chicago—and the FBI had traced the young thug to Cleveland, where he was supposedly holed up with a girlfriend. When Agent Johnnie L. Oliver and his partner, Agent William Tenwick, burst in, they found Guyon, shirtless and shoeless, and surrounded by children.

Guyon went for a pistol.

The first shot went wild. But the second blasted through Oliver's chest. Oliver, only 35, would die from the wound. Tenwick returned fire, but Guyon ducked the bullet, dove out of the bedroom window, and started to run, bleeding profusely from cuts made by the shattered glass. Agents squeezed off more shots at the fleeing killer, but none appeared to hit their target. Police and G-men stopped a city bus after someone matching the description was reported riding it, but not Guyon. Ditto for a house-to-house search that closed one Cleveland street. (It was later revealed that Guyon had stolen a bicycle 30 blocks away and used that to make his escape.) The next day a $10,000 reward was announced for Guyon's capture. "He's the number one priority in Cleveland," said FBI spokesman Anthony T. Riggio.

Guyon stayed elusive for a few days, and then reports came in that Guyon was holed up in Youngstown, a steel town 70 miles southeast of Cleveland. On August 16, Special Agent Tom Bader led a 34-man team to Youngstown, where some agents spied a man who looked like Guyon inside a phone booth. One agent casually strolled past the phone booth to make a positive ID, then gave the signal. It was Guyon.

A hasty plan was hatched to pin Guyon in the booth by tipping it over with an FBI van. But the booth wouldn't tip, and Guyon started blasting away again. Agents fired back, but Guyon managed to slip away once again and disappeared into the darkness. He broke into a private home and curled up into a ball on a chair, shaking uncontrollably. Guyon hadn't been hit in the recent gun battle, but he was still recovering from cuts and bruises and gunshot wounds he received in Cleveland a week earlier. The owner of the home Guyon had broken into convinced the bleeding fugitive to go to the hospital, and there he finally gave up the fight. "I'm Melvin Guyon," he told Cleveland police. "I'm hurt. I'm tired of running."

"This guy was scared to death," said a Youngstown cop, Wesley V. Merritt, who was moonlighting

211

at the hospital when Guyon was brought in. "He told us, 'I don't want to die.'"

Guyon was treated, then returned to Cleveland to face state and federal charges, which now included murder, attempted murder, and aggravated robbery. He was held on $1.3 million bond and eventually sentenced to life in prison.

INTERESTING FUGITIVE FACT:
The same day that Guyon blasted Agent Oliver, a man named James Maloney walked into FBI offices in El Entro, California, and shot two agents, J. Robert Porter and Charles W. Elmore, before shooting himself. (Maloney had said he wanted to see files investigating his past with groups such as the Weathermen.) It was the bloodiest day in Bureau history.

369. GEORGE ALVIN BRUTON, burglar and kidnapper

LISTED: September 28, 1979
CAUGHT: December 14, 1979
DESCRIPTION: Born 1943 in Swann, Missouri.

Bad Houseguest. George Bruton spent six years at the U.S. penitentiary at Leavenworth. His time there wasn't a cakewalk, but he did manage to make a few friends. Bruton was paroled on November 22, 1978, and immediately looked up an old cellmate buddy of his, Steven Scott Pannell. The two got right back into the business that landed Burton in prison in the first place: robbing and stealing.

Following a short crime spree of knocking over a drug store and stealing cars, Bruton and Pannell took hostages at a home in Davis County, Utah, a few days before Christmas 1978. Police cornered the duo inside the home, but Bruton and Parnell managed to shoot their way out, and two law enforcement officers were left wounded. A few days later, Pannell was captured, but Bruton stayed on the lam. He made his way to Kansas City, Missouri, and looked up yet another prison buddy, Michael Walker. Burton moved in with Walker and his girlfriend. Apparently Bruton skipped his hospitality classes at Leavenworth. Rule #1 of being a houseguest: It is not considered polite to shoot your host in the head, leaving his body in an abandoned car, then strangling your host's girlfriend and dumping her body outside city limits. But that's what authorities believed Bruton did, and six

months later, Bruton was named to the Ten Most Wanted list.

The FBI traced Bruton to a mobile home in Fort Smith, Arkansas, on December 14. Around noon Bruton climbed into his pickup truck, and immediately FBI vehicles swarmed in around him. But Bruton was not ready to surrender without a fight. He hammered the gas pedal and rocketed straight into one of the FBI vehicles. Then Bruton grabbed his gun and opened fire at an agent. G-men returned the favor, and Bruton was taken down with a shotgun blast to the leg. He was taken to the hospital to undergo surgery and to await his return to Utah to face felony charges.

INTERESTING FUGITIVE FACT:
Bruton was responsible for an important legal precedent, one that fans of *Law & Order* and other TV courtroom dramas would find very familiar. Basically, thanks to *Bruton vs. the United States* (1968), a defendant in a federal case can't be convicted on the testimony of a co-defendant if that co-defendant isn't cross-examined on the witness stand first.

370. EARL EDWIN AUSTIN, bank robber

LISTED: October 12, 1979
CAUGHT: March 1, 1980
DESCRIPTION: Born in Tacoma Park, Maryland. Reportedly a compulsive gambler.

"Very Cool." Darrell Brubaker was standing in the lobby of the Arapahoe National Bank in Boulder, Colorado, when a stranger in sport clothes and a hat walked in. Brubaker was the bank's president, and the stranger identified himself as a member of the FDIC (Federal Deposit Insurance Corporation). "He said he wanted to speak to me about a private matter," Brubaker recalled to an AP reporter.

After the two entered Brubaker's office, the stranger asked Brubaker to close the door. The stranger announced that he was here to rob the bank and that he had accomplices armed with hand grenades outside, just waiting for a signal. "He showed me a gun," Brubaker said. "He never took it out of the holster. He was soft-spoken, very cool, very collected—a lot cooler than I was." Then, almost as an afterthought, the stranger told Brubaker his name. "I'm Earl Austin," he said. "I'm on the Ten Most Wanted list."

Austin wasn't bragging. Just six days before, he had been named to the Top Ten list and apparently was quite proud of it. That, or he thought bank presidents would take him more seriously. Brubaker certainly did. He asked two of his employees to help open the vault, where Austin helped himself to a canvas bag with $250,000, which had been prepared for shipment to the Federal Reserve Bank in Denver. "He told us to go out in front of him," said Brubaker, "and that once he was outside and gone we could do whatever we wanted to but not to follow him."

Authorities, however, had been following Austin's career for quite some time. His rap sheet stretched back to 1958, and in two decades the bank robber had racked up convictions for grand larceny, forgery, aggravated assault and battery, escape, and oddly enough, threatening the life of the president of the United States. (See "Interesting Fugitive Fact," below.) As he got older, he got better. By early 1979 Austin had perfected his heist technique: Pose as a FDIC investigator, ask to see the bank president, show him the gun tucked in a trouser waistband, then empty the vault and split. This worked in six banks in Florida, Alabama, Texas, and Kentucky, netting Austin an estimated $270,000. Considering that Austin had been paroled from prison just before embarking on this recent heisting spree, and that he had a nasty habit of firing on police officers when cornered, the FBI decided to name him to the Ten Most Wanted list on October 12, 1979.

A tipster lead FBI agents to Austin's apartment in Tucson, where they were waiting. As Austin emerged from his apartment and headed to his car, G-men and local cops pounced. "We didn't give him an opportunity to resist," said an FBI spokesperson. Austin was carrying $18,000 in cash and a loaded 9 mm pistol at the time.

INTERESTING FUGITIVE FACT:
Before making the Top Ten list, Austin was convicted of an odd crime: threatening the president of the United States. It happened in 1967, when Austin was serving time at the county jail in Boise, Idaho, and wrote an angry letter to President Lyndon B. Johnson from his cell. The threat cost him five additional years in prison.

371. VINCENT JAMES RUSSO, armed robber

LISTED: December 24, 1979
CAUGHT: January 4, 1985
DESCRIPTION: Born July 1954 in St. Albans, New York. Alias: Sonny Brainerd.

"Merry Christmas." Three days before Christmas 1978, Vincent Russo decided to do a little holiday shopping for himself. He burst into a liquor store in Ramona, California, cleaned $500 out of the cash register, then abducted the lone clerk on duty—a 21-year-old named Dale Scott Eaton. Russo then drove Eaton 40 miles out to the deserted countryside of Valley Center and instructed the clerk to lie on the ground, facedown. "Merry Christmas," Russo said, then started blasting away at the prone clerk with a .45 pistol. Thinking Eaton dead, Russo kicked his bleeding body over into a ditch. Amazingly, Eaton survived his five gunshot wounds—bullets to the back of his head, face, and both arms—and waited in that ditch until a passing car finally stopped and the driver called the police. Eaton managed to give the cops a complete description of his would-be killer. Russo was identified as the shooter, and the FBI promoted him to the Top Ten list a little more than a year later. Happy holidays, indeed.

Still, Russo managed to evade the FBI—who made their list and surely checked it more than twice—for more than five years. Finally, the G-men discovered that Russo was using the alias "Sonny Brainerd," but didn't know where. That changed when "Brainerd" registered a 1985 Pontiac in Beaver Falls, Pennsylvania, a town about 20 miles northwest of Pittsburgh. There, Russo/Brainerd was living with his girlfriend, Ann, and their two children, and working at a local fast food restaurant. He was arrested on January 4, 1985, without incident and immediately brought to a U.S. magistrate's office to determine his true identity. From there, Russo was flown back to California to face felony charges from that bloody Christmas Eve five years previous.

INTERESTING FUGITIVE FACT:
Before he broke the law, Russo *was* the law. The fugitive used to be a cop in Gainesville, Georgia, and later, a U.S. Marine Corps sergeant.

FUGITIVES
OF THE 1980s

Introduction

If there's one name that is vital to the Ten Most Wanted list, it is John Walsh. No, Walsh isn't one of the criminal kingpins or drug dealers who made the list. He's the creator of the groundbreaking *America's Most Wanted* television show, which helped bring the Top Ten list—along with other wanted lists—out of post offices and precinct lobbies and directly into American homes. The first Top Tenner to be caught thanks to *AMW* was murderer David James Roberts, who was featured on the show's very first broadcast on February 7, 1988. Within minutes of the show's end, tips began flooding the show's hotline, and one of those tips ended up leading the FBI right to Roberts, who had been living under the name "Bob Lord" in Staten Island. Four days after the broadcast he was in custody. That was the beginning of an astounding run for *AMW*, which, as of early 2003, had caught over 740 fugitives.

Other notable fugitives of this decade include the longest-running Top Tenner, Donald Webb (#375); armed robber—and stepfather of the late rapper Tupac—Mutulu Shakur (#380); psycho Christopher Bernard Wilder (#385); mobster Carmine Persico (#390); sleepover bandits Joe Dougherty (#397) and Terry Lee Conner (#402); spree killer Mike Wayne Jackson (#406); husband-and-wife terrorists Claude Daniel Marks (#411) and Donna Jean Willmott (#412); and muscle-bound drug dealer Gus Farace (#426).

372. ALBERT LOPEZ VICTORY, cop killer

LISTED: March 14, 1980
CAUGHT: February 24, 1981
DESCRIPTION: Born 1941 in Coney Island, New York.

The Phantom Gunmen. Correction officers Roger McGibney and John J. Panarello Jr. had quite a story to tell the night of May 5, 1978. That day the officers had been ambushed while escorting prisoner Albert Victory back to Green Haven Correctional Facility at Stormville, New York, from a dental appointment. Three gunmen, armed to teeth, threatened to shoot McGibney and Panarello unless they released Victory. If it hadn't been for the intervention of another convict, Joseph Tremarco, Victory's trigger-happy henchmen would have surely killed them.

Thing is, there weren't any gunmen.

Instead, Victory had bribed McGibney and Panarello $500 each to escort him to a lawyer girlfriend, who had taken a room at a nearby motel. (Presumably, oral surgery wasn't on the agenda that day.) But Victory double-crossed the officers and slipped away while the two were sipping cocktails in the adjoining bar. McGibney and Panarello, realizing they had been double-crossed, concocted the gunman tale and even bribed Tremarco to go along with the story, promising him a parole recommendation for having "saved their lives." Both were found guilty of perjury in July 1980, but by that time Victory had already made the Most Wanted list.

Victory was the wrong guy to be given a get-out-of-jail-free card. He was a longtime mob associate who in 1968 ran a red light in New York City. When Officer John Varecha pulled Victory and his buddy Robert Bornholdt over, Victory urged Borndholt to take the cop out. Varecha was shot point-blank in the face. Both Victory and Bornholdt were convicted of murder; Victory was given a 25-year-to-life jolt at Green Haven. (A lucky assignment for Victory, as it turned out—a state commission found Green Haven at the center of many charges of favoritism and corruption in the early 1980s.)

Almost three years after his escape, Victory was traced to a posh neighborhood near San Francisco. DEA wiretaps nailed down Victory's new number and linked it to a swank rental—complete with swimming pool and gold Mercedes-Benz parked out front—then surprised him before breakfast on the morning of February 24. Victory was theirs.

INTERESTING FUGITIVE FACT:
A criminal buddy of Victory's, Robert Wyler—who allowed Victory to crash at his pad after the 1978 escape—would later be at the center of his own weird escape attempt. Friends stole a chartered helicopter at gunpoint, then tried to pluck Wyler from the roof of a Manhattan federal jail. (It didn't work.)

373. RONALD TURNEY WILLIAMS, cop killer, robber

LISTED: April 16, 1980
CAUGHT: June 8, 1981
DESCRIPTION: Born 1943 in West Virginia.

Misfire in the Lobby. The prison barber started the whole thing. It was early November 1979, and inmate/hair-trimmer Jack Hart surprised a West Virginia penitentiary at Moundsville prison guard with a gun, allowing an accomplice to sneak in with a knife, which in turn allowed them access to a waiting room, which in turn allowed them to bargain access to outside gates. Prison officials begrudgingly popped them open—and seemingly out of nowhere, 13 other prisoners appeared and made their escape. Ronald Turney Williams was one of them.

For Williams a prison break was nothing new. He had spent half his life behind bars and escaped them five times before the Moundsville break. He had been last sent up the river in 1975 for killing West Virginia police sergeant David Lilly. Two years later, Williams pulled a fast one while being treated at a local hospital and escaped, but was quickly recaptured. That wouldn't be the case during the 1979 Moundsville break.

The gods had an odd sense of irony that day, for the first vehicle that passed by the Moundsville prison was driven by an off-duty state trooper. The 15 escapees overpowered and killed him—but not before that trooper, Philip Kesner, managed to take one prisoner down himself. A few of the sharper escapees hopped into the car and sped away, leaving their buddies behind. A month later, only one fugitive remained at large: Williams. He was named to the Top Ten list the following April, after fingerprints linked him to a murder in Scottsdale, Arizona.

Williams seemed to delight in being one of the most hunted men in the country. He would send taunting letters to law enforcement and mail postcards to con buddies still at Moundsville, signing

"Wish you were here." Once a tip came in that Williams would be in a Charleston, West Virginia, bus station, disguised as a woman. A squad of local cops and state troopers pounced on the scene and nabbed a suspicious-looking woman, but upon further investigation, she turned out to be a real woman. Williams also sent letters to Rev. Tom Cook, who comprised the entire staff of the West Virginia Department of Corrections Fugitive Department. Cook was known for talking fugitives into turning themselves in, but that wouldn't be the case with Williams.

In June 1981 another tip came in, and Williams was finally pinned down by the Feds in the lobby of the Hotel George Washington in Manhattan. An agent had been set up as the clerk, and just after noon on June 8 Williams showed up as expected. He and the clerk made small talk, but Williams must have sensed something odd, because he whipped out his .38 caliber pistol. The clerk/FBI agent showed his own gun, shouting, "FBI! Drop the weapon!"

"Drop dead!" Williams said. "Drop yours!"

And then the fugitive pulled the trigger.

Amazingly, the gun failed to fire.

The agent pumped his own gun three times, catching Williams in the face, chest and arm. Williams survived his wounds and was soon returned to prison.

INTERESTING FUGITIVE FACT:
Williams was the son of a West Virginia coal miner and had a tested IQ of 145.

374. DANIEL JAY BARNEY, rapist, robber

LISTED: March 10, 1981
CAUGHT: April 19, 1981
DESCRIPTION: Born 1953 in Idaho Falls, Idaho.

"Time to Go." The Barney Brothers had a creepy hobby: They would find single women, break into their apartments, bind them, rape them for hours, then steal anything that looked valuable and make their escape. Joseph Lawrence usually played the apologetic, oh-so-sorry-I'm-assaulting-you role; his brother, Daniel Jay, usually played the violent, abusive role. Or perhaps it wasn't just a role. Daniel Barney was jailed in Jeffrey County, Wisconsin, but broke out in late February 1980 and was named to the Top Ten list a little over a year later.

On April 19, 1981, Daniel Barney played his last sick game.

He broke into a Denver condominium at 5 A.M., finding 28-year-old Paul Debroeck and his girlfriend asleep in bed. Barney quickly subdued and bound Debroeck, then took the woman into another room to rape her. Debroeck, however, managed to cut himself loose with a small blade in his key chain, then ran for police. A bizarre two-hour standoff followed, with Barney holed away in the spare bedroom, refusing to come out, with his .38 cocked and pointed not at his female victim, *but at his own chest*. The police urged Barney to let the woman go and surrender himself, but Barney refused and asked police to give a message to his mother. "We don't know your name," said one officer. "You will soon enough," said Barney.

Barney then went into the bathroom, donned a shirt, and came back to the top of the stairs, presumably to turn himself in. Instead, he went down on his knees, checked his watch—it was 8:20 A.M.—and shot himself in the head. Police identified Barney after fingerprinting his corpse.

INTERESTING FUGITIVE FACT:
Barney was a karate expert—a skill that apparently failed to endear him to the ladies.

375. DONALD EUGENE WEBB, alleged cop killer

LISTED: May 4, 1981
STILL ON LIST (as of this printing)
DESCRIPTION: Born July 14, 1931, in Oklahoma City. Five feet nine inches tall, 165 pounds, with gray-brown hair and brown eyes. He might have a small scar on his right cheek and right forearm, as well as two tattoos: "DON" on the web of his right hand and "ANN" on his chest. He is reportedly allergic to penicillin. Occupations: butcher, car salesman, jewelry salesman, real estate salesman, restaurant manager, vending machine repairman. Aliases: A.D. Baker, Donald Eugene Perkins, Donald Eugene Pierce, John S. Portas, Stanley John Portas, Bev Webb, Eugene Bevlin Webb, Eugene Donald Webb, and Stanley Webb. Current bounty on Webb's head: $50,000.

The Holy Grail. As of this writing, Donald Webb is the Top Ten list's worst nightmare, the nagging fugitive who refuses to be caught, and now, past the age of 70, threatens to escape the FBI by dying before he is apprehended. Webb has been on the list for over 20 years, giving him the dubious distinction of having the longest Top Ten run in its 50-year history. "He might be dead right now," said Larry Likar, special

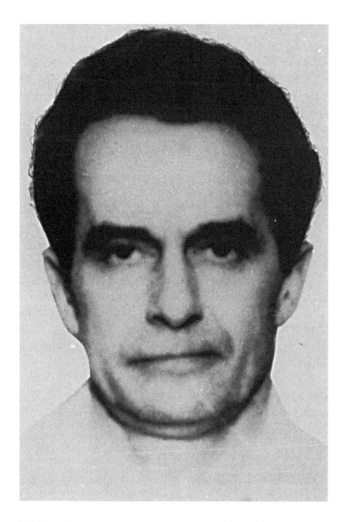

Webb is being sought in connection with the December 1980 murder of a Saxonburg, Pennsylvania, police chief.

agent at the FBI's Pittsburgh field office, in an interview for *Details Magazine* in 1997. "He might be in Mexico. He might be sitting on a beach in Rio. I'd like to know where that bastard is right this minute. But we haven't forgotten him. We still get several tips on him a year, and we follow each one of them up."

Oddly enough, the most wanted of the Most Wanted wasn't that big a deal—in and out of prison a couple of times for robbery—until one fateful December day in Pennsylvania. Webb had been a member of the Fall River Gang, an infamous ring of jewelry thieves based in New England. They were particularly fond of "hick" towns, ones with slow-witted cops and easily frightened citizenry. A town like Saxonburg, Pennsylvania, for instance, which Webb thought of as the perfect spot for an ice boost. He spent late November and early December 1980

casing the town and, in particular, Saver's Jewelers, and then was ready to make his move. "No muss no fuss," Likar told *Details*, putting himself in Webb's mind. "Hit the jewelry store, in and out, and back to Massachusetts on our fine federal highway system in six, seven hours tops."

But that wasn't to be. While Webb was tooling around Saxonburg in his Mercury Cougar, getting a feel for the joint, Chief of Police Greg Adams had noticed him. On December 4, at 3 P.M., Adams pulled Webb over. Webb freaked and pulled a .25 pistol on the cop, then forced him across a shopping mart parking lot and into the backyard of a private home. Webb smashed his gun butt on Adams's head, apparently hoping to send the cop to bye-bye land long enough to hightail it out of Saxonburg. But Adams was a tough officer and refused to be knocked out. In desperation Webb blasted away at Adams four times; Adams managed to fire his .45 back at Webb once.

The Saxonburg chief of police would later die en route to the hospital. Webb escaped, despite his gunshot wound, and abandoned his car in Warwick, Rhode Island. "[There was] blood all over the place," said Likar. "Webb's blood. There's been no trace of him since." Webb's Wanted poster hasn't changed much in the intervening years—although his photo has been computer-aged recently to show how the fugitive might look today. *(See page 295 in Appendix II for information on how to report a Top Tenner to the FBI.)*

INTERESTING FUGITIVE FACT:
Webb is reportedly a flashy dresser, a big tipper, and a dog lover.

376. GILBERT JAMES EVERETT, bank robber, drug dealer

LISTED: May 13, 1981
CAUGHT: August 12, 1985
DESCRIPTION: Born June 26, 1939, in Hamilton, Ohio. Five feet seven inches tall, 185 pounds, with brown hair streaked with gray, brown eyes, and a ruddy complexion. He has a two-inch scar on his right wrist.

The Man Who Wouldn't Quit. Even though one of Gilbert Everett's earliest tastes of bank robbery ended in his arrest, he couldn't get enough of it. Everett broke out of Knox County Jail on October 26, 1980, and went on to rack up dozens of additional bank heists, even though his name was on the Ten Most Wanted list for most of them.

Following the jail break, warrants for Everett's arrest were issued in quick succession: one in Greenville, Tennessee, for the escape; another in Birmingham, Alabama, for two counts of interstate transportation of a stolen vehicle; and another in Orlando, Florida, charging him with bank robbery. The following May, Everett hit the big time: the Top Ten list. But that only seemed to encourage him. Everett moved from Nashville to Denver to Placerville, California, under as many as 14 aliases and swore that he would never be taken alive. He even hid out in Alaska for a time after one Sacramento, California, robbery in 1983. (Clearly, Everett knew his way around the country and how to provide himself with free transportation: Before he turned to crime, he had been a map maker and a car salesman.)

Everett usually knocked over banks using the same M.O.: He'd pick a small financial office with female tellers. During one heist in Florida in 1985, Everett held up the American Federal Saving and Loan Association office in Broward County, walking in at 2:54 P.M., approaching a teller, and asking for change for foreign money. The teller looked up and saw a chrome-plated revolver staring back at her, Everett's finger on the trigger. He then handed her a 9-by-12-inch bank bag and told her to fill it. He did the same thing to the next teller, then made his escape after ordering both women to the back of the bank. This routine worked for as many as 40 armed robberies across the country.

The law finally caught up with Gilbert Everett in the town of Bismarck, Arkansas. Everett was speeding down a road and was spotted by two young cops, who immediately rocketed after him and radioed ahead for a roadblock. Everett, who must have known that his luck had finally run out, surrendered—but didn't admit to his identity at first. However, the stacks of sequential bills found in his car, along with identifying scars and tattoos, gave Everett no choice but to admit to being one of the Most Wanted. The only question remaining: Where to extradite him? "Where to is much in question," an FBI agent in the Little Rock field office told a reporter. "There are so many charges against him all over the country."

INTERESTING FUGITIVE FACT:
Everett had been known to carry a .38 caliber pistol inside a hollowed-out book.

377. LESLIE EDWARD NICHOLS, murderer, drug dealer

LISTED: July 2, 1981
CAUGHT: December 17, 1981
DESCRIPTION: Born in 1943 in Little Rock, Arkansas. A dark-skinned black man of medium build, he has a dollar sign tattooed on his right arm. Aliases: Leslie Murphy, Trainer Barnes, Less Trainer.

Hangover from Hell. Clearly, Leslie Nichols was a talented killer-for-hire, but he was a bit lackluster when it came to disposing his victims' bodies. They kept popping up everywhere. Used-car dealer John Phelan was found on June 15, 1980, limbs bound with boot laces, gagged, beaten, and wire-garroted in an abandoned mining area near Little Rock. Months later, Sheila Bishop was found in a patch of woods, her hands bound with wire coat hangers and a bullet in her brain. She had been in the witness protection program and moved to Little Rock after testifying in a Maryland drug trial. Later still, two men were found in the trunk of a car: Carl Jackson and Leonard Jones, both former cons involved in the Arkansas drug scene. They had also been bound with wire coat hangers and shot in the backs of their heads. Two days later, police found Jones's wife, Rosemary, in a roadside ditch, the method of murder exactly the same.

All of these bodies allowed the police to fit together the real story—Phelan had been killed for robbery; the others had been killed on command from drug lords—and the evidence pointed to one man, Leslie Nichols, along with a group of thugs who had assisted him: Billy Gene Stephenson, Charles V. Moorman, and Luther Hall. The underlings were soon rounded up and given a variety of life sentences (in Stephenson's case, six consecutive ones). But Nichols—the leader of the killing crew, who had been working for drug gangs since he was a teenager—remained at large and was bumped up to the Top Ten list two days before Independence Day 1981.

Nichols's run didn't last very long. As Christmas 1981 approached, Nichols must have felt at ease enough to throw himself a little all-night holiday party at his new apartment in South Central Los Angeles. He must have wished he'd not partied so hard that night, for the next morning the FBI and LAPD came to crash the party. Nichols was too smashed to put up a fight. He was later sent back to Arkansas to face trial.

INTERESTING FUGITIVE FACT:
Coincidentally, Nichols's arrest came the same day as the arrest of another member of the Most Wanted, JOHN WILLIAM SHERMAN (#367). It was the first time two unrelated Top Tenners were caught on the same day.

378. THOMAS WILLIAM MANNING, cop killer, terrorist

LISTED: January 29, 1982
CAUGHT: April 24, 1985
DESCRIPTION: Born June 1946 in Beverly, Massachusetts.

The Family That Runs Together. In October 1984 the arrest of one Top Tenner from the 1970s, RAYMOND LUC LEVASSEUR (#350), inadvertently triggered the end for Thomas Manning, who'd been hiding out with his family under an assumed name for years. In Levasseur's apartment police found Manning's number, traced it back to an address in New Lyme, Ohio, and in mid-November sent a squad of agents out to pay a visit. But by the time the FBI arrived, the Mannings—or as they were known around the neighborhood, the "Carrs"—had already split. They apparently hadn't been gone long; the family's Great Dane had been left behind in one of the bedrooms. The children were said to be model students, and the parents had seemed like such good people.

But the Mannings were far from "good people." Since the 1970s Thomas had been a member of a radical group called the Sam Melville-Jonathan Jackson Unit of the United Freedom Front, a terrorist cell that killed, bombed, and robbed in an effort to overthrow the U.S. government. Manning took part in a September 1976 bank heist in Portland, Maine, and the stolen funds were used for United Freedom Front terrorist acts, including dynamite bombs set at IBM, Union Carbide, General Electric, and three military facilities. But what catapulted Manning to the Top Ten list were his actions on the night of December 21, 1981. Manning and a fellow radical, Richard Williams, were caught speeding in Warren County, New Jersey, by a state trooper named Philip Lamonaco. Lamonaco had discovered that Manning had weapons in the car and began to arrest him when Williams started blasting away, leaving the state trooper with eight bullets in his body. Manning and Williams sped away. Mannings' bloody fingerprint was found in an abandoned car just three miles from where Lamonaco had died.

The gun used to shoot Lamonaco wouldn't be found until that mid-November raid on the Mannings' quiet hideaway in Ohio. (It had been stashed in a trunk in the bedroom.)

After the Mannings fled Ohio, they found a new suburban home to rent in Norfolk, Virginia, and tried to reestablish their quiet lives. It must not have been easy, especially when Manning would read in March 1985 that five of his brethren in the United Freedom Front, along with Thomas himself and wife, Carol Ann, were indicted in New York City for 10 bombings. The heat was turning up. Finally, in April 1985 the FBI closed in on the Mannings for the last time. It was obvious that they hadn't expected to be found so soon. Thomas was nabbed lounging on his front lawn with his five- and three-year-old kids. "We caught him unawares," said Jack Wagner, special agent in charge of the FBI's Norfolk field office. "It was an easy apprehension." Carol Ann was trailed to a nearby grocery store and arrested the moment she stepped out of the car. The kids were placed with Norfolk Social Services pending placement with relatives.

Upon their arrest, Col. Clinton Pagano, head of the New Jersey state police, said that he had been confident that Trooper Lamonaco's killer would be found, since Manning was traveling with his children. "I know that both of them lead that sedentary life when they're not out robbing or doing whatever else they do," he said. "But the bottom line is this: You don't murder a New Jersey state trooper and walk away from it."

INTERESTING FUGITIVE FACT:
The Mannings' final hiding place, Wards Corner in Norfolk, is home to many families of enlisted men at Norfolk Naval Base. In other words, home to the defenders of the very government Manning was so desperate to overthrow.

379. DAVID FOUNTAIN KIMBERLY JR., robber

LISTED: January 29, 1982
CAUGHT: July 8, 1982
DESCRIPTION: Born in 1946 in Nashville, Tennessee. May be traveling in a 1980 dark brown van with orange stripes and "Day Cruiser" on the side of the van. Reward for information leading to arrest: $5,000.

The Stubborn Fugitive. On October 5, 1981, U.S. Park Police officer Keslo David Wallace pulled over a Datsun 280-Z on the Baltimore-Washington Parkway for a routine traffic violation. The passengers of that car were far from ordinary, however. David Kimberly, the driver, had a week before he broke his 21-year-old common-law wife, Sandra Lynn Whatley, out of a Tennessee prison. The two boosted a car in Decatur, Alabama, and were headed up the East Coast when Wallace stopped them. Kimberly was apparently, growing nervous with the line of questioning and decided to shoot his way out of the situation with a .38 caliber pistol. Wallace received bullets in the neck, stomach, and head. Kimberly and Whatley sped away from the scene, later commandeering a second car from a couple in Prince George's County and resuming their getaway.

Fortunately, Wallace survived his injuries—with permanent, partial paralysis—and was able to give investigators the name "Billy Hindman," which was matched to a list of Kimberly's known aliases. A manhunt was on. In mid-December a tip came in that a man in a Washington, D.C., bar was bragging about taking down that Park cop before Halloween. Within minutes police surrounded the bar and began a person-by-person search of the patrons. A man fitting Kimberly's description, however, had already left. There's nothing like a cop killing, even an *attempted* cop killing, to sped one garden-variety thug to the top of the charts. A little over a month later, Kimberly was named to the Ten Most Wanted list.

Kimberly had a decent run—nearly nine months from the time of the Wallace shooting—but in the end was nabbed in Key West, Florida, just as he was about to enter a real estate office. He refused to identify himself to the arresting officers, and even before a federal magistrate. But to no avail: Kimberly's fingerprints bore him out, and later Kimberly was sentenced to 20 years in jail—10 for assaulting a federal officer and 10 for assault resulting in serious bodily injury.

INTERESTING FUGITIVE FACT:
Kimberly was originally wanted for holding up an antiques shop in Mobile, Alabama.

380. MUTULU SHAKUR, murderer, racketeer, armed robber

LISTED: July 23, 1982
CAUGHT: February 11, 1986
DESCRIPTION: Born Jeral Wayne Williams in Baltimore, Maryland, in 1951.

The Big Dance. The Brink's job on October 20, 1981, had the mark of professionals: carefully timed, forcefully executed. The truck was in the Nanuet Mall in Rockland County, New York, making the day's final stop. Out of nowhere a red Chevy van pulled up to the armored car, and gunmen started blasting away at the guards—coolly, professionally. One guard was killed, another wounded, and a handcart containing $1.6 million was stolen. The heist team dumped the Chevy and switched to a U-Haul truck, but encountered a roadblock at the entrance to the New York State Thruway in Nyack. Two police officers had walked to the back of the truck to inspect it when the doors swung open and gunfire erupted. Sgt. Edward O'Grady and Patrolman Waverly Brown were killed in the barrage of bullets, and the crooks split up by commandeering cars from bystanders at the scene. One crook, however, was nabbed at the scene. Once police realized who they had arrested, it became clear that this wasn't just another professional score. The Brink's job was an act of revolution.

Katherine Boudin, a Weather Underground fugitive who'd been wanted for a Greenwich Village bomb blast more than a decade earlier, was taken into custody at the scene, and a short while later, her revolutionary compatriots—Judith Clark, James Lester Hackford, and Solomon Quienes—were rounded up. Once their homes had been searched, and fingerprints, plans, and bomb parts were found, more ex-Weathermen were implicated in the crime, until finally it became clear that the job was the brainchild of Mutulu Shakur, a leader of the Black Liberation Army enclave called "The Family." Shakur dubbed the robbery "The Big Dance" and planned to use the $1.6 million to fund their revolutionary efforts, and perhaps pump some money back into his Harlem detox and acupuncture clinic, which "The Family" used as headquarters. Federal warrants for Shakur's arrest were issued, and he made the Top Ten list in July 1982.

As Shakur stayed on the lam, his fellow Family members faced arrests and convictions galore. One of these arrests gave FBI agents the idea that Shakur might be in Los Angeles, and in early 1986 a team of G-men and police officers spotted the fugitive at the intersection of Packard Street and Spaulding Avenue in West L.A. Shakur tried to run for it, but was hit with a flying tackle and wrestled to the ground. The revolutionary acupuncturist was extradited to New York, where he was found guilty of eight counts of armed robbery, racketeering, and murder and slapped with 60 years in jail.

INTERESTING FUGITIVE FACT:
Shakur is the stepfather of late outlaw rapper Tupac Shakur. His song, "White Man'z World," was dedicated to Mutulu.

381. CHARLES EDWARD WATSON, cop killer, rapist

LISTED: October 22, 1982
CAUGHT: October 25, 1983
DESCRIPTION: Born on October 23, 1946, in Johnson City, Tennessee. Five feet 10 inches tall, 168 pounds, with brown hair, blue or hazel eyes, and a deformed right thumb. He also has a heart-shaped tattoo between his right thumb and index finger, as well as "ED" tattooed on his right forearm. Watson is violently irrational under the influence of alcohol.

Happy Birthday, Fugitive. Watson was another Top Tenner who ignored the unspoken criminal code of "never kill a cop"—in this case a Maryland state trooper. Sgt. Wallace J. Mowbray was patrolling the area near his own home in August 1975, when he spied a suspicious blue van with Virginia dealer tags parked at Wheeler Baker's liquor store. As Mowbray approached the van, the barrel of a sawed-off shotgun appeared in the window. The left side of the trooper's face was torn away from the blast. Only an hour before, he had stopped home to see his wife and to tell her that he'd be in the area if she needed anything.

There were four men in that van: Charles Edward Watson, brothers Richard and Raymond Patterson, and Albert White. Richard Patterson was the one holding the shotgun, and he and Watson subsequently fled to a nearby restaurant, where they kidnapped a couple, stole their car, and raped the woman. A few hours later, police captured them at a bridge toll plaza. The other two, meanwhile, had commandeered a boat and tried to make their getaway by sea, but were picked up two days later.

Watson was sentenced to life in prison plus 95 years for his role in Mowbray's murder, kidnapping, rape, and weapons violations. (He had a record dating back to 1963, when he got sent up the river for armed robbery.) But Watson walked away from a work detail at Patuxent Correctional Institution in Maryland on June 22 after serving only six years and

change. He was named to the Top Ten list on October 22, 1982, the day before his 36th birthday. As it turned out, Watson had fled north and tried to establish himself as a construction worker for hire in the mountain town of Slatington, Pennsylvania. But the FBI tracked him down on October 25, 1983—just two days after his 37th birthday—and arrested him without incident.

There is a twisted footnote to Watson's story. A retrial in 1991 awarded Watson a reduced sentence, and in 1993 early release from prison, much to the outrage of Sgt. Mowbray's family. "He didn't even serve a quarter of his sentence," said Robin Bell, daughter of the slain trooper in a 1999 interview. "It is a slap in the face for my family." As it turned out, justice slapped back: Watson was returned to prison in early 1999 for trying to steal a jar of charity money from a restaurant in Glen Burnie, Maryland.

INTERESTING FUGITIVE FACT:
Many years later, Watson encountered his own son, Charles Edward Watson Jr., in a Maryland jail. The younger Watson was serving time for assault, theft, and forgery, and he told one reporter that he didn't really get to know his father until they were in stir together.

382. LANEY GIBSON JR., murderer, rapist, kidnapper

LISTED: November 28, 1983
CAUGHT: December 18, 1983
DESCRIPTION: Born on August 28, 1950, in Clay County, Kentucky.

The Ceiling's the Limit. Seems that Laney Gibson Jr. couldn't stop killing, raping, or escaping. On August 7, 1983, Gibson got himself, his brother Stanley, and two other cons—armed robber Jerry Hinkle and murderer Larry Knuckles—out of the Clay County jail by beating a guard and locking him in a cell. Gibson had been awaiting trial for a murder in which he had blasted a Manchester, Kentucky, man in the head with a 9 mm pistol. The man was paralyzed and clung to life for nearly a year before dying, at which point Gibson was slapped with his third murder charge. (He'd already been in jail for two other slayings.)

Brother Stanley, Hinkle, and Knuckles were rounded up quickly, but Gibson stayed at large. A little more than a month later, he abducted a female postal employee from Elgin, Ohio. At first the only trace of the woman was the contents of her purse, spread over the post office counter not far from a cash drawer and safe that both had been emptied. Only later was her dead body, clearly tortured and raped, found by the side of a road. Obviously, Gibson was a threat to anyone he encountered, which undoubtedly propelled his name to the Top Ten list a few days after Thanksgiving 1983.

Just three weeks later, Gibson was tracked to a motel in suburban Montgomery, Alabama, and he surrendered without a fight. But it wasn't as if he were sorry and learned a lesson. Gibson would escape again in September 1984 and would be found hiding out behind a false ceiling in a relative's house.

INTERESTING FUGITIVE FACT:
Laney's brother Stanley hadn't been quite as evil as his brother—he'd only been in jail for drunk driving.

383. GEORGE CLARENCE BRIDGETTE, mass murderer

LISTED: January 10, 1984
CAUGHT: January 30, 1984
DESCRIPTION: Born July 1946 in Long Beach, California. Five feet 10 inches tall, 190 pounds, with black hair, brown eyes, and blemishes on his forehead. He has worked as a baker, laborer, and maintenance man. Aliases: George Flap, Kenneth Polee Jr., William Kevin Polee, Ali Rashid, and George Wilkinson.

The Most Wanted Court Employee. George Bridgette's capture was a Most Wanted cliché. A citizen in Miami recognized his face on a sheet at a local post office, and that very afternoon the FBI sent a team to a rooming house to pick up the man. But the man, dressed in designer jeans and a button-down shirt, insisted he wasn't a fugitive. "I don't know nothing," he said when arrested. Later, after asking for a public defender, the man protested: "My real name is Odell Davis. You got me down as George Bridgette."

Fingerprints, however, confirmed that man was George Bridgette The same George Bridgette who, along with accomplices James E. Cade and Willie Thomas, broke into a Long Beach home to settle a drug-related debt and ended up gunning down five people at close range. One of the victims was three-year-old Chinue Cade, daughter of victim Pamela Cade, ex-wife of one of the assailants. Another

daughter of Cade's, 15-year-old Carolyn Ferguson, managed to survive and later identified her would-be killers. Cade and Thomas were rounded up quickly and later convicted of the ghastly slaying, but Bridgette managed to hide. His rap sheet included armed robbery, parole violation, forgery, and auto theft. Now murder was added to the list. Authorities in Long Beach hunted him for years and finally convinced the FBI to name him to the Top Ten list in early January 1984.

Meanwhile, Bridgette had stayed hidden long enough to set up a new life for himself in Miami under his "Odell Davis" identity, marrying and having a child. He found a variety of odd jobs, including baker, maintenance man, and driver for the Florida Department of Health and Rehabilitative Services. In April 1983, however, "Davis" was hired by the Dade County Juvenile Center to drive teenage felons-in-training back and forth to court dates, hospitals, and schools. (It was an irony he must have appreciated: One of the most wanted men in the country responsible for the safety of dozens of kids who had the potential to turn out like him someday.) The job could have been full-time, according to Doris Capri, Bridgette's boss at the Dade County juvie center, except that he couldn't seem to turn up a high school diploma with his name on it. "If he had been able to produce the document, I would have hired him," Capri told a reporter in 1984.

INTERESTING FUGITIVE FACT:
According to Capri, the Top Tenner always "carried a Bible and quoted from the Bible." (Apparently he skipped over the part about "Thou shall not kill three-year-old girls with a shotgun.")

384. SAMUEL MARKS HUMPHREY, murderer, bank robber

LISTED: February 29, 1984
CAUGHT: March 22, 1984
DESCRIPTION: Born August 1949 in Detroit, Michigan. Six feet three inches tall, 175 pounds with black hair and brown eyes. Humphrey is reported to be a heavy drug user and known to carry more than one weapon at a time. He is also believed to drive rented or leased autos. Aliases: Eddie Joe Alston, Leon Archie, Michael Gordy, Kenneth Gregory, Kenneth Smith, and Henry D. Seyferth.

The New Bonnie and Clyde. Transport Bonnie Parker and Clyde Barrow to the mid-1980s, give them chic heroin and coke habits, and you might have the Samuel Humphrey/Luvenia Carter story. Humphrey started out as a loner, racking up a record of postal fraud, aiding and abetting, forgery, bond-jumping, all along using coke and heroin. On March 17, 1977, Humphrey added murder to his résumé after allegedly killing a Detroit man whose home he'd been robbing. At some point Humphrey hooked up with Luvenia Marie Carter, a young Louisville native who used to work as a cocktail waitress and shared her new boyfriend's interest in recreational narcotics. Together they knocked over a series of banks and stores: in mid-November 1982 a jewelry store in San Diego; two days after New Year's 1983 two banks in Rochester, New York; on March 8 another bank in Atlanta. That time Humphrey and Carter took a teller hostage. But it was Humphrey's early murder warrant from 1977 that gave the FBI reason to charge him with unlawful flight to avoid prosecution. Humphrey hopped on the Most Wanted list on Leap Day 1984.

The pair didn't last long after Humphrey became one of the most wanted men in the country. And they were denied a flashy, blood-soaked Hollywood ending—no Bonnie and Clyde–style shoot-out on a dusty country road. Instead, mere weeks after being named to the Top Ten list, Humphrey decided to visit an inmate buddy at a Portland, Oregon, jail. A touching thought, but stupid. Humphrey was nabbed by eagle-eyed prison employees who recognized the fugitive. Luvenia Carter, who had been waiting for Humphrey in the car a block away, was apprehended minutes later. At least the love-birds received a pair of matching sentences: 24 years for bank robbery, followed by additional sentences of 15 years apiece after a second conviction in Rochester, New York.

INTERESTING FUGITIVE FACT:
Humphrey used to work as a meat cutter.

385. CHRISTOPHER WILDER, serial killer

LISTED: April 5, 1984
SHOT DEAD: April 13, 1984
DESCRIPTION: Born on March 13, 1945, in Sydney, Australia. Five feet 11 inches to six feet, 175 to 180 pounds, with brown hair (balding), blue eyes, and a medium build. Occupations: carpenter, contractor, part-time photographer, and Grand Prix–type race car driver. Usually wears trimmed beard and mustache, may be clean shaven, well spoken and presents a neat appearance. He is a habitual fingernail biter and has a five-inch scar on his right ankle.

Driven. Sixteen-year-old Tina Marie Risico couldn't believe what Christopher Bernard Wilder was saying. He had driven her to Logan International Airport in Boston and given her a one-way ticket to Los Angeles, plus $100 cash. Wilder made her promise that she wouldn't tell anyone that he'd shaved off his beard, then said, "I'm going to set you free, since I don't want you to be around when the end comes." Wilder made her kiss him on the cheek and then said: "All you gotta do, kid, is write a book." Then she was free.

Risico didn't believe him. For the past nine days she had been Wilder's captive, subject to brainwashing, repeated rapes, forced lesbian acts, sodomy, torture by electric shocks, and more brainwashing. She had been worn down to the point where she even helped Wilder procure another victim—one he left for dead, stabbed multiple times, in the middle of a park. And now he was letting Risico go? She didn't quite know reality from fantasy until her plane started to take off at 2:10 A.M., and it finally began to dawn on her: She *was* truly free.

In Colebook, New Hampshire, state police attempted to arrest Wilder and a gun battle ensued. Wilder died of gunshot wounds.

Risico never did write a book about her nightmarish days as a captive of one of the weirdest, most violent serial killers in U.S. history. But if she had, where would she have begun? With her own abduction in a Lomita, California, shopping mall on April 4, 1984? Or would she start with the disappearance of Rosario Gonzalez, Wilder's first victim of the rampage that began on Saturday, February 26? Or with Wilder's multiple rapes and assaults, both here and in his native Australia?

Perhaps she would have started with Wilder's birth—an event practically steeped in death. The newborn son of an American serviceman and Australian mother who almost didn't live; the doctor even called in a priest to perform last rites. But Wilder's father insisted that the child would live and told the doctor not to worry about young Christopher's soul. The infant survived. The boy had two more near-death experiences, almost drowning in a pool as a toddler, and lapsing into a bizarre, unexplained six-hour coma at age five. It was a childhood worthy of a Dean Koontz thriller.

As a Navy brat Wilder grew up in a variety of places: the Philippines, San Francisco, Albuquerque, Norfolk, Las Vegas, and finally Sydney again. Only two things seem to capture his interest, girls and cars. The former led to his first criminal conviction in 1963 at the young age of 17, when Wilder and some friends gang-raped a teenage girl they encountered on a Sydney beach. The budding psycho was given a light sentence—a year's probation—but also sex therapy, which included a round of painful electroshock sessions, à la *A Clockwork Orange*, in which he was shown porn, then zapped whenever he became excited. (Years later, the experience would affect him in ways no one could have possibly predicted.)

Three years later, Wilder married, but his wife left after a bizarre abuse session and discovering ladies' lingerie, not her own, around their house. After their breakup Wilder began to experiment with the technique he would use the rest of his criminal life: the photographer-seeking-model scam. He would stroll beaches, camera draped over his suntanned neck, offering young, large-breasted girls the chance at freedom. One of his first victims was an 18-year-old nurse-in-training, who Wilder coerced into posing nude before raping and eventually blackmailing her. Police were summoned, but for some reason the woman declined to press charges. Wilder sold some family property and bought a ticket to South Florida, where he took advantage of a construction boom and soon had his own business.

Wilder continued to pursue his hobby, but for the most part managed to keep his activities on the Q.T. In 1971 Wilder was fined $25 for asking women on the beach to pose nude. Five years later, he abducted a 50-year-old woman with her twin 10-year-old boys at gunpoint, forcing the three to perform sexual acts on Wilder and one another, but the woman never called police, fearful that Wilder would return to kill them.

Law enforcement became familiar with Wilder in 1976, after a 16-year-old girl accused him of assault and forcing her to have oral sex. This time Wilder caught a lucky break—after 55 minutes the jury acquitted him. In June 1980 Wilder was arrested once again, this time for abducting two teenage girls and raping one of them. Once again he beat the rap, pleading to reduced charges of sexual battery and ending up with five years of probation.

One would think Wilder might have given up, or at least lain low for a while. Instead he paid a visit to his homeland of Australia and kidnapped and sexually assaulted two 15-year-olds in late December 1982. This time it wouldn't be so easy for him to slip away. Wilder was forced to post a bond of $350,000, and a trial date was set for April 1984. Still, fate dealt him an easy hand, for Wilder, amazingly, was allowed to return to Florida to attend to "pressing business affairs." As it turned out, it would be the biggest mistake that the Australian court could have possibly made.

Back in Florida Chris Wilder's construction business had been turning a nice profit, and as a result he owned a number of sports cars, some of which he raced professionally in Grand Prix–style events. He owned a swank canalside house in Boynton Beach, complete with hot tub and swimming pool, which had a map of Australia painted on the bottom, complete with kangaroos and koalas. He donated to Save-the-Whales funds and once spent $143 to nurse a sick raccoon back to health. Some knew Wilder as a rich Australian playboy who loved the fast life. A lot of it was a front. After all, he had quite a bit of debt stacked up, and the diamond he wore on his pinky ringer was an obvious fake. But it was nothing that would cause anyone to raise an eyebrow.

However, as his 1984 trial date in Australia approached, something in Wilder must have snapped.

February 26, 1984. Twenty-year-old Rosario Gonzalez disappears after the 1984 Miami Grand Prix. She had been there to glad-hand samples of a painkiller and had been last seen talking to Chris Wilder, who had competed in the race that day.

March 5. Teacher and aspiring model Elizabeth Kenyon vanishes after class one day. She is last seen at a Shell gas station with Wilder in a 1982 Chrysler LeBaron, reportedly heading to the airport. Her parents put up a $50,000 reward for her safe return to "any servant of God at any church . . . No questions asked." Kenyon is never seen again.

March 18. Terry Ferguson disappears from the Merritt Square Mall in central Florida. Her beaten body is later found in a swamp.

March 20. Linda Grober, a 19-year-old Florida State University student, is forcibly abducted from Governor's Square Mall by a man calling himself "Lynn Bishop." She is tortured with a 15-foot extension cord that "Bishop" has converted into a makeshift electroshock device, raped, beaten, has her eyes superglued together, but somehow manages to fight her way out of the room and escapes with her life. Grober is able to identify her assailant as Christopher Bernard Wilder, already sought in connection with the disappearances of Gonzalez and Kenyon.

March 23. Terry Walden, a 23-year-old mother and nursing student in Beaumont, Texas, disappears after dropping her four-year-old daughter at nursery school. Three days later, her body is found floating in a canal. She had been beaten, stabbed, and strangled.

March 25. Suzanne Logan, a 21-year-old newly-wed and aspiring model, is last seen at Oklahoma City's Penn Square Mall, buying a present for her husband. Her beaten, stabbed, and bound body is found the next day by a fisherman in the Milford Reservoir, over 270 miles away.

March 29. Sheryl Bonaventure, an 18-year-old student at Grand Junction High in Colorado—and another aspiring model—fails to meet her friends in the afternoon. Her abandoned Mazda is found in the parking lot. Her body wouldn't be found until May 3, long after Wilder's rampage had come to its bloody conclusion.

April Fool's Day. Seventeen-year-old Michelle Korfman competes in a *Seventeen* magazine cover-model competition at the Meadows Mall in Las Vegas. Self-conscious, she asks her family to stay home. She isn't seen again until June 1984, Jane Doe #39 in a Los Angeles morgue.

April 4. In Lomita, California, Wilder meets Tina Marie Risico, a 16-year-old girl with a troubled childhood who was looking for a way to earn extra money. She is tortured, beaten, raped, and made to swear allegiance to Wilder.

April 5. Risico is watching TV in her motel prison when she learns that her abductor, Christopher Bernard Wilder, has just been named to the FBI's Ten Most Wanted list. Wilder freaks, shaves his beard, then packs up Risico and flees to Arizona.

April 6–9. There are a few near-misses, as authorities pick up men fitting Wilder's description, but no luck. The FBI broadcasts a tape of Wilder, made when he joined a Florida dating service a few years back. Wilder, looking at the camera, says: "I want to meet and enjoy the company of a number of women."

April 10. With Risico's help Wilder abducts Dawnette Sue Wilt near Gary, Indiana. Over the next two days both captives are raped, shocked, beaten, and transported to upstate New York.

April 12. Wilder turns on the TV in the morning to see Tina Marie Risico's mother, Carol Sokolowski, on *Good Morning America,* pleading for her daughter's life. Later that day he stabs Wilt in an isolated park in upstate New York, then leaves her for dead. Miraculously, she would survive her wounds and escape. Later still, he abducts Beth Dodge in Victor, New York, then shoots her in the heart and steals her gold 1982 Pontiac Firebird. That night, he allows Tina Marie Risico to leave, buying her a plane ticket back to Los Angeles. "I don't want you to be around when the end comes," Wilder says.

April 13. The end comes. After abducting a woman near Boston who manages to leap out of the moving vehicle and escape, Wilder pulls into a Getty station 12 miles from the Canadian border. There two New Hampshire state troopers Leo Jellison and Wayne Fortier notice the 1982 gold Pontiac. Alarm bells go off in their heads. There had been a bulletin issued after Beth Dodge's murder, describing the car. "That's the son-of-a-bitch we're looking for," Jellison thinks. He pulls over and tells Wilder he wants to talk to him.

Wilder knows the gig is up. He races for the passenger door, which is locked. He spins on his heels and runs around to the driver's side, then lunges into the car, desperately trying to reach his gun. Jellison in the meantime lands on Wilder's back, trying to pin the man down. Wilder has managed to reach his gun by this point, and the men struggle. The gun goes off. Jellison leans back, shocked to see that he had been shot.

But the bullet didn't have much punch by the time it reached Jellison; it had already blasted through Wilder's heart, obliterating it completely. Wilder's muscles involuntarily twitched a moment later, and he shot himself again, the impact jolting the psycho's body two inches off the car seat. The rampage was over.

However, grisly discoveries were yet to be made in the coming weeks and months—more bodies, both in America and Australia, linking Wilder to murders as far back as 1965. With Wilder dead, no one will ever know exactly how many lives he took. If Tina Marie Risico had written that book, she'd be missing many chapters.

INTERESTING FUGITIVE FACT:

After Wilder's death pathologists removed his brain from his corpse to see if he had any unusual lesions or tumors that might explain why he did what he did. There were none. Days later, a call came in from Harvard University—seems they wanted to analyze the brain as well. The pathologist in charge agreed, pending written request. The letter never came, and when the pathologist followed up, it turned out that Harvard denied asking for the brain in the first place. Wilder, presumably, had a fan.

386. VICTOR GERENA, armed robber

LISTED: May 14, 1984
STILL ON LIST (as of this printing)
DESCRIPTION: Born on June 24, 1958, in New York City. Five
    feet six inches tall, 160 to 169 pounds, with brown hair
    and green eyes. He has a one-inch scar and a mole on
    his right shoulder blade. Occupations: machinist, security
    guard. Aliases: Victor Ortiz, Victor M. Gerena Ortiz. Reward:
    $50,000.

The Security Guard.   On the morning of September 12, 1983, Wells Fargo bank guard Victor Gerena reportedly borrowed 75 cents from his fiancée for bus fare. Later that day, money wouldn't be an issue.

Out of nowhere, Gerena pointed a gun at two coworkers—branch manager James S. McKeon and fellow guard Timothy R. Girard—telling them, "I am tired of working for other people. I have nothing against you. Do what I say, and you will not get hurt." Then Gerena bound them, drugged them, draped jackets over their heads, and proceeded to help accomplices relieve the West Hartford, Connecticut, depot of $7 million. At the time it was the second-largest cash theft in U.S. history.

Authorities were baffled at first; Gerena had a spotless record. But later, it was revealed that Gerena

had been leading a double life: mild-mannered bank guard by day, member of Puerto Rican terrorist group Los Macheteros by night. And his accomplices were believed to be Juan Enrique Palmer and Filiberto Ojeda Rios, members of Puerto Rico's Armed Forces of National Liberation (also known as FALN), a group dedicated to shaking their homeland free of American control. On August 23, 1985, a federal grand jury indicted Gerena, Palmer, and Rios for the crime, for which Los Macheteros had taken credit a year before. Seven days later, Palmer and Rios were rounded up in a bloody dragnet, along with a dozen other suspects believed to have played a part in the Wells Fargo job. But Gerena remained on the lam.

As of this printing, Gerena—and most of the $7 million—is believed to be hiding out in Cuba, protected by Fidel Castro. And spending. *(See page 295 in Appendix II for information on how to report a Top Tenner to the FBI.)*

INTERESTING FUGITIVE FACT:

Timothy Girard says that he and Gerena used to joke that "if we were to take off with the money, we'd go to Canada."

387. WAI-CHIU NG, armed robber

LISTED: June 15, 1984
CAUGHT: October 4, 1984
DESCRIPTION: Born on November 26, 1956, in Hong Kong.
    Nickname: Tony.

Clubbed to Death.   The old man was lucky. He'd caught a bullet in the neck and somehow managed to crawl out of the blood-soaked club and into a dirty alley. He had been gambling at the Wah-My Club, a private (and illegal) gambling den nestled in Seattle's Chinatown district. The clientele was exclusively Asian high-rollers, most of them elderly . . . but none of them expecting an invasion from three armed robbers.

Twentysomething heisters Kwan Mai "Willie" Mak, Benjamin Ng, and Wai-Chui "Tony" Ng (no relation), all of them Seattle residents, all of them Asian, forced their way into the club on February 19, 1983, and proceeded to hog-tie their 14 victims. Then after being robbed, each of the prone patrons received a .22 slug in the back of their heads, execution-style. It would be the worst mass murder in Seattle history. Ng and his gang didn't count on a lone survivor, 61-year-old Wai Y. Chin, to identify the bandits. Mak and Benjamin Ng were rounded up within a day and received a sentence of death and life in prison, respectively. Ng stayed at large, however, and was named to the Top Ten list the following June.

Meanwhile, Ng had fled to his native Hong Kong, then to Canada, hiding out under an alias in a high-rise apartment complex in Calgary, Alberta. The Royal Canadian Mounted Police found and arrested him in early October 1984, and Ng was subsequently sentenced to 13 consecutive life sentences—but for assault and 13 counts of first-degree robbery, not murder.

INTERESTING FUGITIVE FACT:
Ng was the first Asian criminal to make the Top Ten.

388. ALTON COLEMAN, serial killer, rapist

LISTED: July 11, 1984
CAUGHT: July 20, 1984
DESCRIPTION: Born November 1955 in Waukegan, Illinois. Five feet 10 inches tall, 145 pounds, with black hair and brown eyes. He is believed to be traveling with 21-year-old Debra Denise Brown, his companion for the last two years.

"I Am a Dead Man." It's rare that the FBI feels the need to expand the Top Ten list, but if anyone deserved special inclusion as a Number 11, it was Alton Coleman. Even as he was named to the list, Coleman continued his horrific spree across the Midwest, prompting some to compare him to fellow Top Tenner and serial killer CHRISTOPHER WILDER (#385), who had embarked on his own rape and murder rampage just months before.

Coleman was born to a prostitute in 1955, and as a toddler would often watch as his mother plied her trade. When he turned five, Coleman's mother abandoned him, sending him off to be raised by his grandmother. Growing up, he was tormented by classmates who called him "Pissy" because he used to wet himself. His late teens and early 20s were full of rapes, robberies, and assaults, but especially rapes. One prison shrink described Coleman as a "pansexual, willing to have intercourse with any object, women, men, children, whatever." Coleman served some time, was paroled, then committed more rapes and "deviant sexual assaults" as the police termed it. He was married to a teenage girl

briefly, but she left after realizing that Coleman seemed obsessed with bondage and violent sex. In 1980 Coleman was accused of raping a girl at knifepoint and was later released on reduced bail. That would turn out to be a huge mistake.

In 1984 Coleman hooked up with Debra Denise Brown, a 21-year-old from a middle-class family in Waukegan who had ditched her fiancé to be with Coleman. (Later, the FBI would call theirs a "master-slave" relationship.) Together, Coleman and Brown started a multiple-state rampage reminiscent of Mickey and Mallory Knox's in *Natural Born Killers*. Their first victim: nine-year-old Vernita Wheat, who had willingly climbed into Coleman's car when the duo promised the girl a stereo system she could give her mom as a Mother's Day present. She would be found strangled to death in an abandoned building on June 19. The day before, Coleman and Brown had used similar lure to abduct two more little girls. Coleman strangled the seven-year-old to death, then raped and tried to kill her nine-year-old aunt. (She would escape and be able to identify Coleman.) On the afternoon of the 19th, a missing persons' bulletin was issued in Gary, Indiana, for Donna Williams, a young woman who was last seen picking up a "nice young couple" who wanted to see her church. Coleman and Brown were identified as that couple.

Over the next month Coleman and Brown continued a reign of terror through six states: murders, abductions, home invasions, assaults, rapes, shootouts, thefts, and more murders. Donna Williams's body was discovered on the morning of July 11; by that afternoon Coleman had made the Top Ten list. The announcement didn't seem to affect Coleman whatsoever. Two days later, he bludgeoned a 44-year-old woman in front of her husband. (Incidentally, that woman would be Coleman's first white victim; the previous victims were all black, and Coleman complained that he was compelled to kill members of his own race.) Four days later, Coleman nearly beat to death an elderly minister and his wife. The next day a car wash owner was found shot and stabbed to death. The American Midwest had never seen anything like it.

The killing came to an end on July 20, when a tip came in that Coleman and Brown would be in a park in Evanston, Illinois. Officers converged on the scene and arrested Coleman without incident, finding two knives—still slick with blood—on his person. Brown tried to walk away, but was also arrested and found to be carrying a .38 in her purse.

Bail was set at $25 million by a federal magistrate who declared Coleman had held "a nation under siege."

In some ways Coleman's subsequent trials—in Illinois, Ohio, Indiana—were as unpredictable as his rampage. During his trial in Illinois, Coleman dismissed his court-appointed attorneys and received permission to represent himself. A month later, Coleman fired himself, saying, "I'm coming down with a headache. I don't know what medical attention I am going to need." After the original attorneys were reappointed and prosecution challenged it, the judge asked Coleman if he believed one of his lawyers to be competent.

Alton Coleman, left, and Debra Brown stand before the bench during their arraignment in Cincinnati, in this January 10, 1985, photo.

"There is no question she is competent," said Coleman. "At this point, my mind is exhausted. I think she's Perry Mason right now."

Despite the endorsement, Coleman was eventually convicted and sentenced to death. After hearing that, Coleman moaned in horror. "I am a dead man. I am dead already. I was a fool to represent myself and I admit it."

INTERESTING FUGITIVE FACT:
At the time Coleman was the only man in the United States slapped with four separate death sentences in Ohio, Indiana, and Illinois.

389. CLEVELAND McKINLEY DAVIS, murderer

LISTED: October 24, 1984
CAUGHT: January 25, 1985
DESCRIPTION: Born April 1942 in Enfield, North Carolina. Six feet three inches tall, 200 pounds. Davis has a tattoo "LOVE" on his left wrist, as well as knife scars on his left leg and right shoulder. A reported narcotics user, Davis has been employed as a barber, beautician, electrician, mechanic, truck driver, and maintenance worker. Aliases: Jumbo Davis, Jumo Davis, Cleveland Gaynes, Jomo Jaka Omowale, Eric Scott, Eric Thompson, and Erick Thompson.

The Shadow of Attica. A life of relentless crime—convictions for armed robbery, malicious assault, coercion and unlawful imprisonment, burglary, breaking and entering, possession of a sawed-off shotgun, parole violation—landed Cleveland Davis at one of the most infamous prisons at its most infamous time in history, Attica prison during the 1971 riot. Davis was allegedly the ringleader of the hellstorm that would eventually take the lives of 43 inmates and guards.

Davis had been shipped to Attica in 1970 after pulling two armed robberies in the Big Apple. Before that he had escaped from a Virginia prison after holding up a grocery store in Virginia Beach in 1968. Virginia authorities had still been looking for him when the NYPD picked him up. After receiving seven gunshot wounds during the Attica revolt and surviving, Davis was released from Attica and sent back to Virginia to finish the time he had waiting for him. Luck intervened two years later, when Davis protected his warden from a prisoner who was trying to stab him, and the governor of Virginia rewarded his efforts with a full pardon in 1976. Cleveland Davis,

after nearly a decade of trouble with the law, finally had a clean slate.

That lasted until April 2, 1978, when Davis found himself in the middle of yet another battle between cops and a fellow ex-Attica con. What happened on that Bedford-Stuyvesant street that day is still up for debate. The prosecution claimed that Davis saw two cops scuffling with one of his prison buddies, Mariano Gonzalez, and started blasting away with a 9 mm automatic pistol. Davis, however, claimed that another friend of Gonzalez came to his aid. Nevertheless, the end result was clear, Gonzalez and the two cops died from their gunshot wounds. Davis was arrested for the crime.

Nearly ten years later, after his third trial, Davis was found not guilty on all charges. (The first two times the juries deadlocked.) Davis and his wife, Elizabeth Gaynes, a lawyer who fell in love with Davis while representing him, wanted to celebrate, but there was the possibility that he might need to serve more time in Virginia. It was embarrassing to the governor that a man he pardoned not only violated parole by being in Brooklyn, but was involved in the slayings of two cops. It was especially not great for his reelection campaign that year.

It was another break, but Davis couldn't help himself. On March 11, 1984, he and two accomplices broke into the Virginia Beach home of Raymond Stith, hoping to score some cash and drugs. But Stith fought back, stabbing Davis and getting a bullet in the brain for his efforts—courtesy of Curtis Norfleet, one of Davis's accomplices. His other buddy, Robert Green, fixed up Davis's knife wounds before he split, alone, for New York. It was a smart move on Davis's part; Norfleet and Green were nabbed a month later and got slapped with lengthy jail terms. Davis stayed at large and made the Top Ten list by October of that year. Reportedly, he swore not to be taken alive. (Killing Davis would be quite a feat, considering the man had survived seven gunshots, a stabbing, and a prison riot.)

Thankfully, it wouldn't come to more bloodshed. FBI agents and members of the NYPD captured Davis at his new hideout, an apartment in New York, and the fugitive surrendered peacefully. He was sent back to Virginia one more time, where he received a 25-year sentence.

INTERESTING FUGITIVE FACT:
In his early criminal career Davis was treated for severe depression.

390. CARMINE JOHN PERSICO, mob boss

LISTED: January 31, 1985
CAUGHT: February 15, 1985
DESCRIPTION: Born in 1934 in Brooklyn, New York. Five feet seven inches, 150 pounds, with brown hair and eyes and a scar on his right wrist. He also has partial use of his right arm because of a stroke. Aliases: John Persico Carmine, "Junior," Alphonse Persica, Carmine J. Persica, and "Snake."

Trapping the Snake. One common misconception about the Ten Most Wanted list is that it must have been full of Mafia capos and wise guys over the years; it hasn't been. (Hoover didn't officially recognize the mob until quite late in the game.) The point of the Top Ten list was to shine a harsh light on thugs who have stayed hidden and need flushing out; most times mobsters already have plenty of light shining their way.

Nonetheless, Carmine Persico, reputed boss of one the biggest crime families in New York, was named to the list in late January 1985 at age 51. It was at a time when the FBI was cracking down on the mob through new use of the old RICO (Racketeer-Influenced and Corrupt Organizations) act, which allowed the government to dole out hefty prison terms if it could prove a mobster belonged to a criminal "enterprise" or "commission." Persico certainly qualified. He started his dubious career as an enforcer for Brooklyn don Joe Profaci, but later conspired with the Gallo brothers to overthrow his old boss. In the middle of the mob war, which inspired the "mattress war" in *The Godfather*, Profaci convinced Persico to backstab the Gallos. He tried to strangle Larry Gallo in a bar, but was caught by a cop before the deed could be done. The act earned Persico the nickname "The Snake."

By 1971 an elderly mobster had taken control of Profaci's family, stepping aside three years later to let Persico, the former turncoat, rule the roost. But much of his rule was spent behind bars, after Persico was convicted of hijacking in 1972. He was paroled in 1984 . . . just when a federal grand jury indicted him on racketeering charges. Instead of allowing himself to be arrested again, Persico went into hiding. He was named to the Top Ten list on January 31, 1985.

The day after Valentine's Day 1985, agents followed up on a tip that Persico was holed up in a relative's Long Island house. Twenty-five G-men and cops surrounded the home, then picked up the phone. "We simply called him and told him to come out," said FBI assistant director Lee Laster. "He really wasn't very happy, but he came out." Persico was later tried with eight other heads of mob families and acted as his own legal counsel. (At one point the angry boss yelled, "Without the Mafia, there wouldn't even be no case here!") The Snake received a 100-year sentence for murder and conspiracy.

INTERESTING FUGITIVE FACT:

Like many made men, Persico had a skewed view of morality. After hiding a Mafia hood named Joseph Russo who had murdered two black servants in the middle of a dinner party in 1971, Persico reportedly observed, "The guy's all right. He just blew his top and killed two blacks."

391. LOHMAN RAY MAYS JR., murderer, armed robber

LISTED: February 15, 1985
CAUGHT: September 23, 1985
DESCRIPTION: Born on February 19, 1943, in Dallas, Texas. Six feet tall, 170 pounds, with brown hair, hazel eyes, a dark complexion, and slender build. Mays had reportedly shot and wounded a police officer in the past and may travel with an attack dog.

Loose Luggage. Sgt. Dan Gifford, a Missouri state trooper, thought he was doing a good deed when he pulled over a mobile home on I-70 in Kansas. He'd noticed a piece of luggage on the vehicle's roof rack was about to jiggle loose and fall to the mercies of the busy highway.

He didn't know that the mobile home contained Lohman Mays, an unrepentant criminal with a violent record reaching back into the 1960s, when he was convicted of armed robbery, aggravated assault, receiving stolen property, firearms violations, and wounding a police officer. A little over a year earlier, Mays had broken out of a prison in Only, Tennessee, and had been knocking over banks—one in Spartansburg, South Carolina, one in Orleans, Vermont, one in Eagle Rock, Missouri—ever since. Along with him for the ride was his new 28-year-old girlfriend and another unidentified white male.

Gifford was promptly kidnapped and taken to a farmhouse where he was tied up with the family of three that lived there. Mays and accomplices took off in the family car. After Gifford freed himself and checked the mobile home, he learned that it had been stolen in Salt Lake City the week before. Mays's bold moves of the past year had propelled his name to the Top Ten list in February; now his abduction of a state trooper only turned up the heat.

The heat caught up with Mays at his hideout in Wyoming by late September, and he was shipped back to prison to finish the life sentence he had waiting for him—not to mention time for his extracurricular activities as of late.

INTERESTING FUGITIVE FACT:
Reportedly, Mays was extremely soft-spoken. (It *is* the quiet ones you have to worry about.)

392. CHARLES EARL HAMMOND, murderer

DESCRIPTION: Born on December 16, 1942, in Seattle, Washington. Five feet seven inches, 140 pounds, with brown hair and hazel eyes. He reportedly walks with a slight limp. Previously convicted of assaulting a federal officer, burglary, credit fraud, illegal use of firearms, and narcotics violations.

393. MICHAEL FREDERIC ALLEN HAMMOND, murderer

BOTH LISTED: March 14, 1985
BOTH REMOVED FROM LIST: August 4, 1986
DESCRIPTION: Born on January 3, 1945, in Redding, California. Five feet five inches, 150 pounds, with red hair, blue eyes, and tattoos on his arms. Previously convicted of burglary, assaulting a federal officer, and theft from interstate shipment.

The Bruise Brothers.   According to their FBI hot sheet, both Hammond brothers were users and dealers of narcotics and both used .45 caliber handguns. Drugs and weaponry weren't the only common interests. Allegedly, the two were the triggermen in a drug-related bloodbath in Kansas that produced five shot-up corpses and one badly injured near-corpse. The massacre occurred on May 29, 1980, and the Hammond boys remained at large long enough for Kansas police to petition the FBI to name them to the Top Ten list. That finally happened in March 1985.

Seventeen months later, the hunt was called off at the request of Kansas City prosecutors, and the brothers were removed from the list. This doesn't happen very often, and it's not necessarily good news for the fugitive. Sometimes it can mean that evidence or witnesses have been lost, making prosecution an impossible course of action. Sometimes it can mean the fugitive (or fugitives) are believed dead.

INTERESTING FUGITIVE FACT:
The Hammond were the fourth pair of brothers named to the Top Ten list since it began in 1950.

394. ROBERT HENRY NICOLAUS, child killer

LISTED: June 28, 1985
CAUGHT: July 20, 1985
DESCRIPTION: Born in 1933 in California. Occupations: author, economic analyst, and gardener. Nicolaus is reportedly familiar with rifles and shotguns and is an avid jogger and weight lifter and frequent patron of health food stores.

"Better Off in Heaven."   On a spring day in 1964 Robert Nicolaus gathered up his children—his seven-year-old daughter, five-year-old son, and two-year-old daughter—and drove them to a toy store in Sacramento. It must have been exciting for the kids; Daddy bought all kinds of neat toys for them. Afterward, Nicolaus drove his children to a vacant lot and pulled over. Seems there was trouble; Daddy had lost an important key in the trunk. Would his kids mind helping him try to find it? Still giddy with the thoughts of toys, the children happily agreed. As they climbed into the trunk, Nicolaus pulled out his 5-shot .38 revolver and started blasting away at the backs of their heads. When his bullets ran out, he stopped, reloaded, and fired five more shots.

When police arrested Nicolaus, he told them that the kids would be "better off in heaven." The previous day, May 23, Nicolaus's second wife, Charlyce, the mother of the youngest girl, had left him. Rather than see any of his children end up with either of his ex-wives, Nicolaus decided to murder them. The child killer was sentenced to death exactly four months later. But three years later, California State Supreme Court reduced the sentence, reasoning that Nicolaus could not have possibly understood what he had been doing. And shockingly, in 1977, when his children would have been young adults, had they lived, Nicolaus was given a full pardon.

The intervening years did nothing to help Nicolaus come to terms with his crimes. He was still angry—angry with his ex-wives, angry with people who had wronged him. During his trial in 1964 Nicolaus had claimed to be a godlike figure who could perform miracles. Now he must have considered himself an avenging angel, out for the blood of the guilty, and the blood of his ex-wife, Charlyce M. Robinson, specifically. On February 22, 1985, Nicolaus cornered her in an alley in Sacramento, his car trapping hers. Nicolaus shot his second ex twice in the chest as her three-year-old daughter watched. Charlyce died soon after, but was able to tell police who did it. Nicolaus's apartment was searched. A hit list was found, with the names of his first ex-wife and another couple (who had reported Nicolaus for welfare fraud) on it. Nicolaus was named to the Top Ten list four months later.

Nicolaus, meanwhile, decided to attend the funeral of the founder of the York Barbell Company in York, Pennsylvania. (Aside from having some eccentric ideas about his own divinity, Nicolaus was a huge fan of working out.) On July 19 he took a bus from Charlottesville, Virginia, and checked into the local YMCA, where a local citizen recognized him from a Wanted poster hanging at a nearby post office. The next morning the FBI was waiting for him and arrested him without a fight. "He seemed very polite," said YMCA receptionist Barbara Keister to a *San Diego Union-Tribune* reporter at the time. "We didn't know he was on the lam."

Months later, Nicolaus was sentenced to death for the second time.

INTERESTING FUGITIVE FACT:
Nicolaus's major in college was child psychology.

395. DAVID JAY STERLING, armed robber, rapist

LISTED: September 30, 1985
CAUGHT: February 13, 1986
DESCRIPTION: Born January 1945 in Vancouver, Washington. Five feet 10 inches, 180 pounds, with gray black hair and brown eyes, and has scars on his right thigh and lower left leg. Sterling has been diagnosed in the past as having skin rash conditions. He formerly served in the U.S. Marines and previously had worked as a building maintenance man, computer service engineer, electronic repairman, fireman, and pilot.

The Hazel Dell Rapist. When David Sterling walked away from the grounds of Western Washington State Hospital in Steilacoom, he had served only three years of five consecutive life sentences for a series of rapes and assaults in the Hazel Dell area of Washington in 1982. (His escape would prompt the state legislature to move all sex offender treatment *behind* bars.) Sterling had been an unrepentant rapist, and authorities were worried that he would immediately pick up where he left off, which no doubt sped his way to the Top Ten list six months later.

By the time he had made the list, however, Sterling had picked up a new diversion, bank robbery, as well as a partner, 23-year-old Ronald Johnson, from Green Cove Springs, Florida. Together they knocked over a series of banks in Nevada, then fled to Covington, Louisiana, where they were picked up by a state trooper after a routine traffic violation. Troopers found marijuana, burglary tools, a 9 mm semi-automatic, a .38 caliber snub nose revolver, and a .223 caliber semi-automatic rifle in the car. Sterling was returned to Washington, this time in a maximum-security wing.

INTERESTING FUGITIVE FACT:
Sterling would later allege that a law officer intentionally lost a duffel bag full of personal items, and he sued the office in a Pennsylvania court. The first suit was pending when Sterling broke out of jail, so a judge tossed it out. Sterling had the nerve to file *another* suit after his recapture, and a judge threw this suit out as well. But later, the Seventh U.S. Circuit Court of Appeals reversed that decision, saying that Sterling's second suit shouldn't have been automatically tossed out because the first had been, creating a minor footnote in law journals in 1996.

396. RICHARD SCUTARI, armed robber, neo-Nazi

LISTED: September 30, 1985
CAUGHT: March 19, 1986
DESCRIPTION: Born 1948 in Fort Jefferson, New York. Five feet 11 inches, 180 pounds, with brown hair and eyes. He has a tattoo "U.S. NAVY" on his upper right arm and has been known to wear a mustache and beard. A former karate instructor, Scutari is reportedly armed with unlimited ammunition, weapons, and is known to use bulletproof vests. He has vowed not to be taken alive.

Meet Mr. Black. Consider it the crème de la crème of white supremacists everywhere: the Bruder Schweigen ("Silent Brotherhood") was the hardcore "special ops" unit of the Order, which itself was a paramilitary group formed to eradicate Jews and blacks and obliterate the so-called Zionist Occupational Government in Washington, D.C. (This was the same Order believed to be connected to the shooting death of Denver talk radio host Alan Berg.) Richard Scutari, nicknamed "Mr. Black" for his black belt in karate, was a charter member of the Bruder Schweigen and allegedly lent a hand in a series of armored car and bank heists between December 1983 and July 1984—fundraisers for the Order. Scutari and the Order patterned their crimes after a novel, *The Turner Diaries,* in which Aryan warriors finance their coup of the U.S. government with armored car heists.

The biggie: the bold boost of $3.6 million from a Brink's armored truck near Ukiah, California, for which the Silent Brotherhood had a brother on the inside, helping them plot the caper. That insider, Charles Ostrout, later betrayed the Bruder Schweigen when he testified against his former members. He revealed that Scutari was considered the Brotherhood's internal security agent, giving new members voice stress analyzer tests to make sure they weren't government moles, and in some cases recommending the assassinations of Order members he considered "security risks." In April Scutari and others were indicted on charges of racketeering, conspiracy, transporting stolen goods across state lines, and interfering with interstate commerce by means of threats of violence.

In March 1986 FBI agents had traced Scutari— hiding under the name "Larry Cupp"—to a brake shop in San Antonio, Texas. (Scutari's wife was also arrested for her role in trying to hide a cut of the money from the Brink's job in Ukiah.) He had a .45 automatic hidden in his car, but the fugitive didn't take the chance and surrendered peacefully. Six months later, Scutari pleaded guilty to racketeering and robbery and received 40 to 100 years in prison.

INTERESTING FUGITIVE FACT:
Even Scutari was long thought to have had a hand in the murder of Alan Berg, and as the last surviving suspect, he would later be acquitted of the charges.

397. JOSEPH WILLIAM DOUGHERTY, armed robber

LISTED: November 6, 1985
CAUGHT: December 19, 1986
DESCRIPTION: Born 1940 in Philadelphia. Six feet two inches, 230 pounds, with blue eyes, graying black hair, and a ruddy complexion. He has a scar on the back of his right hand and has been known to wear a beard in the past.

Dougherty may be accompanied by Terry Lee Conner, who is also being sought by the FBI for bank robbery. They are alleged narcotics users and reportedly armed with handguns and automatic weapons. They have vowed not to be taken alive.

Partners in Crime. Raymond and Verona Deering had a car for sale in their driveway and were happy when two men interested in the car came knocking the night of June 30, 1986. Raymond and the men haggled for a while, at which point the two buyers pulled out .45 caliber pistols from their jackets and put a small submachine gun on a chair next to the dining room table.

"Okay," blurted Thomas, the Deerings' 19-year-old son. "You can have the car."

But the two men, Joseph Dougherty and TERRY LEE CONNER (#402), weren't in the market for new wheels.

"Sit down," Dougherty said.

Raymond Deering said, "I don't have any money."

"I don't want your money," Dougherty. "I want the bank's money."

At the time Deer was assistant manager and assistant vice president at a First Independent Bank branch in Hazel Dell, Washington. Dougherty and Conner had developed a new way of knocking over banks: Hold a bank employee and his family hostage the night before, show up at the bank the next morning bright and early, and have their hostage open the vault for them. It had worked before—just that past September the two had held a Wisconsin bank manager hostage and helped themselves to $574,119 at his workplace the next day. (They forced their way into the manager's house with FBI badges, and when asked to see ID, one of them said, "We're not here to display badges. We're here to rob banks.") And back in 1982 a similar hostage stunt had worked in Oklahoma City, netting the duo $706,000.

That 1982 job had ended badly for Conner. He was arrested and received a 25-year jail term. Dougherty kept up the work, knocking over banks in Phoenix, Salt Lake City, and Reno before his own arrest. On June 19, 1985, the two found themselves on the same prisoner transport bus. Conner spit out a handcuff key he'd hidden in his mouth, followed by a razor blade. In a scene right out of *The Fugitive,* Conner used the key to free himself, then held the blade to the neck of a deputy U.S. marshal and commandeered the transport bus, then forced it to make an early stop. Dougherty and

Conner stole their captors' badges, handcuffed them to a tree, and made their escape in a stolen truck. Later, they used their new badges to force their way into a house, where they helped themselves to new clothes.

The boys were back in business. They stole $27,000 from a St. Louis bank and soon after pulled the Wisconsin hostage job. Dougherty was named to the Top Ten list that following November. The FBI would have liked to have included his buddy, Conner, but there weren't any other spots open at the time.

Dougherty, in fact, bragged to the Deerings about being on the Top Ten list. "We can leave our prints everywhere, and within 20 minutes, they will know who we are." Interestingly, the Deerings came to sympathize with their captors, according to interviews with *The Oregonian* after the incident. "I felt sorry for them," said Thomas Deering. "They were unable to have a normal family life." Added Verona: "I told them they didn't seem like criminal types. They said they were victims of circumstances, and were just playing out roles." Dougherty and Conner played their roles well. They suited up in business attire—and bulletproof vests—and forced Raymond Deering to open the vault at 7:05 A.M. and took $225,000. The Deerings, along with six other bank employees, were locked in a storage room as their captors made their escape.

The crime team didn't last too long after the Deering heist. Dougherty was trapped by the FBI and U.S. marshals after they started trailing one of his prison friends, Robert Butcher, and captured him as they met in a laundromat in Antioch, California, possibly to plan another caper. More jail time was piled on Dougherty, who told a judge that he already had enough time to last until his 193rd birthday.

As for what happened to Conner, see his profile (#402) below.

INTERESTING FUGITIVE FACT:
Dougherty and Conner were two of the few fugitives to make the Top Ten list and the U.S. Marshal's Top Fifteen list at the same time.

398. BRIAN PATRICK MALVERTY, murderer, drug dealer

LISTED: March 28, 1986
CAUGHT: April 7, 1986
DESCRIPTION: Born in 1959.

"The Fugitive Asked Me Out on a Date!" To most of the residents of the San Diego condo at 8300 Regents Road, "Tommy Louzzi" was a nice, social kind of guy who worked as a carpet layer. "He lived two doors down from me," neighbor Shelley Kilbourne told the *San Diego Union-Tribune*. "I used to see him all the time. Whenever I was out by the pool, he'd come over and talk to me about his ex-wife and kids in Georgia. He asked me out, but I never went out with him."

Good thing. "Tommy" was actually Brian Malverty, wanted in Georgia for the murder of two men who were bound, shot in the chest, neck, and head, then soaked in gasoline and set on fire on April 23, 1985. Allegedly, Malverty had two accomplices on that execution-style murder, and one of them, Tony Albertson, got a case of verbal diarrhea and started blabbing about the murders. Weeks later, in early summer 1985, two joggers in Queens got the surprise of their lives: two guys digging what appeared to be a grave for a corpse wrapped up in a sleeping bag. The joggers were beaten with shovels, but managed to get away. Police later identified the body in the sleeping bag as Albertson. He had two .25 slugs in his brain.

By the time Malverty made the Top Ten list, he had started a new life for himself in San Diego as "Tommy Louzzi," renting a condo that he said he planned to buy someday. Once, "Tommy" even went drinking with some of his neighbors, but for some odd reason couldn't produce a driver's license. "He said he'd lost it for drunk driving," said neighbor Barrie Stiller. "I feel a bit shaken, because he didn't turn out to be who he said he was. He used to talk to me and my roommate all the time, come over and watch TV, and even fixed our carpet in our unit. He was friendly."

Friendly, and also hanging on the walls of local post offices. That's how one anonymous tipster recognized Malverty, prompting FBI to pounce on him at 7:50 A.M. Monday morning at his own apartment. Malverty didn't put up a fight.

Added Art Glassman, another condo neighbor: "About six months or a year ago, an international jewel thief was arrested here. He robbed and burglarized a lot of people who lived here. Now this."

INTERESTING FUGITIVE FACT:
Malverty is one of the few fugitives who didn't bother to disguise his appearance after his face appeared on a Most Wanted poster.

399. BILLY RAY WALDON, murderer, rapist, arsonist

LISTED: May 16, 1986
CAUGHT: June 16, 1986
DESCRIPTION: Born 1952 in Tahlequah, Oklahoma. Six feet two inches, 160 pounds with brown hair and eyes. Waldon speaks Esperanto, Spanish, French, Italian, Japanese, Cherokee and has worked as an electronic warfare technician and deep sea diver. He has also traveled extensively in Europe and the Far East.

Out of Nowhere. No one can explain why a brilliant, compassionate ex-navy man would embark on a relentless, bloody crime spree in the fall of 1985. No one, that is, except Billy Ray Waldon himself, who claims he was set up by the CIA and FBI because he was a quarter Cherokee Indian. "It was my Cherokee identity that caused me to be the target of a COINTELPRO," he said, referring to the FBI's counterespionage program started in 1956.

Whether you believe Waldon's conspiracy theory or not, his case is a strange one. Waldon is believed to have lived a crime-free life until 1985, when his grandmother, who had raised him since he was five years old, passed away. Soon after, Waldon was sought in connection with a series of crimes in Tulsa: the shooting of a senior citizen outside a grocery mart on October 10, a shopping mall robbery on the 11th, another robbery attempt on the 15th, the attempted murder of a 28-year-old woman on November 15, the murder of a 52-year-old woman on the 17th, and another wounding/robbery on the 23rd. Tulsa police began to gather evidence pointing to Waldon.

Sometime after Thanksgiving 1985 Waldon traveled to Gardenia, California, where his ex-wife lived with their two kids, and then moved on to San Diego, where he had spent time serving in the navy. That's when the mayhem started again: the murders of a mother and daughter, the murder of a retired carpenter, the rape of an elementary schoolteacher, and 20 other assorted burglaries, robberies, and rapes. The double murder was particularly brutal; 42-year-old Dawn Ellerman was shot in the neck with a .25-caliber pistol, then was locked in her own bathroom with her dogs, whose skulls had been crushed. The house was set on fire, at which point Ellerman's 13-year-old daughter, who had just returned home from babysitting, valiantly tried to save her mother, but died in the fire.

The murder of the retired carpenter, Charles Wells, spawned a massive manhunt involving more than 150 people that failed to snag Waldon. They did find evidence, however, linking him to the Ellerman murders, and once authorities in San Diego traded notes with those in Tulsa, a federal warrant for Waldon's arrest was issued on January 3, 1986, and he made the Top Ten list five months later.

If it wasn't for broken taillights, Waldon may have remained at large. At 3:50 A.M. on Monday, June 16, San Diego police pulled over a man driving a 1965 Ford Mustang with its taillights on the fritz. The cops planned to give a friendly warning, but then the man bolted, dropping a dagger on the ground. The man who would later identify himself as "Steven Midas" was taken down and thrown in the slammer. The guy bugged San Diego detective Gerald Berner, though. Something about him looked familiar. In the middle of the night it came to him. *Billy Ray Waldon.* The next morning, fingerprints revealed the truth. Midas was Waldon. Good thing they checked—Midas would probably have been arraigned and set free in a few days' time. (Oddly enough, the San Diego PD discovered Midas's true identity the same day they opened a new fugitive-apprehension unit. "It was pretty ironic," noted one cop.)

The weirdness was far from over. Waldon insisted on representing himself in his murder trial, at one point eerily reading questions from a sheet, pausing, turning his head, then answering them. The judge who sentenced Waldon to die in the gas chamber was almost "moved to tears" when he reminded the jury how Waldon calmly ate microwaved pizza while watching a news report of the Ellerman murders on TV.

"Only an innocent man could have done that," Waldon said.

"You are not an innocent man," the judge replied. "I'm convinced of that."

INTERESTING FUGITIVE FACT:
According to Waldon, his Cherokee name "Nvwtohiyada Idehesdi Sequoyah" translates into "Let us live in peace, harmony, and good health."

400. CLAUDE LAFAYETTE DALLAS JR., murderer

LISTED: May 16, 1986
CAUGHT: March 8, 1987
DESCRIPTION: Born on March 11, 1950, in Winchester, Virginia. Five feet 10 inches tall, with brown hair and eyes and a ruddy complexion. He wears glasses occasionally and has a scar on his left calf.

The Folk Hero. Before the two game wardens approached Claude Dallas Jr. on that fateful January day in 1981, the hard-working hunter/trapper had butted heads with the Idaho Fish and Game Department a number of times. Dallas didn't give much credence to limits or conservation or seasons; he believed he had a right to hunt and trap from the land as much as he saw fit. So when Bill Pogue and Conley Elms dropped in on Dallas at his southwestern Idaho trapping camp, the hunter was ready for a fight. When he began to believe that the wardens were fixing to arrest him, Dallas opened fire with a .357 Ruger pistol, dropping both men. "Oh, no!" one of the men could be heard to scream. Then he calmly retrieved his .22 Marlin rifle from a tent and pumped a shell into the space behind each man's left ear—just to make sure.

Then Dallas recruited a friend—who had seen the whole thing—to help him hide his tracks. "I've got to get rid of the bodies, and you've got to help me."

The two strapped the bodies to mules, but Warden Elms proved too heavy for the animal, and his body ended up dumped in a nearby river. The two packed up Pogue's body and drove five hours to another friend's house. "We're in trouble," Dallas said. "I dusted two Fish and Game." After borrowing a pickup truck and shovel, Dallas set off to the desert to bury Pogue in secret. Dallas returned the truck, then disappeared into the county.

A manhunt ensued, but authorities were playing on Dallas's game board. Friends would help Dallas stay on the run, leaving food and gas and vehicles in the Nevada desert. He stayed at large for 14 months before he was apprehended in a scene worthy of an action thriller. FBI agents in a helicopter and speeding cars pursued the fugitive in his pickup through the scorching desert. The ensuing gun battle wounded Dallas, but he was brought in alive. He was found guilty of two counts of voluntary manslaughter and given 30 years in jail. But by that time Dallas had become a weird western folk hero to people who believed that the hunter had acted only in self-defense to protect his life and property. One book about Dallas even cast him as a romantic hero straight out of the Old West. He received piles of fan mail while at Idaho State Penitentiary.

But Dallas didn't stay in prison long. On Easter Sunday 1986 he managed to cut his way through two chain link fences and escaped. The FBI named him to the Top Ten list 47 days later.

Dallas's second run was much different from the first. Instead of living off the land, he fled to Mexico for plastic surgery. He shaved his beard, ditched his glasses and trademark cowboy hat, and started calling himself "Al Shrank." After that, he spent time in San Francisco, Los Angeles, and Eugene, Oregon, before heading to Riverside, California, where an old ranching buddy had rented a house. And that's how the G-men caught him. They'd kept careful tabs on all of Dallas's friends, especially ones who had testified on his behalf at his trial. On March 8, 1987, Dallas was spotted leaving a convenience store with groceries and a Dr Pepper. He was surrounded and taken down for the second time.

Amazingly, Dallas never received any additional time for his prison break. The jury in Idaho seemed genuinely moved by Dallas's story that he'd escaped prison in the first place to escape murder at the hands of prison guards, who considered him a cop killer. He returned to finish his original sentence and continued to receive fan mail.

INTERESTING FUGITIVE FACT:
The FBI had a run-in with Dallas long before he met Pogue and Elms. The survivalist hunter had dodged the Vietnam draft in 1970 and was arrested in October 1973. The U.S. attorney later dropped the charges when the draft board couldn't prove that Dallas had received a second notice to appear for induction.

401. DONALD KEITH WILLIAMS, bank robber

LISTED: July 18, 1986
CAUGHT: August 20, 1986
DESCRIPTION: Born 1929 in Lincoln, Nebraska.

The Veil Bandit. In comic books some arch-villains adopt a clever disguise to hide a hideous physical defect. Williams's defect—a muscular defect that caused his right eye to squint—wasn't all that hideous, but it would be troublesome in his chosen profession, bank robber. ("Yep—right there, officer. The squinty one. He's the guy.") So Williams wore a cloth veil draped over the visor of a baseball cap for many of the 34 bank heists he pulled during the mid-80s.

But Williams's criminal career dated back to 1952, when he was convicted of larceny and burglary in Missouri. Same thing happened in 1961, and Williams was sent to the slammer, then paroled in 1968, only to violate the terms of his parole later that year by committing armed robbery. But Williams's streak starting in 1983 was his career peak: more than $100,000 netted from 34 banks in Colorado, Illinois, Minnesota, Oregon, Washington, and California. (Fifteen jobs alone were pulled in Los Angeles). When he was named as the 401st addition to the Top Ten list in July 1986, Williams was 57 years old.

Fortunately, Williams was stopped before he hit retirement age and collected his gold watch from bank robbers' guild. A citizen spied Williams's face on a Wanted poster and directed officials to his house in the Mar Vista section of West Los Angeles, according to a spokesman from the FBI's L.A. office. The veil was ripped away; FBI agents raided the place. Williams had three handguns stashed at his pad, but didn't go for any of them and surrendered peacefully. He went on to face up to 950 years of prison time.

INTERESTING FUGITIVE FACT:
In true comic book arch-villain fashion, Williams also wore body armor and ear phones tuned to police frequencies.

402. TERRY LEE CONNER, bank robber

LISTED: August 8, 1986
CAUGHT: December 9, 1986
DESCRIPTION: Born 1943 in Terre Haute, Indiana. Six feet one inch tall, 190 pounds, with blue eyes and balding brown hair. He may be wearing a toupee.

Partners in Crime, Part 2. When we last left Terry Lee Conner, he was awaiting two things—his own spot on the Top Ten list and capture by the FBI. (See the profile of his partner, JOSEPH WILLIAM DOUGHERTY, #397, for full story.) Both came within months of each other.

One week after the crime duo forced the Deering family to help them rob a Hazel Dell, Washington, bank, Conner earned his own place on the Top Ten list. The FBI focused part of their search on Chicago, where Conner was believed to have friends and family, and, word had it, a big bank caper was in the works, involving hostages and explosives. An anonymous phone tip directed agents to a Red Roof Inn in suburban Arlington Heights, Illinois, and Conner was picked up after he left his room to find a cup of joe. He surrendered without a fight. At the time G-men and U.S. marshals thought his partner-in-crime might be nearby. "They work together, but stay apart when planning to rob a bank," FBI spokesman Robert

Long told the *Chicago Tribune*. (As it turned out, Dougherty would be caught 10 days later on the West Coast.) Conner received life in prison for his crimes.

INTERESTING FUGITIVE FACT:
Conner and Dougherty had identical tattoos of a purple rose with green leaves on their upper arms.

403. FILLMORE RAYMOND CROSS, extortionist

LISTED: August 8, 1986
CAUGHT: December 23, 1986
DESCRIPTION: Cross is an avid weight lifter, trained in the martial arts, and is known to carry a gun in his ankle holster. Previous jobs include bail bondsman, car salesman, collector, construction worker, import business owner, real estate investor, and tree surgeon. Aliases include Fill Raymond Close, Fillmore Cross, Phillip Raymond Cross, Gary Greenfest, Phillip Louis Long, Walter Lee McMillen, Carl Westmore, Fill, and Pierre.

Crazy in California. In October 1984 real estate agent James Eberhardt found himself being beaten within an inch of his life by two men who wanted $100,000. No, they weren't looking for the return of a security deposit—allegedly, the thugs were under the employ of Fillmore Cross, an influential Hell's Angels member who had been trying to extort the money from Eberhardt.

His biker buddies nicknamed him "Crazy," and Cross's prior run-ins with the law—including charges of rape, and convictions of battery, assault, and conspiracy to deal coke and amphetamines—only bolstered that opinion. The manhunt for Cross began shortly after the assault of Eberhardt, but it took nearly two years to make the Top Ten list. A few months later, Cross decided to turn himself in, and this began six weeks of "delicate, tedious, and secret negotiations," said Santa Cruz County assistant D.A. Gary Fry. Odd that it took so long, since Cross's only request was that his bail be lowered to $250,000. (It was.) In fact, A.D.A. Fry wasn't sure why Cross was named to the list in the first place. "I'm baffled by that," he told a reporter in 1986. "It was like a little fish caught with a big hook." FBI spokeswoman Ellen Knowlton said that Cross made the Top Ten list because he was considered a danger to the public.

INTERESTING FUGITIVE FACT:
Among Cross's hobbies: ancient Mexican artifacts, wine, and rattlesnakes.

404. JAMES WESLEY DYESS, burglar, murderer

LISTED: September 29, 1986
CAUGHT: March 16, 1988
DESCRIPTION: Born on June 10, 1956, in Laurel, Mississippi.
   Consider armed and extremely dangerous.

Truck Stop Takedown.   On April 25, 1986, James Dyess was cooling out in a Clarke County, Mississippi, prison, waiting for the bus that would take him away to Mississippi State Penitentiary to serve a seven-year jolt for burglary and other habitual crimes. Dyess wasn't exactly looking forward to the trip, so he teamed up with fellow prisoner Robert S. Minnick and checked himself out of the Gray Bar Hotel.

The next night the pair smashed their way into a Clarke County trailer home to look for guns. Sadly, the owner of that trailer, Donald E. Thomas, along with friend Lamar Lafferty, showed up mid-break-in. Both were gunned down with Thomas's own .22 caliber revolver, and the pair of fugitives fled the scene.

A federal warrant for Dyess was issued a few weeks later, and by September the bloodthirsty escape artist would make the Top Ten list. Minnick was arrested in California not long after, but Dyess stayed on the run for nearly two years, adopting the name "James Nobles" and finding work as a truck driver. He might have stayed hidden, too, if not for that fact that two members of the LAPD spied Dyess in a car at a central Los Angeles truck stop, acting "suspicious." The cops ran the plates; the vehicle popped up as stolen. Dyess was arrested without incident.

INTERESTING FUGITIVE FACT:
Dyess's partner, Minnick, took his case to the U.S. Supreme Court. Minnick claimed that his Miranda rights had been violated when he confessed to killing Lafferty when speaking to a Mississippi sheriff. In 1990 the Supreme Court agreed, granting Minnick a new trial.

405. DANNY MICHAEL WEEKS, murderer, kidnapper, robber

LISTED: September 29, 1986
CAUGHT: March 20, 1988
DESCRIPTION: Born on January 19, 1954, in Roswell, New
   Mexico.

The Roswell Abductor.   It wasn't as if Danny Weeks needed any more time added to his jail term. The baby-faced prisoner was already serving a 99-year sentence for armed robbery along with a life sentence for a December 1981 contract killing of a U.S. Army sergeant. (Weeks had been hired by the sergeant's wife.) But when Weeks and a fellow prisoner, 33-year-old James Lee Colvin, broke out of Louisiana State Penitentiary at Angola in late August 1986, he did the one thing guaranteed to rack up more time; he and Colvin abducted a woman.

They found her in the parking lot of an Alexandria, Louisiana, hospital, and then forced her at knifepoint to drive them to Houston. Eight hours later, she was released unharmed, and the duo picked up another woman—coincidentally, a U.S. Army lieutenant—and forced her to drive them to El Paso over the course of 50 hours. Weeks and Colvin disappeared after leaving their second abductee, also unharmed, in a mall parking lot.

Colvin was nabbed by police not long after, but Weeks stayed at large for more than a few weeks. He was busy, too—accused of robbing banks in San Antonio and Tucson. By early 1988 Weeks had teamed up with a new partner, 56-year-old Jorene H. Florea. Together they nabbed Susan Kathleen Vincent, a 27-year-old sheriff's deputy in Guilford, North Carolina, from a shopping center in Greensboro. Vincent was forced to tap a MAC machine for $208, then watched as Weeks and Florea robbed a bank in Davenport, Iowa, before being released in Chicago.

Meanwhile, there was an unfortunate addition to the weekly television lineup—unfortunate for Weeks and Florea. *America's Most Wanted* debuted in February 1988 and featured Weeks in one of its earliest broadcasts. Sure enough, three weeks later an anonymous tipster informed the FBI that Weeks was in Seattle. A 10-member FBI team—"It was a spur-of-the-moment thing," said a Seattle FBI spokesman later—converged on Weeks and Florea within 30 minutes of the tip being made. Both fugitives were pulled over on a road in a residential neighborhood, agents then looking in the trunk of their car. They were brought in without incident.

"I'm ecstatic," said Susan Vincent days after the capture. "I'm real glad they caught them so soon, before they got out of the country. The worst is over now. All that's left is the court action." And time to be added to Danny Weeks's existing sentences.

INTERESTING FUGITIVE FACT:
As a child, Weeks grew up surrounded by members

of outlaw biker gangs such as Hell's Angels and the Bandidos.

406. MIKE WAYNE JACKSON, spree killer

LISTED: October 1, 1986
CAUGHT: October 2, 1986
DESCRIPTION: Born in Mississippi on September 23, 1945.

Nightmare in Silver. Federal probation officer Thomas Gahl showed up at 8 A.M. on September 22, 1986. It was a routine spot check of recent parolee Mike Wayne Jackson, who had served a hitch at the Medical Center for Federal Prisons in Springfield, Missouri, and now lived in Indianapolis. Gahl didn't expect Jackson to be overjoyed to see him, but he certainly didn't expect what followed, either.

Out of nowhere Jackson whipped out a 12-gauge, pump-action shotgun. "Don't do it! Don't do it!" cried Gahl according to a nearby witness, but Jackson blasted at Gahl anyway. The officer fell to his knees and continued pleading for his life. Jackson ignored him, calmly racking the weapon again, taking careful aim, then shooting Gahl again.

Then things *really* got weird.

Jackson smeared his rough, bearded face with grease, then sprayed silver paint over his face and hair and set out on one of the wildest crime sprees of the 1980s.

Jackson had been in trouble with the law since ninth grade, when he robbed a cab driver. Over the years he had racked up more than 35 arrests in three states for a variety of heinous crimes, including rape, sodomy, assault and battery, kidnapping, and firearms violations. He was institutionalized a few times, but to no avail. When Jackson, an alcoholic and heroin addict, was paroled in early 1986, it was against the advice of staff psychiatrists. The year before, Jackson's own 73-year-old mother pleaded with authorities to commit her son permanently to an institution "where he can be helped mentally and physically."

After shooting Gahl, Jackson went to a local grocery store to rob it. When the owner, Jim Hall, moved too slow to hand over cash, witnesses say, Jackson shot him in the throat, then kidnapped bakery driver Russell Van Osdol and ordered him to take him to the Indianapolis International Airport. Miraculously, the bread guy was allowed to live, as was the driver of another truck that Jackson commandeered. Soon Jackson encountered 27-year-old Jodi Smith

and forced her to drive to Frankfort, Indiana. "He said if I tried to get away, he would kill me," Smith told police later. "I think he would." To save herself, Smith jumped from the moving vehicle, breaking her ankle in the process.

But Jackson's spree was far from over. He then nabbed a mother and child, robbed them, then left them on a country road about five miles away. Not long after, he shot and killed 47-year-old Earl Finn, thinking him to be an undercover cop. (He wasn't.) From there Jackson traveled 250 miles to O'Fallon, Missouri, where he stole another car at gunpoint, then, shortly after, another car by the same method. (The second time, however, he fired a shot at the vehicle's owner through the back window, adding injury to insult.) Jackson's next victim was 26-year-old Rick Darcy, who had been waxing his Cadillac. Jackson forced Darcy into his own trunk, then sped away to Wright City.

Wright City is where it all went wrong for Jackson. Officer Roland Clemonds spotted the Cadillac pulling into a gas station off I-70, then pulled up behind and aimed his gun at Jackson. "He didn't say a word," Clemonds told reporters later. "He just came up with a shotgun and . . . boom. I returned fire and he started to drive away and I fired a second shot." Jackson's stolen Cadillac crashed, forcing the silver-headed psycho to flee the scene on foot. Bloodstains and bullet holes in the car indicated that Clemonds had winged him. A shaken, but otherwise unharmed Darcy was pulled from the trunk. A bullet had grazed Clemonds's face, but he was treated at a hospital and released soon after.

It had been one hell of a Monday.

That night, countless households in the quiet, 1,200-person farming town locked and loaded the family shotgun, and more than 100 lawmen began a house-to-house manhunt for Jackson. "What we fear is, he has someone hostage in a house," said the captain of the Missouri Highway Patrol at the time. "But it's always a possibility that he hit the road and was gone last night." The next day half of Wright City kept their kids home from school, and helicopters and dogs joined the hunt. A new heat-detecting plane would also be employed in the search for Jackson. But nothing worked. Nine days after the shooting, Jackson made the FBI's Top Ten list.

The next day officers heard that a man matching Jackson's description was seen hitchhiking, wearing a blue raincoat. One officer had a brain flash; he had seen a blue raincoat hanging in a nearby abandoned barn. Four officers approached the barn, then heard a shotgun blast. Reinforcements were called in. SWAT teams were deployed. Police used a bullhorn to urge Jackson's surrender. Helicopters covered the area with searchlights. Tear gas was lobbed. Jackson was discovered in the loft, his head blown apart by a self-inflicted shotgun wound. His eyes were open, and his body was emaciated, as if he had gone hungry for days.

To this day no one can explain the silver paint.

INTERESTING FUGITIVE FACT:
Blame it on a mid-life crisis; Jackson began his spree the day before his 41st birthday.

407. THOMAS GEORGE HARRELSON, bank robber

LISTED: November 28, 1986
CAUGHT: February 9, 1987
DESCRIPTION: Born in 1958 in Little Rock, Arkansas. Alias: Paul Milton Fullerton.

White Flight. On August 1, 1986, the doors swung open at the First National Bank of Rossville in Illinois, and in walked two men wearing blue coveralls, construction-style hard hats, and bandannas over their faces. They weren't there to check for asbestos.

Instead, Thomas George Harrelson and his accomplice, both members of the neo-Nazi Aryan Nations group, relieved a bank teller of $44,000, then sped away. One police car pursued them into a cornfield, only to discover too late it was an ambush: Harrelson and partner had stopped their car and were waiting with a 9 mm handgun and 12-gauge shotgun in their hands. They riddled the car, then drove 25 miles across the state line in Indiana and set their own car on fire. (Miraculously, the officers in the police car were unharmed.)

It was all in a day's work for one of Aryan Nations' hardest working fundraisers. Over the course of a year and a half Harrelson had robbed more than six banks in three states, all in the name of defending the white race from the menace of the spawns of Satan (i.e., Jewish and African-American people). Previously, Harrelson had been convicted of robbing a bank in Sacramento, but was paroled in July 1985. He resumed robbing banks just a few short months later. By the time of the Rossville heist, Harrelson had stolen/raised better than $90,000 for the Aryans. His efforts earned him a spot on the Top Ten list that November.

Harrelson's lucrative lucky streak came quite literally to a grinding halt at a February 9th fundraising gig at the Drayton State Bank in North Dakota. Netting only $2,800, Harrelson—along with 22-year-old fiancée Cynthia Ehrlich and 29-year-old Stuart Kenneth Skarda—fled the scene, only to slide into a ditch and get stuck in the mud. The trio hopped out, commandeered a grain truck, took a family of four aboard as their hostages, and continued their escape. But by that time cops had already set up a roadblock ahead, and when officers shot out the grain truck's back tires, Harrelson and company slid into their final ditch. The Aryans did their best to shoot it out, but gave up when they realized they were completely surrounded.

Harrelson later pleaded guilty, to the Rossville heist and all of the others and was given 34 years in Leavenworth.

INTERESTING FUGITIVE FACT:
Harrelson's promotion to the Top Ten list caused him to postpone his wedding. But his blushing (and pregnant) bride-to-be, Cynthia Ehrlich, understood it was for a good cause. Her father was Robert Miles, who had been arrested for bombing school buses in Michigan to protest integration.

408. ROBERT ALLEN LITCHFIELD, bank robber

LISTED: January 20, 1987
CAUGHT: May 20, 1987
DESCRIPTION: Born in 1948.

The Wrong Card. Tip to wannabe bank robbers: Among the many things you might want to pack—a gun, a mask, a sack for the stacks of unmarked bills, tickets to Rio—don't bring the business card of your former federal parole officer.

That's what Robert Litchfield did when he robbed the First Security Bank in Boise, Idaho, on May 14, 1987. By that time Litchfield had already made the Top Ten list for a string of other bank robberies in Florida and Michigan. Before that Litchfield had received a 60-year sentence for robbing 15 banks over the course of two years, but escaped from the federal prison at Talladega, Alabama, in early 1986. You'd think he'd have his routine down pat by then.

Oddly enough, it was his routine that ultimately led to his capture. During the Boise boost Litchfield relied on his usual plan: bring an empty shoe box and a pistol, tell the bank employees that there was a bomb in the shoebox, then leave with a briefcase full of cash. Only this time, Litchfield accidentally dropped a business card when making his getaway—and sadly for the fugitive it wasn't his dry cleaners'. It was the card for his West Palm Beach, Florida, parole officer, who remembered that Litchfield often used a fake bomb scare during robberies.

On May 20, a phone tip came in, saying that Litchfield and his wife were holed up at Lake Tahoe in Zephyr Code, Nevada. Within hours the FBI, along with U.S. marshals and the local sheriff, nabbed him without a fight and sent him back to Alabama to face further charges. He was convicted and sentenced to 140 years at Leavenworth. No parole officers would be giving Litchfield a business card for quite some time.

INTERESTING FUGITIVE FACT:

Two years later, Litchfield escaped from prison again, becoming the first prisoner in 12 years to break out of Leavenworth. Litchfield was caught by U.S. marshals exactly one month later in Pensacola Beach, but by that time he had already undergone surgery to make himself look like his idol, actor Robert De Niro.

409. DAVID JAMES ROBERTS, murderer, arsonist

LISTED: April 27, 1987
CAUGHT: February 11, 1988
DESCRIPTION: Born on January 25, 1944, in Perth Amboy, New Jersey. Six feet three inches tall, 218 pounds, with black hair and brown eyes. He has a small scar on his back near his shoulder blade and a one-inch scar on his right knee. Roberts reportedly also has numerous additional scars from gunshot wounds, knives, and surgery.

America's Most Wanted's **First Catch.** Eight months after being released from jail on parole, David Roberts scammed a set of tires from a shop in White River, Indiana. Manager Bill Patrick signed a formal complaint with the police, and apparently Roberts took it personally. On January 20, 1974, Roberts took a can of gasoline and torched Patrick's home, killing the manager, his wife, and their one-year-old daughter. Investigators determined, however, that the Patricks had been dead prior to the fire.

Roberts was arrested and charged with triple homicide, but released on $10,000 bail. A month and a half later, in November 1974, Roberts grabbed a 19-year-old woman in Indianapolis, raped her in the backseat of her own car, then locked her in the trunk. For Roberts this was a return to form: He had been sent to prison back in the late 1960s for raping women and locking them in the trunks of their cars. (He had served only half his sentence when he was paroled in 1972.) But this time the attack had an even grislier component. Roberts deposited the victim's six-month-old son in a nearby patch of snowy woods, where he crawled for hundreds of yards before dying of exposure. Within the same year Roberts had managed to kill two babies.

Not surprisingly, on January 14, 1977, Roberts was convicted and sentenced to die—a sentence that would later be reduced to six consecutive life terms. In October 1986 Roberts pulled another scam, and this time it wasn't over car tires. On the way back from a medical exam in Indiana, Roberts somehow managed to get hold of a gun and used it to overpower his prison escorts. He escaped shortly after, and he made the Top Ten list the following April.

Meanwhile, a new show, *America's Most Wanted*, was in the works on the fledgling Fox network. The show was to be hosted by John Walsh, whose son Adam had been the victim of a brutal killer back in 1970s, and who dedicated his life to protecting other children from similar fates. The *AMW* staff knew they wanted to feature an FBI Top Tenner on their first broadcast, and Roberts presented himself as a perfect candidate. No one was sure the show would work, or help find a fugitive for that matter, but even host Walsh agreed that there was a certain poetic justice to featuring Roberts. "I'm the father of a murdered child, and here's a guy who killed two kids," said Walsh at the time. "Wouldn't it be great if we caught just one guy?"

Walsh needn't have worried. Even though AMW initially aired only in a handful of cities, tips about Roberts came in within minutes of the broadcast on February 7, 1988. One caller from New York City said that Roberts looked a lot like "Bob Lord," who worked as the director of a Staten Island homeless shelter. Dozens of other calls repeated the tip, and three days later, FBI agents arrested Roberts at his apartment. He was sent back to Indiana State Prison in Michigan City to finish his sentences.

A year after the broadcast Roberts agreed to be interviewed by Walsh for an *AMW* anniversary special. Walsh asked: "When you learned you were going to be profiled on *America's Most Wanted*, what went through your mind?"

"Immediately to flee the area," said Roberts. "In fact, let me correct that. I did not know it was going to be *America's Most Wanted*. I just knew several hours before the program was actually aired that I was going to be profiled."

"So then you decided that it was time to run?"

"Oh," said Roberts, "most assuredly."

A few questions later, Walsh asked, "How do you live with the knowledge [that you murdered two children]?"

"Sir," said Roberts, "I've lived with it because I was convicted of it, not because I'm guilty of it. In fact, which brings me to the question, may I ask you a question along these same lines? How do you feel being part of an instrument that takes people who maybe are not guilty of such heinous crimes and really drives these individuals into prison?"

Walsh responded: "I believe that if people are wanted, they should be brought back and either proven innocent or guilty."

For the FBI and *AMW* it was the beginning of a beautiful relationship.

INTERESTING FUGITIVE FACT:
While a Top Ten fugitive, Roberts—as "Lord"—once had his picture taken with New York City mayor Ed Koch.

410. RONALD GLYN TRIPLETT, rapist, robber, arsonist

LISTED: April 27, 1987
CAUGHT: May 16, 1987
DESCRIPTION: Born in Alabama in July 1949. Triplett used to work as an assembly line worker in Detroit, a spray painter, a health club manager, a landscaper, and an auto mechanic. Alias: James R. Triplett.

Twice Lucky. Ronald Triplett wasn't exactly lucky with the ladies; instead he felt the need to rob and rape them. But he was lucky with the law—exactly twice. The first time came on June 14, 1984, when Triplett escaped from Southern Michigan Prison, where he was serving a sentence for the 1978 robbery of a restaurant in Trenton, Michigan, and the attempted murder of a female employee. Triplett next popped up in the Southwest, where on May 13, 1986, he surprised a young couple in Bernalillo County, New Mexico, locking the man in the trunk, and proceeding to rape the woman. He tried another rape just seven days later, but was caught after a high-speed police chase.

That was the second time Triplett got lucky. The fugitive gave a false name and was allowed to post $100,000 in bail. Only later did the police realize they had a prison escapee in their custody. Of course he didn't show up for his arraignment, and the FBI placed his name on their Top Ten list in April 1987.

Just three weeks later, the FBI found him hiding out as a construction worker named "James R. Triplett" in Tempe, Arizona, and surrounded his car at an intersection. Triplett must have thought about his luck and about the 9 mm pistol he had stashed in his car. But before he was able to roll the dice, the Feds nabbed him.

INTERESTING FUGITIVE FACT:
Triplett was an amateur hockey and softball player.

411. CLAUDE DANIEL MARKS, terrorist

DESCRIPTION: Born Claudio Daniel Makowski on December 31, 1949, in Buenos Aires, Argentina. Six feet tall, 190 pounds, with brown hair and brown eyes and a medium complexion. His build is described as heavy, and he has a mole on his neck. He alternates between glasses and contact lenses and has worked as a fast food cook, radio announcer, auto mechanic, and printer. Aliases: John Chester Clark, Edward Cole, Charles Everett, Michael Hamlin, C. Henly, Dale Allen Martin, Tony McCormick, Michael Prentiss, and Brian Wilcox.

412. DONNA JEAN WILLMOTT, terrorist

BOTH LISTED: May 22, 1987
BOTH CAUGHT: December 6, 1994
DESCRIPTION: Born on June 30, 1950, in Akron, Ohio. Five feet tall, 105 pounds, with brown hair (dyed blonde) and brown eyes, her complexion is described as ruddy. Her build is small. Both Marks and Willmott wear corrective lenses. She has the ability to change her appearance by dyeing her hair or wearing wigs. She has worked as a hospital technician, nurse, lab technician, acupuncturist, and housekeeper. Aliases: J. Billings, Marcie Garber, Marcia Gardner, Jean Gill, Dona J. Krupnick, Donna Wilmiet, and Terry Young.

Nine and a Half Years. Marks and Willmott were not typical fugitives. They didn't kill any cops, boost cars, nor rob banks. In fact, their grand criminal scheme didn't even come to pass. Nevertheless, the two were named to the Top Ten list for their involvement in a conspiracy to use explosives to aid a friend to escape from Leavenworth Prison in Kansas. But this friend, Oscar Lopez, was not a typical convict either. Like Marks and Willmott, he was a member of the terrorist FALN organization, which is dedicated to a free and socialist Puerto Rico. (See VICTOR GENERA, #386 and CARLOS TORRES, #356 for more.) In June 1985 Marks and Willmott purchased $5,000 worth of plastic explosives, planning to fly a helicopter to Leavenworth to forcibly—explosively—liberate Lopez from prison. But after discovering an FBI listening device in the dashboard of Marks's car, the two put the kibosh on their plans and went into hiding. The FBI named Marks and Willmott to the Most Wanted list nearly two years later.

Marks and Willmott might have stayed hidden forever if they hadn't decided to surrender in December 1994, the result of year-long negotiations with the government. Both had been hiding in Pittsburgh for years with their respective families, Marks using the name "Gregory Peters" while Willmott was known as "Jo Elliot." Both lived within blocks of each other. The two went through great pains to demonstrate that they had led peaceful, quiet lives while on the Top Ten list. And by all accounts, they had; Marks had two young children, and Willmott raised one daughter while establishing a program for children with AIDS.

Still, it was a bad time for two people who'd once planned to blow up a federal building to throw themselves at the mercy of the court; the Oklahoma City bombing of the Alfred P. Murrah Federal Building was still fresh in people's minds. Prosecutors didn't think Marks and Willmott deserved a break. "Those contemplating acts of horror like those agreed to by Marks and Willmott must know that they will be hunted and punished to the severest extent of the law," said assistant U.S. attorneys Daniel Gillogly and Deborah Devaney in their case filing. "We owe the victims of terrorism—past and intended—nothing less." Willmott herself said she didn't expect leniency: "I fully expect to go to prison and to spend a long time there."

In the end the U.S. district judge declined to inflict the maximum penalties—10 years for Marks, five for Willmott—and instead gave Marks six years and Willmott three, both eligible for release after serving two-thirds of their time.

INTERESTING FUGITIVE FACT:
Marks and Willmott's announcement to the Top Ten marks the first time a man and woman made the list on the same day. And both were noted martial arts enthusiasts.

413. DARREN DEE O'NEALL, rapist, murderer

LISTED: June 25, 1987
CAUGHT: October 25, 1987
DESCRIPTION: Born on February 26, 1960, in Albuquerque, New Mexico. O'Neall is a chain smoker and a pathological liar and has often been known to obtain rides from cross-country truckers and reside at city missions and flop houses. Aliases: Mike James Johnson, Jerry Zebulan, Macranahan, Zebulan J. Macranahan, Larry Sackett, Buppy, and Zeb.

The Last Round-Up. Few people know how most Top Tenners think up their fugitive aliases. Darren O'Neall's aliases could be found in dozens of books available in nearly every bookstore in the United States. O'Neall was a huge fan of the western novels of Louis L'Amour and would adopt favorite character names as he galloped across his own twisted version of the wild American west.

But instead of cattle, O'Neall was a cowboy rounding up innocent women.

In early 1987 a trucker from Nampa, Idaho, gave a young man with long, wild blond hair a ride and was kind enough to offer him a place to crash for the night. It was a mistake. The young man, who had "JUNE" tattooed across the knuckles of his left hand, boosted the trucker's car and Ruger .357 Magnum revolver.

In March 1987, two months later, a man calling himself "Herb Johnson" picked up a 22-year-old woman named Robin Smith at a Puyallup, Washington, bar, promising to take her to a cooler party. She made it to the all-night party, but never made it home. A few days later, police found an abandoned car containing Smith's bloodstained jacket and a handful of her teeth. (Smith's remains would be found two months later. Thirteen years later, the Discovery Channel would reenact the discovery of her body on location in Washington for the series *FBI Files*.)

A check on the car traced it back to that trucker from Idaho, who told authorities about the man with the "JUNE" tattoo. That rang a bell; a guy named Darren O'Neall, with a similar tattoo, had been ducking child support payments and was currently at large.

He was at large and apparently busy. On April 29 a 29-year-old beauty school student named Wendy Aughe never returned home from a first date with a local bartender named "Mike James Johnson." Johnson was new, as it turned out—in fact, it had been his first day on the job. When his prints were lifted from the bartop, they belonged to one Darren O'Neall. But by then O'Neall had already fled. In early June a woman named Lisa Szubert disappeared from a truck stop in Idaho; her body was found four days later. A week later, a woman fought off an abductor—one with the "JUNE" tattooed on the knuckles of his last hand. Authorities in Salt Lake City began to suspect that O'Neall might be responsible for the shooting deaths of three women in 1985 and 1986.

On June 25 the FBI slapped O'Neall's face on Wanted posters from coast to coast, making him one of the baddest outlaws in the country. (O'Neall might have been pleased to think of it like that.) During the summer of 1987 O'Neall was spotted applying for work as a landscaping contractor in Ketchum, Idaho, but must have felt something was odd because he split soon after. By late fall of 1987 the FBI had lost track of him completely.

That's because O'Neall was already in jail.

On October 25 a man named "John Mayeaux" was arrested for stealing a car and $500 in cash in a Louisiana suburb. He was fingerprinted and sent to a New Orleans jail. It wasn't until February 3, 1988, when Kathleen Gremillion of the State Police Bureau of Criminal Investigation in Baton Rouge compared "Mayeaux's" fingerprints with various federal fugitive fingerprints, did she realize that Mayeaux was indeed the man with the "JUNE" tattoo on the knuckles of his left hand.

Edna Smith, mother of victim Robin Smith, told a reporter she was "ecstatic" to hear that O'Neall was in custody. "It's been pure, pure hell, because my concern was always knowing what my daughter went through," said Smith. "Everyday I kept thinking, Dear God, protect any other girl that may come into contact with him, because he's a very sick man."

Smith won't have to worry. O'Neall was convicted of multiple crimes—including kidnapping, rape, and sodomy—and sentenced to more than 150 years in jail. He won't be riding off into any sunset, except the kind that flicker between the bars of a jail cell.

INTERESTING FUGITIVE FACT:
O'Neall was such a huge L'Amour fan, the FBI asked the author himself to turn over fan letters O'Neall had written him in hopes of finding clues.

414. LOUIS RAY BEAM JR., white supremacist

LISTED: July 14, 1987
CAUGHT: November 6, 1987
DESCRIPTION: Born on August 20, 1946, in Lufkin, Texas. Beam may be traveling with his wife, Sheila Marie Beam, also known as Sheila Marie Toohey, 20, and a seven-year-old daughter from a previous marriage, Sarah Hadassah Beam. He was last seen publicly in the Houston area in December 1985 as he came out of a public library.

Clash with the Titan. On April 21, 1987, the federal government cracked down on 15 militant white supremacists, charging some of the biggest names in hate-mongering—David Lane, Andrew Barnhill, RICHARD SCUTARI (#396), David Snell, Richard Butler, and other members of Aryan Nations and the Ku Klux Klan—with seditious conspiracy to overthrow the government of the United States via murder, armed robbery, and sabotage. Eleven of them were snared by an FBI dragnet, but Louis Ray Beam Jr., former Grand Titan of the Texas Klan, slipped through. Three months later, he was named to the Top Ten list.

Beam had left the Klan in 1980 for bigger things—namely, the Order, an extremist group dedicated to overthrowing the government and replacing it with Aryan leaders. Beam was known as something of an innovator in white supremacist circles; he was among the first to utilize the pre-Internet computer bulletin board systems (BBS) to link hate groups across the country and give them a space to complain about "mud people" and the "Zionist Occupational Government" in Washington, D.C. Beam's group was alleged to have perpetrated more than 100 crimes, including attempted assassinations of judges and FBI agents, destruction of public utilities, pollution of water supplies, and the founding of illegal guerrilla training camps.

Two weeks before the indictment, Beam had married 20-year-old Sheila Marie Toohey in rural Pennsylvania. Too bad their honeymoon consisted of ducking G-men and fleeing to Mexico. In early November 1987 the FBI traced the happy couple to Guadalajara and surrounded their house with the help of Mexican federales. Beam gave up quietly, but his new bride wasn't about to let the FBI ruin her first year of marriage. She whipped out a pistol and started blasting away, pumping four bullets into a Mexican cop before she was forcibly disarmed.

Bail was denied Beam upon his return to the United States. As the charges were being read, Beam told the U.S. magistrate: "To me, what I'm charged with is an honor, sir." Justice Department prosecutor Markton Carlson cross-examined Beam about his beliefs, asking, "Who would you kill?"

"International bankers, international politicians of some weight, that kind of thing," replied Beam. "Most of them white—just like you. My duty is to absolutely oppose them and remove them from being a threat."

"You would commit murder for those reasons?" asked Carlson.

"It's not murder when you kill an enemy," said Beam.

In April 1988 an all-white jury surprised most by acquitting Beam and his fellow white supremacists of all charges. Beam gloated on the steps of the courthouse. "I want to say to hell with the federal government," he said. Sheila Beam—who had in the meantime been released from Mexican prison—fainted moments later.

INTERESTING FUGITIVE FACT:
Beam often used the name of Ku Klux Klan founder and Confederate general Nathan Bedford Forrest as his alias.

415. TED JEFFREY OTSUKI, murderer, robber

LISTED: January 22, 1988
CAUGHT: September 4, 1988
DESCRIPTION: Born 1953 in Harlingen, Texas.

The Cop Killer. When Ted Otsuki was sprung from a Texas federal penitentiary in 1986, he came to Boston with big plans. He had the idea to kidnap bank execs and demand outrageous amounts of ransom. Otsuki even knew some ex-cons who might want a piece of the action. In the meantime, there were funds to raise.

So, early on the morning of October 2, 1987, Otsuki found himself busy robbing an apartment building in the Back Bay section of Boston. A pair of cops appeared, and Otsuki bolted down an alley and started to scale a 12-foot fence. Rookie Jorge L. Torres, 21, along with his partner, Chris Rogers, yanked Otsuki down from the fence and began to arrest him. But while being frisked, Otsuki's hand found his secret 9 mm handgun tucked away in his coat. He fired at Torres's chest, then spun around and blasted away four times at Rogers, finally spinning back and nailing Torres again. Then Otsuki ran again. At the end of the alley another cop, Roy J. Sergei, a 17-year veteran, blocked Otsuki's escape path. Sergei's partner, William Kennedy, recalled the scene for a *Boston Globe* reporter: "The suspect came running out of the alley, shooting at us."

Luckily, Officers Kennedy and Rogers escaped unharmed. But Officer Torres was hospitalized for his wounds and later quit the force. Officer Sergei took bullets in his chest, buttocks, and right arm; the Vietnam vet died three weeks later from a heart attack related to his wounds.

Otsuki disappeared. A search of his apartment led to a murder warrant for his arrest, and his name was added to the Top Ten list a few months later.

It wasn't Otsuki's first violent run-in with the police. Back in 1979 he pulled off an audacious robbery in Los Fresnos, Texas, where he donned a motorcycle helmet with a visor, strolled into the local police station, then proceeded to beat and handcuff the two on-duty cops. After whipping out a semiautomatic weapon and blowing the police communications console to bits, Otsuki walked across the street and relieved the town bank of $70,000. Maybe he thought the world owed him something. Reportedly, Otsuki was still angry over not inheriting his family's 2,000-acre farm along the Rio Grande, and he probably felt cheated that a cerebral hemorrhage had taken his mother when he was still a teenager. "Ted Otsuki became a career criminal after his mother died," said one police officer in his south Texas hometown of Harlingen. After the Los Fresnos boost Otsuki was caught and sentenced to 15 years, winning conditional release after seven. It was a release that the parole board would soon regret.

After the Back Bay shoot-out, authorities received tips that Otsuki might be in the San Francisco area, but the only trace found was an abandoned car in the fugitive's name and two pipe bombs in a storage locker, thought to be rented by him. A break came when the FBI began interviewing old friends and family in Harlingen, which led them to Mexico City, then finally to Guadalajara, where he'd been hiding out. A motley band of law enforcement officers, including FBI agents, Boston dicks, and Mexican federales surprised Otsuki just as he was about to enter his swank condo. The fugitive looked shocked and perhaps thought about shooting his way past police once again—after all, he was carrying a .45 semiauto. But he never reached for his gun and allowed himself to be taken in. When the news hit police airwaves in Boston, cheers and shouts of

"Hallelujah" could be heard. Otsuki was later extradited to Boston and received a life sentence.

INTERESTING FUGITIVE FACT:
Otsuki was only the second Asian American to make the list since it began in 1950.

416. PEDRO LUIS ESTRADA, murderer, drug enforcer

LISTED: April 15, 1988
CAUGHT: October 1, 1989
DESCRIPTION: Born on November 17, 1963, in Brooklyn, New York. Between five feet 10 inches and six feet tall, 160 pounds, with brown hair and eyes. He has a one-inch tattoo with "PE" on his upper left arm. Estrada was a one-time professional boxer and has also worked as a cab driver and construction worker. Aliases: Pablo Estrada, Pedro Epstrade, Junior Rivera, Pablo Rivera, Pete Rivera, "Moe," and "Pistola." Last seen in New York City and believed to be traveling with his girlfriend and their two-year-old son.

Rocky's Evil Twin. Toward the beginning of the 1976 movie *Rocky*, the titular boxer played by Sylvester Stallone works as hired muscle for a bunch of Philadelphia gangsters. If Rocky had descended further into that underworld, he might have ended up like Pedro Luis Estrada.

Estrada used to be a pro boxer, winning 48 knockouts as an amateur and eight more wins as a pro. But during a 1984 fight at Madison Square Garden, Estrada was knocked out. Soon after, he found himself in the employ of a New York City drug ring named "Checkmate." In June 1986 Checkmate—which reportedly earned $122 million a year—caught word that a former member was hanging out his own shingle as a crack dealer. Checkmate wasn't fond of competition. So Estrada and two buddies stopped by the competitor's Bronx apartment, tied him and a partner up, then put a bullet in each of their throats, execution-style. Then Estrada turned his gun on two female witnesses: Esther Rodriguez and Jacqueline Cardona. Rodriguez died, but Cardona escaped and would later identify Estrada, who disappeared from New York in November. A year and a half later, Estrada was named to the Top Ten list.

The FBI eventually found Estrada in Harrisburg, Pennsylvania, thanks to tips from viewers of *America's Most Wanted*. According to Wayne R. Gilbert,

special agent in charge of the Philadelphia FBI office, Estrada was nabbed on a pleasant Sunday afternoon just as he was about to go for his daily bike ride. A year later, a Bronx court gave Estrada his final TKO: convictions of murder and attempted murder.

INTERESTING FUGITIVE FACT:
Estrada's boxing nickname was "The Pistol."

417. JOHN EDWARD STEVENS, bank robber

LISTED: May 29, 1988
CAUGHT: November 30, 1988
DESCRIPTION: Born May 22, 1953.

"You'll Never Catch Me." John Stevens thought of himself as a criminal genius, the kind the world hadn't seen since the days of WILLIE SUTTON (#11). But Stevens was no gentleman. During bank heists Stevens adopted the persona of a mad dog bandit, just itching to blow someone's head off. He would enter a bank in a mask, announce that he was robbing the place, then start to wig out, barking at employees, threatening to pump bullets into their bodies if they failed to cooperate, then finally lose it completely, leaping over the counter to help himself to piles of cash. Not only did Stevens think he was a master actor, he also thought he was dozens of IQ points above the average law enforcement official. After many robberies—and there were 22 of them, scattered throughout eight states, in which Stevens took home close to a cool half million—he would call FBI agents and taunt them. "You'll never catch me."

Ohio police lieutenant Jim Whitney just so happened to be vacationing in Clearwater, Florida, when he saw a TV news story about a bank robbery suspect, along with the perp's blurry image caught by a security camera. Whitney recognized the suspect as the same guy who had knocked over a bank in his Ohio hometown of Westerville not long before. That gave the FBI the link they needed, and eventually they tracked Stevens down to a motel outside of Cincinnati and arrested him a few days after Thanksgiving 1988, along with his 30-year-old girlfriend.

INTERESTING FUGITIVE FACT:
Stevens, along with JACK FARMER (#418) and ROGER JONES (#419) were personally announced by FBI director William Sessions on *America's Most Wanted*.

418. JACK FARMER, murderer, drug dealer

LISTED: May 29, 1988
CAUGHT: June 1, 1988
DESCRIPTION: Born in Chicago in 1953.

The Wrong Kind of Retainer. Jack Darrell Farmer knew he was facing serious time. He had been accused of running Chicago's "Little Mafia," a gang accused of drug trafficking, extortion, murder, home invasions, and false credit transactions. Worse yet, he had threatened to kill someone set to testify against him at his upcoming trial. Farmer had even been denied bail. His only taste of freedom were his day trips to see his lawyer to plan his defense.

That gave Farmer an idea. In April 1987, along with his wife, Pamela, Farmer subdued, tied, and gagged his own lawyer. The couple escaped. Authorities were looking for Farmer for more than a year when he made the Most Wanted list on May 29, 1988. His run from Chicago may have lasted a while, but his time as a Top Tenner was anything but. Just three days after his mug was highlighted by FBI director William Sessions on *America's Most Wanted,* a call came in from a Florida resident who said that Farmer looked an awful lot like a guy named Robert J. Niewiadomski, who was working in a Deerfield Beach supermarket warehouse. Agents traced "Niewiadomski" to his new residence in nearby Lantana, Florida. Pamela was nabbed first, and Farmer tried to make his getaway moments later, but there were no match for the nine G-men and SWAT team that had surrounded the house. The couple was arrested and returned to Chicago, where Farmer was sentenced to 40 years in federal prison.

INTERESTING FUGITIVE FACT:
Farmer claimed that he had been framed by the FBI.

419. ROGER JONES, child molester

LISTED: May 29, 1988
CAUGHT: March 4, 1989
DESCRIPTION: Born in 1946. Six feet one inch, 180 pounds. Jones is very cunning and knowledgeable in changing his identity. He frequents auto auctions, adult bookstores, and topless bars. He also allegedly endears himself to neighborhood children, then lures them into increasingly higher levels of sexual contact.

Playback. In August 1986 Roger Jones was charged with three counts of sexual battery, three counts of lewd and lascivious conduct, and one count of sexual performance by a child. All throughout that summer he had been luring neighborhood kids to his Venice, Florida, trailer home and forcing them to have sex with him, taping it to later trade or sell to other pedophiles. A judge granted him bail, and Jones used the opportunity to flee Sarasota County. Jones was spotted in West Virginia the following March, giving the authorities opportunity to charge him with interstate flight to avoid prosecution—a federal charge. His continuing threat to children propelled him to the Most Wanted list in May 1988, making him the first Top Tenner sought for sexual crimes against children.

Jones stayed hidden until he made the mistake of trying to sell a truck. In early 1989 he was hiding out at a Butte, Montana, campground as "Mike Andrews," and had a red pickup truck to sell. A local forest ranger was interested in the truck, but noticed that the vehicle and tags didn't match the paperwork, so he called it in. The local computer system was down, so the ranger called the police department in Great Falls to use their system. In the conversation that followed, the ranger and the police officer he'd reached started to suspect that "Mike Andrews" actually might be "Don Hamilton," wanted for burglary in Great Falls. Back in Butte authorities searched the man's trailer at the campground and were startled to find not only evidence of the Great Falls burglaries, but also 60 child porn videotapes and articles. They also found phony birth certificates, a family photo album, and newspaper clips about other FBI fugitives.

On the way to the station Jones admitted his identity as a Top Tenner, but at first the officers didn't believe him. Fingerprints confirmed his identity, and the following years Jones was convicted of four counts of lewd and lascivious or indecent acts, facing a maximum sentence of 60 years in jail.

INTERESTING FUGITIVE FACT:
Jones's ex-wife, Faye Yager, made headlines in the late 1980s for founding an "underground railroad" shelter for sexually abused children. Yager started it a few years after Jones allegedly abused her daughter Michelle.

420. TERRY LEE JOHNSON, murderer, drug dealer

LISTED: June 12, 1988
CAUGHT: August 17, 1988
DESCRIPTION: Born 1949 in Madison County, Alabama.

Crash Landing. Terry Lee Johnson, an ex-marine and current drug addict, showed up on his neighbor's property one day in 1976 and asked for permission to hunt. James J. Crowson, a farmer, said no. So Johnson returned later in the day with a high-powered rifle and decided he'd go hunting after all. He shot and killed Crowson. Johnson fled Alabama and managed to stay hidden for five years before authorities caught up with him, armed to the teeth, in South Pittsburgh, Tennessee. He was extradited to Alabama, but before he could be tried, he escaped. FBI agents recaptured him in Blountsville, Alabama, where again Johnson was loaded down with weapons. Finally, he was dragged into court, convicted of murder, and sentenced to life in prison at Limestone Correctional Facility at Elmore, Alabama. Five years later, however, Johnson bolted again.

After the 1986 prison break Johnson hid out in Montana, where he set up a marijuana farm. Oddly enough, he was actually arrested for it, but the officers never realized his true identity and let him go after two weeks. He frustrated law enforcement officials to the point where he was named to the Top Ten list in the summer of 1988. *America's Most Wanted* highlighted Johnson's case on the day he was announced, and a tip came in that Johnson might be in California.

Johnson, however, gave himself away a little more than two months later. On August 17, 1988, Johnson got into an argument with a man in San Diego and subsequently relied on his old debate trick; he pulled out a shotgun and stuck it in his opponent's face. The cops arrived soon after, and Johnson ran for his white pickup truck and rocketed away from the scene. The ensuing chase was worthy of a block-buster action flick: speeds of up to 80 miles per hour, ending in an six-vehicle chain-reaction crash on I-8. Johnson's camper shell even flew off and smacked into two parked cars. When police dug Johnson out of the wreckage, they found $1,800 in cash, a shotgun, and narcotics. Police, however, thought they had arrested a 29-year-old Canadian man named David Roy More. (This would be Johnson's fourth arrest—but only two were under his birth name.) Luckily, three weeks later, someone ran a check on his fingerprints, and the name Terry Lee Johnson popped up, and soon he was awaiting his third extradition to Alabama.

INTERESTING FUGITIVE FACT:
Like fugitives before (CLAUDE LAFAYETTE DALLAS, #400) and after (ERIC ROBERT RUDOLPH, #454), John-son was adept at wilderness survival. It seems to be a required skill to elude the FBI for any period of time.

421. STANLEY FAISON, murderer

LISTED: November 27, 1988
CAUGHT: December 24, 1988
DESCRIPTION: Born in 1942. Five feet five inches tall, 140 pounds, with brown eyes and black hair. Faison has a tattoo of a cross over a boxed "C" on his upper left arm and may have a shaved head. He reportedly uses drugs and is considered "armed and extremely dangerous." Alias: Basil Samseh Bilal.

Violent Holiday. On June 6, 1987, Stanley Faison beat Ophilena Edwards with a tire iron, then waited for her boyfriend, Sylvester Wilson, to show up. Wilson was promptly stabbed with a butcher knife; Faison fled the east side of Detroit and never looked back, running through Georgia, Florida, and Washington, D.C. Faison knew what he faced if he was ever caught—after all, he'd spent 19 of 46 years in prison, according to Anthony Riggio, then FBI assistant special agent-in-charge in Michigan. Faison had started his criminal career at the tender age of 18, when he was sent to prison for breaking and entering, car theft, manslaughter, and armed robbery. He had been most recently paroled in April 1985.

A federal warrant was issued for his arrest in August 1987, but few leads came in, prompting the FBI to name him to the Most Wanted list. Faison ended up being caught when he succumbed to the holiday spirit, taking a break from a life on the run to visit family in Detroit. Agents found him hiding in the basement of a Detroit home, where he was arrested.

INTERESTING FUGITIVE FACT:
Faison used to work as an interior decorator.

422. STEVEN RAY STOUT, murderer

LISTED: November 27, 1988
CAUGHT: December 6, 1988
DESCRIPTION: Born in Webster Springs, West Virginia, in 1956.

"I Didn't Think It Would Be So Soon." Many American workers dread Sunday night because it means the grinding workweek is just around the corner. Steven Stout had a different reason for dreading

Sunday night. That was the night a new show, *America's Most Wanted*, aired, and in late November 1988 Stout had reason to believe they'd feature him sooner or later, since he'd brutally butchered his ex-mother-in-law and her 19-year-old daughter with a hammer and knife in West Valley City, Utah. Ever since, Stout had gone into hiding as a construction worker in Gulfport, Mississippi.

Shortly after Stout first heard about the show, he would watch nervously every week. "I knew that I would be on eventually," he told a reporter from *American Lawyer* magazine. "I didn't think it would be so soon." On November 27 Stout was at a coworker's room, borrowing money, when the show came on and began previewing that night's lineup. "At the beginning of the show, when they show who's going to be on? I was the last one." Stout rushed to his new girlfriend's house and found her watching the show. "I tried to get her to watch something else," he said, but the girlfriend kept watching. Stout missed his own debut on national TV—he was hiding in the bathroom, waiting for the other shoe to drop.

The girlfriend didn't mention anything right away, but it became clear that her friends knew and tipped off the FBI. Stout was arrested at the hotel where he worked nine days later, and later pled guilty to capital and second-degree murder.

INTERESTING FUGITIVE FACT:
After his conviction Stout told *American Lawyer* that he has "nothing against" *AMW*, and in fact, watches it in jail. "There's no doubt that most of the people on the show need to be off the streets."

423. ARMANDO GARCIA, drug dealer

LISTED: January 8, 1989
CAUGHT: January 18, 1994
DESCRIPTION: Born on January 20, 1962, in Cuba. Five feet nine inches tall, 180 pounds, with brown hair and eyes. He has a burn scar on his left cheek and is a former police officer. Aliases: Aramando Gracia, "Scarface."

The River Cops. In the summer of 1985 the words *Miami Vice* took on an entirely different meaning when seven Miami cops were accused of killing drug dealers so they could set up their own criminal empire. They earned the nickname "River Cops" after three drug smugglers jumped from their own boat to escape the crooked cops and drowned in the

Miami River. Within a few years most of the River Cops had been rounded up, but Garcia, along with his father and another accused officer, escaped while awaiting trial. Garcia was named to the Top Ten list in early January 1989.

Garcia was featured on *America's Most Wanted* a total of seven times, but an August 1990 show generated what would turn out to be the most useful tip: Garcia was hiding in Ecuador. Eventually, the FBI traced him to Colombia, where he was arrested after leaving his apartment in Cali—at the time home to the world's largest cocaine-trafficking cartel. The Colombian government deported Garcia, who faced three counts of murder and multiple counts of drug trafficking.

INTERESTING FUGITIVE FACT:
In 1992 a man thought to be Garcia was arrested after the case was again highlighted on *AMW*. Robin John Delgado, a 29-year-old Los Angeles resident, said he lost his job after the mix-up.

424. MELVIN EDWARD MAYS, gang leader

LISTED: February 7, 1989
CAUGHT: March 9, 1995
DESCRIPTION: Born on September 7, 1957, in Chicago, Illinois. Five feet nine inches, 165 pounds, with black hair and brown eyes. He may have a beard and mustache. He is missing several upper left front teeth and stutters when he speaks. Aliases: Melvin Mays, Melvin E. Mays, "Maumee," and "Maumie."

Terror for Hire. Law enforcement officials dubbed El Rukn—Arabic for "the foundation"—"the ultimate street gang," formed from a confederation of Chicago gangs that had operated since the late 1960s. But perhaps *gang* is too light a word for a criminal enterprise that once conspired with the government of Libya to perform terrorist acts in exchange for a reported $2.5 million. Melvin Mays played a huge role in that conspiracy and was indicted in August 1986 for negotiating to buy anti-tank rocket launchers to bomb U.S. targets. Mays stayed hidden, however, while his El Rukn comrades were indicted in a massive racketeering case in 1989. Mays made the list in February of that same year.

Mays managed to stay on the lam for close to a decade, but was eventually found in an apartment on Chicago's South Side by the Chicago Terrorism Task Force, a group made up of FBI agents, Secret Service, and ATF officers. A year later, Mays was convicted of racketeering, drug, and murder conspiracies, and sentenced to three life terms in prison, with no chance of parole. After sentencing, Mays rambled, and then said, "In the name of God, I seek him in refuge from Satan."

INTERESTING FUGITIVE FACT:
At his trial Mays renounced his U.S. citizenship, claiming to be a citizen of "New Afrika."

425. BOBBY GENE DENNIE, rapist

LISTED: February 24, 1989
CAUGHT: October 29, 1989
DESCRIPTION: Born in 1950 in Falmouth, Kentucky. Dennie has a tattoo "Sandy" on his left forearm.

In the Name of the Wife. In early 1988 Bobby Dennie robbed a female bartender in western Missouri, but he wasn't satisfied with the cash from the till. He raped the 37-year-old woman at knifepoint, forced her to drive him 200 miles to St. Louis, raping her again along the way. The woman was finally allowed to leave, and she immediately called the police, who captured Dennie as he was climbing into a cab. When he later escaped from a Kansas City mental clinic, more than just the St. Louis police were looking for him: Dennie was wanted in Vegas for rape and murder, in Kentucky for rape and parole violation, and in Ohio for writing rubber checks. On February 24, 1989, Dennie was named to the Top Ten list.

Later that year, FBI director William Sessions appeared on *Unsolved Mysteries*, showing photographs of Dennie and laying out his sordid case history. The photo did the trick: Police in Miami recognized Dennie under the alias Daniel Geno DeAngelo. Seems that "DeAngelo" raped and tried to kill another woman, but was careless enough to leave his driver's license behind. The two photos matched. The FBI learned something else; Dennie, as DeAngelo, had married a 27-year-old woman named Janet Tubbs while on the lam.

Ultimately, Tubbs would lead them to her—and the FBI's—man. In late October 1989 the Florida Highway Patrol stopped her on I-95, and Tubbs claimed she was going to visit friends in Lake Wales and had no idea where Dennie was. But later, her truck was spotted at the Traveler's Inn near Lake Wales, where she had registered under her own name.

Inside Tubbs's room was Dennie. He was arrested and jailed without bond to await trial.

INTERESTING FUGITIVE FACT:
Dennie used to work as a laborer and a cook.

426. COSTABILE "GUS" FARACE, murderer, drug dealer

LISTED: March 17, 1989
KILLED: November 17, 1989
DESCRIPTION: Born on June 21, 1960, in Brooklyn. Six feet two inches tall, 220 pounds, with brown hair and eyes. Farace has tattoos of a rose and "Mom" and "Dad" on his upper left arm, a girl on the lower calf of his right leg, and a butterfly on his stomach. Former occupation: grocery man.

As the Mob Turns. Undercover DEA agent Everett Hatcher didn't like the way small-time pusher Gus Farace had been acting lately. Farace—a member of the Bonanno crime family coke ring Everett had been trying to break up—hadn't been returning calls, seemingly avoiding him. Something was up. Even Everett's wife had a bad feeling and begged him to stay home.

But a big coke buy was already set up, and three squads of back-up agents were ready to pounce, so on February 28, 1989, Agent Hatcher decided to meet with Farace anyway and drove his Buick Regal to a quiet overpass in Staten Island. Farace and a few buddies soon drove up in a van and told Hatcher they were going to a diner. It was a bad move. Somehow the back-up teams lost both the Buick and the van in traffic, and to make matters worse, Hatcher's radio transmitter died. The back-up teams scrambled across Staten Island, trying to find Hatcher and Farace. An hour later, a few agents returned to the original overpass and found Hatcher slumped over the wheel of his still-running car. He had been shot three times in the head and chest.

The slaying of Hatcher would spark one of the most intense manhunts in New York history, a mob civil war, even angry comments from then-president George Bush. All of this for a low-level "coke cowboy" from Staten Island, who one agent said had "been a dirtbag from day one."

Farace didn't exactly pop out of his mother's womb, causing trouble, but it wasn't too long after. By age 15 he was already running with a Staten Island gang called the "Bay Boys" who enjoyed taunting and beating innocent people. Two years later, he was pulled over for reckless driving and arrested for possession of a firearm. He was also arrested for forgery three weeks later. Farace hit the big time in October 1979, when an old Bay Boy buddy of his and two other thugs abducted two black teenagers in Greenwich Village and drove them out to a quiet park in Staten Island. There Farace forced one of the victims to perform oral sex on one of Farace's buddies, and then beat and shot the teen. The other teenager escaped to identify Farace and his gang, and Farace was sentenced to seven to 21 years in jail. The slammer was one of the best things that could have happened to Farace. There he received a new tooth to replace one he'd broken in a car wreck. He bulked up in the prison gym. And he eventually met Gerry Chilli, a captain in the Bonanno crime family. Upon his release from prison after serving exactly seven years, Farace went to work for the Bonanno family, which ultimately led him to that fateful meeting with DEA agent Hatcher.

Immediately after the shooting, local DEA head Robert M. Stutman deployed 500 men and tightened the vise on the Bonanno family—and all New York mob families—in an effort to find Farace. Gus's brother Dominick was picked up for parole violation; Gus's pregnant wife was arrested for possession of pot; Gus's Bonanno mentor, Gerry Chilli, was indicted for loansharking; bookie joints throughout South Brooklyn were raided and closed. (At one point Stutman even drove out to the Queens residence of John Gotti, head of the Gambino crime family, to implore him to cough up Farace. Gotti answered the door himself in his bathrobe and told Stutman, "There is little I can say, but of course, I am sorry.") At first no one would give "Gussie" up. But as the pressure rose, mob families started to respond. When the Luchese family learned that one of their own, John Petrucelli, had helped Farace stay hidden, they implored their man to turn him over. Petrucelli refused and got whacked, allegedly for his loyalty to Gus. "It was getting to be like the Civil War," said one DEA agent to writer Eric Pooley in a story about Farace in *New York* magazine.

Meanwhile, Farace had been bopping around New York, counting on the kindness of family and Family to stay hidden. He dyed his hair, grew a beard, and spent most of his time eating fattening Italian food and watching rented videos. On November 17, the day after he watched *The Godfather* for the umpteenth time, Farace drove out to meet Louis

Tuzzio, a buddy who had been passing messages along and helping Farace find new hideouts. That wouldn't be the case this time. Authorities believe that Tuzzio, acting on orders from Gerry Chilli himself, set Farace up. It was a turkey shoot: one man behind a park bench, two gunmen in a van, all blasting away at Farace as he pulled up in his 1982 Pontiac to meet Tuzzio. Innocent bystanders ducked for cover; neighbors reported hearing *pop! pop! pop!* sounds up and down the block. Farace's driver, 29-year-old Joey Sclafani, tried to return fire, but received three slugs in his own chest for his trouble.

At the scene Sclafani pointed to the bloodied, bearded man and told police, "That's my friend Gus." Farace had taken eight bullets, and despite being placed in a pressure suit to stabilize the trauma, died on the way to the hospital. "Mob justice isn't always swift," said James Fox, head of the New York FBI office the day after the incident, "but it's always deadly, and this may be an example of deadly mob justice."

INTERESTING FUGITIVE FACT:
In eighth grade Farace was voted "class flirt."

427. ARTHUR LEE WASHINGTON JR., attempted murderer

LISTED: October 18, 1989
REMOVED FROM LIST: December 27, 2000
DESCRIPTION: Born on November 30, 1949, in Neptune, New Jersey. Six feet one inch tall, 200 pounds, with black hair and brown eyes. He has scars on the back right side of his neck, his left and right wrist, and his upper leg. He has needle track marks on both arms. Washington has been associated in the past with militant black prison groups and the Black Liberation Army.

The Out Is Death. In the spring of 1989 two-time convicted armed robber Arthur Washington was in a car that had been pulled over by a New Jersey state trooper. As Michael J. Clayton approached the vehicle, intending to give the operator a ticket for an expired registration sticker, Washington jumped out of the passenger seat and started walking away. Clayton ordered him to stop. Washington turned and opened fire with a .45 caliber semiauto pistol, then ran away. Luckily, Clayton was uninjured. It's no wonder Washington was skittish; he was more than just another armed robber. He was also a member of the Black Liberation Army, which had a long history of shoot-outs with police up and down the East Coast. Washington was named to the Top Ten list in October 1989.

As the hunt for Washington progressed, however, fewer and fewer tips, sightings, and leads came in, prompting the FBI to think that their fugitive may have died due to complications from AIDS. (Washington had a long history of intravenous drug use.) Finally, a few days after Christmas 2000, Washington was dropped from the list. But even if Washington is still alive, his removal from the list doesn't mean the FBI will forget about him. "All available resources are being utilized in order to apprehend him," said Michelle L. Walensky, a spokesperson in the FBI's fugitive section in D.C. "He's still a wanted fugitive." And the New Jersey state police said that he would stay on their own 12 Most Wanted list until they produced a capture or a dead body.

INTERESTING FUGITIVE FACT:
Washington was the first Top Tenner in history to be dropped because he is *believed* to be dead. (Other fugitives who escaped the list due to death were actually verified to be dead.)

428. LEE NELL CARTER, murderer

LISTED: November 19, 1989
CAUGHT: November 20, 1989
DESCRIPTION: Born on May 10, 1956, in Alabama.

Give Me a Break. There have been many daring, lengthy runs from the FBI in the history of the Most Wanted list. Lee Carter's run, however, ain't one of them.

Carter lasted a mere two hours after being named to the Top Ten. Then again, he had been on the run since November 15, 1986, when he gunned down an ex-girlfriend and two others in Mobile, Alabama. (Previously, Carter had been convicted and paroled for murdering his own father.) He was indicted on one count of murder and two attempteds, but through some horrible mistake, Carter was set free eight days later. He ran for three years before the FBI placed his name on the Most Wanted list, with FBI director William Sessions personally announcing him to the list on *America's Most Wanted* on Sunday, November 19, 1989. Right after the show aired, calls came pouring in, pinpointing Carter in Detroit, where he had been working at an auto body shop. "We had no idea he

was in the Detroit area," said an FBI spokesman the next day. Carter was arrested on the east side of Detroit and extradited to Alabama.

INTERESTING FUGITIVE FACT:
In Detroit Lee Carter lived under the brilliant alias of "Lee Carter."

429. WARDELL DAVID FORD, murderer, armed robber

LISTED: December 20, 1989
CAUGHT: September 17, 1990
DESCRIPTION: Born in 1955.

Sub Rosa. Over a period of six years Wardell Ford mastered the art of hiding behind paper—fake birth certificates and driver's licenses. He even managed to produce the documents necessary to get a painting job in Connecticut at General Dynamic Corporation's Electric Boat Division—makers of nuclear submarines for the U.S. Navy. His bosses had no idea that "Michael Collins" was actually a man wanted by the FBI for a violent armored car heist that went awry in Detroit back in 1983. In the shoot-out that followed the heist, Ford's accomplice, David Temple, was killed, along with a guard. Ford took more than $40,000 in cash and fled the scene.

Six years later, *America's Most Wanted* re-created the grisly heist, and tips came in, saying that Ford looked an awful lot like a guy painting subs over at Electric Boat. FBI agents were dispatched to analyze Ford's job application, and while the fugitive had become quite skilled at forging official documents, he couldn't disguise his own handwriting. Company security was sent to bring Ford in, and he was subsequently fingerprinted and arrested. Electric Boat, for their part, seemed dreadfully embarrassed to have employed a Top Ten fugitive and issued a statement stressing that Ford "was hired in accordance with all Department of Defense and Electric Boat Division security procedures." Ford's arrest was the ninth Top Ten arrest due to contributions from *AMW* viewers. He was held without bail and extradited to Michigan.

INTERESTING FUGITIVE FACT:
Ford knew to aim low. If Ford had applied for a slightly better job—one that demanded a higher security clearance—his fingerprints would have been sent to the FBI for double-checking.

FUGITIVES
OF THE 1990s

Introduction

The FBI's Ten Most Wanted list has always relied on the media. Early on, newspapers and magazines carried mug shots and grisly rap sheets; eventually radio and TV were enlisted. And then, in the mid-1990s, the FBI Ten Most Wanted list hit the Internet, and the results were immediate. A bank robber named Leslie Isben Rogge holed up in a country (Guatemala) far, far away from the scenes of his crimes and thought he was escaping public view. He was wrong. A new neighbor saw Rogge's photo on the FBI's new website, and within weeks Rogge was in custody. Today citizens don't have to rely on trips to the post office to check out the latest crop of Top Tenners. They can simply log on to the FBI's website (www.fbi.gov) and view Wanted posters and read bulletins at their whim. They can even leave a tip with a handy online form.

At first glance it might seem that the Top Ten list slowed down in its fifth decade—much the way people tend to. This would be misleading. The FBI didn't take it easy; it turned its attention to more complex and difficult fugitives. The most notable fugitives of this decade were truly the worst of the worst, including CIA shooter Mir Aimal Kansi (#435); original World Trade Center bomber Ramzi Ahmed Yousef (#436); Pan Am Flight 103 bombers Abdel Bassett Ali Al-Megrahi (#441) and Lamen Khalifa Fhimah (#442); and the modern-day embodiment of evil, Usama bin Laden (#456). Other infamous members of the 1990s Top Ten list include spree killer Andrew Cunanan (#449), bomber Eric Robert Rudolph (#454), and Irish mobster James J. Bulger (#458). Be warned: There are no car thieves here, folks.

430. LESLIE IBSEN ROGGE, bank robber

LISTED: January 24, 1990
CAUGHT: May 19, 1996
DESCRIPTION: Born on March 8, 1949, in Seattle. Five foot 11 inches tall and 160 pounds, with brown hair and blue eyes. Tattoos include a seahorse and dragon on his left shoulder, an eagle on his right, and a devil with "Les" on his right forearm. Fond of Foster Grant wire-rimmed glasses, Rogge is also an expert recreational sailor.

The First Internet Capture.   At first Leslie Ibsen Rogge must have thought he beat the system. He had robbed a bunch of banks with a handgun, made the Top Ten list, robbed even more banks, then eventually holed up in Antigua, one of the oldest cities in Guatemala. It was a clever move: the Feds, knowing that Rogge was a die-hard sailor, wouldn't think to look for him in a land-locked city like Antigua. "Rogge was smart like that," admits Miami Bureau special agent Fernando Rivero.

During the six years Rogge was hiding out—as "Bill Young," along with his wife, "Anna"—his story was featured repeatedly on *America's Most Wanted*, as well as placed on that show's website and the FBI's fledgling Top Ten site. Nothing. Then Guatemala got access to the Internet in the mid-1990s, and Rogge made the mistake of helping a neighbor and his 14-year-old son make their first trip into cyberspace. Two weeks later, the teenager logged on to the FBI home page and was shocked to discover that "Bill Young"—a friendly handyman who never forgot to buy him a birthday present—was actually a wily thief who'd broken out of an Idaho prison and robbed banks all across the United States. "He just flipped out," said John Biskovich of his son's reaction. "But he insisted we turn him in."

The capture, however, wasn't as easy as point and click. Agent Rivero followed up the Internet lead personally in Antigua, but by that time Rogge was on the run again. More tips indicated that Rogge was now in the port town of Puerto Barrios, and with the help of the Guatemalan police Rivero eventually found the fugitive's new address. The Feds began round-the-clock surveillance.

Rogge, knowing he was about to be thrown off-line for good, called his American lawyer and arranged for a surrender at the U.S. Embassy in Guatemala. "When I took him into custody,"

Rivera says, "he just said, 'Hey, I've had it.' He told me he was tired of running, tired of the pressure." According to the *Washington Post*, Rogge also later admitted that he was afraid that the trigger-happy Guatemalan police might shoot first and ask questions later after his true identity had been revealed.

INTERESTING FUGITIVE FACT:
After Rogge's arrest, the local paper, *The Guatemala Weekly*, published a heartfelt editorial titled, "Adios, Bill and Anna," which described the town's mixed emotions after discovering their beloved handyman "Bill" was actually a Top Ten fugitive: "All the people who knew Anna and Bill were torn between their personal feelings of friendship and their sense of social responsibility."

431. KENNETH ROBERT STANTON, child molester

LISTED: October 24, 1990
CAUGHT: October 31, 1990
DESCRIPTION: Born in 1939 in Huntington, Indiana.

Nothing Good on TV.   In late October 1990 Kenneth Stanton was relaxing at home in the quiet suburbs of Dayton, Ohio, catching a little television after dinner. He flipped to his local NBC station and saw the start of the show *Unsolved Mysteries*.

Then he saw himself. The 51-year-old quickly flicked off the TV.

Stanton told his wife he had to meet someone at work, then left home. Janet Leggett Stanton, curious, turned the TV back on and caught the remainder of the segment. It detailed how her new husband of four weeks was wanted for the molestation of two sisters in Leesburg, Georgia, in August 1998, as well as a 10- and an 11-year-old girl in nearby Warner Robins, and an eight-year-old girl in Douglas County.

In each case Stanton relied on the same ruse. He would scope out a home where a young girl was alone. Then Stanton would knock on a door and present himself as a plainclothes cop, complete with phony badge. He'd hold up a joint and tell the girl he found it in the backyard and needed to perform a drug test, otherwise she'd be in big trouble. Once he was inside, Stanton would squeeze drops into his victim's eyes, blindfold her, then molest her. Afterward, he would tell the girl to count to 100, and he'd make his escape.

Stanton had a molestation record as long as his arm, it turned out, beginning with charges in the early 1960s, followed by years in a mental hospital until his release in the mid-1970s, followed by even more molestations—possibly in the hundreds, FBI profilers estimated.

It wasn't quite the TV show Stanton's new bride had expected to see.

Janet immediately called the FBI. So did a bunch of Stanton's coworkers who also happened to be watching the show, along with 240 other random tipsters. But Stanton had been prepared. He kept a packed suitcase and $20,000 in his car in case of emergencies. He'd also shaved his beard since moving to Ohio and hoped that would help him stay under the radar. For a while it worked; Stanton managed to elude the FBI dragnet that quickly surrounded his hometown.

But days later, an 11-year-old Mississippi boy named John Corcoran saw something funny going on in his neighborhood: a strange-looking guy knocking on doors up and down his block. "There just wasn't something right with that picture," Corcoran later told the *York Observer*. "He was saying he was from the police, and he was going around the neighborhood checking eyes. It sounded kind of silly." The young boy wrote down Stanton's license plate number and gave it to a neighbor, who forwarded it to police.

"If it weren't for him writing that number down, we would have had zero," said Sgt. Randall Banks of the Houston County, Georgia, Sheriff's Department. Using that number, the FBI finally tracked him down to a motel near Rock Hill, South Carolina, and arrested him without incident.

Stanton was a new kind of criminal to be added to the Top Ten list, a child molester. "The fact that we have a child molester on the Ten Most Wanted list will help increase public awareness that this is a major crime against the innocence of children," said Meg Couillard, executive director of a Georgia home for sexually abused children, just two days before Stanton's arrest. "Often, it's not a one-time incident like a lot of people think."

Nine months later, Stanton was sentenced to 60 years in a Georgia prison.

INTERESTING FUGITIVE FACT:
Stanton also had another wife—and a child—in Mobile, Alabama. He split in 1989 after cops called his then-employer, trying to locate him as a suspect in another child molestation case.

432. PATRICK MICHAEL MITCHELL, bank robber

LISTED: November 23, 1990
CAUGHT: February 22, 1994
DESCRIPTION: Born on June 25, 1942, in Ottawa, Ontario. Five feet nine inches tall, 165 pounds, with light brown hair and blue eyes. He has a scar between his eyebrows, an appendectomy scar, a tattoo of "Helen-Pat" on his upper left arm, a cross in the middle of his chest, and five dots on his thumb. Aliases: "Paddy" Mitchell, Richard Jordon Baird, Michael Baxter, Gary Blackstone, Michael Brewer, Michael Lawrence Garrison, Gilbert Keyes, Richard Joseph Landry, Roger L. Lanthorn, Gary Stone.

America's Best Bank Robber. Patrick "Paddy" Mitchell's last heist on February 22, 1994, wasn't the score of a lifetime—the one he always hoped would be enough to let him and his buddies retire. It was just another random job: a small bank in sleepy Southaven, Mississippi, a suburb of Memphis. "This bank, my sister could have robbed," Mitchell told a reporter from the Associated Press. "It was an easy, easy bank. There was nothing to it, but I was too much in a hurry."

Mitchell was in a hurry because he had been featured on *America's Most Wanted*, and figured he had better strike and split quick. So for the Southaven heist, Mitchell fell back on an oldie-but-goodie ploy: Call City Hall and threaten to blow the place to kingdom come, wait for every black-and-white in the area to scramble to City Hall, then hit the bank and be out before the cops had time to respond. (Top Tenner Al Nussbaum, #168, pioneered this stunt in the 1960s.) But the Southaven police chief was wise to the trick. When the bomb threat was called in, the chief sent a car to every bank. "There are only nine banks in town," said Mitchell. "I was out in about 45 seconds. I scooped up the money bags and left, but the police were waiting."

Until then, Mitchell's so-called "Stopwatch Gang" was grade-A Hollywood caper movie material: They were cool, polite professionals who prided themselves on being in and out of a bank in less than two minutes. They also were fond of wearing masks of ex-presidents, and they never fired a single shot during any caper. "I've never even had a bullet in the chamber," said Mitchell, who in his prime bore a resemblance to actor Tom Selleck. Even his dogged pursuers fell for his charm. "There is a rare quality to him," said U.S. Marshall David Crews. "He has a certain kind of old-style integrity, a criminal ethic you don't see much these days." America hadn't seen such a gentleman robber since Willie Sutton.

Mitchell's professional, polite attitude paid off. Between 1974 and his arrest in 1994, Mitchell estimates that he and his associates robbed 40 banks, with a tally reaching into the millions. The team started small. After getting laid off from his job as a delivery man for Pure Spring Bottling on Ottawa, Ontario, in the early 1970s, Mitchell received a call from an old friend named Lionel Wright. Seems Wright, who had a foolproof method for tampering with seals and boosting goods from the trucking company where he worked, needed help moving the merchandise. "I have never done another day's work since that night Lionel called me," says Mitchell today. "Over the next couple of years, we stole everything from the company but the kitchen sink. Come to think of it, we did steal a load of plumbing supplies and, if I remember correctly, there were some kitchen sinks included."

But Mitchell dreamed of a big score that would let him retire, and he cooked up a $750,000 gold heist—six 65-pound gold bars—at the Ottawa International Airport. Along for the gig were Wright and Stephen Reid, a Canadian bank robber who had escaped prison the year before. It was indeed a score to retire on, but Mitchell and Wright were caught in 1976 and sentenced to 17 years in prison, but not for the gold heist. Instead, Mitchell was convicted of conspiring to import cocaine—a crime Mitchell insists he didn't commit. (He claims he took the fall for a buddy.)

Three years later, Mitchell started gasping and clutching at his chest. Prison guards figured he was having a heart attack. An ambulance was summoned, and two attendants strapped him to a stretcher and rushed him away to a hospital. Only Mitchell never quite made it to the hospital. Three men, dressed in hospital masks and carrying pistols, were waiting outside the hospital to take Mitchell away. One of those men was Stephen Reid, who had busted out of prison himself. (The other two have never been positively identified.) Mitchell and Reid crossed the border into the United States, met up with Lionel Right, and started robbing dozens of banks with precise, carefully timed operations. Thus was born the Stopwatch Gang, which earned the nickname after Mitchell's habit of timing every heist. Mitchell and the boys eventually had enough money to lie low in a gorgeous cedar-and-glass home in Sedona in the Arizona mountains, where they all posed as eccentric rock concert staging experts. Even the local sheriff bought the act, and made the Stopwatch Gang his bridge partners.

But in 1980, time ran out for Reid and Wright. They were caught at their hideout and charged with the gang's latest hit, a $283,000 bank heist in San Diego, and each sentenced to 20 years in prison. Mitchell was now on his own—and without a hideout. He moved operations to Florida and started all over again. In his memoir, *This Bank Robber's Life,* Mitchell details his lone-wolf years, a life of fine restaurants and romantic encounters sandwiched between expertly timed robberies. In 1982 Mitchell visited a Florida honky-tonk bar and met a teenaged girl named Janet Rush who claimed to be 21; the 40-year-old Mitchell claimed he was only 31. The two hit it off over white wine and expensive marijuana, and eventually Rush confided to Mitchell that her last boyfriend had been carted away by the FBI when it turned out that he was a bank robber.

"When I saw you come in," Janet said, "I knew you were different from those other hayseeds." Then she added, half-joking: "I hope you're not a bank robber!"

Mitchell assured her he was no such thing. The next morning, he kissed her goodbye, then drove 60 miles to Ocala, Florida, to case a bank. "In my business, it wasn't wise to live and work in the same town."

Mitchell and Rush moved in together, all without Rush knowing what her new boyfriend did for a living. "I would venture to say that I was probably the happiest, most contended man on the planet," writes Mitchell. "I had the prettiest lady in town, the greatest sex in the universe, and we never had an argument or cross words." But three months later, she came from work to find the man she knew as "Richard John Baird" sitting on their couch in handcuffs.

"Do you know this man?" asked the FBI agent, who strangely enough, had been on hand to arrest Rush's previous bank robber boyfriend.

"Yes, I know him," Rush said, horror building on her face. "Now what the hell is going on here?"

"What's going on here, Janet," continued the agent, "is that this man is an escaped convict who is also wanted for robbing a couple dozen banks between here and California. This man is Patrick 'Paddy' Mitchell."

"It's all a mistake, Janet," explained Mitchell. "I'll get this cleared up and be back in time to cook you dinner."

"Yeah, you'll be back in time to cook her dinner, all right," said the FBI agent. "In about 20 years."

Mitchell was indeed sent back to prison, but it did not take 20 years for him to become a free man again. He escaped from Arizona State prison on May 9, 1986, by sawing through steel bars and crawling through an air-conditioning duct with two other inmates. (The duct ran straight above the warden's office.) Mitchell began another impressive run, robbing more banks with the two men he had helped break out of Arizona State—Cecil Kinkaid and Johnny Stuart. But by 1990 Mitchell had been named to the FBI's Ten Most Wanted list, so he moved to the Philippines under the alias Gary Wayne Weber. There, he remarried, sired a son, and tried to live a normal life.

The FBI nearly nabbed him in a 1993 raid; a relative of his new wife had snitched after seeing *America's Most Wanted,* and Mitchell escaped only hours before agents broke down his front door. He flew back to the United States. He was down to his last $12,000. Next came the ill-fated Southaven heist, and the end of the line for Mitchell. Today, 59-year-old Mitchell is serving out a 30-year-sentence at Leavenworth.

INTERESTING FUGITIVE FACT:

The Stopwatch Gang was the inspiration for the 1991 Keanu Reeves/Patrick Swayze heist movie *Point Break.*

433. JON PRESTON SETTLE, murderer

LISTED: August 9, 1991
CAUGHT: August 6, 1991
DESCRIPTION: Born in 1961.

Steel Cage Hit. Jon Settle was the gunman for a San Fernando Valley crack ring one D.A. called "the biggest, most ruthless drug organization you wished you never heard of." The D.A. wasn't exaggerating.

The Bryant Family Gang was a notorious cocaine ring based in the San Fernando Valley. It was a 200-man organization run by brothers Stanley and Jeff Bryant, who raked in an estimated $500,000 from the eight crack houses they ran. Such a large organization is prone to internal squabbles, however. Family hit man Andre Armstrong had spent some time in the slammer for murder and thought the family owed him some money for his trouble. The Bryants refused. Armstrong threatened to take over some of the business for himself. So the family decided to take care of the Armstrong problem in-house. Literally.

On the evening of August 28, 1988, Armstrong and his partner, James Brown, walked into one of the family crack houses. They were buzzed into the front door and stepped into a steel cage, one of the house security features. That's when two of their coworkers, Settle and Donald Franklin Smith, pulled out shotguns and semiautomatic pistols and proceeded to blast both Armstrong and Brown to death. The unarmed men had no chance.

The bloodshed didn't end there. Brown's girlfriend, Loretha Anderson, had been waiting outside the house in a car with her two-year-old daughter and 18-month-old son. As soon as the men were dead, another family employee, LeRoy Wheeler, went outside and saw Anderson. "There's a bitch in the car!" Wheeler shouted, according to one witness. Wheeler used his shotgun on Anderson and her daughter at point-blank range. The son was cut by flying glass, but somehow escaped death and fled the scene.

The men were dumped in Lopez Canyon. Anderson and her daughter were dumped around the corner. In-house problem solved.

But the solution didn't stay in-house.

The quadruple killing at the crack house opened up the floodgates. Law enforcement officials set out gunning for a dozen Bryant family members—ones who were directly or indirectly responsible for the Armstrong and Brown slaying. (Cops also had 11 other murders on the books that they attributed to the Bryant Family.) Within a year the ensuing manhunt rounded up 11 Bryant family members—everyone but Settle, who managed to elude them. When cops burst into his last known address, they discovered a virtual arsenal of handguns and weapons.

Almost a year later, Settle was caught by members of the LAPD and San Fernando PD. "We were playing a hunch," said one detective. "It was a 50-50 chance whether he would be there, and he showed up." Turned out, Settle went back to his own home at 2800 Leeward Avenue in Los Angeles and was caught driving away with his wife, Norma Ramirez Settle, in a beat-up station wagon.

Out of all of the Bryant Family Gang members, Settle had been the luckiest in avoiding arrest. In late January 1996 Settle got lucky again; as the result of a plea bargain, he was sentenced to 21 years and four months in prison. His three codefendants received death sentences.

INTERESTING FUGITIVE FACT:
Settle is one of those rare Top Tenners who were named to the list but caught before the formal announcement. Settle had been nabbed on a Tuesday, and FBI special agent Scott Hanley was supposed to make the announcement the following Friday.

434. ROBERT MICHAEL ALLEN, murderer

LISTED: September 13, 1991
FOUND DEAD: December 23, 1992
DESCRIPTION: Formerly a reserve law enforcement office in Spokane, Washington. Aliases: Robert Michael Suggs, Robert M. Sugs.

True Hollywood Story. Robert Michael Allen was a bit of a Hollywood cliché—a down-on-his-luck private eye who'd come to Southern California with a murky past and a taste for violence—even before he met producer Jon Emr.

But when he met Emr, Allen probably thought his luck was about to turn around. Emr convinced him to close his Scottsdale, Arizona, private eye business to move to California to work as his personal bodyguard and to serve as the associate producer of a hot James Dean biopic. Perhaps L.A. dreams do come true, after all.

Alas, Emr was another Hollywood cliché: the producer/scam artist, complete with silky smooth pitches, cocktail in hand, and Hawaiian shirt on his back. At least four people accused Emr of conning them out of thousands of dollars after he promised them producer credits—and thereby, silver screen immortality—that never materialized. "It's amazing how gullible people will be when Hollywood is concerned," said writer/director Rod Lurie, who wrote about Emr and Allen in his 1995 book, *Once Upon a Time in Hollywood: Movie Making, Con Games and Murder in Glitter City.* "It's not just the money issue—it's fame, celebrity, skiing in Aspen."

Emr's L.A. con games, however, came to end on July 11, 1991, after Allen followed him to the corner of Slauson Avenue and Sepulveda Boulevard in Culver City, drove up next to Emr's Lincoln Town Car, and then blasted his .22-caliber revolver, killing Emr and his 19-year-old son, Roger. Allen fled the scene. Oddly enough, a few days later, Allen took a friend to Disneyland.

It had been the culmination of a really strange week for Allen. Suspicion about Emr's empty promises had been growing through the summer of 1991.

Money got tight, real tight. Allen desperately wanted the $30,000 that Emr owed him. It all boiled to a head after Allen was kicked out of his apartment and his girlfriend, 28-year-old Susan Lynn Calkins, split. "He placed all of this on Emr," said Culver City police sergeant Hank Davies, who started the job just four days before the Emr shooting. "[Allen] thought there was nothing else to live for anymore, and he wanted to take everyone else with him."

Over the Fourth of July weekend, Allen is alleged to have killed Calkins—and, in some sick fit of spite, her dog—then packed both corpses into his car. He drove to desert lands in San Bernardino County and then buried his ex-girlfriend and her pet in a shallow grave. Next, Allen hit the road again, to a suburb of Phoenix, where he had planned to grease Emr's teenage boys. The kids weren't home, but Emr's 71-year-old father was. Allen pumped five bullets into the man's head. Days later, Allen staked out Jon Emr's rental office in Culver City, then finished his twisted job.

Afterward, Davies petitioned the FBI to name Allen to the Top Ten list, where he remained for over a year until some hikers stumbled upon Allen's remains in the California desert—right next to the white bones of Susan Calkins and her dog. It is thought that right after his Disneyland trip, Allen went back to the burial site and killed himself.

INTERESTING FUGITIVE FACT:
Fittingly, Allen's debut on the Ten Most Wanted list was timed to coincide with his debut on the 8 P.M. broadcast of *America's Most Wanted*—the first time such an announcement had been timed to accommodate the television show. Allen got his big break after all.

435. MIR AIMAL KANSI, assassin

LISTED: February 9, 1993
CAUGHT: June 17, 1997
DESCRIPTION: Born on February 10, 1964, in Pakistan. Five feet five inches tall, 154 pounds, with black hair and black eyes. Last seen wearing a tan jacket and dark-colored pants, driving a dull medium-brown 1970s or early 1980s compact station wagon. Aliases: Mir Aimal Kanci, Mir Aimal Kasi, Mohammed Alam Kasi, Mir Aman Qazi, Mir Amial Qansi, Amial Khan.

The Man Who Went Gunning for the CIA. Employees of the CIA know the risks of their job. The front lobby of CIA headquarters in Langley, Virginia, has rows of black stars on a white marble wall, commemorating the agents and operatives who were killed in service to their country. But most never thought the risk would hit so close to home, as it did in early 1993.

Five days after Bill Clinton was sworn in as president, a man took a Chinese-made AK-47 and opened fire at eight in the morning, right in front of the gates at CIA headquarters.

Operative Frank Darling and his new bride, Judy Becker, were driving their Volkswagen Golf past the main gate when their back window exploded. Frank's body was hurled forward into the steering wheel. "My God, get down, Judy!" he yelled. "I've been shot!" Judy hid under the dashboard, but could only watch in slack-jawed horror as the gunman doubled back, poked the business end of the AK-47 into their car, and finished off her husband with another burst of bullets. Across the highway Lansing Bennett, a 66-year-old CIA doctor, was mortally wounded. Three other employees were also shot and bleeding badly. And then the gunman disappeared.

Soon after, a Pakastani living in Virginia called police and told them that the shooter just might have been his roommate, Mir Aimal Kansi, who had been bragging about making a "big statement" at the CIA and had recently purchased an AK-47. But by the time the cops and FBI tossed the apartment and found the murder weapon—fingerprints and all—Kansi had already hopped a plane back to Quetta, Pakistan, to see his family. Then he disappeared again, kicking off one of the trickiest international manhunts in recent memory.

It wasn't so much that the FBI didn't know where he'd gone. "We pretty much knew the area of the world where he was located," said FBI deputy director William Esposito in an interview with NPR. That area was Pakistan. The problem: The United States and Pakistan weren't exactly buddies back in the mid-90s. "Their attitude was basically, who cares about a crazy guy who killed a couple of CIA guys in Washington?" an FBI agent told writer Jeff Stein for a feature in GQ magazine. "A couple of infidels are dead—so what?" Complicating matters further was the fact that Kansi was from a region of Pakistan that was big on self-policing and not so big on helping government investigators. He would be well hidden by his own people.

Several FBI raids into Pakistan came up with nothing. Posters and matchbooks with Kansi's photo were spread throughout the Middle East, but no

dice. According to the GQ article, there was even a notion to send retired CIA specialists to find Kansi—an idea right out of a Robert Ludlum novel, it would seem—that also stalled. The waters of international politics were too tough to navigate.

Finally, in June 1997, the CIA told the FBI that they had a lead on Kansi—a tip that he'd be in a certain hotel on a certain day. Special Agents Brad Garrett and Jimmy Carter from the Washington Bureau were dispatched to Pakistan by an Air Force C-141 transport, and more than a week later, joined by a team of Pakistani commandos to descend upon the town of Dera Ghazi Khan. They found Kansi in a third-floor room in the cheap hotel their tipster had named. Carter and Garrett and their team knocked at 4:30 A.M., when they found Kansi on a prayer rug. Kansi was immediately cuffed.

Garrett asked, "Who are you?"

"Fuck you," Kansi said, then began to yell for help.

After a quick fingerprint check—it was indeed Kansi—a hood went over Kansi's head and the mad gunman was whisked away. The FBI squad hit two road blocks on the way out. On the way back from the hotel a Pakistani police barricade had to be ordered away, and then two days later, after Pakistani officials refused to let Kansi go, the FBI took him and fired up their C-141 anyway, but the plane was refused clearance for takeoff. It took a phone call from U.S. Secretary of State Madeleine Albright to convince Prime Minister Nawaz Sharif that it was in his best interests to let that plane take off.

On the flight home Kansi signed a confession.

Kansi's motive? That remains a mystery. The GQ article quotes an intelligence officer who says that Kansi, along with other members of his family, had been formerly employed by the CIA. (Which would make sense; his hometown of Quetta has long been an intelligence hub, since it sits near the Afghanistan border.) Other officials, on the record and off, steadfastly deny this, and maintain that he acted alone. There's no denying that Kansi was anti-American; he once fired a pistol into the air to scare off two visiting American professors at his university. But was that enough to make him initiate a bloodbath in broad daylight at the front gates of the world's most powerful intelligence organization?

In January 1998, nearly five years after the shooting, Kansi was sentenced to death. "I don't feel proud for it," Kansi told the courtroom. "This is the result of the wrong policy toward Islamic countries." Kansi was executed by lethal injection in November 2002.

INTERESTING FUGITIVE FACT:
Kansi has a master's degree in English literature from Baluchistan University in Pakistan.

436. RAMZI AHMED YOUSEF, terrorist

LISTED: April 21, 1993
CAUGHT: February 7, 1995
DESCRIPTION: Born on May 20, 1967, in Iraq. Six feet tall, 180 pounds, with brown hair and brown eyes. Usually clean shaven. Previously arrested for "knowingly and willfully making false statements on documents."

The Evil Genius. On February 26, 1993, Ramzi Ahmed Yousef stood on the waterfront near Jersey City and watched the smoke rise from the southern tip of Manhattan. He was disappointed. The twin towers of the World Trade Center were still standing. This wasn't the way it was supposed to have happened. The Great Satan needed to feel the pain equivalent to a Hiroshima or Nagasaki. Nothing less was acceptable. But from the looks of things, his plan to shear through the steel columns of one tower—sending it crashing into the other, killing 250,000 people—had failed.

But there was no time for regrets. Yousef went back to his Jersey City safe house, packed, then took a $30 cab ride to JFK airport and waited for his first-class trip to Pakistan.

Meanwhile, chaos reigned back in lower Manhattan. Six people had been killed by the blast, and more than a thousand sustained injuries. At the same time that rescue crews scrambled to extinguish the fire and evacuate the towers, the New York–based Joint Terrorist Task Force (JTTF)—a squad made up of FBI, NYPD, ATF, INS, among other groups—scrambled to answer the questions: Who? And why?

The answer to that first question came with a bit of luck and a whole lot of old-fashioned investigative drudge work. The luck came in the form of a VIN (vehicle identification number), which workers found beneath 6,000 tons of rubble. That led investigators to the Ryder rental agency in Jersey City, where the van had been originally rented. Would the driver be foolish enough to come back and seek his deposit? In this case, he was—another bit of luck. Mohammed Salameh, one of Yousef's henchman, not only came back to claim the $400 deposit, but also bickered angrily with the Ryder rental agent when he was offered only half. Out-

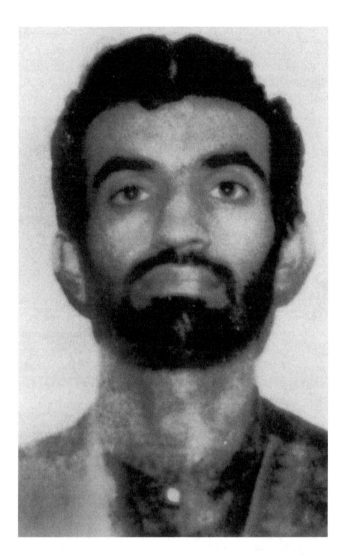

Yousef was apprehended in Pakistan. He was convicted of the 1993 bombing at New York's World Trade Center.

side the Ryder office agents nabbed Salameh. The man was a walking jackpot: ID, credit cards, addresses, which in turn led to phone records and more contacts, all of which eventually led investigators to the bombing mastermind, Ramzi Yousef. It was an astounding run of detective work, and it all started with a tiny piece of metal found in the debris.

And as for the why? Yousef was a new kind of terrorist: one with a murky background and unclear allegiances. "In the past we were fighting terrorists with an organizational structure and some attainable goal," said Oliver "Buck" Revell, former FBI deputy director. "But Yousef is the new breed, who are more difficult and hazardous. They want nothing less than the overthrow of the West, and since that's not going to happen, they just want to punish—the more casualties the better." Yousef became a special addition to the Top Ten list in April 1993, bumping the list up to 11.

For Yousef, the fun was just beginning. He had many places to go, many people to blow up. He first fled to Baluchistan—the same area where gunman MIR AIMAL KANSI, #435, hid after his attack on CIA headquarters—and later hopped around the globe: Egypt, mainland Asia, Manila, among other destinations. In late 1994 Yousef planted a bomb on a Philippine Airlines flight that left one passenger dead and forced the plane to make an emergency landing. Later, U.S. intelligence officers told *Time* magazine they suspect this was Yousef doing a test run to see if he could sneak a bomb on a U.S. airliner. One report said that Yousef had planned to blow up 10 airplanes at the same time.

In the end Yousef was turned in by a snitch who was eyeing a $2 million reward (apparently the going rate for international terrorists in the early 1990s; Kansi also had a $2 million bounty slapped on his head). He was captured at the Su Casa Guest House in Pakistan at 9:30 in the morning. "I'm innocent! Where are you taking me?" Yousef yelled, insisting that he was a businessman named "Ali Mohammad." Later, officials opened two large suitcases "Mr. Mohammad" had brought with him. They contained bomb parts, flight schedules for United and Delta airlines, and, creepily enough, two remote-controlled toy cars loaded with explosives. He was later returned to the United States to stand trial.

In early January 1998 Yousef was sentenced to solitary confinement for the rest of his life. "Yes, I am a terrorist and proud of it," said Yousef in the courtroom. "I support terrorism as long as it used against the United States and Israel. You are more than terrorists. You are butchers, liars and hypocrites."

After sentencing, U.S. district judge Kevin Duffy said that solitary confinement was historically reserved for those "who spread plague and pestilence throughout the world." Yousef is currently housed at the "Supermax" prison in Florence, Colorado, known as the most secure jail in the world.

INTERESTING FUGITIVE FACT:
In early 1995 Yousef plotted to assassinate Pope John Paul II in Manila, but never had the chance to follow through.

437. JOSEPH MARTIN LUTHER GARDNER, rapist, murderer

LISTED: May 25, 1994
CAUGHT: October 19, 1994
DESCRIPTION: Born on January 30, 1966, in Detroit, Michigan. Five feet eight inches tall, 145 pounds with black hair and brown eyes. Aliases: Joseph M. L. Gardner, Joe Gardner.

The New Year's Resolution. On December 30, 1992, Melissa McLauchlin had been out drinking and found herself wandering along a street in North Charleston, South Carolina. Three young men in a car pulled up next to her and said they'd give her some crack cocaine in exchange for sex. McLauchlin agreed and hopped into the car.

But the men—among them Joe Gardner, a 23-year-old Detroit native and enlisted navy sailor—had something else in mind. Witnesses would later testify that Gardner and a friend named Matthew Carl Mack, 21, had been talking for weeks about torturing, raping, and murdering a white woman "for 400 years of oppression," Mack would later tell police. In fact, the idea was kind of a New Year's resolution. Just two days before New Year's, Gardner and Mack got their chance to keep that resolution.

The group drove to a nearby mobile home and took McLauchlin inside. The 25-year-old may have consented at first, but things soon spiraled out of control. At one point, testified a witness, Gardner forced McLauchlin to have anal sex at gunpoint. Another witness claimed that Mack held a kitchen knife and said he was going to stab her to death. After repeated rapes, Gardner and Mack forced McLauchlin to wash her genitals with bleach—to literally burn away the evidence—and then blindfolded her and led her away from the trailer. The group piled back in the car and drove about 15 miles into nearby Dorchester County. Then, without warning, Gardner pulled out a pistol and shot McLauchlin five times in the face, then pushed her out of the car.

Somehow, McLauchlin lived long enough to tell police that she didn't know her attackers, but died soon after. Gardner and friends went on the run.

In a little more than a week, the police rounded up everyone save Gardner—the two who were with him, three who were charged with being accessories after the fact, and one charged with having knowledge of a felony. Gardner stayed at large for more than a year, finally making the Top Ten list in May 1994.

The story of his capture was proof that sometimes old-fashioned ways still work best. "A citizen went to the post office, and it's the classic wanted-poster scene," said Brad Koch, an FBI agent in the Philadelphia branch. "She looks at the Ten Most Wanted pictures and said, 'I know that man, but not by that name. That's Tony.'"

"Tony" worked at a local grocery store. A mix of Philly cops and FBI agents staked out the store; "Tony" was indeed Gardner. The rapist-murderer walked out of the store and down the street and was promptly arrested. At first he held to the claim that his name was "Tony Dawkins," but eventually confessed. He told the arresting agents: "Call the girl's mother and put her mind at rest. I haven't slept in two years."

Gardner was returned to South Carolina for trial, and in December 1995—nearly three years after the McLauchlin murder—was given the death penalty.

INTERESTING FUGITIVE FACT:
At the time of his fugitive run, Gardner was an active-duty sailor aboard the missile cruiser *Richmond K. Turner,* thereby making him both AWOL and Most Wanted at the same time.

438. GARY RAY BOWLES, serial killer

LISTED: November 19, 1994
CAUGHT: November 22, 1994
DESCRIPTION: Born in Clifton Forge, Virginia. Five feet, nine inches tall, 150 pounds with hazel eyes and brown hair. Tattoos on both arms and scars from stab wounds on the left side of his chest.

The One Before Cunanan. In late November 1994 detectives in Jacksonville, Florida, were gathered around a man who they thought had killed his roommate. The suspect was Tim Whitfield, a drifter who was currently working as a pool cleaner a short distance away from his $40-a-week flophouse. The victim: Walter Jammell Hinton, a 42-year-old florist who had been found with his head bashed in with a 40-pound cinderblock. Usually in these cases the roommate is the most likely suspect, so police immediately started looking for Whitfield. A snitch coughed up his current location: an Ameri-Force job center, looking for a day's work.

The detectives had been grilling Whitfield for more than an hour when he finally changed his tune. But not quite the way they expected.

"Look, I'm tired of this," Whitfield said. "Do you really want to know who I am? I'm Gary Ray Bowles."

Whitfield/Bowles asked for a pack of cigarettes, and then started to tell his story.

The gruesome spree started in Daytona Beach earlier that year. Bowles had just served a hitch at a Florida prison for robbery and needed a place to crash. Enter 59-year-old insurance salesman named John Hardy Roberts, whom Bowles met in a gay bar. Roberts let Bowles stay with him and soon came to consider him a boyfriend. Odd, though, that Bowles had a girlfriend—one who got knocked up and soon skipped town, throwing Bowles into a depressive funk. This bothered Roberts, and in March 1994 he gave his younger roommate an ultimatum: "Make up your mind. It's me or her."

Bowles never said "her," but it was clear he didn't want Roberts. Bowles grabbed a lamp and smacked Roberts in the head with it, then continued beating him until he was out cold. Then he rolled up a rag and crammed it down Roberts's throat. That was a precaution: If Roberts somehow regained consciousness, he wouldn't have enough air to live very long.

That murder kicked off a spree of six that spanned Maryland, Georgia, and Florida. All of Bowles's victims were gay, older and lonely, usually picked up in a bar. He'd hustle them for a place to crash and some spending money in exchange for companionship, household chores, and sexual favors. Then, invariably, it got ugly. For each murder the M.O. was the same: a brutal attack, followed by a towel—or in some cases leaves or a dildo—down the throat. Then Bowles would split in their car, using their credit cards and spending their money until he found the next victim.

The spree caused something of a panic in the gay community up and down the East Coast. Oddly enough, Bowles had been arrested and jailed twice, under his Whitfield alias, while police were hunting for him. On November 12, just seven days before he was named to the FBI's Top Ten list, Whitfield/Bowles was arrested for carrying an open container of booze in public. (The arresting officers took fingerprints, but they were only compared with local records. The Bowles connection never hit.) It was the arrest for the Hinton murder, and a tired confession, that finally ended the manhunt.

In that interrogation room in Jacksonville, Bowles recounted every grisly detail of his six murders. "It's time," Bowles said wearily. "I want the killing to stop. I'm either getting six life sentences or the electric chair."

Bowles got the second part of his wish, at least. In a Florida circuit court in September 1999 Bowles was sentenced to death.

INTERESTING FUGITIVE FACT:
Despite working his entire adult life as a male prostitute catering to men, Bowles insisted he wasn't gay. "I just live off these people," he told police.

439. GERALD KEITH WATKINS, murderer

LISTED: March 4, 1995
CAUGHT: May 5, 1995
DESCRIPTION: Born in 1969 in New York. Six feet, three inches tall, 205 pounds. Occupations: Construction worker and union carpenter.

Boom-Boom Explodes. It's a humid night in Pittsburgh, July 1994. Gerald Keith Watkins has a bad temper, and he's having a very bad night. He's just found out that his live-in girlfriend, Beth Anderson, is still legally married to another guy. In a fit of rage he takes his Tec-22 and shoots Anderson to death in front of her nine-year-old son, Kevin Kelly. Watkins doesn't want any witnesses, so he pumps six bullets into Kevin's head, chest, and neck. The boy dies wearing nothing but underwear; he'd been sleeping and cooling off next to a plug-in fan, tired after a playful night of catching fireflies with his buddies.

Then Watkins hears the shrill screams. They're coming from his own baby girl, only 18 days old, lying in her crib. Watkins shoots her, too—eight times in her tiny chest and head.

"It was one of the worst homicide scenes we've had since I've been here," a Pittsburgh detective told the *Pittsburgh Post Gazette*. "It was extremely brutal." It was so gruesome, in fact, that *America's Most Wanted* chose not to stage a re-enactment when featuring Watkins two months later.

Watkins wasn't just the garden variety psycho with a pistol. He was a PCP addict, a nasty drunk with the nickname "Boom Boom," and an enforcer for a coke dealer in the Pittsburgh area. The following March Watkins was nominated to the Top Ten list by Larry Likar, chief of the Pittsburgh Fugitive Task Force. "He was my baby," Likar said in a *Details* magazine article.

Oddly enough, Watkins had been picked up by the NYPD just a few weeks after the murder. The fugitive had been found unconscious on the side of a road in New York. Cops took him to a Bronx hospital, where he recuperated for a while, then split. Days later, hospital staff members recognized Boom Boom on TV. By that time he was gone.

But Likar finally tracked Watkins down, using Watkins's mother's phone records, of all things. "Most fugitive hunts involve real drudge work," Likar told *Details*. "Some of it—going through phone bills, running down DMV records, or shagging half-assed leads from every other Burger King counterman—sometimes seems counterproductive. But then you hit one." Which Likar did. He noticed that a bunch of calls had come in to Watkins's mother's phone from New York City, the Bronx specifically.

With this in mind, Likar squeezed a buddy of Watkins, and the guy gave up Watkins's new address. The NYPD and Pittsburgh Fugitive Task Force were there the next morning at 9:45 A.M. FBI agent Robert Bendetson knocked on the door and called out, "Gerald, open up, it's over." An agent out back radioed that Watkins was trying to jump out a window onto a fire escape. The agents at the front door smashed it to pieces. Watkins was caught.

More than a year later, a Pennsylvania Common Pleas judge sentenced Watkins to three consecutive death sentences. In the audience Kevin Kelly's father muttered the word "Yes!" and pumped his fist after the jury forewoman announced each sentence.

As Watkins was led away, he told his victims' family members, "I'll be back."

Kevin Kelly's father shot back: "But not in our lifetime."

INTERESTING FUGITIVE FACT:
At Watkins's trial ministers from New York City testified on the killer's behalf, saying that he had attended church regularly while on the run. One deacon even called him "the sweetest person you could ever know." The prosecutor retorted with a photo of the bloodied corpse of 18-day-old Melanie Watkins, asking, "Did the sweetest person you ever met do anything like this?"

440. JUAN GARCIA-ABREGO, drug lord

LISTED: March 9, 1995
CAUGHT: January 15, 1996
DESCRIPTION: Born on September 13, 1944, in La Paloma, Texas. Five feet nine inches tall, 200 to 220 pounds, with brown hair and brown eyes. Known to frequently travel to Costa Rica, Mexico City, and Monterrey.

Smashing the Doll. "They don't get any bigger than Juan Garcia-Abrego," said Phil Jordan, the former director of the El Paso Intelligence Center, a DEA information clearinghouse. "The guy is what I describe as a malignant cancer."

Garcia-Abrego's "Gulf Cartel" was, at its peak, responsible for about 70 percent of the cocaine that entered the United States. Since the 1980s the man is alleged to have made more than $1 billion shipping coke and weed over the border. And, according to testimony from ex-employees, Garcia-Abrego protected himself by bribing anyone on both sides of the border who might cause him trouble—a customs official here, a deputy attorney general there. There

Juan Garcia-Abrego, one of Mexico's most notorious drug lords, is escorted from the FBI headquarters in Houston by agents Monday, Jan. 15, 1996. He was arrested in Monterrey, Mexico, and later deported to the United States.

were expensive suits, watches, even a twin-engine plane, which allegedly was a gift to a Mexican police commander. And when bribes didn't work, there was always murder. Officials have linked Garcia-Abrego to 50 murders, causing some to liken him to Pablo Escobar, the infamous ultra-violent Colombian drug lord.

The U.S.-born Garcia-Abrego, nicknamed "The Doll" and "The Director," had been indicted in Houston back in 1993 on drug trafficking and money laundering charges. But his announcement to the list in 1995 came after Mario Ruiz Massieu, former Mexican deputy attorney general, was arrested in Newark, New Jersey, where he had stopped after fleeing Mexico. Massieu had been accused of covering up the assassination of two Mexican political figures, one of them his own brother. Officials followed the money, and the trail led back to Garcia-Abrego.

This was an important development. In addition to the political skullduggery, there was growing concern that Mexico wasn't doing all it could to stop the flow of drugs into the United States. (In 1989, in fact, an entire police force in Matamoros, Mexico, was arrested for allegedly protecting Garcia-Abrego.) It was time to see if Mexico was indeed serious about smashing drug cartels.

It was Mexican federal police who finally captured Garcia-Abrego in Monterrey—or so they were quick to claim. "There was no American agent whatsoever," said Juan Rebollevo, the chief of the U.S.-Mexican relations at Mexico's Foreign Ministry. "It was a Mexican operation, fully." (Some, however, maintain that the DEA also had a hand in his capture.) The fugitive was captured after Mexican police staked out some of Garcia-Abrego's favorite spots and then pounced. The fugitive was quickly extradited to Houston after his arrest, a move that many Mexicans questioned—especially since Garcia-Abrego might be able to answer some lingering questions about the two recent political assassinations.

But Mexico's decision to throw Garcia-Abrego on a speeding plane to the United States may have been more about money than about a thirst for justice. At the time of Garcia-Abrego's arrest, Mexico was up for certification as a reliable partner in the War on Drugs. "Certification means that countries will not be able to obtain U.S. international loans and foreign aid unless they actually cooperate in stopping drug trafficking," said Bob Wiener, a spokesperson for the White House Drug Policy Office. What better example of cooperation than

the apprehension of one of the country's most notorious drug kingpins?

On January 31, 1997, Garcia-Abrego was sentenced to life in prison without parole and was ordered to pay half a billion dollars in fines and forfeitures. After the sentence was read, Garcia-Abrego was asked if he had anything to say. "No, señor," was his reply.

INTERESTING FUGITIVE FACT:
On his poster, Garcia-Abrego's occupations were listed as "rancher, drug dealer." Before his arrest he owned more than 250 Mexican ranches.

441. ABDEL BASSETT ALI AL-MEGRAHI, terrorist

DESCRIPTION: Born on April 1, 1952, in Tripoli, Libya. Five feet eight inches tall, 190 pounds with black hair and dark brown eyes. Formerly the director of the Center for Strategic Studies and the chief of airline security for Libyan Arab Airlines. Aliases: Ahmed Khalifa Abdusmad, Abdelbaset A. Mohmed, Abdelbaset Ali Mohmed, Abdelbaset Ali Mohmed Al Megrahi, Abdelbaset El Azzabi, Abd Al Baset Ali, Abd Al Basset Al Megrahi, Abd Al-Basit Ali Mohammed, Mr. Baset.

442. LAMEN KHALIFA FHIMAH, terrorist

BOTH LISTED: March 23, 1995
BOTH CAUGHT: April 5, 1999
DESCRIPTION: Born on April 4, 1956, in Suk Giuma, Libya. Five feet seven inches tall, 190 pounds, with black hair and dark brown eyes. Formerly the airline station manager for Libyan Arab Airlines. Aliases: Lamen Khalifa Al-Fhimah, Al Amin Khalifa Fhimah, Mr. Lamin.

The Brown Suitcase. The price on the suspects' heads: $4 million, then a record. "We want to make sure the citizens of Libya and North Africa are aware of what these men are accused of," said Robert Bryant, the FBI's assistant director for national security, on the day after the two suspects were named to the Most Wanted list. "We want them to know we're not giving up, that we want these people back and that there is a reward for information."

What Al-Megrahi and Fhimah were accused of is the bombing of Pan Am Flight 103 in 1988, which killed 259 passengers—189 of them Americans. Eleven residents of Lockerbie, Scotland, were killed when flaming wreckage crashed into their homes. It was one of the most horrifying terrorist acts in recent memory. And it soon turned into a prolonged wrestling match between the U.N. and Libya.

It all began with a brown Samsonite suitcase that appeared to have been shipped from Malta to Frankfurt, Germany, where it was transferred to a London-bound Pan Am plane. Once at Heathrow, it was transferred again to another Pam Am plane, a 747. Inside the suitcase were some clothes and a radio cassette player—a radio cassette player that actually contained Czech-made plastic explosives and a Mebo MST-13 digital timer.

After the explosion investigators from around the world spent countless hours sifting through evidence, eventually linking Al-Megrahi and Fhimah to the bomb components, piece by piece. On the surface the two claimed to be former Libyan airline employees; investigators suspected they were actually former Libyan intelligence officers. (Either way, the State Department says that Libyan air has long been a front for that country's intelligence organization.)

As the years progressed, Libya would hint that it might know the whereabouts of the two suspects and might even hand them over if sanctions against the country were lifted. When Al-Megrahi and Fhimah were named to the Most Wanted list in 1995, it was meant both to generate new leads and apply pressure to Libyan leader Moammar Kadafi. Finally, in 1999, after $30 billion in sanctions had taken their toll, the Libyan government agreed to hand over the suspects. U.N. sanctions were immediately lifted. Al-Megrahi and Fhimah made V-for-victory signs as they boarded a plane that would take them to the Netherlands for a trial under Scottish law—Kadafi insisted on this, saying that a fair trial was not possible in the United States or England. Both suspects maintained their innocence. "The days will prove what we are saying is true," said Al-Megrahi.

That's not quite how it turned out. The verdict from the Scottish court finally came down on January 31, 2001. While the case was tough—the evidence was more than a decade old, and there were no witnesses who saw either suspect physically place that suitcase bomb on the plane—there was enough to convict Al-Megrahi (confirmed in the trial to be a Libyan intelligence agent) and earn him at least 20 years in prison. "Twenty years for 270 murders is less than a month per victim," said Peter Lowenstein, father of a young American killed in the blast. "It's just not right."

Fhimah, his alleged partner, was set free.

INTERESTING FUGITIVE FACT:
The model of Toshiba radio cassette player that was chosen to hide the explosives was called "Bombeat."

443. O'NEIL VASSELL, drug dealer

LISTED: July 15, 1995
CAUGHT: October 16, 1996
DESCRIPTION: Born on September 27, 1976, in Brooklyn, New York. Five feet 10 inches tall, 180 pounds, with brown hair and brown eyes. Suspect is a drug user and known to carry a 9 mm semiautomatic handgun. Consider armed and extremely dangerous. Nickname: "Yellow."

The Angry Rat. O'Neil Vassell had a temper. Once, after losing a pickup basketball game, Vassell blew away one of his opponents with a 9 mm handgun. Imagine: One minute you're going for a lay-up, the next, you're being laid out.

Vassell had been a member of the "Rats," a Jamaican drug posse that dealt pot and hash along the East Coast, since he was 15 years old. Before he was old enough to vote, he was wanted for slaying three people in a drug gunfight in Bridgeport, Connecticut, during the summer of 1993. Cops in Bridgeport and Durham, North Carolina, also wanted to talk to Vassell about alleged assaults on three other people. He was reported as being last seen in New York.

After two years, the FBI finally received a tip that Vassell was hiding in the Canarsie section of Brooklyn. Agents evacuated apartments and houses around a 93rd Street building, then searched it for two hours, apartment by apartment. They found Vassell behind the last door they checked. It took a while for agents to talk Vassell into giving himself up. "We didn't know if he had hostages in there," explained one agent involved in the stakeout. Fortunately, the young Rat surrendered peacefully.

INTERESTING FUGITIVE FACT:
At 18, Vassell was the youngest fugitive ever to make the Ten Most Wanted list.

444. RICKEY ALLEN BRIGHT, child molester

LISTED: December 15, 1995
CAUGHT: January 7, 1996
DESCRIPTION: Born on January 13, 1954, in South Charleston, West Virginia. Five feet 10 inches tall, 175 pounds, with blue eyes and brownish red hair. He

wears glasses and may have a mustache. Last seen driving a silver 1987 Chevrolet Cavalier with N.C. license tag HVC 9159.

Repeat Offender. In fall 1995 Joel Brown owned the Parkside Male Residential Hotel in Akron, Ohio. Around the middle of October Brown had a new guest, a bowling alley maintenance man named Rickey Bright. "He was a real easygoing guy, an unassuming fellow," Brown recalled to the *Charlotte Observer*. More important, Bright always paid his hotel bill on time. On November 11 Bright moved out and didn't leave Brown a forwarding address.

After a long weekend trip Brown flipped on *America's Most Wanted*. "They flashed his picture on the screen," Brown said, "and I thought I recognized him. Then they said, Rickey Allen Bright. I said, Oh, geez!" Brown immediately called the FBI and told them everything he knew—not much—about his previous tenant.

The FBI, however, knew quite a bit about Rickey Allen Bright.

In January 1979 Rickey Allen Bright was convicted of the kidnapping and attempted rape of a seven-year-old girl from Gastonia, North Carolina, and given a life sentence. Over the years Bright applied for parole twice and was shot down both times. But in 1992 Bright got lucky and was allowed to join a special rehab program for inmates called "Mutual Agreement Parole." As part of the new deal he would enter A.A. and volunteer with church groups in work-release projects. If he kept up his end of the bargain and didn't break a single rule, Bright would be eligible for parole.

In 1995 Bright was sprung. After a few months of electronic house arrest he was a free man again. And a few months after that, on October 8, he kidnapped another little girl.

This time Bright struck in his new neighborhood, a small town in the foothills of the Blue Ridge Mountains of North Carolina. Bright crept into a trailer in the middle of the night and grabbed a nine-year-old girl without her mother, sleeping close by, noticing. Bright took the girl to his Chevy Cavalier and raped her, then kept her by his side for hours. She was allowed to leave only after promising she wouldn't tell anybody what happened. Bright drove her to school, but it was closed. The girl was forced to find her way home alone.

In North Carolina the public outcry was immediate: Why was scum like Bright allowed out of the

slammer after only 15 years? "It's a terrible thing to know he's out there," said 43-year-old Terry Smith, father of the girl who had been attacked in 1979. "What's going to stop him from getting another girl? He's got nothing to lose. I couldn't lay down and sleep at night if I was on the parole board." Some former members of the North Carolina parole commission were just as perplexed. "How the hell did he get out of the prison system?" asked Arlene Pulley, who had served as a board member in 1992. "He's the kind of person you can't ever let out." Pulley didn't know how Bright, being a child sex offender, could have been eligible for MAP—that special program that let Bright out early.

Meanwhile, Bright had skipped town for Kentucky, then West Virginia, to see relatives. Then he ended up at Joel Brown's hotel in Ohio for a few weeks and was spotted in Macomb County, Michigan. Finally, thanks to a tip from *America's Most Wanted* viewers, Bright was arrested at 3 A.M. at the Continental Inn in Nashville, Tennessee. Bright was sentenced to between 127 and 158 years in prison, with little chance of enrolling in any "Mutual Agreement Parole" program.

INTERESTING FUGITIVE FACT:
Bright used to play drums in various country-western bands.

445. AUGUSTIN VASQUEZ-MENDOZA, drug lord

LISTED: August 3, 1996
CAPTURED: July 9, 2000
DESCRIPTION: Born on either October 1, 1969, or October 1, 1972, in Apatzingan, Michoacan, Mexico. Five feet three inches, 110 pounds, with brown hair and eyes. Has a three inch-scar on his right forearm, and two of his front teeth are partially capped with silver. Occupations: laborer, construction worker, mate on fishing boats. Fond of cowboy boots and gold chains. Aliases: Fernando Cruzziniga, Anisito Cruzziniiga, Rogelio Cruz-Sunica, Augustin Mendoza, Fernando Vasquez, P. Agustin Vasquez, Anisito Cruz Zuniga, Fernando Zunica.

Burros and Satellites. June 30, 1994, began as a happy day for DEA agent Richard Fass. His buddies at the Phoenix office threw him a going-away party—Fass was scheduled to leave for a comfy desk gig at a foreign post. But before he packed his bags, Fass had one more local assignment: an undercover "buy-bust" at a strip mall.

A "buy-bust" is when a DEA agent tries to score dope, then arrests the dealers once they sell it. Fass, 37 years old and a father of four, took a bag with $167,000 in cash and headed to his meeting point. Fass's body was covered in the fake tattoos and earrings that he'd adopted over his years as an undercover narc. He was glad to be giving them up soon. His final target: a ring of meth dealers. The 167 Gs were meant to purchase 10 kilos' worth. But the dealers must have known something was odd—that, or they were very stupid and greedy. After a tense exchange in which Fass managed to wound one of his suspects, the DEA agent was disarmed and forced to beg for his life. Then one of the dealers, Juan Rubio Vasquez, shot Fass repeatedly in the face with a .45. He and two accomplices walked away with the money.

Within days the shooter and his buddies were rounded up and indicted. Their boss, however, was another matter.

The boss was Vasquez-Mendoza, a baby-faced drug kingpin who the DEA believed masterminded the robbery. By late July the DEA assumed that Vasquez-Mendoza was headed for Mexico to hide.

Two years after the murder Vasquez-Mendoza made the Top Ten list, and a $50,000 price tag was slapped on his head. Later, the bounty was upped to $250,000, then in 1998 it reached a record $2.2 million. "We are not going to give up," DEA special agent Jim Molesa told *The Arizona Republic*. "If we can't get to him directly, we'll make life extremely uncomfortable for him and the people who are housing him. It's just a matter of turning up the heat."

The joint U.S.-Mexican manhunt was hot, indeed; in something resembling a military operation, helicopters and trucks were deployed to the Vasquez-Mendoza's home state of Michoacan to scour every square foot of earth. (The search was so intense at times that local residents complained to human-rights groups.) Then the manhunt swung into the neighboring state of Campeche on the Yucatán peninsula, then south to the state of Puebla.

That's where they eventually found Vasquez-Mendoza, who had kept on the run from state to state, eventually settling in the most remote corner of Puebla he could think of. He took every precaution, too: no cell phones, no Internet account, no modern communications whatsoever. The land surrounding his hideout was rough and dense, and not easily traveled by car. He had changed his name, married, and had two children. "He was living the life of a Mexican bandit from the last century," said

Michael G. Garland, a DEA agent involved in the manhunt.

Vasquez-Mendoza was finally undone by his in-laws. Nobody ratted him out. He just had the habit of calling his new wife's family from a pay phone every Sunday, like clockwork. After some painstaking electronic detective work ("It was a burros and satellite operation," said one DEA official), the boyish drug lord was nabbed on that pay phone on July 9, 2000, a little more than six years since Fass's grisly murder. "When I saw him, he was terrified," recalled Agent Garland. "His hands and feet were shaking."

As of this printing, Vasquez-Mendoza is awaiting extradition to the United States to stand trial.

INTERESTING FUGITIVE FACT:
While hiding, Vasquez-Mendoza adopted the new surname "Cornejo," which just happened to be the surname of a notorious Mexican drug-trafficking family.

446. THANG THANH NGUYEN, robber, murderer

LISTED: August 3, 1996
CAUGHT: January 6, 1998
DESCRIPTION: Born on March 20, 1969, in Soc Trang, Vietnam. Five feet six inches tall, 135 pounds, with black hair and brown eyes. Formerly a cook and has worked in a gambling house and a Vietnamese restaurant. Suspect frequents casinos and gambling houses and associates with members of Vietnamese crime gangs. He may be living in Portland, Oregon; Vancouver, British Columbia; Fort Worth, Texas; Boston, Massachusetts; New York City; or the state of Minnesota. Nguyen drinks heavily and smokes cigarettes. There are pockmarks on his face and a tattoo on his chest.

On the Lam in Vietnam. Thang Thanh Nguyen's Wanted poster listed a host of possible hiding places. As it turned out, none of them were even close, not by a hemisphere.

Back January 1992 Nguyen decided to tap three buddies and do a little home invasion at his boss's place in Irondequoit, New York, just north of Rochester. Nguyen worked as a cook at Chung Lam's restaurant and had the idea that Lam was holding a nice pile of cash and gold at home. The gang of four showed up, and Lam ended up shot in the stomach and back of the head—in front of his family's horrified eyes. Somehow, one of Nguyen's accomplices also caught a bullet. After the gang split up, two of them were caught when one decided to have his wound treated; another was nabbed in Fort Worth, Texas. Nguyen, however, was nowhere to be found.

In July 1992 Nguyen was indicted for murder by a Monroe County grand jury; he was named to the Ten Most Wanted list a little more than four years later.

Soon, nearly every FBI bureau office was looking for Nguyen. Then came a tip that the fugitive had actually skipped town big time—all the way to Vietnam. At the time Nguyen probably thought it was the safest move he could make. After all, even the FBI would have a hard time penetrating communist Vietnam.

Nguyen didn't count on how determined the FBI can be.

Perhaps he wasn't aware that the FBI had 32 legal attaché offices around the world, meant for cases just like this. Through the legal attaché in Bangkok, the FBI gave Nguyen's vitals to the United States Embassy in Hanoi and the People's Police in Vietnam. All three worked together to track down Nguyen in the Bac Lieu province. He was arrested there on December 22, 1997, and turned over to the U.S. authorities a few weeks later. "The arrest is an exceptional example of the benefits of cooperation in every level of law enforcement—local, state national and international," said FBI director Louis Freeh. Suddenly, the world seemed just a bit small for Top Ten fugitives.

Nguyen was convicted of murder in a Rochester courtroom on July 31, 1998, and faced 25 years to life.

INTERESTING FUGITIVE FACT:
The Lam family had actually befriended Nguyen, but he decided to rob them anyway.

447. GLEN STEWART GODWIN, murderer

LISTED: December 7, 1996
STILL ON LIST (as of this printing)
DESCRIPTION: Born on June 26, 1958. Six feet tall, 170 pounds, with black hair and green eyes. Also goes by the aliases: Michael Carrerra, Miguel Carerra, Michael Carmen, Glen Godwin, Glen S. Godwin, Dennis H. McWilliams, and Dennis Harold McWilliams. Fond of extensive trips, fancy hotels, restaurants, and clothes. Current bounty on his head: $50,000.

The Escape Artist. Of course Shelly DeLeeuw had no idea that her sweet Glen would turn out to be a cold-blooded killer. To her he was simply this charming, good-looking preppie who would often stop by the hamburger stand in Texas where she worked. Glen loved playing tennis and was moderately successful as a salesmen, hawking restaurant supplies and novelties across the state. Even though she was only 16, and Glen was five years older, they started dating. "He was a perfect gentleman all the way," DeLeeuw would later say.

But six months later, Shelly's "perfect gentleman" had to split—his mother needed him back in Palm Springs. The two kept in touch through letters and phone calls, and he stopped back for a visit the following year. But late in 1981 Glen stopped calling. Shelly couldn't figure it out. What had happened? Was it something she said?

Her question was answered in the spring of 1982, with a call from Glen's dad: Her ex-boyfriend was in prison for murder.

A particularly grisly murder, in fact. Godwin had stabbed his drug dealer best friend 26 times, then stuffed his body in a truck and blew it up with dynamite in an effort to hide the evidence. Godwin was caught, convicted, and given 26 years to life. (Apparently Godwin left these details out of his love letters.)

Soon, though, Godwin got back in touch, insisting that the cops had put the wrong guy in jail, and it would all be okay after an appeal. And would she marry him? Shelly, being nobody's sucker, thought no way. But he kept working at her. Finally, after two years of pestering, Shelly agreed to visit him in person. "I still cared for him and what happened to him," she later explained.

But Godwin had already sprung a trap of love: a minister and the Godwin family lying in wait, all of them ready for a good old-fashioned prison wedding. Surprisingly, Shelly said, "I do."

The groom continued to serve time.

Then came the interesting part. Sixteen months to the day after his wedding, June 5, 1987, Godwin escaped from maximum-security lockup at Folsom State Prison. Somehow, he'd seen the blueprints to the joint and realized a drainage system ran from inside to out. Then a former cellmate of Godwin's started to hack away at the 1,000-foot drainage pipe from the outside. Meanwhile, Godwin managed to change his own classification so he was allowed to move to the main yard. "He paid off some inmates to change his records," said Tim Virga, a corrections officer who was on duty during Godwin's escape. "It allowed him to work in Oak Lawn, which is basically on the other side of the building from where he was working and also where a storm drain came to the surface."

In early June the escape hatch was ready. Godwin took it, rode a raft across the river, then hopped into a waiting car. Prison officials say the escape took less than 20 minutes.

Oddly enough, six months later, Godwin was picked up in Mexico for drug trafficking in Jalisco state. He got seven years, and then the police found out he was a Top Tenner. Godwin knew he had to do something, otherwise he was on the fast track back to the States. So he killed one of the inmates, a desperate move that halted his extradition fast. Then Godwin made some buddies on the inside, who helped him break out in September 1991.

The FBI named Godwin to the Top Ten list late in 1996 in an effort to end his decade-long run. Since then he's been spotted in Hawaii and San Francisco. Both tips failed to help the FBI nab Godwin.

And as for Shelly Godwin, neé DeLeeuw? She met up with Godwin after his escape from Folsom State and remained on the lam with him until his arrest in Mexico. DeLeeuw claims she was forced; authorities believe she helped him hide. DeLeeuw divorced her fugitive husband while he was at Jalisco State, and she later moved to East Dallas, where the FBI found her. Some have reported that after breaking out of Jalisco, Godwin ordered a hit on his ex-wife, but it was never carried out. The hunt for Godwin continues. *(See page 295 in Appendix II for information on how to report a Top Tenner to the FBI.)*

INTERESTING FUGITIVE FACT:
Prior to cutting up his best friend, Godwin had been an ordinary citizen with no priors—unusual for a Top Tenner.

448. DAVID ALEX ALVAREZ, murderer

LISTED: December 14, 1996
CAUGHT: May 20, 1997
DESCRIPTION: Born on February 23, 1967, in Los Angeles. Five feet eight inches tall, 180 pounds, with black hair and brown eyes. Alvarez has been known to have tattoos on his chest, right knee, and "Patricia" on his neck. He has scars on his right forearm. He is fluent in English and Spanish. He may wear his hair very short and may be clean shaven. He is believed to have been in parts of Mexico and may also travel extensively along the southwestern U.S. border. Alvarez is believed to be a member of an East Los Angeles gang called "The Avenues." Aliases: David Alejandro Alvarez, Dominic Alex Alvarez, Miguel Alvarez Jr., and "Spooky."

The Ex-ecutioner. Nobody ever taught David Alvarez that violence begets violence. Or if they did, it never sank in.

Alvarez used to beat his wife until he got thrown in jail for it. Two years later, he was out on parole and went back to his estranged wife to kidnap and beat her some more. This time his in-laws got involved and allegedly exacted brutal payback on Alvarez, hoping to teach him that he should keep his fists to himself. But he didn't learn his lesson. On September 29, 1996, Alvarez and an accomplice broke into his ex-wife's peaceful new suburban home, looking to inflict more punishment. But his ex-wife wasn't home. Instead, Alvarez and 21-year-old Trinia Irene Aguirre bound, shot, and stabbed nine-year-old Evelyn Torres and her 12-year-old sister, Massiel. Then they killed the girls' uncle and even an innocent gardener who picked the wrong house to work that afternoon.

"I think any time you talk about an individual that shoots and kills four individuals, two children execution-style, we're talking about a pretty vicious individual," said FBI spokesman John Hoos. There's no surefire way to make the Top Ten list, but killing two children in cold blood certainly eases the process. Alvarez was named to the on list December 14, 1996, and Los Angeles County and Baldwin Park officials offered a $15,000 reward for information leading to his capture.

The cops had nabbed his partner, Aguirre, in late November, but by then Alvarez had already high-tailed to Mexico. He bought contact lenses to make his brown eyes blue and had plastic surgery to change the shape of his nose. But that didn't help him stay hidden very long. According to Tim McNally, the FBI's assistant director in Los Angeles, tips poured in from people who saw Alvarez on the FBI's website, as well as his profile on *America's Most Wanted*. This helped Mexican cops track him to a Chinese restaurant in downtown Tijuana, and then arrest him. At the time, Alvarez claimed that he was innocent and only ran to Mexico (and changed his eyes and nose) because his ex-wife's allegations. "I was a 'three strikes' candidate already," he said.

INTERESTING FUGITIVE FACT:
Alvarez was a professional killer; he used to work as a bug exterminator.

449. ANDREW PHILLIP CUNANAN, murderer

LISTED: June 12, 1997
FOUND DEAD: July 24, 1997
DESCRIPTION: Born on August 31, 1969, in San Diego, California. Five feet, 10 inches tall, 160 pounds, with dark brown hair and brown eyes. May wear prescription eyeglasses. Believed to be driving a red 1995 Chevy pickup truck with dark interior, New Jersey license plate KH993D. Aliases: Andrew DeSilva, Commander Andy Cummings.

A New Kind of Killer. Take a bit of Jeffrey Dahmer, throw in some Gary Ray Bowles, and finally pepper with Charles Manson and you might get a strange dish resembling Andrew Cunanan. Expert profilers are still uncertain how to classify Cunanan, who at times acted like a serial killer (taking delight in torturing his victims), at other times a spree killer (hopping from murder to murder in quick succession) and finally, as a celebrity killer (pumping a bullet into the brain of world-famous clothing designer Gianni Versace).

Cunanan's motive is still uncertain, too. Some suspected he killed just because he enjoyed it; other claim he was seeking revenge on a former lover who may have given him the AIDS virus. What is clear is the bloody trail of murder Cunanan left behind: five dead bodies over a four-month period. At each murder scene Cunanan left so many clues, it was as if he were taunting his pursuers. "His ego is not allowing him to stop killing," said Bill Hagmire, chief of the FBI's child-abduction and serial-killer unit in an interview with the *Los Angeles Times*. "He seems to have a procedure with his victim selection and what some might call a signature."

Cunanan's serial-spree began in late April 1997, when he flew from his hometown San Diego to visit a former lover, 33-year-old David Madson, in Minneapolis. After Madson failed to show up at work for two days, some of his coworkers called his building manager, who discovered a gruesome tableau in Madson's trendy apartment: blood everywhere, a fully clothed dead man rolled up in a plush, bloodied Oriental rug, and a gore-caked claw hammer resting nearby. Nearby was the first Cunanan clue: a nylon gym bag containing an empty gun holster and bearing a name tag—Andrew Cunanan, San Diego.

But the corpse in the carpet turned out not to be Madson, but a Persian Gulf war vet named Jeffrey Trail. The 28-year-old propane company engineer was also a former lover of Cunanan's. At first the police suspected Madson as the killer—his red Jeep Cherokee was missing—then later pieced together that Cunanan and Madson were probably working together. "They intended at some point to get rid of the body," said Minneapolis Police sergeant. Bob Ticich. "They may have been surprised. It's very possible they were in close proximity while we were searching."

Days later, a body was found near shell casings and Jeep tracks some 45 miles north of Minneapolis. It was Madson, who had been shot in the back and the eye. From the defensive wounds found on Madson's fingers, police theorized that he knew it was coming.

Now Cunanan was officially a fugitive. The FBI was brought in to help find him. Gay websites posted Cunanan's photo and warned people of his "chameleon" personality. A bulletin went out for Madson's red 1995 Jeep Cherokee—but it wasn't missing for long. The next day, May 4, it was found outside the posh three-story home of Lee Miglin, a 72-year-old famed Chicago land developer. His wife, Marilyn, had found Miglin's body in their garage, and it was another scene straight out of a horror movie. Miglin had his throat slashed and his chest worked over with a gardening saw, and his body was bound up in masking tape. There was a slit through the tape around Miglin's mouth, presumably so he could breathe. Presumably, so he could live long enough to know he was being tortured.

Outside in the stolen Jeep Cherokee were photos of Cunanan; inside, a half-eaten ham sandwich, which police believe Cunanan made for himself after butchering Miglin. There was also evidence that Cunanan had used Miglin's own razor to shave.

Miglin's green 1994 Lexus was now missing, and police followed Cunanan's trail—by a cellular phone in the Lexus—through Pennsylvania. In Pennsville, New Jersey, Cunanan killed a 45-year-old cemetery worker named William Reese with a single gunshot to the head just to steal his red Chevy pickup truck. At the scene were Cunanan's passport and newspaper clippings about the manhunt. Cunanan was clearly enjoying himself, which frustrated law enforcement officials no end.

In early June Cunanan was named to the Top Ten list. "You newspaper types laugh at that," said one law enforcement officer to the *Los Angeles Times*. "But it helps keep it in front of the public." Over 400 FBI agents were on the hunt for Cunanan, their search largely taking place in his hometown of San Diego. Cunanan, meanwhile, had already driven to Florida and had been living at the Normandy Plaza

Hotel in South Beach—a hotel that caters to a gay clientele. There he holed up, reading about himself in *Time, Newsweek,* and *Vanity Fair*—Cunanan's favorite magazine. The June issue featured a gorgeous spread about Donatella Versace (Gianni's sister) and Casa Casuarina, the family's gorgeous South Beach mansion. Cunanan must have read this with great interest and realized it wasn't very far away.

What was to follow on July 15 would become one of the most infamous murders of the 1990s—the slaying of Gianni Versace. The gun and bullets used—a .40 caliber Taurus semiautomatic, with Golden Saber hollow-point shells—were the same Cunanan had used to kill Madson and Reese. Versace had been bent over, unlocking his front gate, and never knew what hit him, according to police. Cunanan ran. There was no time to leave behind photos or passports this time, but there were witnesses to the murder. And Reese's red pickup truck was found blocks away.

Cunanan fled to a houseboat nearly 40 blocks away. The two-story boat, named *The New Year,* was owned by a German named Frank Matthias Ruehl, who owned a gay club in Las Vegas. He was discovered nine days after the murder by a 71-year-old caretaker named Fernando Carreira. "The door was unlocked," said Carreira during a local television interview. "I walked in and the lights were on. I thought it was a bum, or something." Carreira heard a gunshot on the second floor, then fled to call the police. Authorities found Cunanan dead, propped up on two pillows. He'd shoved the same semiautomatic he'd used to kill Madson, Reese, and Versace in his own mouth, then pulled the trigger.

For all of the clues Cunanan left at various murder sites, none of them clued the FBI or police into his motives. (Rumors floated that Versace may have known Cunanan, but nothing more than chance encounters at gay parties four years in the past could be corroborated.) Immediately after Cunanan was found dead, the FBI and Miami police were criticized for not finding Cunanan fast enough, not alerting the gay community to his presence fast enough, and not following up on leads fast enough. "I don't think law enforcement has anything to be embarrassed about," said Larry Collins, special agent in charge of the FBI's Chicago office. "It's not quite as easy as people might think to locate one individual in 250 million people."

Or one individual like Cunanan, who broke every serial killer mold, driven by desires few can fathom.

INTERESTING FUGITIVE FACT:
Cunanan was voted "Least Likely to Be Forgotten" at the exclusive Bishop's High School in La Jolla, California.

450. PAUL RAGUSA, gangster

LISTED: September 6, 1997
CAUGHT: January 30, 1998
DESCRIPTION: Born on Christmas Day 1970; five feet 10 inches, 170 pounds, light brown hair and hazel eyes. Nickname: "Paulie." Able to speak fluent Italian.

Generation X Goodfella. Paul Ragusa's birthday happened to be Christmas, but he considered the borough of Queens his personal gift sack all year long. He was allegedly the ringleader of a gang of young thugs called the "Giannini Crew," named for the neighborhood café in which the boys met to plot their bloody heists.

Between 1992 and 1996 the crew of teenagers and early twentysomethings allegedly knocked over banks all over Queens—including the same Ridgewood bank three times—and even tried to burn down Ragusa's own pizza shop, which he'd named "Goodfellas." When one crew member knocked up a 15-year-old girl, he ordered her to have an abortion. The girl, then six months pregnant, refused, and the crew pumped a bullet into her stomach. She survived, but her baby didn't.

On the first day of summer 1993, the Crew decided to take on an armored car. The two uniformed guards happened to be retired NYPD officers. Both were shot at with automatic weapons, and one was seriously wounded. By 1996 the gang was charged in a federal indictment with racketeering, armed robbery, armed bank robbery, and arson.

Ragusa and his crew were largely the offspring of the Bonanno and Colombo mob families. Paulie's father, Fillipo Ragusa, was wanted in 1984 for heroin trafficking. He fled the house mere hours before the cops arrived and remained at large for six years before surrendering; his son Paulie pulled off the same trick on June 21, 1996, when authorities came to raid his house. They nabbed 13 members of the Giannini Crew, but missed Ragusa by a matter of minutes. "It's kind of ironic," said FBI special agent Lewis Schiliro in *New York Newsday.* "It was the same thing when we went to arrest the father."

Finally, in September 1997, Ragusa was named to the Top Ten list, and a $50,000 reward was slapped on his head. (A local bankers' organization kicked in an additional $10,000.) Ragusa replaced another violent twentysomething, Andrew Cunanan. "Our belief is that he is still around in the metropolitan area," Schiliro said at the time. "Ragusa and his crew have connections to the Bonanno and Colombo families, either directly or through their parents. They have the resources to hide this guy."

However, the Feds and the NYPD used these family connections to their advantage, squeezing Paulie's relatives until he was forced to show himself, according to FBI agent Jim Margolin. "There couldn't have been any doubt in his mind that we were on to him," he said. According to famed mob columnist Jerry Capeci, the FBI-NYPD task force hunting Ragusa threatened to squeeze the fugitive's father and his sister on a variety of charges if he didn't give himself up. (A few days before Christmas, Ragusa's sister Francesca had been arrested for drug trafficking.)

Apparently the pressure worked. On a Friday morning in late January Ragusa walked into the FBI's Manhattan headquarters and gave himself up. He'd tried to change his appearance, dyeing his brown hair a bright yellow and growing a goatee. Word of the surrender got out to the media fast, and by the time agents were escorting Ragusa out of headquarters, an army of media was there to meet him.

Ragusa reportedly looked around, stunned, and said, "You guys have to let Gotti out, because these guys [obviously] miss him."

INTERESTING FUGITIVE FACT:
Paulie used to work in both a pizza shop and a bakery. (That is, when he wasn't busy trying to burn them down.)

451. RAMON EDUARDO ARELLANO-FELIX, drug lord

LISTED: September 24, 1997
STILL ON LIST (as of this printing)
DESCRIPTION: Born on August 31, 1964. Six feet two inches tall, 220 pounds, with brown hair and brown eyes. Nickname: "El Comandante Mon." Aliases: Gilberto Camacho Rodriguez, Ramon Torres-Mendez, El Walin, and simply "Ray." Current reward: $2 million.

Plata o Plomo. In the mid-1990s the War on Drugs raged on. The infamous Gulf Cartel had been dealt a serious blow with the capture and imprisonment of its leader, JUAN GARCIA-ABREGO (#440). Not long after, the head of the Juarez drug cartel, Amado Carillo Fuentes, died after botched plastic surgery. That left one huge, nasty fish in the sea of drug-trafficking: the Arellano-Felix organization—also known as the Tijuana cartel, and responsible for much of the cocaine supply in the United States. The cartel is run by the seven Arellano-Felix brothers, and its lead enforcer is 33-year-old Ramon—the most brutal man in an already brutal organization. "Not since the Colombian Cali cartel have we seen an organization so willing and quick to use violence," said Bill Gore, the FBI San Diego office chief in an interview with the *Washington Post*.

The Arellano-Felix brothers rule their Tijuana-based organization by *plata o plomo*—translated as "silver or lead," or more to the point, "bribes or bullets." You can agree to turn a blind eye to brothers' activities and become modestly rich, or you can choose to buck the system and get greased. For many it's not a tough decision. (An FBI-DEA task force estimated that the gang pays out $1 million *a week* in bribes to Mexican officials alone.) Even those who aren't on the Arellano-Felix payroll are swayed by the whole romantic ideal of the brothers—much like the Mafia dons and capos who are given a weird form of respect in the United States. And for those officials who refuse to accept the *plata* or former cartel members who chose to snitch? Ramon pays a visit. That's his job; he does it well.

No one knows the exact number of bloodied corpses that lie at Ramon's feet. He is suspected of at least 10 gangland-style slayings of Mexican cops since 1994. In 1993, he is thought to have orchestrated the assassination of Roman Catholic cardinal Juan Jesus Posadas Ocampo. Some estimate Ramon or his enforcement squad have killed more than 200 people for a variety of reasons—snitching to the Feds, maybe, or insulting a member of the cartel. (One poor guy was reportedly killed because he dated one of the Arellano-Felix sisters.) Ramon himself has been racking up indictments since 1980, but many of them have faded, since witnesses have had a funny of way of disappearing.

U.S. authorities see Ramon as the weak link that can be used to blast the Tijuana cartel to pieces. "The point is to highlight this cartel's criminality and make [Ramon] socially unacceptable in the society in which he has operated," said a senior U.S. law enforcement officer in the pages of the *Los Angeles Times*. "No one should be caught dead with him after this." Nonetheless, Ramon has reportedly been seen flaunting himself on both sides of the U.S.-Mexico border—in hotels, restaurants, and discos. As of this printing, he remains at large. *(See page 295 in Appendix II for information on how to report a Top Tenner to the FBI.)*

INTERESTING FUGITIVE FACT:
In addition to being a brutal punisher with seemingly no conscience, Ramon is guilty of appalling taste: He has been known to favor leather pants and disco music.

452. TONY RAY AMATI, murderer, robber

LISTED: February 21, 1998
CAUGHT: February 27, 1998
DESCRIPTION: Born on June 28, 1976, in Carbondale, Illinois. Five feet six inches tall, 145 pounds, with brown hair and green eyes. Aliases: Phillip D. Gitlitz, Anthony Ray Jones, Debon D. Restivito, Shane W. Wade. Reward: $50,000.

"Killa Ray." Three murders in three months. A drywall worker named Michael Matta was shot more than 20 times and died in a parking lot in May 1996. Two months later, 48-year-old John Garcia was shot to death in his own garage, only a block away from where Matta had died. Three weeks later, 49-year-old Keith Dyer was gunned down outside of his apartment when he was walking a coworker, Stacey Dooley, to her apartment. Dyer was shot 13 times in the back—certainly more than was needed to kill the man. Dooley survived the attack and remembers the three black-clad gunmen laughing as they ran away. "It was overkill," said an FBI special agent involved in the case.

What had touched off this bloodbath? Stolen guns and the sick, giddy impulse to take them for a test drive. Tony Amati, along with buddies Troy Sampson and Eddie James, broke into a Vegas gun shop and hauled away 75 weapons, intending to sell them. But police theorize that the trio was also trigger-happy, eager to test the merchandise. They chose Matta as their test dummy. A few months after the Dyer slaying, Amati and crew were arrested after trying to pawn the hot iron off on a pair of undercover detectives. The police searched Amati's home and found the laser-sighted handgun that had been used to kill Dyer, Garcia, and Matta. But by the time ballistics matched the weapon to the three killings, Amati had already jumped bail.

On February 21, 1998, Amati was named to the Top Ten list, and his story was featured on *America's Most Wanted*. Just minutes after the show ended, a tip came in from Knoxville, Tennessee. Amati was hiding out as "Jeff" in Atlanta, working as a door-to-door magazine salesman. Another tipster led the FBI to a motel in Marietta, Georgia, where they nailed Amati. He'd dyed his hair and was wearing glasses.

In a letter to a fellow inmate, Amati signed his name "Killa Ray" and referred to himself as a "Death Row achiever." But in the trial that followed, Amati begged for his life: "I'm sorry this had to happen," Amati told the court. "Let me live." The jury apparently listened. In early December 1999 Amati was sentenced to life in prison, with the possibility of parole in 40 years. Charges against his alleged accomplices, Sampson and James, were dropped.

INTERESTING FUGITIVE FACT:
In court Amati was shown to have "obsessive-compulsive disorder, with excessive tidiness and a preoccupation with detail."

453. HARRY JOSEPH BOWMAN, racketeer, murderer

LISTED: March 14, 1998
CAUGHT: June 7, 1999
DESCRIPTION: Born on July 17, 1949. Five feet 10 inches tall, 190 pounds, with black hair and brown eyes. Bowman has several tattoos reflecting his association with the Outlaws Motorcycle Club: a skull with crossed pistons and "Outlaws" above and "Detroit" below, a swastika on his right forearm, a "Merlin the Magician" figure on his left, and other assorted tattoos. Aliases: Harry Bouman, David Bowman, Harry Bowman, Harry J. Bowman, Harry Joe Bowman, David Charles Dowman, Harry Douman, Harry Tyree, "Taco," and "T." Reward: $50,000.

Taco Hell. In late March 2000, from his jail cell in Tampa, Florida, Bowman managed to have a message posted on the Internet at www.outlawsmc.com, the official website of the Outlaws Motorcycle Club. "I'd like to express my best wishes to all participating in the furtherance of what's closest to all of our hearts, Biking and Brotherhood!"

No doubt, Bowman was serious about the brotherhood—he would seemingly do anything to protect it, even if that meant punishing his own. His string of murders stretched back to 1982, when he was accused of killing a fellow Outlaws member named

Arthur Allen Vincent in Ormond Beach, Florida. Bowman is also thought to have iced another Outlaw in 1995. Authorities also think Bowman killed Raymond Chaffin, president of the rival Warlocks biker club in 1991 and had a hand in bombing two rival biker clubhouses—one in Florida, the other in Chicago. The Chicago blast, which targeted the Hell's Henchmen club, hurt no one, but partially damaged six private homes. The reason? To protest the alliance between the Hell's Henchmen and the Hell's Angels. Aside from killing and bombing, Bowman and the Outlaws were accused of distributing methamphetamine and opium, racketeering, extortion, and robbery.

The Outlaws began as the "McCook Outlaws Motorcycle Club" in a bar outside of Chicago in 1935; their website maintains that they are simply guys who ride Harleys, wear black leather, and have tattoos—and are being persecuted by the federal government. They certainly weren't wrong about the last part. As part of a nationwide push to crack down on the Outlaws, the group was indicted for a laundry list of criminal activity in 1997. Bowman became a fugitive soon after.

A few months after Bowman was named to the Top Ten list, a tip came in: "Taco" was visiting buddies in Sterling Heights, Michigan, a suburb of Detroit. At 9:15 P.M. on Monday, June 7, 1999, a squad of 40 FBI agents, SWAT team members, and local police descended upon the home where Bowman had holed up. They warned neighbors to lock their doors and hide in basements until further notice, then called Bowman. "Our negotiators spoke to him on the phone, and he knew that the house was surrounded," said Nick Walsh, an FBI special agent in charge of the Detroit division in an interview with the *Detroit Free Press*. Bowman surrendered peacefully, much to the relief of neighbors. "I feel a little better knowing that he's not a serial killer," said one woman who lived next door to Bowman's hideout.

Bowman, who was clean-shaved and had trimmed up his hair a bit to differentiate himself from his Most Wanted poster, was extradited to Florida a few days later.

INTERESTING FUGITIVE FACT:
Because the Outlaws suspect the federal government of reading their website's guest book, the following warning appears there: "We ask that you NOT post any references or messages to Taco at this time in the guest book. . . . Please respect this request."

454. ERIC ROBERT RUDOLPH, terrorist

LISTED: May 5, 1998
CAUGHT: May 31, 2003
DESCRIPTION: Born on September 19, 1966, in Merritt Island, Florida. Five feet 11 inches tall, and 165 to 180 pounds with brown hair and blue eyes. Rudolph was once a carpenter and handyman, and has a noticeable scar on his chin.

Fugitive in the Mountains. The last time anyone saw Eric Rudolph alive, he had just purchased $500 worth of supplies: vitamins, food supplements, canned food, dried food, and a five-gallon white plastic tub of honey. His getaway was almost as sweet.

More than 150 people have been injured by the bombs allegedly set by Rudolph. The most famous was the knapsack bomb that exploded right in the middle of the 1996 Olympics in Atlanta's Centennial Park. Others included a double-bombing at a gay bar in Atlanta, and an abortion clinic in north Atlanta. The most recent was a dynamite-nail bomb that exploded inside the New Woman All Women Health Care clinic in Birmingham, Alabama, on January 20, 1998, killing one off-duty cop named Robert Sanderson and blasting the head nurse, Emily Lyons, with dozens of speeding nails. But as the bomber made his getaway, someone noted his license plate.

That's when the police first learned the name Eric Rudolph, a 32-year-old carpenter and outdoorsman who served time as a demolition expert in the U.S. Army and lived in a $275-a-month trailer in northwestern North Carolina. He'd grown up in this area and was raised in the teachings of "Christian Identity," a movement that believed the country should be run by the Bible, not law; that whites were God's chosen people; and that abortion and homosexuality were aberrations that should be severely punished. (Letters from "God's Army" claimed responsibility for many of Rudolph's bombings.) Extreme forms of protest seem to run in the Rudolph family. Not long after news broke that Rudolph was being pursued by the FBI, his brother Daniel took a power saw and sliced off one of his hands, videotaping the whole gory procedure. "This is for the FBI and the media," he said, looking straight into the camera.

In 1996 Rudolph was living near Murphy, North Carolina, and calling himself "Bob Randolph." Neighbors gave the stereotypical description of the modern psycho. He was quiet and polite and always paid his bills on time (and in cash). In fact, the only thing that seemed to anger him were all of the transplants from Florida who'd moved into the area—he called them "Floridiots."

By the time authorities arrived at the secluded trailer, Rudolph had already started running—in a hurry, too. Lights were on, CNN was blaring on the television, and his front door was ajar. Still, Rudolph had an advantage; he'd slipped into North Carolina's Nantahala mountains, an area Rudolph knew like the back of his hand. The woods in that area are thick, and FBI agents on the hunt said it was hard to see more than a few feet in any direction. "We could have walked within five feet of Rudolph and not seen him," said one agent. Helicopters with infrared scanners flew overhead. Two bloodhounds named Colombo and Quincy were imported from Texas. More than 100 federal agents and local officers poked through every barn, outhouse, and flower pot in the area. Nothing. "The area is vast," said FBI special agent Craig Dahle in *Time* magazine. "And the locals say, 'Lotsa luck.'"

The last person to see him was George Nordmann, the owner of a health food shop in Andrews, North Carolina. Nordmann was a casual acquaintance of Rudolph's and was surprised to see how Rudolph had changed; he'd grown a beard, a ponytail and seemed to have lost some weight. The next day, while Nordmann was at his shop, Rudolph took roughly 50 pounds of groceries from the house and left five $100 bills in exchange. Investigators would find some empty containers now and again—a tuna can, a vitamin bottle, an oatmeal box. But no Rudolph.

On May 31, 2003, a rookie cop named Jeffrey Postell arrested a suspicious character in a camouflage jacket who was digging through a dumpster behind a Save-a-Lot supermarket in Murphy, North Carolina. The man claimed to be "Jerry Wilson" but soon turned out to be 36-year-old Eric Rudolph, who had been on the run for five years. "I didn't have a clue who he was," admitted Postell. Not long after Rudolph's arrest and fingerprint identification check, Rudolph asked for fresh fruit and a Bible.

While in custody, the former fugitive refused to admit his guilt but told his captors stories about his time in the North Carolina woods—which he said he treated as one long, long camping trip. Rudolph claimed he survived by hunting deer, bear, and turkey with a .223-caliber rifle as well as by eating acorns. Even salamanders found their way into his diet. "I just swallowed them whole, like sushi," Rudolph

said. He avoided fishing, for fear the running water would dampen the sound of approaching footsteps. Rudolph also said that he had no help from anyone else; he spent his five years on the run completely alone. He added that he had been without the company of a woman for so long that "even the bears started looking good."

At press time, Rudolph faced the death penalty in two states.

INTERESTING FUGITIVE FACT:
Rudolph was very prompt about returning rented videos—even after allegedly blowing up buildings. Ten hours after the Birmingham blast, Rudolph returned one tape and then rented an action-adventure flick. "He's always been very prompt," said video store clerk Dedra McGrady.

455. JAMES CHARLES KOPP, murderer

LISTED: June 7, 1999
CAUGHT: March 29, 2001
DESCRIPTION: Born on August 2, 1954. Five feet seven inches tall, 150 to 175 pounds, with brownish red hair and blue-gray eyes. Kopp has a long list of aliases, including John Kapp, Clyde Swenson, Jack Crotty, Charles Cooper, John Capp, Jim Cobb, Samuel E. Weinstein, Jaco I. Croninger, Enoch A. Guettler, Jonathan H. Henderson, Soloman E. Aranburg, Dwight Hanson, K. Jawes Gavin, P. Anastation, as well as the nicknames "Atomic Dog" and "Catfish." Kopp wears glasses, may limp, and has a scar on the top of his left hand, near his thumb. Reward: $650,000.

Kopp, Killer. James Kopp couldn't believe that his girlfriend, Jennifer, had an abortion without his consent. "It just broke him," said his stepmother, Lynn Kopp, in *The New York Times Magazine*. "When he found out about it, it just flipped him out." It is uncertain if Jennifer's abortion was the pivotal moment in Kopp's life, one that turned a shy, quiet marine biology major into a man who would use a high-powered rifle to assassinate a father of four as he puttered around his own kitchen. But what is clear is that not long after the incident, Kopp became deeply religious. And deeply, *violently* opposed to the idea of abortions.

Kopp began protesting in 1984 and soon found himself arrested nine times for trespassing and aggravated assault outside San Francisco clinics. By 1988 he had joined Operation Rescue—a group that blockaded abortion clinics—and observed that protesters with their arms linked together would be harder to remove. The group's shining moment came during the 1988 Democratic Convention in Atlanta, where some 100 protesters blocked clinics and were thrown into jail. The protesters refused to give their real names and instead preached and prayed in their holding cells. According to a *New York Times* story, a number of those anonymous protesters would go on to some degree of infamy, including Rachelle Shannon, who would be convicted of shooting and wounding a doctor, and John Arena, later famous for attacking clinics with poisonous butyric acid.

In 1994 it became illegal to block abortion clinic entrances. So Kopp tried a different strategy.

Late in the evening of October 23, 1998, Dr. Bernard A. Slepian was in the kitchen of his Amherst, New York, home. The 52-year-old man was heating up a can of soup and chatting with his wife and one of his kids. Without warning, a bullet came screaming through the window. Dr. Slepian died two hours later. A neighborhood jogger later reported a suspicious vehicle—a black 1987 Chevy Cavalier with Vermont plates—had been parked in the area a few days before. The car was traced back to Kopp and eventually found in a parking lot at Newark Airport that December. Back in Amherst investigators matched a hair from the murder scene to a hair from the Cavalier. Four months later, they found the murder weapon buried in the woods behind the Slepian home.

Kopp, meanwhile, had fled the country. The FBI would eventually track him to Ireland, where he was moving from city to city, working clerical-type jobs and using public phones and anonymous e-mail services to communicate with two anti-abortion activists back in the United States, Dennis J. Malvasi and Loretta Marra, a married couple living in Brooklyn. As of this writing, a federal complaint alleges that Malvasi and Marra plotted to send Kopp enough money to allow him to sneak back into the United States. Wiretaps and intercepted e-mail exchanges helped reveal the plan. One message from Kopp read: "As soon as I get about 1,000, the sooner you will see this smiling face."

However, when Kopp showed up at a village post office in western France to collect $300 of that money, French police were there waiting for him. He was arrested without incident. While French authorities are typically reluctant to extradite suspects who might face the death penalty—as Kopp certainly would—authorities as of this writing were working to bring Kopp back to the United States for a trial.

Canadian authorities might also like a word with Kopp; he's suspected in three nonfatal shootings of doctors in 1994, 1995, and 1997.

INTERESTING FUGITIVE FACT:
Kopp used to be an Eagle Scout and played trombone in his high school band.

456. USAMA BIN LADEN, terrorist

LISTED: June 7, 1999
STILL ON LIST (as of this printing)
DESCRIPTION: Born in 1957 in Saudi Arabia. Six foot four inches to six feet six inches, 165 pounds, with black hair and brown eyes. Bin Laden has a thin build and is known to walk with a cane. Aliases: Usama Bin Muhammad Bin Ladin, Shaykh Usama Bin Ladin, the Prince, the Emir, Abu Abdallah, Mujahid Shaykh, Hajj, and the Director. Current reward: $25 million.

International Public Enemy Number One. If every generation needs a Hitler, the current generation has Usama Bin Laden. Bin Laden has the dubious honor of being the most-feared man in America during the turn of the 21st century. He seems to delight in the idea of punishing the United States for perceived offenses against the Middle East. "If someone can kill an American soldier," said Bin Laden in an interview, "it is better than wasting time on other matters." He has been linked to dozens of terrorist acts, either planned or perpetrated, including the 1993 bombing of the World Trade Center (see RAMZI AHMED YOUSEF, #436), a bombing at the Egyptian Embassy in Pakistan, plots to assassinate Bill Clinton and the Pope, as well as a plan to blast six American 747 planes out of the sky. Bin Laden's bombing of U.S. embassies in Kenya and Tanzania killed more than 200 people and injured an astounding 4,000. But Bin Laden will forever be remembered for his most brazen terrorist act: sending planes to crash into the World Trade Center and Pentagon on September 11, 2001, which killed thousands of innocent people and horrified a nation.

Bin Laden was the 17th of 52 children, born to a rich Saudi builder who had 10 wives. Despite being one of many, Bin Laden inherited about $250 million from his father, which he used to fund his terrorist strikes against the United States. He fought on the side of the American-backed *mujahadeen* ("holy warriors") in the Afghanistan War in the early 1980s, but later came to despise the United States's involvement in the affairs of Middle Eastern countries. He then founded a group called Al Qaeda, which is Arabic for "The Base." Its mission: to repel non-Islamic governments with violence. In the following decade two countries kicked him out for supporting terrorist groups—first Saudi Arabia in 1991, then Sudan in 1996. Back in Afghanistan, Bin Laden started training his troops. War was coming. And he was going to start it.

At 9:30 A.M. on August 7, 1998, a Bin Laden henchman named Rashed Dauoud Al-'Owhali drove to the front doors of the U.S. Embassy in Kenya, armed with a pistol, grenade, and an extremely powerful bomb. Al-'Owhali hurled the grenade at a guard, then hightailed it out of there just before the bomb went off. The blast was enormous, demolishing a nearby school and bank, and even managing to flip off the supposedly bombproof doors of the embassy. Ten minutes later, another bomb went off in a refrigerator truck parked outside the U.S. Embassy in Dar es Salaam, Tanzania, killing 11 people.

Under a year later, Bin Laden made the Top Ten list, along with the largest price ever to be slapped on a fugitive's head, $5 million. The trial of the embassy bombers began in early 2001; by May, all four would be convicted. But by September 11 of that same year, the Kenya bombing would seem like a distant memory as four planes were hijacked early that Tuesday morning, then sent hurling toward their targets: the two towers of the World Trade Center and the Pentagon. (A fourth plane crashed in the middle of Pennsylvania; many believe its target was the White House.) Bin Laden, already a two-year veteran of the Ten Most Wanted list, was quickly named the prime

Usama bin Laden is seen at an undisclosed location in this television image broadcast, Sunday, Oct. 7, 2001. He praised God for the September 11th terrorist attacks. Bin Laden was first wanted in connection with the 1998 bombings of the U.S. Embassies in Dar Es Salaam, Tanzania, and Nairobi, Kenya.

suspect. And for perhaps the first time in Top Ten history, the fugitive eclipsed the list itself. On September 12, everybody knew the name Bin Laden.

The U.S. struck back in late fall, crushing the Al Qaeda–supporting Taliban regime in Afghanistan and disrupting Al Qaeda bases throughout that country. By March 2002, Bin Laden was thought to be cornered in the mountains of eastern Afghanistan, and for a short while, was suspected to have been killed during a wave of air strikes. But U.S. officials admitted they had no proof that Bin Laden perished in the attacks, and Al Qaeda members insisted their leader was alive and well, and planning more strikes. Throughout 2002 and 2003, infrequent radio messages and speeches attributed to Bin Laden would surface, promising America more pain and misery. *(See Appendix II for information on how to report a Top Tenner to the FBI.)*

INTERESTING FUGITIVE FACT:
Bin Laden was only 10 years old when his millionaire father died in a helicopter crash.

457. RAFAEL RESENDEZ-RAMIREZ, serial killer

LISTED: June 21, 1999
CAUGHT: July 13, 1999
DESCRIPTION: Born on August 1, 1960, in Puebla, Mexico. Five feet seven inches tall, 150 pounds, with black hair and brown eyes. He may wear prescription glasses. Resendez-Ramirez has scars on his right ring finger, left wrist, and forehead. He has a snake tattoo on his left arm and may possibly have a flower tattoo on his left wrist. He is believed to be a heavy user of alcohol and drugs and has been known to work as a day laborer and migrant worker. Aliases: Lionzo Angel Reyes-Resendiz, Jose Angel, Jose Konig Angel, Jose R. Angel, Daniel Arnold, Daniel Edward Arnold, Carlos Cluthier Eduardo III, Daniel Eduardo III, Jose Jaramillo, Pedro Angel Jaramillo, Jose Angel Mangele, Jose Konig Mangele, Angel Martinez, Angel Joseph Martinez, Antonio Martinez, Antonio E. Martinez, Pedro Argel Resemez Ramirez, Jose Angel Resendez, Jose Angel Reyes Resendez, Joseph R. Reyes Resendez, Angel Reyes, Angel Joseph Reyes, Angel Martinez Reyes, Antonio Reyes, Daniel Eduardo Resendez Reyes, Jose Angel Reyes, Antonio Rodriguez, Carlos Cluthier Rodriguez, and Carlos Rodriguez. Reward: $50,000.

Working on the Railroad. Rafael Resendez-Ramirez had more aliases or nicknames than any Top Tenner in recent memory. The kicker: Rafael Resendez-Ramirez wasn't even the killer's real name.

Angel Leoncio Reyes Resendez had been a petty thief since childhood, graduating to stealing late-model cars (boosting them in the United States, then driving them right past INS agents and into Mexico, where they'd be delivered to local crime lords), and eventually, home burglary and invasion. In July 1979 Resendez broke into a home near Miami, only to be startled by its female occupant. The two fought; the short and slender Resendez fled, only to be picked up by a roadblock two hours later. Upon his arrest, he gave his uncle's name: Rafael Resendez-Ramirez. That false name would be tied to countless burglaries over the next 20 years and would even be used when Resendez hit the big time as a Top Tenner in the summer of 1999.

Resendez spent the 1980s in and out of various prisons in what became a routine: Hop a freight train, take it to a new part of the United States, steal a car or rob a home, maybe work as a migrant laborer for a while, then start over or get arrested—whichever came first. In 1985, while incarcerated in Florida, Resendez was fascinated by newspaper accounts of another Latino criminal, Richard Ramirez, the "Night Stalker" who raped and murdered 13 victims during the spring and summer of 1985, often leaving Satanic pentagrams scrawled in blood at the murder scene. A little over 13 years later, Resendez allegedly took up a similar, grisly line of work, seemingly for no other reason than personal amusement.

The first alleged victim was 87-year-old Leafie Mason, who was found clubbed to death in her Hughes Springs, Texas, home, which sat near train tracks. The second was Dr. Claudia Benton, a Baylor College of Medicine physician, who was found raped and bludgeoned to death in her suburban Houston home, which also sat within view of train tracks. Resendez's fingerprints were found on a broken steering wheel lock outside the home; the name that popped up, however, was "Resendez-Ramirez." (Satanic drawings reminiscent of the "Night Stalker" killings were also found on the walls.) A few months later, Weimar, Texas, residents Norman and Karen Sirnic were found stabbed and sledgehammered to death. Their home was within earshot of train tracks. A pattern had been firmly established. The last serial killer of the 20th century was using hundred-year-old technology to carry out his brutal slayings.

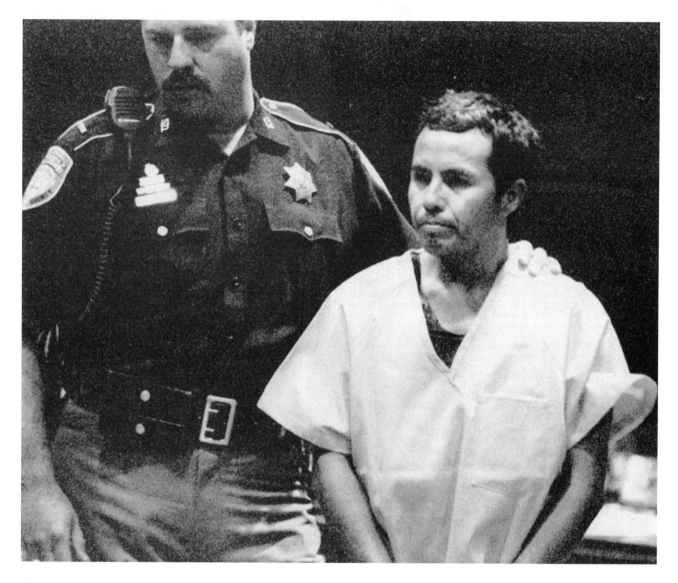

Ramirez was arrested in Houston, Texas, due to the national response of the news media as newspapers, television, and radio gave massive coverage to track down Ramirez. Here he is escorted into a courtroom in Houston on July 14, 1999.

By the time Resendez—make that Resendez-Ramirez—made the Top Ten list, he had allegedly racked up a total of eight murders between August 1997 and June 1999, all following the same M.O.: victims were mercilessly beaten and unlucky enough to live near rail lines, with no apparent motive. There was a near miss in early June 1999. U.S. Border Patrol agents unwittingly captured, then released Resendez to Mexico. He allegedly killed his three final victims in the weeks following this grievous mistake.

And then, seemingly out of nowhere, Resendez had his sister, Julieta Dominguez, broker a surren-

der with the Texas Rangers—and only the Texas Rangers. "There was a feeling of trust," said a Texas Department of Public Safety spokesman in the *Los Angeles Times*. "It was the behind-the-scenes, unsexy background work that ended up paying off. [Texas Ranger] Drew Carter went to Albuquerque within the last month, met with [the killer's] sister, and developed a relationship with her." The surrender took place on a border crossing bridge near El Paso, Texas. Resendez calmly walked across at 9 A.M., as arranged, shook Carter's hand, and then allowed himself to be handcuffed.

At a hearing the next day, Resendez admitted that he was guilty. Some people question why he turned himself in at all—Mexico has no death penalty and is usually reluctant to extradite suspects who might face the death penalty in another country. As of this printing, he is awaiting trial in Texas.

INTERESTING FUGITIVE FACT:
At one point Resendez-Ramirez used to teach nuns and orphans English for only $6 a week—even though Resendez-Ramirez himself hadn't been in school since he was six years old.

458. JAMES J. BULGER, gangster

LISTED: August 19, 1999
STILL ON LIST (as of this printing)
DESCRIPTION: Born on September 3, 1929, in Boston, Massachusetts. Five feet seven inches to five feet nine inches, 150 to 160 pounds, with white/silver hair and blue eyes. Aliases include Thomas F. Baxter, Jimmy-Boy Bulger, Jimmy Blue-Eyes, Whitey, Tom Harris, and Tom Marshall. Bulger currently takes the heart medication Atenolol 50 mg.

In Bed with the Feds. The last Top Ten fugitive of the 20th century was one of its most interesting: the first federal informant to appear on the list. James "Whitey" Bulger had taken advantage of the system, only to have it turn against him with a vengeance.

Bulger's history reads like a Boston-Irish version of *Goodfellas*—only with more head-spinning plot twists. Bulger grew up in a hardscrabble South Boston housing project, the eldest of six children. He was a neighborhood legend by the time he was 17, having run with a gang of hoodlums and eventually getting pinched for unarmed robbery, then attempted car theft, and finally assault with intent to rape. On the other hand, reports Sean Flynn in a *Boston Magazine* article, Bulger was also known as a Robin Hood type—helping old ladies with groceries and buying local kids ice cream. When he was 19, Bulger saved an eight-year-old kid from getting beat up after a baseball field scuffle. Bulger chased the kid's attackers away, then helped the kid to his feet. "You all right, kid?" he asked.

That kid grew up to be FBI agent John Connolly, and it wouldn't be the last time he and Bulger would find themselves in an unlikely partnership.

Bulger went on to join the air force in 1949, but soon went AWOL and was captured. By 1955 he and some buddies had formed a bank heisting team

and relieved banks in Massachusetts, Rhode Island, and Indiana of some $60,000. Bulger—who'd dyed his trademark white hair jet black—eluded capture, while his buddies took a fall. He was caught in 1956 and sent to the infamous Alcatraz prison, where he spent the next nine years. There Bulger caught some luck. In exchange for volunteering to take LSD in controlled experiments for the government, he'd be sprung 11 years early. Bulger dropped the acid and took the parole. When he stepped out of prison in 1965, Bulger walked

Undated FBI handout photo showing reputed Boston mobster and fugitive James J. "Whitey" Bulger. A federal warrant was issued in 1995 charging Bulger with extortion and for violation of the Racketeering and Influenced Corrupt Organization Act (RICO).

right into the middle of a brutal Irish mob war. Seven years later, several dead bodies later, Bulger found himself to be the head of South Boston's Winter Hill Gang.

In 1975 FBI agent Connolly—the kid who Bulger had saved from a vicious pummeling in the 1940s—reintroduced himself into Bulger's life. He wanted Bulger to become an informant, to help smash the Italian mob, which had sworn to grease Bulger. At first Bulger balked, but then saw that it was a way to eliminate some of the competition. So he agreed, just so long as nobody told his brother Bill, who was Whitey's polar opposite: an altar boy, an academic, and by the 70s, a hard-working Massachusetts state senator. The other condition: He wanted to be referred to as a "consultant" or "strategist." "I don't want to be a fuckin' informant or anything," said Bulger, according to the *Boston* article. "I don't want your money, and I'm not going to fuck our friends. I'll only fuck people who try to fuck us."

Connolly also recruited Bulger's gang partner, Steve Flemmi, and for the next 15 years the two helped the FBI smash the Boston-area arm of La Cosa Nostra. Small rumors from Bulger were routinely used by Connolly to cultivate snitches within the Italian mob ranks. By the late 80s more than 34 made guys were put away, and the Mafia was no more. Meanwhile, Bulger and Flemmi were protected, to a degree, by the FBI. The degree of that protection is still being explored as of this printing. Some law enforcement agencies accused Connolly of covering up for Bulger and Flemmi and allowing them to carry out the very same criminal activity that the Italian mob did. Southie favoritism, it was alleged. Connolly, for his part, retired from the FBI in 1990 to become the head of corporate relations at the utility company Boston Edison. He defended his actions to reporter Sean Flynn in *Boston,* saying that using Bulger and Flemmi "was a business decision. This is a business we're in, the business of eradicating crime. And to do that, you need criminal informants. This day, this very moment, law enforcement agents all over the country are making deals with criminals in order to catch other criminals."

Whatever the case, the tide shifted in 1995, when Bulger and Flemmi were indicted on charges of federal racketeering and murder—more than 19 bodies piled up in more than 30 years of mob "business." The night before the indictment, Bulger disappeared and hasn't been seen since. Since Bulger made the Top Ten list in August 1999, the FBI has made it clear that there is nothing wishy-washy about their pursuit of Bulger. "I'm here to tell you we are out to catch him," said Barry Mawn, special agent in charge of the FBI's Boston office, in the pages of the *Boston Globe.* Soon after, Connolly himself was charged with racketeering and obstruction of justice. In an interview with *60 Minutes,* the current head of the FBI's Boston Office, Charles Prouty, said that the office is appalled and that rules for using informants had been dramatically stiffened. (Connolly maintains his innocence and says he was only following guidelines for high-level informants.) In May 2002, Connolly was found guilty of two counts of obstruction of justice as well as making a false statement.

As of this printing, Bulger has been on the lam for six years. He is thought to be traveling in the Southeast, along with his companion, Catherine Elizabeth Greig. Greig was born on April 3, 1951, in Massachusetts. She's five feet six inches, 130 to 140 pounds, with dyed blond hair and blue eyes. She used to be a dental hygienist and is known to frequent beauty salons and has a love for dogs. (In fact, both Bulger and Greig are avowed animal lovers and might be visiting shelters and zoos wherever they may be.) She was indicted in April 1997 for harboring a federal fugitive.

The most recent tip: a man thought to be Bulger, waiting outside a hair salon in Fountain Valley, California. He was thought to be waiting while Greig had her blond dye-job touched up. Other law enforcement officials suspect Bulger might be hiding out in homosexual communities or nudist resorts—the last place somebody might look for a tough Boston Southie. (See page 295 in Appendix II for information on how to report a Top Tenner to the FBI.)

INTERESTING FUGITIVE FACT:
According to *Boston Magazine,* Bulger enjoys using the pejorative "fuckster."

Appendix I:
Most Wanted Since 2000

It's the start of a new century, and there's a new crop of Top Ten fugitives. The history of the next 50 years of the program is still being written, but here's a sneak preview of who's been appearing on the list lately. (All information on crimes is taken directly from FBI press releases and/or bulletins.)

459. JESSE JAMES CASTON, murderer

LISTED: August 19, 2000
CAUGHT: December 20, 2000
DESCRIPTION: Born on September 19, 1965, in Lake Providence, Louisiana. Five feet 11 inches to six feet one inch tall, 210 pounds, with light brown hair and blue eyes. Caston has a burn scar on his right hand, and two tattoos, "J" on his right forearm and "Angela" on the left side of his chest.

The Crime: Jesse James Caston was sought for the murder of his wife and her female friend, as well as the attempted murder of two police officers in Lake Providence, Louisiana, in April 2000. He's also suspected of abducting a man in Louisiana and forcing him at gunpoint to drive them to Texas.

460. ERIC FRANKLIN ROSSER, child pornographer

LISTED: December 27, 2000
CAUGHT: August 21, 2001
DESCRIPTION: Born on January 17, 1952, in Syracuse, New York. Five feet seven inches tall, 145 pounds, with dark brown hair and blue eyes. Rosser is a professional concert and jazz pianist and piano teacher. He wears prescription glasses and is completely bald. He should be considered a suicide and escape risk. Alias: Rice Sorser. Reward: $50,000.

The Crime: Eric Franklin Rosser was sought in the United States in connection with the international production, distribution, and exchange of child pornography between Bloomington, Indiana, and Bangkok, Thailand. He is also wanted for his alleged molestation of a number of young girls in Thailand.

461. AURLIEAS DAME McCLARTY, bank robber, murderer

LISTED: February 5, 2001
CAUGHT: February 14, 2001
DESCRIPTION: Born in 1979.

The Crime: McClarty was wanted on federal bank robbery charges for the robbery of the Citizens National Bank in Laurel, Maryland, on October 4, 2000. In addition, McClarty was wanted on local charges in Orlando, Florida, for the double homicide of two employees of a truck rental dealership. Those murders occurred on July 18, 2000, and were allegedly committed during the course of an armed robbery that netted only $200. Both victims were shot in the head.

462. HOPETON ERIC BROWN, drug dealer

LISTED: March 17, 2001
STILL ON LIST (as of this printing)
DESCRIPTION: Born on September 26, 1974, (but also has used August 26 as his birthday) in Montego Bay, Jamaica. Five foot eight inches, 175 pounds, with black hair and brown eyes. Brown has a mole below his left eye and possibly a large scar on his chest. He has been known to wear heavy gold jewelry. Aliases: Anthony Brisco, Simon

Eric Franklin Rosser talks to reporters after the extradition order outside a criminal courtroom in Bangkok, August 19, 2002. Rosser was indicted by a federal grand jury in Indianapolis in March 2000 on six counts of producing and distributing child pornography.

Plested, Devon Foster, Eric Brown, Omar Brown, Richard Omar Kennedy, Richard Omar Kennedy Sandokam, "Sando," "Angel," "Shawn."

The Crime: Hopeton Eric Brown is being sought in the United States for his alleged involvement in drug-related activities, as well as for the murder of a man and the attempted murder of a woman in March 1997 in St. Paul, Minnesota. He is also wanted by authorities in Jamaica for allegedly com-

mitting two murders in Montego Bay in January 2001.

463. MAGHFOOR MANSOOR, kidnapper, rapist, robber

LISTED: May 7, 2001
KILLED: May 11, 2001
DESCRIPTION: Born on March 9, 1966. Five feet eight inches

tall, 165 pounds, with black hair and brown eyes. Scars and marks: several scars on left forearm, Arabic letters on right forearm.

The Crime: Maghfoor Mansoor, a convicted sex offender, was wanted in Las Vegas, Nevada, for kidnapping and raping a 17-year-old girl on December 11, 2000, and at least four violent incidents across the country during a "one-man crime spree."

464. FRANCIS WILLIAM MURPHY

No information available as of this writing.

465. DWIGHT BOWEN, alleged arsonist, murderer

LISTED: August 30, 2001
CAUGHT: August 30, 2001
DESCRIPTION: Born in 1976.

The Crime: Dwight Bowen was accused of firebombing a house in North Philadelphia, a crime that resulted in the deaths of two young boys on June 6, 2001.

466. NIKOLAY SOLTYS, alleged murderer

LISTED: August 23, 2001
CAUGHT: August 30, 2001
DESCRIPTION: Born on May 19, 1974, in Ukraine. Six feet tall, 165 pounds, with blond or brown hair and blue eyes. Soltys is a Ukrainian immigrant who has lived in the United States for approximately two years and speaks broken English with an accent. He may seek refuge in a Ukrainian community. Soltys has ties to New York; California; Seattle, Washington; Charlotte, North Carolina; and Canada. Aliases: Mykola Soltys, Nikolay A. Soltys, Nikolay Alekseyevi Soltys.

The Crime: On August 20, 2001, Nikolay Soltys allegedly stabbed his 23-year-old pregnant wife to death in their North Highlands, California, home. He reportedly then drove to the home of his aunt and uncle, where he is suspected of killing the couple and his two young cousins. After the first five murders Soltys allegedly drove to his mother's house and picked up his three-year-old son. Later that evening, Soltys's car was found in the vicinity of his mother's house.

During a search of the vehicle, a note was recovered with information regarding the location of Soltys's son. On August 21, 2001, investigators located the boy's body in an empty field in Roseville California.

467. CLAYTON LEE WAAGNER, bank robber

LISTED: September 21, 2001
CAUGHT: December 5, 2001
DESCRIPTION: Born on August 25, 1956, in North Dakota. Six feet one inch tall, 175 to 220 pounds, with brown-gray hair and green eyes. Scars and marks: Waagner has scars on his right knee, right ankle, and nose. Due to previous frostbite injuries on his hand and toes, Waagner may have limited use of his left hand and may walk with a limp. He is known to be anti-abortion and has, in the past, allegedly made threats against abortion clinics and doctors. He has survivalist skills and may be heavily armed. Aliases: Jack Avery, Mike L. Buchanan, Steve Bruenberg, Randy Miller, Jack Fisher, Kenny Logan, Rick Mullins, Ronald Johnson, Robert Sales, John Roner, Randy Taylor, Steve Vetter, Rex H. Turner (among many others).

The Crime: Clayton Lee Waagner was sought for escaping from federal custody in Illinois, bank robbery charges in Pennsylvania, federal firearms violations in Tennessee, and carjacking in Mississippi. All of these crimes occurred in 2001.

Special Update Information from the FBI, November 29, 2001: During the second week of October 2001, more than 280 letters that threatened to contain anthrax were mailed to women's reproductive health clinics on the East Coast. The envelopes were marked "Time Sensitive" and "Urgent Security Notice Enclosed." The envelopes also bore return addresses of the U.S. Marshals Service or the U.S. Secret Service. During the first week of November 2001, a second series of more than 270 anthrax letters were sent to women's reproductive health clinics via Federal Express. Over Thanksgiving weekend authorities received information that Clayton Lee Waagner had claimed responsibility for sending these letters to women's reproductive health clinics.

468. FELIX SUMMERS, murderer

LISTED: October 30, 2001
CAUGHT: December 14, 2001
DESCRIPTION: Born on May 21 or 28, 1980 or 1981, in Philadelphia, Pennsylvania. Five feet seven inches, 210

pounds, with black hair and brown eyes. Scars and marks: Summers has the following tattoos: "Phil" in cursive writing with quotation marks around it and a line under it on his left arm, and "Sherry" on his chest. Summers has ties to the Statesville, North Carolina, area, and may also have ties to South Carolina. He is known to wear a beard and mustache. Aliases: Larry Alvin, Jamil Russell, Feliv Summers, Larry Faulks, Felix Simms.

The Crime: Felix Summers was wanted for the shooting death of a 16-year-old girl and the wounding of five others in Philadelphia in August 2001. He was also sought in connection with the murder of a witness in a previous Philadelphia murder investigation in 1999.

469. CHRISTIAN MICHAEL LONGO, murderer

LISTED: January 11, 2002
CAUGHT: January 14, 2002
DESCRIPTION: Born on January 23, 1974, in Iowa. Six feet one inch, 150 to 195 pounds, with reddish blond hair and blue eyes. Scars and marks: Longo has surgical scars on his back. Longo is a diabetic and dependent on insulin. In the past he suffered from a form of skin cancer and had skin surgically removed from his back. Longo has ties to the Detroit, Michigan, and Indianapolis, Indiana, areas. He has traveled extensively throughout the United States and Mexico. Longo enjoys living in or near large coastal cities. He has been known to frequent coffeehouses. Aliases: Jason Joseph Fortner, John Thomas Christopher.

The Crime: Christian Michael Long was wanted for the murder of his wife and their three young children in Oregon in December 2001. Considered armed and extremely dangerous and an escape risk.

470. MICHAEL SCOTT BLISS, alleged child molester

LISTED: January 31, 2002
CAUGHT: April 23, 2002
DESCRIPTION: Born on March 4, 1965, in Greenfield, Massachusetts. Five feet 11 inches tall, 195 to 210 pounds, with brown hair and brown eyes. Bliss may limp slightly due to an old injury to his right leg. He is balding, left-handed, and at time may wear glasses. Bliss is known to smoke and rolls his own cigarettes. He is proficient in the use of computers and enjoys baseball and car racing. Bliss has been known to travel throughout northern New

England, the West Coast of the United States, and Canada. He has ties to Vermont, New Hampshire, and the San Diego, California, area.

The Crime: Michael Scott Bliss, a convicted felon, was wanted for the alleged molestation of a young girl on numerous occasions beginning in September 2000. Many of these molestations, which occurred in Vermont, New Hampshire, and Massachusetts, were videotaped. Portions of these tapes were later converted to computer files.

James Spencer Springette, shown in this police photo taken in February 1999, has allegedly been the leader of a Caribbean-based drug-smuggling organization since 1991. He was wanted for allegedly conspiring to import multiton quantities of cocaine into the United States, as well as acts of violence including the attempted murder of a police officer in the British Virgin Islands.

471. JAMES SPENCER SPRINGETTE, alleged drug dealer

LISTED: April 25, 2002
CAUGHT: November 5, 2002
DESCRIPTION: Born on August 16 or 18, 1960, in St. Thomas, U.S. Virgin Islands. Five feet 11 inches, 240 pounds, with black hair and brown eyes. Springette is known to have facial hair. He has ties to the United States and British Virgin Islands, as well as other islands in the Caribbean. Aliases: Elmo Brady, Elmo Brandy, Kyle Pierce, Elmo Spencer, Kent Worwell, Shawn Pickering, Brian Miller, Efram Zoran Johnson, Everson Weberson, "Jimmy," "Juice," "Seagal," "Jimmy the Juice," "Uncle."

The Crime: James Spencer Springette has allegedly been the leader of a Caribbean-based drug-smuggling organization since 1991. He was wanted for allegedly conspiring to import multiton quantities of cocaine into the United States, as well as acts of violence including the attempted murder of a police officer in the British Virgin Islands.

472. RUBEN HERNANDEZ MARTINEZ, alleged serial rapist

LISTED: May 1, 2002
CAUGHT: May 2, 2002
DESCRIPTION: Born on October 31, 1967, in Mexico. Five feet seven inches, 145 pounds, with black hair and brown eyes. Martinez may have a goatee or mustache and shoulder-length hair. He has ties to Houston, Texas, and Rio Bravo, Mexico.

The Crime: Ruben Hernandez Martinez was a suspected serial rapist, wanted for his alleged participation in a series of armed home invasions and sexual assaults in the Nashville, Tennessee, area during 1997 and 1998.

473. TIMMY JOHN WEBER, rapist

LISTED: April 28, 2002
CAUGHT: April 28, 2002
DESCRIPTION: Born on June 3, 1973, in Nevada. Six feet four inches, 200 pounds, with brown hair and hazel eyes. May be clean-shaven, and is known to have rotten teeth, as well as liking remote-controlled racing cars. Alias: "TJ."

The Crime: Timmy John Weber was wanted in connection with a sexual assault on a 14-year-old girl—the daughter of Weber's live-in girlfriend—in Las Vegas, Nevada, on April 4, 2002.

474. RICHARD STEVE GOLDBERG, alleged child molester

LISTED: June 14, 2002
STILL ON LIST (as of this printing)
DESCRIPTION: Born on November 9, 1945, in Brooklyn, New York. Six feet tall, 160 pounds, with black hair and brown eyes. Goldberg has a thick mustache and a receding hairline. He was the president of a gun club in Long Beach, California. Goldberg has ties to, or may have traveled to, New Jersey, Nevada, Colorado, Arizona, and Georgia.

The Crime: From January through May 2001, Goldberg allegedly lured neighborhood girls to his Long Beach, California, home in order to engage in illicit sexual activities with them. Goldberg gained the trust of the parents and then befriended their children. He entertained the girls by allowing them to play with his pets, watch television, and use his computer to play games. Some of these girls also took short trips with him. In July 2001 a state arrest warrant was issued in California charging Goldberg with six counts of lewd acts upon a child and two counts of possession of child pornography.

475. ROBERT WILLIAM FISHER, alleged murderer

LISTED: June 29, 2002
STILL ON LIST (as of this printing)
DESCRIPTION: Born on April 13, 1961, in Brooklyn, New York. Six feet tall, 190 pounds, with brown hair and blue eyes. Fisher is physically fit and is an avid outdoorsman, hunter, and fisherman. He has a noticeable gold crown on his upper left first bicuspid. He may walk with an exaggerated erect posture and his chest pushed out due to a lower back injury. Fisher is known to chew tobacco heavily. He has ties to New Mexico and Florida. Fisher is believed to be in possession of several weapons, including a high-powered rifle.

The Crime: Robert William Fisher is wanted for allegedly killing his wife and two young children and then blowing up the house in which they all lived in Scottsdale, Arizona, in April 2001.

476. MICHAEL ALFONSO, alleged murderer

LISTED: January 23, 2003
STILL ON LIST (as of this printing)
DESCRIPTION: Born on June 26, 1969, in Illinois. Five feet five inches tall, 150 pounds, with black hair and brown eyes. Scars and marks: Alfonso has a scar on his chest under his left arm and a tattoo of "Blanca" on his shoulder blade. Alfonso is a registered sex offender in Illinois. He is fluent in Spanish. Alfonso is known to enjoy working out at gyms. He may wear earrings in both ears. Alfonso has ties to Chicago, Illinois; Phoenix, Arizona; Columbus, Georgia; Memphis, Tennessee; Alabama; and Mississippi. In the past he is known to have traveled to Puerto Vallarta, Mexico.

The Crime: Michael Alfonso is wanted for allegedly stalking and then shooting to death two of his former girlfriends in Illinois in September 1992 and June 2001.

477. GENERO ESPINOSA DORANTES

LISTED: August 14, 2003
STILL ON LIST (as of this printing)
DESCRIPTION: Born June 19 or 29, 1970, in Pachusa, Hidalgo, Mexico. Five feet six inches tall, 170 to 180 lbs, with black hair and brown eyes. Scars and marks: Dorantes has a scar on his face and a tattoo of a heart on his left arm.

The Crime: Genero Espinosa Dorantes is wanted for his alleged participation in the burning, beating, torture, and murder of his four-year-old stepson in Nashville, Tennessee, in February 2003.

Appendix II: The Current Top Ten

As of this printing, here is the current crop of Ten Most Wanted fugitives:

Michael Alfonso *(for more information, see page 294)*

Usama Bin Laden *(for more information, see page 283)*

Hopeton Eric Brown *(for more information, see page 289)*

James J. Bulger *(for more information, see page 287)*

Genero Espinosa Dorantes *(for more information, see page 294)*

Robert William Fisher *(for more information, see page 293)*

Victor Gerena *(for more information, see page 229)*

Glen Stewart Godwin *(for more information, see page 275)*

Richard Steve Goldberg *(for more information, see page 293)*

Donald Eugene Webb *(for more information, see page 219)*

HOW TO REPORT A TOP 10 FUGITIVE

If you see someone you think might be a Ten Most Wanted fugitive, *do not approach or attempt to apprehend him yourself.* Most Wanted posters say that the fugitive is "armed and dangerous" for a reason. Instead, give your tip to the professionals. There are two easy ways.

The Internet. Go to tips.fbi.gov and you'll find a form you can use to report the sighting of a Top Ten fugitive or any other suspicious activity, for that matter.

Field Offices. Call or e-mail your closest FBI field office. There are 56 of them scattered throughout the United States:

FBI Albany
200 McCarty Avenue
Albany, New York 12209
albany.fbi.gov
(518) 465-7551

FBI Albuquerque
Suite 300
415 Silver Avenue, Southwest
Albuquerque, New Mexico 87102
albuquerque.fbi.gov
(505) 224-2000

FBI Anchorage
101 East Sixth Avenue
Anchorage, Alaska 99501-2524
anchorage.fbi.gov
(907) 258-5322

FBI Atlanta
Suite 400
2635 Century Parkway, Northeast
Atlanta, Georgia 30345-3112
atlanta.fbi.gov
(404) 679-9000

FBI Baltimore
7142 Ambassador Road
Baltimore, Maryland 21244-2754
baltimore.fbi.gov
(410) 265-8080

FBI Birmingham
Room 1400
2121 8th. Avenue North
Birmingham, Alabama 35203-2396
birmingham.fbi.gov
(205) 326-6166

FBI Boston
Suite 600
One Center Plaza
Boston, Massachusetts 02108
boston.fbi.gov
(617) 742-5533

FBI Buffalo
One FBI Plaza
Buffalo, New York 14202-2698
buffalo.fbi.gov
(716) 856-7800

FBI Charlotte
Suite 900, Wachovia Building
400 South Tyron Street
Charlotte, North Carolina 28285-0001
charlotte.fbi.gov
(704) 377-9200

FBI Chicago
Room 905
E. M. Dirksen Federal Office Building
219 South Dearborn Street
Chicago, Illinois 60604-1702
chicago.fbi.gov
(312) 431-1333

FBI Cincinnati
Room 9000
550 Main Street
Cincinnati, Ohio 45202-8501
cincinnati.fbi.gov
(513) 421-4310

FBI Cleveland
Federal Office Building
1501 Lakeside Avenue
Cleveland, Ohio 44114
cleveland.fbi.gov
(216) 522-1400

FBI Columbia
151 Westpark Boulevard
Columbia, South Carolina 29210-3857
columbia.fbi.gov
(803) 551-4200

FBI Dallas
One Justice Way
Dallas, Texas 75220
dallas.fbi.gov
(972) 559-5000

FBI Denver
Federal Office Building, Room 1823
1961 Stout Street, 18th Floor
Denver, Colorado 80294-1823
denver.fbi.gov
(303) 629-7171

FBI Detroit
26th Floor, P. V. McNamara FOB
477 Michigan Avenue
Detroit, Michigan 48226
detroit.fbi.gov
(313) 965-2323

FBI El Paso
660 South Mesa Hills Drive
El Paso, Texas 79912-5533
elpaso.fbi.gov
(915) 832-5000

FBI Honolulu
Room 4-230, Kalanianaole FOB
300 Ala Moana Boulevard
Honolulu, Hawaii 96850-0053
honolulu.fbi.gov
(808) 521-1411

FBI Houston
2500 East TC Jester
Houston, Texas 77008-1300
houston.fbi.gov
(713) 693-5000

FBI Indianapolis
Room 679, FOB
575 North Pennsylvania Street
Indianapolis, Indiana 46204-1585
indianapolis.fbi.gov
(317) 639-3301

FBI Jackson
Room 1553, FOB
100 West Capitol Street
Jackson, Mississippi 39269-1601
jackson.fbi.gov
(601) 948-5000

FBI Jacksonville
Suite 200
7820 Arlington Expressway
Jacksonville, Florida 32211-7499
jacksonville.fbi.gov
(904) 721-1211

FBI Kansas City
1300 Summit
Kansas City, Missouri 64105-1362
kansascity.fbi.gov
(816) 512-8200

FBI Knoxville
Suite 600, John J. Duncan FOB
710 Locust Street
Knoxville, Tennessee 37902-2537
knoxville.fbi.gov
(865) 544-0751

FBI Las Vegas
John Lawrence Bailey Building
700 East Charleston Boulevard
Las Vegas, Nevada 89104-1545
lasvegas.fbi.gov
(702) 385-1281

FBI Little Rock
Suite 200
Two Financial Centre
10825 Financial Centre Parkway
Little Rock, Arkansas 72211-3552
littlerock.fbi.gov
(501) 221-9100

FBI Los Angeles
Suite 1700, FOB
11000 Wilshire Boulevard
Los Angeles, California 90024-3672
losangeles.fbi.gov
(310) 477-6565

FBI Louisville
Room 500
600 Martin Luther King Jr. Place
Louisville, Kentucky 40202-2231
louisville.fbi.gov
(502) 583-3941

FBI Memphis
Suite 3000, Eagle Crest Building
225 North Humphreys Boulevard

Memphis, Tennessee 38120-2107
memphis.fbi.gov
(901) 747-4300

FBI North Miami Beach
16320 Northwest Second Avenue
North Miami Beach, Florida 33169-6508
miami.fbi.gov
(305) 944-9101

FBI Milwaukee
Suite 600
330 East Kilbourn Avenue
Milwaukee, Wisconsin 53202-6627
milwaukee.fbi.gov
(414) 276-4684

FBI Minneapolis
Suite 1100
111 Washington Avenue, South
Minneapolis, Minnesota 55401-2176
minneapolis.fbi.gov
(612) 376-3200

FBI Mobile
One St. Louis Centre
1 St. Louis Street, 3rd Floor
Mobile, Alabama 36602-3930
mobile.fbi.gov
(334) 438-3674

FBI Newark
1 Gateway Center, 22nd Floor
Newark, New Jersey 07102-9889
newark.fbi.gov
(973) 792-3000

FBI New Haven
600 State Street
New Haven, Connecticut 06511-6505
(203) 777-6311

FBI New Orleans
2901 Leon C. Simon Dr.
New Orleans, Louisiana 70126
neworleans.fbi.gov
(504) 816-3000

FBI New York
26 Federal Plaza, 23rd Floor
New York, New York 10278-0004
newyork.fbi.gov

FBI Norfolk
150 Corporate Boulevard
Norfolk, Virginia 23502-4999
norfolk.fbi.gov
(757) 455-0100

FBI Oklahoma City
3301 West Memorial Drive
Oklahoma City, Oklahoma 73134
oklahomacity.fbi.gov
(405) 290-7770

FBI Omaha
10755 Burt Street
Omaha, Nebraska 68114-2000
omaha.fbi.gov
(402) 493-8688

FBI Philadelphia
8th Floor
William J. Green Jr. FOB
600 Arch Street
Philadelphia, Pennsylvania 19106
philadelphia.fbi.gov
(215) 418-4000

FBI Phoenix
Suite 400
201 East Indianola Avenue
Phoenix, Arizona 85012-2080
phoenix.fbi.gov
(602) 279-5511

FBI Pittsburgh
3311 East Carson Street
Pittsburgh, PA 15203
pittsburgh.fbi.gov
(412) 432-4000

FBI Portland
Suite 400, Crown Plaza Building
1500 Southwest 1st Avenue
Portland, Oregon 97201-5828
portland.fbi.gov
(503) 224-4181

FBI Richmond
1970 E. Parham Road
Richmond, Virginia 23228
richmond.fbi.gov
(804) 261-1044

FBI Sacramento
4500 Orange Grove Avenue
Sacramento, California 95841-4205
sacramento.fbi.gov
(916) 481-9110

FBI St. Louis
2222 Market Street
St. Louis, Missouri 63103-2516
stlouis.fbi.gov
(314) 231-4324

FBI Salt Lake City
Suite 1200, 257 Towers Building
257 East, 200 South
Salt Lake City, Utah 84111-2048
saltlakecity.fbi.gov
(801) 579-1400

FBI San Antonio
Suite 200
U.S. Post Office Courthouse Building
615 East Houston Street
San Antonio, Texas 78205-9998
sanantonio.fbi.gov
(210) 225-6741

FBI San Diego
Federal Office Building
9797 Aero Drive
San Diego, California 92123-1800
sandiego.fbi.gov
(858) 565-1255

FBI San Francisco
450 Golden Gate Avenue, 13th Floor
San Francisco, California 94102-9523
sanfrancisco.fbi.gov
(415) 553-7400

FBI San Juan
Room 526, U.S. Federal Building
150 Carlos Chardon Avenue
Hato Rey
San Juan, Puerto Rico 00918-1716
sanjuan.fbi.gov
(787) 754-6000

FBI Seattle
1110 Third Avenue
Seattle, Washington 98101-2904
seattle.fbi.gov
(206) 622-0460

FBI Springfield
Suite 400
400 West Monroe Street
Springfield, Illinois 62704-1800
springfield.fbi.gov
(217) 522-9675

FBI Tampa
Room 610, FOB
500 Zack Street

Tampa, Florida 33602-3917
tampa.fbi.gov
(813) 273-4566

FBI Washington
Washington Metropolitan Field Office
601 4th Street, N.W.
Washington, D.C. 20535-0002
washingtondc.fbi.gov
(202) 278-2000

Selected Bibliography

Countless magazine and newspaper clippings were used while researching this book, as well as dozens of other books, videotapes, and websites. It would be impossible to list them all—I've relied on at least three articles for every fugitive, and in some cases, up to 40 different articles. Here is a sample of some of the best general resources I've found; if you're interested in learning more about the Ten Most Wanted program (or fugitives and criminals in general), any of the books, articles, or websites below would be an excellent start.

BOOKS

Breslin, Jack. *America's Most Wanted: How Television Catches Crooks.* New York: Harper Paperbacks, 1990.

Burke, Jan. *Nine.* New York: Simon & Schuster, 2002.

Caren, Eric C. *Crime Extra: 300 Years of Crime in North America.* Edison, N.J.: Castle Books, 2001.

Clarkson, Wensley. *The Railroad Killer: Tracking Down One of the Most Brutal Serial Killers in History.* New York: St. Martin's Paperbacks, 2000.

Clouser, John William, with Dave Fisher. *The Most Wanted Man in America.* New York: Stein and Day, 1975.

Cooper, Courtney Ryley. *Ten Thousand Public Enemies.* Boston: Little, Brown and Company, 1935.

D'Angelo, Laura. *The FBI's Most Wanted.* Philadelphia: Chelsea House, 1997.

Deloach, Cartha D. *Hoover's FBI: The Inside Story by Hoover's Trusted Lieutenant.* Washington, D.C.: Regnery, 1997.

DeSimone, Donald. *"I Rob Banks: That's Where the Money Is!"; The Story of Bank Robber Willie Sutton and the Killing of Arnold Schuster.* New York: Shapolsky, 1991.

Editors of Time-Life Books. *True Crime: Most Wanted.* New York: Time-Life Books, 1993.

Gentry, Curt. *J. Edgar Hoover: The Man and the Secrets.* New York: Norton, 1991.

Helmer, William, with Rick Mattix. *Public Enemies.* New York: Facts On File, 1998.

Hynd, Alan. *We Are the Public Enemies.* New York: Fawcett, 1949.

Hynd, Alan. *Murder, Mayhem and Mystery.* New York: A.S. Barnes, 1958.

Kirchner, L. R. *Robbing Banks: An American History 1831–1999.* New York: Sarpedon, 2000.

Kessler, Ron. *The FBI: Inside the World's Most Powerful Law Enforcement Agency.* New York: Pocket Books, 1994.

Lehr, Dick, and Gerald O'Neill. *Black Mass: The True Story of An Unholy Alliance Between the FBI and the Irish Mob.* New York: Harper Perennial, 2000.

MacDonald, John D. *April Evil.* Greenwich, Conn.: Fawcett Gold Medal, 1956.

MacNee, Marie J. *Outlaws, Mobsters and Crooks: From the Old West to the Internet.* Detroit: UXL, 1998.

Nash, Jay Robert. *Almanac of World Crime.* Garden City, N.Y.: Anchor Press/Doubleday, 1981.

Nash, Jay Robert. *Bloodletters and Badmen: A Narrative Encyclopedia of American Criminals from the Pilgrims to the Present.* New York: M. Evans, 1995.

Newton, Michael, and Judy Ann Newton. *The FBI Most Wanted: An Encyclopedia.* New York: Dell, 1989.

Newton, Michael. *The Encyclopedia of Robberies, Heists and Capers.* New York: Checkmark Books, 2002.

Orth, Maureen. *Vulgar Favors: Andrew Cunanan, Gianni Versace, and the Largest Failed Manhunt in U.S. History.* New York: Delacorte, 1999.

Penzler, Otto and Thomas H. Cook. *The Best American Crime Writing 2002*. New York: Vintage: 2002.

Phillips, Charles, and Alan Axelrod. *Cops, Crooks and Criminologists: An International Biographical Dictionary of Law Enforcement*. New York: Facts On File, 1996.

Powers, Richard Gid. *G-Men: Hoover's FBI in American Popular Culture*. Carbondale: Southern Illinois University Press, 1983.

Reeve, Simon. *The New Jackals: Ramzi Yousef, Osama bin Laden and the Future of Terrorism*. Boston, Mass.: Northeastern University Press, 1999.

Revel, Oliver "Buck" and Dwight William. *A G-Man's Journal: A Legendary Career Inside the FBI—From the Kennedy Assasination to the Oklahoma City Bombing*. New York: Pocket Books, 1998.

Reynolds, Quentin. *I, Willie Sutton*. New York: Farrar, Straus and Giroux, 1953.

Roth, Andrew. *Infamous Manhattan: A Colorful Walking History of New York's Most Notorious Crime Scenes*. New York: Citadel Press, 1996.

Sabljak, Mark, and Martin H. Greenberg. *Most Wanted: A History of the FBI's Ten Most Wanted List*. New York: Bonanza Books, 1990.

Sifakis, Carl. *Encyclopedia of American Crime*. New York: Smithmark, 1982.

Sutton, Willie, with Edward Linn. *Where the Money Was*. New York: Viking, 1976.

Swierczynski, Duane. *This Here's A Stick-Up: The Big Bad Book of American Bank Robbery*. Indianapolis, Ind.: Alpha Books, 2002.

Theoharis, Athan G., with Tony G. Poveda, Susan Rosenfeld, and Richard Gid Powers. *The FBI: A Comprehensive Reference Guide*. New York: Checkmark Books, 2000.

Turner, William. *Hoover's FBI: The Men and the Myth*. Los Angeles: Sherbourne Press, 1970.

Volkman, Ernest, and John Cummings. *The Heist*. New York: Franklin Watts, 1986.

Walsh, John, with Philip Lerman. *No Mercy: The Host of America's Most Wanted Hunts the Worst Criminals of Our Time—In Shattering True Crime Cases*. New York: Pocket Books, 1998.

Welch, Neil, and David Marston. *Inside Hoover's FBI*. New York: Doubleday, 1984.

Wilson, Colin and Damon Wilson. *The Mammoth Book of Illustrated Crime: A Photographic History*. New York: Carroll & Graf, 2002.

Wolf, Marvin J., and Katherine Mader. *Fallen Angels: Chronicles of L.A. Crime and Mystery*. New York: Facts On File, 1986.

SELECTED ARTICLES

Carr, Howie. "Family Tree: Boston's Mob Roots Run Deep." *Boston Magazine,* April 2001.

Conan, Neal. "Organization of FBI's Ten Most Wanted list and placement of fugitives based on each era's trends and politics." National Public Radio, March 18, 2000.

Dove, Donna J. and Jeffrey M. Maynard. "FBI's Ten Most Wanted Fugitives Program: 50th Anniversary 1950–2000." Published by the FBI in commemoration of the 50th anniversary of the program. Available by download at www.fbi.gov.

Drury, Bob. "Ten the Hard Way." *Details,* December 1997.

Epps, Garrett. "Wanted By the FBI: A Better Class of Criminal." *The Washington Post,* January 28, 1979.

Felton, David. "Attention! If You Have Information Concerning Most Wanted Fugitives . . ." *Esquire,* December 1973.

Flynn, Sean. "Good Guy, Bad Guy." *Boston Magazine,* September 2000.

Friedman, David. "Wanted: Lowlifes and High Ratings." *Rolling Stone,* January 12, 1989.

Glasser, Jeff. "In Demand for 50 Years." *U.S. News & World Report,* March 20, 2000.

Greene, Bob. "100 Reasons to Avoid Making This List." *Chicago Tribune,* March 21, 2000.

Haskell, Kari. "Everybody's Got A Price: Hunting Public Enemy No. 1, No. 2 . . ." *The New York Times,* November 25, 2001.

Herbeck, Dan. "FBI's Top 10 Clicks as a Hit List." *Buffalo News,* March 19, 2000.

Ingrassia, Robert. "Milestone for 'Most Wanted': Top Ten List Paying Off for 50 Years." *New York Daily News,* March 16, 2000.

John, Kevin and Gary Fields. "FBI Gets Its Man, But It Didn't Catch Him." *USA Today,* July 15, 1999.

Kolbert, Elizabeth. "The Prisoner." *The New Yorker,* July 16, 2001.

Lukas, J. Anthony. "On the Lam in America." *The New York Times Magazine,* December 13, 1970.

McEvoy, George. "I Could Still Use $50 Gs, If The FBI's Feeling Generous." *The Palm Beach Post,* March 20, 2000.

Metrick, Amy. "FBI Celebrates 50 Years of 'Most Wanted' List." ABCNews.com, March 14, 2000.

Newhouse News Service. "FBI Agents Nab Eight Fugitives on Top 10 List." *The San Diego Union-Tribune,* December 4, 1986.

Pooley, Eric. "Death of a Hood: The Bloody End of Big Bad Gus." *New York,* January 29, 1990.

Pray, Amy. "Unwanted? Posters of Fugitives Can Be Hard to Find At Post Offices." *St. Louis Post-Dispatch,* June 14, 1995.

Prial, Frank J. "Freeze! You're On TV." *The New York Times,* September 25, 1988.

Puente, Maria. "A No Longer Most Wanted List? FBI Top 10 May Be Losing Effectiveness." *USA Today,* July 29, 1997.

Remsburg, Charles, and Bonnie Remsburg. "Roll of Dishonor." *The New York Times Magazine,* January 26, 1964.

Rubin, James H. "Only the Elite Need 'Apply.'" Associated Press, June 19, 1979.

Serrano, Richard A. "Trail of Many Fugitives Has Grown Cold." *Los Angeles Times,* June 12, 1998.

Schipper, Henry. "A Trapped Generation on Trial." *The Progressive,* January 1974.

Shannon, Elaine. "Taking a Byte Out of Crime." *Time,* May 25, 1987.

Solomon, John. "Bush to Unveil New Most Wanted List." Associated Press, October 10, 2001.

Stein, Jeff. "To Catch A Killer." *GQ,* December 1997.

Stewart, Jim. "The 50th Anniversary of the FBI's Ten Most Wanted List." *CBS Early Show,* March 14, 2000.

Stout, David. "Poster Boys of Crime." *The New York Times,* March 19, 2000.

Swierczynski, Duane. "Number One With a Bullet." *Philadelphia Magazine,* March 2002.

[Unsigned.] "Least Wanted." *The New Republic,* November 28, 1970.

Vobejda, Barbara. "FBI Goes Prime Time With 'Most Wanted' Additions, Announcements Coincide With Broadcasts of NBC, Fox Television Programs on Crime." *The Washington Post,* September 16, 1991.

Witkin, Gordon. "45 Years of Bad Guys On the Run." *U.S. News & World Report,* March 13, 1995.

Wittels, David G. "The Ten Most Wanted Men." *The Saturday Evening Post,* November 28, 1953.

USEFUL FUGITIVE WEBSITES

The Federal Bureau of Investigation (main site): www.fbi.gov

The FBI's Ten Most Wanted: www.fbi.gov/mostwant/topten/fugitives/fugitives.htm

America's Most Wanted: www.americasmostwanted.com

Court TV's Most Wanted: www.courttv.com/mostwanted

National Association of Fugitive Investigators: www.nafi-fugitive.com

Index

U

V